'Hard Power' and the European Convention on Human Rights

# International Studies in Human Rights

VOLUME 134

The titles published in this series are listed at brill.com/*ishr*

Frontispiece: Klewang (2nd pattern) 1911 (Author's collection).

The klewang is an infantry sabre developed around the turn of the twentieth century for use by the Royal Netherlands East Indies Army in counter-guerrilla warfare. It takes its name from a weapon native to the Indonesian archipelago. By a historical coincidence, the same weapon was issued to units of the American armed forces during World War II as a cutlass. The klewang is among the last types of sword developed for actual fighting use by the armed forces of any nation and probably the last type of sword to be so used. Even after World War II, it saw service in the Indonesian war of independence (1945-49), and, according to some reports, the Korean War (1950-53).

# 'Hard Power' and the European Convention on Human Rights

*By*

Peter Kempees

BRILL
NIJHOFF

LEIDEN | BOSTON

Typeface for the Latin, Greek, and Cyrillic scripts: "Brill". See and download: brill.com/ brill- typeface.

ISBN 978-90-04-42563-7 (hardback)
ISBN 978-90-04-42565-1 (e-book)

Copyright 2021 by Koninklijke Brill NV, Leiden, The Netherlands.
Koninklijke Brill NV incorporates the imprints Brill, Brill Hes & De Graaf, Brill Nijhoff, Brill Rodopi, Brill Sense, Hotei Publishing, mentis Verlag, Verlag Ferdinand Schöningh and Wilhelm Fink Verlag.
Koninklijke Brill NV reserves the right to protect this publication against unauthorized use. Requests for re-use and/or translations must be addressed to Koninklijke Brill NV, brill.com or copyright.com.

This book is printed on acid- free paper and produced in a sustainable manner.

# Contents

Foreword by the President of the European Court of Human Rights   XI
Preface   XIII
Acknowledgments   XV

**1   Introduction**   1
   1.1   The European Convention on Human Rights and 'Hard Power'   1
   1.2   Understanding of 'Hard Power' for Purposes of this Study   4
   1.3   Object of this Study   13

**2   Problems of Substantive Convention Law in Relation to 'Hard Power'**   18
   2.1   Introduction   18
   2.2   Article 2, Right to Life   19
   2.3   Article 3, Prohibition of Torture   25
   2.4   Article 5, Right to Liberty and Security   28
   2.5   Protection of Home and Property   31
   2.6   Article 13   34
   2.7   The Problem of Proof   35
   2.8   Conclusion   37

**3   Interplay between the Convention and International Humanitarian Law**   38
   3.1   Introduction   38
   3.2   Drafting History   39
   *3.3   Lex Specialis?*   40
   3.4   Case-law of the Court   49
   3.5   Conclusion   63

**4   Derogation**   65
   4.1   Introduction   65
   4.2   The Nature of Derogation   67
   4.3   War   69
   4.4   Legal Consequences of Lawful Derogation in Time of War   89
   4.5   Derogation in Response to an 'Emergency Threatening the Life of the Nation' in Practice   89
   4.6   When Does a Public Emergency Threaten the Life of the Nation?   117

| | | |
|---|---|---|
| 4.7 | Non-Derogable Rights | 122 |
| 4.8 | Strictly Required by the Exigencies of the Situation | 138 |
| 4.9 | Not Inconsistent with the State's Other Obligations under International Law | 139 |
| 4.10 | Formalities | 141 |
| 4.11 | The *Hassan* Judgment | 143 |
| 4.12 | Conclusion | 144 |

**5 Jurisdiction of the Contracting States** 147
- 5.1 Introduction 147
- 5.2 Territorial and Quasi-Territorial Jurisdiction 149
- 5.3 Sea, Airspace and Outer Space under the Sovereignty of States 155
- 5.4 Ships, Aircraft and Spacecraft 162
- 5.5 Extraterritorial Jurisdiction 175
- 5.6 Cases in Which Acts Producing Effects Abroad are Not Exercise of Extraterritorial Jurisdiction 179
- 5.7 Conclusion 182

**6 Typology of Article 1 Jurisdiction in 'Hard Power' Situations** 183
- 6.1 Introduction 183
- 6.2 States Exercising 'Hard Power' on Their Own Territory 183
- 6.3 Foreign State Agents Committing Unlawful Acts with the Acquiescence of Convention State 195
- 6.4 'Hard Power' as Exercise of Extraterritorial Jurisdiction 202
- 6.5 Peacekeeping and Peace-enforcing 235
- 6.6 Exercise of Jurisdiction on Territory of Foreign State with the Latter's Permission 245
- 6.7 The Status of 'Occupying Power' 246
- 6.8 Conclusion 252

**7 Jurisdiction of the European Court of Human Rights** 254
- 7.1 Introduction 254
- 7.2 Territorial Limitations to the Acceptance of Convention Jurisdiction 254
- 7.3 Reservation (Article 57 of the Convention) 256
- 7.4 Conflicting International Obligations 258
- 7.5 Conclusion 265

CONTENTS                                                                                    IX

8   **Attribution**   267
    8.1   Introduction   267
    8.2   'Jurisdiction' and 'Attribution' in the Logic of the Court   267
    8.3   Attribution of the Exercise of 'Hard Power' by the Contracting
          State   272
    8.4   Involvement of Agents Other than Organs of the Contracting
          State   276
    8.5   Subordinate Pseudo-States   308
    8.6   Conclusion   335

**Summary and Conclusions**   338
    9.1   Applicability of the Convention *Ratione Pacis Sive Belli*   338
    9.2   The First Defence: No Violation   339
    9.3   The Second Defence: Denying the Jurisdiction of the Contracting
          State   344
    9.4   The Third Defence: Denying the Jurisdiction of the European
          Court of Human Rights   349
    9.5   The Fourth Defence: Denying Attribution   350
    9.6   Final Observations   353

**References**   357
**Index**   397

# Foreword by the President of the European Court of Human Rights

As we prepare to celebrate the 70th anniversary of the European Convention on Human Rights ('the Convention') in 2020, we are reminded that the text of the Convention was drafted only a few years after the end of the Second World War, the bloodiest conflict in human history so far. So how should we see the Convention? As a peacetime treaty or one marked by the experiences of two World Wars? Conflict and war form the backdrop of this engaging book by a long-serving member of the Registry of the European Court of Human Rights. As President of the Court, I am pleased to be able to provide a foreword to this important piece of legal scholarship on the law of the European Convention on Human Rights.

The book suggests that in making deliberate provision for derogation in time of war or other public emergency threatening the life the nation, the drafters of the Convention were adopting a practical approach appropriate to the reality of warlike Europe. It is worth remembering that the Convention itself entered into force at least a decade and a half before International Covenant on Civil and Political Rights. According to the author many of the drafters would have seen active service themselves in the First World War. He contrasts this position to the drafters of the International Covenant whose idealist quest purported to ban war altogether.

Indeed, when looking at the Court's case-law, we can see that the Court has had to address numerous situations of conflict resulting in the use of military force that have occurred on the continent. Although the vast majority of applications before the European Court of Human Rights are lodged by individuals or groups of individuals, there have also been 24 inter-State cases since the Convention entered into force and at the time of writing 8 such applications are currently pending. A number have concerned situations of crisis or conflict. In addition to these inter-State cases there are thousands of individual applications before the Court related to conflict situations, such the armed conflict between Georgia and Russia in 2008 as well as the events in Crimea and the hostilities in Eastern Ukraine.

Can States resort to 'hard power' and still remain within their obligations under the European Convention on Human Rights when there is legitimate need to do so? Is the Convention relevant to the conduct of hostilities at all? These are important questions which lie at the heart of this work and are answered in the affirmative by the author.

But what is 'hard power'? The author borrows the term from the language of international relations. It encompasses all manner of coercive behaviour exercised by States. The author defines it to include targeted assassinations, UN and other peacekeeping operations, and acts of classic warfare. The main focus on the book is armed conflict, whether international or non-international.

The very applicability of the Convention – 'Article 1 jurisdiction' – takes a prominent place in the analysis. The novelty of this book lies in the attempt to define the coherence between *Banković and Others* on the one hand and *Al-Skeini and Others* on the other.

The book seeks to underline that application of the Convention to 'hard power' has been rather overlooked. Its main importance will be understood as a study of how exactly the Convention applies to the role of the modern soldier. As the author himself states, it is designed to help the reader navigate through the tortuous channels of international human rights law and other branches of international law, such as international humanitarian law.

I would like to finish this foreword with a final word about the intriguing frontispiece. I have been informed that it is a sword, known as a *klewang* (its name in Indonesian). It is a weapon developed by the Dutch army at the turn of the twentieth century for use in counter-guerrilla warfare in what was then the Netherlands East Indies. It is probably the last type of sword issued by any army for use in active hostilities. As a brutal weapon it reminds us of the very serious subject-matter of this book.

Ultimately, the book attempts to convince the reader that the Convention leaves Contracting States room for manoeuvre in pursuing legitimate policy objectives in their use of 'hard power' including in peace-keeping operations. Accordingly, the Convention retains its importance and usefulness in an increasingly dangerous world. This is an important birthday message.

*Linos-Alexandre Sicilianos*
President of the European Court of Human Rights (2019-2020)

# Preface

In June 2015 I took part in an international legal conference in Brugge, Belgium, organised by EUCOM/SHAPE for the military, their legal advisers and students of the international law relevant to armed conflict. I gave a talk on the impact of the European Convention on Human Rights ("the Convention") on combined military operations.

I expected the military and their lawyers to know the classic laws of war, of course; and so they did. Indeed, those were what they knew well. I expected them to be distrustful of human rights law; and again, so they were. Their attitude was not a hostile one: indeed, they knew full well that human rights, democracy and the rule of law were what they had pledged their very lives to protect. Rather, their attitude was one of bewilderment. Having been confronted with decisions and pronouncements of human rights treaty bodies (not least the European Court of Human Rights) finding fault with their actions, always from a safe distance and with the benefit of hindsight, they arrived with the feeling that human rights lawyers were interfering in things they did not even really understand.

I came away with the feeling that human rights law, and perhaps the law of the European Convention on Human Rights in particular, had been too long overlooked in the thinking of military lawyers, and resolved to do something about it.

The first step was a little monograph I wrote about derogation from the Convention in time of war or emergency. Published in early 2017 with the title "Thoughts on Article 15 of the European Convention on Human Rights", it can still be ordered from Wolf Legal Publishers.

The next step was this book. It is, to all intents and purposes, my doctoral thesis, which I defended in the university of Leiden in June 2019, published for a wider audience.

I would suggest that the time has come for human rights law to be made part of the military curriculum. The plain fact is that human rights law is relevant to the decision-making of soldiers, sailors and airmen. What is required is guidance on precisely how human rights law relates to the difficult decisions that have to be taken by service personnel in the field, or at sea, or in the air, and by their democratic political leaders. Focusing on the Convention, that guidance is precisely what I hope this book can offer.

The basic assumption on which this book is based is that the European Convention on Human Rights is well adapted to the needs of the armed forces of European States that respect human rights and the rule of law – indeed, better than other international human rights instruments. In fact, on closer examination it will be seen that, uniquely, the Convention was drafted with armed conflict in mind.

Although the main focus of this book is on national and non-international armed conflict, its subject-matter is broader. It includes such matters as the suppression of terrorism and piracy, which are normally considered in terms of law enforcement; peacekeeping, peace enforcing, and even post-conflict peace-building; and economic sanctions. I have chosen to borrow from the language of diplomacy the expression 'hard power' to include the additional areas covered.

As a serving member of the Registry of the European Court of Human Rights I feel I must add the following. The views expressed in this work are mine alone, as held at the time when they were formulated. They do not necessarily correspond to views held by any other person or institution, including the European Court of Human Rights or any one of its judges, or that Court's Registry or any one of its members other than myself.

*Peter Kempees*

# Acknowledgments

Thanks are due to Roderick Liddell and Françoise Elens-Passos, Registrar and Deputy Registrar of the European Court of Human Rights ('the Court') respectively, for permission to publish this work; to Lawrence Early and Anna Austin, Jurisconsult and Deputy Jurisconsult of the Court respectively, for their support; to Professors Rick Lawson and Helen Duffy, for their inspired and inspiring supervision; to the indefatigable Genevieve Woods, Head of the Court's Library, and her team, for their invaluable assistance; to all the friends and colleagues who gave me their encouragement (they know who they are); and finally, to my wife, Ingrid, for her faith in the project, her patience and her love. To her I dedicate this book.

CHAPTER 1

# Introduction

## 1.1    The European Convention on Human Rights and 'Hard Power'

In Article 1 of the European Convention on Human Rights,[1] the High Contracting Parties undertake to 'secure to everyone within their jurisdiction the rights and freedoms' defined in its Articles 2-11 and, by extension, in the Protocols to the Convention. This very phrasing makes it clear that the primary responsibility to protect human rights rests with the High Contracting Parties themselves. The role of the European Court of Human Rights,[2] defined in Article 19 of the Convention, is essentially supervisory.

In ordinary circumstances the Parties to the Convention expect to entrust compliance with human rights standards to a competent administration faithfully applying domestic law. Contentious human-rights issues will nonetheless arise; these will be dealt with the domestic courts, which in so doing will also apply rules of domestic law subject as necessary to rules of international human rights law. At the same time citizens expect the State to protect them against the violence of others. It is for that reason that the State enjoys a monopoly on the use of force[3] – or, to use an expression that we will introduce presently, 'hard power'.[4]

The armed forces of our countries also protect human rights. This they do at the most basic level possible. Individual freedom, political liberty and the rule of law[5] would not survive for long unless defended by the credible threat – and if necessary, the actual use – of military force: put differently, the exercise of 'hard power' on behalf of the State.[6]

In recent years the European Court of Human Rights has been called to pass judgment on the actions of servicemen doing their duty towards the countries they served. In several such cases the Court has had to find breaches of the Convention. Such findings have sometimes met with a frosty reception from

---

1    Hereafter "the Convention".
2    Hereafter "the Court".
3    *Ramsahai and Others v. the Netherlands* [GC], no. 52391/99, § 325, ECHR 2007-II.
4    See 1.2.3 below.
5    Preamble to the Statute of the Council of Europe, third paragraph.
6    See generally Dwight Raymond, "Military Means of Preventing Mass Atrocities", in *Reconstructing Atrocity Prevention* (Sheri P. Rosenberg, Tibi Galis, Alex Zucker, eds.), Cambridge University Press 2016, pp. 295-318.

© KONINKLIJKE BRILL NV, LEIDEN, 2021 | DOI:10.1163/9789004425637_002

respondent governments. The defence minister of one of the Convention's Contracting States, for example, has gone on record stating that 'the cumulative effect of some of Strasbourg's decisions on the freedom to conduct military operations raises serious challenges which need to be addressed'.[7] In the same country, a member of parliament (a former soldier) has published an article in the press arguing that the 'imposition' of 'complex human rights law' designed, as he sees it, solely for application in peacetime 'changes the conditions of service and hampers the ability of soldiers to fight, because human rights law does not accept that there is anything unique about a military operation'.[8]

Closer to home, the Court has on occasion had to find fault with use of force lawful in terms of domestic law to eliminate a terrorist threat or put an end to a terrorist attack. The public, and especially some sectors of the press, have sometimes been dismissive of such findings.[9]

It is easy to dismiss statements of politicians as mere politics, and the rants of journalists as facile; but even the most ardent human rights defender must at least make an effort to understand the frustration of governments, not to mention their military forces, at being taken to task for having violated the human rights of an often ruthless enemy. One cannot but sympathise with the bewildered soldier and his or her political superiors. Likewise, the view that it is justified to use lethal force to keep the public safe from terrorism is hardly incomprehensible. Even so, it is submitted that those who argue that the European Convention on Human Rights imposes unreasonable constraints on the meaningful use of 'hard power' are wrong.

The first basic supposition defended in this work is that the Convention itself makes sufficient provision for the legitimate use of 'hard power' in difficult situations. It should not be forgotten that the Convention itself was created only a few short years after the Second World War, the bloodiest conflict in hu-

---

7   The Rt Hon Sir Michael Fallon MP, Secretary of State for Defence of the United Kingdom, speaking at the Policy Exchange seminar 'Clearing the "Fog of Law"' on 8 December 2014. See also Haijer, F.A. & Ryngaert, C.M.J., "Reflections on *Jaloud v. the Netherlands* – Jurisdictional Consequences and Resonance in Dutch Society", *Journal of International Peacekeeping* 19 (2015), pp. 174-189, p. 185.

8   Tom Tugendhat MP, "Human rights lawyers now present a real threat to British troops at war", *The Telegraph*, 19 September 2016, http://www.telegraph.co.uk/news/2016/09/19/human-rights-lawyers-now-present-a-real-threat-to-british-troops/.

9   For example, "European Court of Killers' Rights; EXCLUSIVE: Third of cases won by terrorists, murderers and lags", *The Sun*, 17 August 2015, updated 5 April 2016, https://www.thesun.co.uk/archives/politics/204465/european-court-of-killers-rights/ (accessed on 24 August 2018). For a discussion of the phenomenon, see Egbert Myjer, "About court jesters: Freedom of expression and duties and responsibilities of journalists", in *Freedom of expression: Essays in honour of Nicolas Bratza*, Wolf Legal Publishers 2012, p. 111.

INTRODUCTION

man history so far, and after two colonial empires – British India and the Netherlands East Indies – had wrested themselves free from European overlordship: the first of many.[10] Actual drafting took place even as new conflicts threatened to tear Europe apart. NATO, the North Atlantic Treaty Organization, was created on 24 August 1949[11] in response to the perception of a new threat to peace from the Soviet Union. European troops were in transit to Korea to fight with the blessing of the newly-created Security Council of the United Nations.[12] The founding fathers of the Convention were no strangers to the reality of their day; they read the newspapers just as other responsible citizens did. We shall see that they strove to accommodate the need for 'hard power', even active war, more effectively than the United Nations did in their later Covenant on Civil and Political Rights.[13]

Of course, even an observer who recognises that the use of 'hard power' may be inescapable even for the most well-intentioned of political leaders is bound to recognise that the protection of democracy, human rights and the rule of law in the name of their citizens, or even in a more abstract sense the protection of the international legal order, is hardly the only motive for States to resort to the threat or use of force in their domestic and international relations. Whatever the reasons for which the political decision is taken to resort to military force, for the serviceman ordered into action they are of importance only in so far as they may define his operational goals: otherwise, at his level, they matter little, and in so far as the legality of the use of force concerns him it will be at the level of *ius in bello* rather than *ius ad bellum*. These reasons are however relevant to domestic and international courts in that they may engage the State's responsibility for the actions of its servicemen and in some cases the individual criminal responsibility of political decision-makers.

This takes us to the second basic supposition of this work. Human rights law, including the law of the European Convention on Human Rights, is a subdivision of international law. Other such subdivisions include the law of international organisations, most notably the United Nations Organization or UN,

---

10    British India gained independence as two new states, Pakistan (14 August 1947) and India (15 August 1947); the independence of the Netherlands East Indies (minus Netherlands New Guinea) as the Republic of Indonesia was recognised by the Netherlands on 27 December 1949 (in 2005 the Netherlands retrospectively accepted the Indonesian declaration of independence of 17 August 1945).

11    The date of the entry into force of the North Atlantic Treaty ("Washington Treaty"), signed on 4 April 1949.

12    S/Res/83, 27 June 1950, Complaint of aggression upon the Republic of Korea; S/Res/84, 7 July 1950, Complaint of aggression upon the Republic of Korea.

13    See 3.2 below.

and international humanitarian law, also known as the international law of armed conflict or, more traditionally, the laws of war.[14] It is our position that in terms of *ius ad bellum* the law of the United Nations, and in particular Chapter VII of the Charter of the United Nations, while it does not justify or condone violations of human rights, qualifies the way in which the European Convention on Human Rights applies in situations of armed conflict.[15] International humanitarian law is relevant to the Convention applied as *ius in bello*.[16]

## 1.2 Understanding of 'Hard Power' for Purposes of this Study

Since the purpose of this study is to identify the parameters within which the Convention allows States to exercise 'hard power', we must first define our understanding of that concept.

### 1.2.1 *Armed Conflict*

The classical use of 'hard power' involves the use of military force in an armed conflict.

A Vice-President of the Court, speaking in 2015, has used the expression 'conflict' in noting that the Court has had to address in one way or another all instances of the use of military force that have occurred on the continent, at least since 1990. The examples he mentions include the situations in Northern Cyprus and Transdniestria, the dispute between Armenia and Azerbaijan over Nagorno-Karabakh, the events of 2008 in northern Georgia, the dissolution of the former Socialist Federative Republic of Yugoslavia and its aftermath, and the NATO intervention in Kosovo. He also refers to the involvement of European Contracting States, as members of the American-led force, in events in Iraq.[17] He is right; and we shall come across all of these 'conflicts' below.

The Convention nowhere uses the expression 'conflict'. The word 'war' appears in only one Article of the Convention – namely, in Article 15 (derogation in time of emergency) – and in no other Protocols than Protocols Nos. 6 and 13, which concern the abolition of the death penalty. We will discuss the mean-

---

14 The expression "international humanitarian law", which has much the same meaning as "laws of war" or "law of armed conflict", has gained currency in recent decades.
15 See 4.3 and 8.4.5.2 below.
16 See 4.9, 4.11 and 6.7 below.
17 Linos-Alexandre Sicilianos, "The European Court of Human Rights at a time of crisis in Europe", SEDI/ESIL Lecture, European Court of Human Rights, 16 October 2015, p. 10.

# INTRODUCTION

ing of the expression 'war' as used in that particular context when we come to derogations from Convention rights.[18]

The Convention was first drawn up in the immediate aftermath of the Second World War. A field of international law intended to rid warfare of the worst excesses of inhumanity existed already then, in the form of a body of treaty law that largely codified the customary 'laws of war' – the best known of the treaties being the Hague Conventions of 1899 and 1907, the Geneva Conventions of 1929 that had served the world as well as they could during the Second World War, and most recently the four Geneva Conventions of 1949. The understanding of 'conflict' that then prevailed was kinetic warfare of the classic kind – 'set-piece'[19] or open-field battles, perhaps guerrilla – between the armed forces of opposing states.[20]

This understanding of 'conflict' has not lost its relevance; neither have the classic laws of war. However, other forms of violence have arisen that cannot be understood in terms of direct confrontation between the armed forces of two or more States but that do not comfortably fit the paradigm of ordinary law enforcement either. For these, a new legal category has been created: the 'non-international armed conflict'. This new category, although foreshadowed by the common Article 3 of the four Geneva Conventions of 1949, has obtained recognition in the second of two Protocols added to those Conventions in 1977. The classical interstate conflict is now dignified by a category of its own: that of 'international armed conflict'.[21]

Non-international armed conflicts are now much more common than classical international armed conflicts. *The War Report 2017*, a paper published by the Geneva Academy of International Humanitarian Law and Human Rights (Geneva Academy),[22] lists six situations in 2017 that could be considered 'in-

---

18    See 4.3 below.

19    An expression apparently first used by Lieutenant General Sir John Monash in *The Australian Victories in France* (London, Hutchinson & Co., 1920), p. 226: "[An operation or a battle] is a 'set-piece' because the stage is elaborately set, parts are written for all the performers, and carefully rehearsed by many of them. The whole performance is controlled by a time-table, and, so long as all goes according to plan, there is no likelihood of unexpected happenings, or of interesting developments."

20    Marko Milanovic, "Extraterritorial Derogations from Treaties in Armed Conflict", in *The Frontiers of Human Rights: Extraterritoriality and its Challenges, Collected Courses of the Academy of European Law*, vol. XXIV/1, p. 55-88 at p. 66-67.

21    See generally Sten Verhoeven, "International and non-international armed conflicts", in *Armed Conflicts and the Law*, Jan Wouters, Philip De Man, Nele Verlinden (eds.), Intersentia, 2016, pp. 151-185 at pp. 156-17 1.

22    Annysa Bellal, *The War Report* 2017, https://www.geneva-academy.ch/joomlatools-files/docman-files/The%20War%20Report%202017.pdf (accessed on 11 August 2018), pp. 9-30

ternational armed conflicts' in the classical sense (some of them short-lived); seventeen cases of 'belligerent occupation'; and no fewer than fifty-five 'non-international armed conflicts' (some unfortunate countries hosted a plurality of such conflicts simultaneously).[23]

States Parties to the Convention are concerned by conflicts in all these categories. For example, the situations identified by the Geneva Academy as arguably active 'international armed conflicts' include Ukraine v. Russia and the international coalition v. Syria – the 'international coalition' being comprised of (in addition to non-European states) European NATO members Belgium, Denmark, France, Germany, Italy, the Netherlands and Turkey. Of the ten 'belligerent occupations' identified by the Geneva Academy, five are to be found on the territory of Convention States: Armenia v. Azerbaijan, Turkey v. Cyprus, Russia v. Georgia, Russia v. Moldova, and Russia v. Ukraine. The Falkland Islands are alleged by Argentina to be under belligerent occupation by the United Kingdom.[24]

Of the thirty-eight 'non-international armed conflicts' identified as such by the Geneva Academy in 2017, two are on the territory of Convention States: that between Ukraine on the one hand and the breakaway 'Donetsk People's Republic' and 'Luhansk People's Republic' on the other (it is not necessary for our purposes to take a position on whether this is one conflict or two), and that between Turkey and the *Partiya Karkerên Kurdistanê* (Workers' Party of Kurdistan, 'PKK'). The others are all to be found outside Europe, mainly in Africa and the Middle East; but Convention States take part in some of them as contributors to United Nations forces (at the time of writing, the United Nations Multidimensional Integrated Stabilization Mission in Mali (*Mission multidimensionnelle intégrée des Nations unies pour la stabilisation au Mali*, MINUSMA) and the United Nations Organization Stabilization Mission in the

---

(up from three, ten and thirty-five the previous year: see Annyssa Bellal, *The War Report* 2016, https://armedgroupsinternationallaw.files.wordpress.com/2017/05/the-war-report-2016.pdf (accessed on 27 May 2017).

23  The present study does not take any position on the classification in international law of any of these alleged conflicts.

24  *The War Report* 2016, p. 28. The General Court of the European Union has held the 'actions and policies of the Russian Government destabilising Ukraine' to constitute 'war or serious international tension constituting threat of war' within the meaning of Article 99(1)(d) of the Agreement on partnership and cooperation establishing a partnership between the European Communities and their Member States, of one part, and the Russian Federation, of the other part, Official Journal of the European Communities L 327, 28 November 1997: see General Court, judgment of 15 June 2017, Case T-262/15, *Kiselev v. Council*, § 33 and *passim*.

INTRODUCTION 7

Democratic Republic of the Congo (*Mission de l'Organisation des Nations unies pour la stabilisation en République démocratique du Congo*, MONUSCO)).[25]

No mention is made in the Geneva Academy's report of the strife in the parts of the northern Caucasus that are under Russian sovereignty. This is not generally considered in terms of 'non-international armed conflict'; that expression is not used by the Russian Government to describe it.[26]

Even so, the sheer scale of the separatist violence in that area – and elsewhere in Russia: the separatists have taken it to Moscow itself[27] – has made its mark, including on the case-law of the Court, which draws a distinction between 'routine police operations' and 'situations of large-scale anti-terrorist operations'.[28] It is accordingly of interest to us for purposes of this study.

No Convention State is understood currently to deploy military force in Iraq; but several have in the recent past, and the case-law of the European Court of Human Rights has had to develop accordingly. Similarly, the involvement of Convention States in Bosnia and Herzegovina during the 1992-95 war and its aftermath and in Kosovo during and after the events of 1999 is of interest from our standpoint. So, potentially, is the military operation briefly undertaken by Turkish forces in the Afrin district of Syria in January 2018, which we mention in passing since it has yet to give rise to Strasbourg case-law.

An 'armed attack' creating for the State under attack the right to defend itself was once thought to be possible only if occurring at the hand of another State. However, as we shall see below,[29] al-Qaeda's 9/11 attack on New York and Wash-

---

25    *The War Report* 2017, pp. 30-31.

26    In a judgment of 31 July 1995 the Constitutional Court of the Russian Federation proceeded on the implicit recognition that Additional Protocol II was applicable to the conflict which was at that time being fought in Chechnya (later to be known as the First Chechen War), and that its provisions were "binding on both parties to the armed conflict". Constitutional Court of the Russian Federation, Judgment of 31 July 1995 on the constitutionality of the Presidential Decrees and the Resolutions of the Federal Government concerning the situation in Chechnya (translation by Federal News Service Group, Washington D.C., published by the Venice Commission on 10 January 1996 as CDL-INF (96) 1). See Bowring, Bill (2008) – "How will the European Court of Human Rights deal with the UK in Iraq?: lessons from Turkey and Russia" – p. 9. London: Birkbeck ePrints. Available at: http://eprints.bbk.ac.uk/859. Large-scale fighting between Chechen insurgents and Russian (and Russian-backed) armed forces, often referred to as the "Second Chechen War", occurred between August 1999 and April 2009. A low-level insurgency continues to the present day. The Russian Federation ratified the Convention (and Protocols Nos. 1, 4, 7 and 11) on 5 May 1998.

27    *Finogenov and Others v. Russia*, nos. 18299/03 and 27311/03, ECHR 2011.

28    *Tagayeva and Others v. Russia*, nos. 26562/07, 14755/08, 49339/08, 49380/08, 51313/08, 21294/11 and 37096/11, § 595, 13 April 2017.

29    See 4.5 below.

ington was sufficient for the NATO members for the first time in history to activate Article 5 of the Washington Treaty, according to which 'an armed attack against one or more of them in Europe or North America shall be considered an attack against them all', and invoke the right to collective self-defence, no less, under Article 51 of the Charter of the United Nations.[30] As is well known, forces of the United States and their allies ran the al-Qaeda leadership to earth in Afghanistan; even today no fewer than thirty-seven Convention States are contributing to the Resolute Support mission in that country.[31]

### 1.2.2 *Other Exercise of 'Hard Power' Relevant to this Study*

Armed conflict in the sense of kinetic military action against another political actor does not exhaust the scope of the expression 'hard power' as used for purposes of this study.

The threat of terrorist attack, and indeed actual terrorist attacks, by al-Qaeda and groups with a similar ideological motivation have induced several European NATO members to allow American intelligence services to undertake covert action on their territory. The measures taken against al-Qaeda and its ideological successors do not fit neatly into any category of armed conflict, whether international in character or not. Even so, politicians and journalists have sometimes been led to dignify them by the expression 'war'. Already by reason of their sheer scale, they are of interest to us – even though the expression 'war' by any conventional legal definition is inappropriate.[32]

The same may be said, *a fortiori*, about the suppression of widespread organised crime. The kind of widespread violence committed by criminal armed groups, as seen in some parts of Latin America, is at the present time not to be found in Europe; but piracy, a similar phenomenon, does concern European States. Like terrorism of the al-Qaeda type, neither is conventionally viewed in terms of international or non-international armed conflict.[33] Nevertheless,

---

30  Helen Duffy, *The 'War on Terror' and the Framework of International Law* (2nd edition 2015), Cambridge University Press, pp. 296-97.

31  Albania, Armenia, Austria, Azerbaijan, Belgium, Bosnia and Herzegovina, Bulgaria, Croatia, Czech Republic, Denmark, Estonia, Finland, the Former Yugoslav Republic of Macedonia (now North Macedonia), Georgia, Germany, Greece, Hungary, Iceland, Ireland, Italy, Latvia, Lithuania, Luxembourg, Montenegro, the Netherlands, Norway, Poland, Portugal, Romania, Slovakia, Slovenia, Spain, Sweden, Turkey, Ukraine and the United Kingdom (*The War Report 2016*, fn. 4 on p. 15).

32  Helen Duffy, *The 'War on Terror' and the Framework of International Law* (2nd edition 2015), Cambridge University Press, p. 2, fn. 3 and pp. 296-97; Luc Reydams and Jan Wouters, "A la guerre comme à la guerre", in *Armed Conflicts and the Law*, Jan Wouters, Philip De Man, Nele Verlinden (eds.), Intersentia, 2016, pp. 1-27 at pp. 22-24.

33  Duffy (2018), p. 21.

INTRODUCTION

combating piracy requires the use of armed force; indeed, it is the traditional preserve of naval forces of the State. Piracy too is therefore worth examining in the present context.

Finally, it is conceivable that States – or rather, Governments – may resort to the covert use of lethal means to further their interests. This study touches briefly on such phenomena, which for present purposes must be treated as relevant though hypothetical.[34]

### 1.2.3    Defining 'Hard Power'

#### 1.2.3.1    Background to the Concept

It is convenient for our purposes to use the expression 'hard power' as a holdall term to cover all instances of the use of force referred to above. The concept is borrowed from the study of international relations.

The definition of 'hard power' used by diplomatists is usually in terms such as

> The coercive use of military or economic means to influence the behaviour or interests of political players[35]

distinguishing it from 'soft power', which is the use of diplomacy, foreign aid and cultural relations to the same end,[36] and 'smart power', which is the judicious use of 'hard' and 'soft' power combined.[37]

---

34    Hypothetical because there is a case pending before the Court that concerns such an allegation and on which the Court has yet to pronounce. See 6.4.6.3 below.

35    *Adviesraad internationale vraagstukken* (Advisory Council on International Affairs), *Azië in opmars: Strategische betekenis en gevolgen* (Asia on the rise: Strategic significance and implications), no. 86, December 2013, appendix 3; compare House of Lords, Select Committee on Soft Power and the UK's Influence – First Report: Persuasion and Power in the Modern World (ordered by the House of Lords to be printed on 11 March 2014), Chapter 3, paragraph 40, '... getting what one wants by using coercion or inducement to force other countries to do what one wants – "hard power", which includes the threat or use of military coercion or of economic coercion through sanctions or boycotts ...'

36    *Adviesraad Internationale Vraagstukken, ibid.*; compare House of Lords, Select Committee on Soft Power and the UK's Influence, *ibid.*: '... getting what one wants by influencing other countries (via their governments and publics) to want the same thing, through the forces of attraction, persuasion and co-option ...'.

37    House of Lords, Select Committee on Soft Power and the UK's Influence, *loc. cit.*, § 61. For more extensive discussion of these three concepts, see Ernest J. Wilson, III, "Hard Power, Soft Power, Smart Power" in *The Annals of the American Academy of Political and Social Science* 2008; 616; p. 110-24, *passim*, and Joseph S. Nye, Jr., 'Hard, Soft, and Smart Power', in *The Oxford Handbook of Modern Diplomacy* (Andrew F. Cooper, Jorge Heine, and Ramesh Thakur, eds.), Oxford University Press 2013, pp. 559-574.

The use of economic means of coercion – boycotts, economic sanctions imposed by a state on another political actor – has rarely been the object of a judgment or decision of the Court or a decision or report of the Commission; there have been only a few such cases.[38] The coercive use of military means is more frequently found in Strasbourg case-law. States Parties to the Convention have taken part in armed conflicts, in some cases on their own territory, in some cases abroad; they have used military force, either to exercise 'hard power' in the above sense themselves or to resist attempts of other political actors to do so.

However, the opponent against whom coercive force is directed is not necessarily a 'political player' in any conventional sense of the word: pirates, for example, are generally viewed as common criminals. Our understanding of 'hard power' is accordingly wider than that of the student of international diplomacy inasmuch as we must also touch on situations of this nature.

### 1.2.3.2 'Hard Power': a Definition

For our purposes, accordingly, 'hard power' means:

- Firstly, the deliberate projection by a Government of coercive force outside the territory of the State, whether the situation concerned constitutes an armed conflict within the meaning of international humanitarian law or not;
- Secondly, the deliberate use (or conscious acceptance) by a Government of coercive force within the State's own borders on a scale necessitating the application either of military force or of non-military force in excess of the requirements of ordinary law enforcement to overcome opposition, whether the situation concerned is admitted by that Government to be an armed conflict within the meaning of international humanitarian law or not;
- Thirdly, the application by a Government of economic sanctions in the international relations of the State.

Such a definition encompasses situations which, from the standpoint of international humanitarian law, would in most cases be seen as law enforcement rather than armed conflict, including counter-insurgency operations, antiterrorist action going beyond ordinary policing, and the suppression of piracy whether in home or international waters.

The above definition is autonomous: it does not depend on any admission or declaration by the Government. Thus, the assumption by the Government of emergency powers is not a part of it.

---

38　See 8.4.5.1 and 8.4.5.2.4 below.

# INTRODUCTION

### 1.2.4 *Problems of Applying the Convention to the Use of 'Hard Power'*

1.2.4.1 Perception of Inapplicability of Human Rights Law to Armed Conflict

No one denies the applicability of human rights law to policing, or law enforcement. In contrast, until recently there was a tendency on the part of decision-makers both military and civilian to pay scant attention to human rights law, Convention law in particular, in relation to 'conflict', whether international or non-international. The writing had been on the wall since 1996 at the latest,[39] but even so their assumption tended to be that human rights law was meant to govern law enforcement only and had little if any relevance to the conduct of hostilities, that being a matter to consider exclusively in terms of international humanitarian law. This can explain, for example, that the Dutch manual on military law (*Handboek Militair Recht*) mentions the Convention and the International Covenant on Civil and Political Rights only in passing, in one brief paragraph, and in its index refers to them not at all.[40] The discovery that the Convention was not merely relevant but applicable to the actions of the armed forces not merely on home territory but also on foreign soil and even at sea[41] would have come as a rude shock.

Military lawyers who take the trouble to study the interaction between human rights law and the law governing the use of 'hard power' – however defined – take the perspective of the confused serviceman trying to predict what the courts will think of next to complicate his life's work; Pouw's dissertation,

---

39 International Court of Justice, *Legality of the Threat or Use of Nuclear Weapons*, Advisory Opinion, I.C.J. Reports 1996, p. 226 at § 25; see also *Legal Consequences of the Construction of a Wall in the Occupied Palestinian Territory*, Advisory Opinion, I.C.J. Reports 2004, p. 176 at § 106; and *Armed Activities on the Territory of the Congo* (*Democratic Republic of the Congo v. Uganda*), Judgment, 19 December 2005, I.C.J. Reports 2005, pp. 242-43 at § 216. The latter judgment is of particular interest in that the International Court of Justice finds Uganda responsible for violations of (*inter alia*) the African Charter on Human and Peoples' Rights, a regional treaty like the Convention, committed on the territory of the Democratic Republic of the Congo (pp. 243-44 at § 217-220). See also D. Murray, *Practitioner's Guide to Human Rights Law in Armed Conflict* (Chatham House/Oxford University Press 2016), pp. v-vi (Foreword by Lord Phillips of Worth Maltravers) and pp. 12-13.

40 *Handboek Militair Recht* (P.J.J. van der Kruit, ed.), published by *Nederlandse Defensie Academie* (Netherlands Defence Academy), 2nd edition 2009, pp. 35-36.

41 See *Al-Jedda v. the United Kingdom* [GC], no. 27021/08, ECHR 2011; *Al-Skeini and Others v. the United Kingdom* [GC], no. 55721/07, ECHR 2011; *Hirsi Jamaa and Others v. Italy* [GC], no. 27765/09, ECHR 2012; *Jaloud v. the Netherlands* [GC], no. 47708/08, ECHR 2014.

which explores the 'outer operational limits' of targeting and detention in a counterinsurgency setting, is an excellent example.[42]

The fact is, however, that international human rights law – for our purposes, the Convention – applies also to the actions of service personnel, even, as we shall see, when they are conducting hostilities. Service personnel are entitled to guidance to help them navigate its tortuous channels.

### 1.2.4.2 Legal Interoperability

In military parlance, 'interoperability' defines

> The ability of systems, units, or forces to provide services to and accept services from other systems, units, or forces, and to use the services so exchanged to enable them to operate effectively together.[43]

Thus defined, it may refer to the capability of diverse military units – formations of land forces, ships, aircraft – to act to a common purpose in the conduct of hostilities. The concept is however not limited to weapons systems and military personnel: the hardware, communications systems and command structures must be compatible, but so must the rulebooks. This may be referred to as 'legal interoperability'.

A problem perceived by at least one military lawyer, the Canadian Colonel Kirby Abbott from whom we borrow the expression, is a loss of legal interoperability within NATO between on the one hand the European NATO members, all of which are parties to the Convention, and the North American NATO members, the United States and Canada, which are not and cannot be. He notes a growing divergence in legal doctrine between the two groups arising from the case-law of the Court. He sees the former increasingly constrained by the restrictive law enforcement paradigm that governs the Convention, whereas the latter remain bound only by the more permissive standards of international humanitarian law. In his words,

---

42 Eric Pouw, *International Human Rights Law and the Law of Armed Conflict in the Context of Counterinsurgency – With a Particular Focus on Targeting and Operational Detention* (diss. UvA 2013), p. 7.

43 Myron Hura, Gary W. McLeod, Eric V. Larson, James Schneider, Dan Gonzales, Daniel M. Norton, Jody Jacobs, Kevin M. O'Connell, William Little, Richard Mesic, and Lewis Jamison, *Interoperability: A Continuing Challenge in Coalition Air Operations*. Santa Monica, CA: RAND Corporation, 2000, https://www.rand.org/pubs/monograph_reports/MR1235.html (accessed on 22 August 2018).

INTRODUCTION 13

> ... there is a real and currently emerging potential for the transatlantic link of legal interoperability between North American and European NATO Member States to be strained or severed, and for divergence among NATO's European members, due to the influence of litigation arising from the European Court of Human Rights (...). This litigation, in turn, is redefining, and has the potential to further redefine, NATO's use of force doctrine and Rules of Engagement (ROE), targeting and detention frameworks. It also has the potential to impact on how NATO Member States, as a matter of law and policy, view the overall relationship between IHL (i.e. international humanitarian law) and IHRL (i.e. international human rights law).

This perception, which is not Colonel Abbott's alone, has to be taken seriously. The issue is not limited to the interaction between NATO member States. The armed forces of NATO members take part in military operations together with non-NATO States, often but not always in an *ad hoc* framework such as United Nations peacekeeping, and indeed so do the armed forces of European States that are not members of NATO.[44]

It seems likely that considerations of interoperability in this sense may have had some influence on the position of some Contracting States that the Convention should not apply extraterritorially to military action (and hence on their failure to make use of Article 15 to derogate from their obligations under the Convention in respect of such action).

It is our belief that the Convention was never intended to stand in the way of the effective operation of any military alliance to which its Contracting States might be parties – indeed, such an aim would be inexplicable in the light of the drafting history of the Convention as briefly described above[45] – and that it need not have that effect either.

## 1.3 Object of this Study

### 1.3.1 *Research Question*

Since as we have briefly mentioned in 1.2.4.1 above the Convention can, and does, continue to protect human rights in the direst of circumstances, even

---

44 Cordula Droege and Louise Arimatsu, "The European Convention on Human Rights and international humanitarian law: Conference report", *Yearbook of International Humanitarian Law* volume 12 – 2009 – pp. 435-449 at pp. 446-449.

45 See 1.1.

in wartime, the question arises whether the Convention leaves Contracting States the latitude needed to deal with situations in which a legitimate need to resort to the use of 'hard power' in the sense corresponding to our definition may arise.

Our assumption is that the latitude available to Contracting States will be sufficient if despite the obligations which they have assumed upon ratifying the Convention States retain access to means enabling them to pursue policy objectives that are legitimate in terms of international law.

### 1.3.2 Method and Approach

To answer the above question, this study investigates precisely what latitude Contracting States have to tailor their Convention obligations to the situation in which the need to exercise 'hard power' presents itself to them. To that end, it identifies the limits both of the applicability of the Convention and of attribution of the use of 'hard power' to Contracting States.

It is important to reiterate in this connection that – quite contrary to the suppositions of the domestic politicians cited above[46] and perhaps others – the Convention is not to be applied only in times of peace: it has relevance also to situations of conflict, even international armed conflict. As we will see,[47] this was actually envisaged from the very outset by the drafters of the Convention; the Strasbourg institutions – the European Commission and Court of Human Rights – recognised it in their practice and case-law and strove from a very early date to accommodate the various competing interests. More recently the Council of Europe's Steering Committee for Human Rights has recognised the Court's role in this domain as 'pivotal'.[48]

This study is essentially a survey of the relevant case-law of the Court and the Commission with a view to identifying the resulting jurisprudential principles. Our intention is to state the law (as it stands in 2019) as comprehensively as possible. The Court and Commission case-law cited is all accessible through the Court's own searchable database HUDOC.

The case-law considered relevant is that in which the Court was called upon to determine whether the use of 'hard power' was in breach of the Convention. Additionally, cases are analysed where the Court developed general principles or interpretations with the potential to have a bearing on such cases in the fu-

---

46    Notes 7 and 8 above.

47    See 4.3.1 below.

48    Council of Europe, *The longer-term future of the system of the European Convention on Human Rights*, Report of the Steering Committee for Human Rights (CDDH) adopted on 11 December 2015, p. 52; Alice Donald and Philip Leach, "A Wolf in Sheep's Clothing: Why the Draft Copenhagen Declaration Must be Rewritten", *EJIL:Talk!,* 21 February 2018.

ture. It will be attempted to relate this case-law to other fields of international law, international humanitarian law and general international law in particular. This will require us to examine a variety of treaties other than the Convention; judgments and decisions of treaty bodies other than the Court and the Commission; documents from a variety of international bodies; domestic legislation and judicial decisions and other domestic legal documents; and finally, selected writings of learned authors.

The perspective of an individual applicant before the Court is necessarily that of an aggrieved victim who feels entitled to redress. As in all litigation, the terms of the dispute are dictated by the party with whom the initiative lies.

The perspective chosen for this study is the opposite: that of the respondent Contracting State. This is the most obvious choice, since only States (and then only Members of the Council of Europe) are Parties to the Convention[49] and within the legal space of the Convention[50] only they may lawfully resort to the use of force.

The extent to which non-State actors may be bound by human rights law is an interesting one,[51] but from our perspective it is of little relevance since they cannot be respondents before the Court. Moreover, even though they may have the potential to violate human rights on a scale comparable to that of a Contracting State, as many armed groups now do, none have so far committed themselves to abide by Convention standards of human rights. A non-governmental structure (of the Geneva Call type)[52] that would make it possible for them to register such a commitment, and perhaps enhance their legitimacy, does not exist at this time.

Nonetheless, the position of applicants cannot and will not be overlooked: it takes two, at least, to litigate, and for applicants (whether Contracting States themselves – in interstate cases –, individuals or groups of individuals, or strategic litigators) it is of interest to study possible defences precisely to overcome them. In the European Court of Human Rights as in any other court, the way in which a case is introduced can decide its fate at the outset.

---

49  Article 59 of the Convention. The European Union may accede, but has yet to do so.

50  The space within which Contracting States enjoy territorial and quasi-territorial jurisdiction. See Chapter 5.1-5.4 below.

51  See generally Liesbeth Zegveld, *The Accountability of Armed Opposition Groups in International Law*, Cambridge University Press 2002, and Katharine Fortin, *The Accountability of Armed Groups under Human Rights Law*, diss. Utrecht 2015.

52  https://genevacall.org/. According to its mission statement, 'Geneva Call is a neutral and impartial non-governmental organization dedicated to promoting respect by armed non-State actors (ANSAs) for international humanitarian norms in armed conflict and other situations of violence, in particular those related to the protection of civilians'.

The method chosen is to identify the basic types of legal argument that a respondent Government may make before the Court when it is faced with complaints under the Convention arising from the use of 'hard power'. Since the perspective chosen is the defensive position of the respondent Contracting State they may also be described as 'defences', if one will:

- Once the facts have been established, the first line of defence is to argue that no violation can be found on the facts of the case; in other words, that there has been no violation of the Convention in the first place. This is the most obvious solution: it amounts to persuading the Court that the Contracting Party has remained in compliance with the obligations which it took upon itself in ratifying the Convention. Much of the relevant case-law has been developed over the years in situations of normality; the principles developed, however, are of general application. Its relevance to situations involving the use of 'hard power' will be the subject of Chapter 2.
- Reliance on a prior derogation under Article 15 of the Convention is a special sub-type of the first type of defence; it depends on a prior choice to recognise publicly that a problem exists that is insuperable as long as ordinary Convention standards are maintained. This will be discussed in Chapter 4. However, since, as is apparent from its very wording, Article 15 is of particular relevance to situations of 'war', an understanding of the interrelation between human rights law – for our purposes, Convention law in particular – and international humanitarian law is necessary before we can enter into the subject of derogation. This will be examined in Chapter 3.
- The second defence is that the matters complained of fall outside the 'jurisdiction' of the Contracting Party within the meaning of Article 1 of the Convention. This will be the object of Chapter 5, which explores the limits of what we will term Article 1 jurisdiction, and Chapter 6, which studies its actual exercise in situations of the use of 'hard power'.
- The third defence is that the matters complained of fall outside the competence of the European Court of Human Rights itself. This will be considered in Chapter 7.
- The fourth defence is that the matters complained of are not attributable to the Contracting Party but to some other State or entity if to anyone at all. This will be the focus of in Chapter 8.

All have been considered by the Commission and the Court at various times. Sometimes they have been argued by a respondent. Sometimes the Commission and Court have applied them of their own motion and declared applications inadmissible *de plano*. In the latter situation it is, strictly speaking, more appropriate to use the expression 'ground of inadmissibility' than 'defence';

but this distinction, which goes to the subtleties of Convention procedure, is not relevant to the purpose of this study.

Some 'defences' have been accepted by the Court in certain conditions; some have not. The interest of this study lies in the supposition that much has been said on these subjects but by no means all; that new problems will arise to which existing case-law may be applied; that the possibilities of presenting new positions have not yet been exhausted; and even, perhaps to the surprise of some, that the Convention itself actually has a role to play in furthering the very aims pursued by Contracting States in their use of 'hard power' – as a help, not a hindrance.

CHAPTER 2

# Problems of Substantive Convention Law in Relation to 'Hard Power'

## 2.1 Introduction

As mentioned, the most obvious defence available to a respondent is to persuade the Court that there is no substantive violation of the Convention at all. Let us therefore first examine the types of cases that experience shows are most liable to give rise to a finding of violation in our particular field of interest.

In times of normality, it is the police who exercise the State's monopoly on the use of force, not the military. On the whole, the Commission and the Court have developed the applicable jurisprudential standards on the basis of unspectacular cases: the kind of issues that can and will arise even in a society at peace – the arrest, questioning and detention of criminal suspects; the fairness and length of judicial proceedings; the enforcement of domestic decisions and judgments; conditions of detention in police stations and prisons; and so on.

Since the latter decades of the twentieth century, applications complaining about Government measures to combat terrorism and even armed insurgency have increased in absolute numbers (though not necessarily as a proportion of the Court's case-load). Previously, cases of this nature arose almost invariably from the actions of the United Kingdom, first in Cyprus (a British colony at the time) and later in Northern Ireland; but the United Kingdom has been joined by Turkey, which seeks to assert its sovereignty in the south-eastern parts of its territory, and Russia, whose central Government as we have seen is opposed by separatist forces in parts of the Northern Caucasus under its sovereignty.

More recently applications have reached Strasbourg arising from the exercise of 'hard power' in situations that cannot be seen in terms of terrorism or insurgency, to which the expression 'international armed conflict' is more appropriate. Events of such a nature have taken place in Iraq and Syria, in the former Yugoslavia, in Moldova, in the Caucasus, and on the island of Cyprus after it achieved statehood.

The challenge was, and is, to apply the substantive standards developed over the years to the use of 'hard power' in a way that neither diminishes the protection of the rights of the individual nor prevents Contracting States from acting effectively.

© KONINKLIJKE BRILL NV, LEIDEN, 2021 | DOI:10.1163/9789004425637_003

The case-law that has developed is extensive and detailed. Since the main focus of this work is elsewhere, we will confine ourselves to a selection of the most important cases that have arisen under substantive Convention law, concentrating on their relevance to the legal questions here in issue. We will revisit many of them later on.

## 2.2 Article 2, Right to Life

The use of lethal force by Government operatives, be they military or police, is covered by Article 2 of the Convention.[53]

### 2.2.1 *Substantive Obligations*

2.2.1.1    Active Deprivation of Life

It can happen that forces on the ground are faced with a situation in which they see no alternative to the use of force. The European Convention on Human Rights does not prevent the use of force in all circumstances: it makes express provision for the use of lethal force where such is absolutely necessary for law enforcement purposes.[54] On the whole the Court will try to avoid second-guessing the actions of the law enforcer on the spot as long as there is a proper regulatory framework in place, the planning and control of the operation are designed to avoid the use of lethal force, the actual decision to use force is reasonable and the force used is not disproportionate. This is apparent from *McCann and Others*, the case of the shooting dead in Gibraltar of Provisional IRA (Irish Republican Army – 'IRA') operatives by the British Special Air Service (SAS),[55] and confirmed by the multitude of judgments and decisions in which the Court has had to consider the use of lethal force by police. The Court is prepared to make allowances for mistakes made in good faith.[56] It is comparatively rare for the Court to find a violation on account of the actual use of force in a genuine violent confrontation unless there is evidence of bad faith or of serious deficiencies in planning and control.[57]

---

53    The second sentence of Article 2 § 1, which permits the execution of the death penalty, is now a dead letter (see Protocols 6 and 13 and 4.7.5 below).

54    Article 2 § 2 of the Convention.

55    *McCann and Others v. the United Kingdom* [GC], no. 18984/91, §§ 192-193, Series A no. 324.

56    See, for example, *McCann and Others*, § 200; *Bubbins v. the United Kingdom*, no. 50196/99, § 139, ECHR 2005-II; and *Giuliani and Gaggio v. Italy* [GC], no. 23458/02, §§ 178-179, ECHR 2011.

57    See, for example, *Ramsahai and Others v. the Netherlands* [GC], no. 52391/99, § 288, ECHR 2007-II; *Mulder-van Schalkwijk v. the Netherlands* (dec.), no. 26814/09, §§ 107-114, 7 June

The test, as required by the words 'absolutely necessary', is one of strict proportionality to the achievement of the aims set out in sub-paragraphs 2 (a), (b) and (c) of Article 2.[58] It is therefore required that there be an appropriate legal and administrative framework defining the limited circumstances in which law enforcement officials may use force and firearms, in the light of the relevant international standards. In line with the principle of strict proportionality, the national legal framework must make recourse to firearms dependent on a careful assessment of the situation. Furthermore, the national law regulating policing operations must secure a system of adequate and effective safeguards against arbitrariness and abuse of force and even against avoidable accident. The Court sees these requirements as part and parcel of the 'primary duty on the State to secure the right to life'.[59]

### 2.2.1.2 Positive Obligations

The Court has interpreted the first sentence of Article 2 § 1, which states simply that '[e]veryone's right to life shall be protected by law', to require the State not only to refrain from the intentional and unlawful taking of life, but also to take appropriate steps to safeguard the lives of those within its jurisdiction. The State's obligation in this respect involves putting in place effective criminal-law provisions to deter the commission of offences against the person backed up by law-enforcement machinery for the prevention, suppression and sanctioning of breaches of such provisions and may also imply in certain well-defined circumstances a positive obligation on the authorities to take preventive operational measures to protect an individual whose life is at risk from the criminal acts of another individual.[60] It cannot however be required that the State provide absolute safety: inevitably, there are operational choices to be made in terms of priorities and resources, and there is a trade-off in terms of due process and other guarantees which legitimately place restraints on the scope of police action to investigate crime and bring offenders to justice, including the guarantees contained in Articles 5 and 8 of the Convention. An applicant

---

2011; and *Finogenov and Others v. Russia*, nos. 18299/03 27311/03, §§ 226 and 235. For examples of violation, see *Nachova and Others v. Bulgaria* [GC], nos. 43577/98 and 43579/98, §§ 99-109, ECHR 2005-VII, and *Tagayeva and Others v. Russia*, nos. 26562/07, 14755/08, 49339/08, 49380/08, 51313/08, 21294/11 and 37096/11, §§ 540-611, 13 April 2017. See generally Clare Ovey, "Application of the ECHR during International Armed Conflicts", in *The UK and European Human Rights: A Strained Relationship?* (Katja S Ziegler, Elizabeth Wicks and Loveday Hodson, eds.), Hart Publishing, 2015, pp. 225-245 at pp. 233-237.

58 See *McCann and Others*, § 149; more recently and among many other examples, *Giuliani and Gaggio v. Italy* (GC), no. 23458/02, § 176, ECHR 2011.

59 *Giuliani and Gaggio*, § 209.

60 *Osman v. the United Kingdom* (GC), no. 23452/94, §§ 115-16, *Reports* 1998-VIII.

complaining of a lack of adequate protection must satisfy the Court that the authorities knew or ought to have known at the time of the existence of a real and immediate risk to the life of an identified individual or individuals from the criminal acts of a third party and that they failed to take measures within the scope of their powers which, judged reasonably, might have been expected to avoid that risk. This is a stricter test than one of 'gross negligence or wilful disregard' of the right to life.[61]

It has been rightly pointed out that while this positive obligation imposes a duty on the State to protect the public against possible terrorist acts, States are not allowed to combat international terrorism at all costs. They must not resort to methods which undermine the very values they seek to protect.[62]

### 2.2.2  *Procedural Obligations*

It does not end there. The obligation to protect the right to life under Article 2, read in conjunction with the State's general duty under Article 1 of the Convention to 'secure to everyone within their jurisdiction the rights and freedoms defined in [the] Convention', requires by implication that there should be some form of effective official investigation when individuals have been killed as a result of the use of force by, *inter alios*, agents of the State.[63] The State must therefore ensure, by all means at its disposal, an adequate response – judicial or otherwise – so that the legislative and administrative framework set up to protect the right to life is properly implemented and any breaches of that right are repressed and punished.[64] Moreover, where there has been a use of force by State agents, the investigation must also be effective in the sense that it is capable of leading to a determination of whether the force used was or was not justified in the circumstances. An effective enquiry is one that is:[65]

---

61    *Osman*, §§ 115-116.
62    *Saadi v. Italy* [GC], no. 37201/06, ECHR 2008, concurring opinion of Judge Myjer, joined by Judge Zagrebelski.
63    *McCann and Others*, § 161.
64    *Armani da Silva v. the United Kingdom* (GC), no. 5878/08, § 230, ECHR 2016.
65    Useful summaries are given in *Mustafa Tunç and Fecire Tunç v. Turkey*, no. 24014/05, §§ 171-182, 25 June 2013, and *Armani da Silva v. the United Kingdom* (GC), no. 5878/08, §§ 231-239, ECHR 2016. See generally D.J. Harris, M. O'Boyle, E.P. Bates and C.M. Buckley, *Harris, O'Boyle & Warbrick: Law of the European Convention on Human Rights*, 3rd edition Oxford University Press 2014, pp. 214-218; Clare Ovey, "Application of the ECHR during International Armed Conflicts", in *The UK and European Human Rights: A Strained Relationship?* (Katja S Ziegler, Elizabeth Wicks and Loveday Hodson, eds.), Hart Publishing, 2015, pp. 225-245 at pp. 237-239; and Bernadette Rainey, Elizabeth Wicks, and Clare Ovey, C., *Jacobs, White, and Ovey, The European Convention on Human Rights*, 7th edition Oxford University Press 2017, pp. 168-177.

22                                                                                                              CHAPTER 2

- adequate: that is, it must be capable of leading to the establishment of the facts and, where appropriate, the identification and punishment of those responsible. This means decent police work: all reasonable efforts must be made to collect the evidence needed, and the evidence must be properly assessed. In particular, the investigation's conclusions must be based on thorough, objective and impartial analysis of all relevant elements;
- independent: that is, from anyone implicated or likely to be implicated in the events. This means not only a lack of hierarchical or institutional connection but also a practical independence;
- accessible: that is, to the victim's family and to public scrutiny. This does not mean that the victim's family and the public should have access to the investigation file whenever they like, but it does mean that there should be a procedure for them to be properly informed and for their interests to be properly protected.

What is at stake here is nothing less than public confidence in the State's monopoly on the use of force.[66]

It should be added that the circumstances of the case may dictate an investigation into possible nefarious motives that may have led to the use of unnecessary or excessive force, racist sentiment for example.[67]

One writer, Olga Chernishova, reminds us that the procedural requirement of Article 2 should be placed against the background not merely of repression and prevention, but also against that of the right of surviving kin to know the truth about what happened to their loved ones.[68]

It is worth mentioning here that the Government of the United Kingdom has created an organisation, Iraq Historic Allegations Team (IHAT), to review allegations of abuse of Iraqi civilians by UK armed forces personnel in Iraq during the period of 2003 to July 2009. The alleged offences range from 'murder to low-level violence' from the start of the military campaign in Iraq, in March 2003, through the major combat operations of April 2003 and the following years spent maintaining security as part of the Multi-National Force and men-

---

66    *Ramsahai and Others*, § 325; *Armani da Silva*, § 232.

67    *Nachova*, § 164. For a critical appraisal of the Court's case-law on the distribution of the burden of proof in this case and similar ones see Jasmina Mačkić, "Het onzichtbare bewijzen: Over de mogelijkheden om de bewijslast te verschuiven van klager naar de verwerende staat in zaken van discriminatoir geweld voor het Europese Hof voor de Rechten van de Mens", *NTM/NJCM-bulletin* jrg. 42 [2017], nr. 4, pp. 477-494.

68    Olga Chernishova, "Right to the truth in the case-law of the European Court of Human Rights", in in *The Right to Life under Article 2 of the European Convention on Human Rights: Twenty Years of Legal Developments since McCann v. the United Kingdom (In honour of Michael O'Boyle)*, pp. 145-160.

# SUBSTANTIVE CONVENTION LAW IN RELATION TO 'HARD POWER'    23

toring and training Iraqi security forces. The Ministry of Defence funded the IHAT, 'consistent with its obligations to ensure that allegations were investigated in compliance with the European Convention of Human Rights'. Of the approximately 3,400 complaints received, some 1,400 have been or are being investigated.[69]

If an application is presented in Strasbourg, the Court usually avoids second-guessing the domestic investigating authorities. That said, experience shows that this is where in practice violations of Article 2 have proved to be the most likely.

Thus, in *al-Skeini and Others v. the United Kingdom*, the military police investigators reported to the commanding officer of the suspects instead of directly to the prosecutors. The criminal investigation was therefore not independent.[70] The case concerned a number of fatal shootings by British servicemen in Iraq.

In *Jaloud v. the Netherlands*, another case arising from a fatal shooting in Iraq (this time involving the Dutch Royal Army), it turned out that there were documents that had gone missing from the investigation file; the Dutch soldier suspected of having fired at least some of the fatal shots had not been kept separate from other witnesses (not that there was any appearance of collusion, but as a safety measure his separation would have been necessary); the autopsy had been carried out by an Iraqi doctor whose qualifications were unknown; the report of the autopsy was very flimsy indeed; and the bullet fragments taken from the body of the deceased had been allowed to disappear.[71] On the subject of the autopsy, the Court suggested that if the Dutch armed forces had not the facilities in Iraq then perhaps it ought to have been carried out by another of the Coalition powers.

It has been suggested that the standards resulting from *Jaloud* would not impose too onerous a burden on a peacekeeping force.[72] However, a minority

---

69    https://www.gov.uk/government/groups/iraq-historic-allegations-team-ihat (accessed 4 September 2018). See also the paper "De Britse reactie op claims van mensenrechtenschendingen door Britse militairen gedurende de militaire aanwezigheid in Irak: een analyse van het Iraq Historic Allegations Team" (The British reaction to claims of human rights violations by British military personnel during the military presence in Iraq: an analysis of the Iraq Historic Allegations Team), published by the Dutch Ministry of Defence, http://puc.overheid.nl/doc/PUC_88361_11 (accessed on 4 September 2018).

70    *Al-Skeini and Others v. the United Kingdom* [GC], no. 55721/07, §§ 172-174, ECHR 2011.

71    *Jaloud v. the Netherlands* (GC), no. 47708/08, §§ 203, 208, 211, 213-15 and 219, ECHR 2014.

72    Jane M. Rooney, "Extraterritorial derogation from the European Convention on Human Rights in the United Kingdom", E.H.R.L.R. 2016, 6, pp. 656-663, at pp. 657-58 and *passim*.

of the Grand Chamber thought the majority judgment too harsh on the merits, especially in relation to the autopsy.[73]

An example worth mentioning of compliance with investigative obligations under Article 2 is the case of *Mustafić-Mujić and Others*. The case concerned attempts by surviving kin of some of the victims of the Srebrenica massacre to have the leadership of the Dutch peacekeeping force prosecuted as alleged accomplices of the Bosnian Serb perpetrators. The Dutch court refused to order any prosecution, finding the facts to be such that convictions were highly unlikely to result.

In dismissing the applicants' complaints against this refusal, the Court found that it was 'not possible for the Court to find that the investigations [had been] ineffective or inadequate'. The information available included a report on the Srebrenica massacre by the Secretary General of the United Nations; several judgments of the International Tribunal for the Prosecution of Persons Responsible for Serious Violations of International Humanitarian Law Committed in the Territory of the Former Yugoslavia since 1991 (International Criminal Tribunal for the former Yugoslavia, 'ICTY') convicting Bosnian Serb accused; a report of debriefing of all returning Dutch military personnel who had lived through the events; a parliamentary enquiry; an extensive and detailed report by an independent domestic body, the NIOD Institute for War, Holocaust and Genocide Studies, running to thousands of pages; and evidence produced by the applicants themselves in parallel civil proceedings.[74] This decision illustrates that an investigation satisfying the procedural requirements of Article 2 does not have to be carried out under the sole responsibility of the authorities of the Convention Party concerned: it is acceptable to rely on information obtained by a competent international body. Nor does it have to be specifically criminal in nature, as long as it is independent and thorough and yields the necessary facts.

The mass murder at Srebrenica has aroused horror in many parts of the world, not least in the Netherlands owing precisely to the presence of Dutch peacekeeping troops. The existence of extensive and well-researched domestic material is therefore not surprising.

---

73    *Jaloud*, joint concurring opinion of Judges Casadevall, Berro-Lefèvre, Šikuta, Hirvelä, López Guerra, Sajó and Silvis.

74    *Mustafić-Mujić and Others v. the Netherlands* (dec.), no. 49037/15, §§ 103-06, 30 August 2016.

## 2.3 Article 3, Prohibition of Torture

### 2.3.1 *Substantive Obligations*

2.3.1.1 'Inhuman or Degrading Treatment' and 'Torture'

Article 3 of the Convention, which in the present redaction of the Convention bears the title 'prohibition of torture', in actual fact is wider in scope than that: it forbids torture or inhuman or degrading treatment or punishment. The Court's classical formulation, frequently repeated, is that any recourse to physical force which has not been made strictly necessary by the victim's own conduct diminishes human dignity and is in principle an infringement of the right set forth in Article 3 of the Convention.[75]

The fact that the victim is in possession of information that he or she refuses to disclose does not constitute 'conduct' justifying the use or threat of force. In *Gäfgen v. Germany* the Court reinforced the absolute nature of Article 3 to the point of finding that it prevented the use of torture even when human life was at stake.[76] The case was one in which police subjected a suspected kidnapper to treatment contrary to that provision in the sincere but mistaken belief that his victim, a young child, was still alive and forcing him to divulge the child's whereabouts might save the child's life. On occasion the Court has held that the use of a confession or a witness statement extracted under torture to ground a criminal conviction constitutes a violation of Article 6 of the Convention.[77]

The protection of Article 3 is equally absolute in expulsion cases. In *Chahal* the Court, invited by the Government of the United Kingdom to permit the handover of a suspected terrorist to India, held, although well aware of 'the immense difficulties faced by States in modern times in protecting their communities from terrorist violence', that the activities of the individual in question, 'however undesirable or dangerous', could 'not be a material consideration'.[78]

Physical violence does not exhaust the applicability of Article 3. Even in the absence of actual bodily injury or intense physical or mental suffering, where

---

75  See, among many other authorities, *Ribitsch v. Austria*, no. 18896/91, § 38, Series A no. 336; *Selmouni v. France* (GC), no. 25803/94, § 99, ECHR 1999-V; *El-Masri v. "the Former Yugoslav Republic of Macedonia"* (GC), no. 39630/09, § 207, ECHR 2012; and *Bouyid v. Belgium* (GC), no. 23380/09, § 88, ECHR 2015.

76  *Gäfgen v. Germany* (GC), no. 22978/05, § 107, ECHR 2010.

77  *Harutyunyan v. Armenia*, no. 36549/03, § 65, ECHR 2007-III; *Othman (Abu Qatada) v. the United Kingdom*, no. 8139/09, § 267, ECHR 2012.

78  *Chahal v. the United Kingdom* (GC), no. 22414/93, § 80, Reports 1996-V. For a detailed statement of the Court's approach to cases of this type, see *Othman (Abu Qatada) v. the United Kingdom*, no. 8139/09, §§ 183-89, ECHR 2012 (extracts).

treatment humiliates or debases an individual, showing a lack of respect for or diminishing his or her human dignity, or arouses feelings of fear, anguish or inferiority capable of breaking an individual's moral and physical resistance, it may be characterised as degrading and also fall within the prohibition set forth in Article 3. It may well suffice that the victim is humiliated in his own eyes, even if not in the eyes of others.[79]

In the context of this study, issues under Article 3 are most likely to arise in relation to the interrogation of captives, terrorist suspects or prisoners of war for example. Interrogation techniques found to have violated that provision have included the 'five techniques' used by the United Kingdom authorities in Northern Ireland in the 1970s, during a particularly troubled period: these were the use of stress positions, sensory deprivation, white noise, deprivation of sleep and deprivation of food and drink,[80] which were designed to keep the victim in a prolonged state of state of anguish and stress by means other than bodily assault.[81]

The distinction between actual torture and 'mere' inhuman or degrading treatment is stated by the Court as follows:

> In order to determine whether any particular form of ill-treatment should be classified as torture, the Court must have regard to the distinction drawn in Article 3 between this notion and that of inhuman or degrading treatment. This distinction would appear to have been embodied in the Convention to allow the special stigma of "torture" to attach only to deliberate inhuman treatment causing very serious and cruel suffering (see [*Aksoy v. Turkey*, no. 21987/93, § 62, Reports 1996-VI]). In addition to the severity of the treatment, there is a purposive element, as recognised in the United Nations Convention against Torture and Other Cruel, Inhuman or Degrading Treatment or Punishment, which came into force on 26 June 1987, which defines torture in terms of the intentional infliction of severe pain or suffering with the aim, *inter alia*, of obtaining information, inflicting punishment or intimidating (Article 1 of the United Nations Convention) (see *İlhan v. Turkey* [GC], no. 22277/93, § 85, ECHR

---

79    *Bouyid*, § 87.
80    *Ireland v. the United Kingdom*, judgment of 18 January 1971, §§ 96 and 167, Series A no. 25. Judgment of 20 March 2018, revision request dismissed; referral request dismissed on 10 September 2018.
81    *El-Masri*, § 202.

# SUBSTANTIVE CONVENTION LAW IN RELATION TO 'HARD POWER'

2000-VII; and [*El-Masri v. the Former Yugoslav Republic of Macedonia* [GC], no. 39630/09, § 197, ECHR 2012]).[82]

Acts found by the Court to have amounted to actual torture have included, among others, 'Palestinian hanging', the victim being stripped naked, with his arms tied together behind his back, and suspended by his arms;[83] rape;[84] severe beating and sodomy with an object;[85] and the use of 'enhanced interrogation techniques' by the American CIA including the now-infamous waterboarding.[86]

### 2.3.1.2 Positive Obligations

As in the case of Article 2, States are required to take measures designed to ensure that individuals within their jurisdiction are not subjected to torture or inhuman or degrading treatment or punishment, including ill-treatment administered by private individuals. Children and other vulnerable individuals, in particular, are entitled to State protection, in the form of effective deterrence.[87] The mere fact that a victim (or potential victim) withdraws a criminal complaint against the perpetrator does not relieve public authority of its duties to act effectively and prevent recurrence.[88]

### 2.3.2 *Procedural Obligations*

As in the case of Article 2, where an individual raises an arguable claim that he or she has been seriously ill-treated by the police or other such agents of the State unlawfully and in breach of Article 3, that provision, read in conjunction with the State's general duty under Article 1, requires by implication that there should be an effective official investigation. The principles are, to all intents

---

82 *Al Nashiri v. Poland*, no. 28761/11, § 56, 24 July 2014; *Husayn (Abu Zubaydah) v. Poland*, no. 7511/13, § 500, 24 July 2014.

83 *Aksoy v. Turkey*, no. 21987/93, § 64, Reports 1996-VI.

84 *Aydın v. Turkey*, no. 23178/94, § 86, Reports 1997-VI.

85 *El-Masri*, §§ 205 and 211.

86 *Al Nashiri v. Poland*, §§ 401 and 516; *Husayn (Abu Zubaydah) v. Poland*, §§ 416 and 511. On the CIA rendition programme as a violation of the *ius cogens* prohibition of torture, see generally Vincent Charles Keating, "The anti-torture norm and cooperation in the CIA black site programme", *The International Journal of Human Rights*, 2016, Vol. 20, No. 7, 935-955.

87 *Opuz v. Turkey*, no. 33401/02, § 159, ECHR 2009.

88 *Opuz*, § 168.

and purposes, the same as those governing the procedural aspect of Article 2 and need not be repeated.[89]

## 2.4 Article 5, Right to Liberty and Security

### 2.4.1 *Substantive Obligations*

#### 2.4.1.1 Deprivation of Liberty

Short of the use of force, it may be necessary to arrest and detain people. Arrest and detention are covered by Article 5 of the Convention, which guarantees the right to liberty and security of person. The first paragraph of the Article provides that no one may be deprived of their liberty save in accordance with a procedure prescribed by law, and on the grounds specified. It was for a long time held that the enumeration of permitted grounds of detention – which covers all conceivable cases in which detention may be used for purposes of law enforcement – was exhaustive;[90] however, since *Hassan v. the United Kingdom*, it would appear that an exception now exists for the detention of prisoners of war, in accordance with the Third Geneva Convention, and the detention of persons whose internment is necessary for imperative reasons of security, in accordance with the Fourth Geneva Convention, in the event of an international armed conflict.[91] We will consider this particular judgment in greater depth below, as part of our discussion of the interrelation of the Convention and international humanitarian law.[92]

The Court has developed a vast body of case-law under this Article, some of which is directly relevant to our subject.

For anyone arrested and detained, here should normally be access to family or some other support network. There should be supervision by a judge or a similarly qualified functionary who has the power to order release. *Habeas corpus* is basic to every civilised detention system, but supervision by a judge also helps to prevent, for example, torture. So does access to a doctor or a lawyer.

---

89 See, among other authorities, *Mocanu and Others v. Romania* (GC), nos. 10865/09, 45886/07 and 32431/08, §§ 314-325 and 2.2.1.2 above.

90 Among many other authorities, *Del Río Prada v. Spain* (GC), no. 42750/09, § 123, ECHR 2013.

91 *Hassan v. the United Kingdom* (GC), no. 29750/09, ECHR 2014; see also *Merabishvili v. Georgia* (GC), no. 72508/13, § 298, ECHR 2017 (extracts). The statement that the list of exceptions set out in Article 5 § 1 is an exhaustive one reappears, however, in *Mehmet Hasan Altan v. Turkey*, no. 13237/17, § 123, 20 March 2018, and *Şahin Alpay v. Turkey*, no. 16538/17, § 102, 20 March 2018.

92 See 3.4.2 below.

SUBSTANTIVE CONVENTION LAW IN RELATION TO 'HARD POWER'

Both were found lacking in *Aksoy v. Turkey*, the first case in fact in which the Court found that there had been torture as distinct from 'ordinary' inhuman or degrading treatment.[93]

The Court's judgment in *Ibrahim and Others v. the United Kingdom*, although it concerned a case decided under Article 6 not Article 5, strongly suggests that holding a detainee incommunicado – denying them contact with their support network and even legal advice – may be justified only in exceptional circumstances amounting to 'compelling reasons' and for the briefest of periods, and must be based on an individual assessment of the particular circumstances of the case. The existence of 'an urgent need to avert serious adverse consequences for life, liberty or physical integrity in a given case' could amount to 'compelling reasons'.[94]

The dangers of incommunicado detention are well illustrated by the *El-Masri* case, which we will examine in greater depth later. The applicant in that case was taken prisoner in the territory of the Former Yugoslav Republic of Macedonia and held in unacknowledged detention in a hotel room for three weeks of brutal questioning. He was then handed over to American CIA agents who whisked him off to Afghanistan for four more months of unsavoury treatment. Had not the country's Minister of the Interior of the day, who was later to become its Prime Minister, had the courage to break his silence, the Court would have had to rely entirely on the applicant's own statement backed up only by circumstantial evidence.[95]

Worse still, of course, is when people are arrested and then disappear without trace. *Kurt v. Turkey*[96] and *Bazorkina v. Russia*[97] are both cases in which the applicant was the mother of a young man last seen surrounded by soldiers.

In *Al-Jedda* the applicant was kept in internment by British forces in Iraq for three years. The United Kingdom Government tried to argue that they were duty bound under United Nations Security Council Resolution 1546 to exercise their power of detention where this was necessary for imperative reasons of security. The Court restated its own case-law according to which Article 5 of the Convention does not authorise preventive detention without charge (in

---

93 *Aksoy*, §§ 64 and 83-84.

94 *Ibrahim and Others v. the United Kingdom* (GC), nos. 50541/08, 50571/08, 50573/08 and 40351/09, §§ 258-259, ECHR 2016.

95 *El-Masri*, §§ 161-164. See also Helen Duffy and Stephen A. Kostas, "'Extraordinary Rendition': A Challenge for the Rule of Law", in *Counter-Terrorism: International Law and Practice* (Ana María de Frías, Katja L.H. Samuel, Nigel D. White, eds.), Oxford University Press, 2011, p. 539 at pp. 564-566.

96 *Kurt v. Turkey*, 25 May 1998, Reports 1998-III.

97 *Bazorkina v. Russia*, no. 69481/01, 27 July 2006.

fact, this is a rule stated by the Court in the very first case decided by it, back in 1961: *Lawless v. Ireland*).[98] It then took a close look at the Charter of the United Nations and Resolution 1546. According to the first Article of the Charter, the United Nations existed to maintain peace and security, but also to 'achieve international cooperation in … promoting and encouraging respect for human rights and for fundamental freedoms'. That being so, the Court found a presumption that the Security Council Resolution had to be interpreted so as to avoid conflict with obligations under human rights law. Since there was nothing in Resolution 1546 to suggest that the Security Council intended the United Kingdom to violate the European Convention on Human Rights or any other human rights document, it followed that there was no justification for failing to comply with Article 5.[99]

In *Hassan v. the United Kingdom* the Court was prepared to follow the argument of the respondent Party that in situations of international armed conflict the guarantees of Article 5 should be read in the light of the Third and Fourth Geneva Conventions. This takes us outside the safe enclosure of Convention law and into a minefield that we will enter warily.[100]

### 2.4.1.2 Positive Obligations

In *Storck v. Germany*, the Court held that Article 5 § 1, first sentence, of the Convention must be construed as laying down a positive obligation on the State to protect the liberty of its citizens. The case concerned the detention of a person in a private psychiatric clinic without a judicial decision and without her consent.[101] It goes without saying that this obligation applies all the more when the threat emanates from terrorists or other criminals.

As we will see, it also applies when the threat emanates from foreign governments and when the victims are foreign nationals, as in the CIA rendition cases.[102]

With the deradicalisation of jihadist fighters returning from the Middle East becoming a concern in some countries,[103] it is worth drawing attention briefly

---

98   *Lawless v. Ireland (no. 3)*, 1 July 1961, Series A no. 3.

99   *Al-Jedda v. the United Kingdom* [GC], no. 27021/08, §§ 99-110, ECHR 2011; see also 8.4.5.2.3 below. See also Clare Ovey, "Application of the ECHR during International Armed Conflicts", in *The UK and European Human Rights: A Strained Relationship?* (Katja S Ziegler, Elizabeth Wicks and Loveday Hodson, eds.), Hart Publishing, 2015, pp. 225-245 at pp. 240-241.

100  See 3.4.2 below.

101  *Storck v. Germany*, no. 61603/00, § 102, ECHR 2005-V.

102  See 6.3 below.

103  The United Kingdom, for example. *The Daily Telegraph*, 1 September 2014, "British jihadists to be forced to attend deradicalisation programmes, says Cameron", http://www.tel-

SUBSTANTIVE CONVENTION LAW IN RELATION TO 'HARD POWER'

to the judgment *Riera Blume and Others v. Spain*. The applicants in that case were believed to have been brainwashed by a religious or pseudo-religious sect; at the behest of their families and with the assistance of the police, they had been taken to a hotel where they had been held against their will for 'deprogramming'. The Court found that the applicants had been detained without any legal basis. Although direct responsibility lay with private actors (the applicants' families and a private association), Spain had violated Article 5 of the Convention by dint of the active support lent by its authorities.[104]

### 2.4.2   *Procedural Obligations*

Article 5 itself lays down procedural obligations. A right 'to take proceedings by which the lawfulness of [one's] detention shall be decided speedily by a court and [one's] release ordered if detention is not lawful' – often referred to by the mediaeval Latin phrase of English law *habeas corpus* – is to be found in Article 5 § 4.

The fifth paragraph of Article 5 provides that anyone arrested or detained in contravention of the provisions of Article 5 shall have an enforceable right to compensation.

## 2.5   Protection of Home and Property

Article 1 of Protocol No. 1 protects property rights. In the situations relevant to our study, complaints about violations of this provision frequently coincide with complaints under Article 8, right to respect for one's home, because they concern homes and real estate.

The Court has received many applications from Greek Cypriots turned out of their homes in Northern Cyprus.[105] There has also been an interstate case before the Court, in addition to three before the Commission, brought by the Cyprus Government against Turkey.[106] The Turkish Government has had to pay large amounts in compensation.[107]

---

egraph.co.uk/news/uknews/terrorism-in-the-uk/11068878/British-jihadists-to-be-forced-to-attend-deradicalisation-programmes-says-Cameron.html (accessed 26 August 2017)

104   *Riera Blume and Others v. Spain*, no. 37680/97, §§ 31-35, ECHR 1999-VII.

105   Among many others, *Loizidou* and *Xenides-Arestis*, note 5 above.

106   *Cyprus v. Turkey* (merits) (GC), no. 25781/94, ECHR 2001-IV.

107   For example, *Xenides-Arestis v. Turkey* (just satisfaction), no. 46347/99, §§ 42 and 48 and operative provision no. 1, 7 December 2006 (800,000 euros for pecuniary damage, 50,000 for non-pecuniary damage, plus costs and expenses); *Cyprus v. Turkey* (just satisfaction)

Other aspects of the Turkish occupation of Northern Cyprus include the isolation of the Karpas peninsula and its inhabitants. This too has resulted in awards totalling a considerable sum of money.[108]

The problems encountered by persons wishing to regain possession of homes from which they have been driven by military action are at the core of *Chiragov and Others* and *Sargsyan*. The cases are each other's mirror image: both arise from the conflict between Armenia and Azerbaijan over Nagorno-Karabakh, but Armenia is the respondent in the former and Azerbaijan in the latter. Substantive violations were found of both Article 8 of the Convention and Article 1 of Protocol No. 1.[109] The applicants' claims for restitution and compensation for damage were decided in separate judgments on what the Convention terms 'just satisfaction' (Article 41).[110]

Beyond the immediate scope of direct application of the Convention (and of the jurisdiction of the European Commission and Court of Human Rights) the importance of the rights guaranteed by Articles 8 of the Convention and 1 of Protocol No. 1, as they relate to housing, are well illustrated by the wars that raged in the former component republics of the Socialist Federative Republic of Yugoslavia between early 1992 and the end of 1995. Millions of people were driven from their homes – over 2.2 million persons in Bosnia and Herzegovina alone – by 'ethnic cleansing' or generalised violence. Most fled to areas controlled by their own ethnic group; their homes were quickly taken over by others who had been forced to flee from elsewhere.[111] After the end of the hostilities, most wished to return to their original homes.[112] Many who sought to return to their pre-war properties found them occupied by others who, displaced themselves, had nowhere to return to. Others, wishing to sell their original dwellings to finance a new home in a different location, were unable to because occupancy, and in many cases title, had been transferred to someone else while they were displaced. There followed a flurry of litigation that carried on until well after the various former Yugoslav republics had been

---

(GC), no. 25781/94, §§ 58 and operative provisions nos. 4 and 5, ECHR 2014 (a total of 90 million euros for non-pecuniary damage).

108   *Cyprus v. Turkey* (just satisfaction) [GC], no. 25781/94, § 58 and operative provision no. 5, ECHR 2014 (sixty million euros).

109   *Chiragov and Others v. Armenia* (GC), no. 13216/05, ECHR 2015; *Sargsyan v. Azerbaijan* (GC), no. 40167/06, ECHR 2015.

110   *Chiragov and Others v. Armenia (just satisfaction)* (GC), no. 13216/05, 12 December 2017; *Sargsyan v. Azerbaijan (just satisfaction)* (GC), no. 40167/06, 12 December 2017.

111   *Đokić v. Bosnia and Herzegovina*, no. 6518/04, § 7, 27 May 2010.

112   Commission for Real Property Claims of Displaced Persons and Refugees and United Nations High Commissioner for Refugees, *Return, Local Integration and Property Rights* (Sarajevo, November 1999), http://www.unhcr.org/3c3c42794.pdf (accessed 25 April 2017).

admitted to the Council of Europe and joined the Convention and continues even to the present day.[113]

The most thorough attempt to remedy this situation at the domestic level by encapsulating the standards of the Convention in domestic law was made in the armistice agreement that put an end to the war in Bosnia and Herzegovina, the Dayton Peace Agreement (or to give it its official title, the General Framework Agreement for Peace in Bosnia and Herzegovina), which entered into force on 14 December 1995. Annexed to it was an 'Agreement on Refugees and Displaced Persons' (Annex 7), which in the first paragraph of its first Article provided that

> All refugees and displaced persons have the right freely to return to their homes of origin. They shall have the right to have restored to them property of which they were; deprived in the course of hostilities since 1991 and to be compensated for any property that cannot be restored to them. The early return of refugees and displaced persons is an important objective of the settlement of the conflict in Bosnia and Herzegovina. The Parties confirm that they will accept the return of such persons who have left their territory, including those who have been accorded temporary protection by third countries.

The reality was that many were prevented shortly after the end of the war from making use of this right. The Commission for Real Property Claims of Displaced Persons and Refugees set up under Annex 7 could recognise title but not enforce it;[114] for that, other bodies had to be created. Most notable among these, for our purposes, were the Constitutional Court of Bosnia and Herzegovina, set up under the new Constitution (Annex 4 to the Dayton Peace Agreement)[115] and the Commission on Human Rights, consisting of an Ombudsperson and a Human Rights Chamber, set up under the Agreement on Human Rights, Annex 6.[116] We will address the functioning of these externally-imposed quasi-indigenous institutions later.[117] The remit of both the Constitutional Court and

---

113    See, for example, *Blečić v. Croatia* (GC), no. 59532/00, ECHR 2006-III; *Brezovec v. Croatia*, no. 13488/07, 29 March 2011; *Mago and Others v. Bosnia and Herzegovina*, nos. 12959/05, 11706/09, 19724/05, 47860/06, 8367/08 and 9872/09, 3 May 2012.

114    Antoine Buyse, *Post-Conflict Housing Restitution: The European human rights perspective, with a case study on Bosnia and Herzegovina* (diss. Leiden 2008), Intersentia, 2008, pp. 275-281; see also *Janković v. Bosnia and Herzegovina* (dec.), no. 5172/03, 16 May 2006.

115    Buyse (2008), pp. 281-284.

116    Buyse (2008), pp. 284-301.

117    See 8.5.5.2 below.

the Commission on Human Rights included the Convention and its Protocols as their primary source of substantive law,[118] which were thus fully applied for over six and a half years before Bosnia and Herzegovina became a party to the Convention on 12 July 2002.

The pattern is the same after all wars. When the fighting stops, ordinary people tend to want to resume normal life and leave quarrelling to the politicians. Their order of priorities is well described by Maslow's famous hierarchy of needs: once their immediate physiological needs are met, their next priorities are their homes and their livelihoods.

## 2.6 Article 13

As we mentioned right at the outset,[119] it is in the first place the responsibility of the Contracting States to secure the rights and freedoms defined in the Convention and its Protocols. It is therefore no surprise to find that Article 13 of the Convention provides that '[e]veryone whose rights and freedoms as set forth in [the] Convention are violated shall have an effective remedy before a national authority notwithstanding that the violation has been committed by persons acting in an official capacity'.

The existence of an actual violation has never been a prerequisite for the applicability of Article 13. It has long been recognised that 'a person cannot establish a "violation" before a national authority unless he is first able to lodge with such an authority a complaint to that effect'; rather, 'Article 13 requires that where an individual considers himself to have been prejudiced by a measure allegedly in breach of the Convention, he should have a remedy before a national authority in order both to have his claim decided and, if appropriate, to obtain redress'.[120] However, the Court does not interpret Article 13 so as to require a remedy in domestic law in respect of any supposed grievance under the Convention that an individual may have, no matter how unmeritorious his complaint may be: the grievance must be an arguable one in terms of the Convention.[121]

In many if not most cases of the actual exercise of 'hard power' it will be difficult for aggrieved individuals to prove their case without the assistance of an official inquiry of some sort. The significance of the procedural requirements

---

118  Article II (2) of Annex 4; Article I of Annex 6.

119  See 1.1 above.

120  *Klass and Others v. Germany*, no. 5029/71, § 64, Series A no. 28.

121  *Boyle and Rice v. the United Kingdom*, 27 April 1988, § 52, Series A no. 131.

of Articles 2 and 3, as outlined above, is therefore wider than merely to satisfy the need for a criminal remedy: it is also to enable use to be made of other remedies, such as a claim for compensation.[122]

## 2.7    The Problem of Proof

Regardless of the context of the case, it is standing case-law of the Court that parties must substantiate their factual arguments before it by providing the necessary evidence.[123]

In cases of the types here in issue it will often be difficult for the applicant to prove the facts underlying his complaint. The Court has accordingly developed evidentiary principles in its case-law under Articles 2, 3 and 5 of the Convention to the effect that, as summarised in *El-Masri*:

> In cases in which there are conflicting accounts of events, the Court is inevitably confronted when establishing the facts with the same difficulties as those faced by any first-instance court. It reiterates that, in assessing evidence, it has adopted the standard of proof "beyond reasonable doubt". However, it has never been its purpose to borrow the approach of the national legal systems that use that standard. Its role is not to rule on criminal guilt or civil liability but on Contracting States' responsibility under the Convention. The specificity of its task under Article 19 of the Convention – to ensure the observance by the Contracting States of their engagement to secure the fundamental rights enshrined in the Convention – conditions its approach to the issues of evidence and proof. In the proceedings before the Court, there are no procedural barriers to the admissibility of evidence or pre-determined formulae for its assessment. It adopts the conclusions that are, in its view, supported by the free evaluation of all evidence, including such inferences as may flow from the facts and the parties' submissions. According to its established case-law, proof may follow from the coexistence of sufficiently strong, clear and concordant inferences or of similar unrebutted presumptions of fact. Moreover, the level of persuasion necessary for reaching a particular conclusion and, in this connection, the distribution of the burden of proof,

---

122    *Taş v. Turkey*, no. 24396/94, § 93, 14 November 2000; *Aktaş v. Turkey*, no. 24351/94, §§ 329-333, ECHR 2003-V (extracts).

123    See, for example, *Lisnyy and Others v. Ukraine and Russia* (dec.), nos. 5355/15, 44913/15 and 50853/15, 5 July 2016.

are intrinsically linked to the specificity of the facts, the nature of the allegation made and the Convention right at stake. The Court is also attentive to the seriousness that attaches to a ruling that a Contracting State has violated fundamental rights (...).[124]

That said,

> where the events in issue lie within the exclusive knowledge of the authorities, as in the case of persons under their control in custody, strong presumptions of fact will arise in respect of injuries and death occurring during that detention. The burden of proof in such a case may be regarded as resting on the authorities to provide a satisfactory and convincing explanation. In the absence of such explanation, the Court can draw inferences which may be unfavourable for the Government.[125]

The *Jaloud* judgment illustrates the difficulties that may be involved in arguing on the facts that there is no substantive violation. We have seen that the failings in the autopsy proceedings were found by a majority of the Grand Chamber to have violated Article 2 under its procedural head. The Dutch Government had in fact submitted that the Dutch Royal Military Constabulary (*Koninklijke Marechaussee*, military police) had been compelled to entrust the body to the care of the Iraqi authorities, and it was they who had prevented any Dutch officials from attending the autopsy; in addition, Iraqi nationals in attendance had threatened to take Dutch personnel hostage, forcing them to leave.[126]

No finding that Royal Military Constabulary personnel were excluded from the autopsy and threatened with capture is to be found in the judgment. Brief statements to this effect appear in the Government's written memorial, unsupported by any official record or other evidence of any description; the applicant's counsel, speaking at the hearing, stated that the applicant and his family had been present but denied that any attempt was made to prevent the autopsy from going ahead.[127] As so often in judicial practice, the question was

---

124 *El-Masri*, § 151.

125 *El-Masri*, § 152; see also Helen Duffy and Stephen A. Kostas, "'Extraordinary Rendition': A Challenge for the Rule of Law", in *Counter-Terrorism: International Law and Practice* (Ana María de Frías, Katja L.H. Samuel, Nigel D. White, eds.), Oxford University Press 2011 p. 539 at p. 574.

126 Joint concurring opinion of Judges Casadevall, Berro-Lefèvre, Šikuta, Hirvelä, López Guerra, Sajó and Silvis, § 6.

127 Government's memorial, §§ 51 and 59; see also the webcast of the hearing, available on the Court's web site.

SUBSTANTIVE CONVENTION LAW IN RELATION TO 'HARD POWER'

who must shoulder the burden of proof:[128] while one can understand how the majority judgment might appear unreasonable to the serviceman whose duty it is to create a semblance of law and order in a plainly hostile environment,[129] in fairness to the majority it needs to be pointed out that like every other court of law in the world the Court must apply the law to established fact.[130]

## 2.8    Conclusion

Even in ordinary times, there is scope aplenty for any person wielding the powers of the State to violate the Convention rights of the individual. Such however is the nature of 'hard power' that its exercise only makes violations more likely. That said, even in situations of armed conflict, the serviceman on the ground remains no less duty bound than his political leaders to be aware of the human rights obligations of his State: any failure to comply with them is likely to engage the responsibility of the State which he serves.

It is possible, albeit within limits, for the State to adapt its liabilities under the Convention to the possibilities which it has to meet them. First, however, we must turn to the interrelation between the Convention and international humanitarian law in general.

---

128    Compare, for example, *D.H. and Others v. the Czech Republic* (GC), no. 57325/00, § 179, ECHR 2007-IV.

129    See, for example, Francoise J. Hampson, "Article 2 of the Convention and military operations during armed conflict", in *The Right to Life under Article 2 of the European Convention on Human Rights: Twenty Years of Legal Developments since McCann v. the United Kingdom (In honour of Michael O'Boyle)*, p. 191 at p. 207.

130    *Jaloud*, § 223.

CHAPTER 3

# Interplay between the Convention and International Humanitarian Law

## 3.1 Introduction

If one considers only the text itself of the Convention, the applicability of international humanitarian law passes through Article 15, where it refers to the Contracting State's 'other obligations under international law' – an expression that, as we will see in the following chapter, refers specifically to international humanitarian law inasmuch as Article 15 provides for derogation 'in time of war'.[131] For that reason, and even though Article 15 is not limited to 'war', we should at this point touch briefly on the way in which the Convention and international humanitarian law interact in general before turning to the narrower subject of derogation.

It should be noted at the outset that there is no equivalent reference to international humanitarian law in the International Covenant on Civil and Political Rights. This means, in our submission, that the interrelation between international humanitarian law and international human rights law is necessarily different if the question is considered under the Covenant rather than the Convention.[132]

We will first consider how this difference came to be. As we shall see, it was not an oversight on the part of one group of drafters as compared to the other: the two groups were working from very different premises.

We will then examine the interrelation between international humanitarian law and international human rights law as developed in case-law and doctrine.

---

131 See 4.3 below; see also Linos-Alexandre Sicilianos, "La Cour européenne des droits de l'homme et le droit international humanitaire : une ouverture progressive", in *Human Rights in a Global World: Essays in Honour of Judge Luis López Guerra* (Guido Raimondi, Iulia Motoc, Pere Pastor Vilanova, Carmen Morte Gómez, eds.; Wolf Legal Publishers, 2018), pp. 373-386 at p. 376.

132 The American Convention on Human Rights includes a derogation provision similar to Article 15 of the Convention. The African Charter on Human and People's Rights does not provide for derogation. To clarify our point, it is sufficient for present purposes to compare the Convention and the Covenant.

© KONINKLIJKE BRILL NV, LEIDEN, 2021 | DOI:10.1163/9789004425637_004

## 3.2 Drafting History

An interesting insight into the thinking of the drafters of the Convention is offered in the *travaux préparatoires* of the International Covenant on Civil and Political Rights. The Secretary General of the United Nations, in an annotation to the draft of that document published in 1955, differentiated between 'war' and 'instances of extraordinary peril or crisis, not in time of war', in which measures derogating from the rights guaranteed in normal times might be required.[133] It may be assumed that the drafters of the Covenant primarily had in mind the cataclysmic kind of conflict that wars on European or North American territory had been in modern times: the Napoleonic Wars, the American Civil War, the First and Second World Wars, and others. Eventually, as we know, Article 4 § 1 of the United Nations Covenant came to provide for derogation 'in time of public emergency which threatens the life of the nation and the existence of which is officially proclaimed'. It appears from the above-mentioned annotation of 1955, which reflects the drafting history of the Covenant, that its drafters were unwilling to envisage, even by implication, the possibility of war, that being a phenomenon which the United Nations was intended above all else to prevent.[134]

In stark contrast, the drafters of the Convention seem to have had no such inhibitions. In 1950 the memory of the Second World War, the bloodiest conflict in human history, was still fresh; in addition, many of them had seen active service in the First World War (René Cassin, for example, won the Croix de Guerre in the trenches in 1914). Presumably, therefore, they had fewer qualms about calling war by its ugly name and differentiating it from a mere 'public emergency'. It can accordingly be assumed that they intended derogation to be possible in the event of *any* war, since all major European wars in living memory – the Franco-Prussian war of 1870, the two world wars, indeed the Spanish Civil War – had constituted an existential threat to some nation or other.

---

133    *Travaux préparatoires* of the Convention, DH (56) 4, Annex I: Extract from the annotations on the draft International Covenants prepared by the United Nations Secretary-General (Doc. A/2929, pp. 65-69, at §§ 37 and 39).

134    Annotations on the draft International Covenants prepared by the United Nations Secretary-General (Doc. A/2929), § 39; Marko Milanovic, "Extraterritorial Derogations from Treaties in Armed Conflict", in *The Frontiers of Human Rights: Extraterritoriality and its Challenges, Collected Courses of the Academy of European Law*, vol. XXIV/1, p. 55-88 at p. 63. It has also been suggested that the Covenant's drafters believed that during armed conflict the Covenant should not apply at all: see Christian Tomuschat, "Human Rights and International Humanitarian Law", *EJIL* (2010), Vo. 21 No. 1 15-23 at p. 16.

In making provision for the eventuality of 'war', the drafters of the Convention were adopting a practical approach appropriate to the reality of warlike Europe. The drafters of the Covenant were engaged on a different, more idealistic quest: the Covenant was to be part of a global experiment under the umbrella of the Charter of the United Nations, which purported to ban war altogether.[135]

## 3.3 *Lex Specialis?*

### 3.3.1 *Is International Humanitarian Law* Lex Specialis *in Relation to Human Rights Law?*

When it is argued on the subject of the interplay between international human rights law and international humanitarian law that in relation to the former, the latter is the *lex specialis* applicable in situations of armed conflict, what is meant is probably that if in case of armed conflict international human rights law imposes greater restrictions on the State than international humanitarian law, then the burdensome constraints of human rights law should be left aside, defined as they are to fit a 'law enforcement paradigm', and the more broadly permissive provisions of humanitarian law should prevail.[136] That position has been defended by at least one Government before the Court, to wit, the United Kingdom Government in *Hassan*.[137]

A suggestion to this effect appears in a dissenting opinion attached to the Commission's report in the first *Cyprus v. Turkey* case;[138] but as we will see below,[139] a considerable majority of the Commission preferred the way of formal derogation.

The International Court of Justice famously held in its advisory opinion on the *Legality of the Threat or Use of Nuclear Weapons* that the protection of the International Covenant on Civil and Political Rights did not cease in time of

---

135   Charter of the United Nations, Preamble and Article 2 §§ 3 and 4.

136   Kirby Abbott, "A brief overview of legal interoperability challenges for NATO arising from the interrelationship between IHL and IHRL in light of the European Convention on Human Rights", *International Review of the Red Cross*, vol. 96, no. 893, pp. 107-37 at p. 115.

137   See 3.4.2 below.

138   *Cyprus v. Turkey*, nos. 6780/74 and 6950/75, Commission report of 10 July 1976, Dissenting opinion of Mr G. Sperduti, joined by Mr S. Trechsel, on Article 15 of the Convention (pp. 168-71); see also Jean-Paul Costa and Michael O'Boyle, "The European Court of Human Rights and International Humanitarian Law", in *The European Convention on Human Rights, a living instrument, Essays in Honour of Christos L. Rozakis* (Bruylant, 2011), p. 107 at p. 120.

139   See 4.10 below.

war, except in so far as particular provisions might be derogated from under Article 4 of the Covenant. Next noting that under the Covenant the right to life was non-derogable, it stated that the right not arbitrarily to be deprived of one's life applied also in hostilities. The test of what constituted an arbitrary deprivation of life then fell, however, to be determined

> by the applicable *lex specialis*, namely, the law applicable in armed conflict which [was] designed to regulate the conduct of hostilities.[140]

In its advisory opinion on the *Legal Consequences of the Construction of a Wall in the Occupied Palestinian Territory* it identified three different ways in which IHL and human rights law might interrelate:

> ... some rights may be exclusively matters of international humanitarian law; others may be exclusively matters of human rights law; yet others may be matters of both these branches of international law. In order to answer the question put to it, the Court will have to take into consideration both these branches of international law, namely human rights law and, as *lex specialis*, international humanitarian law.[141]

That begs the question precisely what it means that international humanitarian law is a *lex specialis* in relation to international human rights law. In *Armed Activities on the Territory of the Congo* the International Court of Justice quoted the above passage word for word, then went on to find Uganda internationally responsible for violations of both human rights instruments and international humanitarian law instruments concurrently – which is no answer.[142]

For all that the Latin in which the expression *lex specialis derogat legi generali* is cast suggests a venerable rule of Roman law, it is not. The origins of the adage have actually been traced to mediaeval canon law. Whether in contemporary legal practice it is a rule of conflict avoidance (a legal principle) or a rule of interpretation, and in either case, in what situation it is applicable is open

---

140  International Court of Justice, *Legality of the Threat or Use of Nuclear Weapons*, Advisory Opinion, I.C.J. Reports 1996, p. 226 at § 25.

141  *Legal Consequences of the Construction of a Wall in the Occupied Palestinian Territory*, Advisory Opinion, I.C.J. Reports 2004, p. 176 at § 106.

142  *Armed Activities on the Territory of the Congo (Democratic Republic of the Congo v. Uganda)*, Judgment, 19 December 2005, I.C.J. Reports 2005, pp. 242-45 at §§ 216-20.

to debate.[143] It is absent from any basic international legal text.[144] The Court has never resorted to it in relation to international humanitarian law, although applicant and respondent parties have sometimes invoked it.[145]

As a matter of logic, it must be so that the *lex specialis* properly governs a circumscribed part of the *lex generalis*. In any system of civil law, for example, the specific rules that govern the relationship between seller and purchaser, or between landlord and tenant, or between employer and employee, constitute *leges speciales* in relation to the general law of contract. This is also the way in which the Court has used the expression *lex specialis*, as when defining the relationship between Article 5 §§ 4 and 5 and Article 6 (under its criminal head) on the one hand and Article 13 on the other: there is a more precise definition of the right to an effective remedy in particular situations.[146]

There is no such relationship of specificity between the Convention, or any other system of international human rights law, and international humanitarian law.[147] It is not enough simply to point out that human rights law applies all the time, even in 'a context of armed conflict'[148] (subject to derogation in time of 'war or other public emergency threatening the life of the nation'),[149] whereas international humanitarian law is limited to cases of international or non-international armed conflict and is not needed in peacetime.

To begin with, the two were never conceived of as interrelated in the sense that one was a subdivision of the other. Rather, they were thought of as entirely separate from each other. International humanitarian law had its origins in general international law and developed as a subdivision of that, from the nineteenth century onwards if not much earlier; it imposed duties on states vis-

---

143  Vincent Correia, "L'adage *lex specialis derogat generali*: Réflexions générales sur sa nature, sa raison d'être et ses conditions d'application", https://www.academia.edu/25191057/L_adage_lex_specialis_derogat_generali_R%C3%A9flexions_g%C3%A9n%C3%A9rales_sur_sa_nature_sa_raison_d_%C3%AAtre_et_ses_conditions_d_application (accessed on 13 August 2018); Milanovic (2011/13), p. 250.

144  Unlike the basic *lex posterior derogat legi priori*: see Article 28 of the Vienna Convention on the Law of Treaties.

145  Including the Russian Federation in an interstate case brought by Georgia: see *Georgia v. Russia* (II) (dec.), no. 38263/08, § 69, 13 December 2011, and the United Kingdom in *Hassan* (see 3.4.2 below).

146  See, among many other examples, *A. and Others v. the United Kingdom* (GC), no. 3455/05, § 202, ECHR 2009 (Article 5 § 4); *Kolanis v. the United Kingdom*, no. 517/02, § 88, ECHR 2005-V (Article 5 §§ 4 and 5); Yankov v. *Bulgaria*, no. 39084/97, § 150, ECHR 2003-XII (extracts).

147  Milanovic (2011/13), p. 251.

148  *Al-Skeini*, § 164.

149  Article 15 of the Convention. Compare Article 4 of the International Covenant on Civil and Political Rights.

INTERPLAY BETWEEN THE CONVENTION AND IHL

à-vis each other (and later, in non-international armed conflicts, on non-state organised armed groups). In modern times, its guardian was the International Committee of the Red Cross – a non-political private organisation. In contrast, human rights law as we know it came into being only after the Second World War; it was intended from the very outset as a catalogue of rights enjoyed by the individual vis-à-vis the state simply by virtue of the fact of being human. Its guardians were the United Nations, an intensely political international inter-governmental organisation, and regional organisations such as the Council of Europe.[150] The two converged only gradually, starting in 1968 when the International Conference on Human Rights and later the General Assembly of the United Nations adopted resolutions on 'Human Rights in Armed Conflicts'.[151]

For another thing, the vexed question of jurisdiction is central to human rights law in that, to enjoy its protection, any potential victim must be within the 'jurisdiction' of the Contracting State concerned; conversely, the question of 'jurisdiction' does not arise in international humanitarian law, since the authority of the state over its armed forces is a given and its duty to ensure their compliance with the applicable standards exists without limitation in any international or non-international armed conflict.[152]

Accordingly, even though the basic aims of the two – at least in relation to armed conflict – are arguably the same, namely to attenuate the barbarism of war, the differences remain and they cannot coherently merge into a single body of law.

---

150 Louise Doswald-Beck and Silvain Vité, "International Humanitarian Law and Human Rights Law", *International Review of the Red Cross*, 30 April 1993, no. 293; Robert Kolb, "The relationship between international humanitarian law and human rights law: A brief history of the 1948 Universal Declaration of Human Rights and the 1949 Geneva Conventions", *International Review of the Red* Cross, September 1998, no. 324, pp. 409-419, *passim*; Cordula Droege, "Elective affinities? Human rights and humanitarian law", *International Review of the Red Cross*, September 2008, vol. 90, no. 871, pp. 501-547 at pp. 503-04; Cordula Droege and Louise Arimatsu, "The European Convention on Human Rights and international humanitarian law: Conference report", *Yearbook of International Humanitarian Law* volume 12 – 2009 – pp. 435-449 at pp. 436-438; Robert Kolb, "Human Rights and Humanitarian Law", *Max Planck Encyclopedia of Public International Law* (2012).

151 Human Rights in Armed Conflicts, Resolution XXIII adopted by the International Conference on Human Rights, Teheran, 12 May 1968; United Nations General Assembly, Resolution 2444 (XIII), Respect for Human Rights in Armed Conflict, 19 December 1968.

152 Article 3 of Hague Convention (IV) Respecting the Laws and Customs of War on Land; Common Article 1 of the 1949 Geneva Conventions (I)-(IV); Article 91 of the Additional Protocol (I) to the Geneva Conventions of 12 August 1949, and relating to the Protection of Victims of International Armed Conflicts (both taken alone and, in relation to non-international armed conflict, read in conjunction with common Article 3).

So, how then is international humanitarian law a *lex specialis* in relation to human rights law? Hampson, writing in 2008, suggests that the International Court of Justice meant to say, firstly, that where both international humanitarian law and human rights law applied, priority should be given to international humanitarian law, and secondly, a human rights body should in such cases make a finding based on international humanitarian law and expressed in the language of international human rights law.[153] That, however, raises as many problems as it solves, as Hampson also notes.

One way to understand this suggestion is in the sense that international humanitarian law should *displace* human rights law when the two are at variance. This cannot in all logic have been the International Court of Justice's intention, given its explicit ruling that human rights law continued to apply except in so far as derogated from.[154]

A second possibility might be that international humanitarian law would take precedence where it contained an express provision which addressed a similar field to that of a norm of human rights law. In practical terms, this might mean that the limitation clauses attached to certain rights – Articles 18 § 3; Article 19 § 3; Article 21, second sentence; Article 22 § 2 of the Covenant[155] – would be interpreted in the light of international humanitarian law governing the exercise of the rights concerned. Article 6 of the Covenant, for example, limits the right to life only in that it forbids 'arbitrary' killing and provides for the penalty of death; in an armed conflict properly so called, whether a killing was 'arbitrary' would depend on the interpretation of international humanitarian law.[156]

A third solution might be to let the applicability of international humanitarian law or international human rights law depend on the issue at stake. This might mean, however, that international human rights law – with its far more

---

153    Françoise Hampson, "The relationship between international humanitarian law and human rights law from the perspective of a human rights treaty body", *International Review of the Red Cross*, September 2008, vol. 90, no. 871, pp. 549-572 at p. 559.

154    Cordula Droege, "Elective affinities? Human rights and humanitarian law", *International Review of the Red Cross*, September 2008, vol. 90, no. 871, pp. 501-547 at p. 507; Françoise Hampson, "The relationship between international humanitarian law and human rights law from the perspective of a human rights treaty body", *International Review of the Red Cross*, September 2008, vol. 90, no. 871, pp. 549-572 at pp. 559-62.

155    The equivalent provisions of the Convention would be the 'paragraphs 2' of Articles 8, 9, 10 and 11 of the Convention, and the limitation clauses of certain rights defined in the Protocols.

156    Françoise Hampson, "The relationship between international humanitarian law and human rights law from the perspective of a human rights treaty body", *International Review of the Red Cross*, September 2008, vol. 90, no. 871, pp. 549-572 at p. 560.

detailed provisions on certain matters, such as fair trial guarantees – would add guarantees to international humanitarian law, in some cases turning international human rights law into a *lex specialis* in relation to international humanitarian law.[157]

True it is that the *lex specialis* relationship between international human rights law and international humanitarian law was originally developed by the International Court of Justice in the context of the right to life:

> The Court observes that the protection of the International Covenant on Civil and Political Rights does not cease in times of war, except by operation of Article 4 of the Covenant whereby certain provisions may be derogated from in a time of national emergency. Respect for the right to life is not, however, such a provision. In principle, the right not arbitrarily to be deprived of one's life applies also in hostilities. The test of what is an arbitrary deprivation of life, however, then falls to be determined by the applicable *lex specialis,* namely, the law applicable in armed conflict which is designed to regulate the conduct of hostilities. Thus whether a particular loss of life, through the use of a certain weapon in warfare, is to be considered an arbitrary deprivation of life contrary to Article 6 of the Covenant, can only be decided by reference to the law applicable in armed conflict and not deduced from the terms of the Covenant itself[158]

– the point being that the right to life is non-derogable, under Article 4 § 2 of the Covenant as under Article 15 § 2 of the Convention, but that unlike Article 15 § 2 of the Convention the Covenant does not make any exception for deaths resulting from 'lawful acts of war'.[159] Although, as mentioned, in the Palestinian Wall opinion the International Court of Justice broadened the scope of *lex*

---

157  Françoise Hampson, "The relationship between international humanitarian law and human rights law from the perspective of a human rights treaty body", *International Review of the Red Cross*, September 2008, vol. 90, no. 871, pp. 549-572 at pp. 561-62.

158  International Court of Justice, *Legality of the Threat or Use of Nuclear Weapons, Advisory Opinion*, I.C.J. Reports 1996, p. 226 at § 25.

159  On the interrelation generally between international humanitarian law and international human rights law, see Terry D. Gill, "Some Thoughts on the Relationship Between International Humanitarian Law and International Human Rights Law: A Plea for Mutual Respect and a Common-Sense Approach", in [2013] 16 *Yearbook of International Humanitarian Law* p. 251 ff., and Fortin, pp. 38-42.

*specialis* to include other rights, it has been suggested that the International Court of Justice has abandoned this approach since.[160]

### 3.3.2    *If Not* Lex Specialis, *Then What?*

It is very difficult to give a coherent theoretical answer to how international humanitarian law is a *lex specialis* in relation to human rights law; and in our submission, the inclusion of 'war' in Article 15 of the Convention makes it unnecessary for our purposes as long as Contracting States are prepared actually to make use of that Article.

In contrast, in terms of the Covenant, the problems raised by the dual applicability of the two regimes are insoluble: the absence of any provision for war in the Covenant, even a 'war' that would be lawful in *ius ad bellum* terms under the Charter of the United Nations, is an omission that has not only the International Court of Justice but also practitioners of military law tying themselves in knots. Attempts have been made, prompted by the difficulties inherent in the *lex specialis* approach, to develop theories of 'complementarity' and 'systematic integration';[161] the Human Rights Committee, for example, has stated that 'while, in respect of certain Covenant rights, more specific rules of international humanitarian law may be specially relevant for the purposes of the interpretation of Covenant rights, both spheres of law are complementary, not mutually exclusive'.[162]

The *Leuven Manual on the International Law Applicable to Peace Operations*, a practical work aimed primarily at civilian and military decision-makers and their advisers, puts it as follows:

> It suffices for the purposes of the present Manual therefore to note that, according to current legal interpretations, if a Peace Force becomes involved in an armed conflict, IHRL [international human rights law] and IHL [international humanitarian law] should be viewed as complementary bodies of law. In determining which particular rules of law will ap-

---

160    Tanja Fachataller, "Hassan v. United Kingdom and the Interplay Between International Humanitarian Law and Human Rights Law in the Jurisprudence of the European Court of Human Rights", EYIL 2016 p. 345 at p. 346, referring to International Court of Justice, *Armed Activities on the Territory of the Congo (Democratic Republic of the Congo v. Uganda)*, Judgment, I.C.J. Reports 2005, p. 168, § 216.

161    For a brief overview, see Vito Todeschini, 'The ICCPR in Armed Conflict: An Appraisal of the 'Human Rights Committee's Engagement with International Humanitarian Law', in *Nordic Journal of Human Rights* (2017) Vol. 35, Issue 3.

162    Human Rights Committee, General Comment No. 31, The Nature of the General Legal Obligation Imposed on States Parties to the Covenant, CCPR/C/21/Rev.1/Add.13, 26 May 2004, § 11.

ply to specific activities associated with the armed conflict, it should be recognised that some situations will call for the exclusive application of law of armed conflict rules, some will require the exclusive application of human rights norms, and some will be regulated by a combination of the two. In the latter case, it will need to be determined how IHL and IHRL rules interact when they both apply. In principle, the more specific rule will prevail (*lex specialis*) but there may also be cases where the more recent rule will prevail.[163]

Interestingly, the *Leuven Manual* uses the expression '*lex specialis*' to refer to 'the more specific rule' – which may be a rule of international human rights law – but again, this is not enough to guide us out of the quagmire.

Duffy, citing Murray (2016), evokes a form of 'weighted co-applicability' of the two fields of law in which the first question asked would be whether the conduct in issue falls within an 'armed hostilities' or a 'security operations' framework. The former would be 'primarily' guided by international humanitarian law, the latter primarily by international human rights law. In general, the closer to 'active hostilities', the greater the weight afforded to international humanitarian law; the further from them, the greater the emphasis given to international human rights law. However, as Duffy is careful to point out, while this approach is a well-intentioned attempt to avoid the blunt instrument that is the *lex specialis* approach described in the previous section, it may be no easy matter to situate the conduct in issue on the sliding scale between the two extremes; nor is it clear precisely how conflicts between permissions under international humanitarian law and duties under human rights law would be resolved.[164]

A solution was suggested, 'by way of bold assertion', by Hampson at an ICRC expert meeting in January 2012:

– Where IHL is applicable but a State denies its applicability and/or does not invoke it, a human rights body should confirm its applicability as a matter of law but state that the respondent State has chosen to be

---

163 *Leuven Manual on the International Law Applicable to Peace Operations* (Terry D. Gill, Dieter Fleck, William H. Boothby and Alfons Vanheusden, general eds; Marco Benatar and Remy Jorritsma, assistant eds.), Cambridge University Press 2017, pp. 89-90. Elsewhere, the Manual advises States to "consider derogations from human rights obligations to the extent that this is considered necessary to achieve the mandate." (p. 87; see also the following chapter).

164 Duffy (2018), pp. 63-64 and 86.

judged by a higher standard and should then apply human rights law, with the benefit of derogation if applicable;

– Where the victim was, at the time of death, in detention or in the physical control of State agents, a human rights body should apply human rights law. It can reinforce its analysis by reference to IHL;

– Where the killing occurred in the context of ordinary policing, even if against the background of an armed conflict, a human rights body should apply human rights law. When applying necessity and proportionality, the human rights body can take account of the context of conflict (not the same as applying IHL);

– Where the killing occurred in the context of a military operation but the intensity of the fighting is not such as to cross the threshold of applicability of Additional Protocol II, a human rights body should apply both human rights law and IHL prohibitions but not IHL permissions;

– Only where a killing occurs in a military operation in a non-international armed conflict which would satisfy the substantive conditions of applicability of Additional Protocol II should a human rights body only find a violation of human rights law if there is a violation of IHL;

– In the case of killings during military operations (i.e. not policing operations) during an international armed conflict, a human rights body should only find a violation of human rights law where there would be a violation of IHL.[165]

Such a formula might provide a practical way out in many if not most cases. The fact remains that the two bodies of law are not 'complementary' in the sense that they fit neatly together so that each covers gaps left by the other. They may clash, most inconveniently when core human rights such as the right to life and the right to liberty and security of person are in issue. When they do, the choice is either to apply international human rights law – which is notably stricter especially in relation to the right to life – or to choose the expedient solution and apply the generally more permissive standards of international humanitarian law. If the latter, then whatever the name given to it there is no other practical way to proceed than simply to allow international humanitarian law to override human rights law – perhaps least objectionably, in accordance with a 'rule of the road' such as that proposed by Hampson – and let the theory take care of itself.

---

165    Written statement by Françoise Hampson, in *The use of force in armed conflicts: interplay between the conduct of hostilities and law enforcement paradigms*, Expert meeting held in 2012, ICRC, November 2013, pp. 69-80 at p. 79.

## 3.4 Case-law of the Court

The Court itself has said relatively little about the interplay between Convention law and international humanitarian law.[166] That is only to be expected. The Court is a specialised jurisdictional body, whose task is '[t]o ensure the observance of the engagements undertaken by the High Contracting Parties in the Convention and the Protocols thereto'[167] and whose competence *ratione materiae* is limited to 'all matters concerning the interpretation and application of the Convention and the Protocols thereto'.[168] True, the Court has the power itself to decide the limits of its jurisdiction,[169] but that does not free the Court from the constraints imposed by its governing text which remains the Convention.

Depending on the demands of a particular case before it, the Court may *interpret* the Convention in the light of another body of international law.[170] Even then, the Court will be applying the Convention alone. It will not apply international humanitarian law directly.[171] This applies even where a Contract-

---

166  Larissa van den Herik and Helen Duffy, *Human Rights bodies and International Humanitarian Law: Common but Differentiated Approaches*, Grotius Centre Working Paper 2014/020-IHL, pp. 17-21. Writing before the delivery of the *Hassan* judgment, they describe the Court's approach to international humanitarian law as "myopic, or at least opaque".

167  Article 19 of the Convention.

168  Article 32 § 1 of the Convention. See also Evangelia Vasalou, "Les rapports normatifs entre le droit international humanitaire et la Convention européenne des droits de l'homme : Le droit international humanitaire, une lex specialis par rapport a la Convention européenne des droits de l'homme ?", *Revue trimestrielle des droits de l'homme* (112/2017), pp. 953-987 at p. 972 and Linos-Alexandre Sicilianos, "La Cour européenne des droits de l'homme et le droit international humanitaire : une ouverture progressive", in *Human Rights in a Global World: Essays in Honour of Judge Luis López Guerra* (Guido Raimondi, Iulia Motoc, Pere Pastor Vilanova, Carmen Morte Gómez, eds.; Wolf Legal Publishers, 2018), pp. 373-386 at p. 374-375.

169  Article 32 § 2 of the Convention.

170  For example, the law of the United Nations: see *Behrami and Behrami v. France and Saramati v. France, Germany and Norway* (dec.) (GC), nos. 71412/01 and 78166/01, 2 May 2007; or the law of the sea: see *Hirsi Jamaa and Others v. Italy* [GC], no. 27765/09, ECHR 2012; or the law of State immunity: see, for example, *Al-Adsani v. the United Kingdom* (GC), no. 35763/97, ECHR 2001-XI, and *Jones and Others v. the United Kingdom* (GC), nos. 34356/06 and 40528/06, ECHR 2014.

171  Evangelia Vasalou, "Les rapports normatifs entre le droit international humanitaire et la Convention européenne des droits de l'homme : Le droit international humanitaire, une lex specialis par rapport a la Convention européenne des droits de l'homme ?", *Revue trimestrielle des droits de l'homme* (112/2017), pp. 953-987 at p. 965; Linos-Alexandre Sicilianos, "La Cour européenne des droits de l'homme et le droit international humanitaire : une ouverture progressive", in *Human Rights in a Global World: Essays in Honour of Judge*

50                                                                                                CHAPTER 3

ing State makes use of Article 15 and derogates in response to a situation that can reasonably be described as an 'armed conflict', be it international or non-international.

Only on a few occasions has the Court resorted to international humanitarian law actually to interpret the Convention.

### 3.4.1   *Article 2*

Although the exceptions provided for by Article 2 are written for a law enforcement paradigm rather than an armed conflict paradigm,[172] the Court has, in *Varnava and Others*, made it clear that international humanitarian law has its role to play:

> Article 2 must be interpreted in so far as possible in light of the general principles of international law, including the rules of international humanitarian law which play an indispensable and universally accepted role in mitigating the savagery and inhumanity of armed conflict (see [*Loizidou v. Turkey (merits*), § 43, *Reports* 1996-VI]). The Court therefore concurs with the reasoning of the Chamber in holding that in a zone of international conflict Contracting States are under obligation to protect the lives of those not, or no longer, engaged in hostilities. This would also extend to the provision of medical assistance to the wounded; where combatants have died, or succumbed to wounds, the need for accountability would necessitate proper disposal of remains and require the authorities to collect and provide information about the identity and fate of those concerned, or permit bodies such as the ICRC to do so.'[173]

–      quite regardless of whether or not Article 15 has been invoked. As Sicilianos points out, this is a situation in which Convention law and IHL converge.[174]

---

*Luis López Guerra* (Guido Raimondi, Iulia Motoc, Pere Pastor Vilanova, Carmen Morte Gómez, eds.; Wolf Legal Publishers, 2018), pp. 373-386 at p. 377.

172    Françoise Hampson, "The relationship between international humanitarian law and human rights law from the perspective of a human rights treaty body", *International Review of the Red Cross*, September 2008, vol. 90, no. 871, pp. 549-572 at p. 564.

173    *Varnava and Others v. Turkey* (GC), nos. 16064/90, 16065/90, 16066/90, 16068/90, 16069/90 16070/90, 16071/90, 16072/90 and 16073/90, § 185, ECHR 2009 (with a footnote referring, for an understanding of 'international humanitarian law', to the four Geneva Conventions of 1949 and their three Protocols); see also *Georgia v. Russia* (II) (dec.), no. 38263/08, § 72, 13 December 2011.

174    Linos-Alexandre Sicilianos, "La Cour européenne des droits de l'homme et le droit international humanitaire : une ouverture progressive", in *Human Rights in a Global World:*

INTERPLAY BETWEEN THE CONVENTION AND IHL 51

This, incidentally, is not a finding that international humanitarian law reduces or limits the guarantees offered by the Convention. Rather, it specifies and refines the modalities of the exercise, in situations of international armed conflict, of certain duties that Article 2 imposes on Contracting States. That said, the Court has shown itself willing on occasion to take account of the practical difficulties that may be encountered in a post-conflict situation, as in *Palić v. Bosnia and Herzegovina*.[175]

### 3.4.2 *Article 5*

In one case thus far, *Hassan v. the United Kingdom*, has the Court given a radically novel interpretation of the Convention in the light of international humanitarian law with the practical effect of limiting the protection offered by the Convention.

The case derives from the arrest and detention, by United Kingdom forces in Iraq, of the brother of a high-ranking Ba'ath party member in circumstances that ordinarily would presumably have engaged the responsibility of the United Kingdom under Article 5. As we will see when we come to discuss the issue of 'jurisdiction', the Court found the United Kingdom to have had jurisdiction (in the sense of Article 1) by virtue of the actual detention – the 'physical power and control' exercised over the victim, that is to say, 'State agent authority and control'.[176]

The United Kingdom Government argued that '[w]here provisions of the Convention fell to be applied in the context of an international armed conflict, and in particular the active phase of such a conflict, the application had to take account of international humanitarian law, which applied as the *lex specialis*, and might operate to modify *or even displace* [emphasis added] a given provision of the Convention'. It could not be, and it was not so, that a Contracting State, when its armed forces were engaged in active hostilities in an armed conflict outside its own territory, had to afford the procedural safeguards of Article 5 to enemy combatants whom it took as prisoners of war, or suspected enemy combatants whom it detained pending determination of whether they were entitled to such status, nor to civilians whose detention was 'absolutely necessary' for security reasons, in accordance with Article 42 of the Fourth Geneva Convention. In the alternative, if the Court were to find that Article 5

---

     *Essays in Honour of Judge Luis López Guerra* (Guido Raimondi, Iulia Motoc, Pere Pastor Vilanova, Carmen Morte Gómez, eds.; Wolf Legal Publishers, 2018), pp. 373-386 at p. 377.

175   *Palić v. Bosnia and Herzegovina*, no. 4704/04, 15 February 2011, judgment and joint partly dissenting opinion of Judges Bratza and Vehabović. The case did not concern the application of international humanitarian law.

176   *Hassan*, § 76.

applied and was not displaced or modified in situations of armed conflict, the Government submitted that the list in Article 5 § 1 of permissible purposes of detention had to be interpreted in such a way that it took account of and was compatible with the applicable *lex specialis*, namely international humanitarian law. The taking of prisoners of war pursuant to the Third Geneva Convention, and the detention of civilians pursuant to the Fourth Geneva Convention, had to be a lawful category of detention under Article 5 § 1; it fell most readily as a 'lawful detention' within Article 5 § 1 (c). In this special context, the concept of 'offence' within that provision could correctly be interpreted to include participation as an enemy combatant and/or challenging the security of the Detaining Power within Article 42 of the Fourth Geneva Convention. On this premise, the United Kingdom Government argued that there had been no need for the United Kingdom to derogate under Article 15. The inclusion of Article 15 in the Convention 'in no sense indicated that, in time of war or public emergency threatening the life of the nation, obligations under the Convention would at all times be interpreted in exactly the same way as in peacetime'.[177]

The Court did not find that 'detention under the powers provided for in the Third and Fourth Geneva Conventions [was] congruent with any of the categories set out in subparagraphs (a) to (f)'. Article 5 § 1 (c), relied on by the Government, was inapposite already because 'there [did] not need to be any correlation between security internment and suspicion of having committed an offence or risk of the commission of a criminal offence'; with particular regard to enemy combatants, the Court pointed out that they committed no crime by taking part in hostilities.[178]

The Court took as its starting point Article 31 § 3 of the Vienna Convention on the Law of Treaties, according to which there shall, in interpreting treaties, be taken into account ('together with the context') '[a]ny subsequent practice in the application of the treaty which establishes the agreement of the parties regarding its interpretation' (sub-paragraph (b)), and '[a]ny relevant rules of international law applicable in the relations between the parties' (sub-paragraph (c)).[179] It then noted that while there had been a number of military missions involving Contracting States acting extra-territorially after ratifying the Convention, the practice of the States Party to the Convention was 'not to derogate [under Article 15] from their obligations under Article 5 in order to detain persons on the basis of the Third and Fourth Geneva Conventions during international armed conflicts'. This practice was mirrored by State practice

---

177    *Hassan*, §§ 87-90.
178    *Hassan*, § 97.
179    *Hassan*, § 100.

INTERPLAY BETWEEN THE CONVENTION AND IHL 53

under the International Covenant on Civil and Political Rights: in the Court's words,

> [a]lthough many States have interned persons pursuant to powers under the Third and Fourth Geneva Conventions in the context of international armed conflicts subsequent to ratifying the Covenant, no State has explicitly derogated under Article 4 of the Covenant in respect of such detention (see paragraph 42 above), even subsequent to the advisory opinions and judgment referred to above, where the International Court of Justice made it clear that States' obligations under the international human rights instruments to which they were parties continued to apply in situations of international armed conflict'[180]

The Court then reiterated that 'the Convention must be interpreted in harmony with other rules of international law of which it forms part' – including international humanitarian law. Having held in *Varnava and Others* that Article 2 should 'be interpreted in so far as possible in light of the general principles of international law, including the rules of international humanitarian law which play an indispensable and universally-accepted role in mitigating the savagery and inhumanity of armed conflict',[181] it then considered that 'these observations apply equally in relation to Article 5'. Referring to case-law of the International Court of Justice, according to which 'some rights [might] be exclusively matters of international humanitarian law; others [might] be exclusively matters of human rights law; yet others [might] be matters of both these branches of international law', it concluded that it 'must endeavour to interpret and apply the Convention in a manner which is consistent with the framework under international law delineated by the International Court of Justice'.[182]

The Court was thus led to accept the Government's argument that the lack of a formal derogation under Article 15 did not prevent the Court from taking account of the context and the provisions of international humanitarian law when interpreting and applying Article 5 in this particular case.[183] It continued:

---

180    *Hassan*, § 101.

181    *Varnava and Others*, § 185.

182    *Hassan*, § 102, referring to International Court of Justice, *Armed Activities on the Territory of the Congo* (*Democratic Republic of the Congo v. Uganda*), Judgment, I.C.J. Reports 2005, p. 168, § 216.

183    *Hassan*, § 103.

Nonetheless, and consistently with the case-law of the International Court of Justice, the Court considers that, even in situations of international armed conflict, the safeguards under the Convention continue to apply, albeit interpreted against the background of the provisions of international humanitarian law. By reason of the co-existence of the safeguards provided by international humanitarian law and by the Convention in time of armed conflict, the grounds of permitted deprivation of liberty set out in subparagraphs (a) to (f) of that provision should be accommodated, as far as possible, with the taking of prisoners of war and the detention of civilians who pose a risk to security under the Third and Fourth Geneva Conventions. The Court is mindful of the fact that internment in peacetime does not fall within the scheme of deprivation of liberty governed by Article 5 of the Convention without the exercise of the power of derogation under Article 15 (...). *It can only be in cases of international armed conflict, where the taking of prisoners of war and the detention of civilians who pose a threat to security are accepted features of international humanitarian law, that Article 5 could be interpreted as permitting the exercise of such broad powers.*[184] (emphasis added).

Taking the view that 'the detention must comply with the rules of international humanitarian law and, most importantly, that it should be in keeping with the fundamental purpose of Article 5 § 1, which is to protect the individual from arbitrariness', the Court was satisfied that the procedural guarantees available under the Third and Fourth Geneva Conventions sufficed for purposes of Article 5 §§ 2 and 4.[185]

However, the court added a caveat:

Finally, although, for the reasons explained above, the Court does not consider it necessary for a formal derogation to be lodged, *the provisions of Article 5 will be interpreted and applied in the light of the relevant provisions of international humanitarian law only where this is specifically pleaded by the respondent State.* It is not for the Court to assume that a State intends to modify the commitments which it has undertaken by ratifying the Convention in the absence of a clear indication to that effect.[186] (emphasis added)

---

184    *Hassan*, § 104.
185    *Hassan*, §§ 105-106.
186    *Hassan*, § 107.

This in effect allows States to choose *post factum* the legal standard by which they wish to be judged: the more permissive one of Article 5 of the Convention in the light of international humanitarian law or the stricter one of Article 5 in its classical interpretation.

For extensively-reasoned criticism of the *Hassan* judgment one need look no further than the powerful dissent of Judge Robert Spano, which is joined by Judges Nicolaou, Bianku and Kalaydjieva.[187]

Spano starts by pointing out the scope of the powers granted the Detaining Power under the Third and Fourth Geneva Conventions. Once the status of prisoners of war has been determined in accordance with Article 5 of the Third Geneva Convention, they can be detained under the Third Geneva Convention for the duration of hostilities without any review of their detention. Civilians detained (or assigned to a particular residence) for security purposes under the Fourth Geneva Convention are entitled to twice-yearly review, it is true, but the sole test is the security of the Detaining Power (Articles 42 and 78 of the Fourth Geneva Convention) and detention can be prolonged indefinitely. This Spano finds impossible to subsume under any of the exceptions provided for by Article 5 § 1 (a)-(f) of the Convention. Next, he adds that this 'novel understanding of the exhaustive grounds of detention under Article 5 § 1' cannot be confined to acts on the territory of States not Parties to the Convention in circumstances in which a Contracting State exercises jurisdiction under Article 1, but must, 'conceptually and in principle', also apply in an international armed conflict taking place *within* the Convention's legal space – including in an international armed conflict between two Contracting Parties. In such a situation, effectively, the belligerents would have the right to detain persons indefinitely without going through the 'openly transparent and arduous process of lodging a derogation from Article 5 § 1, the scope and legality of which is then subject to review by the domestic courts, and if necessary, by this Court under Article 15.'

Spano continues:

> 8. The Convention applies equally in both peacetime and wartime. *That is the whole point of the mechanism of derogation provided by Article 15 of the Convention.* There would have been no reason to include this structural feature if, when war rages, the Convention's fundamental guarantees automatically became silent or were displaced in substance, by granting the Member States additional and unwritten grounds for limiting fun-

---

187  *Hassan*, partly dissenting opinion of Judge Spano, joined by Judges Nicolaou, Bianku and Kalaydjieva.

damental rights based solely on other applicable norms of international law. Nothing in the wording of that provision, when taking its purpose into account, excludes its application when the Member States engage in armed conflict, either within the Convention's legal space or on the territory of a State not Party to the Convention. The extra-jurisdictional reach of the Convention under Article 1 must necessarily go hand in hand with the scope of Article 15 (see *Banković and Others v. Belgium and Others* [GC], no. 52207/99, § 62, 12 December 2001).

9. It follows that if the United Kingdom considered it likely that it would be "required by the exigencies of the situation" during the invasion of Iraq to detain prisoners of war or civilians posing a threat to security under the rules of the Third and Fourth Geneva Conventions, *a derogation under Article 15 was the only legally available mechanism for that State to apply the rules on internment under international humanitarian law without the Member State violating Article 5 § 1 of the Convention.* It bears reiterating that a derogation under Article 15 will not be considered lawful under the first paragraph of that provision if the measures implemented by the Member State are "inconsistent with its other obligations under international law". In reviewing the legality of a declaration lodged by a Member State to the Convention within the context of an international armed conflict, the domestic courts, and, if need be, this Court, must thus examine whether the measures in question are in conformity with the State's obligations under international humanitarian law. (emphasis added)

Spano dismisses the argument based on State practice subsequent to ratification of the Convention. In the first place, he argues that the practice of not lodging notices of derogation has hitherto been predicated on the fundamental assumption that Article 1 jurisdiction cannot arise in extra-territorial situations – an assumption that has been shown to be incorrect in a series of judgments including *Al-Skeini, Al-Saadoon and Mufdhi* and *Medvedyev and Others*. Secondly, the said practice is not 'common to all Parties', nor is it 'concordant, common and consistent'. More importantly in his view, he identifies a fundamental distinction between 'on the one hand, ... a State practice clearly manifesting a concordant, common and consistent will of the Member States to collectively modify the fundamental rights enshrined in the Convention, towards a *more expansive or generous understanding of their scope than originally envisaged,* and, on the other, a State practice that *limits or restricts those rights,* as in the present case, in direct contravention of an exhaustive and narrowly tailored limitation clause of the Convention protecting a fundamental right.' In the third place, derogation from Article 5 of the Convention is fundamentally different from derogation from Article 9 of the International Covenant on Civil and Political Rights in application of its Article 4: Article 9 of the Covenant does not, like Article 5 of the Convention, set out an *exhaustive* list of *permitted* grounds of detention, but only sets out a general prohibition of 'arbitrary arrest or detention'.

Spano dismisses the possibility of applying international human rights law and international humanitarian law on an equal footing, arguing that they 'exhibit quite extensive differences both methodologically and structurally'. Although the positive obligation under Article 2 to protect life is 'flexible enough to take account of the relevant rules of international humanitarian law so as to create a more robust and coherent regime of protection under the Convention', international humanitarian law does not provide safeguards comparable to those set out in Article 5 § 1: 'On the contrary, indefinite and preventive internment in wartime flatly contradicts the very nature of the grounds found in sub-paragraphs (a) to (f) ...'.

The method chosen to 'accommodate' the grounds of detention permitted by Article 5 § 1 with the powers of internment under international humanitarian law, while intended to avoid 'disapplying' Article 5 in the absence of a valid derogation under Article 15, is in Spano's assessment a novelty in the Court's case-law and an undesirable one at that. Not only does it create uncertainty as to the interpretation of Article 5 § 1, but its effect actually is to disapply or displace the fundamental safeguards underlying that Convention provision.

Spano concludes:

> 19. In conclusion, on the facts of this case, the powers of internment under the Third and Fourth Geneva Conventions, relied on by the Government as a permitted ground for the capture and detention of Tarek Hassan, are in direct conflict with Article 5 § 1 of the Convention. The Court does not have any legitimate tools at its disposal, as a *court of law*, to remedy this clash of norms. It must therefore give priority to the Convention, as its role is limited under Article 19 to "[ensuring] the observance of the engagements undertaken by the High Contracting Parties in the Convention and the Protocols thereto". By attempting to *reconcile the irreconcilable*, the majority's finding today does not, with respect, reflect an accurate understanding of the scope and substance of the fundamental right to liberty under the Convention, as reflected in its purpose and its historical origins in the atrocities of the international armed conflicts of the Second World War.

With a few exceptions,[188] the reception given to the Hassan judgment by commentators has, on the whole, been lukewarm at best. Most note, with thinly-disguised disapproval, the audacity of the United Kingdom in suggesting that the Court disapply Article 5 of the Convention altogether – a first in the history of the Court – and express satisfaction at the Court's dismissal of it.

Some congratulate the Court for not holding international humanitarian law to displace human rights law as *lex specialis* in cases of armed conflict.[189] One, Cedric De Koker, offers limited defence to the judgment for coming up with a 'nuanced, well-balanced solution to an old and heavily disputed issue' – the interrelation between human rights law and international humanitarian law.[190] A similar view is expressed by Linos-Alexandre Sicilianos, who recognises that the Court has reduced the standard of protection offered by the Convention for reasons of expediency:

> On notera que – tout comme la CIJ dans l'*Affaire des activités armées sur le territoire du Congo* – la Cour évite de se référer au DIH en tant que *lex specialis*, les ambiguïtés de ce terme n'échappant à personne. Elle préfère procéder à une application simultanée de la Convention et du droit humanitaire. Elle s'assure que l'objectif primordial de l'article 5 de la Convention est atteint. Elle exige également que l'Etat défendeur invoque explicitement le DIH. En même temps, la Cour fait preuve de pragmatisme en acceptant de baisser quelque peu le standard de protection prévue par la Convention pour tenir compte de la situation qui prévaut dans le contexte d'un conflit armé international.[191]

---

188    Sir Daniel Bethlehem, "When is an act of war lawful?", in *The Right to Life under Article 2 of the European Convention on Human Rights: Twenty Years of Legal Developments since McCann v. the United Kingdom (In honour of Michael O'Boyle)*, p. 231, *passim*.

189    Marko Milanovic, "A Few Thoughts on Hassan v. United Kingdom", *Ejil:talk!* 22 October 2014; Cedric De Koker, "Hassan v United Kingdom: The Interaction of Human Rights Law and International Humanitarian Law with regard to the Deprivation of Liberty in Armed Conflicts", *Utrecht Journal of International and European Law*, http://www.utrechtjournal. org/article/10.5334/ujiel.db/.

190    Cedric De Koker, *ibid.*

191    Linos-Alexandre Sicilianos, "La Cour européenne des droits de l'homme et le droit international humanitaire : une ouverture progressive", in *Human Rights in a Global World: Essays in Honour of Judge Luis López Guerra* (Guido Raimondi, Iulia Motoc, Pere Pastor Vilanova, Carmen Morte Gómez, eds.; Wolf Legal Publishers, 2018), pp. 373-386 at p. 86. A judge of the Court as well as an academic, Linos-Alexandre Sicilianos was not a member of the Grand Chamber that delivered the *Hassan* judgment.

Criticism, however, predominates in academic circles. Philip Czech states that '[t]he Court's modification of the obligations under the ECHR through state practice amounts to allowing member states to lower the standards of human rights protection through simply disobeying them' and describes the judgment as a whole as 'an attempt to avoid a norm conflict at any price'.[192] Silvia Borelli calls the *Hassan* solution 'no more and no less than an exercise in *contra legem* interpretation'.[193] Dario Rossi d'Ambrosio is of the opinion that 'the right to liberty has suffered a severe blow in the context of IACs [international armed conflicts]'.[194] Beatrice Pastre-Belda considers that 'Bien que limitant cette interprétation de l'article 5 aux « cas de conflit armé international » (...), la Cour offre malgré tout aux Etats la possibilité de contourner le mécanisme de dérogation en temps de crise spécialement prévu à l'article 15, § 1, de la Convention EDH ...'[195] – a point also made by Tanja Fachataller.[196] Philippe Frumer goes further still, boldly stating that Article 15 has been 'rendu inopérante' in cases of international armed conflict[197] while suggesting that the Court might have adopted a 'constructive and dynamic interpretation' of Article 15.[198] Lawrence Hill-Cawthorne feels 'left with the question of whether the alternative approach, of demanding the Contracting Parties to derogate in order to access rights under IHL that the text of the Convention does not appear to permit, might eventually have been accepted by States and created a more robust mechanism for protecting rights'.[199]

More than one commentator has obliquely suggested that the Court was cowed into an accommodating attitude by the outspoken directness of the United Kingdom Government in this case, which takes on all its meaning if

---

192    Philip Czech, "European Human Rights in International Military Operations", 15 *European Yearbook on Human Rights* (2015) p. 391 at p. 402

193    Silvia Borelli, "*Jaloud v. Netherlands* and *Hassan v. United Kingdom*: Time for a principled approach in the application of the ECHR to military action abroad", *QIL, Zoom-in* 16 (2015) 25-43 at p. 39.

194    Dario Rossi d'Ambrosio, *Hassan v. the United Kingdom*, 23 European Human Rights Advocacy Centre Bulletin (Summer 2015) p. 4 at p. 5;

195    Beatrice Pastre-Belda, « L'interprétation surprenante de l'article 5 a la lumière du droit international humanitaire », *La semaine juridique* 2014, page 1796.

196    Tanja Fachataller, *op. cit.* at pp. 355-56.

197    Philippe Frumer, « Quand droits de l'homme et droit international humanitaire s'emmêlent – Un regard critique sur l'arrêt Hassan c. Royaume-Uni », *Rev. tr. d.h.* 102/2015 p. 481 at p. 506.

198    Frumer, *op. cit.* at p. 501.

199    Lawrence Hill-Cawthorne, "The Grand Chamber Judgment in Hassan v UK", *Ejil:talk!* 16 September 2016.

60 CHAPTER 3

seen in the light of the vocal, even hostile, opposition to the Court's supervision sometimes expressed in the United Kingdom.[200]

As it is, the Court itself has acknowledged in a later judgment, *Merabishvili v. Georgia*, that the enumeration given in Article 5 § 1 (a)-(f) of aims capable of justifying detention, hitherto exhaustive,[201] has been expanded by one additional ground created by its case-law (case-law references omitted):

> The list of situations in which Article 5 § 1 of the Convention permits deprivation of liberty is likewise exhaustive (...), except when it is being applied, in the context of an international armed conflict, to the detention of prisoners of war or of civilians who pose a threat to security (see *Hassan v. the United Kingdom* [GC], no. 29750/09, § 104, ECHR 2014).[202]

What consequences this may have remains to be seen. For example, the Court has until now condemned incommunicado detention as contrary to Article 5 of the Convention even when applied in a counterterrorism context.[203] In the light of *Hassan* as construed by the Court itself in *Merabishvili*, the provision in Article 5 of the Fourth Geneva Convention, which permits a spy or a saboteur in occupied territory to be regarded as 'having forfeited rights of communication under [that] Convention', might require this case-law to be revisited.

In the meantime, the Supreme Court of the United Kingdom has relied on *Hassan* as authority to find that a resolution of the United Nations Security Council under Chapter VII of the Charter can modify Article 5 § 1 of the Convention to justify detention in a non-international armed conflict.[204]

### 3.4.3    *Article 7*
There have been a few cases in which the Court has had to assess the facts constitutive of a criminal charge in light of international humanitarian law.

---

200    See, in particular, Philippe Frumer, *op. cit.*, at p. 506; Nicolas Hervieu, « La jurisprudence européenne sur les opérations militaires à l'épreuve du feu », *La Revue des droites de l'homme* (en ligne), §§ 89-90, placed online on 20 October 2014, accessed 22 May 2016.

201    See, for example, *Del Río Prada*, § 123, and *Khlaifia and Others v. Italy* (GC), no. 16483/12, § 88, ECHR 2016, and see also 2.4.1.1 above.

202    *Merabishvili*, § 298.

203    *Aksoy*, § 84; *El-Masri* §§ 236-37; and 2.4.1.1 above.

204    United Kingdom Supreme Court, *Abd Ali Hameed Al-Waheed (Appellant) v Ministry of Defence (Respondent) and Serdar Mohammed (Respondent) v Ministry of Defence (Appellant)* (per Lord Sumption), 17 January 2017, [2017] UKSC 2. For a critical appraisal, see Admas Habteslasie, "Detention in times of war: Article 5 of the ECHR, UN Security Council Resolutions and the Supreme Court decision in Serdar Mohammed v. Ministry of Defence", E.H.R.L.R. 2017, 2, 180-191.

INTERPLAY BETWEEN THE CONVENTION AND IHL 61

So it was in *Korbely v. Hungary*, which concerned the prosecution of a former Hungarian serviceman who in 1956 had killed an insurgent who at the time was taking an active part in the uprising;[205] in *Kononov v. Latvia*, which concerned the prosecution of a Red Partisan who in 1944 had taken part in an attack on a village whose inhabitants were suspected of collaboration with the Nazi German occupying forces;[206] and in *Van Anraat v. the Netherlands*, which concerned the prosecution of a Dutch businessman who had sold an ingredient of a chemical weapon to the Iraqi regime during the Iraq-Iran War, eventually becoming the regime's sole supplier of the substance.[207]

*Stricto sensu* these were not cases in which the interpretation of international humanitarian law was central to the interpretation of the Convention itself. Rather, the assessment of whether international humanitarian law had been correctly applied was relevant to the validity of the interpretation of the definition of the 'criminal offence' by the domestic courts.[208]

### 3.4.4 *Article 4 of Protocol No. 7*

In one judgment, *Marguš v. Croatia*, the Court has relied on international humanitarian law to clarify a duty to prosecute that already existed under Convention law. The case was one that fell to be decided under Article 4 of Protocol No. 7 – the *ne bis in idem* Article – which in its second paragraph makes provision for the reopening of criminal cases 'if there is evidence of new or newly discovered facts, or if there has been a fundamental defect in the previous proceedings, which could affect the outcome of the case'.

In late 1991, shortly after the outbreak of fighting in Croatia following that country's declaration of independence, the applicant in that case killed, maltreated and robbed civilians, for which after the closure of hostilities he was prosecuted under ordinary criminal law. He was however allowed to benefit from an amnesty by the domestic criminal courts in 1997. In 2006 he was indicted afresh on the same charges, this time defined as war crimes contrary to the Fourth Geneva Convention and Additional Protocol No. 1, and in 2007 he was convicted. The conviction survived an appeal to the Supreme Court and a complaint to the Constitutional Court to become final in 2009.

---

205 *Korbely v. Hungary* (GC), no. 9174/02, §§ 78-94, ECHR 2008.
206 *Kononov v. Latvia* (GC), no. 36376/04, §§ 196-227, ECHR 2010.
207 *Van Anraat v. the Netherlands* (dec.), no. 65389/09, 6 July 2010.
208 Linos-Alexandre Sicilianos, "La Cour européenne des droits de l'homme et le droit international humanitaire : une ouverture progressive", in *Human Rights in a Global World: Essays in Honour of Judge Luis López Guerra* (Guido Raimondi, Iulia Motoc, Pere Pastor Vilanova, Carmen Morte Gómez, eds.; Wolf Legal Publishers, 2018), pp. 373-386 at pp. 378-380.

The Court pointed out the following:

> The possibility for a State to grant an amnesty in respect of grave breaches of human rights may be circumscribed by treaties to which the State is a party. There are several international conventions that provide for a duty to prosecute crimes defined therein (see the Geneva Conventions of 1949 for the Protection of Victims of Armed Conflicts and their Additional Protocols, in particular common Article 3 of the Geneva Conventions; Articles 49 and 50 of the Convention (I) for the Amelioration of the Condition of the Wounded and Sick in Armed Forces in the Field; Articles 50 and 51 of the Convention (II) for the Amelioration of the Condition of Wounded, Sick and Shipwrecked Members of Armed Forces at Sea; Articles 129 and 130 of the Convention (III) relative to the Treatment of Prisoners of War; and Articles 146 and 147 of the Convention (IV) relative to the Protection of Civilian Persons in Time of War. See also Articles 4 and 13 of the Additional Protocol (II) to the Geneva Conventions (1977), relating to the Protection of Victims of Non-International Armed Conflicts; Article 5 of the Convention on the Prevention and Punishment of the Crime of Genocide; and the Convention Against Torture and Other Cruel, Inhuman, or Degrading Treatment or Punishment).[209]

We have seen above[210] that the State's procedural obligations under Article 2 of the Convention include the duty to ensure, by all means at its disposal, an adequate response – judicial or otherwise – so that the legislative and administrative framework set up to protect the right to life is properly implemented and any breaches of that right are repressed and punished – in other words, in the case of a violation of the right to life, to bring the perpetrators to justice.[211] As we shall see below, no derogation from Article 2 is possible except in respect of deaths resulting from 'lawful acts of war'[212] – which the murder of civilians plainly is not – and no derogation from Article 3 is possible at all.[213] Thus the Court was able to hold that

> ... by bringing a fresh indictment against the applicant and convicting him of war crimes against the civilian population, the Croatian authori-

---

209 *Marguš v. Croatia* (GC), no. 4455/10, § 132, ECHR 2014.
210 See 2.2.2 above.
211 See 2.2.2 above.
212 See 4.7.1 below.
213 See 4.7.2 below.

ties acted in compliance with the requirements of Articles 2 and 3 of the Convention and in a manner consistent with the requirements and recommendations of the above-mentioned international mechanisms and instruments[214]

– effectively using international humanitarian law to reinforce the protection of those two Articles.[215]

## 3.5 Conclusion

The Court has held in its admissibility decision in *Georgia v. Russia II* that 'the question of the interplay of the provisions of the Convention with the rules of international humanitarian law in the context of an armed conflict belongs in principle to the merits stage of the procedure';[216] presumably, therefore, the definitive word on the subject – if there can ever be one – will only be spoken when the Grand Chamber seized of that case delivers its judgment.

We would conclude, provisionally, that international humanitarian law and the Convention are conceptually distinct. It is submitted that neither is a *lex specialis* to the other. Even in *Hassan* the Court has eschewed such a finding.

Although on its facts and reasoning *Hassan* only concerns Article 5, the question is whether the approach it introduces is capable of application to other Convention Articles guaranteeing substantive rights – most notably Article 2. At least one author has suggested that future case-law might develop in that direction.[217] We would submit that whatever flexibility may be possible under other provisions of the Convention and Protocols, most notably the Articles with open-ended limitation clauses such as Articles 8-11, it would be difficult to justify interpreting Article 2 'in the light of international humanitarian law' without jurisprudentially transferring the 'lawful acts of war' clause from Article 15 § 2 to Article 2, effectively turning it into a fourth sub-paragraph

---

214   *Marguš* § 140.

215   Duffy (2018), pp. 80-81, takes the opposite view that the Court's interpretation of the Convention "lent weight to the existence of [a duty to prosecute]" under international humanitarian law.

216   *Georgia v. Russia* (II) (dec.), § 71.

217   Francoise J. Hampson, "Article 2 of the Convention and military operations during armed conflict", in *The Right to Life under Article 2 of the European Convention on Human Rights: Twenty Years of Legal Developments since McCann v. the United Kingdom* (*In honour of Michael O'Boyle*), p. 191 at p. 195.

64                                                                    CHAPTER 3

of Article 2 § 2, and effectively removing the need to derogate in time of war altogether.[218]

What is safe to say at this point is that the Convention, through its requirement of a domestic remedy and especially its own procedure before the European Court of Human Rights, offers protection additional to that provided by international humanitarian law in that individual victims are expressly given standing before a treaty body invested with the power to give binding judgments on the merits.[219]

It goes without saying that such protection will be most effective if Convention standards are not allowed to be eroded by the exigencies of what may admittedly be a disastrous situation. In our view, this was precisely the purpose of the drafters of the Convention in making express provision for derogation in time of war or other public emergency threatening the life of the nation – and as we shall see in the next chapter, subject always to the supervision of the Court.

---

218   This consequence is accepted by Sir Daniel Bethlehem. As he puts it: "If the Convention is to apply in armed conflict, and is not to be fundamentally at odds with IHL [i.e. international humanitarian law], an armed conflict exception to the Article 2 § 1 prohibition must be located in Article 15 § 2. Although Article 15 § 2 is cast as a derogation provision, it should properly be read as an exception to the Article 2 § 1 prohibition, beyond the exceptions contained in Article 2 § 2." See Sir Daniel Bethlehem, "When is an act of war lawful?", in *The Right to Life under Article 2 of the European Convention on Human Rights: Twenty Years of Legal Developments since McCann v. the United Kingdom (In honour of Michael O'Boyle)*, p. 231 at p. 237. See also Daragh Murray, *Practitioner's Guide to Human Rights Law in International Armed Conflict*, (Chatham House/Oxford University Press 2016, p. 105: "The Court stated [in *Hassan*] that it would permit such reliance on the law of armed conflict, in the absence of a derogation, only in the case of international armed conflicts. Derogation was not required in light of the existence of explicit law of armed conflict rules, designed for the situation under consideration. The reasoning underpinning this conclusion would appear to apply more broadly in international armed conflict, and should include, for example, permissive rules relating to the use of force."

219   Cordula Droege, "Elective affinities? Human rights and humanitarian law", *International Review of the Red Cross*, September 2008, vol. 90, no. 871, pp. 501-547 at pp. 545-46.

CHAPTER 4

# Derogation[220]

## 4.1    Introduction[221]

The State may be faced with a situation in which it is not possible fully to secure the rights and freedoms which it guarantees – not even using the limitation clauses which the Convention itself attaches to a number of its provisions.[222] The Convention itself recognises this and therefore offers its High Contracting Parties a certain latitude to reduce the level of protection they have bound themselves to guarantee if such a situation arises.

This latitude must be circumscribed: emergency powers of all kind lend themselves to abuse if they are not subordinated to democratic or judicial review. In the words of the European Commission for Democracy through Law ('Venice Commission'):

> The security of the State and of its democratic institutions, and the safety of its officials and population, are vital public and private interests that deserve protection and may lead to a temporary derogation from certain human rights and to an extraordinary division of powers. However, emergency powers have been abused by authoritarian governments to stay in power, to silence the opposition and to restrict human rights in general. Strict limits on the duration, circumstance and scope of such powers is [sic] therefore essential. State security and public safety can only be effectively secured in a democracy which fully respects the Rule of Law. This requires parliamentary control and judicial review of the existence and duration of a declared emergency situation in order to avoid abuse.[223]

---

220    An earlier version of this part was published separately as a monograph entitled *Thoughts on Article 15 of the European Convention on Human Rights*, Wolf Legal Publishers, 2017.

221    See generally *Derogation in time of emergency*, factsheet by the Press Unit of the Court's Registry, July 2016.

222    J.P. Loof, *Mensenrechten en staatsveiligheid: verenigbare grootheden?* (diss. Leiden 2005), Wolf Legal Publishers, p. 379

223    European Commission for Democracy through Law (Venice Commission), Rule of Law Checklist, CDL-AD(2016)007, § 51.

---

© KONINKLIJKE BRILL NV, LEIDEN, 2021 | DOI:10.1163/9789004425637_005

With particular reference to the Convention, one might add that its very nature as a human rights instrument marrying a catalogue of rights to supervision by an international organism dictates a restrictive approach.

The terms and conditions setting out the extent of the latitude left to the State as well as its exercise are set out in Article 15, which reads as follows:

> 1. In time of war or other public emergency threatening the life of the nation any High Contracting Party may take measures derogating from its obligations under this Convention to the extent strictly required by the exigencies of the situation, provided that such measures are not inconsistent with its other obligations under international law.
>
> 2. No derogation from Article 2, except in respect of deaths resulting from lawful acts of war, or from Articles 3, 4 (paragraph 1) and 7 shall be made under this provision.
>
> 3. Any High Contracting Party availing itself of this right of derogation shall keep the Secretary General of the Council of Europe fully informed of the measures which it has taken and the reasons therefor. It shall also inform the Secretary General of the Council of Europe when such measures have ceased to operate and the provisions of the Convention are again being fully executed.

This part sets out by exploring the limits of the very concept of 'derogation'.

It next suggests a Convention-relevant definition of 'war', an expression that has never been given any construction in the case-law of the Court and the Commission, and examining the circumstances in which a Convention State may be entitled to invoke the existence of a 'war' in support of derogating measures. The suggestion is that the definition of 'war' for the purposes of Article 15 should be tied to the concept of 'armed conflict', as that expression is used in fields of international law other than international human rights law.

It continues by examining the cases in which the Commission and the Court have been required to review States' use of Article 15, all of which occurred in the context of a claimed 'public emergency'.

It studies the limitations on measures derogating from particular Convention rights – the so-called non-derogable rights – and the substantive, legal and formal requirements to which derogation is subject.

It briefly considers one case (*Hassan v. the United Kingdom*, which we examined in depth in the previous chapter) in which the Court was faced with the consequences of a Contracting State's spectacular *failure* to make use of Article 15, devoting some thought to what might have been if the understanding of Article 15 here suggested had been prevalent from the outset and the Contracting State concerned had acted accordingly.

## 4.2    The Nature of Derogation

The basic principle is that the Convention remains fully applicable even in time of war or other public emergency threatening the life of the nation. That much is clear from the very structure of Article 15 § 1: should such a dire eventuality materialise, Contracting Parties are permitted, subject to certain conditions, to take measures derogating from their obligations. Nonetheless their obligations remain unaffected unless and until they do.[224]

As used in legal parlance, the meaning of 'to derogate' is 'to repeal or abrogate in part (a law etc.); destroy or impair the force, effect, or authority of'.[225]

It is therefore implicit in the expression 'derogation' that Contracting States are given a measure of latitude, in certain circumstances, to limit the exercise of substantive rights guaranteed by the Convention.

On a substantive level, the conditions governing derogation under Article 15 are the following:
- Firstly, derogation under Article 15 is only permitted in time of 'war or other public emergency threatening the life of the nation'.
- Secondly, there are rights from which derogation is not permitted in even the direst of circumstances (usually referred to as the 'non-derogable rights').
- Thirdly, any measures taken must be 'strictly required by the exigencies of the situation'.
- Fourthly, they must not be inconsistent with the State's other obligations under international law.

There is in addition a formality to be observed, namely notification to the Secretary General of the Council of Europe – a 'formal and public act' which is a necessary requirement for any Article 15 derogation to be valid.[226]

---

224    Louise Doswald-Beck, *Human Rights in Times of Conflict and Terrorism* (Oxford University Press 2011) p. 5; Eric Pouw, *International Human Rights Law and the Law of Armed Conflict in the Context of Counterinsurgency – With a Particular Focus on Targeting and Operational Detention* (diss. UvA 2013), pp. 71-72; see also International Court of Justice, *Legality of the Threat or Use of Nuclear Weapons*, Advisory Opinion, I.C.J. Reports 1996, p. 226 at § 25 (although strictly speaking this passage concerns Article 4 of the International Covenant on Civil and Political Rights, the reasoning is directly transposable to Article 15 of the Convention).

225    *The New Shorter Oxford English Dictionary* (1993 ed.).

226    *Cyprus v. Turkey*, nos. 6780/74 and 6950/75, Commission report of 10 July 1976, § 528; see also *Cyprus v. Turkey*, no. 8007/77, Commission report of 4 October 1983, §§ 67-68.

It should be noted already at this point that derogation under Article 15 does not dispense the Court from considering whether or not the measure complained of was *per se* permissible under the Convention. Only if it is not will the Court consider whether the derogation invoked by the respondent Government is, firstly, valid, and secondly, sufficient to restore to that measure its acceptability.[227] Moreover, the Court will not examine the application of Article 15 of its own motion if the parties themselves do not ask it to.[228]

The effect of Article 15 derogation is thus not to limit the jurisdiction of the Court. Indeed, the latter would sit ill with Article 32 of the Convention, which extends the Court's jurisdiction to 'all matters concerning the interpretation of the Convention and the Protocols thereto', including the question whether the Court has jurisdiction at all. Already for this reason a Government cannot use Article 15 to 'switch off' the powers of the Court when they become an inconvenience, as some writers and at least one Government seem to have suggested.[229]

Nor does derogation limit the rights derogated from as such, but only the protection of their exercise. In the words of Loof, if a Convention State makes use of the possibility to derogate from certain of its obligations under the Convention, all that is excluded is State liability for the failure fully to meet those obligations.[230] This is illustrated by the fact that States may lodge notices of derogation but are not for that reason obliged to make full use of the possibilities offered – and indeed, sometimes they have not.[231]

However grave the crisis, an obligation to make use of the possibilities offered by Article 15 does not exist. For example, the Russian Federation has been locked in a bitter struggle against a murderous foe in the Northern Causasus. The weapons resorted to by the Russian armed forces have included Sukhoi

---

227   *Ireland v. the United Kingdom*, § 191; *A and Others v. the United Kingdom* (GC), no. 3455/05, § 161, ECHR 2009.

228   *Georgia v. Russia* (II) (dec.), §§ 72-73; *Khlebik v. Ukraine*, no. 2945/16, § 82, 25 July 2017.

229   Richard Ekins, Jonathan Morgan, Tom Tugendhat, *Clearing the Fog of Law: Saving our armed forces from defeat by judicial diktat*, Policy Exchange, 30 March 2015, available on http://www.policyexchange.org.uk; Gov.uk, "Government to protect Armed Forces from persistent legal claims in future overseas operations", 4 October 2016, https://www.gov.uk/government/news/government-to-protect-armed-forces-from-persistent-legal-claims-in-future-overseas-operations (accessed 29 August 2018). For the contrary view, see "UK Armed Forces Personnel and the Legal Framework For Future Operations", Written Evidence from Dr Aurel Sari, Lecturer in Law University of Exeter, submitted to the House of Commons (Session 2013-2014), http://www.publications.parliament.uk/pa/cm201314/cmselect/cmdfence/writev/futureops/law10.htm (accessed 16 February 2016).

230   Loof, pp. 347-358.

231   For examples, see Loof, fn. 10 on p. 358.

DEROGATION                                                                                      69

SU-24M and SU-25 attack aircraft armed with large numbers of 250-270 kg bombs. Even so, the Russian Government have not seen fit to lodge a notice of derogation. Consequently, the Convention remains fully applicable and is fully applied by the Court – the only restriction being defined by the reservation made by the Russian Federation at the time of ratification (which relates to Article 5 §§ 3 and 4).[232]

## 4.3   War

It has become clear that the age of armed conflict, whether international or not, is not yet behind us. The question what constitutes 'war' for purposes of Article 15, and what the significance of the use of that expression should be, has therefore lost none of its importance.

It is submitted that, for our purposes, the expression 'war' makes no sense divorced from its ordinary meaning in international humanitarian law – that is, if it does not mean either an international armed conflict or an armed conflict not of an international character between a State and a non-State armed group but reaching the minimum intensity needed to trigger the applicability of international humanitarian law.[233]

---

232   See, in particular, *Isayeva and Others v. Russia*, nos. 57947/00, 57948/00 and 57949/00, 24 February 2005; *Isayeva v. Russia*, no. 57950/00, 24 February 2005; *Khashiyev and Akayeva v. Russia*, nos. 57942/00 and 57945/00; *Khamzayev and Others v. Russia*, no. 1503/02, 3 May 2011; and *Kerimova and Others v. Russia*, nos. 17170/04, 20792/04, 22448/04, 23360/04, 5681/05 and 5684/05, 3 May 2011; all of which note the absence of any derogation under Article 15. For the text of the reservation, see the web site of the Council of Europe Treaty Office. See also Cordula Droege, "Elective affinities? Human rights and humanitarian law", *International Review of the Red Cross*, September 2008, vol. 90, no. 871, pp. 501-547 at p. 507; Françoise J. Hampson, "The relationship between international humanitarian law and human rights law from the perspective of a human rights treaty body", *International Review of the Red Cross*, September 2008, vol. 90, no. 871, pp. 549-572 at p. 563; Anne-Marie Baldovin, "Impact de la jurisprudence récente de la Cour européenne des droits de l'Homme sur la planification et l'exécution des opérations militaires à venir : Application extraterritoriale de la Convention, imputabilité des faits des troupes et fragmentation du droit international", in *Military Law and the Law of War Review* 50/3-4 (2011), pp. 369-418 at p. 405; and Linos-Alexandre Sicilianos, "La Cour européenne des droits de l'homme et le droit international humanitaire : une ouverture progressive", in *Human Rights in a Global World: Essays in Honour of Judge Luis López Guerra* (Guido Raimondi, Iulia Motoc, Pere Pastor Vilanova, Carmen Morte Gómez, eds.; Wolf Legal Publishers, 2018), pp. 373-386 at p. 375.

233   See also Sir Daniel Bethlehem, "When is an act of war lawful?", in *The Right to Life under Article 2 of the European Convention on Human Rights: Twenty Years of Legal Developments since McCann v. the United Kingdom (In honour of Michael O'Boyle)*, p. 231 at p. 236.

### 4.3.1 Defining a 'War'

Article 1 of the Hague Convention (III) on the Opening of Hostilities (1907) requires 'previous and explicit warning, in the form either of a reasoned declaration of war or of an ultimatum with conditional declaration of war' before hostilities are permitted to commence.[234] Since 1941 there has been no declaration of war in such terms,[235] although as all the world knows there have been serious and violent conflicts between States involving the deliberate use of force by one to overcome resistance by another.

If one conveniently overlooks the Greek law of 1940 declaring war on Albania, which created a state of war that apparently continues to the present day (much to the embarrassment of all concerned),[236] then probably the closest to a declaration of war in the classical sense by a Convention State was the United Kingdom's declaration with effect from 12 April 1982, in response to the Argentinian invasion of the Falkland Islands, of a 'Maritime Exclusion Zone' two hundred miles wide around a point defined in the centre of that territory. Within this zone, Argentinian warships and naval auxiliaries would be treated as hostile and liable to attack by British forces. Towards the end of April this zone became a 'Total Exclusion Zone', from which Argentinian aircraft both military and civil were excluded in addition to naval forces. On 7 May 1982 the zone was extended to cover all Argentinian military vessels and aircraft found more than twelve miles from the Argentinian coast – in other words, units of the Argentinian navy and air force might be attacked without warning anywhere in the world beyond the outer limits of the Argentinian territorial sea. Argentina followed suit by declaring comparable zones of her own.[237] Both States however stopped short of taking the conflict to each other's home land territory.

Nevertheless, while in terms of classical law of war hostilities between States are only permitted following a declaration of war (whether conditional or not), permissibility is not a prerequisite to the existence of a state of war.

---

234    Hague Convention (III) of 1907 on the Opening of Hostilities, Article 1.

235    The Georgian declaration of a 'state of war' of 9 August 2008 applied in the territory of Georgia and for fifteen days only: see *Georgia v. Russia (II)* (dec.) (GC), no. 38263/08, § 1, 13 December 2011.

236    *Balkan Insight*, 22 March 2016, http://www.balkaninsight.com/en/article/albania-and-greece-agree-to-abolish-the-war-law-03-22-2016 (retrieved 6 November 2016); *Tirana Times*, 25 March 2016. It would appear that the state of war still exists at the time of writing.

237    Commander Timothy C. Young, *Maritime Exclusion Zones: A Tool for the Operational Commander?*, Naval War College, Newport, Rhode Island, USA, 18 May 1992, pp. 6-7 and Appendix II.

DEROGATION                                                                71

To begin with, the expression 'war' has never been limited to conflicts between sovereign States. Already Hugo Grotius, in *De iure belli ac pacis*, reminds us that wars may be 'public, private or mixed' depending on the nature of the parties:

> Publicum bellum est quod auctore eo geritur qui iurisdictionem habet; privatum, quod aliter; mixtum, quod una ex parte est publicum, ex altera privatum.[238]

To define a contemporary understanding of the concept of war, one that is appropriate to international human rights law, it would appear sensible to turn to the field of international law that actually regulates its conduct – namely, international humanitarian law, also referred to as the law of armed conflict, or the law of war (the terms are synonymous).[239]

Modern international humanitarian law is based on the same understanding of war as that of Grotius. The four Geneva Conventions of 1949, for example, apply to

> all cases of declared war or of any other armed conflict which may arise between two or more of the High Contracting Parties, even if the state of war is not recognized by one of them[240]

– thus making it clear that a state of 'armed conflict' relevant to those Conventions does not depend on a formal declaration of war – and to

> all cases of partial or total occupation of the territory of a High Contracting Party, even if the said occupation meets with no armed resistance[241]

as well as to

> armed conflicts not of an international character occurring in the territory of one of the High Contracting Parties[242]

---

238   Hugo Grotius, *De iure belli ac pacis* (1625), Book I, Chapter III, paragraph 1.
239   Frits Kalshoven and Liesbeth Zegveld, *Constraints on the waging of war: an introduction to international humanitarian law* (fourth edition), Cambridge University Press/ICRC 2011, p. 1.
240   Common Article 2 of the 1949 Geneva Conventions, first paragraph.
241   *ibid.*, second paragraph.
242   Common Article 3 of the 1949 Geneva Conventions.

72 CHAPTER 4

– which by definition, if the conflict is not to be international, implies either that the High Contracting Party concerned is in conflict with at least one non-State organised armed group or that non-State organised armed groups are fighting each other.[243]

Article 1 of Additional Protocol II to the 1949 Geneva Conventions develops and supplements common Article 3, rendering the Protocol applicable to armed conflicts

> which take place in the territory of a High Contracting Party between its armed forces and dissident armed forces or other organized armed groups which, under responsible command, exercise such control over a part of its territory as to enable them to carry out sustained and concerted military operations and to implement this Protocol[244]

while specifically excluding

> situations of internal disturbances and tensions, such as riots, isolated and sporadic acts of violence and other acts of a similar nature, as not being armed conflicts[245]

The International Criminal Tribunal for the Former Yugoslavia gives the following definition of 'armed conflict':

> An "armed conflict" is said to exist "whenever there is a resort to armed force between States or protracted armed violence between governmental authorities and organised armed groups or between such groups within a State"[246]

– which definition

---

243  *How is the Term "Armed Conflict" Defined in International Humanitarian Law?*, International Committee of the Red Cross (ICRC) Opinion Paper, March 2008, page 1, https://www.icrc.org/eng/assets/files/other/opinion-paper-armed-conflict.pdf (accessed 19 August 2015.

244  Protocol Additional to the Geneva Conventions of 12 August 1949, and relating to the Protection of Victims of Non-International Armed Conflict (Protocol II), 8 June 1977, Article 1 § 1.

245  *ibid.*, Article 1 § 2.

246  International Criminal Tribunal for the Former Yugoslavia (ICTY), Appeals Chamber, *Prosecutor v. Kunarac, Kovač and Vuković*, Cases Nos. IT-96-23 and IT-96-23/1, judgment, 12 June 2002, § 56.

DEROGATION 73

focuses on two aspects of a conflict; the intensity of the conflict and the organization of the parties to the conflict. In an armed conflict of an internal or mixed character, these closely related criteria are used solely for the purpose, as a minimum, of distinguishing an armed conflict from banditry, unorganized and short-lived insurrections, or terrorist activities, which are not subject to international humanitarian law.[247]

The International Committee of the Red Cross, in an Opinion Paper of March 2008, summarises the distinction between an armed conflict not of an international character (Non-International Armed Conflict, 'NIAC') and 'mere' internal disturbances and tensions, riots or acts of banditry, in the following terms:

> First, the hostilities must reach a minimum level of intensity. This may be the case, for example, when the hostilities are of a collective character or when the government is obliged to use military force against the insurgents, instead of mere police forces.
> Second, non-governmental groups involved in the conflict must be considered as "parties to the conflict", meaning that they possess organized armed forces. This means for example that these forces have to be under a certain command structure and have the capacity to sustain military operations.[248]

In its 2016 Commentary on the First Geneva Convention, the International Committee of the Red Cross (ICRC) describes an 'armed conflict not of an international character' as follows:

> A situation of violence that crosses the threshold of an "armed conflict not of an international character" is a situation in which organized Parties confront one another with violence of a certain degree of intensity. It is a determination made based on the facts.[249]

It is submitted that the understanding of the expression 'armed conflict' as used in the four Geneva Conventions and their Additional Protocols, whether of an international character or not, is equally appropriate to the understand-

---

247    ICTY, Appeals Chamber, *Prosecutor v. Duško Tadić*, IT-94-1-T, judgment, 7 May 1997, § 561.
248    *How is the Term "Armed Conflict" Defined in International Humanitarian Law?*, International Committee of the Red Cross (ICRC) Opinion Paper, March 2008, p. 3.
249    International Committee of the Red Cross, Convention (I) for the Amelioration of the Condition of the Wounded and Sick in Armed Forces in the Field, Commentary of 2016, § 387.

ing of the expression 'war' for purposes of Article 15 of the Convention, it being understood that in the case of an armed conflict not of an international character one of the protagonists must be the State; in other words, that the expressions 'war' and 'armed conflict' are interchangeable.[250]

### 4.3.2 *Use of the Expression 'War' in Practice*

#### 4.3.2.1 International Armed Conflict

The classical understanding of 'war' as a legal concept encompasses only armed conflict between two or more states (or alliances). It is to this concept that the classical laws of armed conflict, or laws of war, are applicable – the Hague Conventions of 1899 and 1907 including their protocols and all the Geneva Conventions entered into between 1864 and 1949.

To date Article 15 has never been invoked in response to a 'war' between States, however defined. In its notice of derogation of 5 June 2015, Ukraine refers to the 'annexation and temporary occupation by the Russian Federation of the integral part of Ukraine – the Autonomous Republic of Crimea and the city of Sevastopol' as the result of 'armed aggression against Ukraine' involving 'both regular Armed Forces of the Russian Federation and illegal armed groups guided, controlled and financed by the Russian Federation', but shrinks from using the expression 'war'. Although the military occupation of part of the territory of a State by a neighbouring State (or by irregular forces under the latter's control), as posited by Ukraine, is surely *casus belli* – and the Ukrainian *note verbale* does mention Article 51 of the United Nations Charter – Ukraine describes the situation as 'a public emergency threatening the life of the nation' and its response as 'an anti-terrorist operation'. Interestingly, however, reference is made to 'war crimes and crimes against humanity' allegedly committed by Russian regular armed forces and by irregulars under Russia's control.[251]

Neither, in Strasbourg case-law, has the expression 'war' been applied to military operations involving Contracting States acting extra-territorially, as

---

250   Kalshoven and Zegveld, *supra* note 239, *ibid.*; see generally Marko Milanović and Vidan Hadži-Vidanović, *A Taxonomy of Armed Conflict* (January 20, 2012). *Research Handbook on International Conflict and Security Law*, Nigel White, Christian Henderson, eds., Edward Elgar, 2012, p. 256.

251   *Note verbale* from the Ukrainian Permanent Representative to the Secretary General of the Council of Europe, 5 June 2015, Council of Europe treaty office web site, http://www.coe.int/en/web/conventions/full-list/-/conventions/treaty/005/declarations?p_auth=oM51wfc3. An identical document was lodged with the Secretary General of the United Nations under Article 4 § 1 of the International Covenant on Civil and Political Rights on the same day (UN Doc. C.N.416.2015.TREATIES-IV.4). See also Marko Milanović, "Ukraine Derogates from the ICCPR and the ECHR, Files Fourth Interstate Application against Russia", *EJIL:Talk!*, 5 October 2015.

DEROGATION

in Afghanistan, Bosnia and Herzegovina, Kosovo or the Middle East.[252] In *Banković*[253] and *Hassan*,[254] the Court notes that 'although there have been a number of military missions involving Contracting States acting extra-territorially since their ratification of the Convention, no State has ever made a derogation pursuant to Article 15 of the Convention in respect of these activities'.

However, in *Varnava and Others* the Court implicitly recognised that an international armed conflict had existed between Cyprus and Turkey at the time of the disappearance of the victims of the violation found (although this fell outside the Court's jurisdiction *ratione temporis*).[255]

On the one occasion when a Contracting State relied on the existence of an 'international armed conflict' in a context relevant to Article 15 of the Convention – *Hassan* – the Court deferred to the Government's view[256] rather than follow that of the applicant, who considered the conflict to be a non-international one fought on foreign territory.[257]

### 4.3.2.2   Non-international Armed Conflict

As we have seen, there are situations on the continent that arguably constitute 'non-international armed conflicts'[258] and accordingly, for our purposes, 'wars'; but Article 15 has never been invoked in respect of these either.

The expression 'war' is rarely, if ever, used by States in relation to internal conflicts on their own territory. It has been suggested, not implausibly, that Governments may be reluctant to admit that a non-state organised armed group has acquired the potential to challenge their monopoly on the use of force, and especially to recognise that the situation of violence has reached the high threshold of application of Additional Protocol II to the Geneva Conventions.[259] The latter in particular, despite its reassuring recognition of the State's right to strive to reimpose its rule,[260] implies recognition that the armed group is not merely organised, but under responsible command and exercises control over territory allowing it to conduct sustained and concerted military operations[261] – an admission of weakness, on the part of the State, that can fairly be

---

252   *Hassan v. the United Kingdom* (GC), no. 29750/09, § 42, ECHR 2014.

253   *Banković and Others v. Belgium and Others* (dec.) (GC), no. 52207/99, § 62, ECHR 2001-XI

254   *Hassan*, § 101.

255   *Varnava and Others* § 185.

256   *Hassan, passim.*

257   *Hassan, passim.*

258   See 1.2.1 above.

259   On the interpretation of the expression "non-international armed conflict", see generally Milanović and Hadži-Vidanović, pp. 282 *et seq.*

260   Article 3 of the 1977 Additional Protocol.

261   Article 1 of the 1977 Additional Protocol.

described as a *testimonium paupertatis*[262] – and enjoins the State to vouchsafe to its opponents, whom it would otherwise be entitled to try as rebels or traitors, the 'widest possible amnesty'.[263] Worse still, conferring any such degree of legitimacy on an armed group might amount to constructive recognition of the latter as a 'liberation movement' possessed of rights of its own under international law, including the right of a disgruntled ethnic minority to 'self-determination' or to the protection of a foreign power invested with a corresponding 'responsibility to protect'.[264]

An expression more frequently applied to armed non-state opponents of Government – with the active or tacit endorsement of the Court – is 'terrorist', even when the opponents pose a significant armed threat and expressly intend to wrest control over part of the territory of the state from the Government.[265] It is submitted that as a legal categorisation of armed opponents use of this expression is unsatisfactory. The word terrorism describes a tactic that can be loosely defined as 'criminal acts intended or calculated to provoke a state of terror in the general public, a group of persons or particular persons for political purposes'[266] and that may be resorted to not only by renegades

---

262 Françoise J. Hampson, "The relationship between international humanitarian law and human rights law from the perspective of a human rights treaty body", *International Review of the Red Cross*, September 2008, vol. 90, no. 871, pp. 549-572 at p. 556; Anna Austin, Contribution to a seminar held at the University of Toulouse in March 2016. See also Harris, O'Boyle and Warbrick, *Law of the European Convention on Human Rights* (Oxford University Press, 3rd edn. 2014), p. 825.

263 Article 6 § 5 of the 1977 Second Additional Protocol. As the term 'amnesty' indicates, the existence of a non-international armed conflict does not of itself prevent States from bringing prosecutions under ordinary criminal law: see, for example, Supreme Court of the Netherlands (*Hoge Raad*), judgment of 7 May 2004, ECLI:NL:HR:2004:AF6988, also published in NJ 2007/276 with an annotation by A.H. Klip; and Supreme Court of the Netherlands, judgments of 4 April 2017, ECLI:NL:HR:2017:574, also published in NJ 2018/106, ECLI:NL:HR:2017:574, also published in NJ 2018/107, and ECLI:NL:HR:2017:577, also published in NJ 2018/108, with an annotation by E. van Sliedregt after NJ 2018/2018.

264 Elizabeth Chadwick, *Self-Determination, Terrorism and the International Humanitarian Law of Armed Conflict*, Martinus Nijhoff 1996, pp. 41-42 and 82.

265 See, among many other examples, *Sakık and Others v. Turkey*, nos. 23878/94, 23879/94, 23880/94, 23881/94, 23882/94 and 23883/94, Reports 1997-VII; *Öcalan v. Turkey* (GC), no. 46221/99, ECHR 2005-IV; and *Finogenov and Others v. Russia*, nos. 18299/03 and 27311/03, ECHR 2011.

266 Working definition taken from the *Declaration to Supplement the 1994 Declaration on Measures to Eliminate International Terrorism*, A/RES/51/210, 16 January 1997. Compare Article 2 § 1 (b) of the International Convention for the Suppression of the Financing of Terrorism, 10 January 2000: (in addition to acts which constitute offences within the scope of and as defined in specific named treaties), 'Any other act intended to cause death or serious bodily injury to a civilian, or to any other person not taking an active part in the

DEROGATION 77

and religious fanatics but also by Government forces.[267] On this view, the so-called 'war on terror' declared by the Bush Administration in the USA is not a 'war' properly so-called; the paradigm is one of law enforcement, not armed conflict, whether international or non-international.[268]

In a judgment of 10 January 1996 the Constitutional Court of the Russian Federation proceeded on the implicit recognition that Additional Protocol II was applicable to the conflict which was at that time being fought in Chechnya (later to be known as the First Chechen War), and that its provisions were 'binding on both parties to the armed conflict'.[269] However, Russia became a party to the Convention only on 5 May 1998, by which time the First Chechen War had been over for nearly two years.

*Korbely v. Hungary* remains to date the only case in the Court's history in which the Government of a State Party to the Convention has recognised a situation on its own territory as amounting to a non-international armed conflict.[270] The situation was, in fact, the 1956 uprising against Soviet-imposed Communist rule, which the post-Communist Government of Hungary could safely recognise as legitimate.

### 4.3.3 *Must a 'War' Constitute a 'Threat to the Life of the Nation' for Derogation under Article 15 to be Possible?*

4.3.3.1 Why it Matters

It does not follow as night follows day that 'the life of the nation' will be 'threatened' by the existence of a conflict, whether of an international character or

---

hostilities in a situation of armed conflict, when the purpose of such act, by its nature or context, is to intimidate a population, or to compel a government or an international organization to do or to abstain from doing any act.'

267 See generally Jelena Pejic, "Armed Conflict and Terrorism: There Is A (Big) Difference", in *Counter-Terrorism: International Law and Practice* (Ana María de Frías, Katja L.H. Samuel, Nigel D. White, eds.), Oxford University Press 2011 p. 171.

268 Helen Duffy, *The 'War on Terror' and the Framework of International Law* (2nd edition 2015), Cambridge University Press, pp. 566-567.

269 Constitutional Court of the Russian Federation, Judgment of 31 July 1995 on the constitutionality of the Presidential Decrees and the Resolutions of the Federal Government concerning the situation in Chechnya (translation by Federal News Service Group, Washington D.C., published by the Venice Commission on 10 January 1996 as CDL-INF (96) 1). See Bowring, Bill (2008) – "How will the European Court of Human Rights deal with the UK in Iraq?: lessons from Turkey and Russia" – London: Birkbeck ePrints. Available at: http://eprints.bbk.ac.uk/859 at p. 9.

270 *Korbely* § 61.

not.[271] A limited war fought far away on foreign soil, for example, need not constitute a vital danger. Many (though not all) conflicts fought against non-European indigenous peoples during the colonial period served the establishment of a European State's power and influence beyond its borders but were not a response to any direct existential threat to the State concerned. Similarly, the question may well be asked to what extent the armed extraterritorial operations that have taken place since 2001 constituted a response to a genuine threat to the 'life of the nation'.[272]

The question is therefore whether such a 'threat' should be required for Article 15 derogation to be permissible in time of 'war', as distinct from a mere 'public emergency' – in other words, whether (and if so, to what extent) the words 'threatening the life of the nation' qualify 'war' as they do the words 'other public emergency'. The retrospective assessment to be made under the Convention of wartime acts and decisions depends on it.

### 4.3.3.2    On the Territory of the Home Country

The first question is what constitutes the territory of the Convention State. Undoubtedly the secession of Algeria (1954-62) was felt in metropolitan France as a 'war' on French soil, and one that threatened the life of the nation at that. Nonetheless, it has to be said that the French Republic has survived, magnificently, despite the loss of the Algerian *départements*. Be that as it may, the Convention could not apply to that particular conflict: France ratified it only in 1974. Moreover, the *guerre d'Algérie* was only officially declared to have been a 'war' *post factum*, in 1999.[273]

While the expression 'war' will not be as quickly resorted to by Governments (or courts, whether domestic or international) as by journalists, the question whether a conflict worthy of that name must also constitute a threat to 'the life of the nation' before Article 15 can be brought into play is, in our submission, pointless if the conflict results from a conventional kinetic conflict on the home territory of a Convention State. It is difficult to conceive of a situation in

---

271    Jean-Paul Costa and Michael O'Boyle, "The European Court of Human Rights and International Humanitarian Law", in *The European Convention on Human Rights, a living instrument, Essays in Honour of Christos L. Rozakis* (Bruylant, 2011), p. 107 at p. 116.

272    Helen Duffy, *The 'War on Terror' and the Framework of International Law* (2nd edition 2015), Cambridge University Press, p. 587.

273    "*Guerre d'Algérie*" (Algerian war) is now the expression approved by law; formerly the official appellation was "operations carried out in North Africa" (Loi n° 99-882 du 18 octobre 1999 relative à la substitution, à l'expression « aux opérations effectuées en Afrique du Nord », de l'expression « à la guerre d'Algérie ou aux combats en Tunisie et au Maroc », *Journal officiel* no. 244, 20 October 1999).

DEROGATION

which an actual 'war' being fought on home territory does not also constitute an 'emergency threatening the life of the nation'; most likely, therefore, the very intensity of the conflict will provide the answer.

The right of a Contracting State to fight a defensive war against a foreign attacker on its home territory pending action by the United Nations Security Council will be governed, in principle, by Article 51 of the Charter of the United Nations. We do not doubt that such a Contracting State would be entitled to avail itself of Article 15 in any case.

### 4.3.3.3    Hybrid Warfare

The question whether a conflict is international in character or not, and if not, sufficient to justify the expression 'war' is of great practical importance when considered in the context of what is now called hybrid warfare. A definition of 'hybrid warfare' appears not to exist, but until now the expression has been used to describe a combination of conventional kinetic warfare and unconventional tactics such as cyber-attacks and the covert use of irregulars who may have been recruited from among the population of the State under attack (members, perhaps, of a minority of the same ethnicity as the population of the attacking state). Typically the attacker is expected to limit the intensity of the conflict and make it appear non-international, so as to reduce the likelihood of triggering a military response by an existing military alliance – such as NATO, under Article 5 of the Washington Treaty – and create a *fait accompli*.[274]

The leaders of the State under attack will need both the perception to identify the threat as coming from abroad and the courage to say so in public – for only thus can they be sure that a low-intensity conflict that, to a superficial observer, may appear to be a mere internal disturbance that offers no particular threat to the life of the nation will entitle them to invoke Article 15 of the

---

[274]    "Hybrid war – does it even exist?", NATO review, http://www.nato.int/docu/review/2015/ Also-in-2015/hybrid-modern-future-warfare-russia-ukraine/EN/index.htm (accessed 7 June 2016). The closest NATO has come appears to be a paragraph of the Wales Summit Declaration of 5 September 2014: "We will ensure that NATO is able to effectively address the specific challenges posed by hybrid warfare threats, where a wide range of overt and covert military, paramilitary, and civilian measures are employed in a highly integrated design. ..." NATO press release (20014)120, 5 September 2014, https://www.nato.int/cps/ en/natohq/official_texts_112964.htm (accessed on 27 November 2017). See generally Andres B. Munoz Mosquera and Sascha Dov Bachmann, "Lawfare in Hybrid Wars: The 21st Century Warfare", in *Journal of International Humanitarian Legal Studies* 7 (2016) 63-87. See also Martin Murphy, Frank G. Hoffman, Gary Schaub, Jr., *Hybrid Maritime Warfare and the Baltic Sea Region*, University of Copenhagen, Centre for Military Studies, November 2016, p. 3.

80                                                                    CHAPTER 4

Convention (not to mention, in the case of NATO members, Article 5 of the Washington Treaty).[275]

### 4.3.3.4 Outside the Territory of the Home Country

It has been suggested that a Contracting State acting extraterritorially, as several have done in Iraq and Afghanistan, should not be allowed to derogate from the Convention under Article 15; but conversely, the Court's observation that the United Kingdom 'did not purport to derogate under Article 15', which appears in *Hassan*[276] but also in *Al-Jedda*,[277] has been construed *a contrario* by at least one author as suggesting that it would have been possible for the United Kingdom to derogate in respect of its operations in Iraq.[278]

We consider that since – as we will see below[279] – the Convention is capable of applying extraterritorially to the use of 'hard power', the corresponding availability of Article 15 is a necessary corollary.

We would however add the caveat that the position on whether a 'war' must also threaten the 'life of the nation' for Article 15 to apply may well be different if a State Party to the Convention engages in a 'war' *outside* its own home territory rather than on its home territory in self-defence.

#### 4.3.3.4.1 *Colonies and Dependencies*

Between 1947 and 1949 the Netherlands embarked on 'policing operations' – counter-guerrilla offensives – in its East Indies, and later, in 1962, defeated an Indonesian naval attack on Netherlands New Guinea; in the 1950s the United Kingdom suppressed uprisings in northern Borneo, Kenya and elsewhere;[280]

---

275    With regard to cyber-attacks, see Jack Goldsmith, "How Cyber Changes the Laws of War", EJIL (2013), Vol. 24 No. 1, 129-138 at pp. 133-34; Lieutenant Ken M. Jones, USN, *Cyber War: The Next Frontier For NATO*, Progressive Management, 2016, pp. 20-23; Christian Henderson, "The use of cyber force: Is the *jus ad bellum* ready?", in *QIL*, Zoom-in 27 (2016), pp. 3-11 at p. 7; and International Committee of the Red Cross, Convention (I) for the Amelioration of the Condition of the Wounded and Sick in Armed Forces in the Field, Commentary of 2016, § 254. See also *Military and Paramilitary Activities in and against Nicaragua (Nicaragua v. United States of America)*, Merits, Judgment, 27 June 1986, I.C.J. Reports 1986, § 195.

276    § 98.

277    § 100.

278    Helen Duffy, *The 'War on Terror' and the Framework of International Law* (2nd edition 2015), Cambridge University Press, p. 587.

279    See Chapter 6 below.

280    The United Kingdom derogated under Article 15 in respect of these; the derogations were either withdrawn eventually or came to an end when the territory concerned gained independence. Information available from the web site of the Council of Europe Treaty Office. See also Bart van der Sloot, "Is All Fair in Love and War? An Analysis of the Case Law

DEROGATION

and until 1975 Portugal fought bitterly to retain control of Angola, Mozambique and Portuguese Guinea. Colonial wars eventually went out with colonialism; and as France weathered the loss of Algeria, so also European colonial powers overcame the loss of possessions that had often been sources of prosperity for centuries. It may therefore be argued that the secession of overseas territories did not, in retrospect, affect the home country to the point of 'threatening the life of the nation'. Nevertheless, just as the United Kingdom was permitted to invoke Article 15 in respect of a mere 'emergency' in Cyprus – then still one of its remaining Crown Colonies – the mother country would surely have been entitled to make use of Article 15. It was, after all, the life of the colony or territory *itself*, as an integral part of the State, which was threatened.

It is worth noting in this connection that the Convention does not comprise any provision that can be construed as permitting territorial or ethnic entities to secede. In particular, it has no provision comparable to, for example, Article 1 § 1 of the International Covenant on Civil and Political Rights, which recognises to 'all peoples' a right of 'self-determination'. This is perhaps just as well, since the 'self-determination' argument can be wielded in support of diametrically opposed interests even within the jurisdiction of a single Contracting State.[281] In any event, it is by no means certain that 'outside the context of non-self-governing territories and peoples subject to alien subjugation, domination and exploitation, the international law of self-determination confers upon part of the population of an existing State a right to separate from that State'.[282]

The availability of Article 15 in the event of a foreign attack on an overseas colony (or other non-self-governing territory) is a matter on which there can be no controversy. Had the Convention applied in 1942, no right-thinking person would have thought ill of the United Kingdom Government for derogating under Article 15 in respect of Hong Kong or British Malaya, or of the Dutch Government (then in exile in London) for doing so in respect of the Netherlands East Indies.

---

on Article 15 ECHR", in *Military Law and the law of War Review* 53/2 (2014), pp. 319-358 at p. 344, who considers it "highly questionable whether it [was] in the interest of the rebelling indigenous population ... to limit their rights and freedoms by invoking the state of necessity."

281    Contrast *Cyprus v. Turkey*, § 69, with *Öcalan*, § 78.

282    *X v. Germany*, no. 6742/94, Commission decision of 10 July 1974, p. 98 at p. 101; International Court of Justice, *Accordance with International Law of the Unilateral Declaration of Independence in Respect of Kosovo, Advisory Opinion, I.C.J. Reports* 2010 p. 403, §§ 82-83; see also Crawford (2012), pp. 141-142. For a contrary view, see Bart van der Sloot, "Is All Fair in Love and War? An Analysis of the Case Law on Article 15 ECHR", in *Military Law and the law of War Review* 53/2 (2014), pp. 319-358 at p. 344.

Even so, the Argentinian attack on the Falkland Islands in 1982 did not induce the United Kingdom Government to invoke Article 15. In an opinion submitted to the British House of Commons a legal scholar states, though he does not explain, that in the Falklands crisis 'the legal conditions for invoking Article 15 were undoubtedly satisfied'.[283] Indeed, if the British claim to sovereignty over the Falkland Islands is valid in international law (and it has never been called into question in the case-law of either the Commission or the Court), it is difficult to argue that the United Kingdom was not entitled to rely on Article 51 of the Charter of the United Nations – as in fact the United Kingdom did throughout the conflict.[284]

#### 4.3.3.4.2 A Historical Example: the Korean War

In terms of international law, the Korean War (1950-1953) was a conflict unlike any other. It remains, so far, the only 'war' dignified by that name fought with the prior authorisation of the Security Council of the United Nations.[285] Since therefore, in strictly formal terms, there can be little doubt as to its legality, there would be little point in posing any requirement that it constitute a direct threat to the life of the nation – which indeed, remote as the conflict was from Europe, it arguably did not for the European States that took part under the flag of the United Nations.[286] It would however have been incongruous to deny the availability of Article 15 had the Convention been in force at the time.

#### 4.3.3.4.3 Contemporary Practice: Peace Operations

More Contracting States now participate in peace operations on foreign soil than take part in international or non-international armed conflicts as belligerents in their own name. Peace operations may be based on the consent of the host State, or they may be mandated by the Security Council[287] – peacekeeping under Chapter VI of the United Nations Charter, or peace enforcing under Chapter VII[288] – or both.

---

283 Sari, *supra* note 229.

284 Young, *supra* note 237, Appendix II.

285 UNSC Resolutions 83 (1950), 27 June 1950, and 84 (1950), 7 July 1950 (Complaint of aggression upon the Republic of Korea).

286 Principally Belgium, France, Greece, Luxembourg, the Netherlands, Turkey and the United Kingdom (Denmark, Italy, Norway and Sweden sent humanitarian aid but not combat forces).

287 *Leuven Manual on the International Law Applicable to Peace Operations*, p. 27.

288 A distinction made by Tristan Ferraro in "The applicability and application of international humanitarian law to multinational forces", in *International Review of the Red Cross* (2013), 95 (891/892), pp. 561-612 at p. 565.

DEROGATION

A peace operation is not necessarily an armed conflict, whether international or non-international; but even if it does not start out as one, it may degenerate into one, either because an already tense situation escalates or because the peacekeepers or peace enforcers are dragged into a conflict between others. Such may be the case, for example, when peacekeepers are attacked by insurgents or when they intervene on the side of one or other of the parties to an existing conflict.[289] Whether there is an armed conflict, international or not, is a matter to be assessed in the light of the relevant criteria of international humanitarian law discussed above;[290] but when such a situation develops, there is a 'war' for purposes of Article 15 of the Convention.

Until now, Contracting States have not derogated under Article 15 in respect of such operations. There is, however, no reason why they should not be entitled to. It is in the logic of things that the right, in principle, to make use of Article 15 should follow the existence of Article 1 jurisdiction.[291]

The question arises in particular in respect of peace operations that are not subsidiary organs of the United Nations. With a few early exceptions, peace operations mandated by the Security Council have been its subsidiary organs;[292] such operations are subject to a regime of their own, which may preclude attribution of violations of the Convention altogether.[293]

### 4.3.3.4.4   *Responsibility to Protect*

In recent years, the concept of 'responsibility to protect' has emerged.[294] First formulated in a report of an expert body set up by the Canadian Government to attempt to identify principles governing 'humanitarian intervention'[295] – an

---

289  For an overview, see Ferraro, *loc. cit.,* pp. 561-612.

290  See 4.3.1 above.

291  Kjetil Mujezinović Larsen, *The Human Rights Treaty Obligations of Peacekeepers*, Cambridge University Press 2012, pp. 312-13.

292  Articles 7 § 2 and 29 of the Charter of the United Nations. See also Lotten Paulsson, *Delegation of powers to United Nations Subsidiary organs* (Master's thesis, Lund 2004), p. 24.

293  Compare *Behrami and Behrami v. France and Saramati v. France, Germany and Norway* (dec.) (GC), nos. 71412/01 and 78166/01, § 143, 2 May 2007 (*"Behrami and Saramati"*); see also 8.4.5.2 below.

294  For a description of the emergence of the concept and a critical appraisal, see Carlo Focarelli, "The Responsibility to Protect Doctrine and Humanitarian Intervention: Too Many Ambiguities for a Working Doctrine", *Journal of Conflict and Security Law* (2008), Vol. 13 No. 2, 191-213, and Nienke van den Have *The prevention of gross human rights violations under international human rights law* (diss. Amsterdam 2017), pp. 209-214.

295  International Commission on Intervention and State Sovereignty, *The Responsibility to Protect*, Ottawa (issued by the International Government Research Centre, December 2001). Note however that "humanitarian intervention" was the international legal ground invoked by the Government of the United Kingdom in justification of participation by

idea that was, and remains, controversial as it is perceived by some as difficult to reconcile with State sovereignty and by others as a contradiction in terms[296] – it found its first expression in an official legal text in 2005, when the United Nations General Assembly adopted the outcome of the World Summit:

> The international community, through the United Nations, also has the responsibility to use appropriate diplomatic, humanitarian and other peaceful means, in accordance with Chapters VI and VIII of the Charter of the United Nations, to help protect populations from genocide, war crimes, ethnic cleansing and crimes against humanity. In this context, *we are prepared to take collective action, in a timely and decisive manner, through the Security Council, in accordance with the Charter, including Chapter VII, on a case-by-case basis and in cooperation with relevant regional organizations as appropriate, should peaceful means be inadequate* and national authorities are manifestly failing to protect their populations from genocide, war crimes, ethnic cleansing and crimes against humanity. We stress the need for the General Assembly to continue consideration of the responsibility to protect populations from genocide, war crimes, ethnic cleansing and crimes against humanity and its implications, bearing in mind the principles of the Charter and international law. We also intend to commit ourselves, as necessary and appropriate, to helping States build capacity to protect their populations from genocide, war crimes, ethnic cleansing and crimes against humanity and to assisting those which are under stress before crises and conflicts break out.[297] (emphasis added)

---

United Kingdom forces in the attack on Syrian targets on 14 April 2018 in response to an attack by the Syrian regime in the Syrian town of Douma on 7 April 2018 allegedly using chemical weapons: see *Syria action – UK government legal position*, policy paper published on 14 April 2018.

296 The position of the International Committee of the Red Cross, for example, is that "[i]nternational humanitarian law cannot serve as a basis for armed intervention in response to grave violations of its provisions" and that the expression "armed intervention in response to grave violations of human rights and of international humanitarian law" is to be preferred. See Anne Ryniker, 'The ICRC's position on "humanitarian intervention"', *International Review of the Red Cross*, June 2001, vol. 83, no. 842, pp. 527-532 at p. 527 and *passim*.

297 UNGA Res. 60/1, 2005 World Summit Outcome, § 139.

DEROGATION

The United Nations Security Council reaffirmed this paragraph in April of the following year[298] and in November 2009,[299] and actually referred to it in a resolution of August 2006 authorising action under Chapter VII of the UN Charter in Darfur.[300]

In this light, it would be difficult to deny the applicability of Article 15 of the Convention if the Security Council, having found that national authorities of a State, perhaps a State that is not a party to the Convention, are 'manifestly failing to protect their populations from genocide, war crimes, ethnic cleansing and crimes against humanity' and peaceful means are inadequate, authorises 'collective action' to be taken by Contracting Parties in application of Chapter VII.

### 4.3.3.4.5    *Aggressor States*

What if an *aggressor* State seeks to rely on Article 15 of the Convention?[301] Wars may turn against the aggressor State, which may end up seeing its very existence threatened. Examples abound, including in recent history. As the expression is, *ex iniuria ius non oritur*: surely it would offend against the very principles on which human rights law is built[302] if such a State could get away with limiting the substantive protection which it has undertaken in the Convention to protect.[303] Had the Convention existed in 1944, no one in their right mind would have wished to vouchsafe the right to derogate to Nazi Germany.

Of course, the aggression of Nazi Germany is the obvious example – and to date the only such case (in Europe at least) that is not denied by the successor State. Even in interstate or pseudo-interstate cases, the Court has never found any other State to have committed an act of 'aggression' though aggrieved Governments have sometimes made suggestions of that nature.[304]

---

298    S/Res/1674, 28 April 2006.

299    S/Res/1894, 11 November 2009.

300    S/Res/1706, 31 August 2006.

301    For a definition of "aggression" in international law, see UNGA Res. 3314 (XXIX) (1974).

302    "Reaffirming the profound belief in those fundamental freedoms which are the foundation of justice and peace in the world and are best maintained on the one hand by an effective political democracy and on the other by a common understanding and observance of the human rights on which they depend; ..." (Preamble to the Convention, fourth paragraph).

303    Compare Articles 17 and 18 of the Convention; see also *De Becker v. Belgium*, no. 214/56, Commission report of 8 January 1960.

304    *Demopoulos and Others v. Turkey* (dec.) (GC), nos. 46113/99, 3843/02, 13751/02, 13466/03, 10200/04, 14163/04, 19993/04 and 21819/04, § 67 and 99, ECHR 2010 (Cyprus, intervening, in relation to Turkey); *Kononov*, § 179 (Lithuania, intervening, in relation to both the Soviet Union and Nazi Germany).

86 CHAPTER 4

As it is, Article 2 § 4 of the United Nations Charter requires States to

> refrain in their international relations from the threat or use of force against the territorial integrity or political independence of any state, or in any other manner inconsistent with the Purposes of the United Nations.

This is accepted as a rule of *ius cogens*.[305] That leaves only 'demonstrations, blockade, and other operations by air, sea, or land forces of Members of the United Nations' sanctioned by the Security Council (Article 42 of the Charter) and individual or collective self-defence (Article 51), both set out in Chapter VII of the Charter, as permissible instances of the 'threat or use of force' in international relations, and perhaps, in some situations, enforcement action as part of a regional arrangement (Chapter VIII of the Charter) – again, provided that it be sanctioned by the Security Council (Article 54). Other than these, non-consensual military adventures abroad without the blessing of the Security Council, even well-intentioned ones, are not permitted.[306]

Superfluously perhaps, Article 103 of the Charter provides that obligations under the Charter itself override obligations under any other treaty. As a necessary corollary, obligations under the Charter negate any rights under such another treaty with which they are incompatible.[307] That would include, in the event of such incompatibility, any right to derogate from the Convention.

### 4.3.3.4.6 *A Problematic Case: the United Kingdom in Iraq*

On 6 July 2016 a Committee of British Privy Council members under the chairmanship of Sir John Chilcot published a report (the Report of the Iraq Inquiry, known as the 'Chilcot Report') on the decision-making that led to the military involvement of the United Kingdom in Iraq starting in 2003.

The stated intention of the report is not to express an opinion on the legality in terms of international law of the decision of the United Kingdom to take part in the American-led invasion and occupation of Iraq, although it notes, unambiguously, that the United Kingdom did so without the authorisation of

---

305 Bruno Simma, "NATO, the UN and the Use of Force: Legal Aspects", in *EJIL* 10 (1999), 1-22, pp. 1-6.

306 Simma, *ibid.*; Antonio Cassese, "*Ex iniuria ius oritur*: Are We Moving towards International Legitimation of Forcible Humanitarian Countermeasures in the World Community?", in *EJIL* 10 (1999), 1-22, pp. 23-40 at p. 25; Crawford (2012), p. 757.

307 See also Article 75 of the Vienna Convention on the Law of Treaties.

DEROGATION

the Security Council and before the point was reached where military action was the last resort,[308] and that

> Unlike other instances in which military force has been used, the invasion was not prompted by the aggression of another country or an unfolding humanitarian disaster.[309]

It has been suggested that in the circumstances the United Kingdom would not have been entitled to derogate under Article 15 in respect of an elective overseas operation.[310]

The Chilcot Report reassures the reader that

> The decision to join the US-led invasion of Iraq in 2003 was the product of a particular set of circumstances which are unlikely to be repeated[311]

– which is just as well.

### 4.3.4   *Provisional Conclusion*

We have no doubt that a Contracting State making use of its right to individual and collective self-defence under Article 51 of the United Nations Charter may avail itself of Article 15 of the Convention.

If the Contracting State resorts to the use of 'hard power' outside its own territory in compliance with a mandate of the Security Council under Article 42 or Article 54 of the Charter, as in the case of the Korean war of 1950-1953 or a peace operation mandated by the Security Council, it is in our opinion open to that State to make use of Article 15.

Provisionally, one must conclude that the expression 'threatening the life of the nation' does not qualify 'war' as long as the 'war' is being fought in accordance with the Charter of the United Nations: that is, either in pursuance of a

---

308   Report of the Iraq Inquiry ("Chilcot Report"), Executive Summary, §§ 338-39. Similar conclusions have been reached elsewhere; for example, for the Netherlands, see the Report of the Committee to Investigate Decision-Making concerning Iraq (*Commissie van onderzoek besluitvorming Irak*, known as the "Davids Committee", after its chairman), Uitgeverij Boom 2010, p. 145.

309   Chilcot Report, Executive summary, § 826.

310   Eirik Bjorge, "What is living and what is dead in the European Convention on Human Rights? A Comment on Hassan v. United Kingdom", *Questions of International Law Zoom-In* 15 (2015), 23-36 at 26-28; see also *R (on the application of Al-Jedda) (FC) (Appellant) v Secretary of State for Defence (Respondent)*, [2007] UKHL 58, [2008] 1 AC 332, § 38 (per Lord Bingham).

311   Chilcot Report, Executive summary, *ibid.*

decision of the Security Council (Article 42 or Article 54) or, pending action by the Security Council, for individual or collective self-defence (Article 51).

Interestingly, support for this view can be drawn from the drafting history of Article 4 of the International Covenant on Civil and Political Rights. Even though the drafters of the Covenant refused to countenance the possibility of war in the text of the instrument itself, they did consider the legality of war in the context of the 'other obligations under international law' with which derogating measures must be consistent:

> The opinion was expressed that reference to the Charter [of the United Nations] would ... make it clear that war was recognized only in case of self-defence or for other reasons consonant with the Charter. It was pointed out, however, that the principles of the Charter were part of international law ...[312]

This, however, does not tell us what the law is when Article 51 of the Charter does not apply and the Security Council has not, or not yet, explicitly authorised military action under Chapter VII or Chapter VIII.

For all that it finds no violation of Article 5 despite the absence of a derogation under Article 15, the *Hassan* judgment gives us some indication of what the position might be. It will be remembered that UNSC Resolution 1441 (2002) of 8 November 2002 referred to Chapter VII of the Charter but did not in terms authorise the use of force against Iraq (although it did reiterate warnings that Iraq would 'face serious consequences as a result of its continued violations of its obligations').[313] Having established the jurisdiction of the United Kingdom (in terms of Article 1 of the Convention), the Court referred to case-law of the International Court of Justice to find that 'the protection offered by human rights conventions and that offered by international humanitarian law [coexisted] in situations of armed conflict'.[314] The Court's willingness to construe the guarantees of Article 5 in the light of provisions of the Third and Fourth Geneva Conventions, which cover the detention of prisoners of war and the internment of civilians for security reasons respectively in situations of international armed conflict, suggests that *a fortiori* the Court might not have been disinclined to give favourable consideration to a notice of derogation had one been in place – at least, not at that time.[315]

---

312    UN Doc A/2929, § 43.

313    S/RES/1440 (2002), § 13.

314    *Hassan*, § 102.

315    See the following sections.

DEROGATION 89

## 4.4 Legal Consequences of Lawful Derogation in Time of War

The effect of derogation under Article 15 is not to make the rights derogated from entirely inoperable. No measures derogating from the Convention may go further than 'strictly required by the exigencies of the situation'; and moreover, they must not be 'inconsistent with [the State's] other obligations under international law'.

Views can – and do – differ from case to case, and depending on standpoint, as to what is 'the extent strictly required by the exigencies of the situation'.[316] So do views on what constitute 'other obligations under international law'.[317] There is however no room for discussion on the applicability in an armed conflict, be it international or non-international, of international humanitarian law. The importance of this statement derives from the fact that international humanitarian law admits of no further derogation: by its very nature, when it applies it sets the lowest permissible legal standard of rights protection.[318]

## 4.5 Derogation in Response to an 'Emergency Threatening the Life of the Nation' in Practice

Ireland derogated from the Convention in the 1950s, when the IRA was causing trouble; the United Kingdom did so, also in the 1950s, to deal with EOKA insurgents in what was then its 'Crown Colony' of Cyprus; the Greek colonels did so, to counter the political threat from the left; the United Kingdom did so again, for a while, in respect of Northern Ireland; Turkey did so at the height of the troubles with the PKK; and as we shall see, the United Kingdom did so, yet again, after the 9/11 attacks.

In recent years, internal turmoil led Albania to enter a derogation in 1997 referring to a 'constitutional and public order crisis'[319] and riots induced the Armenian Government in 2008 to declare a state of emergency in the capital Yerevan in 2008 requiring it to derogate from freedom of information, assem-

---

316 See 4.8 below.

317 See 4.9 below.

318 Doswald-Beck, pp. 79-80; Helen Duffy, *The 'War on Terror' and the Framework of International Law* (2nd edition 2015), Cambridge University Press, pp. 480-481; Austin, *supra* note 262; Marko Milanovic, "Extraterritorial Derogations from Treaties in Armed Conflict", in *The Frontiers of Human Rights: Extraterritoriality and its Challenges, Collected Courses of the Academy of European Law*, vol. XXIV/1, p. 55-88 at p. 60.

319 Harris, O'Boyle and Warbrick (3rd edn. 2014), p. 824, fn. 6.

bly and movement for twenty days.[320] An outbreak of bird flu caused by the H5N1 virus caused Georgia to derogate for a short period in 2006,[321] as did an attempted *coup d'état* in 2007,[322] but the Russian incursion into Abkhazia and South Ossetia in 2008 did not.

The most recent notices of derogation are that submitted by Ukraine on 10 June 2015, which as already mentioned is based on what Ukraine submits to be the unlawful Russian occupation and annexation of Crimea and the separatist violence in the Ukrainian east; that of France, lodged on 24 November 2015 in the wake of the terrorist attacks in Paris of the preceding 13 November, extended several times since; and yet another lodged by Turkey, this time on 21 July 2016 after the attempted *coup d'état* of 15 July 2016.[323] The French derogation was terminated in November 2017.[324] The Turkish state of emergency was terminated on 19 July 2018; the Turkish derogation was formally withdrawn by *note verbale* of 8 August 2018.[325] The Ukrainian derogation remains in force at the time of writing.

The attacks of '9/11' prompted the North Atlantic Council to state the very next day that

> if it [was] determined that this attack was directed from abroad against the United States, it [should] be regarded as an action covered by Article 5 of the Washington Treaty, which states that an armed attack against one or more of the Allies in Europe or North America shall be considered an attack against them all" and that "the United States' NATO Allies [stood] ready to provide the assistance that [might] be required as a consequence of these acts of barbarism.[326]

---

320  Notification - JJ6631C Tr./005-175 04 March 2008.

321  from freedom of movement in a particular district. Notification - JJ6239C Tr./005-166, 13 March 2006, withdrawn by Notification - JJ6268C Tr./005-168 07 April 2006.

322  Notification - JJ6565C Tr./005-173 09 November 2007, withdrawn by Notification - JJ6566C Tr./005-174 20 November 2007.

323  Quoted in *Mehmet Hasan Altan v. Turkey*, no. 13237/17, § 81, 20 March 2018, and *Şahin Alpay v. Turkey*, no. 16538/17, § 65, 20 March 2018. See also 4.5.1.9 below.

324  The French state of emergency, and hence the French derogation, ended on 1 November 2017. Annex to Notification JJ8525C Tr./005-213, 7 November 2017; see also the web site of the Council of Europe's Treaty Office, https://www.coe.int/en/web/conventions/full-list/-/conventions/treaty/005/declarations?p_auth=8PL9eBer (accessed on 12 April 2018).

325  Letter from the Turkish Permanent Representative to the Secretary General withdrawing the derogation notified on 21 July 2016, 8 August 2018.

326  Statement by the North Atlantic Council, NATO press release (2001)124, 12 September 2001, http://www.nato.int/docu/pr/2001/p01-124e.htm (accessed 28 July 2015). See also UNSC Resolution 1368 of the same date.

DEROGATION

It was soon suspected, and later confirmed, that the attacks were directed from Afghanistan by al-Qaeda.[327] To this day this remains the only occasion on which Article 5 of the Washington Treaty has been activated.

Yet despite the magnitude of the attack on a major ally whose support was essential to their own security and the resulting certain need for a robust military response, not one of the European NATO members – all of which are Contracting Parties to the Convention – derogated from the Convention under Article 15 on that ground alone. At this remove, one can only surmise that if this failure was not a massive oversight, which seems unlikely, none of them was willing either to declare war or to recognise publicly the capability of a non-state actor to cause 'a public emergency threatening the life of the nation'.

We cannot know now what view the Court would have taken of any derogation announced in reliance on the statement of the North Atlantic Council. That said, it is apparent that Governments of Contracting States do not view the activation on Article 5 of the Washington Treaty by itself as evidence of a situation requiring derogating measures. Accordingly, should any Contracting State in future wish to derogate from the Convention following a decision to activate Article 5 of the Washington Treaty, it will presumably be necessary to identify features distinguishing the new situation from the immediate aftermath of the 9/11 attacks.

In fact, only the United Kingdom derogated under Article 15 of the Convention in the wake of the 9/11 attacks – but only from its obligations under Article 5 § 1 (f), with a view to enhancing its powers to detain suspect foreign nationals and remove them from its territory.[328] This derogation accordingly bore no direct relation to the 9/11 attacks themselves, nor to the military activity that would soon follow.

### 4.5.1 Commission and Court Case-law

#### 4.5.1.1 Greece v. the United Kingdom (the 'First Cyprus Case')

Having been a part of the Ottoman Empire since the sixteenth century and placed under British administration after the Congress of Berlin in 1878, Cyprus was made a British Crown Colony during the First World War. After the Second World War, a Greek Cypriot movement sprouted which sought unity with the Kingdom of Greece (*enosis*). This led to the founding, in 1955, of the EOKA movement, which sought to bring about such unity by armed struggle.

---

327  US Government, National Commission on Terrorist Attacks Upon the United States, *The 9/11 Commission Report*, pp. 145-169, http://govinfo.library.unt.edu/911/report/911Report. pdf (accessed 28 July 2015).

328  *A. and Others v. the United Kingdom* § 11.

The British colonial government responded by enacting emergency legislation and deporting the Greek Cypriot leader, Archbishop Makarios III, and three of his followers to the Seychelles. The United Kingdom Government transmitted *notes verbales* giving notice of derogation under Article 15 to the Secretary General of the Council of Europe on 7 October 1955 and 13 April 1956.

In May 1956 the Kingdom of Greece brought an interstate application against the United Kingdom, which responded by invoking its derogation.

Losing little time, the Commission declared the application admissible less than a month later,[329] holding among other things that 'the effects of derogations made by the Government of the United Kingdom under Article 15 of the Convention relate[d] to the merits of the case and not to the admissibility of the application'. It then appointed a 'Sub-Commission' from among its members to establish the facts.

The Commission, in plenary formation once more, adopted its report[330] on 26 September 1958. It is a bulky document, published in two volumes. The first volume deals with the preliminary issues, namely whether there was a 'public emergency threatening the life of the nation' and whether the notice given to the Secretary General of the Council of Europe was sufficient in its terms. The second goes into the substance of the derogating measures.

In considering whether there was a 'public emergency threatening the life of the nation', it first determined that the expression 'nation' meant not the United Kingdom itself or the Commonwealth, but 'the people and its institutions, even in a non-self-governing territory, or in other words, the organised society, including the authorities responsible both under domestic and international law for the maintenance of law and order'. Any other interpretation would have made nonsense of the 'colonial clause' contained in then Article 63 of the Convention (now Article 56) by hindering a colonial power in taking measures aimed at preventing the violent overthrow of a subordinate government.[331]

The Commission next noted that during the year 1955 until the state of emergency was proclaimed (on 26 November 1955), EOKA violence had killed 11 persons and wounded 74 more. There had been 185 bomb explosions, 20 cases of arson and 3 'raids on police stations etc.' From the proclamation of the state of emergency until 14 March 1957 when EOKA declared a truce there were a further 245 killed and 636 wounded, 866 bomb explosions, 251 cases of arson, and 57 raids. These figures had to be seen against the background of the popu-

---

329  *Greece v. the United Kingdom*, no. 176/56, Commission decision of 2 June 1956.
330  Article 31 of the Convention (1950 text).
331  *Greece v. the United Kingdom*, § 130.

DEROGATION

lation of Cyprus, which at the time numbered only some 500,000 souls. During EOKA's self-declared truce the occurrence of incidents involving violence was reduced, but strikes, riots, demonstrations and 'reported threats and intimidation' continued.

The Commission was unwilling to accept the Greek argument that there was no 'emergency threatening the life of the nation' during the first period, up to 26 November 1955. Such a conclusion might have been justified if only the number of incidents were taken into account; however, 'these incidents emanated from a fast-growing and militant organisation which, according to its own statements, aimed at obtaining self-determination for Cyprus by all possible means, including force and violence'. The existence of such a threat already at that time was accordingly 'at least plausible'. The Commission continued:

> The assessment whether or not a public danger existed is a question of appreciation. The United Kingdom Government made such an assessment of the situation prevailing at that time and concluded that there existed a public danger threatening the life of the nation. That this appreciation by the British Government was correct was subsequently proved by the great increase of violence which occurred between November 1955 and March 1957.[332]

There could, however, be no doubt that such a threat existed during the second period (November 1955-March 1957), when the threat perceived earlier materialised.

During the remaining period, other developments had included the emergence of a Turkish Cypriot counter-movement opposed to unification with Greece, which also threatened to turn violent, and tensions between the political right, represented by EOKA and related organisations, and the political left, which was said by the United Kingdom Government to have links to the Communist movement.

All these factors together led the Commission, with one dissenting vote (that of its Greek member, Mr C.Th. Eustathiades),[333] to express the following opinion:

> The Commission of Human Rights is authorised by the Convention to express a critical opinion on derogations under Article 15, but the Government concerned retains, within certain limits, its discretion in appre-

---

332    *ibid.*, § 132.
333    *ibid.*, § 139.

ciating the threat to the life of the nation. In the present case the Government of Cyprus has not gone beyond these limits of appreciation.[334]

The substance of the complaints made by the Greek Government concerned the use of curfews, allegedly imposed on communities by way of collective punishment; arrest without warrant and detention for up to sixteen days before the detainee was brought before a court; detention without trial of terrorist suspects; the deportation of Archbishop Makarios and the others; the infliction of corporal punishment on male juvenile offenders (whipping); the application of collective punishments (other than curfews); and the existence and use of powers to search and censor, control burials, prevent processions and meetings, close schools and restrict the right to strike.

A majority of the Commission was unable to find that the curfews had been anything other than necessary measures to maintain order.[335] As to arrest without warrant, the Commission noted that it was not prohibited by the Convention. As regards administrative detention for up to sixteen days, the Commission noted that this measure was not mentioned in the notice of derogation but found nonetheless that since a notice of derogation had been lodged which covered detention without trial the omission was 'a technical rather than a substantive departure from the term of the Convention'.[336] On the subject of detention without trial of suspected terrorists, a majority of the Commission recognised that this was an extraordinarily far-reaching measure but accepted that it was necessary in an environment where the intimidation of witnesses made it unlikely that a conviction could be secured at trial, and also that safeguards existed, in the form of a *habeas corpus* procedure, to prevent abuse.[337] Archbishop Makarios and the three others having been released from detention in the Seychelles, the remaining issues were their removal from Cyprus and the order preventing their re-entry; these a majority of the Commission did not find to violate Articles 5 and 8 of the Convention as such.[338] The other measures complained of were grouped together and accepted as legitimate within the terms of the second paragraphs of Articles 9, 10 11, respectively, simply in the light of the established existence of a 'public emergency threatening the life of the nation'.[339] The Commission did not find it necessary to express a view on corporal punishment, the United Kingdom Government

---

334    *ibid.*, § 136.
335    *ibid.*, § 287.
336    *ibid.*, § 297.
337    *ibid.*, § 318.
338    *ibid.*, § 337.
339    *ibid.*, § 363.

DEROGATION

having agreed to discontinue the practice (though it survived a while longer in parts of the British Isles[340]); nor, for the same reason, did it give a legal opinion on collective fines.[341]

This report, the very first published by the Commission, unites all the elements of the later case-law under Article 15 of the Convention: the concept of a 'nation'; the question whether there is a 'public emergency' threatening its 'life'; whether the matters in issue were 'strictly required by the exigencies of the situation'; whether there was adequate notice given to the Secretary General of the Council of Europe; and whether there was compliance with 'other obligations under international law'.

The case came to be known as the *First Cyprus Case*. There is, of course, a Second Cyprus Case; but the Commission's report in that case merely closes the file and is of no substantive interest whatsoever.[342]

### 4.5.1.2 *Lawless v. Ireland (No. 3)*

Mr Gerard Lawless, a national and resident of the Republic of Ireland, was arrested in September 1956 with two others on suspicion of firearms offences, the group having been found in possession of a Thompson sub-machine-gun, six army rifles, six sporting guns, a revolver, an automatic pistol and 400 magazines. He admitted on that occasion having taken part in an armed raid in which guns and revolvers had been stolen. Put on trial for unlawful possession of firearms, he was however acquitted, the trial judge directing the jury that (in the words of both the Commission and the Court) 'it had not been conclusively shown that no competent authority had issued a firearms certificate authorising him to be in possession of the arms concerned'.[343] Lawless was arrested a second time in May 1957, having been found in possession of documents implicating him in the planning of attacks to be carried out by the IRA on border posts and military and civilian targets in Northern Ireland. He was tried and sentenced to a brief term of imprisonment, which he served.

On 8 July 1957, after a series of IRA attacks on targets in both the Republic of Ireland and Northern Ireland and shortly before the annual Orange Processions, the Irish Government activated the Offences against the State (Amendment) Act, 1940, giving Ministers of State the power to order the detention without trial of 'any particular person (...) engaged in activities which, in his

---

340   *Tyrer v. the United Kingdom*, no. 5856/72, §§ 14-15, Series A no. 26.

341   *Greece v. the United Kingdom*, § 235.

342   *Greece v. the United Kingdom (no. 2)*, no. 299/57, Commission report of 8 July 1959.

343   *Lawless v. Ireland*, no. 332/57, Commission report of 19 December 1959, § 2; *Lawless v. Ireland* (No. 3), judgment of 1 July 1961, § 19, Series A no. 3.

opinion, are prejudicial to the preservation of public peace and order or to the security of the State'. The Irish Government informed the Secretary General of the Council of Europe accordingly on 20 July, invoking Article 15 of the Convention.

A few days later, on 11 July, Lawless was again arrested as being a suspected member of an unlawful organisation, namely the IRA. His detention was ordered by the Minister of Justice. He unsuccessfully challenged his detention in *habeas corpus* proceedings; he was released in December 1957 after giving an undertaking 'not to engage in any illegal activities under the Offences against the State Acts, 1939 and 1940'.

The Court, like the Commission before it, held that Article 5 §§ 1 (c) and 3 allowed the arrest and detention of a criminal suspect only for the purpose of bringing him before a judge and entitled him to trial within a reasonable time. These provisions therefore could not justify Lawless's detention between July and December 1957.[344] The question therefore became whether any other Convention provision – Article 15 – could serve instead.

The Court interpreted the words 'other public emergency threatening the life of the nation' as meaning 'an exceptional situation of crisis or emergency which affects the whole population and constitutes a threat to the organised life of the community of which the State is composed', and concluded, given the attacks that had taken place and the violence to be expected around the time of the Orange Processions (12 July), that the Irish Government had been entitled to invoke Article 15. As to whether the measures taken were 'strictly required by the exigencies of the situation', the Court accepted that IRA activities were mainly intended to produce effects across the border, in Northern Ireland, and were extremely difficult to prevent from within the Republic applying ordinary criminal law. Short of sealing the border entirely, which would have had serious repercussions on 'the population as a whole', administrative detention appeared an adequate response. Moreover, safeguards were in place in the form of a (non-judicial) Detention Commission that was accessible to the detainee and had the power to order release, and could in fact be ordered to do so by the courts. Finally, release could be obtained by means of an undertaking to desist from unlawful activity.[345]

### 4.5.1.3   The *'Greek Case'*

On 21 April 1967 a group of senior officers of the Greek armed forces deposed the constitutional government of the Kingdom of Greece and, by Royal De-

---

344   *Lawless (No. 3)*, §§ 9 and 15.
345   *Lawless (No. 3)*, §§ 36-37.

DEROGATION

cree, suspended certain provisions of the Greek Constitution guaranteeing basic rights. Over the following months the revolutionary government, as they styled themselves, disbanded Parliament and dissolved political parties; gave themselves sweeping powers of arrest, detention and search; introduced trial of political offences by military courts; imposed censorship on the media; suspended trade union freedoms; and replaced the Constitution. On 3 May 1967 the permanent representative of Greece transmitted a French translation of the Royal Decree to the Secretary General of the Council of Europe. On 27 September 1967 the permanent representative again wrote to the Secretary General, stating that the letter of 3 May had constituted a notice of derogation under Article 15 of the Convention and setting out the view of his masters that a public emergency existed that threatened the life of the nation: the letter made reference to anarchist demonstrations, revolutionary activity by Communist sympathisers and other left-wing movements, strikes called by trade unions and an alleged plot to subvert the armed forces. The letter added that there was no infringement of any of the non-derogable rights set out in Article 15 § 2.

Interstate applications against Greece were lodged by the governments of Denmark, Norway, Sweden and the Netherlands.[346]

The Commission gave a first decision on 24 January 1968, declaring the applications admissible; after the Danish, Norwegian and Swedish Governments submitted additional complaints, the Commission gave a follow-up decision on 31 May 1968 declaring these admissible also.

The Commission adopted its report on 5 November 1969.[347] Considering, firstly, the argument of the Greek government that in applying Article 15 they were entitled to special consideration (in the form of a wider margin of appreciation) as a 'revolutionary' government, the Commission, referring to its first admissibility decision, reiterated that a revolutionary government was not absolved from its obligations under the Convention. That said, such a government 'established in a High Contracting State, and recognised as representing this State in international relations', might in principle invoke Article 15 provided that the conditions laid down in that Article were fulfilled[348] – which, however, was not the case. The Commission found on the facts that the circumstances cited – the danger of a Communist takeover, the existence of a constitutional crisis and a breakdown in law and order – were not established: while undoubtedly there had been some political unrest in the years preced-

---

346    Nos. 3321/67, 3322/67, 3323/67 and 3344/67 respectively.

347    *Denmark, Norway, Sweden and the Netherlands v. Greece*, nos. 3321/67, 3322/67, 3323/67 and 3344/67 (the *"Greek Case"*), Commission report of 5 November 1969.

348    *ibid.*, §§ 27 and 49.

ing the coup, to all appearances the cataclysmic events feared by the colonels had not been imminent and the constitutional Government had remained in firm control of the country until ousted.[349] Although after the coup there had been a number of violent incidents and a number of illegal organisations had been formed, the Commission was not convinced that 'either factor [was] beyond the control of the public authorities using normal measures, or that they [were] on a scale threatening the organised life of the community'.[350]

Nevertheless, the Commission decided to consider whether the measures taken could have been said to have been 'strictly required by the exigencies of the situation' had the derogation been valid. It came to the conclusion that the restrictions on the rights protected by Articles 5 and 6 did not meet that requirement, and that restrictions on the rights protected by Articles 8, 9, 10, 11 and 14 could not be considered 'necessary' within the substantive meaning of those Articles given the absence of any corresponding emergency threatening the life of the nation.[351] A remedy within the meaning of Article 13 appropriate to complaints of torture had been lacking. Finally, there had been no need to suspend Parliament, in violation of Article 3 of Protocol No 1. In contrast, there had been no violation of Article 7 of the Convention,[352] and there was no need to address issues raised under Article 1 of Protocol No. 1.[353]

The 'Greek Case', as the case came to be called, remains the only one to date in which either Strasbourg institution has refused to accept the Government's assessment that an existential threat to the nation was sufficiently great to justify the taking of derogating measures in reliance on Article 15.

The case did not reach the Court. In the system as it existed at the time, either the Commission or an applicant or respondent Contracting State had to refer the case to the Court within three months from the date on which the Commission's report was transmitted to the Committee of Ministers of the Council of Europe (Articles 32 and 48 of the 1950 Convention); this did not happen. It therefore fell to the Committee of Ministers to express its opinion in the matter. On 15 April 1970 the Committee of Ministers adopted a resolution in which it adopted the Commission's views as its own.[354]

---

349    *ibid.*, §§ 115-125.

350    *ibid.*, §§ 142-144.

351    *ibid.*, §§ 198-201 (Article 5); §§ 231-234 (Article 6); § 251 (Article 8); §§ 274-276 (Articles 9 and 10); §§ 296-300 (Article 11); § 305 (Article 13); §§ 319-320 (Article 3 of Protocol No. 1).

352    *ibid.*, §§ 327-328.

353    *ibid.*, § 329.

354    *The "Greek Case"*, nos. 3321/67, 3322/67, 3323/67 and 3344/67, Committee of Ministers resolution DH (70)1 of 15 April 1970.

DEROGATION                                                                    99

### 4.5.1.4    *Brannigan and McBride*

It is not necessary here to chart the background of the internecine conflict in Northern Ireland frequently referred to as 'the Troubles'. Suffice it for present purposes that the United Kingdom sought to contain it by enacting, from 1974 on, a series of Prevention of Terrorism (Temporary Provisions) Acts proscribing certain named Irish Republican underground organisations that had a history of violence, broadening the powers of the police to arrest terrorist suspects and extending the permitted length of police custody, normally forty-eight hours, by a further five days.

In its *Brogan and Others* judgment of 29 November 1988, the Court held that there had been a violation of Article 5 § 3 of the Convention in respect of each of the applicants, all of whom had been detained under the Act in its redaction of 1984. The Court held that even the shortest of the four periods of detention concerned, namely four days and six hours, fell outside the constraints as to time permitted by the first part of Article 5 § 3.[355]

Less than a month later, on 23 December 1988, the United Kingdom lodged a notice of derogation with the Secretary General of the Council of Europe. As relevant to our discussions, it read as follows:

> ... Following [the *Brogan and Others* judgment], the Secretary of State for the Home Department informed Parliament on 6 December 1988 that, against the background of the terrorist campaign, and the over-riding need to bring terrorists to justice, the Government did not believe that the maximum period of detention should be reduced. He informed Parliament that the Government were examining the matter with a view to responding to the judgment. On 22 December 1988, the Secretary of State further informed Parliament that it remained the Government's wish, if it could be achieved, to find a judicial process under which extended detention might be reviewed and where appropriate authorised by a judge or other judicial officer. But a further period of reflection and consultation was necessary before the Government could bring forward a firm and final view. Since the judgment of 29 November 1988 as well as previously, the Government have found it necessary to continue to exercise, in relation to terrorism connected with the affairs of Northern Ireland, the powers described above enabling further detention without charge, for periods of up to 5 days, on the authority of the Secretary of State, to the extent strictly required by the exigencies of the situation to enable nec-

---

355    *Brogan and Others v. the United Kingdom,* nos. 11209/84, 11234/84, 11266/84 and 11386/85, §§ 55-62, Series A no. 145-B.

essary enquiries and investigations properly to be completed in order to decide whether criminal proceedings should be instituted. To the extent that the exercise of these powers may be inconsistent with the obligations imposed by the Convention the Government have availed themselves of the right of derogation conferred by Article 15(1) of the Convention and will continue to do so until further notice ...[356]

Messrs Brannigan and McBride were arrested in January 1989. They were kept detained for six days, fourteen hours and thirty minutes, and four days, six hours and twenty-five minutes respectively without being brought before a magistrate. They complained of this under Article 5 § 3 of the Convention.

Given the precedent established by *Brogan and Others*, the United Kingdom Government were not in a position to dispute that the requirement of 'promptness' contained in Article 5 § 3 had not been met. Discussion therefore focused on the validity of the derogation.

The applicants, supported by a group of NGOs as intervening third parties (Amnesty International, Liberty, Interights and the Committee on the Administration of Justice), argued that the margin of appreciation left to the respondent Government in the matter should be a narrow one, especially since the state of emergency giving rise to the use of the special powers in issue had already been in existence for a very long time. The Court responded as follows:

> The Court recalls that it falls to each Contracting State, with its responsibility for 'the life of [its] nation', to determine whether that life is threatened by a 'public emergency', and, if so, how far it is necessary to go in attempting to overcome the emergency. By reason of their direct and continuous contact with the pressing needs of the moment, the national authorities are in principle in a better position than the international judge to decide both on the presence of such an emergency and on the nature and scope of derogations necessary to avert it. Accordingly, in this matter a wide margin of appreciation should be left to the national authorities (see the *Ireland v. the United Kingdom* judgment of 18 January 1978, Series A no. 25, pp. 78-79, § 207).
>
> Nevertheless, Contracting Parties do not enjoy an unlimited power of appreciation. It is for the Court to rule on whether inter alia the States have gone beyond the 'extent strictly required by the exigencies' of the crisis. The domestic margin of appreciation is thus accompanied by a Eu-

---

356     Quoted in *Brannigan and McBride v. the United Kingdom*, nos. 14553/89 and 14554/89, § 31, Series A no. 258-B.

ropean supervision (ibid.). At the same time, in exercising its supervision the Court must give appropriate weight to such relevant factors as the nature of the rights affected by the derogation, the circumstances leading to, and the duration of, the emergency situation.[357]

The majority of the Court had little difficulty accepting the existence of a public emergency 'threatening the life of the nation'. That was clear enough in view of its own earlier case-law – *Lawless, Ireland v. the United Kingdom* – and from 'all the material before it as to the extent and impact of terrorist violence in Northern Ireland and elsewhere in the United Kingdom'; the latter reflected that there had since the early 1970s been over forty thousand terrorist shooting and bombing incidents in Northern Ireland alone leaving over thirty-five thousand people injured.

As to whether the absence of judicial control of extended detention was justified, the United Kingdom Government relied heavily on the need to withhold classified information from detainees and their legal advisers. In the Court's paraphrase,

> ... the Government had reluctantly concluded that, within the framework of the common-law system, it was not feasible to introduce a system which would be compatible with Article 5 § 3 but would not weaken the effectiveness of the response to the terrorist threat. Decisions to prolong detention were taken on the basis of information the nature and source of which could not be revealed to a suspect or his legal adviser without risk to individuals assisting the police or the prospect of further valuable intelligence being lost. Moreover, involving the judiciary in the process of granting or approving extensions of detention created a real risk of undermining their independence as they would inevitably be seen as part of the investigation and prosecution process

– which conclusion was supported by Government-commissioned reports submitted to Parliament each time the Act came up for renewal.[358]

The Court was prepared to accept the Government's argument. In so doing, it made reference to the specific context of Northern Ireland, 'where the judiciary [was] small and vulnerable to terrorist attacks', and that accordingly

---

357    *Brannigan and McBride,* § 43.

358    *ibid.,* § 56.

102                                                                    CHAPTER 4

'public confidence in the independence of the judiciary [was] understandably a matter to which the Government [attached] great importance'.[359]

In addition, 'basic safeguards against abuse' were available in the form of the common-law remedy of *habeas corpus* and access to a solicitor (after an initial period of detention of forty-eight hours – any denial of access to a solicitor beyond that was reviewable by the courts); and the operation of the legislation was kept under regular independent review. Further protection was offered by the entitlement of detainees to inform a relative or friend about their detention and to have access to a doctor.[360]

There remained some discussion as to whether the reference to 'other obligations under international law' in Article 15 § 1 meant that a state of emergency must be 'officially proclaimed', that being a requirement set out in Article 4 of the International Covenant on Civil and Political Rights. For its part, the Court, while declining to give an interpretation of the terms 'officially proclaimed' in Article 4 of the Covenant, declared itself satisfied with the statement made by the Secretary of State for the Home Department to the House of Commons explaining in detail the reasons underlying the Government's decision to derogate and announcing that steps were being taken to give effect to that decision.[361]

#### 4.5.1.5    *Marshall*

The notice of derogation in issue in *Brannigan and McBride* was again put to the test in 2001. The applicant, Mr Marshall, had been arrested in February 1998. The situation was, in its essentials, identical to that in issue in *Brannigan and McBride*. The complaint, for our purposes, was essentially that the continued existence of the powers of detention resulting from the maintenance in force of the Prevention of Terrorism Act, which had been renewed each year since 1989, could no longer be justified with reference to Article 15 of the Convention.

After announcing its intention to apply *Brannigan and McBride* while noting that it 'must at the same time address with special vigilance the fact that almost nine years separate the prolonged administrative detention of the applicants Brannigan and McBride from that of [Mr Marshall]', the Court held:

> The Court does not agree with the applicant's submission that the security situation in Northern Ireland at the time of his detention had

---

359    *ibid.*, §§ 58-59.
360    *ibid.*, § 64.
361    *ibid.*, § 73.

DEROGATION

improved to the point where it was no longer justified to refer to it as a public emergency "threatening the life of the nation". It notes that the authorities continued to be confronted with the threat of terrorist violence notwithstanding a reduction in its incidence. It cannot but note that the weeks preceding the applicant's detention were characterised by an outbreak of deadly violence. This of itself confirms that there had been no return to normality since the date of the *Brannigan and McBride* judgment such as to lead the Court to controvert the authorities' assessment of the situation in the province in terms of the threats which organised violence posed for the life of the community and the search for a peaceful settlement. It recalls in this connection that by reason of their direct and continuous contact with the pressing needs of the moment, the national authorities are in principle better placed than the international judge to decide both on the presence of such an emergency and on the nature and scope of the derogation necessary to avoid it (...).

As to the decision to prolong the applicant's detention in the absence of judicial intervention, the Court observes that the Government rely on the same justifications for this measure which they advanced in the *Brannigan and McBride* case. Those justifications were accepted by the Court in that case on the basis that it was not its role to substitute its view as to what measures were most appropriate or expedient at the relevant time in dealing with an emergency situation for that of the Government which have direct responsibility for establishing the balance between the taking of effective measures to combat terrorism on the one hand, and respecting individual rights on the other. ...

Going on to find that the reasoning on which *Brannigan and McBride* had been decided remained pertinent, the Court declared the application inadmissible.[362]

In actual fact, by the time the Court gave its decision in this case the United Kingdom Government had withdrawn their notice of derogation. They had done so on 19 February 2001, with effect from 26 February 2001.

The Court adopted its decision on 10 July 2001, two months and one day before the attacks of 9/11 which changed the world's conception of terrorism completely.

---

362    *Marshall v. the United Kingdom* (dec.), no. 41571/98, 10 July 2001.

## 4.5.1.6    *Aksoy*

The case of *Aksoy v. Turkey* is generally remembered as the first in which the Court reached a finding that treatment contrary to Article 3 of the Convention amounted to 'torture'. Tortured Zeki Aksoy certainly was, but what is more is that this this this happened during a fourteen-day stretch of detention without his being brought before a magistrate.

Turkey too had derogated under Article 15 at the time.[363] The legislative measure relevant to Article 5 of the Convention read as follows:

> The Governor of the state of emergency region can order persons who continuously violate the general security and public order, to settle at a place to be specified by the Minister of the Interior outside the state of emergency region for a period which shall not exceed the duration of the state of emergency ...[364]

The Court was willing to accept that 'the particular extent and impact of PKK terrorist activity in South-East Turkey [had] undoubtedly created, in the region concerned, a "public emergency threatening the life of the nation"'.[365] It did not, however, accept that the measures taken were 'strictly required by the exigencies of the situation', and moreover found that even the most basic safeguards were lacking:

> 77. In the *Brannigan and McBride* judgment (...), the Court held that the United Kingdom Government had not exceeded their margin of appreciation by derogating from their obligations under Article 5 of the Convention to the extent that individuals suspected of terrorist offences were allowed to be held for up to seven days without judicial control.
>
> In the instant case, the applicant was detained for at least fourteen days without being brought before a judge or other officer. The Government have sought to justify this measure by reference to the particular demands of police investigations in a geographically vast area faced with a terrorist organisation receiving outside support (...).
>
> 78. Although the Court is of the view – which it has expressed on several occasions in the past (see, for example, the ... *Brogan and Others* judg-

---

363    Letters of the Permanent Representative of the Turkish Republic to the Secretary General of the Council of Europe, 6 August 1990 and 5 May 1992; *Aksoy v. Turkey*, no. 21987/93, §§ 31-33, Reports 1996-VI.

364    *Aksoy*, § 31.

365    *ibid.*, § 70.

DEROGATION 105

ment) – that the investigation of terrorist offences undoubtedly presents the authorities with special problems, it cannot accept that it is necessary to hold a suspect for fourteen days without judicial intervention. This period is exceptionally long, and left the applicant vulnerable not only to arbitrary interference with his right to liberty but also to torture (...). Moreover, the Government have not adduced any detailed reasons before the Court as to why the fight against terrorism in South-East Turkey rendered judicial intervention impracticable.'[366]

#### 4.5.1.7 Sakık and Others

In *Sakık and Others* the Turkish Government sought to rely on the same derogation in respect of the trial and detention of a number of former members of the Grand National Assembly found to be of a separatist bent. However, the trial and detention having taken place in Ankara not in the South-Eastern Anatolian provinces covered by the derogation, the derogation could not apply.[367]

This judgment demonstrates that the scope and extent of a derogation under Article 15 is limited by the terms in which it has been couched in the notice to the Secretary General of the Council of Europe.[368]

#### 4.5.1.8 A. and Others v. the United Kingdom

As we have seen, the United Kingdom was the only State party to the Convention to derogate from the Convention under Article 15 in the aftermath of the 9/11 attacks on the United States. In its relevant parts, the notice of derogation lodged with the Secretary General of the Council of Europe on 18 December 2001 read as follows:[369]

---

366 *Aksoy*, §§ 77-78. See also *Demir and Others v. Turkey*, nos. 21380/93, 21381/93 and 21383/93, §§ 49-57, Reports 1998-VI (incommunicado detention for at least sixteen or twenty-three days); *Nuray Şen v. Turkey*, no. 41478/98, §§ 25-29, 17 June 2003 (eleven days before the applicant was brought before a judge or other judicial officer); *Elci and Others v. Turkey*, nos. 23145/93 and 25091/94, § 684, 17 June 2003 (detention not "in accordance with a procedure prescribed by law" in that the lawful authority of a "judge or other officer" was entirely lacking); and *Bilen v. Turkey*, no. 34482/97, §§ 44-50, 21 February 2006 (eighteen days before the applicant was brought before a judge or other judicial officer).

367 *Sakık and Others v. Turkey*, nos. 23878/94, 23879/94, 23880/94, 23881/94, 23882/94 and 23883/94, § 39, Reports 1997-VII. See also *Sadak v. Turkey*, nos. 25142/94 and 27099/95, § 56, 8 April 2004; *Yurttas v. Turkey*, nos. 25143/94 and 27098/95, § 58, 27 May 2004; and *Abdülsamet Yaman v. Turkey*, no. 32446/96, § 69, 2 November 2004.

368 Loof, p. 625.

369 Quoted in *A. and Others v. the United Kingdom*, § 11.

### Public emergency in the United Kingdom

The terrorist attacks in New York, Washington, D.C. and Pennsylvania on 11 September 2001 resulted in several thousand deaths, including many British victims and others from seventy different countries. In its Resolutions 1368 (2001) and 1373 (2001), the United Nations Security Council recognised the attacks as a threat to international peace and security.

The threat from international terrorism is a continuing one. In its Resolution 1373 (2001), the Security Council, acting under Chapter VII of the United Nations Charter, required all States to take measures to prevent the commission of terrorist attacks, including by denying safe haven to those who finance, plan, support or commit terrorist attacks.

There exists a terrorist threat to the United Kingdom from persons suspected of involvement in international terrorism. In particular, there are foreign nationals present in the United Kingdom who are suspected of being concerned in the commission, preparation or instigation of acts of international terrorism, of being members of organisations or groups which are so concerned or of having links with members of such organisations or groups, and who are a threat to the national security of the United Kingdom.

As a result, a public emergency, within the meaning of Article 15 § 1 of the Convention, exists in the United Kingdom.

and

### Article 5 § 1 (f) of the Convention

It is well established that Article 5 § 1 (f) permits the detention of a person with a view to deportation only in circumstances where "action is being taken with a view to deportation" (*Chahal v. the United Kingdom* (1996) 23 EHRR 413 at paragraph 112). In that case the European Court of Human Rights indicated that detention will cease to be permissible under Article 5 § 1 (f) if deportation proceedings are not prosecuted with due diligence and that it was necessary in such cases to determine whether the duration of the deportation proceedings was excessive (paragraph 113).

In some cases, where the intention remains to remove or deport a person on national security grounds, continued detention may not be consistent with Article 5 § 1 (f) as interpreted by the Court in the Chahal case. This may be the case, for example, if the person has established that removal to their own country might result in treatment contrary to Article 3 of the Convention. In such circumstances, irrespective of the gravity of the threat to national security posed by the person concerned, it is

DEROGATION

well established that Article 3 prevents removal or deportation to a place where there is a real risk that the person will suffer treatment contrary to that Article. If no alternative destination is immediately available then removal or deportation may not, for the time being, be possible even though the ultimate intention remains to remove or deport the person once satisfactory arrangements can be made. In addition, it may not be possible to prosecute the person for a criminal offence given the strict rules on the admissibility of evidence in the criminal justice system of the United Kingdom and the high standard of proof required.

*Derogation under Article 15 of the Convention*
The Government has considered whether the exercise of the extended power to detain contained in the Anti-terrorism, Crime and Security Act 2001 may be inconsistent with the obligations under Article 5 § 1 of the Convention. As indicated above, there may be cases where, notwithstanding a continuing intention to remove or deport a person who is being detained, it is not possible to say that "action is being taken with a view to deportation" within the meaning of Article 5 § 1 (f) as interpreted by the Court in the *Chahal* case. To the extent, therefore, that the exercise of the extended power may be inconsistent with the United Kingdom's obligations under Article 5 § 1, the Government has decided to avail itself of the right of derogation conferred by Article 15 § 1 of the Convention and will continue to do so until further notice.

British immigration law, like the immigration laws of other countries, provided for the detention of non-nationals pending deportation. However, detention was not permissible under the ordinary law where deportation was known to be impossible, whether because there was no country willing to take the person in question or because there would be a risk of torture or other serious ill-treatment to the proposed deportee in his or her country of origin – and accordingly, as in *Chahal*,[370] a prospective violation of Article 3 of the Convention.[371]

The legislation enacted in derogation of the ordinary law provided that a 'suspected international terrorist' might be detained despite the fact that his removal or departure from the United Kingdom was prevented by 'a point of law which wholly or partly relates to an international agreement' – such as,

---

370    *Chahal* §§ 79-80.
371    Immigration Act 1971 and *R. v. Governor of Durham Prison, ex parte Hardial Singh*, [1984] 1 Weekly Law Reports 704, cited in *A. and Others*, § 87.

presumably, the assessment that the person's removal would be in violation of Article 3 of the Convention – or 'a practical consideration'.[372] It is implicit that persons detained under this legislation could obtain release if they left of their own accord for another country – as indeed several of the applicants later did.

From the outset, both the legislation and the derogation were criticised within the United Kingdom and internationally. A Review Committee consisting of Privy Councillors (the 'Newton Committee', after its chairman) pointed out that a considerable proportion of terrorist suspects had been British citizens, which justified doubts as to both the principle and the efficacy of a measure aimed solely at foreign nationals.[373] Similar concerns were voiced by a British Joint Parliamentary Committee on Human Rights.[374] Outside the United Kingdom, the European Commissioner for Human Rights queried the need for derogating from the Convention at all, pointing out that no other European State – not even States 'long faced with recurring terrorist activity' – had found such a course needful.[375] He also observed that deporting suspected terrorists – or allowing them to leave of their own volition – left them 'at liberty to plan and pursue, albeit at some distance from the United Kingdom, activity potentially prejudicial to its public security'.[376] The United Nations Committee on the Elimination of All Forms of Racial Discrimination was concerned that the measures provided for discriminated against non-nationals.[377]

In the light of such forceful criticism, it could have been no surprise to the Government of the United Kingdom that their derogating measures were challenged both in the English courts and in Strasbourg.

Of the eleven applicants in *A and Others v. the United Kingdom* one was stateless (he had been born in a Palestinian refugee camp); the others were of various nationalities, all of states in North Africa and the Middle East. All were identified by the Secretary of State for the Home Department as 'suspected

---

372 Section 23 of the Anti-terrorism, Crime and Security Act 2001, quoted in *A. and Others*, § 90.

373 Privy Councillor Review Committee, Anti-terrorism, Crime and Security Act 2001 Review, Ordered by The House of Commons to be printed 18th December 2003, §§ 193-94; see *A. and Others*, §§ 98-99.

374 Joint Parliamentary Committee on Human Rights, Second Report of the Session 2001-02, § 38, and Sixth Report of the Session 2003-04, §§ 42-44, quoted in A. and Others, § 100.

375 Opinion of the European Commissioner for Human Rights, Mr Alvaro Gil-Robles, on certain aspects of the United Kingdom 2001 derogation from Article 5 par. 1 of the European Convention on Human Rights, 28 August 2002, CommDH(2002)7, § 33).

376 *ibid.*, § 37.

377 Concluding observations of the Committee on the Elimination of Racial Discrimination, United Kingdom of Great Britain and Northern Ireland, CERD/C/63/CO/11, § 17.

DEROGATION

international terrorists' and made subject to deportation orders. All were accordingly placed in detention ostensibly for the purpose of deportation.

The applicants appealed, first to the Special Immigration Appeals Commission (SIAC), then to the Court of Appeal. Ultimately they were granted leave to appeal to the House of Lords.[378]

SIAC and the Court of Appeal both found it established that the terrorist threat identified constituted a 'public emergency threatening the life of the nation'. They differed, however, in their views of whether the legislation enacted in derogation of ordinary immigration law was 'strictly required by the exigencies of the situation'. SIAC found it to discriminate unjustifiably against foreign nationals, in violation of Article 14 of the Convention. The Court of Appeal took the contrary view: it found that British nationals suspected of being terrorists were not an analogous situation to foreign nationals who could not be deported because to do so would place them in danger, the latter having no right to remain in the country but merely a right not to be removed for their own safety.

The House of Lords, by eight to one, accepted the assessment that there was a 'public emergency threatening the life of the nation'. It found this to be based on the very real threat posed by the presence of a 'significant body' of foreign nationals in the United Kingdom who had the will and the capability of mounting coordinated attacks such as those the world had just witnessed in the United States. The lone dissenter, Lord Hoffmann, accepted that there was credible evidence of a threat of serious terrorist attack within the United Kingdom but considered that it would not destroy the life of the nation, since the threat was not so fundamental as to threaten, in his words, 'our institutions of government or our existence as a civil community'. He concluded that 'the real threat to the life of the nation ... [came] not from terrorism but from laws such as these'.[379]

In broad agreement with SIAC but differing from the Court of Appeal, the House of Lords nonetheless held that the legislation in issue did not satisfy the requirements of Article 15 § 1. To begin with, the Law Lords found on three principal grounds that it was not a proportional response: firstly, in that the detention scheme applied only to non-nationals suspected of international terrorism and did not address the threat which came from United Kingdom nationals who were also so suspected; secondly, in that it left suspected international terrorists at liberty to leave the United Kingdom and continue their threatening activities abroad (perhaps in a country 'as close as France'); and

---

378    For a summary of the domestic proceedings, see *A. and Others*, §§ 14-23.

379    *A. and Others*, § 18.

thirdly, in that the legislation was drafted too broadly, so that it could, in principle, apply to individuals suspected of involvement with international terrorist organisations which did not fall within the scope of the derogation.[380]

In addition, they found that the legislation in issue was discriminatory and inconsistent with Article 14 of the Convention, from which there had been no derogation. The applicants were in a comparable situation to United Kingdom nationals suspected of being international terrorists, with whom they shared the characteristics of being irremovable from the United Kingdom and being considered a threat to national security. Since the detention scheme was aimed primarily at the protection of the United Kingdom from terrorist attack, rather than immigration control, there was no objective reason to treat the applicants differently on grounds of their nationality or immigration status.[381]

The House of Lords gave a declaration under section 4 of the Human Rights Act of 1998 that the legislation in issue – Section 23 of the Anti-terrorism, Crime and Security Act 2001 – was incompatible with the Convention in so far as it was disproportionate and permitted discriminatory detention of suspected international terrorists.[382] This did not, however, avail the applicants, such declarations being neither binding on the parties to the proceedings in which they are made nor capable of affecting the validity, continuing operation or enforcement of the provision in respect of which they are given.[383] Thus it was that the case was able to reach the Court in Strasbourg.

Among the wider issues raised – which included complaints under Articles 3 and 13 (in respect of which no violation was found)[384] – that which interests us is the way the Court dealt with the applicants' detention and the Government's derogating measures.

Most unusually, the Government found themselves in disagreement with the highest judicial authority of their own State and the applicants submitted preliminary objections calling into question the Government's right to challenge the House of Lord's findings. This situation is, to date, unique in the case-law of the Court. This, however, was neither a case of a Government taking a position inconsistent with that which they had defended at the domestic level[385] nor one of estoppel; nor, more generally, was there 'any prohibition on a Government making such a challenge, particularly if they [considered] that the national Supreme Court's ruling is problematic under the Convention and

---

380    *ibid.*, § 20.
381    *ibid.*, § 21.
382    *ibid.*, § 23.
383    United Kingdom, Human Rights Act 1998, section 4 (6) (a) and (b).
384    *A. and Others*, §§ 130-136.
385    cf. *Pine Valley Developments Ltd. and Others v. Ireland*, no. 12742/87, § 47, Series A no. 222.

DEROGATION 111

that further guidance is required from the Court'. Moreover, since the Lords' declaration of incompatibility with the Human Rights Act 1998 had not had the effect of making it unnecessary for the applicants to lodge their application, there was no reason in principle why the Court should not consider the case in its entirety, which meant that the Government should not now be prevented from raising all arguments open to them to defend their position.[386]

The Court had first to consider whether the detention of the applicants was in accordance with Article 5 § 1 (f) of the Convention. In accordance with existing case-law, this involved examining the question whether action was actually being taken against the applicants with a view to their deportation.[387] As regards two of the applicants, it found that there actually had been: in a matter of no more than a few months, one had left for Morocco, the other for France.[388] In the cases of the others, however, the Court found that their deportation was not being actively pursued: instead, it was clear from the terms of the derogation notice and the legislation in issue that their detention was based on the suspicion that they were 'international terrorists' and the belief that their presence in the United Kingdom gave rise to a threat to national security. Dismissing the Government's argument that a balance should be struck between the individual's right to liberty and the State's interest in protecting its population from terrorist threat, it reiterated that Articles 5 § 1 (a) – (f) amounted to an 'exhaustive list of exceptions and that only a narrow interpretation of these exceptions was compatible with the aims of Article 5'. If detention did not 'fit within the confines of the subparagraphs as interpreted by the Court, it could not be made to fit by an appeal to the need to balance the interests of the State against those of the detainee'. Referring to earlier findings in *Lawless* and *Ireland v. the United Kingdom* to the effect that 'internment and preventive detention without charge' were incompatible with Article 5 § 1 absent a valid derogation under Article 15, the Court then had to consider the validity of the derogation.[389]

In considering whether there was a 'public emergency threatening the life of the nation', the Court was once again willing to grant the domestic authorities a wide margin of appreciation. In the words of the Court:

> 177. Before the domestic courts, the Secretary of State adduced evidence to show the existence of a threat of serious terrorist attacks planned

---

386   *A. and Others*, §§ 153-59.
387   See, among many other authorities, *Chahal*, § 113.
388   *A. and Others*, § 168.
389   *ibid.*, §§ 170-172.

against the United Kingdom. Additional closed evidence was adduced before SIAC. All the national judges accepted that the danger was credible (with the exception of Lord Hoffmann, who did not consider that it was of a nature to constitute "a threat to the life of the nation" ...). Although when the derogation was made no al-Qaeda attack had taken place within the territory of the United Kingdom, the Court does not consider that the national authorities can be criticised, in the light of the evidence available to them at the time, for fearing that such an attack was "imminent", in that an atrocity might be committed without warning at any time. The requirement of imminence cannot be interpreted so narrowly as to require a State to wait for disaster to strike before taking measures to deal with it. Moreover, the danger of a terrorist attack was, tragically, shown by the bombings and attempted bombings in London in July 2005 to have been very real. Since the purpose of Article 15 is to permit States to take derogating measures to protect their populations from future risks, the existence of the threat to the life of the nation must be assessed primarily with reference to those facts which were known at the time of the derogation. The Court is not precluded, however, from having regard to information which comes to light subsequently (see, *mutatis mutandis, Vilvarajah and Others v. the United Kingdom*, 30 October 1991, § 107(2), Series A no. 215).

...

180. As previously stated, the national authorities enjoy a wide margin of appreciation under Article 15 in assessing whether the life of their nation is threatened by a public emergency. While it is striking that the United Kingdom was the only Convention State to have lodged a derogation in response to the danger from al-Qaeda, although other States were also the subject of threats, the Court accepts that it was for each Government, as the guardian of their own people's safety, to make their own assessment on the basis of the facts known to them. Weight must, therefore, attach to the judgment of the United Kingdom's executive and Parliament on this question. In addition, significant weight must be accorded to the views of the national courts, which were better placed to assess the evidence relating to the existence of an emergency.[390]

The Court accordingly endorsed the view of the House of Lords that there had been a 'public emergency threatening the life of the nation' within the meaning of Article 15 § 1.

---

390 *ibid.*, §§ 177-180.

DEROGATION

This meant that the Court had to address the question whether the measures taken against the applicants had been strictly required by the exigencies of the situation – the precise question on which the Government had found itself at variance with the House of Lords.

At the outset, the Court took the view that:

> ... it should in principle follow the judgment of the House of Lords on the question of the proportionality of the applicants' detention, unless it can be shown that the national court misinterpreted the Convention or the Court's case-law or reached a conclusion which was manifestly unreasonable.[391]

Dismissing the Government's suggestion that the House of Lords should have left it greater latitude, the Court held:

> As the House of Lords held, the question of proportionality is ultimately a judicial decision, particularly in a case such as the present where the applicants were deprived of their fundamental right to liberty over a long period of time. In any event, having regard to the careful way in which the House of Lords approached the issues, it cannot be said that inadequate weight was given to the views of the executive or of Parliament.[392]

Further endorsing the House of Lords' use of its powers to give a general decision on the application of Article 15, the Court held:

> The Court, however, considers that the House of Lords was correct in holding that the impugned powers were not to be seen as immigration measures, where a distinction between nationals and non-nationals would be legitimate, but instead as concerned with national security. Part 4 of the 2001 Act was designed to avert a real and imminent threat of terrorist attack which, on the evidence, was posed by both nationals and non-nationals. The choice by the Government and Parliament of an immigration measure to address what was essentially a security issue had the result of failing adequately to address the problem, while imposing a disproportionate and discriminatory burden of indefinite detention on one group of suspected terrorists. As the House of Lords found, there was no significant difference in the potential adverse impact of detention

---

391    *ibid.*, § 182.
392    *ibid.*, § 184.

without charge on a national or on a non-national who in practice could not leave the country because of fear of torture abroad.

Finally, and dismissing for lack of evidence the suggestion that British Muslims were 'significantly more likely to react negatively to the detention without charge of national rather than foreign Muslims reasonably suspected of links to al-Qaeda' and that foreign nationals posed a significantly greater threat to national security than United Kingdom nationals, the Court, like the House of Lords, found that the derogating measures were 'disproportionate in that they discriminated unjustifiably between nationals and non-nationals.' From this it followed that there had been a violation of Article 5 § 1 in respect of the applicants affected.[393]

### 4.5.1.9    *Mehmet Hasan Altan* and *Şahin Alpay*

During the night of 15 to 16 July 2016 a group of members of the Turkish armed forces attempted a *coup d'état*. Although the attempt was unsuccessful, more than 300 people were killed and more than 2,500 were injured.

In the wake of the coup attempt, on 20 July 2016 the Turkish Government declared a state of emergency for a period of three months as from 21 July 2016; the state of emergency was subsequently extended for further periods until it was finally terminated in 2018.[394]

On 21 July 2016 the Permanent Representative of Turkey to the Council of Europe sent the Secretary General of the Council of Europe the following notice of derogation:

> I communicate the following notice of the Government of the Republic of Turkey.
>
> On 15 July 2016, a large-scale coup attempt was staged in the Republic of Turkey to overthrow the democratically-elected government and the constitutional order. This despicable attempt was foiled by the Turkish state and people acting in unity and solidarity. The coup attempt and its aftermath together with other terrorist acts have posed severe dangers to public security and order, amounting to a threat to the life of the nation in the meaning of Article 15 of the Convention for the Protection of Human Rights and Fundamental Freedoms.
>
> The Republic of Turkey is taking the required measures as prescribed by law, in line with the national legislation and its international obliga-

---

393    *ibid.*, §§ 187-190.
394    See 4.5 above.

DEROGATION

tions. In this context, on 20 July 2016, the Government of the Republic of Turkey declared a State of Emergency for a duration of three months, in accordance with the Constitution (Article 120) and the Law No. 2935 on State of Emergency (Article 3/1b). ... The decision was published in the Official Gazette and approved by the Turkish Grand National Assembly on 21 July 2016. Thus, the State of Emergency takes effect as from this date. In this process, measures taken may involve derogation from the obligations under the Convention for the Protection of Human Rights and Fundamental Freedoms, permissible in Article 15 of the Convention.

I would therefore underline that this letter constitutes information for the purposes of Article 15 of the Convention. The Government of the Republic of Turkey shall keep you, Secretary General, fully informed of the measures taken to this effect. The Government shall inform you when the measures have ceased to operate. ...[395]

The applicants in these two cases were journalists with a record of public criticism of the serving government. Both were arrested as suspected members of FETÖ/PDY ('Gülenist Terror Organisation/Parallel State Structure'), which was stated by the national authorities to be a terrorist organisation led by Fetullah Gülen, a Turkish citizen living in the USA, to which organisation the coup attempt was imputed. Both were placed in detention. Both were charged with trying to overthrow the constitutional order. Mehmet Hasan Altan was sentenced at first instance to 'aggravated life imprisonment'. Criminal proceedings remain ongoing against both applicants at the time of writing.

Both applicants applied to the Turkish Constitutional Court for their release. On 11 January 2018 the Constitutional Court gave judgment in both applicants' cases holding that '"strong evidence that an offence had been committed" had not been sufficiently established'; there had accordingly been violations of the right to liberty and security and the right to freedom of expression and of the press. The judgments were transmitted to the trial courts in order that they take 'the necessary action'. The applicants' counsel applied to those courts for the applicants' release the same day. However, the trial courts, in open defiance of the Constitutional Court, decided that the applicants' detention on remand should continue.

The Government submitted, and the Court accepted, that the coup attempt and its immediate aftermath had constituted a 'public emergency threatening

---

395   *Mehmet Hasan Altan*, § 81; *Şahin Alpay*, § 65. See also the web site of the Council of Europe's Treaty Office, https://www.coe.int/en/web/conventions/full-list/-/conventions/treaty/005/declarations?p_auth=8PL9eBer (accessed on 12 April 2018).

116                                                                        CHAPTER 4

the life of the nation'; so indeed had the Constitutional Court, and the applicants had not suggested otherwise.[396]

The Court noted that the Turkish Constitutional Court formed an integral
part of the judiciary within the constitutional structure of Turkey and that it
played an important role in protecting the right to liberty and security under
the Turkish Constitution and Article 5 of the Convention by offering an effective remedy to individuals detained during criminal proceedings. On that basis, the Court found that the refusal of the courts below to order the applicants'
release was arbitrary, and therefore in violation of Article 5 of the Convention:

> For another court to call into question the powers conferred on a consti-
> tutional court to give final and binding judgments on individual applica-
> tions runs counter to the fundamental principles of the rule of law and
> legal certainty. The Court reiterates that these principles, inherent in the
> protection afforded by Article 5 of the Convention, are the cornerstones
> of the guarantees against arbitrariness (...). Although the Constitutional
> Court transmitted its judgment to the Assize Court so that it could take
> "the necessary action", the Assize Court resisted the Constitutional Court
> by refusing to release the applicant, with the result that the violation
> found by the Constitutional Court was not redressed.[397]

Echoing the finding of the Turkish Constitutional Court, the Court went on to
hold 'that a measure of pre-trial detention that [was] not "lawful" and [had]
not been effected "in accordance with a procedure prescribed by law" on account of the lack of reasonable suspicion [could not] be said to have been
strictly required by the exigencies of the situation'; the same applied to the
concomitant interference with freedom of expression.[398]

However, no violation of Article 5 § 4 was found in respect of the duration
of the appeals before the Constitutional Court: fourteen months and three
days in the case of Mehmet Hasan Altan, sixteen months and three days in the
case of Şahin Alpay. The Court accepted that the applicants' cases were among
the first of a series of cases raising new and complicated issues concerning
the right to liberty and security and freedom of expression under the state
of emergency following the attempted military coup. Moreover, bearing in
mind the Constitutional Court's case-load following the declaration of a state
of emergency, the Court accepted that this was an exceptional situation. Al-

---

396    *Mehmet Hasan Altan* § 93; *Şahin Alpay*, § 76.
397    *Mehmet Hasan Altan*, §§ 138-139; *Şahin Alpay*, §§ 117-118.
398    *Mehmet Hasan Altay*, §§ 140 and 213; *Şahin Alpay*, §§ 119 and 183.

DEROGATION

though proceedings as protracted as these 'could not be described as "speedy" in an ordinary context', in the 'specific circumstances of the [cases]' they were nonetheless acceptable.[399]

## 4.6    When Does a Public Emergency Threaten the Life of the Nation?

The concept of 'public emergency threatening the life of the nation' is of necessity more vague than that of 'war'. In a report which it published in 2006, the Venice Commission, referring to the Commission's decision in the *'Greek Case'* and to the Court's *Lawless* judgment, summarised the characteristics of such an emergency as follows:

(1) It [i.e. the emergency] must be actual or imminent;
(2) Its effects must involve the whole nation;
(3) The continuance of the organised life of the community must be threatened;
(4) The crisis or danger must be exceptional, in that the normal measures or restrictions, permitted by the Convention for the maintenance of public safety, health and order, are plainly inadequate. In 1961 the ECtHR stressed that there must be a *"threat to the organised life of the community"*.[400]

Thus far, in the cases that have reached the Commission and the Court, such an emergency has been found to exist when an organised armed group arose with the aim of overthrowing and replacing, at least locally, the existing governmental structures of the Convention State concerned and whose actions reflected both the will and the ability to use force effectively in the process. Such situations, of course, come close to a non-international armed conflict or may develop into one if left unchecked.

One might imagine 'the life of the nation' being threatened by hostile action that need not necessarily involve any direct danger to the State's control over its land territory. For example, many if not most European countries would be crippled by sustained interference with shipping, air traffic or energy supply,

---

399    *Mehmet Hasan Altay*, §§ 165-167; *Şahin Alpay*, §§ 137-139.
400    Venice Commission, Opinion on the protection of human rights in emergency situations, CDL-AD(2006)015, § 10. Emphasis in the original.

or even by action directed against the country's communications (in the form, perhaps, of sustained cyber-attacks).[401]

We have seen that the Court is prepared to leave the State a wide margin of appreciation in deciding on the need for derogation – indeed, the concept of 'margin of appreciation' was first developed in that precise context,[402] and it has been observed that 'this is the area in Convention law where the margin is at its widest'.[403]

There would therefore be nothing to prevent the Court from accepting the existence of an 'emergency threatening the life of the nation' if the crisis were caused not by a conflict but by a natural disaster, uncontrollable immigration (or emigration), an epidemic or even an economic or monetary crisis that proves beyond the capacity of government to contain by ordinary means.[404] The existence of such an emergency requiring derogating measures might also be found to exist in a particularly chaotic post-war situation, to which the expression 'war' would no longer be appropriate.

While the effects of the emergency situation must involve the whole nation, it is not a requirement that the emergency itself cover the entire territory of the State. The Court has accepted the existence of emergencies affecting only the six counties of Northern Ireland and certain named provinces in south-eastern Turkey.[405] However, as we have seen, it would fly in the face of the purpose of Article 15 to allow the Contracting State to make use of derogating measures outside the territory covered by the derogation.[406]

---

401    With regard to cyber-attacks, see generally Jack Goldsmith, *How Cyber Changes the Laws of War*, EJIL (2013), Vol. 24 No. 1, 129-138, and Lieutenant Ken M. Jones, USN, *Cyber War: The Next Frontier For NATO*, Progressive Management, 2016.

402    J.G.C. Schokkenbroek, *Toetsing aan de vrijheidsrechten van het Europees verdrag tot bescherming van de rechten van de mens* (diss. Leiden 1996), pp. 15-18; Michael O'Boyle, "The Margin of Appreciation and Derogation under Article 15: Ritual Incantation or Principle?", 19 *HRLJ* (1998) p. 23. For a critical appraisal, see Gross, O., and Ní Aoláin, F., "From Discretion to Scrutiny: Revisiting the Application of the Margin of Appreciation Doctrine in the Context of Article 15 of the European Convention on Human Rights", *Human Rights Quarterly* 23 (2001) 625-649, *passim*; see also Bart van der Sloot, "Is All Fair in Love and War? An Analysis of the Case Law on Article 15 ECHR", in *Military Law and the law of War Review* 53/2 (2014), pp. 319-358 at pp. 325-326.

403    Michael O'Boyle, *ibid.*, at p. 25 (citing R. St.J. Macdonald, "The Margin of Appreciation in the Jurisprudence of the European Court of Human Rights", *Collected Courses of the Academy of European Law* (1990), Vols. I-II).

404    Jean-Paul Costa and Michael O'Boyle, "The European Court of Human Rights and International Humanitarian Law", in *The European Convention on Human Rights: a living instrument, Essays in Honour of Christos L. Rozakis* (Bruylant, 2011), pp. 107-129 at p. 115.

405    *Ireland v. the United Kingdom*, § 205; *Brannigan and McBride*, § 47; *Aksoy*, § 70.

406    *Sakık and Others*, § 39.

DEROGATION

There is no temporal limit to the validity of a derogation. As the Court expressed it in *A. and Others*:

> While the United Nations Human Rights Committee has observed that measures derogating from the provisions of the International Covenant on Civil and Political Rights must be of '"an exceptional and temporary nature" (...),[407] the Court's case-law has never, to date, explicitly incorporated the requirement that the emergency be temporary, although the question of the proportionality of the response may be linked to the duration of the emergency. Indeed, the cases cited above,[408] relating to the security situation in Northern Ireland, demonstrate that it is possible for a "public emergency" within the meaning of Article 15 to continue for many years.

Ronald St. John Macdonald, a long-serving judge in the Old Court, points out that an interpretation of the concept of emergency wide enough to include economic crises carries certain dangers in that it might be abused, for example, to justify the introduction of repressive measures inimical to civil and political rights. The example he gives is forced labour.[409] He is, of course, right; but whatever the nature of the emergency, the Court – and presumably the domestic courts[410] – would not be precluded from considering the validity of any such derogation in terms of whether the measures taken are strictly required by the exigencies of the situation.

Macdonald suggests an additional test in that the State must be found to be acting in good faith. Citing another author, he suggests 'distrust of the motivations of the Greek military government and revulsion against its anti-democratic character' as the real explanation (or at least part of it) for the Commission's refusal to accept the Greek Government's derogation in the *'Greek Case'*. Indeed, as he puts it,

> [t]he Convention is founded on a commitment to preserve and strengthen democratic systems of government. A state of emergency declared not to further democracy, but to destroy or repress it, would be invalid under

---

407    Reference to United Nations Human Rights Committee, General Comment No. 29 on Article 4 of the ICCPR (24 July 2001), paragraph 2.

408    *Ireland v. the United Kingdom, Brannigan and McBride, Marshall.*

409    R. St.J. Macdonald, "Derogations under Article 15 of the European Convention on Human Rights", [1997] 36 *Columbia Journal of Transnational Law* p. 225 at p. 236.

410    cf. Article 13 of the Convention. See also Michael O'Boyle, "Emergency Government and Derogation under the ECHR", [2016] E.H.R.L.R. p. 331 at p. 333.

article 15. Such a condition is explicit in article 17, which provides that no state may "perform any act aimed at the destruction of any of the rights and freedoms set forth [in the Convention]".[411]

This view is certainly correct.

The United Kingdom withdrew the derogation of 18 December 2001 with effect from 14 March 2005. Only four months later, on 7 and 21 July 2005, Muslim terrorists launched attacks on the public transport system of London; the first succeeded, the second did not. As well it might, the Court took these attacks as proof that the terrorist threat had at all relevant times been real.[412]

Nonetheless, at the present remove an observer cannot help noting that despite the two attacks of July 2005, and despite further terrorist incidents including the car bomb attack on Glasgow International Airport in 2007, the murder of a soldier in broad daylight in the streets of Woolwich in 2013, a stabbing at a tube station in London's East End in December 2015, a suicide bomb attack on visitors of a pop concert in Manchester in May 2017, and in March and June 2017, two attacks carried out in central London using vehicles to attack pedestrians, for the vast majority of the British population – who were neither perpetrators nor victims of the actual attacks themselves – normal life continued much as it had done, as did the business of Government and the law. While it can accordingly be accepted that on any reasonable view there was a threat of terrorist attack in the early years of the present century, we cannot of course know whether the use of the powers granted the Government by Part 4 of the Anti-terrorism, Crime and Security Act 2001 were effective to prevent such an attack while the grant remained in force. More to the point, neither do we know what terrorist attacks may have been prevented, both before and after withdrawal of the notice of derogation on 14 March 2005, by ordinary police work, or by the use of methods that have yet to be considered under the Convention but are not the object of any derogation. All that can be said with the knowledge we have is that, in retrospect, Lord Hoffmann – no friend of the Court he, but no enemy of freedom either – may well have had a point worth pondering in doubting the existence of a genuine threat to 'the life of the nation'.[413]

---

411    Macdonald (1997), at p. 249; Loof, p. 386.

412    *A. and Others*, § 177.

413    See also Bart van der Sloot, "Is All Fair in Love and War? An Analysis of the Case Law on Article 15 ECHR", in *Military Law and the law of War Review* 53/2 (2014), pp. 319-358 at p. 348. For a very different view, see Michael O'Boyle, "Emergency Government and Derogation under the ECHR", [2016] E.H.R.L.R. p. 331 at p. 336.

DEROGATION

Absent any suggestion of bad faith, the Court's willingness to accept the assessment of the domestic authorities comes close to complete deference, as the *A. and Others* judgment shows.

This apparent passivity has been criticised by academics. Thus, Oren Gross and Fionnuala Ní Aoláin argue that the Court is better placed than domestic authorities to consider the need for derogating measures, not worse:

> ... it may well be that the supranational Court, detached and further removed from the immediate turmoil, reviewing the relevant issues post facto rather than at the time of their occurrence, is able to judge matters more clearly and more accurately.[414]

Criticism of the Court's deferential attitude has also come from within the Court itself. In his dissenting opinion in *Brannigan and McBride*, Judge Martens, expressing agreement on this point with arguments submitted by *amici curiae* Amnesty International, Liberty, Interights and the Committee on the Administration of Justice, put it as follows:

> Inevitably, in this context, a certain margin of appreciation should be left to the national authorities. There is, however, no justification for leaving them a wide margin of appreciation because the Court, being the "last-resort" protector of the fundamental rights and freedoms guaranteed under the Convention, is called upon to strictly scrutinise every derogation by a High Contracting Party from its obligations.[415]

While it is undoubtedly true that an urgent need to stave off disaster may arise on the spur of the moment, as time goes on the executive arm of Government may continue to restrict human rights – and limit judicial and even legislative scrutiny of its choices – based on a state of 'emergency' that no longer so justifies. There is force in the suggestion, made by Gross and Ní Aoláin already in 2001, that '[a] government's attempt to justify or excuse a perceived violation of human rights in terms of exigency and derogation ought to be treated as a suspect classification that calls for a stricter scrutiny of the government's case'.[416]

---

414    Gross, O., and Ní Aoláin, F., "From Discretion to Scrutiny: Revisiting the Application of the Margin of Appreciation Doctrine in the Context of Article 15 of the European Convention on Human Rights", *Human Rights Quarterly* 23 (2001) 625-649 at p. 639.

415    *Brannigan and McBride*, dissenting opinion of Judge Martens, § 4.

416    Gross, O., and Ní Aoláin, F., "From Discretion to Scrutiny: Revisiting the Application of the Margin of Appreciation Doctrine in the Context of Article 15 of the European Convention

122                                                                      CHAPTER 4

For the present, however, the Court seems disinclined to alter its position. The Turkish notice of derogation lodged on 21 July 2016, quoted above in the context of the *Mehmet Hasan Altan* and *Şahin Alpay* judgments,[417] refers only to the 'coup attempt and its aftermath' which 'together with other terrorist acts have posed severe dangers to public security and order, amounting to a threat to the life of the nation'. While there can hardly be any dispute about the finding that the coup attempt itself threatened 'the life of the nation', it is arguably not self-evident that such a threat persisted during its aftermath – and the notice of derogation was sent to the Secretary General several days after the coup attempt had been well and truly crushed. One might also question whether the acts in issue could properly be called 'terrorist': since the aim of the coup attempt seems to have been the direct overthrow of President Erdoğan and the incumbent Government themselves, it is not immediately obvious that the acts in issue, unlawful though they undoubtedly were, fit our working definition of 'terrorism' as being 'criminal acts intended or calculated to provoke a state of terror in the general public, a group of persons or particular persons for political purposes'.[418] Nevertheless, in the two judgments, which were handed down nearly two years later, the Court does not question the position of the Turkish Government: it is worth noting however that the applicants do not seem to have argued either point and the Chamber has confined itself to taking note of their silence.[419]

## 4.7    Non-Derogable Rights

Even though the situation may be dire to the point of admitting of derogation from the Convention, there are rights from which no derogation is permitted in any circumstances.

Article 15 § 2 sets out the following: the right to life (Article 2), except in respect of deaths resulting from 'lawful acts of war' (a concept which we will briefly explore); the prohibition of torture (Article 3); the prohibition of slavery or servitude (Article 4 § 1); and the principle *nulla poena sine lege* (Article 7). Additional non-derogable rights created subsequently include the prohibition

---

on Human Rights", *Human Rights Quarterly* 23 (2001) 625-649 at p. 642. The point is also made in Mariniello, T., "Prolonged Emergency and Derogation of Human Rights: Why the European Court Should Raise Its Immunity System", to appear in *German Law Journal* (forthcoming 2019), available on https://www.academia.edu/ (last accessed 26 June 2018).

417    See 4.5.1.9 above.

418    For this definition of terrorism, see 4.3.2.2 and footnote 266 above.

419    *Mehmet Hasan Altan,* § 92; *Şahin Alpay,* § 76.

DEROGATION 123

of the death penalty (Article 3 of Protocol No. 6 and Article 2 of Protocol No. 13) and the right not to be tried or punished twice (Article 4 of Protocol No. 7).

### 4.7.1 *Article 2*

Article 2 protects the right to life. It provides in its first paragraph that no one shall be deprived of his life intentionally except consequent on a lawful sentence of death handed down by a court.[420] Other than that, deprivation of life is not to be regarded as contrary to that Article

> when it results from the use of force which is no more than absolutely necessary:
> (a) in defence of any person from unlawful violence;
> (b) in order to effect a lawful arrest or to prevent the escape of a person lawfully detained;
> (c) in action lawfully taken for the purpose of quelling a riot or insurrection.[421]

There is no mention of deaths occurring in an international or non-international armed conflict. Article 2 was written for, and fits, a law-enforcement paradigm exclusively. In this it differs from Article 6 § 1 of the International Covenant on Civil and Political Rights, Article 4 § 1 of the American Convention on Human Rights and Article 4, third sentence, of the African Charter on Human and People's Rights, all of which provide that no one shall be 'arbitrarily' deprived of their life – an expression that admits of far broader interpretation.[422]

It is therefore entirely conceivable that killing a combatant during an international armed conflict in accordance with international humanitarian

---

420 Cases in which the death penalty is in issue are very rare in the case-law of the Commission and the Court, most Contracting States having ceased executing it or abolished it altogether before ratifying or acceding to the Convention or accepting the right of individual petition. An exception is Turkey, which became a Party to Protocol No. 6 only on 1 December 2003. On 30 November 1999 the Court indicated a provisional measure to Turkey under Rule 39 of the Rules of Court to the effect that the death sentence imposed on Abdullah Öcalan should not be carried out pending the outcome of the proceedings before it (*Öcalan v. Turkey* (GC), no. 46221/99, § 5, ECHR 2005-IV). See also *leges posteriores* Articles 1 and 2 of Protocol No. 6 and Articles 1 and 2 of Protocol No. 13, discussed in 4.7.5 below.

421 Article 2 § 2 of the Convention.

422 Kirby Abbott, "A brief overview of legal interoperability challenges for NATO arising from the interrelationship between IHL and IHRL in light of the European Convention on Human Rights", *International Review of the Red Cross*, vol. 96, no. 893, pp. 107-37 at p. 127.

law might have to be found in violation of Article 2 of the Convention[423] – a position that Colonel Abbot, whom we encountered above,[424] has labelled 'absurd'.[425] No doubt many others would agree with him.[426]

In its second paragraph, however, Article 15 lists Article 2 as non-derogable 'except in respect of deaths resulting from lawful acts of war'. This means that the meaning of the expression 'war' is relevant not only to the applicability of Article 15 as a whole, but also to the interpretation of the specific right guaranteed by Article 2.

It is likely that the drafters of this provision were concerned with *ius in bello*: a death resulting from a lawful act committed in a lawful war would be covered by the derogation but a death resulting from an unlawful act surely would not. One obvious consequence would be that the procedural obligations immanent in Article 2[427] could be derogated from in the former case but not in the latter: the duty to investigate and, if necessary, prosecute deaths resulting from unlawful acts would continue to flow from Article 2.[428]

It is probably a mistake to understand the expression 'war' in this context as referring to international armed conflicts only, as has been suggested.[429] Already for purposes of Article 15 § 1 we have defined our understanding of that expression so as to include an armed conflict not of an international character between a State and a non-State organised armed group but reaching the minimum intensity needed to trigger the applicability of international humanitarian law; there is no good reason not to do so for purposes of Article 15 § 2 as well.

---

423   Evangelia Vasalou, "Les rapports normatifs entre le droit international humanitaire et la Convention européenne des droits de l'homme : Le droit international humanitaire, une lex specialis par rapport a la Convention européenne des droits de l'homme ?", Revue trimestrielle des droits de l'homme (112/2017), pp. 953-987 at p. 960.

424   See 1.2.4.2 above.

425   Kirby Abbott, "A brief overview of legal interoperability challenges for NATO arising from the interrelationship between IHL and IHRL in light of the European Convention on Human Rights", *International Review of the Red Cross*, vol. 96, no. 893, pp. 107-37 at p. 124.

426   A similar view is expressed by Anne-Marie Baldovin, "Impact de la jurisprudence récente de la Cour européenne des droits de l'Homme sur la planification et l'exécution des opérations militaires à venir : Application extraterritoriale de la Convention, imputabilité des faits des troupes et fragmentation du droit international", in *Military Law and the Law of War Review* 50/3-4 (2011), pp. 369-418 at p. 404.

427   See 2.2.2 above.

428   And indeed from international humanitarian law, on which subject, see 4.9 below. Compare International Committee of the Red Cross, IHL Database, https://ihl-databases.icrc.org/customary-ihl/eng/docs/home, Rule 158, with further references (accessed on 5 September 2018).

429   Nils Melzer, *Targeted killing in international law*, Oxford University Press 2008, p. 122.

DEROGATION

It is tempting to include *ius ad bellum* in the definition of 'lawful acts of war': on this view, deaths resulting from acts committed in an unlawful war would *ipso iure* be excluded from the protection of the derogation. Admittedly such an interpretation sits well with the 'profound belief in those fundamental freedoms which are the foundation of justice and peace in the world'.[430] It does not, however, accord with the actual text of Article 15 § 2 of the Convention: the French text, arguably less ambiguous than the English version, has '*actes licites de guerre*' – which renders more accurately, if more cumbersomely, as 'legally permitted acts of war'.[431]

All agree that under the law of armed conflict, in international armed conflict at least, combatants are liable to lethal attack at any time without warning.[432] Under human rights law, in principle, no one is and the status of combatant does not exist. It is submitted, accordingly, that the expression 'lawful acts of war' should be interpreted as meaning that the legality of the taking of life is governed by international humanitarian law.[433]

The use of the expression 'war' must not necessarily be understood in the same sense for the first paragraph of Article 15 and for the second. For one thing, it is difficult to see how the procedural requirements of Article 2 – that is the duty officially to investigate a death and, if appropriate, prosecute its author[434] – could apply to every single death occasioned in a war of doubtful legality by hostile action that was, from an operational perspective, legitimate: such a view would place the individual serviceman in the impossible position of having to question the political decision to go to war before obeying an order given by his lawful superior. Different considerations may well govern the right to derogate *per se*. Admittedly this leaves us with the *non sequitur* of a death sanctioned by Article 15 § 2 occurring in a war not meeting the requirements of Article 15 § 1; but the distinction will be dictated by the stark reality of the situation.

Absent a genuine state of war, there is no getting away from Article 2. This has been rightly noted in the United Kingdom by the Joint Committee on Human Rights of the House of Lords and the House of Commons:

---

430 Preamble to the Convention.

431 See also Bethlehem, *supra* note 233, at p. 237.

432 For example, Yoram Dinstein, *The Conduct of Hostilities under the Law of International Armed Conflict* (Cambridge University Press, 3rd ed. 2016), p. 42, § 116.

433 cf. *Varnava and Others*, § 185, ECHR 2009; see also Bethlehem at p. 239 and Sicilianos (2015) at p. 12.

434 For example, *Kasap and Others v. Turkey*, no. 8656/10, § 58, 14 January 2014, and *Armani da Silva*, § 238.

126                                                                CHAPTER 4

We note that any future derogation from the ECHR will not affect the Government's policy in relation to the use of lethal force abroad outside of armed conflict. Derogation from the right to life in Article 2 ECHR is only possible in relation to "deaths resulting from lawful acts of war". States can therefore choose to be bound by the more permissive rules of the Law of War, rather than the more restrictive rules of human rights law, in times of war or public emergency. However, the Government will not be able to derogate from the right to life in Article 2 where it uses lethal force abroad outside of armed conflict: such deaths will not be the result of "acts of war" because by definition they will have taken place outside armed conflict. The right to life in Article 2 ECHR therefore inescapably applies to uses of lethal force abroad outside of armed conflict.[435]

It is submitted that it is not inconceivable that human rights law – even Article 2 of the Convention outside the strict confines of 'legitimate acts of war'[436] – might admit of targeted killing without warning (a drone strike for example),[437] but the justification offered would surely have to be the most persuasive imaginable.[438] Otherwise, it has been suggested that a targeted killing might be brought within the scope of an armed conflict if a nexus between the two could be shown[439] – which might allow the Contracting State to avail itself of Article 15 of the Convention.

### 4.7.2    *Article 3*
Article 3 of the Convention prohibits torture and inhuman or degrading treatment or punishment in absolute terms. As the Court was careful to point out in *Ireland v. the United Kingdom*, 'there can be no derogation therefrom even

---

435    House of Lords and House of Commons, Joint Committee on Human Rights, *The Government's policy on the use of drones for targeted killing*, Second Report of Session 2015–16, paragraph 3.62.

436    See 4.9 below.

437    *Contra* Helen Duffy, *The 'War on Terror' and the Framework of International Law* (2nd edition 2015), Cambridge University Press, p. 577.

438    Christof Heyns, Dapo Akande, Lawrence Hill-Cawthorne and Thompson Chengeta, "The International Framework Regulating the Use of Armed Drones", *ICLQ* vol 65, October 2016, pp. 791-827 at pp. 818-821. See also PACE Resolution 2051 (2015) on Drones and targeted killings: the need to uphold human rights and international law (23 April 2015), paras 6.3 and 6.4.

439    Milanović and Hadži-Vidanović, *supra* note 250, p. 309; see also Helen Duffy, *The 'War on Terror' and the Framework of International Law* (2nd edition 2015), Cambridge University Press, pp. 417-420.

DEROGATION

in the event of a public emergency threatening the life of the nation'[440] – nor even, we would add, in the event of war.

For present purposes, one obvious corollary of the non-derogability of Article 3 is that resorting to torture or, for that matter, the use of force short of torture in interrogating prisoners, even enemy agents or spies, is not permissible however grave the situation and is likely to engage the responsibility of the Contracting State under the Convention. The same applies to the use of weapons or tactics that cause unnecessary human suffering. The standards to be applied under the Convention are free-standing and do not necessarily depend on the corresponding standards of the law of armed conflict, although the latter will be helpful in setting the threshold.[441]

### 4.7.3   *Article 4*

Only the first paragraph of Article 4 is listed in Article 15 § 2. It provides that '[n]o one shall be held in slavery or servitude'. The Court has defined 'slavery' in the terms of the 1926 Slavery Convention as 'the status or condition of a person over whom any or all of the powers attaching to the right of ownership are exercised',[442] and 'servitude' as 'an obligation, under coercion, to provide one's services', the latter concept being linked with that of 'slavery'.[443]

The second paragraph of Article 4 provides that '[n]o one shall be required to perform forced or compulsory labour'. For 'forced or compulsory labour' to arise, the Court has held that there must be 'some physical or mental constraint, as well as some overriding of the person's will'.[444]

This paragraph is immediately qualified by the third paragraph of Article 4, which provides that certain duties that the State may impose shall not count as 'forced or compulsory labour'. These are duties which the State may impose in the absence of a 'war or other public emergency threatening the life of the nation'.

For the purposes of our discussions, the pertinent exceptions are 'any service of a military character' (or 'in case of conscientious objectors in countries where they are recognised, service exacted instead of compulsory military service') and 'any service exacted in case of an emergency or calamity threatening the life or well-being of the community'.

---

440   *Ireland v. the United Kingdom*, § 163; see also Andrew Drzemczewski, "Ireland v. U.K.", [1978] 12 *The Law Teacher* 1 p. 49 at p. 52.

441   cf., *mutatis mutandis, Van Anraat*, §§ 89-91.

442   *Siliadin v. France*, no. 73316/01, § 122, ECHR 2005-VII; *Rantsev v. Cyprus and Russia*, no. 25965/04, § 276, ECHR 2010, with further references.

443   *Rantsev, ibid.*

444   *Rantsev, ibid.*

No derogation under Article 15 is necessary for either of these exceptions to apply (nor indeed for the two other exceptions provided for by Article 4 § 3, namely prison work and work or service which forms part of 'normal civic obligations' – e.g. service in a fire brigade[445] or on a jury[446]).

As we have seen, an exception for service exacted instead of military service applies 'in case of conscientious objectors in countries where they are recognised' (Article 4 § 3 (b)). On the face of it, this wording leaves it to the countries themselves whether to recognise conscientious objections to military service. However, in its *Bayatyan* judgment, the Court recognised a general right to claim exemption from military service provided that it be based on serious and convincing conscientious objections, as protected under Article 9 – the right to freedom of thought, conscience and religion.[447] It remains to be seen whether such a right will survive actual war: the letter of the Convention does not prevent Contracting States from derogating from it under Article 15. Nevertheless, on any reasonable view, one would imagine so. To recognise a right of conscientious objection in peacetime but deny it in wartime would defeat its very purpose. It is submitted, therefore, that the *Bayatyan* judgment has created a new non-derogable right.

### 4.7.4 *Article 7*

Article 7 – which enshrines the *nulla poena sine lege* principle – is listed in Article 15 § 2 as non-derogable. However, a derogating clause is contained in the very Article itself, in that its second paragraph states that it 'shall not prejudice the trial and punishment of any person for any act or omission which, at the time when it was committed, was criminal according to the general principles of law recognised by civilised nations'.

The applicant in *Korbely* was an officer in the Hungarian army in 1956. During the uprising, he killed an insurgent; for this act, classed as a 'crime against humanity' rather than common murder, he was put on trial in the 1990s. The Court found a violation of Article 7 in that the understanding of the expression 'crime against humanity' in 1956 did not – at the time – encompass ordinary murder without the presence of additional elements, in particular that the crime 'should form part of "State action or policy"' or of a widespread and systematic attack on the civilian population'; it was therefore not enough to find,

---

445   *Karlheinz Schmidt v. Germany*, no. 13580/88, § 23, Series A no. 291-B.

446   *Zarb Adami v. Malta*, no. 17209/02, § 47, ECHR 2006-VIII.

447   *Bayatyan v. Armenia* (GC), no. 23459/03, §§ 123-127, ECHR 2011; see Petr Muzny, "*Bayatyan v Armenia*: The Grand Chamber Renders a Grand Judgment", *Human Rights Law Review* 12:1(2012), 135-147.

DEROGATION

as the domestic courts had done, that the victim had come within the scope of protection of Common Article 3 of the Geneva Conventions.[448]

The second paragraph of Article 7 has its origins in an amendment to the provision later to congeal as Article 15 § 1 of the International Covenant on Civil and Political Rights. It was suggested by the British Government, which pointed out that without it that provision 'might be thought to impugn the validity of the judgments of the Nuremberg Tribunal'.[449] Article 15 of the Covenant is identical word for word with Article 7 of the Convention (except for punctuation).

Given the context for which it was drafted, the application of Article 7 § 2 in respect crimes committed during the Second World War by the Nazis and their henchmen raises no complicated questions.[450] In contrast, the Court has held that it also applies to crimes committed by others than Nazi collaborators – in particular Soviet Communists.

The applicants in *Kolk and Kisliy* were found guilty in the early years of the 21st century by Estonian courts of having participated, in March 1949, in the deportation of Estonian civilians to remote areas of the Soviet Union. The criminal legislation applied had been enacted only in 1994, after Estonia had successfully regained its independence. The applicants had argued that their actions had been legal under the law of the Soviet Union. The Estonian courts had rejected that defence referring to Article 7 § 2.

Declaring the application inadmissible *de plano*, the Court held as follows:

> The Court notes that deportation of the civilian population was expressly recognised as a crime against humanity in the Charter of the Nuremberg Tribunal of 1945 (Article 6 (c)).[451] Although the Nuremberg Tribunal was established for trying the major war criminals of the European Axis countries for the offences they had committed before or during the Second World War, the Court notes that the universal validity of the principles concerning crimes against humanity was subsequently confirmed by, *inter alia*, resolution 95 of the United Nations General Assembly (11 Decem-

---

448   *Korbely*, §§ 81-85.
449   UN Doc. E/CN.4/353/Add.2 (Comments of Governments on the draft International Covenant on Human Rights and measures of implementation), quoted in the Preparatory Work on Article 7 of the European Convention on Human Rights, Council of Europe document DH (57) 6).
450   *Touvier v. France*, no. 29420/95, Commission decision of 13 January 1997, DR 88-B p. 148 at p. 161; *Papon v. France* (dec.), no. 54210/00, ECHR 2001-XII.
451   Charter of the International Military Tribunal (Nuremberg Tribunal), annexed to the London Agreement of 8 August 1945, 82 UNTS 280.

ber 1946)[452] and later by the International Law Commission.[453] Accordingly, responsibility for crimes against humanity cannot be limited only to the nationals of certain countries and solely to acts committed within the specific time frame of the Second World War. ...

It was thus established, at the very least, that though Article 7 § 2 had been written with a particular view to punishing the crimes of the Nazis its applicability was not limited to them alone. The Nuremberg Charter and the affirmation by the General Assembly of the United Nations of its principles were taken as indicative of the 'general principles of law' and, what was more, their actual recognition by the Soviet Union by 1949.

The Nuremberg Principles, adopted in 1950, codify 'crimes against peace', 'war crimes' and 'crimes against humanity' and set out the principle of international criminal responsibility in a form applicable to those States that are not party to the Rome Statute of the International Criminal Court.[454] Other documents relevant to this discussion include the Genocide Convention[455] and the Convention against Torture,[456] both of which have been ratified or acceded to by all Council of Europe Member States.

### 4.7.5 *The Death Penalty*

Article 3 of Protocol No. 6 adds prohibition of the death penalty to the list of non-derogable rights. However, Article 2 of Protocol No. 6 permits States to 'make provision in its law for the death penalty in respect of acts committed in time of war or of imminent threat of war'. The use of the expression 'war' implies that the death penalty may not be imposed in any other emergency threatening the life of the nation. Thus, for example, the venerable practice of shooting rioters or looters out of hand in a calamity falling short of war is effectively rendered legally impossible.

---

452  UNGA Res. 95 (I), 11 December 1946 (Affirmation of the Principles of International Law recognized by the Charter of the Nürnberg Tribunal).

453  Nuremberg Principles, *Yearbook of the International Law Commission*, 1950, Vol. II, pp. 374-378.

454  Rome Statute of the International Criminal Court, circulated as document A/CONF.183/9 of 17 July 1998 and corrected by *proces-verbaux* of 10 November 1998, 12 July 1999, 30 November 1999, 8 May 2000, 17 January 2001 and 16 January 2002. Available for download on the web site of the International Criminal Court.

455  Convention on the Prevention and the Punishment of the Crime of Genocide, 78 UNTS 277.

456  Convention against torture and other cruel, inhuman or degrading treatment or punishment, 1465 UNTS 85.

DEROGATION

Protocol 13 takes matters still further. Born of the realisation that Protocol No. 6 'does not exclude the death penalty in respect of acts committed in time of war or of imminent threat of war' and the resolve 'to take the final step in order to abolish the death penalty in all circumstances',[457] it removes the option left to States by Article 2 of Protocol No. 6 to make provision for the death penalty even in wartime. As a matter of logic, the second Article of that Protocol – 'No derogation from the provisions of this Protocol shall be made under Article 15 of the Convention' – would seem redundant, but it serves the useful purpose of driving home the point that abolition of the death penalty is now absolute.

At least for the vast majority of European States, that is. To date, Protocol No. 13 has been signed but not ratified by Armenia, and neither signed nor ratified by Azerbaijan and Russia. Russia is not even a party to Protocol No. 6. This is worrying given that these are States that have strained relations with some of their neighbours, in some cases to the point of maintaining a military presence on territory over which their sovereignty is disputed.

It is however arguable in the light of the reasoning developed by the Court in *Öcalan* that the ratification of Protocol No. 13 by the overwhelming majority of Contracting States coupled with the practice of the remaining Contracting States, at least as far as is known, of not carrying out executions even in cases where such would be permitted under the terms of Protocol No. 6 can now be construed as the *de facto* abolition of the death penalty in all circumstances, and thus as evidence of the emergence of a corresponding rule of customary international law broadening the protection of the Convention system in that respect.[458]

### 4.7.6    *Article 4 of Protocol No. 7*

Article 4 of Protocol No. 7 guarantees, in respect of those States that have ratified the Protocol, the right not to be tried or punished again in criminal proceedings under the jurisdiction of the same State for an offence for which one has already been finally acquitted or convicted in accordance with the law and penal procedure of the State concerned. It admits of reopening of the proceedings only if there is evidence of new or newly discovered facts, or if there has

---

457    Preamble to Protocol No. 13, paragraphs 3 and 4.

458    *Öcalan v. Turkey* [GC], no. 46221/99, §§ 162-165, ECHR 2005-IV; see also *Al-Saadoon and Mufdhi*, § 120 ("These figures, together with consistent State practice in observing the moratorium on capital punishment, are strongly indicative that Article 2 has been amended so as to prohibit the death penalty in all circumstances.")

132                                                                                    CHAPTER 4

been a fundamental defect in the previous proceedings, which could affect the outcome of the case.

This Article is non-derogable by virtue of its third paragraph.

The practical importance of the non-derogable nature of this provision is illustrated by the Court's judgment in *Marguš v. Croatia* which we have examined in the previous chapter.[459]

It is true that there was no derogation under Article 15 in this case (nor could there be), but had there been, its effect would have been identical to that of the amnesty: to shield war criminals from a second prosecution after escaping accountability for their crimes through abuse of law. Understood in this sense, Article 4 § 3 of Protocol No. 7 can be seen as a useful companion provision to Article 7 § 2 of the Convention.

### 4.7.7    *Implied Non-derogable Rights*

We have seen that a non-derogable right to claim exemption from military service, provided that it be based on serious and convincing conscientious objections, is implied by the logic of the right itself.[460]

Some authors have identified other rights as non-derogable based on their essential importance or on their connection with the rights recognised as non-derogable by Article 15. These would include Article 13,[461] which would be non-derogable in so far as it is interlinked with non-derogable substantive rights, and the procedural provisions contained in the Convention itself – most notably the right of individual petition (Article 34).[462] Others would derive non-derogable status from their being rules of either *ius cogens* or international humanitarian law.[463] An example of the latter would be the guarantees of trial by an independent and impartial tribunal, attended by all appropriate guarantees, which is guaranteed by Common Article 3 of the Geneva Conventions and Article 6 of Additional Protocol No. II to the Geneva Conventions.[464]

Let us consider these suggestions in the light of the Court's case-law.

### 4.7.7.1    Freedom from Discrimination

Freedom from discrimination is largely non-derogable under the International Covenant on Civil and Political Rights ('provided that such measures ... do not involve discrimination solely on the ground of race, colour, sex, language,

---

459    *Marguš*; see paragraph 3.4.4 above.
460    See 4.7.3 above.
461    Loof, p. 530, with further references.
462    Loof, p. 538.
463    Loof, p. 540-550.
464    Loof, p. 543.

DEROGATION

religion or social origin', Article 4 § 1 of the Covenant)[465] and the American Convention on Human Rights (Article 27 § 1, which uses the same terms as the Covenant bar the word 'solely'). There is nothing in the text of Article 15 of the Convention to suggest that the principle of non-discrimination is non-derogable. Nonetheless, the suggestion that that requirement is subjacent is not new.[466]

In *A. and Others*, as we have seen, the Court found that the measures complained of were 'disproportionate in that they discriminated unjustifiably' between nationals and foreigners, without finding it necessary to delve separately into the complaint brought under Article 14 taken together with Article 5.[467] This could be understood to suggest that there is now a separate non-derogable right to be protected against discrimination under the Convention also.

A separate requirement that any derogating measures taken not be discriminatory was formulated by Judge Matscher in his separate opinion in *Ireland v. the United Kingdom*. He phrases it as follows:

> If the authorities deemed it necessary in order to combat terrorism to take emergency measures which weighed heavily on the population concerned, and if these measures were applied to only one section of the population whereas, in order to combat a comparable terrorist campaign originating from the other side – insofar as it was seriously combated –, they thought that they could confine themselves to the ordinary means of prevention and punishment, the question also arises whether the emergency measures were really indispensable within the meaning of Article 15 of the Convention.[468]

Discrimination is covered by Articles 14 of the Convention and 1 of Protocol No. 12. Article 14 of the Convention protects only against discrimination in 'the rights and freedoms set forth in the Convention', whereas Article 1 of Protocol No. 12 forbids discrimination in 'the enjoyment of any right set forth by law' and 'by any public authority'. The test is the same:

> The notion of discrimination has been interpreted consistently in the Court's jurisprudence concerning Article 14 of the Convention. In par-

---

465 Article 26 of the Covenant is not among the non-derogable Articles enumerated in Article 4 § 2.
466 Macdonald (1997) at p. 264.
467 *A. and Others*, §§ 190 and 192.
468 *Ireland v. the United Kingdom*, separate opinion of Judge Matscher, *in fine*.

ticular, this jurisprudence has made it clear that "discrimination" means treating differently, without an objective and reasonable justification, persons in similar situations (...). The authors used the same term, discrimination, in Article 1 of Protocol No. 12. Notwithstanding the difference in scope between those provisions, the meaning of this term in Article 1 of Protocol No. 12 was intended to be identical to that in Article 14 (see the Explanatory Report to Protocol No. 12, § 18). The Court does not therefore see any reason to depart from the settled interpretation of "discrimination", noted above, in applying the same term under Article 1 of Protocol No. 12 (...).[469]

Consequently, if there *is* objective and reasonable justification for the difference in treatment in issue (or for the failure to treat differently persons whose situations are significantly different),[470] there is no discrimination and hence no violation of either Article.

It is submitted that there is no need to formulate non-discrimination as a separate non-derogable right. A distinction that is objectively and reasonably justified, and for that reason not discriminatory, may well come within the protection of Article 15 § 1: for example, it is difficult to argue that in time of international armed conflict aliens who owe allegiance to the enemy should be treated the same as nationals in all things. Conversely, if objective and reasonable justification cannot be established, there will in any event be a violation of Article 14 of the Convention taken together with the substantive Article (or Article 1 of Protocol No. 12 as the case may be): absent such justification, it is logically impossible to argue that the measure in issue is 'strictly required by the exigencies of the situation'.

### 4.7.7.2    Article 5

In *Hassan*, the Court defined the limits of the protection of Article 5 in international armed conflict in accordance with Articles 4A and 21 of the Third Geneva Convention and Articles 42 and 78 of the Fourth Geneva Convention.[471] This necessarily implies the same limits when Article 44 § 4 of Additional Protocol No. I to the Geneva Conventions applies.

To that extent it can be said that the rights guaranteed by Article 5 are, in part, non-derogable by virtue of international humanitarian law.

---

469    *Sejdić and Finci v. Bosnia and Herzegovina* [GC], nos. 27996/06 and 34836/06, § 55, ECHR 2009.

470    *Thlimmenos v. Greece* (GC), no. 34369/97, § 44, ECHR 2000-IV.

471    *Hassan*, §§ 105-107.

DEROGATION

It is also interesting to compare Article 43 of the Fourth Geneva Convention with Article 5 § 4 of the Convention. The former vouchsafes to any alien 'protected person who has been interned or placed in assigned residence' the entitlement to have such action 'reconsidered as soon as possible by an appropriate court or administrative board', followed, if necessary, by periodic review at twice-yearly intervals. This suggests that Article 5 § 4 of the Convention is non-derogable at least as far as alien civilians caught up in an international armed conflict are concerned.[472]

### 4.7.7.3    Article 6

Although Article 6 is not specifically mentioned in Article 15, it is difficult to conceive of circumstances that might justify restrictions on the right of everyone to a 'fair and public hearing within a reasonable time by an independent and impartial tribunal established by law', at the very least when the case concerns the determination of a 'criminal charge'.

It would be all the less reasonable to countenance such restrictions given that the Third Geneva Convention provides, in its Article 84, that

> In no circumstances shall a prisoner of war be tried by a court of any kind that does not offer the essential guarantees of independence and impartiality as generally recognized, and, in particular, the procedure of which does not afford the accused the rights and means of defence provided for in Article 105.

Article 105 of the Third 1949 Geneva Convention sets out in considerable detail rights of the defence that are, for the most part, equivalent to the catalogue of rights set out in Article 6 § 3; the only one that seems to be lacking is the right to call defence witnesses under the same conditions as prosecution witnesses (Article 6 § 3 (d) of the Convention). The right to call witnesses is, however, mentioned in the Commentary of 1960.[473] Although there is no requirement that the trial of a prisoner of war be public, an equivalent purpose is served by notification of the Protecting Power and by allowing that Power to attend the trial as long as the detaining Power's security is not at risk.

The Fourth Geneva Convention, in its Article 71 and 72, also sets out fair trial guarantees largely corresponding to those provided by Article 6 §§ 1 and 3 (d) of the Convention. Article 71, in its opening words, sets out the requirement of

---

472    See 4.9 below.

473    International Committee of the Red Cross, Convention (III) relative to the Treatment of Prisoners of War. Geneva, 12 August 1949, Commentary of 1960 (Article 105).

a 'regular trial'. Under the terms of Article 5 of that Convention, these requirements are non-derogable even in respect of spies and saboteurs.

The ICRC Commentary of 1958 adds the following:

> The inclusion in the Convention of the express rule that no sentence may be pronounced by the competent courts of the Occupying Power except after "a regular trial" introduces into the law of war a fundamental notion of justice as it is understood in all civilized countries.
>
> The safeguards provided in the Articles dealing with penal legislation, which we have just discussed, and those prescribed elsewhere, particularly in Article 32, which prohibits torture and all other forms of brutality, obviously represent conditions which must be fulfilled if a trial is to be regular; but there are other rules relating to penal procedure which are not expressly laid down in the Convention, but must nevertheless be respected as they follow logically from its provisions. One is the principle that any accused person is presumed to be innocent until he is proved guilty. This essential rule remains fully valid in occupied territory.[474]

As regards armed conflicts not of an international character, the second paragraph under (d) of Article 3 common to all four 1949 Geneva Conventions prohibits 'at any time and at any place whatsoever'

> the passing of sentences and the carrying out of executions without previous judgment pronounced by a regularly constituted court, affording all the judicial guarantees which are recognized as indispensable by civilized peoples.

For the interpretation of this provision, the ICRC Commentary of 2016 refers to '[t]he 1966 International Covenant on Civil and Political Rights and other human rights treaties'. It also mentions treaty bodies having 'stated that the fundamental principles of fair trial and the requirement that courts be independent and impartial can never be dispensed with'.[475] Although the Court is not among the 'treaty bodies' having expressed itself in quite such sweeping

---

474  International Committee of the Red Cross, Convention (IV) relative to the Protection of Civilian Persons in Time of War. Geneva, 12 August 1949, Commentary of 1958 (Article 71).

475  International Committee of the Red Cross, Convention (I) for the Amelioration of the Condition of the Wounded and Sick in Armed Forces in the Field, Commentary of 2016 (Article 3).

DEROGATION

terms,[476] in a footnote the Commentary refers to the requirements of independence and impartiality set by the Court's *Findlay* and *Belilos* judgments.[477]

The conclusion can be none other than that the fair trial guarantees set out in Article 6 are non-derogable in cases of international and non-international armed conflict; in our submission, it is therefore difficult to see how they are not non-derogable in any lesser emergency.

4.7.7.4    Other Implied Non-Derogable Rights

The Human Rights Committee, in its General Comment No. 29 on States of Emergency, signals the existence of other rights that, in its opinion, cannot be made subject to derogation under Article 4 of the Covenant. These are derived from the Covenant itself and from other norms of customary and treaty law. They include such matters as the right of all persons deprived of their liberty to be treated with humanity and with respect for the inherent dignity of the human person (Article 10 of the Covenant itself); the prohibition on the taking of hostages, abductions or unacknowledged detention, which are described as 'norms of general international law'; certain aspects of minority rights; the deportation or forced displacement of populations; and propaganda for war or advocacy of national, racial or religious hatred that would constitute incitement to discrimination, hostility or violence; the right to an effective remedy; and procedural guarantees including the presumption of innocence and the right of *habeas corpus*.[478]

The Court does not issue general comments such as this; indeed, precisely because it is a court, that would not be proper. Courts set substantive standards through their case-law. Nonetheless we would consider it highly unlikely that the Court would accept measures such as those proscribed by the Human Rights Committee, if only because it would be difficult to justify them as justified by the 'exigencies of the situation'.

---

476    The Court goes no further than to refer to "the prominent place held in a democratic society by the right to a fair trial", as for example in *Al-Dulimi and Montana Management Inc. v. Switzerland* (GC), no. 5809/08, § 127, ECHR 2016.

477    *loc. cit.*, footnote 562: *Belilos v. Switzerland*, no. 10328/83, § 64, Series A no. 132; *Findlay v. the United Kingdom*, no. 22107/93, Reports 1997-I, §§ 73-77, Reports 1997-I.

478    Human Rights Committee, General Comment no. 29, States of Emergency (Article 4), CCPR/C/21/Rev.1/Add.11, 31 August 2001, §§ 13-16 and footnote 9.

138                                                                                          CHAPTER 4

## 4.8     Strictly Required by the Exigencies of the Situation

The requirement that the measures taken be 'strictly required by the exigencies of the situation' suggests a strict necessity test. In fact, however, the State has until now been allowed greater discretion than that.

It is a reasonable requirement that any measures taken correspond in some way to the crisis which they are intended to address.[479] The Court implies as much in *A and Others* in criticising the choice of 'an immigration measure to address what was essentially a security issue', which 'had the result of failing adequately to address the problem' and moreover was discriminatory in its effects.[480]

In its report in the *'First Cyprus Case'*, which admittedly is now sixty years old, the Commission was prepared to accept such interferences with ordinary life as curfews, prolonged periods of administrative detention, censorship and controls on burials and religious ceremonies. In *Lawless*, its very first case, the Court accepted administrative detention, though subject to a safeguard in the form of the possibility to seek review before a non-judicial body and of a way out in the form of a binding undertaking to renounce the use of violence. In *Brannigan and McBride*, the Court was marginally less accommodating: it accepted extended periods of detention without access to a magistrate, but only subject to safeguards both procedural (a remedy in the form of *habeas corpus*) and physical (including access to a doctor and the right to notify someone on the outside).

Nonetheless, the existence of safeguards does not exhaust the margin of appreciation in this respect: it is also a reasonable requirement that the respondent State be in a position to satisfy the Court that the measures resorted to are of a nature to assist efforts towards a return to normality – and therefore temporary.[481] Indeed, the expression 'strictly required by the exigencies of the situation' would have no meaning if it did not encompass such a requirement.

Judge Martens, dissenting in *Brannigan and McBride*, doubts that the strict necessity test leaves Governments any margin of appreciation. In his words:

> The second question [i.e. once it is determined that there is a threat to "the life of the nation"] is whether the derogation is to "the extent strict-

---

479    Macdonald (1997), p. 243.

480    *A. and Others*, § 186.

481    Loof, p. 379; Gross, O., and Ní Aoláin, F., "From Discretion to Scrutiny: Revisiting the Application of the Margin of Appreciation Doctrine in the Context of Article 15 of the European Convention on Human Rights", *Human Rights Quarterly* 23 (2001) 625-649 at p. 644.

DEROGATION

ly required by the exigencies of the situation". The wording underlined clearly calls for a closer scrutiny than the words "necessary in a democratic society" which appear in the second paragraph of Articles 8-11. Consequently, with respect to this second question there is, if at all, certainly no room for a wide margin of appreciation.[482]

It is a view that undeniably sits well with a grammatical interpretation of Article 15.[483]

## 4.9    Not Inconsistent with the State's Other Obligations under International Law

We have seen that the expression 'other obligations under international law' relevant to the interpretation of Article 15 primarily include those arising from the Charter of the United Nations, including those that govern the legality of war (Chapter VII of the Charter of the United Nations).

However, once war becomes a reality, other international legal obligations that become pertinent are those that are part of international humanitarian law which, as we have seen, on the one hand are generally more permissive *vis-à-vis* public authority – although not in all cases: sometimes they are noticeably stricter[484] – but on the other hand generally admit of no derogation at all. Consequently, where provisions of international humanitarian law coincide with rights guaranteed by the Convention, their effect is actually to make those rights by implication non-derogable.[485]

It is not necessarily the case that those 'other obligations under international law' offer less protection to the individual than the Convention itself. For example, Article 43 of the Geneva Convention relative to the Protection of Civilian Persons in Time of War (Geneva Convention (IV)) prescribes twice-yearly review of internment (Article 43) – such frequency of review being far more generous than that vouchsafed to long-term detainees ('persons of unsound mind' detained in accordance with Article 5 § 1 (e), for example) by the case-law of the Court.[486] Similarly, Article 73 of Geneva Convention (IV) – and let us recall that the four Geneva Conventions enjoy universal ratification – ex-

---

482    *Brannigan and McBride*, dissenting opinion of Judge Martens, § 4.
483    See also O'Boyle (2016), p. 339.
484    See 6.7 below.
485    See 4.7.7 above.
486    See the summary set out in *Abdulkhanov v. Russia*, no. 14743/11, § 212, 2 October 2012.

140                                                                          CHAPTER 4

tends the right to an appeal in criminal matters even to territories occupied by
Convention States that have not ratified Protocol No. 7.[487]

The expression 'other obligations under international law' may also be relevant to calamities not of a hostile nature that involve more than one country,
a major natural disaster or an economic crisis perhaps, to which customary or
conventional rules of international law may apply.[488]

Obligations relevant to this provision identified in doctrine include the so-
called 'basic human rights conventions' of the International Labour Organisation (ILO).[489] It would appear obvious that rights corresponding to the prohibitions set out in the Rome Statute of the International Criminal Court also
fall within this category, such as the destruction and seizure of property not
justified by military necessity (Article 8 § 2 (a) (iv) and (xiii)); the destruction
of religious buildings and hospitals that are not military objectives (Article 8
§ 2 (a) (ix)); declaring abolished, suspended or inadmissible in a court of law
the rights and actions of the nationals of the hostile party (Article 8 § 2 (a)
(xiv)); and pillaging (Article 8 § 2 (a) (xvi)) – at the very least, as conventional
obligations in respect of those States that have ratified the Rome Statute.[490]

As a matter of common sense, it must be a mistake to interpret 'other obligations under international law' so as to import into Article 15 substantive
provisions from other human rights treaties offering greater protection than
the Convention itself, as is sometimes suggested.[491] Article 4 § 2 of the International Covenant on Civil and Political rights, for example, has a broader catalogue of non-derogable rights than the Convention – including for example
the right to freedom of thought, conscience and religion (Article 18).

The requirement that the measures concerned be not 'inconsistent with
[the State's] other obligations under international law' is a difficult one for the
Court to monitor, since the Court is not set up to rule on any rules of international law other than the Convention. Even so, the Court is prepared to do so to
the extent that the facts of the case make it inevitable, as for example the *Van
Anraat*[492] and *Stichting Mothers of Srebrenica and Others*[493] decisions demon-
strate. In relation to Article 15, the question has thus far only been raised in

---

487    See Article 2 of Protocol No. 7.
488    Loof, p. 388-389.
489    Loof, p. 592.
490    *supra* note 454.
491    Loof, p. 592.
492    *Van Anraat v. the Netherlands*, *supra* note 207.
493    *Stichting Mothers of Srebrenica and Others v. the Netherlands* (dec.), no. 65542/12, ECHR
       2013.

DEROGATION

relation to formal requirements. In that respect the Court has eschewed extremes of formalism.[494]

## 4.10 Formalities

France proclaimed a state of emergency in November 2015, in the wake of the terrorist attacks in Paris, as we know; so did Turkey, in July 2016, after the attempted *coup d'état*. Unlike Article 4 § 1 of the International Covenant on Civil and Political Rights, Article 15 of the Convention does not require that a state of emergency (or, for that matter, war) be officially declared. Ireland and the United Kingdom did not do so before lodging their notices of derogation.

In the *'First Cyprus Case'*, the Greek Government disputed the validity of the *notes verbales* transmitted to the Secretary General. The Commission stated the importance of giving notice in accordance with Article 15 § 3 in the following terms:

> It follows from the above-mentioned provisions of Articles 19, 24 and 25 [now Articles 19, 33 and 34] that, when one High Contracting Party exercises its right to take measures under Article 15 derogating from its obligations under the Convention, the other High Contracting Parties have a legal interest in being informed of those measures since temporarily their own rights under Article 24 of the Convention [now Article 33] are *pro tanto* curtailed. It equally follows from the provisions of Articles 19, 24 and 25, that the position of the Commission (and, ultimately, of the European Court of Human Rights) in applying the Convention is directly affected by the fact that a High Contracting Party has taken measures under Article 15 which derogate from its obligations under the Convention. It further follows, in the case of a State which has recognised the competence of the Commission to receive petitions from individuals and groups under Article 25 [now superseded by Article 34], that the work of the Commission in determining the admissibility of such petitions may be impeded if it does not receive timely and definite information concerning any measure derogating from its obligations under the Convention which a State claims to have taken in reliance on Article 15.

The obvious implication was that notice to the Secretary General had to be given 'without any unavoidable delay' and must contain sufficient information

---

494  *Brannigan and McBride*, § 73.

to allow the other Contracting States and the Commission itself 'to appreciate the nature and extent of the derogation of the provisions of the Convention which the measures involve'.[495]

The Commission considered that the *note verbale* had been transmitted to the Secretary General with excessive delay – nearly three months after the measures derogating from Article 5 of the Convention had been introduced. Its content, nevertheless, was deemed 'sufficient to indicate in a general way the nature of the measures taken' although lacking in detail and precision. This being the first instance of derogation under Article 15, the Commission was unwilling to find it insufficient on that ground but noted for future reference that it required 'rather fuller information' in order satisfactorily to discharge its functions.

In the *'Greek Case'*, in contrast, the Commission found that not only had the Greek rulers failed to give adequate notice of their derogating measures to the Secretary General of the Council of Europe: notice of many of the measures adopted – including the promulgation of the new Constitution – was given either with several months' delay or not at all.[496]

The most recent notice of derogation, that of Turkey of 21 June 2016, again lacked specificity: in the Court's words, it indicated merely

> that a state of emergency has been declared in order to tackle the threat posed to the life of the nation by the severe dangers resulting from the attempted military coup and other terrorist acts, [and did] not explicitly mention which Articles of the Convention [were] to form the subject of a derogation. Instead, it simply [announced] that "measures taken [might] involve derogation from the obligations under the Convention".

Even so, since

> none of the parties [had] disputed that the notice of derogation by Turkey satisfied the formal requirement laid down in Article 15 § 3 of the Convention, namely to keep the Secretary General of the Council of Europe fully informed of the measures taken by way of derogation from the Convention and the reasons for them ... [the Court was] prepared to accept that this formal requirement has been satisfied.[497]

---

495    *Greece v. the United Kingdom*, § 158.
496    The *'Greek Case'*, § 46.
497    *Mehmet Hasan Altan*, § 89; *Şahin Alpay*, § 73.

DEROGATION

What is required by Article 15 § 3 is a statement of the measures taken and the reason therefor. There is no requirement that the notice of derogation specify the Articles actually derogated from – although, as the former Deputy Registrar of the Court points out, this is obviously desirable from the point of view of legal certainty.[498]

In *Mehmet Hasan Altan* and *Şahin Alpay* the Court declared itself satisfied with the bald statement of the Turkish Government that

> [t]he coup attempt and its aftermath together with other terrorist acts have posed severe dangers to public security and order, amounting to a threat to the life of the nation in the meaning of Article 15 of the Convention for the Protection of Human Rights and Fundamental Freedoms.[499]

– which suggests that as the case-law of the Court currently stands, it is not required either that the nature of the threat be specified in detail.

Nor is there a requirement that the existence of a public emergency be officially proclaimed, as in Article 4 § 1 of the International Covenant on Civil and Political Rights. One may assume, however, that in practice such an official proclamation will often be made, if only because States derogating under Article 15 of the Convention are likely to lodge the same derogation under Article 4 of the Covenant at the same time.[500]

It is submitted that Contracting States derogating in order for their armed forces to participate in joint military operations with the forces of States that are not Parties to the Convention might consider including in their notice of derogation a statement of, or at least a reference to, the standing or *ad hoc* rules governing the joint enterprise, such as memoranda of understanding.[501] This might help to allay the problems of 'legal interoperability' mentioned in our opening chapter.[502]

## 4.11    The *Hassan* Judgment

In *Hassan* the Court stretched the margin of appreciation of the Contracting State to its logical extreme by denying the necessity to seek the application

---

498    O'Boyle (2016), p. 335.

499    *Mehmet Hasan Altan*, § 89; *Şahin Alpay*, § 73.

500    As Ukraine did (see footnote 251 above).

501    Compare *Jaloud*, §§100-103 and 138.

502    See 1.2.4.2 above.

144                                                                    CHAPTER 4

of Article 15 at all – at least, as the Court's case-law now stands, in respect of Article 5 of the Convention in case of international armed conflict. We have seen that the Court was favourable to the United Kingdom Government's argument that there had been no need for the United Kingdom to derogate under Article 15.[503] One author has called the *Hassan* judgment a 'final blow'.[504]

It was perhaps not inevitable that the Court should bypass Article 15 as it did. As outlined above, the applicability of Article 15 need not have depended on the 'war' in Iraq 'threatening the life of the nation'. On this view, the United Kingdom might well have given prior expression to its will to be bound only to apply international humanitarian law.[505]

Even better – and it is only right at this point to refer to a paper by Tugendhat and Croft published by the British think tank Policy Exchange in 2013 – the United Kingdom might have lodged a notice of derogation under Article 15 of the Convention *and* sought 'explicit language in future Chapter VII United Nations Security Council Resolutions in order to provide a legal basis for detention or internment acceptable to the ECHR'.[506] That is sound advice for the future.

## 4.12    Conclusion

*Impossibilium nulla obligatio est.*[507] Article 15 was included in the Convention precisely for that reason. It offers Contracting States the possibility to reduce their substantive Convention liabilities in appropriate cases while yet remaining within their Convention obligations.

It is submitted that Article 15 has not yet been tested to its limits. In particular, the cases considered by the Commission and the Court have only ever concerned the threat of terrorist attack (Ireland, United Kingdom, France) or

---

503    See 3.4.2 above.

504    Bart van der Sloot, "Is All Fair in Love and War? An Analysis of the Case Law on Article 15 ECHR", in *Military Law and the law of War Review* 53/2 (2014), pp. 319-358 at p. 350.

505    In a similar sense, see Marko Milanovic, "Extraterritorial Derogations from Treaties in Armed Conflict", in *The Frontiers of Human Rights: Extraterritoriality and its Challenges, Collected Courses of the Academy of European Law*, vol. XXIV/1, p. 55-88 at p. 71. See also *Leuven Manual on the International Law Applicable to Peace Operations* (Terry D. Gill, Dieter Fleck, William H. Boothby and Alfons Vanheusden, general eds; Marco Benatar and Remy Jorritsma, assistant eds.), Cambridge University Press 2017, pp. 85-88.

506    Tugendhat and Croft, *The Fog of Law: An introduction to the legal erosion of British fighting power*, https://policyexchange.org.uk/wp-content/uploads/2016/09/the-fog-of-law.pdf (last accessed on 16 October 2016) pp. 12 and 58-60.

507    Corpus Iuris Civilis, D.50.17.185.

DEROGATION

direct attempts to displace the Government (Cyprus, Greece, Turkey). As we have seen, however, the occasion to apply Article 15 may conceivably arise in situations not readily definable in terms of conflict, for example an environmental disaster or economic collapse.

Equally, from the Court's perspective the time may have come to reassess the limits themselves. Thus far application of Article 15 has been found impermissible only once in Strasbourg case-law: in the *Greek case*, in which as we have seen the bad faith of those who had usurped the powers of government was considered manifest.[508] Rarely until now have there been prolonged states of emergency in place, with corresponding Article 15 derogations, and rarely have they covered the entire territory of the State. The Turkish derogations in issue in *Sakık and Others* and other cases of the period covered only certain provinces in the southeast of the country; the United Kingdom derogations covered only the six counties of Northern Ireland. Between July 2016 and November 2017 there were for the first time three sweeping notices of derogation in place simultaneously, all of them for prolonged periods: that of Ukraine (lodged on 5 June 2015), that of France (lodged on 25 November 2015) and that of Turkey (lodged on 21 July 2016). The French and Turkish notices have been withdrawn. Of the three, only the Ukrainian derogation does not apply to the whole of the country. The continent of Europe appears to be heading towards more instability and crisis, not less; it may well be that more governments succumb to the temptation to solve their domestic problems by limiting substantive Convention rights. If they do, the day will surely come when the Court must consider critically, firstly, whether the situation so justifies, and secondly, whether the derogating measures themselves are – or continue to be – justified.

A further point to be made is that Contracting States have thus far eschewed its use in situations that could properly be described as 'war'. One reason for this, pointed out above,[509] may be that Governments are unwilling both to acknowledge their own inability to contain the situation and to recognise to their opponents combatant status within the meaning of international humanitarian law – especially if the conflict is a non-international one fought on the territory of the Contracting State itself. Another may be a fear of criticism of their unwillingness fully to comply with Convention standards.[510]

The time may soon come for them to reconsider this stand. At all events, if it proves necessary to see current events in Crimea and Eastern Ukraine as oc-

---

508   See 4.6 above.

509   See 4.3.2.2 above.

510   Kjetil Mujezinović Larsen, *The Human Rights Treaty Obligations of Peacekeepers*, Cambridge University Press 2012, pp. 312-13.

146                                                                                                    CHAPTER 4

curring within an 'international armed conflict',[511] then the Ukrainian notice of derogation of 5 June 2015 suggests that the practice of not lodging derogations under Article 15 in situations where the Third and Fourth Geneva Conventions can apply, as identified in *Banković* and *Hassan*, is no longer universal.[512]

In another interesting development, several Convention States – Germany, Belgium, Denmark, the Netherlands, the United Kingdom and Norway – have sent letters to the Security Council justifying military action targeting Islamic State on the territory of Iraq and Syria in terms of 'collective self-defence' within the meaning of Article 51 of the United Nations Charter.[513] Recently, also, Turkey invoked Article 51 of the United Nations Charter (as well as a number of existing Security Council resolutions) in justification of military action in the Afrin region, just across the border in Syria, and directed against 'Deash and the PKK/KCK Syria affiliate, PYD/YPG'.[514]

---

511    There are interstate cases between Ukraine and the Russian Federation pending before the Court: these include, among others, *Ukraine v. Russia* (re *Crimea*), no. 20958/14, communicated on 25 November 2014 and 29 September 2015, and *Ukraine v. Russia* (re *Eastern Ukraine*), no. 42410/15, communicated on 29 September 2015.

512    cf. International Criminal Court, Office of the Prosecutor, Report on Preliminary Examination Activities 2016, §§ 158 ("The information available suggests that the situation within the territory of Crimea and Sevastopol amounts to an international armed conflict between Ukraine and the Russian Federation") and 169 ("Additional information, such as reported shelling by both States of military positions of the other, and the detention of Russian military personnel by Ukraine, and vice-versa, points to direct military engagement between Russian armed forces and Ukrainian government forces that would suggest the existence of an international armed conflict in the context of armed hostilities in eastern Ukraine from 14 July 2014 at the latest, in parallel to the non-international armed conflict.") See also footnotes 24 and 25 above and Sergey Sayapin, "Russia's Withdrawal of Signature from the Rome Statute Would not Shield its Nationals from Potential Prosecution at the ICC", *EJIL:Talk!*, 21 November 2016.

513    S/2015/928, 3 December 2015 (United Kingdom); S/2015/946, 10 December 2015 (Germany); S/2016/34, 13 January 2016 (Denmark); S/2016/132, 10 February 2016 (Netherlands); S/2016/513, 3 June 2016 (Norway); S/2016/523, 9 June 2016 (Belgium). See Marko Milanovic, http://www.ejiltalk.org/belgiums-article-51-letter-to-the-security-council/ (accessed on 19 June 2016) and Monica Hakimi and Jacob Katz Cogan, http://www.ejiltalk.org/a-role-for-the-security-council-on-defensive-force/ (accessed on 22 November 2016).

514    Identical letters dated 20 January 2018 from the Chargé d'affaires a.i. of the Permanent Mission of Turkey to the United Nations addressed to the Secretary-General and the President of the Security Council, S/2018/53. See also Anne Peters, "The Turkish Operation in Afrin (Syria) and the Silence of the Lambs", *EJIL:Talk!*, 30 January 2018.

CHAPTER 5

# Jurisdiction of the Contracting States

## 5.1 Introduction[515]

Article 1 of the Convention makes the Contracting States promise to secure the rights and freedoms to 'everyone within their jurisdiction'. Contracting States may sometimes seek to render the Convention inapplicable to their predicament by evading Article 1 jurisdiction altogether: it is therefore necessary to understand the meaning of the expression.

When the Convention was being negotiated in 1949 and 1950, the first draft held the promise of the Contracting States to guarantee human rights to their nationals; then to everyone 'domiciled' in their territory; later this was widened to 'residents', later still to 'all persons within the territory'. The formulation 'within their jurisdiction' was copied from an early draft of an International Covenant on Human Rights, which was then being prepared for the United Nations at Lake Success, New York. It was accepted apparently without discussion.[516]

What precisely the expression meant was not defined. It was left to the Court to construe it.

In general international law, 'jurisdiction' is in many respects an emanation of 'sovereignty'. 'Sovereignty' is an expression of 'legal personality of a certain kind, that of statehood'.[517] The expression 'jurisdiction' then refers to certain attributes of sovereignty: namely, the right and the power unilaterally to exercise legislative, executive and judicial power to prescribe conduct, whether it be to act in a particular way, to desist from particular action, or to suffer particular action by another.[518] Jurisdiction in this sense is asserted as a right.

---

515 An earlier version of the text contained in 5.1 – 5.4 appeared in *Human Rights in a Global World: Essays in Honour of Judge Luis López Guerra* (Guido Raimondi, Iulia Motoc, Pere Pastor Vilanova, Carmen Morte Gómez, eds.; Wolf Legal Publishers, 2018), pp. 69-88, with the title "The Convention a 'regional' instrument? Territorial and quasi-territorial scope of Article 1 jurisdiction".

516 Collected edition of the *Travaux Préparatoires*, Article 1, Cour (77) 9. For more extensive descriptions, see Lawson (1999), pp. 250-51 and Eric Pouw, *International Human Rights Law and the Law of Armed Conflict in the Context of Counterinsurgency – With a Particular Focus on Targeting and Operational Detention* (diss. UvA 2013), pp. 61-62.

517 Crawford (2012), p. 204.

518 Crawford (2012), p. 456; Jankowska-Gilberg, Magdalena, *Extraterritorialität der Menschenrechte: Der Begriff der Jurisdiktion im Sinne von Art. 1 EMRK* (diss. Regensburg 2007), No-

---

© KONINKLIJKE BRILL NV, LEIDEN, 2021 | DOI:10.1163/9789004425637_006

In contrast, the expression '[t]he High Contracting Parties shall secure', as used in Article 1 of the European Convention on Human Rights, imposes on States a *duty*, or as it has been expressed, a 'one-way obligation', towards individuals[519] – namely to secure the rights and freedoms which the Convention guarantees. The expression 'to everyone within their jurisdiction' defines the circle of those towards whom this obligation exists. Jurisdiction in this sense is borne as a responsibility.

The two concepts of 'jurisdiction' are interrelated. The link between the two is that the State has both the right *and* the duty to exercise its legislative, executive and judicial powers to secure human rights.[520]

Despite their interrelation, the difference between the two concepts of 'jurisdiction' predicates a difference in approach to the limits to be imposed.

Where the expression 'jurisdiction' refers to the powers that international law recognises to States to impose their will on the individual, the limits will be such as to impose restrictions on the State's liberty to act. These are generally limits flowing from the existence of other States enjoying the same powers; the 'jurisdiction', in this sense, of one State ends where that of another begins.

Conversely, where 'jurisdiction' refers to the obligation of the State to secure rights and freedoms to the individual, the limits will be on the scope of the State's duties and, as a corollary, the possibility of applicant States or individuals[521] to hold States responsible for violating these rights and freedoms. The

---

mos, 2008, pp. 25-29; Alex Mills, "Rethinking Jurisdiction in International Law", *The British Yearbook of International Law* (2014), Vo. 84 No. 1, 187-239 at pp. 194-200; Marko Milanovic, *Extraterritorial application of human rights treaties*, Oxford University Press 2011/2013, pp. 23-26; Michael Duttwiler, "Authority, Control and Jurisdiction in the Extraterritorial Application of the European Convention on Human Rights, *Netherlands Quarterly of Human Rights*, Vol. 30/2, 137-162, 2012, at p. 157.

519    *Ireland v. the United Kingdom*, § 239; Maarten den Heijer and Rick Lawson, "Extraterritorial Human Rights and the Concept of 'Jurisdiction'", in M. Langford a.o. (eds.), *Global Justice, State Duties* (Cambridge University Press 2013), p. 153, at paragraph 3.1; see also Rick Lawson, "Out of Control: State Responsibility and Human Rights: Will the ILC's Definition of the 'act of State' meet the Challenges of the 21st Century?" In M. Castermans, F. van Hoof and J. Smiths (eds.), *The Role of the Nation State in the 21st Century – Essays in Honour of Peter Baehr* (Kluwer Law International, 1998).

520    Milanovic (2011/13), p. 53; Angelika Nußberger, "The Concept of 'Jurisdiction' in the Jurisprudence of the European Court of Human Rights", [2012] Current Legal Problems 65 p. 241 at p. 249 (footnote 19). Compare Article 2 § 1 of the Convention against Torture and Other Cruel, Inhuman or Degrading Treatment or Punishment: "Each State Party shall take effective legislative, administrative, judicial or other measures to prevent acts of torture in any territory under its jurisdiction."

521    Articles 33 and 34 of the Convention respectively.

JURISDICTION OF THE CONTRACTING STATES                                    149

latter is what is meant when the Court states, as it has done on several occasions in recent years, that Article 1 jurisdiction is a 'threshold criterion'.[522]

There is an obvious tension between the two understandings of 'jurisdiction'. *Raison d'état* may induce Contracting States to seek to enjoy 'jurisdiction' in the first sense to the greatest possible extent and at the same time limit the responsibilities attending 'jurisdiction' in the second sense when they impose unwelcome constraints on the business of government.

The first step is therefore to consider the scope of 'jurisdiction' understood as the exercise of sovereignty. That will be the focus of this chapter.

In normal circumstances the territorial and quasi-territorial limits on the powers of the State define the limits *ratione loci* on its Convention undertakings. We will examine these in 5.2-5.4. Further down, in 5.5, we will see that States exercise 'jurisdiction' in this sense beyond their borders as well; and in 5.6, that the exercise of domestic jurisdiction may produce Convention-relevant effects abroad.

The next chapter, Chapter 6, will focus more closely on the other aspect of 'jurisdiction', namely jurisdiction in the sense of 'accountability' – the sense in which it is understood for purposes of Article 1 of the Convention in 'hard power' situations.


## 5.2    Territorial and Quasi-Territorial Jurisdiction

As the European Court of Human Rights has construed 'jurisdiction', the concept is 'primarily territorial'.[523] There is thus no doubt that the European Convention on Human Rights applies throughout the European land territory of the various Contracting States. However, as a matter of international law other than Convention law the exercise of domestic 'jurisdiction' outside the metropolitan land territory of the State is by no means unusual; this part of our study will therefore investigate the implications for the exercise of 'Article 1 jurisdiction'.

---

522   See, among other authorities, *Al-Jedda*, § 74; *Al-Skeini*, § 130; *Nada v. Switzerland* (GC), no. 10593/08, § 118, ECHR 2012; *Djokaba Lambi Longa v. the Netherlands* (dec.), no. 33917/12, § 61, ECHR 2012; *Catan and Others v. the Republic of Moldova and Russia* (GC), nos. 43370/04, 18454/06 and 8252/05, § 103, ECHR 2012.

523   *Soering v. the United Kingdom*, 7 July 1989, § 86, Series A no. 161; *Banković and Others v. Belgium and 16 Other Contracting States* (dec.) [GC], no. 52207/99, §§ 59 and 61, ECHR 2001-XII; *Kalogeropoulou and Others v. Greece and Germany* (dec.), no. 59021/00, ECHR 2002-X.

### 5.2.1 *The 'Colonial Clause'*

Article 56 § 1 of the Convention provides that

> [a]ny State may at the time of its ratification or at any time thereafter declare by notification addressed to the Secretary General of the Council of Europe that [the] Convention shall ... extend to all or any of the territories for whose international relations it is responsible.

In other words, applicability of the Convention to territorial possessions outside the European land mass is not automatic. Neither is the right of individual application: according to the fourth paragraph of that Article, it too must be extended separately.

For all that Article 56 is sometimes referred to as the Convention's 'colonial clause', at the time when it was drafted – as Article 63 of the Convention of 1950 – it did not refer to 'colonies' – territorial possessions – alone. After the Second World War and the creation of the United Nations Organisation, certain States held territories in trust under Chapter XII of the Charter of the United Nations; the territories in question, most of them former German colonies and protectorates until 1918, had generally been League of Nations mandate territories until the League of Nations ceased to exist in 1946. The former German colonies in Africa were placed under French or British administration (with the exception of Rwanda-Urundi, which was entrusted to Belgium). Italy was entrusted with its own former colony of Italian Somaliland until this territory was merged with British Somaliland to become what is now Somalia.

It is to a large extent a matter of opinion whether Article 56 allows the scope of the Convention's territorial protection to be extended beyond European land borders or, conversely, restricts it to the territory of the mother country and allows Governments to choose carefully the dependencies to which they consider it can safely apply.

The classical view is that Article 63 of the Convention of 1950 – as mentioned, the predecessor to the present Article 56 – was drafted in recognition of the inappropriateness of a colonial power assuming treaty obligations without the say-so of the 'fledgling democratic institutions' of a soon-to-be-independent territory.[524] This is the view espoused by the Court itself: in *Tyrer*, it noted that 'the system established by Article 63 was primarily designed to meet

---

524   Catherina Meredith and Theodora Christou, "Not in my Front Yard: Security and Resistance to Responsibility for Extraterritorial State Conduct", in *War or Crime? National Legal Challenges in Europe to the War in Iraq* (Elspeth Guild, editor), Wolf Legal Publishers, 2009, at p. 404.

the fact that, when the Convention was drafted, there were still certain colonial territories whose state of civilisation did not, it was thought, permit the full application of the Convention'.[525]

On a more mistrustful view, it has been suggested that regardless of the wording of Article 56, its intended effect is the fruit of cynical politics, British in particular. Marko Milanovic, for example, paints a dark picture of shadowy figures in the British Colonial Office conspiring to withhold the protection of the Convention, and in particular the right of individual petition, from 'large swathes' of the then still-to-be-dismantled British Empire.[526]

There is merit in the traditional view as expressed by the Court in *Tyrer*. In the mid-twentieth century traditional practices incompatible with the Convention survived in some overseas territories under European colonial sovereignty, for example head-hunting and cannibalism in Western New Guinea.[527] While the Dutch, until 1962 the colonial overlords of that particular territory, were certainly concerned to put a stop to these, it is beyond dispute that they could not in reason have been expected to enforce Article 2 of the Convention there as they could in Europe. Similarly, female genital mutilation – an acknowledged violation of Article 3[528] – was, and remains to this day, an indigenous custom accepted and widespread in parts of Africa and the Middle East that in the 1940s and 50s were still under British or French administration.

Article 56 in its present redaction empowers Contracting States to extend the applicability of the Convention to 'all or any' of the territories for whose international relations they are responsible.

France did so, at the time of ratification, for 'the whole territory of the Republic' – that is, including all of its overseas departments and territories, while specifying that due regard should be had to 'local requirements'. However, Saarland, a French protectorate from 1947 until 1956 (now a federal state of Germany), was a Party to the Convention in its own right even though representation of its interests abroad was entrusted to France.[529]

---

525   *Tyrer*, § 38.

526   Milanovic (2011/13), pp. 14-16, citing L. Moore and A.W.B. Simpson, 'Ghosts of Colonialism in the European Convention on Human Rights', (2006) BYIL 121, at 136-58. In a similar sense, Marco Duranti, *The Conservative Human Rights Revolution*, Oxford University Press 2017, pp. 197-205.

527   For a graphic eyewitness account from the 1950s, see http://www.papuaerfgoed.org/en/ Head_Hunting_on_the_South_Coast (translated from the Dutch) (retrieved on 3 April 2016).

528   *Collins and Akaziebie v. Sweden* (dec.), no. 23944/05, 8 March 2007.

529   Constitution of Saarland of 15 December 1947, Preamble (http://www.verfassungen.de/ de/saar/saarland47-index.htm, accessed 22 April 2017).

152                                                                                          CHAPTER 5

The Netherlands extended the applicability of the Convention to overseas territories that were part of its Kingdom (Suriname and the Netherlands Antilles but not Netherlands New Guinea) though some time after ratifying; the Netherlands declaration is still valid for the Caribbean islands of Aruba, Curaçao, and the Netherlands part (just under half) of Sint Maarten/Saint Martin.[530]

In contrast, the Convention was never made to apply in the Belgian Congo.[531]

The United Kingdom, at the time of ratification of the Convention in 1953, extended the applicability of the Convention (though not the right of individual petition) to

> Aden Colony [now part of Yemen], The Bahamas, Barbados, Basutoland [now Lesotho], Bechuanaland [now Botswana], Bermuda, British Guiana [now Guyana], British Honduras [now Belize], British Solomon Islands [now Solomon Islands], Channel Islands: The Bailiwick of Jersey, The Bailiwick of Guernsey [which includes the Channel islands Alderney and Sark], Cyprus, Falklands Islands, Fiji, Gambia, Gilbert and Ellice Islands [Gilbert Islands, now Kiribati; Ellice Islands, now Tuvalu], Gold Coast [now Ghana], Jamaica, Kenya, Gibraltar, Leeward Islands, Federation of Malaya [now absorbed into Malaysia], Malta, Isle of Man, Mauritius, Nigeria, Northern Rhodesia [now Zambia], North Borneo [now absorbed into Malaysia], Nyassaland [or Nyasaland, now Malawi], St. Helena, Sarawak [now absorbed into Malaysia], Seychelles, Sierra Leone, Singapore, Somaliland [now absorbed into Somalia], Swaziland, Tanganyika [now absorbed into Tanzania], Trinidad, Uganda, Windward Islands: Dominica, Grenada, St. Lucia, St. Vincent, Zanzibar [now absorbed into Tanzania], and at the request of the Government of that Kingdom, for whose international relations Her Majesty's Government in the United Kingdom is responsible, Kingdom of Tonga.

Most of the lands mentioned are now independent. Cyprus and Malta are parties to the Convention in their own right. It remains interesting to see that for a

---

530   It extended to Suriname until 25 November 1975 when that country became independent from the Kingdom. The islands of Bonaire, Saba and St Eustatius, formerly part of the Netherlands Antilles, are now administratively part of the Netherlands proper (the Realm in Europe).

531   See *X, Y and Z v. Belgium*, Commission decision of 30 May 1961, Yearbook 1961 p. 260-70.

JURISDICTION OF THE CONTRACTING STATES 153

brief period of perhaps ten years the Convention applied, via the United Kingdom, in much of continental Africa, South-East Asia and the Pacific Ocean.

The presence of the Kingdom of Tonga on this list is especially noteworthy. Between 1900 and 1970 Tonga (a Polynesian archipelago) was a self-governing British 'protected state'. This remarkable case of application of the Convention to a wholly non-European State retaining its own international legal personality remains unique.

Other British colonies and British-governed territories, however, were not offered the protection of the Convention. One example is Southern Rhodesia, where white minority rule prevailed. This territory was later to gain independence as Zimbabwe. Another is Hong Kong, which was to revert to Chinese sovereignty after a century and a half as a British Crown Colony. To date, no territorial declaration has been made in respect of the British Antarctic Territory, the British Indian Ocean Territory (the Chagos Islands) and the Pitcairn Islands.[532]

Only sixteen non-self-governing territories remain on the United Nations list. Of these, eleven are administered by States Parties to the Convention: one by France (New Caledonia) and ten by the United Kingdom (Anguilla, Bermuda, the British Virgin Islands, the Cayman Islands, the Falkland Islands, Montserrat, St Helena, the Turks and Caicos Islands, Gibraltar and Pitcairn). Other offshore territories of European states form a single constitutional entity with the mother country, such as Greenland and the Faeroe Islands (Denmark), Jan Mayen Island and Svalbard (Norway), and the island regions of Portugal (the Azores and Madeira Islands) and Spain (the Balearic and Canary Islands), even though they may have internal self-government within the structures of the State; for these, applicability of the Convention is axiomatic.

It should be pointed out that a territorial extension applicable to the Convention itself does not *ipso iure* also cover any of the Protocols: as is apparent from the decision of inadmissibility in *Quark Fishing Ltd. v. the United Kingdom*, either the Protocols included in the extension are specified, or for each Protocol a separate specific territorial extension is needed.[533] Indeed, each of

---

532   For the text of these declarations, see the web site of the Council of Europe's Treaty Office, http://conventions.coe.int/Treaty/Commun/ListeDeclarations.asp?NT=005&CM=8 &DF=20/06/2015&CL=ENG&VL=1 (English; also available in French). With respect to the British Indian Ocean Territory in particular, for which the point was disputed, see *Chagos Islanders v. the United Kingdom* (dec.), no. 35622/04, §§ 61-62, 11 December 2011.

533   *Quark Fishing Ltd. v. the United Kingdom* (dec.), no. 15305/06, ECHR 2006-XIV; see also *Gillow v. the United Kingdom*, no. 9063/80, § 63, Series A no. 109.

154 CHAPTER 5

the Protocols that contain substantive guarantees (Protocols 1, 4, 6, 7, 12 and 13) has its own colonial clause.[534]

Similarly, although in respect of the mother country the right of individual petition is automatic by virtue of Article 34, in respect of territories for whose international relations the mother country is responsible a separate declaration accepting the right of individual petition remains a requirement (Article 56 §§ 1 and 4).

In addition to the United Kingdom, two other Contracting States (France and Norway) lay claims to territory on the continent of Antarctica. No territorial extensions under Article 56 of the Convention covering those areas appear to be in force and it will have to be seen if the question ever presents itself whether, and to what extent, the Convention applies there. It should however be observed that the Antarctic Treaty, which according to its preamble is intended to ensure that Antarctica 'shall continue forever to be used exclusively for peaceful purposes and shall not become the scene or object of international discord' and to establish scientific cooperation, includes a provision requiring its Contracting Parties 'to exert appropriate efforts, consistent with the Charter of the United Nations, to the end that no one engages in any activity in Antarctica contrary to [its] principles and purposes ...'[535] – that is, to assert their legislative and, if necessary, judicial and executive jurisdiction for the purposes stated.

The question has been raised before the Court whether the two principal exceptions to territoriality identified in *al-Skeini and Others v. the United Kingdom*, namely 'State agent authority and control' and 'effective control over an area',[536] can create a jurisdictional link for purposes of Article 1 over an overseas territory even in the absence of a declaration under Article 56. In the one case where it arose (the *Chagos Islanders* case), the Court recognised the anomaly that would result from accepting Article 1 jurisdiction in areas for whose international relations the Contracting State *was not* responsible while making applicability of the Convention to legitimate overseas territories of the State itself ('anachronistic colonial remnants'[537] though they be) conditional on a declaration to that effect. Nevertheless, the Court did not on that occasion find

---

534 Article 4 of Protocol No. 1; Article 5 of Protocol No. 4; Article 5 of Protocol No. 6; Article 6 of Protocol No. 7; Article 2 of Protocol No. 12; Article 4 of Protocol No. 13.

535 Article X of the Antarctic Treaty (Washington, 1 December 1959). For a Norwegian view, see Magne Frostad, "The 'Colonial Clause' and Extraterritorial Application of Human Rights: The European Convention on Human Rights Article 56 and its Relationship to Article 1", *Arctic Review on Law and Politics*, vol. 4, 1/2013 pp. 21-41.

536 *Al-Skeini*, §§ 133-140; see below.

537 *Chagos Islanders v. the United Kingdom* (dec.), no. 35622/04, § 74, 11 December 2012.

JURISDICTION OF THE CONTRACTING STATES

it necessary to provide an answer because the application was in any event inadmissible for reasons quite unrelated to the exercise of jurisdiction.[538]

In *Ilaşcu and Others* the Moldovan Government tried to rely on the declaration made by Moldova at the time of ratification of the Convention, to the effect that it was unable to guarantee compliance with the Convention 'omissions and acts committed by the organs of the self-proclaimed Trans-Dniester republic within the territory actually controlled by such organs', and suggested that the Court could interpret Article 56 *a contrario* so as to permit a restriction of Moldova's Article 1 jurisdiction in relation to the parts of its territory on which its writ did not run. The Court rejected this argument, holding

> that neither the spirit nor the terms of Article 56, which provides for extending the Convention's application to territories other than the metropolitan territories of the High Contracting Parties, could permit of a negative interpretation in the sense of restricting the scope of the term "jurisdiction" within the meaning of Article 1 to only part of the territory.[539]

## 5.3    Sea, Airspace and Outer Space under the Sovereignty of States

### 5.3.1    *Sea*

#### 5.3.1.1    Applicable Regime

Of the Council of Europe Member States, only Andorra, Azerbaijan, San Marino and Turkey are not signatories to the United Nations Convention on the Law of the Sea of 1982 (hereafter UNCLOS). Liechtenstein is a signatory, but not a party. The Member States of the European Union are dually bound by the European Union's ratification and by their own.

Andorra, Liechtenstein and San Marino are landlocked; Azerbaijan borders on an inland sea (the Caspian); Turkey has direct access to the high seas. Both Azerbaijan and Turkey have naval forces and a merchant fleet; Andorra, Liechtenstein and San Marino have neither. None of these five States is a party to the four Law of the Sea Conventions of 1958 (the Convention on the Territorial Sea and the Contiguous Zone; the Convention on the High Seas; the Convention on Fishing and Conservation of the Living Resources of the High Seas; and the Convention on the Continental Shelf), although these remain in force as

---

538    *Chagos Islanders*, no. 35622/04, §§ 82, 85 and 86.
539    *Ilaşcu and Others v. Moldova and Russia* (GC) (dec.), no. 48787/99, 4 July 2001.

156                                                                                    CHAPTER 5

between those parties that have not chosen to join UNCLOS (most notably the United States).

Turkey's position stems from its dispute with Greece over the Aegean. Turkey claims a 6-mile territorial sea there and recognises Greek jurisdiction to the same distance from the shore, opposing Greek claims based on UNCLOS.[540]

The status of the Caspian Sea is disputed between its littoral states, which include Iran, Kazakhstan, Russia and Turkmenistan in addition to Azerbaijan. The Caspian Sea is only accessible by water from the Baltic, Black and White Seas, and then only via internal waters indisputably Russian – the river Volga and the Russian inland canal system. The first question, which to date remains unanswered, is whether the law of the sea applies at all, or whether alternatively the Caspian should be viewed as an international lake; if the latter, the next question goes to the current status of existing treaties entered into over the centuries by imperial Persia and imperial Russia (and later by the Soviet Union).[541]

Since it cannot be the purpose of this study to take a position on the delimitation and use of disputed stretches of water, this section will focus on the application of UNCLOS.

### 5.3.1.2    Sovereignty and 'Sovereign Rights' over Marine Areas

The baseline from which the various maritime zones are measured is, in principle, the low-water line along the coast, as marked on large-scale charts officially recognised by the coastal State[542] (or along the seaward low-water line of fringing reefs,[543] or around archipelagos[544]); however, straight baselines may be drawn along heavily indented coast or highly unstable coastlines.[545]

Internal waters – that is, those waters that lie landwards of the baseline (special rules apply to archipelagic States[546]) – are within the territorial ju-

---

540     Turkey: "The Breadth of Territorial Waters", website of the Ministry of Foreign Affairs of the Republic of Turkey, http://www.mfa.gov.tr/the-breadth-of-territorial-waters.en.mfa; "The Delimitation of the Aegean Continental Shelf", *ibid.*, http://www.mfa.gov.tr/the-delimitation-of-the-aegean-continental-shelf.en.mfa; Greece: "Territorial sea – Casus belli", web site of the Ministry of Foreign Affairs of the Hellenic Republic, http://www.mfa.gr/en/issues-of-greek-turkish-relations/relevant-documents/territorial-sea-casus-belli.html; all accessed on 6 October 2015.

541     Hanna Zimnitskaya, James von Geldern, "Is the Caspian Sea a sea; and why does it matter?", *Journal of Eurasian Studies* 2 (2011) 1-14.

542     Article 5 UNCLOS.

543     Article 6 UNCLOS.

544     Article 47 UNCLOS.

545     Article 7 UNCLOS.

546     Article 50 UNCLOS.

# JURISDICTION OF THE CONTRACTING STATES

risdiction of the coastal state.[547] There is no doubt that the State exercises its jurisdiction there as it does on its land territory, and accordingly undertakes the corresponding obligations pursuant to Article 1 of the Convention.

Articles 2 and 3 UNCLOS allow those Contracting States with a sea coast to extend their national sovereignty – and therefore their jurisdiction – up to twelve miles offshore, into their territorial sea.[548] Article 2 § 3 UNCLOS provides that sovereignty over the territorial sea shall be exercised not only subject to that Convention, but also to 'other rules of international law' – a formulation that cannot in reason exclude duties assumed under human rights treaties.

The *Women on Waves* judgment can be construed as an illustration of this. Portugal prevented the entry into its territorial sea of a vessel offering aid and information related to voluntary abortion. Abortion being then illegal in Portugal, the Government argued before the Court that actively supporting it was inconsistent with 'innocent passage' within the meaning of Articles 19 and 25 UNCLOS. While recognising the Portuguese interest in enforcing its laws, the Court nonetheless found the interference with the applicants' right to freedom of expression (Article 10 of the Convention) disproportionate.[549] Thus, in the Court's view as expressed in this judgment at least, the rights and freedoms secured by the Convention, understood as 'other rules of international law' in the sense of Article 2 § 3 UNCLOS, can be seen to have a certain bearing on what constitutes 'innocent passage'. The door would seem to be open to other Convention-compliant interpretations of definitions contained in UNCLOS.

Article 33 of UNCLOS allows a coastal State, within an additional twelve-mile zone (the 'contiguous zone'), to

> exercise the control necessary to:
> (a) prevent infringement of its customs, fiscal, immigration or sanitary laws and regulations within its territory or territorial sea;
> (b) punish infringement of the above laws and regulations committed within its territory or territorial sea.

This too necessarily entails the applicability of any human rights treaties to which the coastal State is party.

Up to two hundred miles offshore, in the exclusive economic zone, the coastal state enjoys 'sovereign rights' to regulate and police the use and har-

---

547  Articles 2 § 1 and 8 UNCLOS.
548  Articles 2 and 3 UNCLOS.
549  *Women on Waves and Others v. Portugal*, no. 31276/05, 3 February 2009.

158                                                                                                          CHAPTER 5

vesting of living and non-living resources, the construction and use of marine installations and artificial islands, scientific research and environmental protection.[550] If the coastal state has a continental shelf extending further than that, it enjoys sovereign rights up to 350 miles from its coast for the purpose of exploring and exploiting its resources.[551] Again, the exercise of sovereignty – which involves legislating and policing, and potentially the exercise of jurisdictional powers – necessarily entails the applicability of human rights law.

A special regime applies to straits that are used for international navigation between one part of the high seas or an exclusive economic zone and another part of the high seas or an exclusive economic zone. The basic status of the waters of such a strait is that of the normal category to which they otherwise belong – territorial sea, contiguous zone, etc., as the case may be – but the rights of transit are not identical. For present purposes, it is noted that States bordering such straits may designate sea lanes and prescribe traffic separation schemes and otherwise legislate in order to protect safety and the marine environment, to regulate fishing and to enforce customs tax, immigration and sanitary laws.[552]

Within archipelagic States, another special regime applies, that of 'archipelagic waters'. Within the baselines drawn around the group (or groups) of islands, the State has sovereignty extending to the air space over the archipelagic waters, as well as to their bed and subsoil, and the resources contained therein,[553] albeit that pre-existing submarine cables and fishing rights are to be respected, ships are allowed passage under a regime similar to that applicable to the territorial sea and straits used for international navigation, and special lanes may be created obligatory for both ships and aircraft to use.[554]

It is submitted that the Convention applies to the extent that Convention rights are affected by such exercise of sovereign rights, subject as appropriate to territorial declarations under Article 56 applicable to the relevant coastal land territory.[555] This indeed corresponds to the way the Court has applied the concept of Convention jurisdiction to sea areas delineated in accordance with the United Nations Convention on the Law of the Sea.

In *Drieman and Others* v. *Norway*, a group of Greenpeace protesters complained under Articles 10 and 11 of the Convention about being prosecuted and

---

550    Articles 56 and 57 UNCLOS.
551    Articles 76 and 77 UNCLOS.
552    Articles 41-43 UNCLOS.
553    Article 49 §§ 1 and 2 UNCLOS.
554    Articles 50 -53 UNCLOS.
555    Compare *Quark Fishing Ltd, supra* note 533.

JURISDICTION OF THE CONTRACTING STATES

fined for trying to impede whaling in the Norwegian exclusive economic zone. The Court noted, forthrightly, that

> the applicants' convictions and sentence to pay fines and the confiscation of the first applicant's dinghy were all measures which the respondent State had taken in the exercise of its jurisdiction in the sense of Article 1 of the Convention, and thus were capable of engaging its responsibility under the Convention.[556]

In later cases the exercise of coastal state jurisdiction in the exclusive economic zone was simply taken for granted. Thus it was in *Mangouras v. Spain*, which concerned the modalities of detention on remand of the captain of an oil tanker registered in the Bahamas whose cargo of fuel oil had spilled into the sea and caused an ecological disaster.[557]

*Plechkov v. Romania* was the case of a Bulgarian fisherman prosecuted and sentenced for illegal shark-fishing using long lines twenty-nine nautical miles off the Romanian coast. A legislative decree declaring the Romanian exclusive economic zone in the Black Sea, dating back to 1986, had been repealed shortly before the fisherman's arrest but not replaced by a new one; there being uncertainty as to the delineation of the zone, particularly in the absence of any pertinent agreement between Bulgaria and Romania, there was thus a violation of Article 7 of the Convention.[558] The violation can be said to have resulted from a failure effectively to exercise legislative jurisdiction in pursuance of UNCLOS.

Conversely, in *Quark Fishing v. the United Kingdom* the refusal to extend a licence permitting long-lining for Patagonian toothfish in the exclusive economic zone surrounding South Georgia and the South Sandwich Islands could not be challenged under Article 1 of Protocol No. 1 because, as we have seen, the United Kingdom, being the Contracting State responsible for the international relations of South Georgia and the South Sandwich Islands, had extended the applicability of the Convention itself to that territory but not that of Protocol No. 1.[559]

It is observed that Denmark, Norway and the Russian Federation claim exclusive economic zones and rights to the adjoining continental shelf in the Arctic. At least two of them – the Russian Federation and Denmark – lay com-

---

556  *Drieman and Others v. Norway* (dec.), no. 33678/96, 4 May 2000.

557  *Mangouras v. Spain*, no. 12050/04, 8 January 2009.

558  *Plechkov v. Romania*, no. 1660/03, §§ 71-74, 16 September 2014.

559  *Quark Fishing Ltd, supra* note 533.

peting claims to the continental shelf as far north as the geographical North Pole; these are currently under discussion in the United Nations Commission on the Limits of the Continental Shelf. It was announced in May 2016 that Canada intended to submit claims of its own in 2018.[560]

### 5.3.2 Territorial Airspace

Article 1 of the Chicago Convention on International Civil Aviation provides that every state party to it has 'complete and exclusive sovereignty over the airspace above its territory', 'territory' being defined by its Article 2 as 'the land areas and territorial waters adjacent thereto under the sovereignty, suzerainty, protection or mandate' of the state concerned. The State whose territory is overflown has the right to require aircraft to land in particular places, follow particular routes and comply with regulations governing the loading and unloading of cargo and passengers.[561]

Again, this necessarily brings Article 1 of the Convention into play. However, case-law addressing issues in this respect is rare indeed. In one case only, *P.N. v. Switzerland*, was jurisdiction over airspace in dispute: the applicant, who resided in the canton of Solothurn south of Basel, complained of noise pollution caused by aircraft taking off and landing at Basel-Mulhouse Airport. Switzerland had however delegated control of the airspace over that part of her territory to France. In declaring the application inadmissible, the Commission

---

560 The Danish and Russian claims remain on the agenda of the United Nations Commission on the Limits of the Continental Shelf (CLCS); see UN Doc. CLCS/102, 6 February 2018, Agenda for the forty-sixth session (New York, 29 January-6 March 2018), and Progress of work in the Commission on the Limits of the Continental Shelf - Statement by the Chair - Forty-sixth session, UN Doc. CLCS/103 (8 April 2018) and UN Doc. CLCS/103/Corr.1 (9 May 2018). For the Danish claim, see Partial Submission of the Government of the Kingdom of Denmark together with the Government of Greenland to the Commission on the Limits of the Continental Shelf, The Northern Continental Shelf of Greenland (executive summary, 15 December 2014), https://www.un.org/Depts/los/clcs_new/submissions_files/dnk76_14/dnk2014_es.pdf; for the Russian claim, see the Partial revised submission of the Russian Federation to the Commission on the Limits of the Continental Shelf in respect of the continental shelf of the Russian Federation in the Arctic Ocean (executive summary, 3 August 2015), https://www.un.org/depts/los/clcs_new/submissions_files/rus01_rev15/2015_08_03_Exec_Summary_English.pdf. With respect to the claim intended to be submitted by Canada, see Radio Canada International, 3 May 2016, http://www.rcinet.ca/en/2016/05/03/canada-to-submit-its-arctic-continental-shelf-claim-in-2018/, accessed on 3 September 2016. For a map depicting the present claims, see https://www.dur.ac.uk/resources/ibru/resources/Arcticmap04-08-15.pdf (IBRU Centre for Borders Research, Durham University, accessed on 3 September 2016).
561 Convention on International Civil Aviation (Chicago, 7 December 1944; Ninth Edition, 2006), Articles 3 bis and 5.

JURISDICTION OF THE CONTRACTING STATES

based its decision directly on the inapplicability of Article 6 of the Convention, thus sidestepping the issue of jurisdiction.[562]

### 5.3.3    *Outer Space*

In the discussions on jurisdiction under the European Convention on Human Rights the Treaty on Principles Governing the Activities of States in the Exploration and Use of Outer Space, including the Moon and Other Celestial Bodies, usually called the 'Outer Space Treaty',[563] is even more marginal than the conventions applicable to the sea and the sky. Assimilated territorial jurisdiction is expressly excluded: it is provided that '[o]uter space, including the Moon and other celestial bodies, is not subject to national appropriation by claim of sovereignty, by means of use or occupation, or by any other means'.[564] A further treaty, the Agreement Governing the Activities of States on the Moon and Other Celestial Bodies, sometimes called the 'Moon Treaty', extends this principle to 'other celestial bodies within the solar system'.[565]

Since, consequently, there can be no quasi-territorial exercise of sovereignty in outer space or on the heavenly bodies, Article 1 jurisdiction also of necessity follows the exercise of sovereignty over individual man-made objects.

States Parties to the Outer Space Treaty bear 'international responsibility' for 'national activities in outer space', including on the Moon, whether such activities are carried out by governmental or non-governmental entities. The activities of non-governmental entities shall require 'authorization and supervision by the appropriate State Party'.

A number of States, including States Party to the Convention, have adopted legislation to regulate the activities of their citizens in outer space and the registration of spacecraft.[566]

We will go into the detail of this below.

---

562   *P.N. v. Switzerland*, no. 26245/95, Commission decision of 11 September 1997.

563   London, Moscow and Washington, 27 January 1967.

564   Outer Space Treaty, Article II; see also Article 11 § 2 of the Agreement Governing the Activities of States on the Moon and Other Celestial Bodies (for the moon in particular). See also Michael N. Schmitt, "International Law and Military Operations in Space", in *Max Planck Yearbook of United Nations Law*, Volume 10, 2006 (A. von Bogdandy and R. Wolfrum, eds.), pp. 89-125 at p. 101.

565   *loc. cit.*, Article 1 § 1.

566   The Parties to the Convention referred to are Austria, Belgium, France, Germany, the Netherlands, Norway, the Russian Federation, Spain, Sweden, Ukraine and the United Kingdom. For a collection of legal texts, see the web site of the United Nations Office for Outer Space Affairs, http://www.unoosa.org/oosa/en/ourwork/spacelaw/nationalspacelaw/index.html.

162 CHAPTER 5

## 5.4 Ships, Aircraft and Spacecraft

In *Assanidze*, the Court stated that in certain 'exceptional cases', a State's jurisdiction is assumed on the basis of 'non-territorial factors'; examples given include 'acts performed on board vessels flying the State flag or on aircraft or spacecraft registered there'.[567]

It is submitted that the jurisdiction of a State over ships flying its flag or an aircraft or spacecraft which it has registered, being exclusive and linked to nationality, is actually exercised *within* that State's domestic limits; it is 'extraterritorial' only in the sense that it is not exercised on that State's land territory. A ship, an aircraft or a spacecraft is not *territorium nullius*; nor, for the flag state or state of registration, is it foreign territory. It follows that the expression 'exceptional cases' is not really appropriate in this context; and in fact, this supposed exception is no longer mentioned in more recent case-law statements.[568]

### 5.4.1 *Ships*

#### 5.4.1.1 Flag State Jurisdiction

Article 91 § 1 UNCLOS provides that ships shall have the nationality of the State whose flag they are entitled to fly; and Article 92 § 1 of that Convention places ships on the high seas under the exclusive jurisdiction of their flag state. Article 94 § 1 requires the flag state effectively to exercise its 'jurisdiction and control in administrative, technical and social matters over ships flying its flag'. The regulation required – which includes registration, the technical state and seaworthiness of ships, the qualifications of the master, officers and crew – is detailed in paragraphs 2 through 7 of that Article. The flag State is also expected to impose on the masters of ships flying its flag a duty to render assistance to persons in distress (Article 98).

There has long been a plethora of international agreements and other legal instruments setting out requirements binding on the flag state to implement these undertakings. For example, the first International Convention for the Safety of Life at Sea (SOLAS), negotiated in the wake of the Titanic disaster of 1912, was adopted in 1914 (although it never entered into force owing to the outbreak of World War I). The current SOLAS Convention was adopted in 1974.[569]

---

567 *Assanidze*, § 137.

568 For example, *Chagos Islanders*, § 70.

569 International Maritime Organization web site, http://www.imo.org/en/KnowledgeCentre/ReferencesAndArchives/HistoryofSOLAS/Pages/default.aspx, retrieved on 10 October 2015.

JURISDICTION OF THE CONTRACTING STATES

Under its Article I, all 'Contracting Governments' undertake to 'promulgate all laws, decrees, orders and regulations and to take all other steps which may be necessary' to give that treaty 'full and complete effect'.[570] Other treaties govern standards of training, certification and watchkeeping for ships' officers and crews[571] and such matters as compulsory insurance of ships against civil liability for oil pollution damage;[572] it goes without saying that these require States parties to legislate and enforce their laws.

In a recent advisory opinion[573] the International Tribunal for the Law of the Sea held that the list of 'administrative, technical and social matters' set out in Article 94 UNCLOS was indicative, not exhaustive.[574] In particular,

> 119. It follows from the provisions of article 94 of the Convention that as far as fishing activities are concerned, the flag State, in fulfilment of its responsibility to exercise effective jurisdiction and control in administrative matters, must adopt the necessary administrative measures to ensure that fishing vessels flying its flag are not involved in activities which will undermine the flag State's responsibilities under the Convention in respect of the conservation and management of marine living resources.
> ...
> 120. ... [T]he flag State is under an obligation to ensure compliance by vessels flying its flag with the relevant conservation measures concerning living resources enacted by the coastal State for its exclusive economic zone because, as concluded by the Tribunal, they constitute an integral element in the protection and preservation of the marine environment.[575]

Elsewhere it is stated that flag States must

---

570    SOLAS, Article I (b).

571    International Maritime Organisation web site, International Convention on Standards of Training, Certification and Watchkeeping for Seafarers (STCW), http://www.imo.org/ en/About/Conventions/ListOfConventions/Pages/International-Convention-on-Standards-of-Training,-Certification-and-Watchkeeping-for-Seafarers-%28STCW%29.aspx, retrieved on 10 October 2015.

572    International Convention on Civil Liability for Oil Pollution Damage (CLC), International Maritime Organisation web site, http://www.imo.org/en/About/Conventions/ListOfConventions/Pages/International-Convention-on-Civil-Liability-for-Oil-Pollution-Damage-%28CLC%29.aspx, retrieved on 10 October 2015.

573    International Tribunal for the Law of the Sea, *Request for an advisory opinion submitted by the Sub-Regional Fisheries Commission (SRFC) (Case No. 21)*, Advisory Opinion, 2 April 2015.

574    *loc. cit.*, § 117.

575    *loc. cit.*, § 119.

164                                                                CHAPTER 5

.... ensure that their nationals engaged in fishing activities within the exclusive economic zone of a coastal State comply with the conservation measures and with the other terms and conditions established in its laws and regulations.[576]

The criminal jurisdiction of the coastal State – if it is not the same as the flag State – may only be exercised within the territorial sea and within strict limits, which for present purposes may be summarised as those cases in which there is a link between the crime committed on board and the coastal state; in which the flag state or the master of the vessel requests the coastal State to exercise criminal jurisdiction; and for the purpose of suppressing the trade in illegal drugs.[577] The exercise of civil jurisdiction on board ship is likewise reserved to the flag State, absent 'obligations or liabilities assumed or incurred by the ship itself in the course or for the purpose of its voyage through the waters of the coastal State' or in order to execute a civil judgment or court order against the ship herself.[578]

The primacy of flag State jurisdiction over coastal State jurisdiction is therefore established.

The admissibility decision in *Xhavara and Others v. Italy and Albania* has been cited in doctrine as an example of Italy's exercise of extraterritorial jurisdiction on the high seas.[579] It is submitted that that is not the case in any relevant respect. The case concerns a collision that took place in March 1997, thirty-five miles offshore (i.e. outside the Italian territorial sea and contiguous zone), between a corvette of the Italian navy and a ship flying the Albanian flag carrying Albanian nationals seeking to enter Italy illegally. The Albanian ship sank; fifty-eight people lost their lives. Italy prosecuted the captain of its corvette for manslaughter. The applicants, survivors of the accident and relatives of some who died, joined the proceedings as civil parties.

The Court found that the collision had been 'directly caused' by the Italian naval vessel. Before the Court the applicants invoked, among other Articles of the Convention, Articles 2 and 3. Since domestic proceedings were, at the time,

---

576    *loc. cit.*, § 123.

577    Article 27 UNCLOS.

578    Article 28 UNCLOS.

579    See, for example, Michael Duttwiler, "Authority, Control and Jurisdiction in the Extraterritorial Application of the European Convention on Human Rights, *Netherlands Quarterly of Human Rights*, Vol. 30/2, 137-162, 2012, at pp. 147 and 157.

JURISDICTION OF THE CONTRACTING STATES

still pending in Italy, the Court declared the application inadmissible on the ground that it was premature.[580]

Admittedly the decision does mention Article 1 of the Convention and the positive obligations of the State under Article 2. Even so, it is difficult to see how it establishes the Article 1 jurisdiction of Italy in the applicants' favour. Italy's right to board the Albanian vessel derived directly from a treaty between the two States concluded four days before the collision.[581] Moreover, Italy was, of course, entirely within its rights to prosecute the captain of one of its own naval vessels – indeed, no other state would have been allowed to do so.[582] However, the applicants' position is hardly the same as that of an Italian naval officer serving on an Italian warship: since the proceedings were pending at the time the application was lodged (and apparently the Italian courts – true to form – had not brought them to a conclusion even at first instance three years later when the decision was adopted), it would not have been unthinkable that the Italian courts might ultimately have declined jurisdiction to entertain the applicants' claims.

The case of *Hirsi Jamaa and Others v. Italy* concerned a group of Somalian and Eritrean refugees intercepted at sea by Italian Revenue Police and Coastguard vessels while attempting to reach the island of Lampedusa. The refugees were transferred to Italian military vessels, from which they were set ashore at Tripoli without having been allowed to seek asylum in Italy.

Before the Court the Italian Government argued that the applicants had been taken on board Italian ships in a rescue operation and then landed in Libya, from which it followed that the applicants had not come within Italian jurisdiction.

The Court replied as follows:

> 77. The Court observes that, by virtue of the relevant provisions of the law of the sea, a vessel sailing on the high seas is subject to the exclusive jurisdiction of the State of the flag it is flying. This principle of international law has led the Court to recognise, in cases concerning acts carried

---

580   *Xhavara v. Italy and Albania* (dec.), no. 39473/98, 20 September 1997; see also *Banković*, § 81, and Michael O'Boyle, "The European Convention on Human Rights and Extraterritorial Jurisdiction: A Comment on Life After Banković", in *Extraterritorial Application of Human Rights Treaties*, Fons Coomans and Menno T. Kamminga, eds., Intersentia, 2004, pp. 125-139 at p. 134.

581   Compare and contrast Article 101 § 1 of the United Nations Convention on the Law of the Sea and Article 22 § 1 of the 1958 Convention on the High Seas. Note that, at the time, Albania was not a party to the former but both were parties to the latter.

582   Article 97 of UNCLOS and Article 11 of the 1958 Convention on the High Seas.

out on board vessels flying a State's flag, in the same way as registered aircraft, cases of extraterritorial exercise of the jurisdiction of that State (...). Where there is control over another, this is *de jure* control exercised by the State in question over the individuals concerned.

...

81. The Court observes that in the instant case the events took place entirely on board ships of the Italian armed forces, the crews of which were composed exclusively of Italian military personnel. In the Court's opinion, in the period between boarding the ships of the Italian armed forces and being handed over to the Libyan authorities, the applicants were under the continuous and exclusive *de jure* and *de facto* control of the Italian authorities. Speculation as to the nature and purpose of the intervention of the Italian ships on the high seas would not lead the Court to any other conclusion.[583]

5.4.1.2    Exercise of Jurisdiction over Foreign Ships with the Permission of the Flag State

In *Rigopoulos v. Spain* the applicant was the master of a vessel flying the Panamanian flag that was intercepted three thousand miles from the Canary Islands pursuant to an order of a Spanish investigating judge. Prior verbal authorisation had been obtained from the Panamanian embassy in Spain, in accordance with Article 17 §§ 3 and 4 of the United Nations Convention against Illicit Traffic in Narcotic Drugs and Psychotropic Substances.[584] The applicant complained, unsuccessfully, of having been kept in detention for sixteen days before being presented to a 'judge or officer authorized by law to exercise judicial power' (Article 5 § 3 of the Convention). No question of jurisdiction was raised.[585]

In contrast, in *Medvyedyev and Others v. France*[586] there was. A merchant ship registered in Cambodia was suspected of carrying large quantities of illegal drugs intended for delivery to Europe. In response to a request from the

---

583    *Hirsi Jamaa and Others v. Italy* [GC], no. 27765/09, §§ 77 and 81, ECHR 2012. See also Violeta Moreno-Lax, "Hirsi Jamaa and Others v. Italy *or the Strasbourg Court versus Extraterritorial Migration Control?*", Human Rights Law Review 12:3(2012), 574-598 at pp. 579-582, and Tullio Treves and Cesare Pitea, "Piracy, International Law and Human Rights", in *The Frontiers of Human Rights: Extraterritoriality and its Challenges, Collected Courses of the Academy of European Law*, vol. XXIV/1, pp. 89-126 at p. 105.

584    Vienna, 20 December 1988.

585    *Rigopoulos v. Spain*, no. 37388/97, Commission decision of 16 April 1998; *Rigopoulos v. Spain* (dec.), no. 37388/97, ECHR 1999-II.

586    *Medvedyev and Others v. France* [GC], no. 3394/03, ECHR 2010.

JURISDICTION OF THE CONTRACTING STATES

French government through the French embassy in Phnom Penh, the Cambodian Minister for Foreign Affairs and International Cooperation granted France permission by diplomatic note to 'intercept, inspect and take legal action against' the vessel.

A frigate of the French navy was given orders to intercept the ship. She put a boarding party on board, after first having had to fire warning shots and use force to overcome the resistance of the ship's crew. One crew member died as a result of an injury sustained in the process. The ship was towed to France by a tug and her crew were confined to their quarters.

The surviving crew members complained before the Court of, among other things, having been arbitrarily detained on board their ship (Article 5 § 1 of the Convention).

In considering whether the events complained of came within French 'jurisdiction', the Court found that, in the circumstances described, France had exercised 'full and exclusive control over the [ship] and its crew, at least *de facto*, from the time of its interception, in a continuous and uninterrupted manner until they were tried in France'.[587] In terms of Article 1 of the Convention, the position is the same as in *Hassan v. the United Kingdom*, since France 'retained authority and control over all aspects of the detention relevant to the [applicants'] complaints under Article 5' regardless of any lack of territorial or quasi-territorial sovereignty.[588]

The question then arose whether the detention of the crew had an adequate legal basis. Cambodia was not a party to either UNCLOS, which in its Article 108 makes provision for the flag State to request the assistance of other States to combat drug trafficking, or the United Nations Convention against Illicit Traffic in Narcotic Drugs and Psychotropic Substances.[589]

The majority of the Grand Chamber found that Article 5 § 1 had been violated. They found that since the diplomatic note permitted France only to 'intercept, inspect and take legal action against' the *ship*, there was no legal authority for action to be taken against the *crew* – which meant that a 'clearly defined' legal basis for the applicants' detention was lacking. Moreover, an agreement made for the nonce and confidentially by diplomatic note did not meet the 'foreseeability' requirement either.

Interestingly, the majority added the following *obiter dictum*:

---

587  *Medvedyev and Others*, § 67.
588  *Hassan*, §§ 78-80; compare also *al-Skeini*, § 136. See also Tullio Treves and Cesare Pitea, "Piracy, International Law and Human Rights", in *The Frontiers of Human Rights: Extraterritoriality and its Challenges, Collected Courses of the Academy of European Law*, vol. XXIV/1, pp. 89-126 at p. 105.
589  Vienna, 20 December 1988.

It is regrettable, in the Court's view, that the international effort to combat drug trafficking on the high seas is not better coordinated bearing in mind the increasingly global dimension of the problem. The fact remains that when a flag State, like Cambodia in this case, is not a party to the Montego Bay or Vienna Conventions, the insufficiency of such legal instruments, for want of regional or bilateral initiatives, is of no real consequence. In fact, such initiatives are not always supported by the States in spite of the fact that they afford the possibility of acting within a clearly defined legal framework. In any event, for States that are not parties to the Montego Bay and Vienna Conventions one solution might be to conclude bilateral or multilateral agreements, like the San José Agreement of 2003, with other States. Having regard to the gravity and enormity of the problem posed by illegal drug trafficking, developments in public international law which embraced the principle that all States have jurisdiction as an exception to the law of the flag State would be a significant step in the fight against illegal trade in narcotics. This would bring international law on drug trafficking into line with what has already existed for many years now in respect of piracy[590]

– thus apparently suggesting that if the crime being committed were one of piracy rather than drug trafficking, universal jurisdiction sufficient for purposes of the Convention would exist under Articles 100-107 UNCLOS applied as customary international law.[591]

A sizeable minority of the Court took a very different view. They considered it 'illogical' to construe the diplomatic note so narrowly that jurisdiction over the crew was dissociated from jurisdiction over the ship. As to the requirement of 'foreseeability', the dissenters accepted that the diplomatic note was not foreseeable in the sense of being 'accessible' to the *applicants*. That said, an exchange of diplomatic notes was usually confidential and necessarily so; in any case, the resistance put up by the crew showed that they at least had enter-

---

590   *Medvedyev and Others*, § 110; see also § 85.

591   Tullio Treves, *Piracy, Law of the Sea, and Use of Force: Developments off the Coast of* Somalia, *EJIL* 2009), Vo. 20 No. 2, 399-414 at p. 401; Stefano Piedimonte Bodini, *Fighting Maritime Piracy under the European Convention on Human Rights, EJIL* (2011), Vol. 22 No. 3, 829-848 at page 832. See also Article 105 of the United Nations Convention on the Law of the Sea; that Article is identical to its predecessor, Article 19 of the 1958 Convention on the High Seas. For a historical view of the development of universal jurisdiction, see Mathilda Twomey, *Muddying the waters of maritime piracy or developing the customary law of piracy? Somali piracy and Seychelles,* (2014) 20 CLJP/JDCP pp. 137 *et seq.* at pp. 139-144.

tained no doubts about the nature of their traffic and had foreseen their own probable fate with complete accuracy.[592]

### 5.4.2 *Aircraft*

Aircraft, like ships, have the nationality of the State in which they are registered.[593] Chapter 5 of the Chicago Convention on International Civil Aviation sets out detailed rules governing such matters as registration, equipment, documents to be carried on board, certification of airworthiness of aircraft and the licensing of aviators.

Some of the rules set out in, or under, the Chicago Convention apply only as long as the aircraft is in flight. The definition of 'flight time' used in Annexes 1 and 6 to the Chicago Convention (on personnel licensing and operation of aircraft, respectively) is 'the total time from the moment an aeroplane first moves for the purpose of taking off until the moment it finally comes to rest at the end of the flight'.[594]

Jurisdiction over crimes committed on board aircraft are the subject of several international treaties. Thus, according to the Tokyo Convention on Offences and Certain Other Acts Committed On Board Aircraft, the State of registration has jurisdiction over crimes committed on board an aircraft while it is 'in flight', even when overflying the territory of another State – 'in flight' being defined as 'from the moment when power is applied for the purpose of take-off until the moment when the landing run ends'.[595]

The Montreal Convention for the Suppression of Unlawful Acts Against the Safety of Civil Aviation is more complicated in that it differentiates between acts committed in or against an aircraft 'in flight' or 'in service'. In the words of that instrument:

> (a) an aircraft is considered to be in flight at any time from the moment when all its external doors are closed following embarkation until the moment when any such door is opened for disembarkation; in the case of a forced landing, the flight shall be deemed to continue until the competent authorities take over the responsibility for the aircraft and for persons and property on board;

---

[592] *Medvedyev and Others*, Joint partly dissenting opinion of Judges Costa, Casadevall, Bîrsan, Garlicki, Hajiyev, Šikuta and Nicolaou.

[593] Convention on International Civil Aviation, Article 17.

[594] For a discussion of these definitions, see generally Sami Shubber, *Jurisdiction over crimes on board aircraft*, Martinus Nijhoff, 1973.

[595] Convention on Offences and Certain other Acts Committed On Board Aircraft (Tokyo, 14 September 1963), Article 1 §§ 2 and 3 and Article 3.

170 CHAPTER 5

(b) an aircraft is considered to be in service from the beginning of the preflight preparation of the aircraft by ground personnel or by the crew for a specific flight until twenty-four hours after landing; the period of service shall, in any event, extend for the entire period during which the aircraft is in flight as defined in paragraph (a) of this Article.[596]

The Montreal Convention requires States to establish their criminal jurisdiction over the offences in issue:

(a) when the offence is committed in the territory of that State;
(b) when the offence is committed against or on board an aircraft registered in that State;
(c) when the aircraft on board which the offence is committed lands in its territory with the alleged offender still on board;
(d) when the offence is committed against or on board an aircraft leased without crew to a lessee who has his principal place of business or, if the lessee has no such place of business, his permanent residence, in that State.[597]

We have already seen that the Court has recognised Article 1 jurisdiction on board aircraft registered in a Contracting State.[598]

The Chicago Convention does not apply to 'State aircraft' – that is, aircraft used in military, customs and police services.[599] Aircraft that play a role in Strasbourg case-law are typically State aircraft. They normally enjoy immunity under customary international law.[600]

In *Öcalan v. Turkey* the applicant, a terrorist leader on the run who had sought refuge in Kenya, was taken onto an aircraft at Nairobi Airport by Kenyan officials and arrested by Turkish officials. The registration of the aircraft does not appear from the Court's judgment. At all events, the Court viewed the handover of the applicant into Turkish control as the fact defining Article 1

---

596 Convention for the Suppression of Unlawful Acts Against the Safety of Civil Aviation (Montreal, 23 September 1971), Article 2.
597 Montreal Convention, Article 5 § 1.
598 *Assanidze*, § 137; *Hirsi Jamaa and Others*, § 77.
599 Convention on International Civil Aviation, Article 3.
600 European Commission for Democracy through Law (Venice Commission), Opinion (no. 363/2005) on the international legal obligations of Council of Europe Member States in respect of secret detention facilities and inter-state transport of prisoners (CDL-AD(2006)009), § 95. For a discussion on the modalities governing the use of State aircraft in foreign airspace, see §§ 86-104.

JURISDICTION OF THE CONTRACTING STATES

jurisdiction, regardless of the nationality or location of the aircraft; for this reason, the exercise of jurisdiction by Turkey was considered 'extraterritorial'.[601] Later, in *Al-Skeini and Others*, the Court gave an interpretation of this finding defining the exercise of jurisdiction in terms of 'State agent authority and control'.[602]

The finding in *Öcalan* nevertheless owes much in the way of inspiration to the then recent Commission decision *Sanchez Ramirez v. France*. The applicant in that case, then a well-known Marxist-Leninist 'professional revolutionary' who had sought refuge in Sudan, was kidnapped, apparently by Sudanese officials – he alleges that he recognised some of them –, bundled onto an aircraft and flown to France where he was served with an arrest warrant. The registration of the aircraft, according to the applicant, was French. In the words of the Commission,

> If this was indeed the case, the applicant was effectively under the authority, and therefore the jurisdiction, of France, even if this authority was, in the circumstances, being exercised abroad (...)[603]

– words taken from an even earlier, again very similar decision, that of *Reinette v. France*, the applicant in that case having been apprehended and unceremoniously handed over on the Caribbean island of Saint Vincent.[604]

The same kind of language appears in *Freda v. Italy*, a case in which the applicant, an Italian criminal on the run, was arrested in Costa Rica and handed over to Italian officers to be flown out on an Italian military aircraft.[605] The aircraft made two stops in foreign countries – we do not know which countries – before reaching Italy. It was alleged that on both occasions the applicant asked to be allowed to leave the aircraft to request asylum and on both occasions he was met with a refusal. This implies that the applicant remained in Italian detention throughout the return journey, even while the aircraft was stationary on foreign territory. The Commission did not find it necessary to devote any discussion to this aspect of the case but nonetheless found that Mr Freda's detention had an adequate basis in Italian law for purposes of Article 5. We do not know whether Italy sought and obtained the permission of the countries

---

601    *Öcalan v. Turkey* [GC], no. 46221/99, § 91, ECHR 2005-IV.

602    *Al-Skeini*, § 136.

603    *Ramirez Sanchez v. France*, no. 28780/95, Commission decision of 24 June 1996, DR86-B p. 155 *et seq.*

604    *Reinette v. France*, no. 14009/88, Commission report of 2 October 1989, DR 63, p. 192 *et seq.*

605    *Freda v. Italy*, no. 8916/80, Commission decision of 7 October 1980, DR 21, p. 254 *et seq.*

172          CHAPTER 5

concerned before landing on their territory, as would normally be required;[606] the decision gives no information about this, and the question may not have been raised by the applicant. If such be not the case, then the Commission's finding, which implied that it was 'lawful' in terms of Article 5 § 1 for Italian agents to detain an individual on board an Italian aircraft even while it was parked on foreign soil, of necessity implies that the Article 1 jurisdiction of Italy, understood in a quasi-territorial sense, followed the registration of the aircraft.[607]

We do not know the registration of the aircraft that conveniently suffered a malfunction in flight from Strasbourg to Luxembourg, forcing it to land at Saarbrücken where the German police were waiting to arrest its passenger Stocké.[608] Presumably however it was a civilian aircraft, which German police officers could in any case board without seeking the permission of any foreign government; only if that be so could the Court *not* find that the circumstances of Mr Stocké's arrest involved 'unlawful activities abroad'.[609]

### 5.4.3   *Spacecraft*

We have seen that in *Assanidze* the Court, in an *obiter dictum*, recognised that '[i]n certain exceptional cases', jurisdiction was assumed on the basis of 'non-territorial factors' including acts performed on board 'spacecraft registered [in the State concerned]'. This is to date the only judgment or decision on record in which the Court has recognised Article 1 jurisdiction in respect of spacecraft.

A State Party 'on whose registry an object launched into outer space is carried' retains 'jurisdiction and control thereof, and over any personnel thereof, while in outer space or on a celestial body'.[610] For present purposes, by far the most numerous category of such objects is made up of unmanned satellites.

Satellites are owned and operated for a variety of uses by European State and non-State actors. Among the better-known of these are INMARSAT, based in the United Kingdom (international telecommunications, especially for marine and aircraft use), and GLONASS (Russian, marine navigation), in addition

---

606    On this subject, see European Commission for Democracy through Law (Venice Commission), Opinion (no. 363/2005) on the international legal obligations of Council of Europe Member States in respect of secret detention facilities and inter-state transport of prisoners (CDL-AD(2006)009), § 18.

607    *Freda v. Italy, loc. cit.*

608    *Stocké* v. Germany, no. 11755/85, Series A no. 199.

609    *loc. cit.*, § 54.

610    Article VIII of the Outer Space Treaty; see also Article II of the Convention on Registration of Objects Launched into Outer Space.

JURISDICTION OF THE CONTRACTING STATES

to a large number of commercial television broadcasters who are household names.

Currently the only manned space station is the International Space Station, which is the fruit of co-operation by Canada, Japan, the Russian Federation, the USA and the Member States of the European Space Agency. Alone among the parties to the European Convention on Human Rights (alone in the world, in fact, since the American space shuttle programme was closed down), Russia operates manned delivery devices.

It would be logical to imagine that in principle both unmanned and manned spacecraft (or other extra-terrestrial human habitations), the latter including their occupants, should, by analogy to more conventional maritime or airborne conveyances and their passengers and crew, be considered for purposes of Article 1 of the Convention to be within the jurisdiction of the State which owns, or whose nationals own, the spacecraft or other extra-terrestrial installation should the question ever arise. In fact, the rights and duties of States would appear to go further: Article VI of the Outer Space Treaty provides that

> States Parties to the Treaty *shall bear international responsibility for national activities in outer space, including the moon and other celestial bodies, whether such activities are carried on by governmental agencies or by non-governmental entities*, and for assuring that national activities are carried out in conformity with the provisions set forth in the present Treaty. The activities of non-governmental entities in outer space, including the moon and other celestial bodies, shall require authorization and continuing supervision by the appropriate State Party to the Treaty. When activities are carried on in outer space, including the moon and other celestial bodies, by an international organization, responsibility for compliance with this Treaty shall be borne both by the international organization and by the States Parties to the Treaty participating in such organization.[611]

It has been pointed out that this creates a form of State responsibility unique to space law in that it makes States directly internationally responsible for the acts and omissions of private parties.[612]

The legal framework governing the International Space Station is constituted by an Intergovernmental Agreement to which Canada, Japan, Russia, the USA and ten European Space Agency member States are parties (or 'partners'),

---

611    Emphasis added.
612    Schmitt (2006), p. 106.

the participating European States delegating their role to the European Space Agency (ESA) as 'the European Partner'.[613] Since each of the partners provides parts of the International Space Station (which it registers as its own), each retains 'jurisdiction and control' over the parts it provides and registers as well as 'over personnel who are its nationals'.[614] This solution should be understood in the light of Article VI of the Outer Space Treaty *in fine*. It remains to be seen how it will work for European nationals in terms of Article 1 of the Convention if the occasion should ever arise, the European Space Agency itself and some of its component 'partners' (Canada, Japan, the USA) not being Contracting Parties and the European Space Agency itself enjoying immunity from suit.[615]

The Galileo project, a European–based global navigation satellite system set up in parallel with the American Navstar GPS system and GLONASS, is funded by the European Union and operated by ESA.[616] The older European Geostationary Navigation Overlay Service (EGNOS) system, which complements GPS, is owned by the European Union.[617] Article 1 jurisdiction in relation to these is likely to arise no sooner than when the European Union overcomes its hesitation to accede to the Convention.[618]

---

613     *Agreement among the Government of Canada, Governments of Member States of the European Space Agency, the Government of Japan, the Government of the Russian Federation, and the Government of the United States of America concerning cooperation on the Civil International Space Station* ("the Intergovernmental Agreement", Washington, 29 January 1998). See also Article VI of the Outer Space Treaty *in fine*.

614     Article 5 of the Intergovernmental Agreement; see also André Farand, *Astronauts' behaviour onboard the International Space Station: regulatory framework*, in legal and ethical framework for astronauts in space sojourns, proceedings of a symposium co-hosted by the European Center for Space Law (ECSL), the Legal department of the European Space Agency (ESA), L'institut du droit de l'espace et des télécommunications de l'Université de Paris XI (IDEST) and United Nations Educational, Scientific and Cultural Organization (UNESCO), (Paris, 29 October 2004), pp. 70-78.

615     *Waite and Kennedy v. Germany* [GC], no. 26083/94, § 57, ECHR 1999-I. See also 8.4.5.1 below.

616     European Space Agency, *Galileo Full Operational Capability Procurement factsheet*, http://download.esa.int/docs/Galileo_IOV_Launch/FOC_factsheet_20111003.pdf, accessed on 5 October 2015.

617     European Space Agency, *EGNOS brochure*, http://www.egnos-pro.esa.int/Publications/ESA_EGNOS_br284_2009.pdf, accessed on 5 October 2015.

618     Article 59 § 2 of the Convention (a provision inserted by Protocol No. 14); but see Opinion 2/13 of the Court of Justice of the European Union on accession to the Convention (18 December 2014).

# JURISDICTION OF THE CONTRACTING STATES

## 5.5 Extraterritorial Jurisdiction

Even in normal circumstances, the State may find itself exercising jurisdiction in respect of matters occurring outside its territorial or quasi-territorial sovereignty. Let us therefore now determine when the exercise of jurisdiction can properly be said to be extraterritorial.

### 5.5.1 *Legal Acts of Domestic Authorities in Another Country, Such as Diplomatic or Consular Activity*

A State may impose on aliens wishing to take up residence on their territory the requirement that they normally apply for permission to do so from their own home country. The decision to grant or refuse permission will be submitted to the diplomatic or consular representatives of the State concerned and decided by the Government in accordance with its own domestic legislation, generally – as in the case of the Netherlands – on its own territory.[619] This does not alter the fact that the victim is – and if permission is refused, remains – resident abroad, which means that to that extent the effects of any resulting violation are extraterritorial. Issues under the Convention, when they occur in this situation, tend to concern the application of Article 8 of the Convention (right to respect for family life). The Court has so far declined to answer the question whether they involve the extraterritorial exercise of Article 1 jurisdiction by the Convention State concerned.[620]

The Commission has held that 'authorised agents of a State, including diplomatic or consular agents bring other persons or property within the jurisdiction of that State to the extent that they exercise authority over such persons or property'.[621] An example of extraterritorial jurisdiction in relation to the acts of diplomatic or consular officials from the Court's case-law is *El Morsli v. France*,[622] the applicant being a woman of Muslim faith who objected to a requirement by the French consular authorities to remove her veil for identity check before being allowed to enter the French consulate general in Marrakech. The assumption that France had Article 1 jurisdiction was implicit: the Court considered, without addressing that or any other preliminary issue, that the application was manifestly ill-founded.

---

619 For example, *Ahmut v. the Netherlands*, no. 21702/93, Reports 1996-VI; and *Tuquabo-Tekle and Others v. the Netherlands*, no. 60665/00, 1 December 2005.

620 *I.A.A. and Others v. the United Kingdom* (dec.), no. 25960/13, § 26, 8 March 2016.

621 See, for example, *X v. the United Kingdom*, no. 7547/76, Commission decision of 15 December 1977, Decisions and Reports (DR) 12, p. 73; for a summary of the Court's case-law on the matter, see, among other authorities, *Assanidze*, § 137.

622 *El Morsli v. France* (dec.), no. 15585/06, 4 March 2008.

176                                                                                          CHAPTER 5

Conversely, while the execution in foreign territory of an agreement with the receiving State can engage the responsibility of the sending Convention State, a unilateral legal act by the receiving State affecting the execution of such an agreement cannot be imputed to the Convention State. An example is *Gentilhomme, Schaff-Benhadji and Zerouki v. France*, which concerned the withdrawal by Algeria from an agreement under which children with dual Algerian and French nationality could be educated in French schools on Algerian territory.[623]

### 5.5.2 *The Exercise of Jurisdiction by a State over its Own Troops Abroad*

#### 5.5.2.1 In General

It is standard practice for States to exercise their jurisdiction over members of their own armed forces when these are engaged in operation abroad.

In *Serves v. France*[624] the applicant was a French officer commanding a company of paratroops in the Central African Republic in the late 1980s. It was brought to his notice that one of his platoon commanders had been responsible for the murder of a native. Captain Serves failed to report the incident to his superiors and ordered his men to say nothing about it to anyone. Ultimately he was sent back to metropolitan France where he was prosecuted for aiding and abetting murder.

Captain Serves's complaint to the Court, which was under Article 6 of the Convention, concerned the alleged violation of his right not to incriminate himself. In the event, no violation was found.

The case concerns the exercise by a State of its criminal jurisdiction over one of its own servicemen in connection with acts suspected to have been committed abroad. It is worth mentioning here for that reason only, even though the question of Article 1 jurisdiction did not need to be addressed by the Court. On a substantive level, it is little different in its essentials from many other cases decided by the Court under the criminal head of Article 6.

#### 5.5.2.2 Under the NATO Status of Forces Agreement

States may exercise their jurisdiction over members of their own armed forces stationed abroad and over any civilian component of their forces including family members of their service personnel. This can include the exercise of criminal jurisdiction by a court martial in the foreign country. Typically there will be an arrangement in place between the States concerned. The legal in-

---

623   *Gentilhomme, Schaff-Benhadji and Zerouki v. France*, no. 48205/99 48207/99 48209/99, § 20, 14 May 2002.

624   *Serves v. France*, 20 October 1997, *Reports of Judgments and Decisions* 1997VI.

JURISDICTION OF THE CONTRACTING STATES                                    177

strument most relevant to European States, the NATO Status of Forces Agreement, provides for the sending State to have primary jurisdiction in situations where jurisdiction is concurrent.[625]

Examples in the Court's case-law include *Coyne v. the United Kingdom*, *Mills v. the United Kingdom and Germany* and *Martin v. the United Kingdom*, the issue being the independence and impartiality of a British court martial called upon to try a British serviceman stationed in Germany (or, in the case of *Martin*, a dependent family member).[626]

The Convention applies in such a situation by virtue of binding the sending State.

### 5.5.3 Ad Hoc *Domestic Tribunal Set Up Abroad with the Permission of the Receiving State*

To date, there has been only one *ad hoc* domestic tribunal created on foreign territory with the permission of the receiving State by any State Party to the Convention, namely the Scottish Court organised in the Netherlands to try the Lockerbie bombing suspects under Scots law and procedure.[627] It was set up at a disused air base near Zeist and existed from 1999 until 2002.

Again, there is no doubt that the Convention applied by virtue of binding the United Kingdom.

### 5.5.4 *Cases in Which the Presence of Foreign Judges is Not Exercise of Extraterritorial Jurisdiction by Another State*

Not all cases involving foreign judges are cases in which a foreign State exercises extraterritorial jurisdiction.

Fomerly, French and Spanish judges sat as members of Andorran courts. In *Drozd and Janousek v. France and Spain*, the question arose whether their acts came within the jurisdiction of France and Spain, respectively: sovereignty over the principality was – and still is – shared by the Co-Princes, the president of the French Republic and the bishop of Urgell in Spain, and Andorra was at the time not yet a party to the Convention in its own right. The Court found that they did not; French or Spanish the nationality of the judges might be but

---

625  *Galić v. the Netherlands* (dec.), § 44; *Djokaba Lambi Longa* (dec.), § 70; NATO Status of Forces Agreement 1951, Article VII.

626  *Coyne v. the United Kingdom*, no. 25942/94, Reports 1997-V; *Mills v. the United Kingdom*, no.35685/97, 5 June 2001; *Martin v. the United Kingdom*, no. 40426/98, 24 October 2006.

627  Mentioned in *Galić*, § 45; *Djokaba Lambi Longa*, § 70. See the Agreement between the Government of the United Kingdom of Great Britain and Northern Ireland and the Government of the Kingdom of the Netherlands concerning a Scottish trial in the Netherlands (with annexes), The Hague, 18 September 1998, UNTS 35699 (vol. 2117).

178                                                                                                                    CHAPTER 5

they sat as Andorran judges applying Andorran law, not as judges of France and Spain. Similarly, as the Court pointed out, Austrian and Swiss jurists sat as judges in Liechtenstein.[628]

The Constitutional Court of Bosnia and Herzegovina is constituted of nine judges, six of them nationals of Bosnia and Herzegovina appointed by the Entities and three appointed by the President of the European Court of Human Rights after consultation with the Presidency of Bosnia and Herzegovina. The three judges appointed by the President of the Court are not allowed to be nationals of Bosnia and Herzegovina or any neighbouring State.[629] An interesting feature of this court is that it is part of an armistice arrangement: the Constitution under which it was set up is an annex to the Dayton Peace Agreement – the agreement that ended the 1992-95 war, that still holds Bosnia and Herzegovina together more than twenty years later and that none dare touch, let alone replace, lest the country unravel. We will discuss the Dayton system in greater detail below.

Kosovo makes extensive use of foreign judges, prosecutors and registry staff in its Specialist Chambers, which are set up to try crimes against humanity and war crimes committed on the territory of Kosovo between 1 January 1998 and 31 December 2000 – most notably trafficking in human organs taken by members of the UÇK (*Ushtria Çlirimtare e Kosovës*, Kosovo Liberation Army (also KLA)) from prisoners during the Kosovo War.[630] The Specialist Chambers are based in The Hague rather than in Kosovo itself to ensure the safety of witnesses. They are attached to every level of the Kosovo judiciary. Although it is provided only that the three members of the Specialist Chamber of the Constitutional Court shall be international judges,[631] in practice not one of the judges of the Specialist Chambers has Kosovo citizenship; neither do the Specialist Prosecutor and the Registrar.[632]

---

628    *Drozd and Janousek v. France and* Spain, no. 12747/87, §§ 91 and 96, Series A no. 240.

629    Article 6 (1)(a)-(b) of the Constitution of Bosnia and Herzegovina (Annex 4 to the General Framework Agreement for Peace in Bosnia and Herzegovina ("the Dayton Peace Agreement").

630    Council of Europe Parliamentary Assembly Report on "Inhuman treatment of people and illicit trafficking in human organs in Kosovo", Doc. 12462, 07 January 2011.

631    Article 162 § 3 of the Constitution of Kosovo (Constitutional Amendment No. 24).

632    See generally the Kosovo Law No. 05/L-53 on the Specialist Chambers and Specialist Prosecutor's Office. For the Roster of International Judges, the Specialist Prosecutor and the Registrar, see also the web site of the Specialist Chambers, https://www.scp-ks.org/en (accessed on 22 April 2017).

## 5.6 Cases in Which Acts Producing Effects Abroad are Not Exercise of Extraterritorial Jurisdiction

### 5.6.1 *Expulsion and Extradition*

As the Court has held many a time, Contracting States have the right, as a matter of well-established international law and subject to their treaty obligations including the Convention, to control the entry, residence and expulsion of aliens.[633] The decision of a competent domestic authority to refuse access to an alien, or to deport an alien, undoubtedly constitutes an exercise of domestic sovereignty. Nevertheless, such a decision, if carried out, can produce effects abroad: for our purposes, this will be the case when persons are extradited to a foreign country where they are exposed to a situation or treatment proscribed by the Convention.

In *Soering v. the United Kingdom* the Court recognised that the Convention did not govern the actions of States not Parties to it, nor did it purport to be a means of requiring the Contracting States to impose Convention standards on other States. Article 1 could not be read as justifying a general principle to the effect that, notwithstanding its extradition obligations, a Contracting State might not surrender an individual unless satisfied that the conditions awaiting him in the country of destination were in full accord with each of the safeguards of the Convention.[634] Even so,

> ... the decision by a Contracting State to extradite a fugitive may give rise to an issue under Article 3, and hence engage the responsibility of that State under the Convention, where substantial grounds have been shown for believing that the person concerned, if extradited, faces a real risk of being subjected to torture or to inhuman or degrading treatment or punishment in the requesting country. The establishment of such responsibility inevitably involves an assessment of conditions in the requesting country against the standards of Article 3 of the Convention. *Nonetheless, there is no question of adjudicating on or establishing the responsibility of the receiving country, whether under general international law, under the Convention or otherwise. In so far as any liability under the Convention is or may be incurred, it is liability incurred by the extraditing Contracting State by reason of its having taken action which has as a direct consequence the exposure of an individual to proscribed ill-treatment.*[635]

---

633    Among other examples too numerous to cite, see *Chahal*, § 73.
634    *Soering*, § 86.
635    *Soering*, § 91. Emphasis added. See also Lawson (1999) pp. 241-48.

180                                                                    CHAPTER 5

Since then, many an applicant has taken a case to the Court alleging that his
or her extradition or deportation to another country would entail violation
of Article 2, Article 3 or Protocols 6 or 13. Cases of this type considered by the
Court now number in their thousands.

Examples relevant to the subject of this study include *Chahal v. the United
Kingdom*,[636] *Saadi v. Italy*,[637] *Othman (Abu Qatada) v. the United Kingdom* and
*Trabelsi v. Belgium*,[638] all of which concern the intended (*Chahal*) or actual
(*Saadi* and *Trabelsi*) extradition or deportation of terrorist suspects.

Applicants fearing criminal prosecution have also sought to prevent their
deportation or extradition on the ground that they would suffer a 'flagrant denial of justice' in the receiving country. Although the possibility that deportation or extradition in such circumstances might violate Article 6 of the Convention has been recognised in the Court's case-law since *Soering*, the test is
a stringent one. To date, the Court has on three occasions found violations on
this ground; the applicant Othman (Abu Qatada) managed to persuade the
Court that he had reason to fear conviction on evidence obtained by torturing
supposed witnesses, and the applicants Al Nashiri and Husayn (Abu Zubaydah), whose cases the Court heard in parallel, were found to have been sent to
face the prospect of criminal proceedings lacking even elementary procedural
guarantees on the American military base at Guantánamo Bay.[639]

There have been several cases in which Contracting States have permitted,
or failed to prevent, the transfer of a person from within their jurisdiction to a
foreign destination where they suffered arbitrary detention. Specifically, these
were prisoners held by the CIA as victims of rendition who were first held on
the territory of the Contracting States concerned and then removed to a place
of detention outside the jurisdiction of any European State. The Court has
found the responsibility of those Contracting States to be engaged.[640]

The Court explicitly linked the issue of extradition or deportation to Article
1 of the Convention in *Loizidou (preliminary objections)*,[641] referring (in addition to *Soering*) to its landmark judgments *Cruz Varas and Others v. Sweden*

---

636   *Chahal v. the United Kingdom* [GC], no. 22414/93, Reports 1996-V.
637   *Saadi v. Italy* [GC], no. 37201/06, ECHR 2008.
638   *Trabelsi v. Belgium*, no. 140/10, ECHR 2014.
639   *Othman (Abu Qatada) v. the United Kingdom*, no. 8139/09, § 285, ECHR 2012; *Husayn (Abu
      Zubaydah) v. Poland*, no. 7511/13, §§ 555-560, 24 July 2014; *Al Nashiri v. Poland*, no. 28761/11,
      §§ 565-568, 24 July 2014; *Abu Zubaydah v. Lithuania*, no. 46454/11, § 657, 31 May 2018; *Al
      Nashiri v. Romania*, no. 33234/12, §§ 719-721, 31 May 2018.
640   *Husayn (Abu Zubaydah) v. Poland*, no. 7511/13, § 525, 24 July 2014; *Al Nashiri v. Poland*,
      no. 28761/11, § 531, 24 July 2014; *Abu Zubaydah v. Lithuania*, no. 46454/11, § 657, 31 May
      2018; *Al Nashiri v. Romania*, no. 33234/12, § 691, 31 May 2018.
641   *Loizidou v. Turkey (preliminary objections)* (GC), no. 15318/89, §§ 61-64, Series A no. 310.

and *Vilvarajah and Others v. the United Kingdom*.[642] In *Cruz Varas* the Court was still careful to point out that it was not the responsibility of the receiving State that was engaged but that of the Convention State only. A statement to similar effect is absent from *Vilvarajah and Others* and indeed from *Chahal*. It only made its reappearance in the Chamber judgment in *Mamatkulov and Abdurasulovic v. Turkey*[643] and in the later Grand Chamber judgment in that case (re-named *Mamatkulov and Askarov v. Turkey*[644]). It has since appeared in *Saadi*, *Al Nashiri*, *Abu-Zubaydah* and *Trabelsi* and may therefore be considered to reflect the current state of the law.[645]

Despite the link to extraterritorial jurisdiction made in paragraph 62 of *Loizidou (preliminary objections)*, deportation and extradition cases do not involve the extraterritorial exercise of territorial jurisdiction properly so-called. Although the danger to the person subject to deportation or extradition may threaten or even materialise abroad, the decision to deport or extradite is taken on the home territory of the State and put into effect there through the person's forcible removal across the border; the Article 1 jurisdiction of the deporting or extraditing State is engaged through the adequacy or otherwise of its assessment of the risks.[646]

### 5.6.2    *Attack on Foreign Territory*

Although undoubtedly an armed attack on a target located on the territory of a foreign State produces effects abroad, the consequence that there is exercise of Article 1 jurisdiction is not inevitable. A cross-border attack does not necessarily constitute the assertion by the attacking State of its 'sovereignty', as the refusal to grant access to an alien (or to remove an alien from the territory of the State) undoubtedly does. The establishment of Article 1 jurisdiction resulting from the exercise of 'hard power' abroad will be examined in detail in Chapter 6 below. We will see, in particular, that the Court has rejected the suggestion that an attack is of itself sufficient to bring its victims within the jurisdiction of the attacking Contracting State (the 'cause and effect' model).[647]

---

642    *Soering*, § 91; *Cruz Varas and Others v. Sweden*, no. 15576/89, Series A no. 201; and *Vilvarajah and Others v. the United Kingdom*, nos. 13163/87 13164/87 13165/87 13447/87 13448/87, Series A no. 215.

643    *Mamatkulov and Abdurasulovic v. Turkey*, nos. 46827/99 and 46951/99, § 66, 6 February 2003.

644    *Mamatkulov and Askarov v. Turkey* (GC), nos. 46827/99 and 46951/99, § 67, 4 February 2005.

645    *Saadi*, § 126; *Al Nashiri v. Poland*, § 457; *Husayn (Abu Zubaydah) v. Poland*, § 454-55; *Trabelsi*, § 119.

646    *Paposhvili v. Belgium* (GC), no. 41738/10, § 184, ECHR 2016.

647    See 6.4.3.1 below.

## 5.7 Conclusion

Man is a land animal, and 'jurisdiction' for purposes of Article 1 of the Convention will for the most part be exercised on land. However, its exercise is not limited to the land territory of the Contracting States, let alone their metropolitan land area. It is also exercised on the sea, in the sky, even in outer space, and in some uncontroversial situations, on the territory of other States. The scope for using 'hard power', as we have defined it – for which the Contracting State may be held accountable as a result – exists in all of these places.

CHAPTER 6

# Typology of Article 1 Jurisdiction in 'Hard Power' Situations

## 6.1 Introduction

Having in the previous chapter explored the exercise of 'jurisdiction' both territorial and extraterritorial in general, we will now explore the limits of jurisdiction in the type of situation that interests us in particular – situations involving the use of 'hard power', as we have defined it for our purposes.[648] The focus of this part is on defining the limits of 'Article 1 jurisdiction' in such situations and hence the answerability of the State under the Convention.

## 6.2 States Exercising 'Hard Power' on Their Own Territory

### 6.2.1 *Acknowledging Jurisdiction*

The least problematic category of cases is that of Contracting States acting within their own territory and acknowledging – indeed, actively asserting – their jurisdiction. There is no doubt in these cases that the Convention applies.

#### 6.2.1.1 Ireland

Thus, in the *Lawless* case, the very first case ever brought before the Court, we find the Republic of Ireland in the 1950s moving to suppress 'armed groups, calling themselves the "Irish Republican Army" (IRA)', formed 'for the avowed purpose of carrying out acts of violence to put an end to British sovereignty in Northern Ireland'.[649] The case concerned an Irish national detained without trial for the sole purpose of preventing him from engaging in terrorist activity. It raised issues mainly under Article 5 of the Convention. In the event, as we have seen, the alleged violation was covered by a notice of derogation submitted by the Irish Government under Article 15 of the Convention.[650]

---

648   See 1.2.3 above.
649   *Lawless v. Ireland (No. 3)*, § 6.
650   See 4.5.1.2 above.

© KONINKLIJKE BRILL NV, LEIDEN, 2021 | DOI:10.1163/9789004425637_007

## 6.2.1.2 United Kingdom

Nearly two decades later, we see the United Kingdom itself acting against individuals and groups possessed of very much the same intentions, both on its own side of the Northern Ireland border[651] and in another territory for whose international relations it is responsible, Gibraltar[652] – and back in Northern Ireland, acting rather more equivocally, it has to be said, against loyalist paramilitaries.[653] *Ireland v. the United Kingdom*, the first interstate case to reach the Court, led to findings of violation of Article 3 of the Convention as a result of treatment meted out by the United Kingdom to suspected IRA terrorists; individual applications in this category tend to involve violations of Article 2.

## 6.2.1.3 Turkey

From at least the mid-1980s onwards Turkey's south-east has been beset by serious disturbances between the security forces and the armed wing of the PKK. It was estimated in 1996 that around 4,000 each of civilians and members of the security forces had been killed and some 1,000 villages had been destroyed and evacuated.[654]

Complaints brought about actions of the Turkish security forces concern such matters as the destruction of houses in a village caught in the crossfire;[655] acts of maltreatment and torture;[656] allegedly unlawful killing;[657] and enforced disappearance.[658]

---

651 Beginning with *Ireland v. the United Kingdom*; *McKerr and Others v. the United Kingdom*, no. 28883/95, Reports 2001-III; *Kelly and Others v. the United Kingdom*, no. 30054/96, 4 May 2001; *Shanaghan v. the United Kingdom*, no. 37715/97, 4 May 2001; *Hugh Jordan v. the United Kingdom*, no. 24746/94, 4 May 2001; *McShane v. the United Kingdom*, no. 43290/98, 28 May 2002; *Finucane v. the United Kingdom*, no. 29178/75, ECHR 2003-VIII; *McCaughey and Others v. the United Kingdom*, no. 43098/09, ECHR 2013.

652 *McCann and Others v. the United Kingdom*, 27 September 1995, Series A no. 324.

653 *Brecknell v. the United Kingdom*, no. 32457/04, 27 November 2007; *McCartney v. the United Kingdom*, no. 34575/04, 27 November 2007; *O'Dowd v. the United Kingdom*, no. 34622/04, 27 November 2007; *Reavy v. the United Kingdom*, no. 34640/04, 27 November 2007; *McGrath v. the United Kingdom*, no. 34651/04, 27 November 2007.

654 *Akdivar and Others v. Turkey*, 16 September 1996, § 13, *Reports of Judgments and Decisions* 1996-IV.

655 *Akdivar and Others.*

656 Among many others, *Aksoy.*

657 Among many others, *Tanrıkulu v. Turkey* [GC], no. 23763/94, ECHR 1999-IV; *Oğur v. Turkey* [GC], no. 21594/93, ECHR 1999III.

658 Among others, *Kurt v. Turkey*, 25 May 1998, *Reports of Judgments and Decisions* 1998-III; *Çakıcı v. Turkey* [GC], no. 23657/94, ECHR 1999IV.

### 6.2.1.4 Russia

Russia has had to contend with varying degrees of unrest in the northern Caucasus ever since that region became part of its empire in the late eighteenth century. Restive though the local population may have been over the years (in particular in the autonomous republics of Ingushetia, Dagestan and especially Chechnya), sovereignty of the Russian Federation over the area is internationally recognised and has never been called into question before the Court.

Trouble flared up yet again in the 1990s, after the collapse of the Soviet Union. The Russian response was robust, which led to many applications to the Court. Russia has been held responsible for, among other things, bombing a civilian refugee convoy[659] and a village;[660] unlawful killing;[661] unacknowledged detention;[662] and enforced disappearance.[663]

Although the Court has found many violations of the Convention by the Russian Federation, it is only fair to add that the Russian Federation is not solely to blame. If one confines oneself to the Court's case-law, the two-sided bitterness of the strife is well illustrated by the attack on the 'Dubrovka' theatre in Moscow carried out by Chechen separatists on 23 October 2002[664] and by the attack, also by a Chechen war band, initiated on 1 September 2004, on a school in the northern Ossetian town of Beslan which reportedly left 334 dead including 86 children.[665] The Court has made no bones about labelling both attacks 'terrorist'.

### 6.2.2 *Denying Jurisdiction*

Somewhat more problematical are the cases in which a Contracting Party accepts its territorial jurisdiction but denies responsibility for ensuring the en-

---

659 *Isayeva and Others v. Russia*, nos. 57947/00, 57948/00 and 57949/00, 24 February 2005.

660 *Isayeva v. Russia*, no. 57950/00, 24 February 2005; *Esmukhambetov and Others v. Russia*, no. 23445/03, 29 March 2011.

661 Among many others, *Khashiyev and Akayeva v. Russia*, nos. 57942/00 and 57945/00, 24 February 2005.

662 *Bitiyeva and X v. Russia*, nos. 57953/00 and 37392/03, 21 June 2007.

663 *Bazorkina v. Russia*, no. 69481/01, 27 July 2006.

664 *Finogenov and Others v. Russia*, no. 18229/03, ECHR 2012; *Sabanchiyeva and Others v. Russia*, no. 38450/05, ECHR 2013.

665 *Maskhadova and Others v. Russia*, no. 18071/05, § 16, 6 June 2013. UNHCR puts the casualty figures at over 430 and over 100, respectively: see "UNHCR Position Regarding Asylum-Seekers and Refugees from the Chechen Republic, Russian Federation" of 22 October 2004, quoted in *Jeltsuyeva v. the Netherlands* (dec.), no. 39858/04, 1 June 2006. For the Court's description of the terrorist attack, see *Tagayeva and Others v. Russia* (dec.), nos. 26562/07, 14755/08, 49339/08, 49380/08, 51313/08, 21294/11 and 37096/11, 9 June 2016, and the ensuing judgment, *Tagayeva and Others v. Russia*, nos. 26562/07, 14755/08, 49339/08, 49380/08, 51313/08, 21294/11 and 37096/11, 13 April 2017.

186 CHAPTER 6

joyment of Convention rights in a part of its territory that is not under its full control. This may be because the region in issue is under the control of a powerful local force or a separatist movement that is in a position to deny the Contracting Party projection of its own power or because the region is occupied by a foreign power.

### 6.2.2.1 Georgia

Thus, we see Georgia being made to answer for the detention of an individual applicant by the local government of Ajaria in open defiance of an order for his release issued by the Georgian Supreme Court. Ajaria itself, though autonomous and to all appearances fiercely independent from the Georgian central government, had no separatist aspirations and remained an integral part of Georgia. It followed that the central government of Georgia were obliged under the Convention actively to assert their authority there, as indeed throughout Georgian territory. A 'presumption of competence' applied.[666] The importance of this presumption is stated by the Court in the following terms:

> Indeed, for reasons of legal policy – the need to maintain equality between the States Parties and to ensure the effectiveness of the Convention – it could not be otherwise. But for the presumption, the applicability of the Convention could be selectively restricted to only parts of the territory of certain States Parties, thus rendering the notion of effective human rights protection underpinning the entire Convention meaningless while, at the same time, allowing discrimination between the States Parties, that is to say beween those which accepted the application of the Convention over the whole of their territory and those which did not.[667]

In the event, it turned out that Georgia was able to comply: Mr Assanidze was released the day after the judgment was delivered. The Georgian Government was eventually in a position to report that:

> [f]ollowing the resignation, on 6 May 2004, of [A.], the former leader of the Autonomous Republic of Ajaria (responsible for the failure to comply with the release order of Mr. Assanidze) and the new legitimate elections on 20 June 2004 in the Autonomous Republic of Ajaria, the difficulties

---

666  *Assanidze*, §§ 139-142. Such a presumption was suggested by Lawson already in 1998: see Lawson (1998), pp. 112-114. See also Lawson (1999) p. 259. Compare *Ilaşcu and Others*, § 312, and *Sargsyan v. Azerbaijan* [GC], no. 40167/06, §§ 149-150, ECHR 2015.

667  *Assanidze*, § 142.

TYPOLOGY OF ARTICLE 1 JURISDICTION IN 'HARD POWER' SITUATIONS    187

encountered in exercising jurisdiction in this region [were] henceforth solved.[668]

### 6.2.2.2    Moldova

The former Moldavian Soviet Socialist Republic (later the Soviet Socialist Republic of Moldova) declared its independence from the Soviet Union in August 1991. So, separately, did the 'Moldovan Republic of Transdniestria', which (although a separate territorial entity until 1940) had previously been the part of Moldavian territory situated on the east bank of the river Dniestr. An armed struggle ensued between the central Moldovan government and a Transdniestrian separatist movement, which continued until a ceasefire agreement was reached in July 1992.

Most of the Soviet 14th Army, which had been present in Moldova, became the Russian Operational Group or 'ROG' following the dissolution of the Soviet Union (a few units elected to join the army of Moldova). As the Court found in *Ilaşcu and Others v. Moldova and Russia* [GC]:

> 380. The Court observes that during the Moldovan conflict in 1991-92 forces of the 14th Army (which owed allegiance to the USSR, the CIS and the Russian Federation in turn) stationed in Transdniestria, an integral part of the territory of the Republic of Moldova, fought with and on behalf of the Transdniestrian separatist forces. Moreover, large quantities of weapons from the stores of the 14th Army (which later became the ROG) were voluntarily transferred to the separatists, who were also able to seize possession of other weapons unopposed by Russian soldiers (...).
>
> The Court notes that from December 1991 onwards the Moldovan authorities systematically complained, to international bodies among others, of what they called 'the acts of aggression' of the 14th Army against the Republic of Moldova and accused the Russian Federation of supporting the Transdniestrian separatists.
>
> Regard being had to the principle of States' responsibility for abuses of authority, it is of no consequence that, as the Russian Government submitted, the 14th Army did not participate as such in the military operations between the Moldovan forces and the Transdniestrian insurgents.
>
> 381. Throughout the clashes between the Moldovan authorities and the Transdniestrian separatists, the leaders of the Russian Federation supported the separatist authorities by their political declarations (...). The

---

668    Committee of Ministers of the Council of Europe, Resolution ResDH(2006)53 (2 November 2006).

CHAPTER 6

Russian Federation drafted the broad lines of the ceasefire agreement of 21 July 1992, and moreover signed it as a party.[669]

Russia ratified the Convention on 5 May 1998. After this happened, the ROG was not withdrawn, although its numbers were reduced; its weapons stocks remained in Transdniestria and some of its weaponry found its way into the hands of Transdniestrian separatist forces. In addition, the 'MRT' received economic and other aid from the Russian Federation. The Government of Moldova was thus prevented from regaining control over Transdniestria. No state has yet recognised the 'MRT' as sovereign and distinct from Moldova even so.

*Ilaşcu and Others* is the case of four Moldovan nationals, residents of Tiraspol (the capital and administrative centre of the 'MRT'). They were arrested in June 1992 and kept in Russian, later in Transdniestrian detention. By the time Russia ratified the Convention the applicants had been handed over to the Transdniestrian separatists. An application complaining of developments after the Court's judgment in this case gave rise to the *Ivanţoc and Others* judgment.[670]

Other complaints concern the denial of education in the Romanian/Moldovan language.[671] In *Mozer* the Court ruled detention ordered by 'MRT' courts illegal on the ground that the judiciary of that entity (which in the submission of the Moldovan Government was still cast in the old Soviet mould) did not 'form part of a judicial system operating on a "constitutional and legal basis" compatible with the Convention'.[672]

It was not in dispute that Moldova was unable to assert its authority over Transdniestria, and we shall see later that Moldova made an unsuccessful attempt to escape Article 1 jurisdiction on that ground. Nevertheless, the facts on the ground '[reduced] the scope of that jurisdiction in that the undertaking given by the State under Article 1 must be considered by the Court only in the light of the Contracting State's positive obligations towards persons within its territory'. In other words, as the only legitimate government of the Republic of Moldova under international law, Moldova still had a positive obligation under Article 1 of the Convention to take the diplomatic, economic, judicial or other measures which it was in its power to take and which were in accordance

---

669    *Ilaşcu and Others*, §§ 380-381.
670    *Ivanţoc and Others v. Moldova and Russia*, no. 23687/05, 15 November 2011.
671    *Catan and Others v. Moldova and Russia* [GC], nos. 43370/04, 18454/06 and 8252/05, ECHR 2012.
672    *Mozer v. Moldova and Russia* (GC), no. 11138/10, § 148, 23 February 2016.

TYPOLOGY OF ARTICLE 1 JURISDICTION IN 'HARD POWER' SITUATIONS 189

with international law to secure to the applicants the rights guaranteed by the Convention.[673]

The applicants in *Pocasovschi and Mihaila* were convicts sentenced by Moldovan courts who were serving their sentences in a prison in Bender, a town in the Transdniestrian region. The prison was situated in a security zone under the control of peacekeepers from Moldova, Russia and the 'MRT'. The prison itself was under the exclusive control of the Moldovan authorities. However, it was dependent on the 'MRT' authorities for electricity, water and heating supplies – and in 2002, the 'MRT' authorities decided to disconnect the prison from them. International pressure led to the temporary resumption of supplies; but in 2003 the 'MRT' authorities disconnected the prison again in order that the Moldovan Government close it down. Conditions of detention deteriorated seriously as a result. The applicants were eventually transferred to other prisons in 2004.

Attempts were made to have the persons who had disconnected the prison from the utilities systems prosecuted in Moldova. This proved impossible because Moldova did not control 'MRT' territory. In parallel with these attempts, the applicants and other prisoners brought civil proceedings in Moldova. These met with marginally greater success: the applicants were awarded limited sums of money. The sums were however too small to deprive them of their status of 'victims' of the violations they alleged.[674]

The applicants lodged an application against both Moldova and the Russian Federation. In so far as directed against the Russian Federation the application was declared inadmissible on the ground that it was out of time: since their transfer, the applicants had no longer been held in allegedly inhuman conditions and more than six months had passed before they applied to the Court.[675] With regard to Moldova, the Court held as follows:

> ... unlike in previous cases concerning alleged breaches of the Convention by the "MRT", the Moldovan authorities in the present case were not limited to only fulfilling their positive obligations as mentioned in the preceding paragraphs. The case is different in that, while not having control over the local authorities in Bender which disconnected prison no. 8 from the utilities, the Moldovan authorities had full control over that prison itself and the detainees there throughout the relevant peri-

---

673   *Ilaşcu and Others*, §§ 333-335; *Ivanţoc and Others*, § 105, 15 November 2011; *Catan and Others*, §§ 109-110; *Ziaunys v. Moldova*, no. 42416/06, § 16, 11 February 2014; *Mozer*, §§ 99-100.

674   *Pocasovschi and Mihaila v. Moldova and Russia*, no. 1089/09, § 66, 29 May 2018.

675   Article 35 § 1. *Pocasovschi and Mihaila*, § 50.

od. They could have taken measures in the prison itself to cope with the effects of the disconnection from the utilities or they could have transferred the prisoners to other prisons at any time. By choosing to continue to detain the applicants in prison no. 8 without immediate action taken to ensure basic conditions of detention, the Moldovan authorities knowingly exposed them to the conditions which prevailed there after the disconnection from all utilities. In addition to the above-mentioned positive obligations, it was therefore also the direct responsibility of the Moldovan authorities to prevent or redress the alleged violation of the applicants' rights in that prison.[676]

### 6.2.2.3    Azerbaijan

Nagorno-Karabakh is an area whose traditional population is overwhelmingly of Armenian ethnicity. It has no common border with the territory of the Republic of Armenia. While the Soviet Union existed it was part of the Azerbaijan Soviet Socialist Republic. Having sought since Soviet times to secede to Armenia, the inhabitants of the region proclaimed the 'Republic of Nagorno-Karabakh' when Azerbaijan itself broke away from the Soviet Union in 1991. In the fighting that ensued, a land corridor was established between Nagorno-Karabakh and Armenia proper under the control of Nagorno-Karabakh separatists. A ceasefire has been in force since 1994.

*Sargsyan v. Azerbaijan* is the case of an Armenian national displaced from a village in the front line between the army of Azerbaijan and the forces of the 'Republic of Nagorno-Karabakh'. Much was in dispute; for example, it was not known whether the Azerbaijan army had an effective military presence in the locality. At all events, it seems that the village was within range of Armenian artillery fire.

In its judgment on the merits, the Court applied the presumption of competence developed in *Assanidze* and *Ilaşcu and Others* that the territorial state was in a position, and as a corollary, under a positive obligation in the light of Article 1 of the Convention to impose its authority. The rebuttable presumption developed in *Ilaşcu and Others*, which limited this obligation in respect of parts of a Contracting State's territory that were occupied by a foreign state or under the effective control of a separatist regime, therefore did not apply. The events complained of were thus found to come within the jurisdiction of Azerbaijan.[677]

---

676    *Pocasovschi and Mihaila*, § 46.

677    *Sargsyan v. Azerbaijan* (dec.) (GC), no. 40167/06, 14 December 2011; *Sargsyan v. Azerbaijan* [GC], no. 40167/06, 15 June 2015.

TYPOLOGY OF ARTICLE 1 JURISDICTION IN 'HARD POWER' SITUATIONS 191

This was not a case of extraterritorial jurisdiction properly so-called. As the Court's own Jurisconsult points out, this case did not concern the jurisdiction and responsibility of a State when it exercised jurisdiction extraterritorially, as did Turkey over Northern Cyprus or Russia over Transdniestria. Nor did it concern the jurisdiction of a State over part of its territory which was under the effective control of another State, as Transdniestria remained under the jurisdiction of Moldova itself. In the words of the Court's Jurisconsult:

> Since Azerbaijan was the territorial State, it was presumed to have jurisdiction and there were no exceptional circumstances (such as the effective exercise of control by another State) to rebut that presumption. The Court therefore found that the impugned facts fell within the jurisdiction of Azerbaijan. The Court acknowledged the difficulties which would inevitably be encountered by Azerbaijan at a practical level in exercising authority over such disputed territory: however, those were matters to be taken into account on the merits of each complaint.[678]

The Jurisconsult continues:

> Consequently, this was the first time the Court had to rule on the merits of Convention complaints against a State which had legal jurisdiction, but which had practical control problems over a part of its territory which was "disputed".[679]

This judgment demonstrates that the presumption of territorial jurisdiction is a presumption of fact, which it is for the Contracting State claiming foreign occupation or separatist secession to disprove.

### 6.2.2.4 Kosovo

In June 1999, following a series of NATO air strikes, an agreement was reached under which the Federal Republic of Yugoslavia (by this time composed of the republics of Serbia and Montenegro) would withdraw from the territory of Kosovo. The United Nations Security Council adopted a resolution (Resolution 1244) according to which an international civil ('United Nations Mission in Kosovo – UNMIK') and security ('Kosovo Force – KFOR') presence would be deployed in Kosovo. A Special Representative would be appointed by the

---

678    Overview of the Court's case-law, January to June 2015 (prepared by the Jurisconsult), page 2.

679    *ibid.*

UN Secretary General to head UNMIK. In the performance of duties entrusted to UNMIK, the Special Representative issued legislative acts in the form of regulations with a view to establishing the governing framework in Kosovo. Section 1 of UNMIK Regulation No. 1999/1 (UNMIK/REG/1999/1) provided that all legislative and executive authority with respect to Kosovo, including the administration of the judiciary, was vested in UNMIK and was exercised by the Special Representative.

Apparently in April 1990 – before the onset of the wars that resulted in the dissolution of the SFRY – a Kosovo resident, Mr Ali Azemi, brought an action in an employment dispute before the competent civil court in Pristina. He won a judgment in his favour, finally, in January 2002. However, the judgment was never enforced.

Kosovo declared independence on 17 February 2008. To date, Kosovo has been recognised as an independent state by a majority of United Nations Member States (which has led to envious statements of support from breakaway entities seeking statehood for themselves), Serbia itself – in common with a number of other Council of Europe Member States – not among them. However, the Serbian Supreme and Constitutional Courts have held that Serbia does not exercise jurisdiction over Kosovo.[680]

The applicant brought an application before the Court against Serbia in February 2009 complaining of the non-enforcement of the judgment delivered in his favour.

The Court declared the application inadmissible on 5 November 2013. As is its usual practice – necessarily so, since the Member States of the Council of Europe do not agree on the matter – it declined to rule on the validity of Kosovo's statehood: the decision carries a footnote stating that '[a]ll reference to Kosovo, whether to the territory, institutions or population, in this text shall be understood in full compliance with United Nations Security Council Resolution 1244 and without prejudice to the status of Kosovo.' Its reasoning on the Article 1 point was as follows:

> 46. On 17 February 2008 Kosovo proclaimed its independence, having been subsequently recognised as independent by at least 89 States. On 15 June 2008 the Constitution of Kosovo was adopted. On 10 September 2012, apart from the exercise of certain "residual responsibilities" by UNMIK, the end of "supervised independence" was declared. In these cir-

---

680 Constitutional Court of Serbia, judgment of 1 April 2010 (case no. 531/2008), cited in *Azemi v. Serbia* (dec.), no. 11209/09, § 29, 5 November 2013; Supreme Court of Serbia, judgment of 23 May 2007 (case no. 1251/07), *ibid.*, § 30.

TYPOLOGY OF ARTICLE 1 JURISDICTION IN 'HARD POWER' SITUATIONS 193

cumstances, the Court is satisfied that there existed objective limitations which prevented Serbia from securing the rights and freedoms in Kosovo. 47. Consequently, Serbia's domestic courts have confirmed that its authorities have not been exercising any effective control in Kosovo since 1999 (...). Moreover, the applicant has not been able to point to a particular action or inaction of the respondent State or substantiated any breach of the respondent State's duty to take all the appropriate measures with regard to his right which are still within its power to take. Having regard to the particular circumstances of this case, the Court cannot point to any positive obligations that the respondent State had towards the applicant (compare and contrast with Moldova's positive obligations in the case of *Ilaşcu and Others* ...).[681]

### 6.2.2.5 Cyprus

Like Moldova and Serbia, the Republic of Cyprus is prevented from exercising its sovereignty over part of its territory – namely, that where a 'Turkish Republic of Northern Cyprus' (or 'TRNC') survives by virtue of the support of the Republic of Turkey. We will discuss the jurisdiction of Turkey with regard to the 'TRNC' in its proper place, that of military action abroad as exercise of extraterritorial jurisdiction.[682] Although there is no suggestion that the Republic of Cyprus is under any obligation to recognise the 'TRNC' *de iure* or *de facto*,[683] nonetheless the question arises whether Cyprus is at liberty to refuse all intercourse with it for reasons of political expediency.

In January 2005 a businessman and his wife and daughter, all three Cypriot nationals of Turkish Cypriot origin, were found murdered by the side of the Nicosia-Larnaca highway, within the borders of the Republic of Cyprus. The ensuing criminal investigation yielded eight suspects; six were Cypriot nationals who also held 'TRNC' citizenship, the remaining two were Turkish nationals. One of the Cypriots was later arrested in Limassol but had to be released for lack of evidence; the others all made their escape across the border into the 'TRNC'. One was later murdered himself.

In September 2008 Cyprus sent a request to Turkey, via the embassy in Athens, to extradite the six remaining suspects. The request was returned to the Cypriot embassy unexecuted.

---

681   *Azemi v. Serbia* (dec.), no. 11209/09, 5 November 2013.
682   See 6.4.1.1 below.
683   *Inter alia, Cyprus v. Turkey*, §§ 61 and 238, Reports 2001-IV; *Demopoulos and Others*, §§ 95-96.

194                                                                 CHAPTER 6

The 'TRNC' does not extradite its own citizens but its criminal courts have jurisdiction to try crimes committed by its nationals abroad. Accordingly, already in January 2005, the 'TRNC' authorities had initiated a criminal investigation of their own and arrested all eight identified suspects. All were charged with premeditated murder and remanded in custody.

Attempts were made via UNFICYP to establish a line of communication between the investigating authorities of the Republic of Cyprus and the 'TRNC', in order for a prosecution to be brought in the 'TRNC'; these were unsuccessful as 'the Cypriot police could not have direct contact with the "TRNC" police' and indeed it was for this reason UNFICYP's intervention had been sought. Eventually, in February 2005, all suspects were released on the ground of a lack of evidence linking them to the crime.

According to UNFICYP's Senior Police Adviser and Commander, the 'TRNC' side were genuinely concerned to resolve this matter, perhaps with the involvement of Interpol, the United Nations or the Turkish Government. They feared 'more crimes of this nature – that is to say criminals going through crossing points, committing crimes and then returning to the other side in order to avoid arrest and punishment'. The Cypriot Government, for their part, refused to cooperate for fear of lending legitimacy to the 'TRNC'.

The surviving kin of the three murder victims, the Güzelyurtlu family, lodged an application to the Court against both the Republic of Cyprus and Turkey complaining under Article 2 of the Convention of the failure to conduct an effective investigation into the crime.

A Chamber of the Court found both Contracting States responsible for violating Article 2 under its procedural head, based on their failure to cooperate with each other. As to Cyprus, it did not accept that cooperation in this case would have amounted either to recognition of Turkish sovereignty over Northern Cyprus or of the 'TRNC' itself; as to Turkey, it found it 'striking' that the extradition requests made by the Cypriot Government, still the sole legitimate government of Cyprus, had been ignored.[684]

At the request of both Governments, the case was referred to the Grand Chamber (Article 43 of the Convention). The Grand Chamber took a view quite different from that of the Chamber:

> In this connection, and besides the fact that Turkey never suggested that possibility when receiving the Cypriot extradition requests in 2008 (…), the Court considers that supplying the whole investigation file to the "TRNC" with the possibility that the evidence would be used for the pur-

---

684    *Güzelyurtlu and Others v. Cyprus and Turkey*, no. 36925/07, 4 April 2017, §§ 291-296.

poses of trying the suspects there, and without any guarantee that they would be surrendered to the Cypriot authorities, would go beyond mere cooperation between police or prosecuting authorities (...). It would amount in substance to a transfer of the criminal case by Cyprus to the "TRNC" courts, and Cyprus would thereby be waiving its criminal jurisdiction over a murder committed in its controlled area in favour of the courts of an unrecognised entity set up within its territory. Indeed, the exercise of criminal jurisdiction is one of the main features of the sovereignty of a State. The Court therefore agrees with the Cypriot Government that in such a specific situation it was not unreasonable to refuse to waive its criminal jurisdiction in favour of the "TRNC" courts.[685]

## 6.3 Foreign State Agents Committing Unlawful Acts with the Acquiescence of Convention State

Terrorism was a fact of life in much of Europe for the latter decades of the twentieth century: in the United Kingdom, Northern Ireland especially, the Irish Republican Army and its offshoots were household names (so indeed were its Loyalist opposite numbers, the Ulster Volunteer Force and the Ulster Defence Association), as were the Red Brigades in Italy, Action Directe in France and the Red Army Faction in Western Germany, to mention but some the better-known. It was not unknown either for groups from the Middle East to hijack European civilian passenger aircraft or even to carry out attacks on European soil, the best-remembered of the latter being the Black September attack on the Olympic games being held in Munich in 1972. In contrast, the terrorist attacks on Washington and New York of 11 September 2001 took the whole world by surprise. The hurt was very deeply felt in the United States itself, whose territory had not been a target for foreign hostility since the Japanese attack on Pearl Harbor in December 1941 (and before that, not on anything like the same scale since the burning of Washington by the British in 1814).

The reaction of the American president George W. Bush to these attacks was to declare a 'war on terror'. This 'war' – which as has been sufficiently pointed out elsewhere was, and is, not a 'war' in any legal sense of the word[686] – was

---

685 *Güzelyurtlu and Others v. Cyprus and Turkey* (GC), no. 36925/07, § 253, 29 January 2019.

686 Helen Duffy, *The 'War on Terror' and the Framework of International Law* (2nd edition 2015), Cambridge University Press, p. 2, fn. 3 and pp. 296-97; Luc Reydams and Jan Wouters, "A la guerre comme à la guerre", in *Armed Conflicts and the Law*, Jan Wouters, Philip De Man, Nele Verlinden (eds.), Intersentia, 2016, pp.1-27 at pp.22-24.

196                                                                    CHAPTER 6

taken afield, not only to al-Qaeda's leadership in Afghanistan but also – even
– to Europe.[687]

In November 2005 it became public knowledge through the American press
that the United States, through its Central Intelligence Agency (CIA), had been
detaining and interrogating terrorist suspects on the territory of some of its
allies, including European states.

As was to be written in later years by the rapporteur appointed by the Parliamentary Assembly of the Council of Europe to look into the matter, Senator
Dick Marty of Switzerland:

> While the states of the Old World have dealt with these threats primar-
> ily by means of existing institutions and legal systems, the United States
> appears to have made a fundamentally different choice: considering that
> neither conventional judicial instruments nor those established under
> the framework of the laws of war could effectively counter the new forms
> of international terrorism, it decided to develop new legal concepts.
> The latter are based primarily on the *Military Order on the Detention,
> Treatment, and Trial of Certain Non-Citizens in the War against Terrorism*
> signed by President Bush on 13 November 2001. It is significant that, to
> date, only one person has been summoned before the courts to answer
> for the 11 September attacks: a person, moreover, who was already in pris-
> on on that day, and had been in the hands of the justice system for sev-
> eral months. By contrast, hundreds of other people are still deprived of
> their liberty, under American authority but outside the national territory,
> within an unclear normative framework. Their detention is, in any event,
> altogether contrary to the principles enshrined in all the international
> legal instruments dealing with respect for fundamental rights, including
> the domestic law of the United States (which explains the existence of
> such detention centres outside the country). ...[688]

In a follow-up report, Senator Marty points out that it is not only American
moral and legal responsibility that is engaged:

---

687   For a description of the American measures relevant to this study (in particular, the "High
      Value Detainee" programme), see *Abu Zubaydah v. Lithuania*, §§ 20-89, and *Al Nashiri v.
      Romania*, §§ 22-97.

688   Parliamentary Assembly of the Council of Europe, Committee on Legal Affairs and Hu-
      man Rights, *Alleged secret detentions and unlawful inter-state transfers involving Council of
      Europe member states* (AS/Jur (2006) 16 part II (first Marty report), 7 June 2006, para. 2.

TYPOLOGY OF ARTICLE 1 JURISDICTION IN 'HARD POWER' SITUATIONS    197

The rendition, abduction and detention of terrorist suspects have always taken place outside the territory of the United States, where such actions would no doubt have been ruled unlawful and unconstitutional. Obviously, these actions are also unacceptable under the laws of European countries, who nonetheless tolerated them or colluded actively in carrying them out. This export of illegal activities overseas is all the more shocking in that it shows fundamental contempt for the countries on whose territories it was decided to commit the relevant acts. The fact that the measures only apply to non-American citizens is just as disturbing: it reflects a kind of "legal apartheid" and an exaggerated sense of superiority. Once again, the blame does not lie solely with the Americans but also, above all, with European political leaders who have knowingly acquiesced in this state of affairs.[689]

The first Marty report, published in June 2006, gave detailed information about the practice referred to as 'rendition' and gave a detailed account of a number of specific cases.

### 6.3.1    *'Former Yugoslav Republic of Macedonia'*

One of the cases singled out by Marty was that of Khaled El Masri, who was later to lodge an application with the Court. A German national of Lebanese descent, he was on holiday in the Former Yugoslav Republic of Macedonia when he was arrested, apparently by mistake, by Macedonian agents. The Macedonians held him incommunicado, questioned him and ill-treated him. After several weeks they handed him over at Skopje Airport to a CIA rendition team who transferred him, on a special CIA-operated flight, to a CIA-run secret detention facility in Afghanistan for further interrogation over a period in excess of four months.

The applicant's detention and treatment by Macedonian agents raised no problem of jurisdiction within the meaning of Article 1 of the Convention. As regards the circumstances of the applicant's handover of the applicant to the CIA rendition team, which was found to have been brutal to the point of torture, the Court considered the Former Yugoslav Republic of Macedonia 'responsible under the Convention for acts performed by foreign officials on its territory with the acquiescence or connivance of its authorities'.[690] The ap-

---

689    Parliamentary Assembly of the Council of Europe, Committee on Legal Affairs and Human Rights, *Secret detentions and illegal transfers of detainees involving Council of Europe member states: second report* (second Marty report), 7 June 2007, para. 4.

690    *El-Masri*, § 206.

plicant's transfer to the CIA by itself constituted an 'extrajudicial transfer of persons from one jurisdiction or State to another, for the purposes of detention and interrogation outside the normal legal system, where there was a real risk of torture or cruel, inhuman or degrading treatment' engaging the responsibility of the respondent Contracting State under the Soering line of case-law[691] – not only under Article 3 of the Convention, but also under Article 5 as regards the detention in Afghanistan.[692]

### 6.3.2 Bosnia and Herzegovina

The case of *Boumediene and Others v. Bosnia and Herzegovina* could have raised similar questions. It concerned a group of Algerian nationals released from prison straight into the hands of American armed forces in open defiance of an order for a provisional measure given by the Human Rights Chamber, a hybrid human rights court then in existence set up under the Dayton Peace Agreement on which we will dwell at greater length below,[693] and removed to the American base at Guantánamo Bay, Cuba. The applicants' handover having taken place before the entry into force of the Convention for Bosnia and Herzegovina, the Court was asked to consider whether it had jurisdiction *ratione temporis* in the case. In the event, the Court did not declare the application inadmissible on the ground that it had not: rather, it went straight to the merits of the case and found that in any event Bosnia and Herzegovina had done what could reasonably be expected of it by interceding with the American authorities, obtaining assurances concerning the treatment of the applicants and facilitating their eventual return.[694]

Where formal admissibility conditions are open to dispute and the facts admit of a finding that an application is manifestly ill-founded, the Court will sometimes opt for the latter ground of inadmissibility rather than commit itself to a decision on preliminary issues that may unnecessarily tie its hands in future cases as precedent.

---

691 See 5.6.1 above.

692 *El-Masri*, §§ 221 and 239.

693 Annex 6 to the General Framework Agreement on Peace in Bosnia and Herzegovina (Agreement on Human Rights), Article VIII. See Human Rights Chamber for Bosnia and Herzegovina, Cases nos. CH/02/8679, CH/02/8689, CH/02/8690 and CH/02/8691, *Had` BOUDELLAA, Boumediene LAKHDAR, Mohamed NECHLE and Saber LAHMAR against Bosnia and Herzegovina and the Federation of Bosnia and Herzegovina*, 11 October 2002; see also J. David Yaeger, "The Human Rights Chamber for Bosnia and Herzegovina: A Case Study in Transitional Justice", 14 *International Legal Perspectives* (Spring 2004), pp. 50-51.

694 *Boumediene and Others v. Bosnia and Herzegovina* (dec.), nos. 38703/06, 40123/06, 43301/06, 43302/06, 2131/07 and 2141/07, §§ 62-67, 18 November 2008.

### 6.3.3 Poland

In *Al Nashiri v. Poland* the applicant was a Saudi Arabian national of Yemenite descent suspected in the United States of the attacks on the American destroyer *USS Cole* in the harbour of Aden, Yemen, in 2000 and on the French oil tanker *Limburg* in the Gulf of Aden in 2002. He was captured in Dubai, United Arab Emirates, in October 2002. After having been held by the CIA in Afghanistan and in Thailand, he was taken to Poland, where he was held for approximately six months in a 'black site' in Stare Kiejkuty. There he was subjected to various forms of ill-treatment including 'water-boarding'. In June 2003 he was taken first to Morocco and then to Guantánamo Bay to be tried before an American Military Commission.

The applicant in *Husayn (Abu Zubaydah) v. Poland* was a stateless Palestinian thought to be a high-ranking member of Al-Qaeda and as such co-responsible for the attacks of 11 September 2001. He was captured in Pakistan in early 2002 and was held there and in Thailand until taken to Poland in November 2002. From early December 2002 until late September 2003 he was held in the Stare Kiejkuty 'black site', the same where Al Nashiri was detained, and suffered much the same ill-treatment as Al Nashiri. From there he was transferred to other sites, ultimately to end up in Guantánamo Bay.

### 6.3.4 Italy

In *Nasr and Ghali* the applicants were Egyptian nationals, an imam (Mr Nasr) and his wife (Ms Ghali). As a member of an Islamist organisation, Jama'a al-Islamiya, that was illegal in his country of origin Mr Nasr had requested, and been granted, Italian asylum, after which he had been joined in Italy by his wife.

It does not seem to be in dispute that Mr Nasri was abducted from the streets of Milan by 'foreign agents' with the assistance of a member of the carabinieri, the latter apparently operating without official sanction, and the active involvement of the Italian intelligence service SISMi. Mr Nasri was taken to Egypt where he was detained and subjected to harsh interrogation. He is still in Egypt; he is forbidden to leave that country.

Criminal proceedings were later brought against a number of American nationals, several of whom were convicted and sentenced in their absence. However, the Italian Government did not actively seek their extradition for trial or execution of sentence; several were later reprieved by the President of the Italian Republic. Prosecutions were also brought against members of SISMi; these however collapsed because the Italian Government refused to declassify 'State

200                                                                    CHAPTER 6

secret' information that would have enabled the criminal courts to establish the facts.[695]

A Chamber of the Court found violations of, *inter alia*, Articles 3 (under both its substantive and its procedural heads), 5, and 8 in respect of Mr Nasri as the direct victim, and separately in respect of Ms Ghali in respect of the wrongs found to have been committed against her. From our perspective, the judgment is interesting in what it says about the involvement of the Italian Government.[696]

To establish the Article 1 jurisdiction of Italy, the Chamber applied the principles set out in *Al Nashiri*, *Abu Zubaydah* and *El Masri* and summarised above.

The case is interesting because of the findings with respect to Article 3 under its procedural head. The Chamber is pleased to acknowledge the quality of the investigations carried out by the Italian courts.[697] It finds a violation on the ground that the splendid work of the courts is deprived of its effect by the failure of the executive arm of government to make those responsible for the substantive breaches – significantly, including foreign State agents – face the criminal sanctions appropriate to their crimes.[698]

The Italian Government has declined to seek referral of the case to the Grand Chamber and in so doing has allowed this judgment to become final.[699]

### 6.3.5    *Lithuania*

Abu Zubaydah alleged that after been taken from Poland to Guantánamo Bay, he had been flown via Morocco to Lithuania and detained in a secret prison on the outskirts of Vilnius, there to be submitted to further brutal questioning. The Lithuanian Government accepted that the applicant had been brutalised but denied that it had happened on Lithuanian soil or with the connivance of Lithuanian authorities.

The Court conducted a joint fact-finding effort in this case and that of *Al Nashiri v. Romania*.[700] It considered evidence already presented in the earlier

---

695   Committee on Legal Affairs and Human Rights, *Abuse of state secrecy and national security: obstacles to parliamentary and judicial scrutiny of human rights violations*, Doc. 12714, 16 September 2011 (third Marty report), § 8.

696   *Nasr and Ghali v. Italy*, no. 44883/09, 23 February 2016.

697   "[La Cour] rend hommage au travail des juges nationaux qui ont tout mis en œuvre pour tenter d''établir la vérité'" (*Nasr and Ghali*, § 265). But see Helen Duffy and Stephen A. Kostas, "'Extraordinary Rendition': A Challenge for the Rule of Law", in *Counter-Terrorism: International Law and Practice* (Ana María de Frías, Katja L.H. Samuel, Nigel D. White, eds.), Oxford University Press 2011 p. 539 at p. 569.

698   *Nasr and Ghali*, §§ 266-74.

699   Article 43 § 1 of the Convention.

700   See 6.3.6 below.

TYPOLOGY OF ARTICLE 1 JURISDICTION IN 'HARD POWER' SITUATIONS     201

cases mentioned above, documentary evidence submitted by the applicant and respondent parties, and affidavits by Senator Marty and the then Council of Europe Commissioner for Human Rights, Mr Thomas Hammarberg. A joint fact-finding hearing was held *in camera*; witnesses heard included Mr Giovanni Claudio Fava, who had been the Rapporteur of the European Parliament's Temporary Committee on the alleged use of European countries by the CIA for the transport and illegal detention of Prisoners, Senator Marty himself, an advisor to Senator Marty and Mr Hammarberg referred to only by initials and an investigative journalist, Mr Crofton Black. The Court was able to find it established beyond reasonable doubt that:

> (a) the Lithuanian authorities knew of the nature and purposes of the CIA's activities on its territory at the material time;
> (b) the Lithuanian authorities, by approving the hosting of the CIA Detention Site Violet, enabling the CIA to use its airspace and airports and to disguise the movements of rendition aircraft, providing logistics and services, securing the premises for the CIA and transportation of the CIA teams with detainees on land, cooperated in the preparation and execution of the CIA rendition, secret detention and interrogation operations on its territory; and
> (c) given their knowledge of the nature and purposes of the CIA's activities on their territory and their involvement in the execution of that programme, the Lithuanian authorities knew that, by enabling the CIA to detain terrorist suspects – including the applicant – on their territory, they were exposing them to a serious risk of treatment contrary to the Convention.[701]

Once all this was established as fact, the question of Article 1 jurisdiction could be answered in the light of the existing case-law, including *Ilaşcu and Others, El-Masri, Al Nashiri v. Poland, Husayn (Abu Zubaydah) v. Poland*, and *Nasr and Ghali*.[702] The Court held as follows:

> Following an extensive and detailed analysis of evidence in the present case, the Court has established conclusively and to the required standard of proof that the Lithuanian authorities hosted CIA Detention Site Violet from 17 or 18 February 2005 to 25 March 2006; that the applicant was secretly detained there during that period; that the Lithuanian authorities

---

701    *Abu Zubaydah v. Lithuania*, § 576.
702    *Abu Zubaydah v. Lithuania*, § 579.

202                                                                 CHAPTER 6

> knew of the nature and purposes of the CIA's activities in their country
> and cooperated in the execution of the HVD Programme; and that the
> Lithuanian authorities knew that, by enabling the CIA to detain terrorist
> suspects – including the applicant – on their territory, they were expos-
> ing them to a serious risk of treatment contrary to the Convention (...).
>
> The above findings suffice for the Court to conclude that the matters
> complained of in the present case fall within the "jurisdiction" of Lithu-
> ania within the meaning of Article 1 of the Convention and are capable
> of engaging the respondent State's responsibility under the Convention,
> and that the applicant can be considered a "victim" for the purposes of
> Article 34 of the Convention. ...

– which, once the reality of the treatment undergone by the applicant was
established, made the unanimous finding of violations of Articles 2, 3, 5, 8 and
13 in conjunction with 3 of the Convention inevitable.

### 6.3.6    *Romania*

It appears that after having been taken from Poland to Guantánamo Bay, the
applicant Al Nashiri was taken to a 'black site' elsewhere – in his case, in Bucha-
rest in Romania. He lodged an application against the latter Contracting State.
His case was considered by the same Chamber of the Court as *Abu Zubaydah v.
Lithuania*, and in parallel with it.

The findings of fact in both cases were in essentially identical terms, only
the proper names of the applicants and the Contracting States being different,
and as in *Abu Zubaydah v. Lithuania*, violations were found of Articles 3, 5, 8
and 13 taken together with 3 of the Convention. Violations were also found of
Articles 2 and 6 § 1 of the Convention and Article 1 of Protocol No. 6 in that
Romania had allowed the applicant to be removed from its territory to face
the distinct possibility of both a trial so grossly inadequate as to amount to a
'flagrant denial of justice'[703] and a death sentence at the end of it.

### 6.4    'Hard Power' as Exercise of Extraterritorial Jurisdiction

The most contentious questions under Article 1 of the Convention to come before the Court thus far have all concerned either the maintenance of a military
presence on territory over which another State claims sovereignty or kinetic
military action taking place, or producing effects, elsewhere than on home ter-

---

703    See, *inter alia, Soering,* § 113; *Saadi v. Italy,* § 158.

# TYPOLOGY OF ARTICLE 1 JURISDICTION IN 'HARD POWER' SITUATIONS    203

ritory. Typically, Contracting States faced with applications relating to such actions will seek to deny having any jurisdiction at all, whereas applicants (and sometimes other Contracting States – generally those whose territory and/or nationals are affected) will posit that the responsibility of the respondent State is well and truly engaged.

'Jurisdiction' in this sense, if jurisdiction there be, may be lawful under international law (meaning that it coincides with 'jurisdiction' understood in terms of sovereignty, as discussed in Chapter 5) – or it may be disputed – or it may even be manifestly unlawful.[704] It may even be questionable in terms of domestic law, as we shall see. Even so, whether or not 'jurisdiction' within the meaning of Article 1 exists – and accordingly, whether the State's responsibility under the Convention is engaged – does not depend on whether 'jurisdiction' (understood as 'sovereignty') is lawful under either general international law or domestic law.

### 6.4.1    *Maintaining a Military Presence on Foreign Territory*
#### 6.4.1.1    Northern Cyprus

Turkish forces entered and took control of the northern part of Cyprus in 1974. By the 1990s the Turkish military presence in Northern Cyprus comprised two divisions of infantry totalling 30,000 personnel plus a naval command and an outpost.[705]

Cyprus responded by lodging two applications with the Commission alleging a large variety of violations of the Convention, ranging from illegal expropriations, destruction of churches and displacing the Greek Cypriot population to rape, forced prostitution, torture and murder. Turkey argued that the Commission had no jurisdiction *ratione loci:* Turkey had 'not extended her jurisdiction to the island of Cyprus since she had neither annexed a part of the island nor established a military or civil government there'.

The Commission found that:

> In Article 1 of the Convention, the High Contracting Parties undertake to secure the rights and freedoms defined in Section 1 to everyone "within their jurisdiction" (in the French text: *"relevant de leur juridiction"*). The Commission finds that this term is not, as submitted by the respondent Government, equivalent to or limited to the national territory of the High

---

704    Samantha Besson, "The extraterritoriality of the European Convention on Human Rights: why human rights depend on jurisdiction and what jurisdiction amounts to", *Leiden Journal of International Law* 2012, 25(4), 857-884 at p. 868.

705    *Loizidou v. Turkey* (merits), 18 December 1996, §§ 16, Reports 1996-VI.

204 CHAPTER 6

> Contracting Party concerned. It is clear from the language, in particular of the French text, and the object of this Article, and from the purpose of the Convention as a whole, that the High Contracting Parties are bound to secure the said rights and freedoms to all persons under their actual authority and responsibility, whether that authority is exercised within their own territory or abroad. ...

It continued:

> The Commission further observes that nationals of a State, including registered ships and aircrafts [sic], are partly within its jurisdiction wherever they may be, and that authorised agents of a State, including diplomatic or consular agents and armed forces, not only remain under its jurisdiction when abroad but bring any other persons or property "within the jurisdiction" of that State, to the extent that they exercise authority over such persons or property. Insofar as, by their acts or omissions, they affect such persons or property, the responsibility of the State is engaged.[706]

The same reasoning was later to reappear in the Commission's admissibility decision in *Chrysostomos, Papachrysostomou and Loizidou v. Turkey* and in its Article 31 report in the case of *Loizidou v. Turkey*.[707]

We shall see elsewhere that Turkey sought, unsuccessfully, to exclude its accountability under the Convention by setting up a nominally independent state[708] and by adding territorial provisos to the declarations accepting the right of individual petition (former Article 25 of the Convention) and the jurisdiction of the Court (former Article 46).[709] In *Loizidou v. Turkey (preliminary objections)*, the Court formulated the following rule:

> Bearing in mind the object and purpose of the Convention, the responsibility of a Contracting Party may also arise when as a consequence of military action – whether lawful or unlawful – it exercises effective control of an area outside its national territory. The obligation to secure, in such an area, the rights and freedoms set out in the Convention derives

---

706 *Cyprus v. Turkey (I) and (II)*, nos. 6780/74 and 6950/75, Commission decision of 26 May 1975, DR 2, p. 125, § 8.

707 *Loizidou v. Turkey*, no. 15318/89, Commission report of 8 July 1993; *Chrysostomos, Papachrysostomou and Loizidou v. Turkey*, nos. 15299/89, 15300/89 and 15318/89, Commission decision of 4 March 1991, DR 68, p. 216.

708 See 6.4.2.1 below.

709 See 7.2 below.

TYPOLOGY OF ARTICLE 1 JURISDICTION IN 'HARD POWER' SITUATIONS    205

from the fact of such control whether it be exercised directly, through its armed forces, or through a subordinate local administration.[710]

In a series of applications brought against Turkey by Cypriot nationals[711] and by the Republic of Cyprus itself,[712] we see Turkey answering for denying displaced Greek Cypriots formerly resident in Northern Cyprus access to immovable property that remains theirs;[713] denying them access to their homes;[714] failing to investigate alleged enforced disappearances;[715] and much else besides.[716]

That is not to say that the violations are all one way. The *Egmez* case concerned a Turkish Cypriot resident in the northern part who was maltreated by police of the Republic of Cyprus trying to coerce a confession out of him.[717] In *Denizci and Others v. Cyprus* we find Turkish Cypriots being maltreated and unlawfully detained by the police of the Republic of Cyprus in the direct vicinity of the demarcation line and their movements monitored to an extent amounting to an unjustified interference with their freedom of movement (Article 2 of Protocol No. 4).[718] In *Aziz v. Cyprus* we see a Turkish Cypriot deprived of his right to vote and stand for election in his chosen state of nationality and residence, the Republic of Cyprus, on account of his ethnicity (Article 3 of Protocol No. 1).[719]

---

710   *Loizidou v. Turkey* (preliminary objections), 23 March 1995, § 22, Series A no. 310.

711   Among many others, *Loizidou v. Turkey* (preliminary objections), 23 March 1995, Series A no. 310, and *Loizidou v. Turkey* (merits), 18 December 1996, *Reports of Judgments and Decisions* 1996-VI; *Cyprus v. Turkey* [GC], no. 25781/94, ECHR 2001IV; *Demades v. Turkey*, no. 16219/90, 31 July 2002; *Xenides-Arestis v. Turkey*, no. 46347/99, 22 December 2005; *Varnava and Others v. Turkey* [GC], nos. 16064/90, 16065/90, 16066/90, 16068/90, 16069/90, 16070/90, 16071/90, 16072/90 and 16073/90, .ECHR 2009.

712   *Cyprus v. Turkey* [GC], no. 25781/94, Reports 2001-IV.

713   *Loizidou v. Turkey* (merits), 18 December 1996, *Reports of Judgments and Decisions* 1996VI; *Demades v. Turkey*, no. 16219/90, 31 July 2002; *Eugenia Michaelidou Developments Ltd and Michael Tymvios v. Turkey*, no. 16163/90, 31 July 2003; *Xenides-Arestis v. Turkey*, no. 46347/99, 22 December 2005.

714   *Demades v. Turkey*, no. 16219/90, 31 July 2002; *Xenides-Arestis v. Turkey*, no. 46347/99, 22 December 2005.

715   *Varnava and Others v. Turkey* [GC], nos. 16064/90, 16065/90, 16066/90, 16068/90, 16069/90, 16070/90, 16071/90, 16072/90 and 16073/90, ECHR 2009.

716   *Cyprus v. Turkey* [GC], no. 25781/94, Reports 2001-IV.

717   *Egmez v. Cyprus*, no. 30873/96, Reports 2000-XII.

718   *Denizci and Others v. Cyprus*, nos. 25316-25321/94 and 27207/95, Reports 2001-V.

719   *Aziz v. Cyprus*, no. 69949/01, Reports 2004-V.

## 6.4.1.2 Western Germany

Following the unconditional surrender of the German High Command on 8 May 1945 the Governments of the four allied occupation forces – France, the Soviet Union, the United Kingdom and the United States – assumed supreme authority with respect to Germany. In October 1949 the Soviet Military Governor decided to transfer to the Provisional Government of the German Democratic Republic the function of administration which hitherto belonged to the Soviet Military Administration. On 5 May 1955 the Convention on Relations between the Three Powers (France, United Kingdom and USA) and the Federal Republic of Germany entered into force terminating the Occupation régime in the Republic. The Three Powers retained however the rights and responsibilities, heretofore exercised or held by them, relating to Berlin, which had since 1948 been exercised with the abstention of the Soviet authorities.

The applicant in the case of *Hess v. the United Kingdom* was the wife of Rudolf Hess, the former deputy of Adolf Hitler, who had been convicted at Nuremberg of conspiracy to wage aggressive war and crimes against peace and sentenced to life imprisonment. At the time when the application was lodged, he was the last remaining Nazi prisoner in Spandau Prison, Berlin. Spandau Prison is located in the British sector of Berlin and was guarded in monthly turns by the United States of America, France, the United Kingdom and the Soviet Union. The Commission observed that the exercise of authority by the United Kingdom took place outside its territory, in Berlin, but was of the opinion that 'there [was] in principle, from a legal point of view, no reason why acts of the British authorities in Berlin should not entail the liability of the United Kingdom under the Convention'.[720]

The applicants in *Vearncombe and Others v. the United Kingdom and the Federal Republic of Germany*[721] were the owners and inhabitants of dwellings situated close to a firing range in the British zone of West Berlin built and operated by the British Army. Relying on Articles 8 of the Convention and 1 of Protocol No. 1 they complained of the noise, and relying on Article 13 they complained that the remedy available was ineffective.

The Commission noted that

---

720  *Hess v. the United Kingdom*, no. 6231/73, Commission decision of 28 May 1975.

721  *Vearncombe and Others v. the United Kingdom and the Federal Republic of Germany*, no. 12816/87, D.R. No. 59, p. 186; see also Magdalena Jankowska-Gilberg, *Extraterritorialität der Menschenrechte: Der Begriff der Jurisdiktion im Sinne von Art. 1 EMRK* (diss. Regensburg 2007), Nomos, 2008, p. 68.

TYPOLOGY OF ARTICLE 1 JURISDICTION IN 'HARD POWER' SITUATIONS 207

... under the existing regulations in the Allied Kommandatura Law German authorities do not exercise any control with regard to the Forces of the Allied Powers in Berlin nor do German courts exercise criminal or civil jurisdiction over the Allied Forces, except when expressly authorised by the Allied Kommandatura or the appropriate Sector Commandant.

The shooting range in question is not only used exclusively by the British Army but it was also constructed entirely under the control of the British Military Government. Although the German authorities in Berlin were informed of the plans for constructing the range and certain consultations took place between British and German authorities, the responsibility for the construction and/or use of the range lies solely with the British Military Government.

With regard to Germany, the application was therefore inadmissible *ratione personae*.

With regard to the United Kingdom, the Commission noted that, unlike in the *Hess* case, the responsibility of the other Occupying Powers was not in issue. Nonetheless it declined to express itself on whether the United Kingdom had Article 1 jurisdiction in the matter because the application was in any event inadmissible on unrelated grounds.

### 6.4.2 *Maintaining a Proxy Government on Foreign Territory*

6.4.2.1 Northern Cyprus (Turkey)

In 1983 the occupied territory declared independence as the 'Turkish Republic of Northern Cyprus' in a move condemned as unlawful secession by, among others, the United Nations Security Council and the Committee of Ministers of the Council of Europe, both of which continue to regard the government of the republic of Cyprus as the sole legitimate government of the island state.[722] To date, the Republic of Turkey remains the only state to recognise the 'TRNC' as a state in its own right.

Turkey sought to argue that far from being a 'puppet' State, the 'TRNC' was a democratic constitutional State with impeccable democratic features and credentials. Basic rights were effectively guaranteed and there were free elections. It followed that the exercise of public authority in the 'TRNC' was not imputable to Turkey. The fact that this State had not been recognised by the international community was not of any relevance in this context.

---

722    United Nations Security Council Resolutions 541 (1983), 18 November 1983; 550 (1984), 11 May 1984; see *Loizidou v. Turkey* (merits), 18 December 1996, §§ 19-23, Reports 1996-VI.

In *Loizidou v. Turkey (preliminary objections)*, the Court answered this argument in the following terms:

> It is not necessary to determine whether, as the applicant and the Government of Cyprus have suggested, Turkey actually exercises detailed control over the policies and actions of the authorities of the "TRNC". It is obvious from the large number of troops engaged in active duties in northern Cyprus ... that her army exercises effective overall control over that part of the island. Such control, according to the relevant test and in the circumstances of the case, entails her responsibility for the policies and actions of the "TRNC" ... Those affected by such policies or actions therefore come within the "jurisdiction" of Turkey for the purposes of Article 1 of the Convention. Her obligation to secure to the applicant the rights and freedoms set out in the Convention therefore extends to the northern part of Cyprus.[723]

In the *Cyprus v. Turkey* interstate judgment, the Court added the following:

> 77. It is of course true that the Court in the *Loizidou* case was addressing an individual's complaint concerning the continuing refusal of the authorities to allow her access to her property. However, it is to be observed that the Court's reasoning is framed in terms of a broad statement of principle as regards Turkey's general responsibility under the Convention for the policies and actions of the "TRNC" authorities. Having effective overall control over northern Cyprus, its responsibility cannot be confined to the acts of its own soldiers or officials in northern Cyprus but must also be engaged by virtue of the acts of the local administration which survives by virtue of Turkish military and other support. It follows that, in terms of Article 1 of the Convention, Turkey's "jurisdiction" must be considered to extend to securing the entire range of substantive rights set out in the Convention and those additional Protocols which she has ratified, and that violations of those rights are imputable to Turkey.
>
> 78. In the above connection, the Court must have regard to the special character of the Convention as an instrument of European public order (*ordre public*) for the protection of individual human beings and its mission, as set out in Article 19 of the Convention, "to ensure the observance of the engagements undertaken by the High Contracting Parties" (see the *Loizidou* judgment (*preliminary objections*) cited above, p. 31, § 93).

---

723     *Loizidou v. Turkey* (preliminary objections), 23 March 1995, § 56, Series A no. 310.

Having regard to the applicant Government's continuing inability to exercise their Convention obligations in northern Cyprus, any other finding would result in a regrettable vacuum in the system of human-rights protection in the territory in question by removing from individuals there the benefit of the Convention's fundamental safeguards and their right to call a High Contracting Party to account for violation of their rights in proceedings before the Court.[724]

There have been many cases brought against Turkey in relation to the acts of its agents in Northern Cyprus. Some, like *Loizidou* and the interstate case *Cyprus v. Turkey*, primarily raise issues of property rights and access by displaced persons to their former homes. Others raise issues under Article 2. Thus, in *Solomou v. Turkey* we see a Greek Cypriot protester who has managed to enter the buffer zone between the 'TRNC' and Cyprus proper across the barbed-wire barrier being shot by a Turkish or Turkish Cypriot soldier while trying to take down a Turkish flag.[725]

In *Djavit An v. Turkey* the applicant was a Cypriot national of Turkish Cypriot ethnicity, a member of a movement set up to create peace between the island's two communities, who was denied permission to enter the 'TRNC' to meet like-minded opposite numbers. The Court found a violation of Articles 10 and 11.[726] Indeed there can be little doubt that a State using a proxy government to monitor persons entering the territory under its control is exercising 'jurisdiction' in every sense of the word.

6.4.2.2     Transdniestria (Russia)

In all of the judgments concerning the Trandsniestrian territory – *Ilaşcu and Others, Ivanţoc and Others, Catan and Others* and *Mozer*, mentioned above – Russia is cited as respondent in addition to Moldova.

As we have seen, when Moldova declared independence from the Soviet Union there was a Soviet army in place that transmogrified *in situ* into an operational group of the Russian army and never left. As the Court has found, the separatist government of the 'MRT' has been allowed to survive thanks to Russian economic and political assistance and the continued Russian military presence on Transdniestrian territory.

In the Court's own words:

---

724    *Cyprus v. Turkey* (merits) [GC], no. 25781/94, §§ 77-78, ECHR 2001-IV.
725    *Solomou v. Turkey, no.* 36832/97, 24 June 2008.
726    *Djavit An v. Turkey*, no. 20652/92, ECHR 2003-III.

210 CHAPTER 6

In the light of all these circumstances, the Court considers that the Russian Federation's responsibility is engaged in respect of the unlawful acts committed by the Transdniestrian separatists, regard being had to the military and political support it gave them to help them set up the separatist regime and the participation of its military personnel in the fighting. In acting thus, the authorities of the Russian Federation contributed both militarily and politically to the creation of a separatist regime in the region of Transdniestria, which is part of the territory of the Republic of Moldova.

The Court also notes that even after the ceasefire agreement of 21 July 1992 the Russian Federation continued to provide military, political and economic support to the separatist regime (…), thus enabling it to survive by strengthening itself and by acquiring a certain amount of autonomy *vis-à-vis* Moldova.[727]

This is in its essentials the application of the reasoning set out in *Loizidou v. Turkey (preliminary objections)*.

### 6.4.2.3 Nagorno-Karabakh (Armenia)

We have seen above that following the dissolution of the Soviet Union war broke out between Armenia and Azerbaijan centred on Nagorno-Karabakh, the area within the territory of Azerbaijan inhabited by ethnic Armenians. The breakaway 'Nagorno-Karabakh Republic' (or 'NKR') now controls some 95% of the original Nagorno-Karabakh oblast as well as a land corridor joining it to the Republic of Armenia. Displaced persons, overwhelmingly Azerbaijani nationals, number in the hundreds of thousands.

The application in *Chiragov and Others v. Armenia*[728] was brought by six Azerbaijani nationals. They were among the many displaced from the Lachin district, which had become part of the land corridor linking the 'NKR' with Armenia proper. They obtained from the Court a judgment finding them to be victims of violations of Article 1 of Protocol No. 1 to the Convention and Article 8 of the Convention itself in that they had been denied the possibility to regain control of their former homes.

The type and level of support given by Armenia to the 'NKR' was disputed. The Court found, on the evidence available (which included reports by NGOs such as Human Rights Watch and the International Crisis Group as well as

---

727  *Ilaşcu and Others*, § 382.
728  *Chiragov and Others v. Armenia* (dec.) (GC), no. 13216/05, 14 December 2011; *Chiragov and Others v. Armenia, (merits)* [GC], no. 13216/05, 16 June 2015.

TYPOLOGY OF ARTICLE 1 JURISDICTION IN 'HARD POWER' SITUATIONS    211

United Nations Security Council resolutions, a treaty setting up a military alliance between the Republic of Armenia and the 'NKR' and most strikingly, statements by an Armenian minister of defence and the incumbent Armenian president), that Armenian military support had been and continued to be 'decisive for the conquest of and continued control over the territories in issue, and the evidence, not the least the 1994 military co-operation agreement, convincingly shows that the armed forces of Armenia and the 'NKR' [were] highly integrated'.[729] Other support offered to the 'NKR' by Armenia included financial support, both public and private; political support; the adoption in the 'NKR' of Armenian legislation and 'the operation of Armenian law enforcement agents and the exercise of jurisdiction by Armenian courts on that territory'.[730]

### 6.4.3    *Air Attack on Foreign Territory*

6.4.3.1    European NATO Members in the Federal Republic of Yugoslavia
6.4.3.1.1    Banković and Others
In March 1999 the North Atlantic Council, the political decision-making body of NATO, decided – unanimously, as it always does – to carry out air strikes against the Federal Republic of Yugoslavia (consisting of Serbia and Montenegro) in order to back up demands of the international community for Kosovo to be granted autonomy. Among the targets was Radio Televizije Srbije ('RTS'), the Serbian state radio and television station, which was later stated by NATO to be a 'dual use' target used both for civilian communication and for purposes of military command and control.

The building was hit by a missile launched from a NATO aircraft on 23 April 1999 at 2.20 a.m. Sixteen persons were killed and another sixteen were seriously injured. Human Rights Watch later reported that the attack had been planned for an earlier date but postponed because of disagreement between the American and French governments regarding the legality and legitimacy of the target.[731]

A 'Committee Established to Review the NATO Bombing Campaign Against the Federal Republic of Yugoslavia', set up to report to the ICTY Prosecutor on questions of legality, found that during the entire air campaign NATO aircraft flew 38,400 sorties, including 10,484 strike sorties, releasing 23,614 munitions.

---

729    *Chiragov and Others (merits)*, §§ 173-180.
730    *Chiragov and Others (merits)*, §§ 181-185.
731    Human Rights Watch, *The Crisis in Kosovo*, http://www.hrw.org/reports/2000/nato/Natbm200-01.htm (retrieved on 5 July 2015).

Comparing these figures with the total number of civilian killed – approximately 500 in total – the Committee considered that

> These figures [did] not indicate that NATO [might] have conducted a campaign aimed at causing substantial civilian casualties either directly or indirectly[732]

NATO later alleged that it made 'every possible effort' to avoid civilian casualties and collateral damage. Timing the attack on the RTS station in the middle of the night, when presumably most civilian personnel would normally be at home in bed, would be consistent with such an aim, although doubts were expressed as to whether NATO had done enough to give advance warning of it.[733]

The Committee concluded that the number of civilian casualties caused by the attack on the RTS station 'were unfortunately high but [did] not appear to be clearly disproportionate'.[734]

In the case brought before the Court against the European NATO member States, which came to be known as *Banković and Others v. Belgium and Others*,[735] the applicants were one direct victim who had been injured in the attack and the surviving kin of three of the people killed. They alleged violations of Articles 2, 10 and 13 of the Convention.

As relevant to this study, the applicants argued from the case-law developed in *Loizidou* and *Cyprus v. Turkey*[736] that jurisdiction followed from 'effective control'. Admittedly the level of control exercised by means of an air strike was not the same as that exercised by Turkey in northern Cyprus, but States that struck a target outside their territory could be held accountable under the Convention for those Convention rights within their control in the situation in question.[737] They further submitted that air attack constituted acts of State that might produce effects in the territory of another State and in that respect similar to the deportation or extradition of aliens to a foreign country

---

732 Final Report to the Prosecutor by the Committee Established to Review the NATO Bombing Campaign Against the Federal Republic of Yugoslavia, § 54. Available from ICTY's web site, http://www.icty.org/x/file/Press/nato061300.pdf (accessed on 20 August 2017).

733 Final Report to the Prosecutor, para. 77. See also Paolo Benvenuti, "The ICTY Prosecutor and the Review of the NATO Bombing Campaign against the Federal Republic of Yugoslavia", in *EJIL* (2001), Vol. 12 No. 3, 503-529, at p. 523.

734 Final Report to the Prosecutor, *ibid.*

735 *Banković and Others v. Belgium, the Czech Republic, Denmark, France, Germany, Greece, Hungary, Iceland, Italy, Luxembourg, the Netherlands, Norway, Poland, Portugal, Spain, Turkey and the United Kingdom* (GC) (dec.), no. 52207/99, ECHR 2001-XII.

736 Footnotes 723 and 724 above.

737 *Banković and Others*, §§ 47-48 and observations of the applicants, §§ 78-80.

TYPOLOGY OF ARTICLE 1 JURISDICTION IN 'HARD POWER' SITUATIONS       213

in which they might be at risk of ill-treatment.[738] The decision-making process that had led to the attack was comparable to acts of diplomatic agents of the State, which also produced extraterritorial effects;[739] and the attack itself had been launched from the land territory of one or more NATO Member States – Italy and elsewhere – and from ships and aircraft that constituted the territory of one or more of such States. Finally, drawing on Article 15 of the Convention, they suggested that that Article would be rendered 'meaningless' if it did not also apply to extra-territorial war or emergencies.[740]

The Governments countered that it was

> ... rather the applicants' novel "cause-and-effect" theory of extra-territorial jurisdiction that would have serious international consequences. Such a theory would, when added to the applicants' assertion concerning the several liability of all respondent States as members of NATO, seriously distort the purpose and scheme of the Convention. In particular, it would have serious consequences for international military collective action as it would render the Court competent to review the participation of Contracting States in military missions all over the world in circumstances when it would be impossible for those States to secure any of the Convention rights to the inhabitants of those territories and even in situations where a Contracting State had no active part in the relevant mission. The resulting Convention exposure would, according to the Governments, risk undermining significantly the States' participation in such missions and would, in any event, result in far more protective derogations under Article 15 of the Convention.[741]

The Court understood the real connection between the applicants and the respondent States to be the 'extraterritorial act' itself; the question was therefore whether the attack itself was sufficient to bring the applicants (and their relatives killed in the attack) within the jurisdiction of those States.[742]

In answering this question, the Court held that

> Article 1 of the Convention must be considered to reflect [the] ordinary and essentially territorial notion of jurisdiction, other bases of jurisdic-

---

738   *Banković and Others*, observations of the applicants, §§ 71-84.
739   *Banković and Others*, observations of the applicants, §§ 85-87.
740   *Banković and Others*, § 49.
741   *Banković and Others*, § 43.
742   *Banković and Others*, § 54.

tion being exceptional and requiring special justification in the particular circumstances of each case.[743]

State practice was 'indicative of a lack of any apprehension on the part of the Contracting States of their extra-territorial responsibility in contexts similar to the present case': although there had been a number of military missions involving Convention States acting extra-territorially, no State '[had] indicated a belief that its extra-territorial actions involved an exercise of jurisdiction within the meaning of Article 1 of the Convention by making a derogation pursuant to Article 15 of the Convention'; all Article 15 derogations made until them having related to 'internal conflicts' (in south-east Turkey and Northern Ireland), there was no basis to accept the applicants' suggestion that Article 15 covered all 'war' and 'public emergency' situations wherever they might arise.[744]

With regard to the arguments drawn from *Loizidou* and *Cyprus v. Turkey*, the Court held that

> the case-law of the Court demonstrates that its recognition of the exercise of extra-territorial jurisdiction by a Contracting State is exceptional: it has done so [i.e. given such recognition] when the respondent State, through the effective control of the relevant territory and its inhabitants abroad as a consequence of military occupation or through the consent, invitation or acquiescence of the Government of that territory, exercises all or some of the public powers normally to be exercised by that Government.[745]

The fact of the attack itself was not sufficient to bring the applicants and their relatives killed by it within the Article 1 jurisdiction of the respondent States. The suggestion that 'anyone adversely affected by an act imputable to a Contracting State, wherever in the world that act [might] have been committed or its consequences felt, [was] thereby brought within the jurisdiction of that State for the purpose of Article 1 of the Convention'[746] was not supported by the text of Article 1. Even the applicants' suggestion that the positive obligation in Article 1 to secure the rights and freedoms defined in Section I of the Convention could be 'divided and tailored in accordance with the particular circumstances of the extra-territorial act in question' failed to sway the Court:

---

743  *Banković and Others*, § 61 (references omitted).
744  *Banković and Others*, § 62.
745  *Banković and Others*, § 71.
746  Also referred to as the 'cause and effect' theory of extraterritorial jurisdiction.

# TYPOLOGY OF ARTICLE 1 JURISDICTION IN 'HARD POWER' SITUATIONS    215

if the drafters of the Convention had wished to ensure jurisdiction as extensive as that advocated by the applicants, they could have adopted a text the same as or similar to the contemporaneous Articles 1 of the four Geneva Conventions of 1949 – which demand respect 'in all circumstances'.[747]

It was true that in *Cyprus v. Turkey* the Court had recognised the need to avoid 'a regrettable vacuum' in the protection offered by the Convention in northern Cyprus, but this related to an entirely different situation: Cyprus was a Party to the Convention, and prevented by the 'effective control' exercised by Turkey from meeting its Convention obligations throughout its territory. In summary,

> [t]he Convention is a multi-lateral treaty operating, subject to Article 56 of the Convention, in an essentially regional context and notably in the legal space (*espace juridique*) of the Contracting States. The FRY clearly does not fall within this legal space. The Convention was not designed to be applied throughout the world, even in respect of the conduct of Contracting States. Accordingly, the desirability of avoiding a gap or vacuum in human rights' protection has so far been relied on by the Court in favour of establishing jurisdiction only when the territory in question was one that, but for the specific circumstances, would normally be covered by the Convention.[748]

The decision has been criticised in academic writing.[749] Much of the criticism has in the meantime been overtaken by subsequent case-law developments on the extraterritorial exercise of Article 1 jurisdiction; it would stretch the scope of this study too far to go into the detail of it. Let us nonetheless consider a few.

---

747    *Banković and Others*, § 75.

748    *Banković and Others*, § 80.

749    See, for example, Matthew Happold, "Banković v. Belgium and the territorial scope of the European Convention on Human Rights", in *Human Rights law Review 2003*, Volume 3, Number 1, pap. 77-90; Rick Lawson, "Life after Banković: On the Extraterritorial Application of the European Convention on Human Rights", in *Extraterritorial Application of Human Rights Treaties* (Fons Coomans and Menno T. Kamminga, eds.), Intersentia, 2004, pp. 83 *et seq.*; Federico Sperotto, "Beyond Banković: Extraterritorial Application of the European Convention on Human Rights", Human Rights & Human Welfare, working paper no. 38, 13 November 2006; Magdalena Jankowska-Gilberg, *Extraterritorialität der Menschenrechte: Der Begriff der Jurisdiktion im Sinne von Art. 1 EMRK* (diss. Regensburg 2007), Nomos, 2008, pp. 42-63; Nienke van der Have, *The prevention of gross human rights violations under international human rights law* (diss. Amsterdam 2017), pp. 100-101 (describing the decision as an "infamous judgment").

Happold, for example, is typical of those who argue that the very fact of causing harm through military action ought to have induced the Court to find Article 1 jurisdiction established. He points out, correctly *per se*, that the extraterritorial exercise of jurisdiction engages the responsibility of a State whether or not it is legal – pointing to *Loizidou* as an example of Article 1 jurisdiction arising from 'effective control' – then turns to the quite different issue of State agent control over the individual and boldly states that 'whether in any given situation a Contracting Party is exercising jurisdiction over an individual is a question of fact, not of law'.[750] This appears to be based on a misunderstanding of *Loizidou*: it is the *effectiveness* of the control *over an area* exercised by a Contracting Party that is a question of fact, not of law.[751] If control is effective, it can amount to the exercise of jurisdiction – but that is not a necessary corollary.

Lawson makes a different argument, for which he points to Article 2 of the International Law Commission's Articles on State Responsibility for Internationally Wrongful Acts. He would have expected the Court to follow the order in which that Draft Article sets out the elements of State responsibility and query first whether the bombing attack was attributable to the respondent States, and only then whether it was in breach of these states' international obligations.[752] This is opposed by Michael O'Boyle, the Deputy Registrar of the Court at that time, who counters that the logic of the Convention is actually the opposite precisely because the existence of jurisdiction is a precondition for the existence of an international obligation.[753]

Some authors simply disagree with the outcome, which they dismiss as politically motivated. Sperotto, for example, calls the *Banković* decision a 'clear symptom of the States' tendency to subordinate human rights protection to political interests or opportunities' and calls on the Court to 'dismiss State practice, when it appears clearly inconsistent with fundamental human

---

750    Happold, p. 87.

751    See *Al-Skeini*, § 132, second sentence: "In each case, the question whether exceptional circumstances exist which require and justify a finding by the Court that the State was exercising jurisdiction extraterritorially must be determined with reference to the particular facts."

752    Rick Lawson, *Life After Banković* , *passim*.

753    Michael O'Boyle, "The European Convention on Human Rights and Extraterritorial Jurisdiction: A Comment on Life After Banković", in *Extraterritorial Application of Human Rights Treaties*, Fons Coomans and Menno T. Kamminga, eds., Intersentia, 2004, pp. 125-139 at pp. 127 and 131.

TYPOLOGY OF ARTICLE 1 JURISDICTION IN 'HARD POWER' SITUATIONS 217

rights'.[754] Lawson suggests that the Court was unwilling to be drawn into politically sensitive discussions on remote conflicts.[755] The fact is that the governments' argument based on the possible international political repercussions of any finding that they had Article 1 jurisdiction was not answered by the Court, which was able to declare the application inadmissible on other grounds.

Ultimately the decision in *Banković* rests on the findings, firstly, that the European NATO members did not exercise 'effective authority and control' over Belgrade, nor intended to; and secondly, that they neither did nor intended to wield legislative, judicial or executive power over the individuals unfortunate enough to be hit in the attack.[756] In other words, what was lacking was the intent on the part of the European NATO members to bend any individuals to their will – that is, the *assertion* of jurisdiction over individuals.

### 6.4.3.1.2 Markovic and Others

In a separate development, a different group of citizens of Serbia and Montenegro brought joint and several civil claims in the Italian domestic courts against the Command of NATO's Allied Forces in Southern Europe (AFSOUTH) and against the Prime Minister's Office and the Ministry of Defence, basing their claim on the fact that the aircraft that had bombed the Belgrade and the RTS television station had taken off from air bases located in Italian territory. The proceedings against AFSOUTH were discontinued by the applicants after NATO invoked the immunity of its headquarters.[757] Those against the Italian Prime Minister's Office and Ministry of Defence ended in a preliminary ruling of the Italian Court of Cassation finding that the applicants' claims were based on alleged violations of public international law which were not reviewable by the Italian domestic courts.

In their application to the Court, the applicants argued that there had been violation of Articles 1, 2, 10 and 17 of the Convention as a result of the actual attack, and of Articles 6 and 13 taken together with Article 1 in that the Court of Cassation had blocked their civil claim for damages.

---

754    Federico Sperotto, "Beyond Banković: Extraterritorial application of the European Convention on Human Rights", in East European Human Rights Review 2008, Vol. 14, No. 1, pp. 131-152 at p. 145.

755    Rick Lawson, *Life after Banković*, p. 116.

756    In the same sense, Eric Pouw, *International Human Rights Law and the Law of Armed Conflict in the Context of Counterinsurgency – With a Particular Focus on Targeting and Operational Detention* (diss. UvA 2013), pp. 158-59.

757    Article VIII § 5 of the NATO Status of Forces Agreement, 19 June 1951.

218 CHAPTER 6

The Court gave a separate decision on admissibility[758] in which it declared the complaints under Articles 1, 2, 10 and 17 inadmissible in view of the *Banković* precedent. The fact that the applicants had brought their case before the Italian courts was not sufficient distinction.

What remained was the applicants' complaint under Articles 6 and 13, taken together with Article 1. The Court redefined this as a complaint concerning the right of access to a court as guaranteed by Article 6 of the Convention, taken together with Article 1.

In the proceedings on the merits, the Italian Government submitted a preliminary objection that the matters complained of fell outside Italy's Article 1 jurisdiction. This was easily disposed of:

> 54. Even though the extraterritorial nature of the events alleged to have been at the origin of an action may have an effect on the applicability of Article 6 and the final outcome of the proceedings, it cannot under any circumstances affect the jurisdiction *ratione loci* and *ratione personae* of the State concerned. If civil proceedings are brought in the domestic courts, the State is required by Article 1 of the Convention to secure in those proceedings respect for the rights protected by Article 6.
>
> The Court considers that, once a person brings a civil action in the courts or tribunals of a State, there indisputably exists, without prejudice to the outcome of the proceedings, a "jurisdictional link" for the purposes of Article 1.
>
> 55. he Court notes that the applicants in the instant case brought an action in the Italian civil courts. Consequently, it finds that a "jurisdictional link" existed between them and the Italian State.'[759]

The Italian Government then sought to argue that the applicants' claim was one to which Article 6 did not apply.

The Court disagreed:

> 101. The Court ... considers that there was from the start of the proceedings a genuine and serious dispute over the existence of the right to which the applicants claimed to be entitled under the civil law. The respondent Government's argument that there was no arguable (civil) right for the purposes of Article 6 because of the Court of Cassation's decision that, as an act of war, the impugned act was not amenable to judicial review,

---

758    *Markovic and Others v. Italy* (dec.), no. 1398/03, 12 June 2003.
759    *Markovic and Others*, §§ 54-55.

TYPOLOGY OF ARTICLE 1 JURISDICTION IN 'HARD POWER' SITUATIONS 219

can be of relevance only to future allegations by other complainants. The Court of Cassation's judgment did not make the applicants' complaints retrospectively unarguable (see *Z and Others v. the United Kingdom* ([GC], no. 29392/95, § 89, ECHR 2001-V). In these circumstances, the Court finds that the applicants had, on at least arguable grounds, a claim under domestic law.'[760]

An arguable 'claim' there might be. However, a 'right' to compensation that could be said, at least on arguable grounds, to be recognised in domestic law was a different matter:

> 113. The Court does not accept the applicants' assertion that the impugned decision constituted an immunity, either de facto or in practice, because of its allegedly absolute or general nature. As the respondent Government rightly noted, the decision concerned only one aspect of the right to bring an action against the State, this being the right to claim damages for an act of government related to an act of war, and cannot be regarded as an arbitrary removal of the courts' jurisdiction to determine a whole range of civil claims (see [*Fayed v. the United Kingdom* (21 September 1994, § 65, Series A no. 294-B]). As was pointed out by the British Government and as the Court observed in paragraph 93 above, it is a principle of Convention case-law that Article 6 does not in itself guarantee any particular content for civil rights and obligations in national law. It is not enough to bring Article 6 § 1 into play that the non-existence of a cause of action under domestic law may be described as having the same effect as an immunity, in the sense of not enabling the applicant to sue for a given category of harm (see *Z and Others v. the United Kingdom*, cited above, § 98).
>
> 114. The Court considers that the Court of Cassation's ruling in the present case does not amount to recognition of an immunity but is merely indicative of the extent of the courts' powers of review of acts of foreign policy such as acts of war. It comes to the conclusion that the applicants' inability to sue the State was the result not of an immunity but of the principles governing the substantive right of action in domestic law. At the relevant time, the position under the domestic case-law was such as to exclude in this type of case any possibility of the State being held liable. There was, therefore, no limitation on access to a court of the kind

---

760 *Markovic and Others*, § 101.

220 CHAPTER 6

in issue in [*Ashingdane v. the United Kingdom*, 28 May 1985, § 57, Series A no. 93][761]

– and consequently no violation of Article 6.

### 6.4.4 *Incursion into Foreign Territory*

6.4.4.1 Turkey in Northern Iraq[762]

In March and April 1995 Turkish troops carried out military operations in Northern Iraq for the purpose of pursuing and eliminating terrorists who were seeking shelter there. The applicants were, variously, wives and mothers of men allegedly last seen in the custody of Turkish soldiers and later found dead. Turkey, for its part, acknowledged the presence of its troops in the area at that time but denied all knowledge of the capture of the applicants' husbands and sons or of their fate.

After restating the principles developed in *Banković and Others, Ilaşcu and Others* and *Assanidze*, the Court made the following statement of principle:

> ... [A] State may also be held accountable for violation of the Convention rights and freedoms of persons who are in the territory of another State but who are found to be under the former State's authority and control through its agents operating – whether lawfully or unlawfully – in the latter State (see, *mutatis mutandis, M. v. Denmark*, application no. 173 92/90, Commission decision of 14 October 1992, DR 73, p. 193; *Illich Sanchez Ramirez v. France*, application no. 28780/95, Commission decision of 24 June 1996, DR 86, p. 155; *Coard et al. v. the United States*, the Inter-American Commission of Human Rights decision of 29 September 1999, Report No. 109/99, case No. 10.951, §§ 37, 39, 41 and 43; and the views adopted by the Human Rights Committee on 29 July 1981 in the cases of *Lopez Burgos v. Uruguay* and *Celiberti de Casariego v. Uruguay*, nos. 52/1979 and 56/1979, at §§ 12.3 and 10.3 respectively). Accountability in such situations stems from the fact that Article 1 of the Convention cannot be interpreted so as to allow a State party to perpetrate violations of the Convention on the territory of another State, which it could not perpetrate on its own territory (*ibid.*).[763]

---

761 *Markovic and Others*, §§ 113-14.
762 *Issa and Others v. Turkey*, no. 31821/96, 16 November 2004.
763 *Issa and Others*, § 71.

TYPOLOGY OF ARTICLE 1 JURISDICTION IN 'HARD POWER' SITUATIONS    221

This, however, was a case that hinged on its facts. The Court defined the essential question as whether at the relevant time Turkish troops conducted operations in the area where the killings took place. Doubt in this respect arose from the absence of any information identifying the soldiers seen as Turkish, such as a description of their uniforms. In the absence of proof 'beyond a reasonable doubt', faced with the Turkish denial and given that the area had been the scene of fierce fighting by Kurdish factions, the Court could not find it established that the men had been within the jurisdiction of Turkey for the purposes of Article 1 of the Convention.[764]

The above-quoted paragraph of *Issa* has often been cited by authors critical of the restrictive approach taken by the Court in respect of the 'cause-and-effect' view of extraterritorial jurisdiction. At this point, however, it must be recognised that that paragraph – taken from a judgment delivered in 2004 by a Chamber – is no longer good law in so far as it purports to extend beyond *Banković*. As Clare Ovey correctly points out, in *Al-Skeini* (a judgment delivered in 2011 and now universally considered leading) the Grand Chamber did not endorse the reasoning set out in *Issa*: instead, it resumed the narrower understanding of State agent authority and control given in *Banković* (as indeed it later did in *Jaloud*) according to which there has to be some prior exertion of State agent authority and control, such as an arrest or detention, for Article 1 jurisdiction to be established.[765] The citation of *Issa* in paragraph 136 of *Al-Skeini*, which includes the qualification 'had it been established that Turkish soldiers had taken the applicants' relatives into custody in northern Iraq, taken them to a nearby cave and executed them', is not inconsistent with this interpretation.

6.4.4.2    Turkey in Northern Iran?
A curious decision is *Pad and Others v. Turkey*.[766] The application was brought by the surviving kin of a group of seven Iranian nationals killed by Turkish armed forces close to the border between Turkey and Iran. The facts, as so often in cases of this nature, were disputed: the applicants claimed that the seven men had gone to look for 'wild vegetables and fruit, such as mushrooms and rhubarb', while the defending government had sent its military to go looking for a 'terrorist group' with arms and equipment.

---

764    *Issa and Others*, §§ 72-81.
765    Clare Ovey, "Application of the ECHR during International Armed Conflicts", in *The UK and European Human Rights: A Strained Relationship?* (Katja S. Ziegler, Elizabeth Wicks and Loveday Hodson, eds.), Hart Publishing, 2015, pp. 225-245 at p. 230.
766    *Pad and Others v. Turkey* (dec.), no. 60167/00, 28 June 2007.

The applicants, relying on *Issa v. Turkey*, argued that the events complained of had occurred within the extraterritorial jurisdiction of Turkey. The Turkish Government 'vigorously denied' having carried out a cross-border operation in Iran, claiming instead that the seven men had been intercepted on Turkish territory after having illegally crossed the border. Ultimately, the Court held that it was 'not required to determine the exact location of the impugned events, given that the Government had already admitted that the fire discharged from the helicopters had caused the killing of the applicants' relatives, who had been suspected of being terrorists'[767] – an unnecessary confession on the part of the respondent government and an unnecessary finding for the Court to make, since in any event the domestic remedies had not been exhausted.

The *Pad and Others* decision has been understood, even welcomed, as the beginning of a reversal of the *Banković* case-law.[768] It is submitted that *Pad and Others* is not that, and it is certainly not the 'outright rebellion' claimed by at least one author;[769] this case stands on its own. Jurisdiction is not contested but is actually recognised by the respondent, though on its own stated facts and on its own terms; if the events complained of had occurred unambiguously on the Iranian side of the border, who can say whether the Turkish Government would have conceded the jurisdiction point so easily, and how the arguments of the parties might have differed from *Issa*?

### 6.4.4.3 Turkey in the Northern Cyprus Buffer Zone

There were no such doubts in the case of *Isaak v. Turkey*. The death in issue in that case was witnessed by many, including UNFICYP personnel, and captured on photograph and film. The case was the subject of reports by UNFICYP and the Secretary General of the United Nations.

---

767    *Pad and Others*, § 54.

768    Rick Lawson, *Really out of sight? Issues of Jurisdiction and Control in Situations of Armed Conflict under the ECHR*, in *Margins of Conflict: The ECHR and Transitions to and from Armed Conflict* (Antoine Buyse, ed.), Intersentia, 2011, pp. 57-76, at pp. 65-66; Marco Sassòli, "The Role of Human Rights and International Humanitarian Law in New Types of Armed Conflicts", in Orna Ben-Naftali (ed.), *International Humanitarian Law and International Human Rights Law: Pas de Deux*, Collected Courses of the Academy of European Law vol. XIX/1, Oxford University Press 2011, pp. 34-94 at p. 65; Louise Doswald-Beck, *Human Rights in Times of Conflict and Terrorism* (Oxford University Press 2011) p. 21; Eric Pouw, *International Human Rights Law and the Law of Armed Conflict in the Context of Counterinsurgency - With a Particular Focus on Targeting and Operational Detention* (diss. UvA 2013), p. 159.

769    Rick Lawson, "The Extra-Territorial Application of the European Convention on Human Rights," *European Yearbook of International Law* 2011, pp. 427-444 at p. 435.

TYPOLOGY OF ARTICLE 1 JURISDICTION IN 'HARD POWER' SITUATIONS 223

The victim was a protester who entered the United Nations buffer zone between the TRNC and the Government-controlled Cyprus – a demilitarized area policed by UNFICYP. He was pounced upon and beaten to death by a group later found to have included Turkish or TRNC soldiers. The Court found the events to come within the Article 1 jurisdiction of Turkey.[770]

### 6.4.5 *Exercise of Jurisdiction in Foreign Territorial Waters*

One case has thus far reached the Court concerning pirates captured at sea, *Hassan and Others v. France.*[771] The pirates had taken a sailing yacht and her crew off the Somalian coast and anchored in Somalian territorial waters. They were attacked by French naval forces who liberated the crew of the yacht, killing one pirate and taking six others prisoner. The international legal basis was Security Council Resolution 1816 (2008), in which the Security Council, acting under Chapter VII of the United Nations Charter, authorised States taking part in anti-piracy operations off Somalia to

> (a) Enter the territorial waters of Somalia for the purpose of repressing acts of piracy and armed robbery at sea, in a manner consistent with such action permitted on the high seas with respect to piracy under relevant international law;
> and
> (b) Use, within the territorial waters of Somalia, in a manner consistent with action permitted on the high seas with respect to piracy under relevant international law, all necessary means to repress acts of piracy and armed robbery

– which had the effect of rendering Articles 100-107 of UNCLOS, which ordinarily apply only on the high seas or 'in a place outside the jurisdiction of any State',[772] applicable by analogy to the Somalian territorial sea.[773]

---

770  *Isaak v. Turkey*, no. 44587/98, 24 June 2008.

771  *Hassan and Others v. France*, nos. 46695/10 and 54588/10, 4 December 2014.

772  Article 101 (a) (i) and (ii), respectively, of UNCLOS.

773  S/RES/1816 (2008) of 2 June 2008, para. 7. See also Tullio Treves and Cesare Pitea, "Piracy, International Law and Human Rights", in *The Frontiers of Human Rights: Extraterritoriality and its Challenges, Collected Courses of the Academy of European Law*, vol. XXIV/1, pp. 89-126 at p. 101. For an overview of the international law and practice governing the combating of Somali piracy in particular, see Tamsin Philippa Paige, "The Impact and Effectiveness of UNCLOS on Counter-piracy Operations", in *Journal of Conflict & Security Law* (2017), Vol. 22 No. 1, pp. 97-123.

224                                                                    CHAPTER 6

In the ensuing proceedings, the Court found that the Security Council resolution constituted an adequate legal basis for the pirates' arrest,[774] but that the lack of any legal provision for their subsequent detention or for any judicial control thereof violated Article 5 §§ 1 and 3.[775] In the light of the above-mentioned *Medvyedyev and Others* judgment, the French Government did not deny that France had jurisdiction from the moment the pirates were under the control of the French armed forces.[776]

It is clear that ensuring swift review of the lawfulness of the arrest and detention of persons taken at sea presents problems of a practical nature, but other Convention States have proved equal to these. When, in 2010, twenty suspected Somalian pirates were captured in the Gulf of Aden by a Dutch naval vessel, judges and a prosecutor of the first-instance criminal court in Rotterdam were flown out to hold hearings *in camera* on board. Of the twenty, fifteen were released as there was insufficient evidence to charge them and five were placed in detention on remand before being sent for trial in the Netherlands.[777]

### 6.4.6    *Targeted Killing Abroad*
6.4.6.1        Shot Fired across the Border

In 1996 Greek Cypriots demonstrating against the Turkish presence in Cyprus on the Greek Cypriot side of the ceasefire line were fired on from the 'TRNC' side. One demonstrator, the applicant, was wounded by a bullet in the abdomen.

After restating the principles set out in case-law including *Banković and Others* and *Issa*, the Court came to the following conclusion on Article 1 jurisdiction:

> The Court reiterates that, in exceptional circumstances, the acts of Contracting States which produce effects outside their territory and over which they exercise no control or authority may amount to the exercise by them of jurisdiction within the meaning of Article 1 of the Convention. The Court notes that, according to UNFICYP's press release and

---

774    *Hassan and Others*, §§ 61-68.

775    *Hassan and Others*, §§ 69-72 and 86-104.

776    *Hassan and Others*, § 39. Compare also *Vassis and Others v. France*, no. 62736/09, 27 June 2013.

777    *Openbaar ministerie* (Dutch public prosecution service), press release 5 December 2010, *Vijf Somaliërs wegens zeeroof vervolgd*, https://www.om.nl/actueel/nieuwsberichten/@28465/vijf-somaliers/; Dutch Ministry of Defence, press release 8 December 2010 (in English), *The Netherlands picks up 5 Somalis*, https://www.defensie.nl/english/latest/news/2010/12/08/the-netherlands-picks-up-5-somalis (both accessed 23 April 2017).

# TYPOLOGY OF ARTICLE 1 JURISDICTION IN 'HARD POWER' SITUATIONS    225

> the UN Secretary-General's report on the events of 14 August 1996, the applicant's injuries were caused by Turkish and/or Turkish Cypriot uniformed personnel, who fired some 25 to 30 rounds into the crowd. These agents of the State were at the time of opening fire in the territory of the "TRNC". The Court further notes that, when she was hit by the bullet, the applicant was standing outside the neutral UN buffer zone and in close vicinity to the Greek-Cypriot National Guard checkpoint. Unlike the applicants in the *Banković and Others* case (...) she was accordingly within territory covered by the Convention.
>
> In these circumstances, even though the applicant sustained her injuries in territory over which Turkey exercised no control, the opening of fire on the crowd from close range, which was the direct and immediate cause of those injuries, was such that the applicant must be regarded as 'within [the] jurisdiction' of Turkey within the meaning of Article 1 and that the responsibility of the respondent State under the Convention is in consequence engaged.[778]

This line of reasoning seems to ignore the fact that the Turkish exercise of jurisdiction in the 'TRNC' is already extraterritorial. If the case is seen in that way, an easier distinction to be made from *Banković and Others* is that the applicant sustained her wound while in 'territory covered by the Convention' – which, as we have seen in *Cyprus v. Turkey*, is sufficient to bring the Convention into play simply in order that there be no gap in its applicability *ratione loci*. Nonetheless, it is submitted that we have here a clear indication that a targeted attack by a Contracting State on an individual situated in the territory of a foreign State engages the Contracting State's Article 1 jurisdiction.

Three weeks after the *Andreou* decision the Court delivered its judgment in the case of *Solomou v. Turkey*. That case concerned a Greek Cypriot demonstrator who had managed to enter the buffer zone between Cyprus Government-held territory and the 'TRNC' and had shinned up a flagpole to try and remove a flag – a Turkish flag, according to the judgment. His attempt was cut short by rifle fire from within the 'TRNC' that proved lethal.

The Court noted that the area in which the acts complained of took place was partly situated in the neutral UN buffer zone and the flagpole on which the victim had been climbing when he was shot was situated in the 'TNRC' territory. Be that as it might – the judgment does not decide whether the *locus in quo* was in the buffer zone or not – it was beyond dispute that the fatal shots

---

778    *Andreou v. Turkey* (dec.), no. 45653/99, 3 June 2008. The Court delivered its judgment on the merits of the case on 27 October 2009.

had been fired, if not by Turkish forces, then by 'TRNC' forces; the Court therefore considered that 'in any event the deceased was under the authority and/or effective control of the respondent State through its agents'.[779]

Pouw sees the distinction between these cases and *Banković* in terms of the difference between use of force that is not 'collective and depersonalised', but 'selective and individualised'.[780] It is submitted that this is inaccurate. Rather, the difference is between an intended victim and an accidental one as we shall see.

### 6.4.6.2 Drone Attack

Unmanned remotely-piloted aircraft known as 'drones' (the ordinary meaning of the word is a male bee) have been used for military purposes, mostly reconnaissance and surveillance, since the Vietnam War. Many European Governments continue to use them in such a role. Civilian police too have adopted them for surveillance and detection.

Drones have been armed with missiles and used as weapons of war since at least the turn of the century. They are known to have been used for the targeted killing of individuals by the United States, Israel and the United Kingdom outside their own territory. The first reported drone strike appears to have been an American attack on a high-level al-Qaeda meeting in Kabul in November 2001.[781]

In September 2015 the British Prime Minister informed the House of Commons that drones operated by the British Royal Air Force had carried out successful targeted strikes in Syria the month before, killing two British nationals. One of the two Britons was reported to have been planning a terrorist attack in the United Kingdom, the other was stated to have been a cyber-warfare expert. In the words of the Prime Minister, this was 'the first time in modern times that a British asset has been used to conduct a strike in a country where [the United Kingdom was] not involved in a war'. The justification cited was 'the "inherent right of self-defence" contained in the Charter of the United Nations, based on

---

779   *Solomou v. Turkey*, no. 36832/97, §§ 48-50, 24 June 2008.

780   Eric Pouw, *International Human Rights Law and the Law of Armed Conflict in the Context of Counterinsurgency - With a Particular Focus on Targeting and Operational Detention* (diss. UvA 2013), p. 160.

781   Stuart Casey-Maslen (Editor), *Weapons Under International Human Rights Law*, Cambridge University Press 2014, pp. 383-385.

TYPOLOGY OF ARTICLE 1 JURISDICTION IN 'HARD POWER' SITUATIONS     227

evidence from intelligence agencies'; the strike was stated to have been authorised by the Defence Secretary.[782]

This attack brings the reality of drone warfare within the scope of our discussion. It is undeniable that the armed drone is a lethal weapon with considerable potential. Its use is likely to increase rapidly as time goes on. European Governments other than that of the United Kingdom are said to be eying the armed drone with covetous interest.[783]

It is no longer inconceivable that one State Party to the Convention may one day launch a drone attack against a target on the territory of another State Party. It is submitted that such a situation will be similar, in terms of Article 1 of the Convention, to *Andreou v. Cyprus* – the case of the fatal rifle shot fired into Cyprus by a serviceman in the 'TRNC'. There is little doubt that the Convention will apply, if only because – under the *Cyprus v. Turkey* rule – there would otherwise be an unconscionable gap in the protection offered by it.

If the drone strike is launched *outside* the territory of any Convention State, then the starting point will probably have to be that there is not 'effective control over an area'. Incidental air attack, whether by manned or unmanned aircraft, cannot be equated to establishing dominion over territory.

The next question is therefore whether to follow *Banković and Others* or, alternatively, the 'State agent authority and control' approach developed in *al-Skeini and Others* and confirmed in *Jaloud*.[784]

We have seen that in *Banković and Others* the Court refused to accept the 'cause-and-effect' model of extraterritorial jurisdiction,[785] according to which the mere fact of being a 'victim' of an act that, viewed in isolation, is incompatible with the Convention was sufficient to bring the Convention itself into play.

---

782    BBC 7 September 2015, http://www.bbc.com/news/uk-34178998, see also dronewars.net, http://dronewars.net/2015/12/14/fallon-to-face-questions-on-drone-targeted-killing-but-will-there-be-answers/ (retrieved on 9 March 2016).

783    The Dutch Government, for example, though for the present it denies any intention to use armed drones. Lower House of Parliament (*Tweede Kamer der Staten-Generaal*), Parliamentary Year 2015-16, appendix to the parliamentary proceedings, no. 2640, question by the Member of Parliament Ms. S. Belhaj to the Minister of Defence (submitted on 3 May 2016) and the Minister's reply (received on 26 May 2016). According to the Minister, other governments expressing a similar interest include the German, French, Italian and Spanish (*ibid.*). See also PACE Resolution 2051 (2015) on Drones and targeted killings: the need to uphold human rights and international law (23 April 2015), § 3.

784    Emanuela-Chiara Gillard, "International Humanitarian Law and Extraterritorial State Conduct", in *Extraterritorial Application of Human Rights Treaties*, edited by Fons Coomans and Menno Camminga (Intersentia, 2004), pp. 25-40 at p. 39.

785    *Banković and Others*, § 75.

228                                                                    CHAPTER 6

Conversely, it may be argued that targeting an individual with lethal force constitutes the ultimate exercise of 'State agent authority and control' – the deliberate assumption of power to dispose of the life of a human being. On this view, it matters little from what precise location the actual weapon is controlled, whether within or outside the territory of the Contracting State responsible: what matters is that the decision to apply selective and individualised lethal force is purposely taken by the authorities of that State.[786] As we must conclude,[787] it is precisely this element of intent that was absent from *Banković and Others*: the attack was not intended to exercise destructive power over individual human beings or otherwise bend them to the will of any one of the Governments involved, but to put beyond use a building and installations housed in it, both belonging to the Federal Republic of Yugoslavia.[788]

In a recent report, the Joint Committee on Human Rights of the House of Lords and the House of Commons stated in so many words that '[o]n the current state of the case-law, the use of lethal force abroad by a drone strike is sufficient to bring the victim within the jurisdiction of the UK' – 'jurisdiction' here meaning Article 1 jurisdiction, which entails the applicability of Article 2 of the Convention.[789]

In November 2015, it was reported in the Dutch news media that two Somalian alleged victims of an American drone strike were bringing an action in the Dutch civil courts against the Dutch Government. The connection with the Netherlands was said to be that the American armed forces had made use of intelligence, so-called metadata, collected by the Netherlands military intelligence service MIVD in the course of the international counter-piracy operation 'Ocean Shield' in which both States took part. The choice of a Dutch forum over an American one was stated to be based on the perception that Dutch

---

786   Nils Melzer, *Targeted killing in international law*, Oxford University Press 2008, p. 137-138.
787   6.4.3.1.1 above.
788   Compare Michael Duttwiler, "Authority, Control and Jurisdiction in the Extraterritorial Application of the European Convention on Human Rights, *Netherlands Quarterly of Human Rights*, Vol. 30/2, 137-162, 2012, at p. 158, and Eric Pouw, *International Human Rights Law and the Law of Armed Conflict in the Context of Counterinsurgency - With a Particular Focus on Targeting and Operational Detention* (diss. UvA 2013), p. 160.
789   House of Lords and House of Commons, Joint Committee on Human Rights, *The Government's policy on the use of drones for targeted killing*, Second Report of Session 2015-16, para. 3.58.

TYPOLOGY OF ARTICLE 1 JURISDICTION IN 'HARD POWER' SITUATIONS 229

courts were more 'amenable to cases that involved innocent victims of war crimes' when the victims were foreign nationals.[790]

### 6.4.6.3 Clandestine Murder

On 23 November 2006 Alexander Litvinenko, a former Russian national who had been granted first British asylum and later British citizenship, died in a hospital in London. Post-mortem examination showed that his death had been caused by an ingestion of a fatal dose of a radioactive substance, polonium-210.

Finding circumstances of Litvinenko's death suspicious, the British authorities began an inquest. When the inquest came to a dead end because the United Kingdom Government refused to divulge information in their possession, invoking 'public interest immunity', Litvinenko's widow obtained an order for a public inquiry to be held in its place. The report of the inquiry was presented to the House of Commons on 21 January 2016.[791] It was based on evidence both public and 'closed', i.e. classified secret by the Home Secretary.

The report reaches the unambiguous finding that Litvinenko died from radiation syndrome caused by the ingestion of a lethal quantity of polonium-210 slipped into his tea by two Russian nationals in the bar of a London hotel.[792]

Discounting alternative suggestions – including that Litvinenko might have been murdered by the British intelligence agencies – the report goes on to find 'strong circumstantial evidence of Russian State responsibility' for Litvinenko's death,[793] the killing having been an 'FSB [Federal Security Service, Russian Federation] operation ... probably approved by Mr Patrushev [Nikolai Patrushev, Head of the FSB in 2006] and also by President Putin [Vladimir Putin, President of the Russian Federation in 2006]'.

The present author stops short of accepting the findings of the British inquiry as fact, let alone assuming that any organ of the Russian Government was in any way responsible for the death of Alexander Litvinenko. One reason

---

790  *De Volkskrant*, 28 November 2015, http://www.volkskrant.nl/buitenland/somali-victims-of-us-drone-strike-take-legal-action-against-the-netherlands~a4196845/ (English), http://www.volkskrant.nl/buitenland/somalische-droneslachtoffers-klagen-nederlandse-staat-aan~a4196859/ (Dutch); RTL Nieuws, https://www.youtube.com/watch?v=CMmu5mPNGic (retrieved 15 March 2016).

791  The Litvinenko Inquiry: Report into the death of Alexander Litvinenko, presented to the House of Commons on 21 January 2016 (HC 695), and Statement by the Chairman; https://www.litvinenkoinquiry.org/report, accessed on 14 February 2016.

792  Litvinenko Inquiry report, pp. 183-207.

793  Litvinenko Inquiry report, p. 240.

230 CHAPTER 6

for this has to be the official Russian denial,[794] which must be taken at face value unless and until it is proven false; the other is that an application has been brought against Russia by Litvinenko's widow (it was communicated to the Russian Government in 2010).[795] Nevertheless, cases in which an official inquiry throws up a suspicion of a targeted assassination by one State Party to the Convention on the territory of another – what is more, without the latter's tacit acquiescence or active connivance – are otherwise unknown, so this case can serve as a hypothetical example if nothing else.

It is argued by at least one author that Russia could not be held to account under the Convention because, applying reasoning based on *Al-Skeini* and *Al-Jedda*,

> Russia did not have effective control over any part of London, it did not exercise public powers in the city, and it seems far-fetched to conclude that Litvinenko was in custody of the Russian agents when he was poisoned.

Moreover,

> To argue that Litvinenko may be considered to be within the "jurisdiction" of Russia because his assassination was in all likelihood *planned* on Russian territory does not seem convincing. After all, there is usually a link between commanders and decision-makers who may be physically located within the state and those state representatives (agents, soldiers, etc.) that act on their commands and orders abroad, and Strasbourg has not yet found that the mere planning of extraterritorial activities is sufficient to close the jurisdictional gap.[796]

One answer to that position might be to suggest that this reasoning is based on a misreading of *Al-Skeini*. Extraterritorial jurisdiction does not exist only with-

---

794 TASS, "Kremlin does not perceive Litvinenko death investigation results as verdict", 21 January 2016, quoting an official spokesperson of the Russian Foreign Ministry; http://tass.com/politics/851376, accessed on 3 September 2016.

795 *Carter v. Russia*, no. 20914/07. "To communicate", as used here and elsewhere, is a term of art meaning "to give notice of the application or part of the application to the respondent Contracting Party and invite that Party to submit written observations thereon" (Rule 54 § 2 (b) of the Rules of Court).

796 Anders Henriksen, "The Poisoning of Alexander Litvinenko and the Geographical Scope of Human Rights Law", *Just Security*, https://www.justsecurity.org/29238/poisoning-litvinenko-scope-human-rights/, accessed 14 February 2016.

# TYPOLOGY OF ARTICLE 1 JURISDICTION IN 'HARD POWER' SITUATIONS    231

in foreign territory under actual the control of the Contracting State, or over persons held as prisoners. It also exists over persons subjected to the authority and control of State agents – and deliberate killing is the ultimate exercise of control over any person. The question where the operation is planned would be irrelevant.

Another answer might be to pray in aid the case-law developed in the context of the Turkish presence in Northern Cyprus – the interstate case, *Cyprus v. Turkey*, and *Andreou v. Turkey,*[797] the case of the rifle shot fired by a Turkish soldier from 'TRNC' territory at a person in territory unambiguously within the jurisdiction of the Republic of Cyprus. In this case, it is after all alleged that a violation of the right to life occurred as a result of an unlawful deed committed with malice aforethought by one Convention State within another's borders.

### 6.4.7    *Cyber-attack*

Between 27 April 2007 and 18 May 2007, distributed denial-of-service (DDoS) cyber-attacks shut down the websites of all Estonian government ministries, two major banks, and several political parties. At one point, hackers even disabled the parliamentary email server. Commentators and even the Estonian Minister for Foreign Affairs were quick to accuse Russia of perpetrating the attacks – linking them to the removal of a Soviet-era war memorial from its previous prominent position, an emotive issue in Russia and among the ethnic Russian minority in Estonia – but the Russian government officially denied it, and neither European Commission nor NATO technical experts were able to find credible evidence linking the Russian Government to the attack.[798] It has been suggested, perhaps more plausibly, that the attack was perpetrated by private actors.[799]

On 13 May 2017 it was reported in the news media that a massive ransomware attack, known as WannaCry, had shut down thousands of computers worldwide. Payment for unlocking the computers was demanded in bitcoin. Among the most prominent victims were British National Health Service practices and hospitals. General practitioners and pharmacies lost access to vital patient information, including medical prescriptions; appointments and even

---

797    *Cyprus v. Turkey*; *Andreou v. Turkey* (dec.), no. 45653/99. See 6.4.6.1 above.

798    Stephen Herzog, "Revisiting the Estonian Cyber Attacks: Digital Threats and Multinational Responses", in *Journal of Strategic Security*, Vol. 2, No. 4 (Summer 2011), pp. 49-60 at p. 51.

799    Bill Brenner, "Experts doubt Russian government launched DDoS attacks", http://searchsecurity.techtarget.com/news/1255548/Experts-doubt-Russian-government-launched-DDoS-attacks (accessed 28 May 2017).

operations were cancelled; and ambulances were diverted.[800] The perpetrators remain unknown at the time of writing.

On 27 June 2017 a computer worm later to be known as 'Petya' (or more accurately, 'NotPetya' or 'Petya2017', so as to disambiguate it from a type of ransomware called 'Petya' of which it is a variant) infected computer systems in dozens of countries. Although major commercial companies were among the most conspicuous victims worldwide, most of the damage was suffered in Ukraine and Russia. Significantly, the radiation monitoring system of the Chernobyl nuclear power plant was knocked out of action and monitoring had to be done manually.[801] However, NotPetya appeared poorly designed for its ostensible purpose of making money for its operators; information technology experts have suggested that it was malware disguised to appear as ransomware.[802]

These three examples of cyber-attacks – perhaps the best-known to have produced effects in Europe – drive home the dangers of this new weapon. The first is the difficulty of attributing responsibility to any particular person, organisation or government. The second, underestimated perhaps until now,[803] is the distinct likelihood that individuals may be directly harmed: banks and their customers in the case of the Estonian attack in 2007; worse, the physical health or even the lives of patients in the case of WannaCry; and NotPetya's

---

800    BBC News, "NHS cyber-attack: GPs and hospitals hit by ransomware", 13 May 2017, http://www.bbc.com/news/health-39899646 (accessed 28 May 2017).

801    The Independent, 27 June 2017, '"Petya" cyber-attack: Chernobyl's radiation monitoring system hit by worldwide hack', http://www.independent.co.uk/news/world/europe/chernobyl-ukraine-petya-cyber-attack-hack-nuclear-power-plant-danger-latest-a7810941.html (accessed 25 August 2017); CNN, 28 June 2017, 'Chernobyl monitoring system hit by global cyber attack', http://edition.cnn.com/2017/06/27/europe/chernobyl-cyber-attack/index.html (accessed 25 August 2017).

802    Comae Technologies, 28 June 2017, 'Petya.2017 is a wiper not a ransomware', https://blog.comae.io/petya-2017-is-a-wiper-not-a-ransomware-9ea1d8961d3b (accessed 25 August 2017); International Business Times, 29 June 2017, 'Petya ransomware: What were the hackers' motives and how much money have they raked in so far?', http://www.ibtimes.co.uk/petya-ransomware-what-were-hackers-motives-how-much-money-have-they-raked-so-far-1628223 (accessed 25 August 2017).

803    One advisory opinion on cyber warfare still focuses on '"cyber warfare' ... defined as 'the conduct of military operations to disrupt, mislead, modify or destroy an opponent's computer systems or networks by means of cyber capabilities'" and '"Cyber terrorism' defined as 'the attempt, using cyber capabilities, to seriously disrupt a society or parts of a society in order to achieve a political objective'" *Cyber Warfare*, Report No 77, AIV (*Adviesraad internationale vraagstukken*, Advisory Council on International Affairs)/ No 22, CAVV (*Commissie van advies inzake volkenrechtelijke vraagstukken*, Advisory Committee on Issues of Public International Law) December 2011, pp. 9-10.

# TYPOLOGY OF ARTICLE 1 JURISDICTION IN 'HARD POWER' SITUATIONS 233

shutting down the radiation monitoring system of the Chernobyl plant presages worse still.

Estonia being one of the most wired countries in the world today, it is perhaps not surprising that NATO decided to base its 'Cooperative Cyber Defence Centre of Excellence' in Tallinn. The concept predates the attack of 2007: the Estonian government proposed it already in 2004, shortly after joining NATO.

A prominent product of the Tallinn centre's work is the 'Tallinn Manual on the International Law Applicable to Cyber Operations' prepared by groups of legal and other experts (technicians, military officers). The first edition ('Tallinn Manual 1.0') appeared in 2013. The second edition ('Tallinn Manual 2.0') was published in 2017.

Tallinn Manual 2.0 purports to identify 'black letter' rules of international law governing cyber operations and provides commentary on them. The international legal sources most prominent in the work are taken from general public international law and international humanitarian law: these include, among others, the Hague and Geneva Conventions and judgments of the ICJ and ICTY. International human rights law is given far less attention: sources referred to include the Convention and a few of the judgments of the European Court of Human Rights.

The definition of a cyber-attack is breathtakingly simple:

> A cyber attack is a cyber operation, whether offensive or defensive, that is reasonably expected to cause injury or death to persons or damage or destruction to objects.[804]

Examples given of a cyber-attack in this sense include an operation that interferes with an electricity grid and causes a fire and an operation that releases dam waters and causes downstream destruction.[805]

Reassuringly, the manual states that '[i]nternational human rights law is applicable to cyber-related activities'.[806] As regards the extraterritorial application of human rights law, the Convention in particular, no general rule is formulated. Note is taken of the case-law of the Court on this point, in particular as developed in *Al-Skeini*,[807] but that is considered to be 'specific treaty

---

804    Tallinn Manual 2.0, Rule 92 (p. 415).

805    Tallinn Manual 2.0, p. 416. Compare Rules 140 and 141 (pp. 529-534) and Articles 56 and 57 of the First 1977 Protocol to the Geneva Conventions.

806    Tallinn Manual 2.0, Rule 34, p. 182.

807    *Al-Skeini*, §§ 130-139.

law' – the Tallinn Manual is intended to be relevant also to States that are not Parties to the Convention. The majority view was that

> ... in the current state of the law, physical control over territory or the individual [was] required before human rights law obligations were triggered. [footnote reference to *Al-Skeini.*] These Experts asserted that the premise of exercising power or effective control by virtual means such that human rights obligations attach runs contrary to both extensive State practice and the paucity of expressions of *opinio juris* thereon. As an example, there [was] little evidence that when States conducted signals intelligence programmes directed at foreigners on foreign territory, they [considered] that their activities implicated the international human right to privacy.[808]

However, a minority of the Experts

> ... took the position that so long as the exercise or enjoyment of a human right in question by the individual concerned [was] within the power or effective control of the State, that State [had] power or effective control over the individual with respect to the right concerned. In other words, if an individual [could not] exercise a human right or enjoy the protection of one because of a State's action, international human rights law [applied] extraterritorially.[809]

The minority position is thus identical to the 'cause-and-effect' view of extra-territorial jurisdiction rejected by the Court in *Banković.*[810]

It is submitted that in the current state of the law, there is no need to distinguish between cyber-attacks and other attacks as regards extra-territorial jurisdiction.[811]

An accepted general definition of an 'attack' is that given in Article 49 § 1 of Additional Protocol 1 (1977):

> "Attacks" mean acts of violence against the adversary, whether in offence or in defence.

---

808    Tallinn Manual 2.0, p. 185.

809    Tallinn Manual 2.0, p. 185.

810    See above 6.4.3.1.1.

811    See also United Nations General Assembly Resolution A/Res/ 3314 (XXIX), 14 December 1974, Definition of Aggression, Articles 3 and 4.

# TYPOLOGY OF ARTICLE 1 JURISDICTION IN 'HARD POWER' SITUATIONS 235

It is on this definition that Rule 92 of the Tallinn Manual 2.0 draws.

In the examples given above – a cyber-attack directed against an electricity grid that causes a fire, or a cyber-attack that releases dam water and causes damage downstream – it is possible, assuming that the effects of the attack are felt on the territory of a State not party to the Convention, that the applicable precedent may be *Banković* not *Al-Skeini*. Should such an attack ever materialise, it will have to be determined on the facts of the case whether it is any different in principle from a missile attack on a radio station carried out in the middle of the night.

## 6.5    Peacekeeping and Peace-enforcing

### 6.5.1    *All European Members of the 'Coalition of the Willing' in Iraq*

After the capture of Baghdad by American forces in April 2003, Iraq's long-time president Saddam Hussein went into hiding. He was captured by American forces in December 2003 near Tikrit, in the Central Zone of occupation (which was garrisoned by American troops). After the transfer of authority from the Coalition Provisional Authority to the interim government of Iraq, Saddam Hussein was handed over to the Iraqi interim government for trial.

On 29 June 2004 – the day before he was to be handed over to the Iraqi authorities – Saddam Hussein lodged an application with the Court complaining that he was likely to face the death penalty after a 'show trial' lacking even the most basic guarantees of fairness. He cited as respondents the Convention States participating in the occupation of Iraq.

It took the Court nearly two years to declare the application inadmissible.[812] The Court found that Saddam Hussein had failed to show that any respondent State had had 'any responsibility for, or any involvement or role in' his capture, detention and handover or that any Convention State had held control over any territory where the events complained of had occurred. The Court's reasoning continues:

> This failure to substantiate any such involvement also constitutes a response to his final submission to the effect that the respondent States were responsible for the acts of their military agents abroad. Finally, there is no basis in the Convention's jurisprudence and the applicant has

---

812    *Saddam Hussein v. Albania, Bulgaria, Croatia, Czech Republic, Denmark, Estonia, Hungary, Iceland, Ireland, Italy, Latvia, Lithuania, the Netherlands, Poland, Portugal, Romania, Slovakia, Slovenia, Turkey, Ukraine and the United Kingdom* (dec.), no. 23276/04, 14 March 2006.

not invoked any established principle of international law which would mean that he fell within the respondent States' jurisdiction on the sole basis that those States allegedly formed part (at varying unspecified levels) of a coalition with the US, when the impugned actions were carried out by the US, when security in the zone in which those actions took place was assigned to the US and when the overall command of the coalition was vested in the US.[813]

One interesting conclusion to be drawn from this decision is that mere participation in a coalition is not sufficient to establish Convention jurisdiction: more direct responsibility is required.

### 6.5.2    *United Kingdom in Iraq*

6.5.2.1    *Al-Saadoon and Mufdhi*

This was precisely the position of the United Kingdom in *Al-Saadoon and Mufdhi*, decided some three years later. The applicants were suspected of involvement in the shooting of two British servicemen in southern Iraq. Arrested by United Kingdom troops, they were, for a while, detained in an American-run facility but later handed back to the British. An investigation by the United Kingdom's Royal Military Police into the deaths of the two British soldiers led to the conclusion that 'the strength of the evidence against the applicants warranted referral of the case to the Iraqi authorities'.[814]

The applicants brought proceedings, first in the Iraqi courts, then in the English courts seeking to prevent their handover for trial by the Iraqi High Tribunal on war crimes charges. After the failure of their appeal in the English Court of Appeal, the Court ordered an interim measure under Rule 39 of the Rules of Court informing the Government that the applicants should not be removed or transferred from the custody of the United Kingdom until further notice. Even so, the applicants were transferred into the physical custody of the Iraqi authorities the following day, that being the last day on which the memorandum of understanding (MOU) under which the United Kingdom was entitled to detain criminal suspects held for trial in Iraqi courts remained in force.[815]

---

813    *ibid.*

814    *Al-Saadoon and Mufdhi*, § 26.

815    *Memorandum Of Understanding Between The United Kingdom Of Great Britain And Northern Ireland Contingent Of Multinational Forces-Iraq And The Ministries Of Justice And Interior Of Iraq Regarding Criminal Suspects*, published by the House of Commons Foreign Affairs Committee with evidence taken jointly with the Defence Committee on Iraq and Afghanistan on 28 October 2008, HC (2007-08) 1145–I, http://www.publications.parlia-

TYPOLOGY OF ARTICLE 1 JURISDICTION IN 'HARD POWER' SITUATIONS 237

The United Kingdom did not at any time deny that it had Article 1 jurisdiction in the case. Rather, the discussion centred on the manner of its exercise, the respondent Government citing its obligations under general international law *vis-à-vis* Iraq and arguing that these overrode the obligations of the United Kingdom under the Convention.

As we will see later on when we discuss this judgment in greater detail, the Court did not so find.

### 6.5.2.2    Al-Skeini and Others

The applicants in *Al-Skeini and Others* were surviving kin of five men and a woman who had died either at the hands of British forces in Iraq or (in one case) in their custody. The deaths had all occurred during the time when the United Kingdom was an occupying power in Iraq under United Nations Security Council Resolution 1483.

The United Kingdom Government tried to argue before the Court that two of the deaths were not attributable to the United Kingdom. Those deaths had occurred after 16 October 2003, the date on which the United Nations Security Council adopted Resolution 1511. Paragraph 13 of that Resolution authorised a Multinational Force to take 'all necessary measures to contribute to the maintenance of security and stability in Iraq'. The argument was that, in conducting the relevant operations in which the two victims were shot, United Kingdom troops had not been exercising the sovereign authority of the United Kingdom but the international authority of the Multinational Force acting pursuant to the binding decision of the United Nations Security Council.

The Court held that the United Kingdom Government were estopped from raising this objection before it, since no corresponding argument had been made before the domestic courts.[816]

The attribution argument having failed, the United Kingdom Government then submitted that – save in respect of one applicant, who had died in British custody – the deaths had occurred outside United Kingdom jurisdiction. This argument was based primarily on *Banković and Others*, in which – as we have seen – the Court had described Article 1 jurisdiction as 'primarily' or 'essentially' territorial; outside the area of the metropolitan State, Article 1 jurisdiction existed only in so far as the State itself had extended it in application of Article 56. The only exception was where 'effective control' was exercised outside the national territory of the State but still within the *'espace juridique'* of

---

ment.uk/pa/cm200708/cmselect/cmdfence/1145/8102807.htm; for relevant excerpts, see *Al-Saadoon and Mufdhi*, § 25.

816    *Al-Skeini*, §§ 97-100.

238 CHAPTER 6

the Convention – the metropolitan territory of the State plus the territory covered by declarations under Article 56 – where, as found in *Cyprus v. Turkey*, a gap in the protection of the Convention would exist if the controlling State did not assume responsibility for securing the entire range of Convention rights. Up until July 2003, government was vested in a Coalition Provisional Authority headed by an American official, Ambassador L. Paul Bremer, and which did not answer to the United Kingdom; after July 2003, a Governing Council of Iraq existed which the Coalition Provisional Authority was required to consult with it on all matters concerning the temporary governance of Iraq.

1.1.1.1 Extraterritorial Jurisdiction: the 'Al-Skeini Rule'

The Court's reasoning setting out the broad principles for the extraterritorial exercise of jurisdiction in conflict or post-conflict situations is what gives this judgment its importance.

The Court starts by stating, in the usual way, the principle of territoriality – as already set out in *Soering, Banković* and *Ilaşcu* – and the exceptional nature of extraterritorial exercise of jurisdiction.[817] It continues:

> In each case, the question whether exceptional circumstances exist which require and justify a finding by the Court that the State was exercising jurisdiction extraterritorially must be determined with reference to the particular facts.[818]

The Court then divides situations in which Article 1 jurisdiction can exist extraterritorially into two main categories: firstly, State agent authority and control, and secondly, effective control over an area.

6.5.2.2.1 *State Agent Authority and Control*

A State exercises extraterritorial jurisdiction through 'State agent authority and control' by way of 'acts of its authorities which produce effects outside its own territory'. It can exercise such authority and control consensually, for example through diplomatic and consular agents of the State stationed on foreign territory in the normal way, or if through the consent, invitation or acquiescence of the foreign Government, it exercises all or some of the public powers normally to be exercised by that Government; in the latter situation, 'the Contracting State may be responsible for breaches of the Convention thereby incurred, as long as the acts in question are attributable to it rather than to the

---

817     *Al-Skeini*, § 131.
818     *Al-Skeini*, § 132.

territorial State'.[819] In addition, in certain circumstances, the use of force by a State's agents operating outside its territory might bring the individual thereby brought under the control of the State's authorities into the State's Article 1 jurisdiction. Citing *Öcalan, Issa* (*a contrario*), *Al-Saadoon and Mufdhi* and *Medvyedyev and Others*, the Court observed that it had applied this principle where an individual was taken into the custody of State agents abroad. It did not consider that jurisdiction in the cases cited arose solely from the control exercised by the Contracting State over the buildings, aircraft or ship in which the individuals were held: what was decisive in such cases is the exercise of physical power and control over the person in question.[820]

It was clear that, whenever the State, through its agents, exercised control and authority over an individual, and thus jurisdiction, the State was under an obligation under Article 1 to secure to that individual the rights and freedoms under Section I of the Convention that were relevant to the situation of that individual. In this sense, therefore, the Convention rights could be 'divided and tailored'.[821]

This last statement has been misunderstood: it has been suggested[822] that it is not consistent with the Court's holding in *Banković and Others* that 'the wording of Article 1 does *not* provide any support for the applicants' suggestion that the positive obligation in Article 1 to secure "the rights and freedoms defined in Section I of this Convention" could be divided and tailored in accordance with the particular circumstances of the extra-territorial act in question'.[823] In fact there is no inconsistency: the statement in *Banković and Others* is an answer to a very different argument. It will be recalled that the Court so held in response to the applicants' suggestion that the extraterritorial exercise of 'effective control' over an individual brought that individual within the State's extraterritorial jurisdiction, but that the State's obligation under Article 1 to secure the rights and freedoms guaranteed by the Convention applied in a manner 'proportionate to the level of control in fact exercised' – i.e. the State was accountable 'for those Convention rights within [its] control in the situation in question'.[824] As noted, the *Banković* applicants were arguing that jurisdiction arose from the very fact that they (or their deceased relatives as the case might be) had been affected by the air strike on the RTS building in Belgrade – a position rejected by the Court, and clearly different from the Court's finding

---

819    *Al-Skeini*, §§ 134-135.
820    *Al-Skeini*, § 136.
821    *Al-Skeini*, § 137.
822    For example, Van den Have, p. 103.
823    *Banković*, § 75. Emphasis added.
824    *Banković*, §§ 46 and 47.

240                                                                 CHAPTER 6

that jurisdiction in the form of 'State agent authority and control' arose from
the deliberate exercise of executive or jurisdictional powers of the State over
the individual. In the case of someone held in detention, for example, the obligation to secure to that person the rights and freedoms relevant to his or her
situation related to the rights and freedoms relevant to that person's situation
*as a detainee*.[825] One may consider relevant, for example, the rights which a detainee enjoys under Article 3, Article 5 (including *habeas corpus*, Article 5 § 4),
Protocols 6 and 13 of course, perhaps also Articles 8 (contact with family, confidentiality of correspondence with legal counsel and with the European Court
of Human Rights) and, if there is a criminal charge, Article 6 under its criminal
head. If the exercise of authority and control takes the form of the lethal use of
force – as was the case in *Al-Skeini* and *Jaloud*, as we shall see – the rights and
freedoms relevant to the situation of the person concerned include, at the very
least, those guaranteed by Article 2 under its procedural head.

#### 6.5.2.2.2   *Effective Control over an Area*

Article 1 jurisdiction also exists when, as a consequence of lawful or unlawful
military action, a Contracting State exercises effective control of an area outside that national territory. The obligation to secure, in such an area, the rights
and freedoms set out in the Convention derives from the fact of such control,
whether it be exercised directly, through the Contracting State's own armed
forces, or through a subordinate local administration. Where the fact of such
domination over the territory is established, it is not necessary to determine
whether the Contracting State exercises detailed control over the policies and
actions of the subordinate local administration. The fact that the local administration survives as a result of the Contracting State's military and other support entails that State's responsibility for its policies and actions. The controlling State has the responsibility under Article 1 to secure, within the area under
its control, the entire range of substantive rights set out in the Convention and
those additional Protocols which it has ratified.[826] The prime indicator for the
existence of 'control over an area' is the strength of the State's military presence in the area; the extent to which its military, economic and political support for the local subordinate administration provides it with influence and
control over the region may also be relevant. Whether a Contracting State ex-

---

825    Clare Ovey, "Application of the ECHR during International Armed Conflicts", in *The UK
       and European Human Rights: A Strained Relationship?* (Katja S Ziegler, Elizabeth Wicks
       and Loveday Hodson, eds.), Hart Publishing, 2015, pp. 225-245 at pp. 229-230.
826    *Al-Skeini*, § 138.

TYPOLOGY OF ARTICLE 1 JURISDICTION IN 'HARD POWER' SITUATIONS       241

ercises effective control over an area outside its own territory is a question of fact, to be decided from case to case.[827]

### 6.5.2.3    The Convention Legal Space[828]

It remains the case that the Convention is a constitutional instrument of European public order. Thus, when one Convention State occupies – and therefore exercises jurisdiction – on the territory of another, the former is responsible under Article 1 of the Convention for securing the rights and freedoms which the Convention guarantees simply because there would otherwise be a 'vacuum' of protection within the 'legal space' or '*espace juridique*' of the Convention. However, it does not follow *a contrario* that jurisdiction under Article 1 of the Convention can never exist outside the territory covered by the Council of Europe member States.[829]

### 6.5.2.4    Application of the 'Al-Skeini Rule' to the Facts of the Al-Skeini Case

The Court took as its starting point that the USA and the UK had entered Iraq with the specific aim of displacing the regime then in power. Having done so, they set themselves up as 'occupying powers' and created a subordinate administration – the CPA – 'to exercise powers of government temporarily'. One of the powers of government specifically referred to was the provision of security in Iraq, including the maintenance of civil law and order. In the Basra area, where the fatalities in issue occurred, the United Kingdom had command of the military presence charged with supporting the civilian administration.[830]

Even so, the Court did not find that the United Kingdom's jurisdiction derived from 'control over an area' – rather, it derived from the exercise of 'authority and control over individuals killed in the course of ... security operations'.[831] Ovey explains that any finding that the United Kingdom had 'effective control' in south-east Iraq at the relevant time would have sat uncomfortably with the evidence led in the domestic proceedings in the UK as to the extreme

---

827    *Al-Skeini*, § 139.
828    An expression that has come to be used to refer to the aggregate of the territorial and quasi-territorial jurisdiction of the Contracting States to which the Convention actually applies. As we have seen above (5.1-5.4), this does not coincide with the Contracting States' metropolitan land territory.
829    *Al-Skeini*, §§ 141-42.
830    *Al-Skeini*, § 143-148.
831    *Al-Skeini*, § 149.

state of violence and anarchy that prevailed in the area during the period of British administration.[832]

As we will see, the Court was later to reach a similar finding in *Hassan*.

#### 6.5.2.5 Domestic Case-law in the Wake of Al-Skeini

There was not long to wait before the impact of the *Al-Skeini* judgment on domestic courts was felt.

On 6 September 2014 the Supreme Court of the Netherlands (*Hoge Raad*) gave judgment in a case brought by the surviving kin of three Bosniak (Bosnian Muslim) men who had been killed in the Srebrenica massacre after having been denied protection as United Nations staff by officers of the Dutch battalion then stationed in the Srebrenica enclave. The Supreme Court's judgment included the following *obiter dictum*:

> 3.17.2 According to the case-law of the European Court of Human Rights it is not excluded that a Contracting State may, in extraordinary circumstances, have jurisdiction as referred to in Article 1 of the Convention even outside its own territory [case-law reference to the Court's *Al-Skeini and Others* judgment].
>
> 3.17.3 In this case, the presence of Dutchbat in Srebrenica and on the compound in Potočari flowed from the participation of the Netherlands in UNPROFOR, UNPROFOR deriving its competence to act in Srebrenica from the Agreement on the status of the United Nations Protection Force in Bosnia and Herzegovina entered into between the United Nations and Bosnia and Herzegovina (...). It follows that the State had competence to exercise jurisdiction within the meaning of Article 1 of the Convention in the compound through Dutchbat.
>
> Furthermore, it cannot be said that after the fall of the enclave on 11 July 1995 and more in particular at the time of the action impugned to Dutchbat the State was in the factual impossibility to exercise jurisdiction as referred to above in the compound. In view of the facts which it has taken as its starting point, the Court of Appeal has proceeded on the assumption that the Bosnian Serb Army respected the authority of Dutchbat on the compound to which Dutchbat had withdrawn until Dutchbat's departure on 21 July 1995. These facts offer a sufficient basis for the finding

---

832    Clare Ovey, "Application of the ECHR during International Armed Conflicts", in *The UK and European Human Rights: A Strained Relationship?* (Katja S Ziegler, Elizabeth Wicks and Loveday Hodson, eds.), Hart Publishing, 2015, pp. 225-245 at p. 230; see also the summary of the domestic proceedings given in *Al-Skeini*, §§ 72-88.

# TYPOLOGY OF ARTICLE 1 JURISDICTION IN 'HARD POWER' SITUATIONS     243

that the State, through Dutchbat, was actually in a position to supervise observance with respect to Muhamed and Ibro Nuhanović of the rights secured in Articles 2 and 3 of the Convention and Articles 6 and 7 of the International Covenant on Civil and Political Rights.[833]

To this already far-reaching statement, the Supreme Court added the following further comment:

> 3.18.3 In so far as the [statement of grounds of appeal] reproaches the Court of Appeal for having failed properly to take into account the importance of reticence in its assessment, [it] also fails, given that no basis for such reticence can be found in customary international law, the Convention or the Covenant, and incidentally, not in the domestic law of the Netherlands either.
>
> The reticent assessment advocated in the [statement of grounds of appeal] would mean that hardly any scope would remain for a judicial assessment of the consequences of the actions of a military force within the framework of a peace mission – in this case: the behaviour impugned to Dutchbat and thus to the State. Such far-reaching reticence is unacceptable. It makes no difference that the State expects harmful consequences [of such an assessment] for the implementation of peace operations by the United Nations and in particular for the willingness of Member States to make available troops for such operations. This, after all, ought not to stand in the way of an *ex post facto* judicial assessment of the conduct of the individual military force. It is correct that in so doing, the court should take into account the fact that the decisions in issue are taken under great pressure in a war situation, but the Court of Appeal has not misunderstood this.[834]

Thus we see that the guardian of at least one domestic legal system is now prepared to adopt a wide view of the extraterritorial jurisdiction of its State.

---

833    Supreme Court of the Netherlands, *State v. Nuhanović*, judgment of 6 September 2014, ECLI:NL:HR:2013:BZ9225. Translation by the author. Identical reasoning appears in the Supreme Court's judgment of the same date in *State v. Mustafić-Mujić and Others*, ECLI:NL:HR:2013:BZ9228, also published in NJ 2015/376 with an annotation by N.J. Schrijver.

834    Supreme Court of the Netherlands, *State v. Nuhanović*, ibid. An identical passage appears in *State v. Mustafić-Mujić and Others*.

244 CHAPTER 6

It is interesting to contrast this approach with the course followed by the Italian Court of Cassation in *Markovic and Others*.[835] One is left to wonder what might have happened if, following the example of its Italian counterpart, the Dutch Supreme Court had thrown these cases out and the relatives of the three victims had applied to the Court in Strasbourg.

### 6.5.3 *The Netherlands in Iraq*

Like *Al-Skeini*, *Jaloud v. the Netherlands* concerned the lethal use of force in south-eastern Iraq. The victim, the applicant's son, was mortally hit by rifle fire as the car in which he was a passenger was fired upon after crashing through a checkpoint manned by Iraqi security forces and Netherlands Royal Army troops commanded by a Dutch officer. The Dutch troops were under the overall command of a British officer as part of one of the multinational divisions existing in Iraq at the relevant time.

The Netherlands Government, supported by the United Kingdom Government which intervened as a third party, argued that the Netherlands had no jurisdiction in the case. The Netherlands Government, in particular, submitted that the Dutch troops had been under the command and control of a British officer. Moreover, primary responsibility for security had rested with the Iraqi forces, the Dutch forces being present merely to observe and advise.

The Court dismissed both arguments. The fact of Dutch troops being under British orders was not sufficient to divest the Netherlands of their Article 1 jurisdiction: the Netherlands had retained 'full command' over their military personnel, as the Ministers of Foreign Affairs and of Defence pointed out in a joint letter to Parliament and as was apparent from what was known of the arrangements – a network of Memoranda of Understanding – defining the interrelations between the various armed contingents.[836] Nor could responsibility be shifted onto the Iraqi forces: pursuant to the relevant order of the CPA, they were supervised by, and subordinate to, officers from the Coalition forces – in this case, a Dutch officer.[837]

It has been suggested that, since there was no 'physical contact with or restraint placed on' the deceased, the decision on jurisdiction in *Jaloud* could be seen as a 'significant extension' of the 'state agent authority' basis of jurisdiction, coming very close to the 'cause and effect' jurisdiction rejected in

---

835 See 6.4.3.1.2 above.
836 *Jaloud*, §§ 143-48.
837 *Jaloud*, § 150.

TYPOLOGY OF ARTICLE 1 JURISDICTION IN 'HARD POWER' SITUATIONS 245

*Banković*.[838] So to argue is to ignore the very purpose for which checkpoints are set up, namely precisely to exercise authority and control over individuals. It will be seen, therefore, that we are no closer to 'cause-and-effect' jurisdiction in *Jaloud* than in *Al-Skeini*; if anything, we are further from it.

## 6.6 Exercise of Jurisdiction on Territory of Foreign State with the Latter's Permission

### 6.6.1 *Turkey in Kenya*

In 1999 Abdullah Öcalan was forced out of Syria, from where he had been directing the struggle of the PKK against Turkey. Accepted nowhere in Europe, he ended up in Kenya where he was not welcome either. Although apparently Öcalan had been given to understand that he would be taken to Nairobi airport and from there flown to the Netherlands, a car driven by a Kenyan official in fact took him to an aircraft in which Turkish officials were waiting for him. Öcalan was arrested immediately after boarding the aircraft. Öcalan was later to be tried for his life in Turkey. He was spared the gallows but is currently serving a sentence of life imprisonment in an island prison in the Bosphorus.

Öcalan maintained that there was *prima facie* evidence that he had been abducted by the Turkish authorities operating abroad, beyond their jurisdiction, and that his arrest was for that reason unlawful. The Court did not so find. Quoting from the Commission's report in *Stocké v. Germany*,[839] it held that an arrest made by the authorities of one State on the territory of another State, without the consent of the latter, affected the individual rights to security under Article 5 § 1 of the person concerned. However, the handover by Kenyan officials to their Turkish counterparts placed Öcalan within Turkish Article 1 jurisdiction.[840] Kenya not being party to the Convention and absent proof that Turkey had acted extraterritorially in a manner inconsistent with Kenyan sovereignty, there was therefore no violation of Article 5 § 1 in that the applicant's arrest and subsequent detention were unlawful.[841]

As we have seen, the Court has taken the view that jurisdiction was established by the handover of the applicant into the control of Turkish state agents. This is not wrong; however, although it is plain that the Turkish aircraft

---

838    Aurel Sari, "Untangling Extra-Territorial Jurisdiction from International Responsibility in *Jaloud v. the Netherlands*: Old Problem, New Solutions?" in *Military Law and the Law of War Review* 53/2 (2014) pp. 287-316 at pp. 300-301.

839    *Stocké v. Germany*, opinion of the Commission, p. 24, § 167, Series A no. 199.

840    *Öcalan*, § 91.

841    *ibid.*, §§ 93-98.

could not have overflown, still less landed in, Kenyan territory without Kenyan authorisation,[842] it is clear that once on board the aircraft Öcalan was within Turkish jurisdiction considered in a territorial sense.

### 6.6.2 *France in Somalia*

In a case that on its facts, and as regards its Convention complaints, was comparable to that of *Hassan and Others v. France*, a group of Somalian pirates had captured a French vessel off the coast of Yemen and taken her crew – some thirty persons – onto land in Somalia. The following day the transitional federal government of Somalia addressed a *note verbale* to France granting the French armed forces permission to enter Somalian waters and air space and to use proportionate force to resolve the crisis. The crew were ransomed. French forces, helicopter-borne, seized six of the pirates and recovered part of the ransom money. The pirates were taken to France for trial. As in *Hassan and Others*, the French Government conceded jurisdiction on the strength of *Medvyedyev and Others*.[843]

## 6.7 The Status of 'Occupying Power'

In the context of international law, the expression 'occupation' is an emotive one. In parts of Europe that were occupied by Nazi Germany during the Second World War especially it has become tainted with the suggestion of unlawfulness, having come to conjure up pictures of Nazi jackboots trampling cherished freedoms, of concentration camps, of heroic resistance and abject collaboration. Although 'occupation' and expressions like it occur in Strasbourg case-law in that narrow context, in old Commission decisions but also in judgments of the Court,[844] it is sometimes difficult to escape the impression that they are now sometimes used for effect with that historical association in mind. For example, individual applicants and the Cypriot Government as

---

842   Article 3(c) of the Convention on International Civil Aviation.

843   *Ali Samatar and Others v. France*, nos. 17110/10 17301/10, § 31, 4 December 2014.

844   E.g. *De Becker v. Belgium*, 27 March 1962, Series A no. 4; *X v. Norway*, no. 2002/63, Commission decision of 2 July 1964, Collection 14, pp. 25-28; *X v. Norway*, no. 2369/64, Commission decision of 3 April 1967, Collection 23, pp. 21-25; *D.G.P. N.V. V. the Netherlands*, no. 5178/71, Commission decision of 12 October 1973, Collection 44, pp. 13-24; *Papon v. France*, no. 54210/00, ECHR 2002-VII; *Kononov v. Latvia* (GC), no. 38376/04, § 195, ECHR 2010.

applicant or intervening third party have sometimes referred to Turkey as the occupying power in northern Cyprus.[845]

So also have Governments of Baltic States applied that expression to the Soviet Union in referring to the latter's relationship with their countries until 1991.[846] The Russian Federation firmly opposes their position.[847]

The Court itself is usually circumspect in its use of language borrowed from the laws of war, although it has been known to use expressions such as 'occupying power' and 'occupation regime' to describe the Soviet Union in relation to the Baltic States.[848] Very forthright views are sometimes expressed by individual judges in separate opinions.[849]

It is submitted that the expression is morally neutral and its identification in the popular mind with the forces of evil is fallacious. Thus, as we have seen, after the Second World War France, the Soviet Union, the United Kingdom and the United States were occupying powers in Germany and Austria until 1955 (in Berlin until 1990).[850]

Expressions such as 'occupation' and 'occupying power' have a technical meaning in international humanitarian law[851] – and actually they are sometimes used in their technical sense in domestic legislation.[852] The importance

---

845    See, for example, *Xenides-Arestis v. Turkey* (dec.), no. 46347/99, 14 March 2005; *Demopoulos and Others* §§ 58, 64 and 67; ECHR 2010; and recently, *Güzelyurtlu and Others v. Cyprus and Turkey*, no. 36925/07, § 237, 4 April 2017 (referred to the Grand Chamber).

846    *Sõro v. Estonia*, no. 22588/08, 3 September 2015 (see the concurring opinion of Judge Pinto the Albuquerque, § 6).

847    *Vasiliauskas v. Lithuania* (GC), no. 35343/05, § 147, ECHR 2015. Compare the joint dissenting opinion of Judges Villiger, Power-Forde, Pinto de Albuquerque and Kūris, § 4.

848    *Puzinas v. Lithuania* (dec.), no. 63767/00, 13 December 2005; *Kolk and Kislyiy v. Estonia* (dec.), nos. 23052/04 24018/04, ECHR 2006-I; *Penart v. Estonia* (dec.), no. 14685/04, 24 January 2006.

849    *Slivenko v. Latvia* (GC), no. 48321/99, ECHR 2003-X (Judge Maruste); *Andrejeva v. Latvia* (GC), no. 55707/00, ECHR 2009 (Judge Ziemele); *Ždanoka v. Latvia* (GC), no. 58278/00, ECHR 2006-IV (Judge Zupančič).

850    *Hess v. the United Kingdom*, Commission decision of 28 May 1975, D.R. 2, p. 72; *Vearncombe and Others v. the United Kingdom and the Federal Republic of Germany*, no. 12816/87, D.R. No. 59, p. 186.

851    See generally Helen Duffy, *The 'War on Terror' and the Framework of International Law* (2nd edition 2015), Cambridge University Press, pp. 382-384, and Hanne Cuyckens, "The Law of Occupation" in *Armed Conflicts and the Law*, Jan Wouters, Philip De Man, Nele Verlinden (eds.), Intersentia, 2016, pp. 417-444.

852    For example, in section 5(5)(d) of the Dutch International Crimes Act (*Wet internationale misdrijven*) of 2003 (quoted in translation in *Van Anraat v. the Netherlands* (dec.), no. 65389/09, § 20, 6 July 2010).

of whether a state is an 'occupying power' or not is not in apportioning opprobrium but in defining its obligations under the Convention.[853]

Articles 42 and 43 of the Hague Regulations on the Laws and Customs of Law on Land (text of 1907) read as follows:

> **Article 42.**
> Territory is considered occupied when it is actually placed under the authority of the hostile army. The occupation extends only to the territory where such authority has been established and can be exercised.'

> **Article 43.**
> The authority of the legitimate power having in fact passed into the hands of the occupant, the latter shall take all the measures in his power to restore, and ensure, as far as possible, public order and safety, while respecting, unless absolutely prevented, the laws in force in the country.'

Other provisions of the Hague Regulations require the occupying power to respect 'family honour and rights, the lives of persons, and private property, as well as religious convictions and practice' and prohibit the confiscation of private property (Article 46); they give detailed regulation for the levying and use of taxes and other contributions and requisitions (Articles 48, 49, 51 and 52); and they prohibit the seizure and destruction of, and damage to, religious, charitable, educational and cultural property (Article 56) – offering the population of an occupied territory a higher level of protection against the enemy, in certain respects, than the Convention does against the peacetime government of the State.

Provisions relevant to the rights and duties of the occupying power are also to be found in other instruments, most notably the fourth of the 1949 Geneva Conventions – Convention (IV) Relative to the Protection of Civilian Persons in Time of War (Articles 41-78). It too enumerates human rights of the classical kind, such as the right to humane treatment and a fair trial even for spies, saboteurs or others suspected of 'activity hostile to the security of the Occupying Power' (Article 5) and to *habeas corpus* (Article 43).

As we have seen, when one State Party to the Convention occupies all or part of the territory of another State Party, the occupant *ipso facto* enters into all the Convention obligations of the occupied Contracting Party.[854] In such

---

853 See *Demopoulos and Others*, § 114; compare *Güzelyurtlu and Others v. Cyprus and Turkey* (GC), § 193.

854 *Cyprus v. Turkey* (merits) § 78; see also *Ilaşcu and Others*, §§ 384-93.

a case, it is irrelevant for purposes of Article 1 jurisdiction whether or not the occupying Contracting State is also an 'occupant' within the meaning of Articles 42 and 43 of the Hague Regulations.

However, as the Court points out in *Al-Skeini and Others*, it does not follow *a contrario* that jurisdiction under Article 1 of the Convention can never exist outside the territory of the Convention States.[855] It needs to be considered whether the question takes on a separate meaning when the territory occupied is outside the territory of any Convention State.

In *Al-Skeini and Others*, the events complained of took place during a period when the United Kingdom alongside the United States was an Occupying Power within the meaning of Article 42 of the Hague Regulations by virtue of United Nations Security Council Resolution 1483. The United Kingdom Government argued at length that the 'effective control of an area' test was not relevant because, firstly, that test could only apply within the Convention legal space; secondly, the United Kingdom's control in south-eastern Iraq was far from effective; and thirdly, governmental authority in Iraq was vested in a Coalition Provisional Authority (CPA), which was governed by an American official. Moreover, the status of Occupying Power, so far from conferring sovereignty or colonial dominion, actually required the domestic law of the occupied country to be respected and left intact as far as possible; the corollary was that the United Kingdom was prevented from imposing Convention standards so as to override Iraqi constitutional law.[856]

In § 143 of *Al-Skeini*, the Court took note of the United Kingdom's status of formal Occupying Power and in the first sentence of § 149 it finds that 'the United Kingdom (together with the United States of America) assumed in Iraq the exercise of some of the public powers normally to be exercised by a sovereign government' and 'authority and responsibility for the maintenance of security in south-east Iraq' – language highly reminiscent of Articles 42 and 43 of the Hague Regulations – but it did not base its finding of Article 1 jurisdiction on that ground, as some of the reasoning in *Banković and Others* might have led one to expect.[857] Instead, in the second sentence of § 149, it concluded that 'the United Kingdom, through its soldiers engaged in security operations in Basra during the period in question, exercised authority and control over individuals killed in the course of such security operations, so as to establish [the required] jurisdictional link'.[858]

---

855    *Al-Skeini*, § 142.
856    *Al-Skeini*, §§ 114 and 117.
857    *Banković and Others*, §§ 60 (second sentence) and 71.
858    *Al-Skeini* §§ 143 and 149-150.

In *Al-Jedda*, the Court also noted the status of the United Kingdom as one of the two Occupying Powers;[859] but *Al-Jedda* being a detention case to be considered under Article 5, it based its decision on jurisdiction on the 'authority and control' exercised over the applicant as a prisoner.[860]

In *Jaloud*, the Netherlands Government (supported by the United Kingdom as intervening party) submitted that the Netherlands was not an Occupying Power within the meaning of Article 42 of the Hague Regulations, that status belonging exclusively to the United States and the United Kingdom; nor had the Netherlands assumed in Iraq any of the public powers normally to be exercised by a sovereign government, these too being vested solely in the Occupying Powers.[861]

The Court pointed out that

> ... the status of "occupying power" within the meaning of Article 42 of the Hague Regulations, or lack of it, is not *per se* determinative. Although it found that concept relevant in *Al-Skeini* (cited above, § 143) and in *Al-Jedda v. the United Kingdom* [GC], no. 27021/08, § 77, ECHR 2011, the Court did not need to have recourse to it in finding that the responsibility of Turkey was engaged in respect of events in northern Cyprus (see, *inter alia*, *Loizidou v. Turkey (preliminary objections)*, 23 March 1995, Series A no. 310, and *Cyprus v. Turkey* [GC], no. 25781/94, ECHR 2001-IV), or that of Russia in respect of the situation in Moldovan territory east of the Dniester (see, inter alia, *Ilaşcu and Others v. Moldova and Russia* [GC], no. 48787/99, ECHR 2004-VII, and *Catan and Others v. the Republic of Moldova and Russia* [GC], nos. 43370/04, 8252/05 and 18454/06, ECHR 2012 (extracts)).[862]

In other words, Article 1 jurisdiction is an autonomous concept not dependent on the status of occupying power. As the use of the word 'relevant' bears out, a Contracting State possessed of it will find it difficult to deny the concurrent possession of 'effective control of an area' or, as the case may be, the 'authority and control' over an individual needed for the Convention to apply; but the absence of that status does not suffice to render the Convention inapplicable extraterritorially.

---

859    *Al-Jedda*, § 77.
860    *Al-Jedda*, § 85.
861    *Jaloud*, §§ 113-114 and 125.
862    *Jaloud*, § 142.

Cases like *Al-Skeini* and *Jaloud* are, of course, different from cases like *Loizidou, Cyprus v. Turkey, Ilaşcu and Others* and *Catan and Others* in that the scene of events is not the territory of another Contracting State. The relevance of the difference is that in the latter situation – where the occupied territory is that of another Contracting State – the entire gamut of Convention rights must be applied in occupied territory as it is in the territory of the occupier, so as to prevent the occurrence of a local vacuum in the protection offered by the Convention; whereas in the former situation – where the scene of events is outside the territory of any Convention State, yet there is Article 1 jurisdiction – there may be scope (albeit limited) for the Convention rights to be 'divided and tailored' in the sense that the State's obligation under Article 1 is to secure to individuals under their 'authority and control' the rights and freedoms under Section I of the Convention (and of course the substantive rights under any Protocols that may be applicable) that are 'relevant to [their] situation'.[863]

It is nonetheless implicit that the obligation on the occupant to '[respect], unless absolutely prevented, the laws in force in the country' does not suffice to displace the obligation to secure to everyone within their jurisdiction the rights and freedoms set out in the Convention – in other words, in an occupation properly so-called within the meaning of Articles 42 and 43 of the Hague Regulations the Convention continues to take precedence over local law.[864] Only derogation under Article 15 of the Convention, when permissible, can change that[865] – and as we have seen, limits are imposed by that Article too.

It is appropriate at this point to draw attention to Article 53 of the Convention, which provides that '[n]othing in this Convention shall be construed as limiting or derogating from any of the human rights and fundamental freedoms which may be ensured under the laws of any High Contracting Party or under any other agreement to which it is a party' – and therefore requires an occupying Convention State to respect those rules of international humanitarian law, but also of its own law and even the domestic law of the occupied country, that offer human rights protection going beyond Convention standards.

---

863   *Al-Skeini*, § 137; *Jaloud*, § 154.

864   *Al-Saadoon and Mufdhi*, § 128.

865   Emanuela-Chiara Gillard, "International Humanitarian Law and Extraterritorial State Conduct", in *Extraterritorial Application of Human Rights Treaties*, edited by Fons Coomans and Menno Camminga (Intersentia, 2004), pp. 25-40 at p. 35.

## 6.8    Conclusion

It is uncontroversial that jurisdiction within the meaning of Article 1 exists when a Contracting State acts within its own territory. Few will dispute the logic of also recognising Article 1 jurisdiction to a Contracting State that actively connives at, or even simply permits, violations of the Convention to be perpetrated within its territorial jurisdiction by agents of a foreign state, or for that matter within its quasi-territorial jurisdiction – perhaps in one of its embassies abroad, or on board of a ship flying its flag or an aircraft bearing its registration. It is entirely conceivable that Article 1 jurisdiction may exist dually if the foreign agents belong to another Convention State.

We have seen how in *Cyprus v. Turkey* the Court was concerned that there be no 'jurisdictional gap', which led it to find that events in Northern Cyprus engaged the responsibility under the Convention of Turkey. We have seen in *Al-Skeini* and *Jaloud* how 'State agent authority and control' and 'control over an area' created extraterritorial jurisdiction within the meaning of Article 1, and hence accountability.

But is it necessary to resort to such reasoning when a State Party to the Convention permits itself to commit acts of violence, perhaps even amounting to murder, abroad?

The solution might be perfectly simple. Martin Scheinin makes the following suggestion, admittedly in the context of the International Covenant on Civil and Political Rights:

> ... the assassination of a targeted individual with a cruise missile, an anthrax letter sent from the neighboring country, a sniper's bullet in the head from the distance of 300 meters, or a poisoned umbrella tip on a crowded street all constitute "effective control" in respect of the targeted individual and his or her enjoyment of human rights when undertaken by agents of a foreign state.[866]

– but similar reasoning might be considered under the Convention. In cases of targeted assassination abroad, Article 1 jurisdiction would then be easy to establish, regardless of whether only the state in whose name the deed is done or both that state and the state in whose territory the deed is done are parties

---

866    Martin Scheinin, "Extraterritorial effect of the International Covenant on Civil and Political Rights", in *Extraterritorial Application of Human Rights Treaties* (Fons Coomans and Menno T. Kamminga, eds.), p. 73 *et seq.* at pp. 77-78.

to the Convention. Such reasoning does not sit ill with the Court's case-law until now.

However, this line of argument could only apply to *the targeted use of force* properly so-called. Once again, the sole fact of being an incidental 'victim' of an extraterritorial attack does not suffice to bring a person within the jurisdiction of the attacking Convention State: so to find would be to accept the kind of 'cause-and-effect' jurisdiction first rejected by the Court in *Banković*.

That is not to say that an innocent victim who becomes a casualty as 'collateral damage' in a targeted attack on an intended victim does not come within the Article 1 jurisdiction of the attacking Contracting State. Indeed, such a view would sit ill with the Court's case-law – specifically *Andreou v. Turkey*, in which Article 2 was held to apply to a person wounded by one of several rifle rounds fired deliberately but indiscriminately into a crowd of bystanders present when a protester was targeted and shot.[867]

The corollary that the targeted victim, even if he has been taken out for good reason, enjoys the protection of the Convention whereas the innocent bystander unfortunate enough to be in the wrong place at the wrong time may not, and that for the sole reason that no one was actually targeted, feels uncomfortable to be sure, but in the current state of the case-law is inescapable.

True it is that an applicant, especially an individual applicant under Article 34 of the Convention, may find it difficult to prove beyond reasonable doubt that the attack was targeted against a particular victim; it may be necessary for the Court, in such a case, to reverse the burden of proof back onto the respondent Government.[868] Conversely, before launching an attack a wise Government will take precautions to minimise – better still, avoid altogether – all danger to other than intended targets and be prepared to offer proof of these precautions afterwards.

---

867   *Andreou*, §§ 45-46.
868   See 2.7 above.

CHAPTER 7

# Jurisdiction of the European Court of Human Rights

## 7.1 Introduction

In the current redaction of the Convention, the Court's jurisdiction is defined by Article 32. That Article provides, firstly, that '[t]he jurisdiction of the Court shall extend to all matters concerning the interpretation and application of the Convention and the Protocols thereto which are referred to it as provided in Articles 33 [inter-State applications], 34 [individual applications], 46 [referrals by the Committee of Ministers of the Council of Europe of problems of interpretation and execution] and 47 [requests by the Committee of Ministers for advisory opinions]' and secondly, that '[i]n the event of dispute as to whether the Court has jurisdiction, the Court shall decide' (that is, the Court enjoys jurisdiction to define the scope of its own competence; this power is sometimes referred to using a German expression, *Kompetenz-Kompetenz*).

This chapter will examine the possibilities for removing the exercise of 'hard power' from the jurisdiction of the Court itself.

## 7.2 Territorial Limitations to the Acceptance of Convention Jurisdiction

Under the Convention of 1950, the right of individual petition to the then European Commission of Human Rights and the jurisdiction of the Court were conditional on specific declarations to be made by the Contracting State concerned (Articles 25 and 46, respectively, of the Convention of 1950).

Former Article 25 admitted of limiting the acceptance of the right of individual petition (at that time, to the Commission) to a specific period. Former Article 46 similarly allowed Contracting States to accept the Court's jurisdiction on condition of reciprocity on the part of several or certain other Contracting States or for a specified period.

In 1987, Turkey accepted the right of individual petition for a period of three years, but only in respect of 'allegations concerning acts or omissions of public authorities in Turkey performed within the boundaries of the territory to which the Constitution of the Republic of Turkey is applicable'. Greece

© KONINKLIJKE BRILL NV, LEIDEN, 2021 | DOI:10.1163/9789004425637_008

JURISDICTION OF THE EUROPEAN COURT OF HUMAN RIGHTS 255

protested; other Contracting States expressed reservations as to the validity of this restriction. Turkey later extended the validity of its declaration for further three-year periods, but again, only in respect of 'allegations concerning acts or omissions of public authorities in Turkey performed within the boundaries of the national territory of the Republic of Turkey'.

In 1990 Turkey made a declaration '[recognising] as compulsory *ipso facto* and without special agreement the jurisdiction of the European Court of Human Rights in all matters concerning the interpretation and application of the Convention which relate to the exercise of jurisdiction within the meaning of Article 1 of the Convention, performed within the boundaries of the national territory of the Republic of Turkey, and provided further that such matters have previously been examined by the Commission within the power conferred upon it by Turkey'. Again, Greece protested.

Given that Turkey recognised the 'Turkish Republic of Northern Cyprus' as a state in its own right, these declarations, taken at face value, excluded the possibility of invoking the Convention against Turkey in respect of matters occurring in northern Cyprus.

An application was brought against Turkey by three Cypriot nationals, one of them Mrs Loizidou, whom we have encountered before: she complained of her arrest and detention by Turkish forces and of denial of access to immovable property of which she claimed ownership. Turkey opposed its territorial restriction.

In its admissibility decision, the Commission '[found] no legal basis in the Convention for a restriction of a declaration under Article 25 other than the temporal limitations provided for in paragraph 2 of this Article'.[869]

Mrs Loizidou's case was later disjoined from those of the two other applicants. After the Commission adopted its report (former Article 31 of the Convention), the Government of Cyprus referred it to the Court.

The Court noted the absence from both Article 25 and Article 46 of any wording providing for territorial restrictions. It continued:

> If, as contended by the respondent Government, substantive or territorial restrictions were permissible under these provisions, Contracting Parties would be free to subscribe to separate regimes of enforcement of Convention obligations depending on the scope of their acceptances. Such a system, which would enable States to qualify their consent under the optional clauses, would not only seriously weaken the role of the Commis-

---

869 *Chrysostomos, Papachrysostomou and Loizidou v. Turkey*, nos. 15299/89, 15300/89 and 15318/89, Commission decision of 4 March 1991, DR 68, p. 216.

sion and Court in the discharge of their functions but would also diminish the effectiveness of the Convention as a constitutional instrument of European public order (*ordre public*).[870]

Continuing this line of reasoning, the Court went on to dismiss the argument of the Turkish Government that the lack of validity of the territorial restrictions invalidated the Turkish acceptance of the right of individual petition and the Court's jurisdiction.[871]

This ruling is now of historical interest only. Upon entry into force of Protocol No. 11 to the Convention, on 1 November 1998, acceptance of the right of individual petition to the New Court which had replaced the former Commission and Court became *de iure* mandatory – as indeed it had been, *de facto*, many a day before then.[872]

## 7.3 Reservation (Article 57 of the Convention)

Article 57 of the Convention (like its predecessor, Article 64 of the Convention of 1950) allows Contracting States to make reservations at the time of signature or ratification. This possibility is not unlimited: reservations must relate to a 'particular provision' of the Convention 'to the extent that any law then in force in [the territory of the Contracting State concerned] is not in conformity with the Convention'. Moreover, reservations of a general character are not permitted.

Obviously, making a reservation is no longer an option for Contracting States once they have submitted their instruments of ratification.[873]

The validity of reservations is within the jurisdiction of the Court to consider. Thus, at the time of its ratification of the Convention on 12 September 1997, Moldova made several declarations and reservations, including the following:

> The Republic of Moldova declares that it will be unable to guarantee compliance with the provisions of the Convention in respect of omissions and acts committed by the organs of the self-proclaimed Trans-

---

870  *Loizidou* (preliminary objections), 23 March 1995, § 75, Series A no. 310.

871  *Loizidou* (preliminary objections), § 91.

872  Protocol No. 11 to the Convention for the Protection of Human Rights and Fundamental Freedoms, restructuring the control machinery established thereby (ETS 155), Explanatory Report, para. 85.

873  See also Article 19 of the Vienna Convention on the Law of Treaties.

JURISDICTION OF THE EUROPEAN COURT OF HUMAN RIGHTS        257

Dniester republic within the territory actually controlled by such organs, until the conflict in the region is finally definitively resolved.

The Court did not accept this. It disposed of the Moldovan declaration in the following terms:

> It is true that in their observations the Moldovan Government maintained that the declaration should be interpreted as a negative declaration under former Article 25 of the Convention and, after 1 November 1998, under Article 34 of the Convention. However, the Court observes that when the present application was lodged, on 5 April 1999, former Article 25 of the Convention was no longer in force. Furthermore, the Court's jurisdiction to entertain an application under Article 34 of the Convention is not subject to acceptance of it by a High Contracting Party, unlike the competence of the Commission under former Article 25, which was subject to such acceptance.
>
> Secondly, the Court notes that the declaration does not refer to a specific law in force in Moldova. The words used by the Moldovan Government – "omissions and acts committed ... within the territory actually controlled by such organs, until the conflict in the region is finally definitively resolved" – indicate rather that the declaration in question is of general scope, unlimited as to the provisions of the Convention but limited in space and time, whose effect would be that persons on that "territory" would be wholly deprived of the protection of the Convention for an indefinite period.[874]

Similarly, Azerbaijan's reservation to the effect that it could not apply the Convention 'in the territories occupied by the Republic of Armenia until these territories [were] liberated from that occupation' failed to find favour in the eyes of the Court, which dismissed it in terms identical to those used in the Moldovan case.[875]

France, when depositing its instrument of ratification in 1974, made a reservation to the effect, firstly, that French constitutional and statutory provisions relating to the proclamation of a state of siege or emergency should be understood as complying with the purpose of Article 15 of the Convention, and secondly, that the expression 'strictly required by the exigencies of the situation' '[should] not restrict the power of the President of the Republic [under the

---

874    *Ilaşcu and Others v. Moldova and Russia* (dec.) [GC], no. 48787/99, 4 July 2001.
875    *Sargsyan v. Azerbaijan* (dec.), §§ 59-76.

258                                                                                                         CHAPTER 7

French Constitution] to take the measures required by the circumstances'.[876]
The state of emergency declared on 14 November 2015, after the terrorist attacks in Paris of the previous day, is stated in the French notice of derogation to
be based on these provisions.[877] However, as is also stated in the notice of derogation, '[t]he extension of the state of emergency for three months, with effect
from 26 November 2015, was authorised by Law No. 2015-1501 of 20 November
2015 [, which] law also amends certain of the measures provided for by the Law
of 3 April 1955 in order to adapt its content to the current context' – and may
therefore affect the validity of the reservation.[878]

   No less an author than Michael O'Boyle, former Deputy Registrar of the
Court and one who has done more to shape Convention law than any person
living, suggests that a reservation intended to 'tie the hands of an international
court from examining the compatibility of derogatory measures with one of
the central provisions of the Convention – in other words to exclude all international control of presidential emergency measures' – may be invalid simply
because it is incompatible with the system itself of the Convention.[879]

### 7.4    Conflicting International Obligations

Governments may occasionally cite conflicting obligations under international law that in their submission prevent them from complying with their obligations under the Convention.

   Article 53 of the Vienna Convention on the Law of Treaties provides that
a treaty is void if it conflicts with a peremptory rule of international law (*ius
cogens*). One such international legal obligation that would in theory override
the Convention is the prohibition of genocide, now generally considered to
be *ius cogens*,[880] and the concomitant obligation to punish or extradite (pref-

---

876    Information taken from the web site of the Council of Europe's Treaty Office, http://
       www.coe.int/en/web/conventions/full-list/-/conventions/treaty/005/declarations?p_
       auth=hZbjvpFr (retrieved on 12 April 2016).

877    Specifically, Law No. 55-385 of 3 April 1955 on the state of emergency. Information taken
       from the web site of the Council of Europe's Treaty Office (see previous footnote). (Re-
       trieved on 5 May 2016)

878    *Fischer v. Austria*, no. 16922/90, § 41, Series A no. 312; *Stallinger and Kuso* v. Austria, nos.
       14696/89 and 14697/89, § 48, Reports 1997-II; *Pauger v. Austria*, no. 16717/90, §§ 53-54,
       Reports 1997-III.

879    O'Boyle (2016) at p. 335. cf. Article 19 (c) of the Vienna Convention on the Law of Treaties.

880    International Court of Justice: *Democratic Republic of the Congo v. Rwanda* (judgment of
       3 February 2006, I.C.J. Reports 2006, p. 6), *Bosnia and Herzegovina v. Serbia and Montene-
       gro* (judgment of 26 February 2007, I.C.J. Reports 2007, p. 43) and *Germany v. Italy* (judg-

JURISDICTION OF THE EUROPEAN COURT OF HUMAN RIGHTS 259

erably to an international tribunal) those who have committed that crime.[881]
Another is the prohibition of torture.[882]

Article 28 of the Vienna Convention on the Law of Treaties provides that treaties shall not bind a party 'in relation to any act or fact which took place or any situation which ceased to exist before the date of the entry into force of the treaty with respect to that party'.

Conversely, Contracting States are considered to retain Convention liability in respect of treaty commitments subsequent to the entry into force of the Convention.[883] It does not follow, however, that the later treaty commitment is thereby extinguished: thus, the effect of Article 3 of the Convention is that in extradition cases where the person to be extradited faces the possibility of an irreducible term of life imprisonment – which would constitute a violation of that provision[884] – the Contracting State is under an obligation to accommodate its duty under a later bilateral extradition treaty to extradite with its prior Convention obligation by ensuring that the risk of such a violation is obviated.[885]

---

ment of 3 February 2012, I.C.J. Reports 2012, p. 99); International Tribunal for Rwanda: *Prosecutor v. Kayishema and Ruzindana* (ICTR-95-1-T, judgment of 21 May 1999) (note however the judgment of the Appeals Chamber in the same case, which avoids the expression *ius cogens* but describes the crime of genocide as "extremely grave": judgment of 1 June 2001, § 367). See *Vasiliauskas v. Lithuania* (GC), no. 35343/05, § 113, ECHR 2015.

881  Convention on the Prevention and Punishment of the Crime of Genocide (9 December 1948), Articles IV-VII. See *Jorgić v. Germany*, no. 74613/01, § 68, ECHR 2007-III, and *Stichting Mothers of Srebrenica and Others v. the Netherlands* (dec.), no. 65542/12, § 157, ECHR 2013.

882  *Al-Adsani v. the United Kingdom* (GC), no. 35763/97, § 61, ECHR 2001-XI; compare *H. and J. v. the Netherlands* (dec.), nos. 978/09 and 992/09, §§ 71-74, ECHR 2014 (which does not use the expression "*ius cogens*" but refers to Articles 146 and 147 of Geneva Convention (IV) on Civilians and Articles 4-8 of the Convention against Torture and Other Cruel, Inhuman or Degrading Treatment or Punishment). See also International Court of Justice, *Questions relating to the Obligation to Prosecute or Extradite (Belgium v. Senegal)*, Judgment, 20 July 2012, I.C.J. Reports 2012, p. 457 at § 99.

883  *Bosphorus Hava Yolları Turizm ve Ticaret Anonim Şirketi v. Ireland* (GC), no. 45036/98, § 154, ECHR 2005-VI; *Prince Hans-Adam II of Liechtenstein v. Germany* [GC], no. 42527/98, § 47, ECHR 2001-VIII.

884  *Vinter and Others v. the United Kingdom* (GC), nos. 66069/09, 130/10 and 3896/10, §§ 119-22, ECHR 2013; *Murray v. the Netherlands* (GC), no. 10511/10, §§ 101-12, ECHR 2016.

885  Lawson (1999), pp. 297-98 (referring to *Soering*, in which the question arose with respect to the conditions of detention on death row in the Commonwealth of Virginia, the extradition treaty applicable dating from 1899); more recently, *Harkins and Edwards v. United Kingdom*, nos. 9146/07 and 32650/07, § 138, 17 January 2012; *Trabelsi*, §§ 136-39.

The United Kingdom successfully invoked a prior treaty obligation before the Commission in the *Hess* case.[886] As we have seen,[887] Rudolf Hess was the last remaining Nazi prisoner in Spandau Prison. Mrs Hess alleged violations of Articles 3 and 8 of the Convention in that his continued imprisonment in a building capable of housing 600 inmates amounted to solitary confinement and in addition interfered with her own right to respect of her family life.

The United Kingdom was however bound by an agreement under which decisions regarding the administration of Spandau Prison had to be taken unanimously by the four Allied Powers – France, the United Kingdom, the USA, and the Soviet Union. The Soviet Union opposed its veto against attempts by the other three Powers to release Hess.

The Four Power Agreement dated from 1945, thus predating the Convention by five years; moreover, as the Commission found, the United Kingdom was not free to withdraw from it unilaterally. It therefore took precedence over the Convention.

A case in which a respondent sought to invoke conflicting international obligations *postdating* the Convention was *Al-Saadoon and Mufdhi v. the United Kingdom*. The applicants were Iraqi Baathists who were suspected of having orchestrated violent resistance against the multinational force. They were held, first by American, then by United Kingdom forces as 'security internees', until the Royal Military Police found indications linking them to the wilful killing of two British servicemen who had been captured by Iraqi forces during the hostilities and had been held as prisoners of war.

Pursuant to United Nations Security Council Resolution 1483, the Coalition Provisional Authority set up 'an Iraqi Special Tribunal (the 'Tribunal' [later to be known as the 'Iraqi High Tribunal' or 'IHT']) to try Iraqi nationals or residents of Iraq accused of genocide, crimes against humanity, war crimes or violations of certain Iraqi laws'. As between Iraq and the United Kingdom, a Memorandum of Understanding on criminal suspects was in force that granted the United Kingdom contingent of the Multinational Force discretion to keep persons wanted for prosecution before the Iraqi High Tribunal in its physical custody.

The validity of this Memorandum of Understanding was dependent on the mandate of the Multinational Force to remain in Iraq; it therefore came to an end on 31 December 2008, the date until which the United Nations Security Council Resolution had extended that mandate.

---

886    *Hess v. the United Kingdom*, no. 6231/73, Commission decision of 28 May 1975.
887    6.4.1.2 above.

JURISDICTION OF THE EUROPEAN COURT OF HUMAN RIGHTS       261

After the cases against the applicants concerning the deaths of the two British servicemen had been referred to the Iraqi courts, the Iraqi High Tribunal made repeated requests for the applicants to be handed over to it. The applicants, for their part, brought proceedings in the English courts seeking to prevent such handover absent assurances that the death penalty, if imposed, would not be carried out. The English courts, however, did not prevent the applicants' handover to the Iraqi authorities, holding (in accordance with their practice at the time – this was before the Court's judgment in *Al-Jedda*) that the United Kingdom's jurisdiction under Article 1 of the Convention was not in issue.

The United Kingdom Government, in the meantime, made representations to the Iraqi Government stating their opposition to the death penalty and asking for assurances that it would not be imposed on the applicants. The President of the IHT, President Aref, invited letters from the victims' families and from the British embassy in Baghdad opposing the imposition of the death penalty in this case, as 'that would be a factor which would be taken into account by the court', and also suggested that it would be helpful if the United Kingdom Government waived its right to civil compensation. Letters of such purport were provided by the British embassy and by the surviving family of one of the two British soldiers; the United Kingdom Government also waived civil compensation.

On 30 December 2008, after the failure of the proceedings brought by the applicants in England, the Court gave an indication under Rule 39 of the Rules of Court,[888] informing the respondent Government that the applicants should not be removed or transferred from the custody of the United Kingdom until further notice. The United Kingdom, however, faced with the expiry of the mandate of the Multinational Force and the Memorandum of Understanding on Criminal Suspects, transferred the applicants into Iraqi custody on the very next day.

The Court held as follows:

> 126. The Government contended that they were under an obligation under international law to surrender the applicants to the Iraqi authorities. In this connection, the Court notes that the Convention must be inter-

---

888   Rule 39 of the Rules of Court provides for the Court to indicate interim measures to the parties. The Court's practice is only to issue an interim measure against a Member State where, having reviewed all the relevant information, it considers that the applicant faces a real risk of serious, irreversible harm if the measure is not applied. See the Practice Direction "Requests for interim measures", available on the Court's Internet web site.

preted in the light of the rules set out in the Vienna Convention on the Law of Treaties of 1969, of which Article 31 § 3 (c) indicates that account is to be taken of "any relevant rules of international law applicable in the relations between the parties". More generally, the Court reiterates that the principles underlying the Convention cannot be interpreted and applied in a vacuum. The Convention should be interpreted as far as possible in harmony with other principles of international law of which it forms part (see *Al-Adsani v. the United Kingdom* [GC], no. 35763/97, § 55, ECHR 2001-XI, and *Banković and Others v. Belgium and Others* (dec.) [GC], no. 52207/99, § 55-57, ECHR 2001XII). The Court has also long recognised the importance of international cooperation (see *Al-Adsani*, cited above, § 54, and *Bosphorus Hava Yolları Turizm ve Ticaret Anonim Şirketi v. Ireland* [GC], no. 45036/98, § 150, ECHR 2005VI).

127. The Court must in addition have regard to the special character of the Convention as a treaty for the collective enforcement of human rights and fundamental freedoms. Its approach must be guided by the fact that the object and purpose of the Convention as an instrument for the protection of individual human beings requires that its provisions be interpreted and applied so as to make its safeguards practical and effective (see, *inter alia, Soering*, cited above, § 87; *Loizidou v. Turkey* (*preliminary objections*), 23 March 1995, § 72, Series A no. 310; and *McCann and Others*, cited above, § 146).

128. It has been accepted that a Contracting Party is responsible under Article 1 of the Convention for all acts and omissions of its organs regardless of whether the act or omission in question was a consequence of domestic law or of the necessity to comply with international legal obligations. Article 1 makes no distinction as to the type of rule or measure concerned and does not exclude any part of a Contracting Party's "jurisdiction" from scrutiny under the Convention (see *Bosphorus*, cited above, § 153). The State is considered to retain Convention liability in respect of treaty commitments subsequent to the entry into force of the Convention (*ibid.*, § 154 and the cases cited therein). For example, in *Soering* (cited above), the obligation under Article 3 of the Convention not to surrender a fugitive to another State where there were substantial grounds for believing that he would be in danger of being subjected to torture or inhuman or degrading treatment or punishment was held to override the United Kingdom's obligations under the Extradition Treaty it had concluded with the United States in 1972.[889]

---

889    *Al-Saadoon and Mufdhi*, §§ 126-128.

JURISDICTION OF THE EUROPEAN COURT OF HUMAN RIGHTS 263

In simple terms, therefore, the Convention ought to have taken precedence, not only because of its particular importance as a human rights instrument (which in itself is a consideration), but also – as a matter of general international law – as an earlier binding document preventing its Parties from subsequently entering into contrary legal obligations. Put differently, notwithstanding the obligations arising from the posterior agreement with Iraq, the United Kingdom remained responsible *ratione materiae* under Article 1 of the Convention.[890]

The irony of this case is that the United Kingdom Government might have won it on its facts: there may not have been any violation of the Convention at all. True, the Memorandum of Understanding on criminal suspects between the United Kingdom and Iraq, unlike a similar agreement with Afghanistan, did not explicitly prohibit use of the death penalty. However, the following curious passage appears in a Human Rights Annual Report for 2008 of the House of Commons Foreign Affairs Committee:[891]

> ... [T]he Government states that it has received *assurances* [emphasis added] in relation to the two men from:
>
> President of the Iraqi High Tribunal, President Aref, that a death sentence would be commuted, as well as written assurances from Deputy Justice Minister Posho that the two detainees will be treated humanely whilst in Iraqi detention. We are satisfied that the Government of Iraq is aware of its earlier assurances and have no reason to believe that they are not being adhered to.[892]

This titbit is not replicated in the Court's judgment, which was adopted on 2 February 2010. The Government's argument, as reflected in the judgment, relies on the limited use of the death penalty made by the IHT, on the various representations made by them to the Iraqi authorities and the president of the IHT and on the request for clemency submitted by the surviving relatives of one of the two victims, all of which reduce the likelihood of the applicants' being sent to the gallows, but it makes no mention of actual 'assurances'. Likewise, it is apparent from the partly dissenting opinion of Judge Sir Nicolas Bratza (who disagrees only with the finding of the majority that the refusal to comply with

---

890    Compare *Matthews v. the United Kingdom* (GC), no. 24833/94, § 33, ECHR 1999-I.
891    House of Commons Foreign Affairs Committee, Human Rights Annual Report for 2008, sent for printing on 21 July 2009 and published on 9 August 2009.
892    Statement by the United Kingdom Government, quoted by the House of Commons Foreign Affairs Committee, Human Rights Annual Report for 2008 (Seventh Report of Session 2008-09), page 49 (http://www.publications.parliament.uk/pa/cm200809/cmselect/cmfaff/557/557.pdf).

the Rule 39 indication violated Article 34 of the Convention) that the existence of 'assurances' was not argued by the respondent Party:

> The fact that, had the United Kingdom obtained the necessary assurances from those authorities some four years before, the applicants could have been safely transferred in December 2008, while undoubtedly relevant in the context of the complaint under Article 3 of the Convention, does not in my view affect the question which falls to be examined under Article 34. As to the latter point, while there are strong reasons to believe that the relevant assurances could have been obtained before the referral of the applicants' case to the Iraqi courts, the lack of success of the efforts made after June 2008 would clearly suggest that there was no realistic prospect of obtaining such assurances or achieving a temporary solution at a time when the expiry of the mandate was imminent, a point confirmed by the evidence of Mr Watkins before the Divisional Court and the Court of Appeal (...).

One is left to wonder whether the language used in the Human Rights Report was inaccurate or, alternatively, whether the respondent Government missed a potentially winning argument. The decision in *Boumediene and Others v. Bosnia and Herzegovina* suggests that the Court might well have reached a different decision under Article 3 of the Convention had it been aware of the promise of the President of the Iraqi High Tribunal: 'subsequent developments and, in particular, the assurances obtained by the [Bosnia-Herzegovina] authorities that the applicants would not be subjected to the death penalty, torture, violence or other forms of inhuman or degrading treatment or punishment' sufficed for the Court to find in that case that the respondent had taken 'all possible steps to the present date to protect the basic rights of the applicants' and accordingly to declare the application inadmissible.[893]

The German academic Peters posits the existence, between Germany and the USA, of secret agreements under which the American National Security Agency is granted access to the personal electronic data of individuals within Germany's jurisdiction. She argues that Contracting States cannot validly agree to, or turn a blind eye to, acts within their jurisdiction by non-Contracting States amounting to violations of rights guaranteed under Article 8 of the Convention. Her view is that such agreements, if they exist, are not necessarily unlawful in international law *per se* but must defer to human rights treaties like the Convention, these constituting international law of a higher order. Moreo-

---

893    *Boumediene and Others v. Bosnia and Herzegovina*, § 67.

# JURISDICTION OF THE EUROPEAN COURT OF HUMAN RIGHTS

ver, although admittedly the fact that they are not recorded in the United Nations Treaty Series does not affect their validity *per se* as between the contracting Parties, '... their secrecy does delegitimise them and makes the argument that they must somehow cede to the human rights treaties more plausible'.[894] Germany being among the first ten States that ratified the Convention, and for which the Convention entered into force on 3 September 1953, it would appear more straightforward at this point in history to argue that any such agreements would have to defer to the Convention on the more basic ground that they postdate the Convention.

Several cases raising precisely the question of 'lawfulness' and 'necessity in a democratic society' of the interception, collection and storage of data by, or on behalf of, a foreign intelligence service have been communicated to the Government of the United Kingdom. The applicants (groups of NGOs and individuals) base their complaints on *inter alia* the absence of an adequate basis in domestic law for the receipt by the United Kingdom security services of foreign intercept material relating to their electronic communications.[895]

## 7.5    Conclusion

General treaty law can be of only limited assistance to the defence of a respondent Contracting State.

The only territorial restrictions conceivable are constituted by the failure to extend the validity of the Convention or its Protocols to territories for whose international relations the Contracting State is responsible – that is, not applying the 'colonial clause' of Article 56.

Reservations can no longer be made now that the Convention is in force; and under ordinary treaty law may not be such as to frustrate the very purpose of the Convention as a treaty.

The substantive rights were first set out in the Convention text of 1950 and remain unchanged. The various Protocols entered into force on later dates.

---

894    Anne Peters, *Surveillance without Borders: The Unlawfulness of the NSA Panopticon, Part II*, EJIL:Talk!, 4 November 2013, http://www.ejiltalk.org/surveillance-without-borders-the-unlawfulness-of-the-nsa-panopticon-part-ii/ (retrieved on 31 March 2016).

895    *Big Brother Watch and Others v. the United Kingdom*, no. 58170/13, communicated on 7 January 2014; *The Bureau of Investigative Journalism and Alice Ross v. the United Kingdom*, no. 62322/14, communicated on 5 January 2015; *10 Human Rights Organisations and Others v. the United Kingdom*, no. 24960/15, communicated on 24 November 2015. See also the ensuing Chamber judgment, *Big Brother Watch and Others v. the United Kingdom*, nos. 58170/13, 62322/14 and 24960/15, 13 September 2018 (referred to the Grand Chamber).

They take priority *ratione temporis* over any treaty obligations entered into subsequently – and treaty obligations so venerable that they might override the substantive provisions of the Convention will now surely be few.

CHAPTER 8

# Attribution

## 8.1 Introduction

The questions of jurisdiction and attribution are not always distinct – especially in the type of situation covered by this study.

Nowhere in the Court's case-law has the distinction been better explained than by Judges Spielmann and Raimondi in their joint concurring opinion in *Jaloud*:

> 3. The concept of "attribution" is indeed to be distinguished from that of "jurisdiction" as the latter has been interpreted in the Court's case-law (see, recently, *Hassan v. the United Kingdom* [GC], no. 29750/09, § 74, 16 September 2014, which essentially reproduces the explanations in the *Al-Skeini* judgment (*Al-Skeini and Others v. the United Kingdom* [GC], no. 55721/07, §§ 130-141, ECHR 2011). The concept of "jurisdiction" essentially refers to the territorial principle, State agent authority and control, effective control over an area and the Convention legal space.
> 4. In contrast, the concept of "attribution" essentially concerns the sensitive issue of the "imputability" of internationally wrongful acts. Salmon's Dictionary has the following entry for the term "attribution":
> > "With regard to international-law responsibility, the fact of ascribing to a subject of international law the acts or omissions of individuals or bodies under its effective authority or acting on its behalf". [Translation]
> > (*Dictionnaire de droit international public*, edited by Jean Salmon, Preface by Gilbert Guillaume, Brussels, Bruylant, 2001).[896]

## 8.2 'Jurisdiction' and 'Attribution' in the Logic of the Court

### 8.2.1 *Relationship to the General Law on State Responsibility for Internationally Wrongful Acts*

As the Court stated in *Catan* and reiterated in *Jaloud* and *Mozer*, 'the test for establishing the existence of "jurisdiction" under Article 1 of the Convention

---

896    *Jaloud*, joint concurring opinions of Judges Spielmann and Raimondi.

© KONINKLIJKE BRILL NV, LEIDEN, 2021 | DOI:10.1163/9789004425637_009

has never been equated with the test for establishing a State's responsibility for an internationally wrongful act under general international law'.[897]

A set of Articles on State Responsibility for Internationally Wrongful Acts were drawn up by the International Law Commission over many years as a codification of existing general international law on the subject of State responsibility and endorsed as such by the United Nations General Assembly in 2001.[898] It has since then acquired increasing authority as an expression of customary international law on the subject.[899]

The first and second of these Articles read as follows:

### Article 1

Every internationally wrongful act of a State entails the international responsibility of that State.

### Article 2

There is an internationally wrongful act of a State when conduct consisting of an action or omission:
(a) is attributable to the State under international law; and
(b) constitutes a breach of an international obligation of the State.

The logic followed by the Commission and Court, which predates the General Assembly's endorsement of the ILC's Articles, is significantly different.

Article 1 of the ILC's Articles does not identify the state or states, or the other international legal persons, to which international responsibility is owed, but it is clear from the international legal context (and indeed, on a systematic reading, from the Articles as a whole) that these 'persons' must be invested with international legal personality; they accordingly do not include individual human beings or non-governmental organisations.[900] Consequently, obligations to make reparation for a breach of an obligation may be owed to 'another State, to several States, or to the international community as a whole'.[901]

---

897    *Catan*, § 115; *Jaloud*, § 154; *Mozer*, § 102.
898    A/Res/56/83. The Articles themselves are appended to that Resolution and quoted in Crawford (2013), pp. 712-723.
899    Crawford (2012), p. 540.
900    Crawford (2013), p. 49.
901    Article 33 § 1 of the Articles on State Responsibility for Internationally Wrongful Acts. Part Two of these Articles, which deals with the "content of the international responsibility of a State", is "without prejudice to any right, arising from the international responsibility of a State, which may accrue directly to any person or entity other than a State" (see Article 33 § 2 of these Articles).

ATTRIBUTION

In contrast, Article 1 of the Convention makes it clear that the obligation to secure the rights and freedoms defined in Section 1 of the Convention and corresponding parts of the Protocols are owed by States to 'everyone within their jurisdiction'. That begs the question who is 'within their jurisdiction'. It is therefore a reasonable corollary that the question whether 'jurisdiction' within the meaning of Article 1 of the Convention exists comes before any question of imputability or attribution.

### 8.2.2 The Concepts of 'Jurisdiction' and 'Attribution' in the Case-law of the Court

Thus, in its admissibility decision in *Chrysostomos, Papachrysostomou and Loizidou* the Commission established that the matters complained of came within the jurisdiction of Turkey.[902] In its report[903] in *Chrysostomos and Papachrysostomou*, adopted after Mrs Loizidou's case had been disjoined from the other two, the Commission considered the issue of attribution – or to use its expression, 'imputability' – separately in the following terms:

> 100. The Commission notes in this connection that Turkish armed forces are normally stationed in uninhabited border areas. It appears that, in the inhabited area of Nicosia close to the site of the demonstration, Turkish Cypriot soldiers were on guard on 19 July 1989. Turkish armed forces, if not present in that area, were elsewhere in or near Nicosia (...) and could thus intervene.
>
> 101. The Commission further notes that the Turkish Cypriot Security Forces are under the command of a General detached from Turkey (...).
>
> 102. In the light of the above elements the Commission, recalling the tactic of disguise pursued in the use of camouflage uniforms by Turkish and Turkish Cypriot soldiers (...) and noting the overall control exercised by Turkey in the border area (...), finds that the applicants' arrest in the border area on 19 July 1989 is imputable to Turkey.

In *Ilaşcu and Others* we find an excellent illustration from contemporary case-law of the Court of how the logic of the Convention bodies works in practice.[904]

It will be remembered that the complaint concerned the detention of persons in the 'Moldovan Republic of Transdniestria', an unrecognised entity ow-

---

902   *Chrysostomos, Papachrysostomou and Loizidou v. Turkey*, DR 68, p. 216; see also 6.4.1.1 above.

903   Article 31 of the Convention (text of 1950).

904   *Ilaşcu and Others*, § 311. See also *Catan and Others*, §§ 74 and 118-122.

270 CHAPTER 8

ing its *de facto* independence from Moldova to Russian military and economic support. With regard to Moldova, the Court held:

> The Court considers that where a Contracting State is prevented from exercising its authority over the whole of its territory by a constraining *de facto* situation, such as obtains when a separatist regime is set up, whether or not this is accompanied by military occupation by another State, it does not thereby cease to have jurisdiction within the meaning of Article 1 of the Convention over that part of its territory temporarily subject to a local authority sustained by rebel forces or by another State.
>
> Nevertheless, such a factual situation reduces the scope of that jurisdiction in that the undertaking given by the State under Article 1 must be considered by the Court only in the light of the Contracting State's positive obligations towards persons within its territory. The State in question must endeavour, with all the legal and diplomatic means available to it vis-à-vis foreign States and international organisations, to continue to guarantee the enjoyment of the rights and freedoms defined in the Convention.[905]

Thus, Moldovan Article 1 jurisdiction over the entirety of its territory does not cease: Moldova retains both the right and the duty to secure to all those within the territory purportedly belonging to the 'MRT' the rights and freedoms defined in Section I of the Convention and the Protocols which it has ratified. With respect to Moldova, the Court considered the case in terms of positive obligations – which were not to be interpreted 'in such a way as to impose an impossible or disproportionate burden'.[906] It would obviously have been unreasonable to require Moldova to attempt to dislodge the Russian army from its Transdniestrian territories or even prosecute individual 'MRT' officials responsible for the violations eventually found, but Moldova's efforts to reassert its authority, to secure the applicants' release – which were successful as regards at least one applicant –, and to guard the applicants' health by providing medical care in detention were found by the Court to be sufficient. However, Moldova was found responsible for failing to act once these efforts had ceased.[907]

Contrast the position with respect to the Russian Federation:

---

905   *Ilaşcu and Others*, § 333.
906   *Ilaşcu and Others*, § 332.
907   *Ilaşcu and Others*, §§ 339-352.

ATTRIBUTION

392. All of the above proves that the "MRT", set up in 1991-92 with the support of the Russian Federation, vested with organs of power and its own administration, remains under the effective authority, or at the very least under the decisive influence, of the Russian Federation, and in any event that it survives by virtue of the military, economic, financial and political support given to it by the Russian Federation.

393. That being so, the Court considers that there is a continuous and uninterrupted link of responsibility on the part of the Russian Federation for the applicants' fate, as the Russian Federation's policy of support for the regime and collaboration with it continued beyond 5 May 1998, and after that date the Russian Federation made no attempt to put an end to the applicants' situation brought about by its agents, and did not act to prevent the violations allegedly committed after 5 May 1998.

Regard being had to the foregoing, it is of little consequence that since 5 May 1998 the agents of the Russian Federation have not participated directly in the events complained of in the present application.

Paragraph 392 establishes the Russian Federation's extraterritorial 'jurisdiction' for purposes of Article 1 of the Convention – understood as arising from 'the fact of ... control, whether it be exercised directly, through its armed forces, or through a subordinate local administration'[908] – or, as in this case, both. Next, paragraph 393 establishes attribution to the Russian Federation.

The Court's admissibility decision in *Behrami and Saramati*, to which we will return below,[909] to all appearances does not fit comfortably into this mould. As we shall see, the Court goes straight to the question of 'attribution' – finding that the matters complained of are attributable to the United Nations – and finally declines to rule separately on Article 1 jurisdiction.[910] One may wonder however whether it would have served any useful purpose for the Court to go to the trouble of first establishing the Article 1 jurisdiction of France and Norway (presumably in terms of 'State agent authority and control'), only to conclude that the matters complained of were not attributable to them.

It is in the interpretation of attribution that the Court is most likely to draw inspiration from general international law, including in particular the case-law of the International Court of Justice and the work of the International Law

---

908  *Ilaşcu and Others*, § 314, citing § 52 of *Loizidou* (merits).

909  *Behrami and Behrami v. France and Saramati v. France, Germany and Norway* (dec.) (GC), nos. 71412/01 and 78166/01, 2 May 2007 ("*Behrami and Saramati*"). See 8.4.5.2.1 below.

910  *Behrami and Saramati*, §§ 151-153.

272                                                                                              CHAPTER 8

Commission, in particular Articles 4-8 of the ILC Articles on the Responsibility of States for Internationally Wrongful Acts.

## 8.3 Attribution of the Exercise of 'Hard Power' by the Contracting State

### 8.3.1 *Attribution of Extraterritorial Exercise of 'Hard Power'*

In judgments postdating *Ilaşcu and Others* in which the question of extraterritorial jurisdiction came up, the Court has generally not needed to devote specific attention to the question of attribution. That was because the facts left little room for doubt on that score.

Thus, in *Al-Skeini and Others*, the Court finds a 'jurisdictional link between the deceased and the United Kingdom for the purposes of Article 1 of the Convention' established through the authority and control exercised though its troops, then goes on in the following paragraph to find a 'jurisdictional link for the purposes of Article 1 of the Convention between the United Kingdom and the deceased'.[911] The violations found, it is recalled, were of Article 2 under its procedural head, so that there is no attribution of the actual deaths to the respondent party.

In *Al-Jedda* the respondent Government conceded the jurisdiction point, since the applicant had been detained in a British-run military prison, but tried to evade attribution by arguing that the British troops had been exercising not the sovereign authority of the United Kingdom but the international authority of the Multinational Force acting pursuant to the binding decision of the United Nations Security Council. The Court disagreed:

> The Court does not consider that, as a result of the authorisation contained in Resolution 1511, the acts of soldiers within the Multinational Force became attributable to the United Nations or – more importantly, for the purposes of this case – ceased to be attributable to the troop-contributing nations. The Multinational Force had been present in Iraq since the invasion and had been recognised already in Resolution 1483, which welcomed the willingness of member States to contribute personnel. The unified command structure over the Force, established from the start of the invasion by the United States of America and the United Kingdom, was not changed as a result of Resolution 1511. Moreover, the United States of America and the United Kingdom, through the CPA which they had established at the start of the occupation, continued to exercise the

---

911    *Al-Skeini*, § 149.

ATTRIBUTION

powers of government in Iraq. Although the United States of America was requested to report periodically to the Security Council about the activities of the Multinational Force, the United Nations did not, thereby, assume any degree of control over either the Force or any other of the executive functions of the CPA.[912]

The situation was distinguishable from that in *Behrami and Saramati*:

> In the light of the foregoing, the Court agrees with the majority of the House of Lords that the United Nations' role as regards security in Iraq in 2004 was quite different from its role as regards security in Kosovo in 1999. The comparison is relevant, since in its decision in *Behrami and Saramati* (...) the Court concluded, *inter alia*, that Mr Saramati's detention was attributable to the United Nations and not to any of the respondent States. It is to be recalled that the international security presence in Kosovo was established by United Nations Security Council Resolution 1244, adopted on 10 June 1999, in which, "determined to resolve the grave humanitarian situation in Kosovo", the Security Council "decide[d] on the deployment in Kosovo, under United Nations auspices, of international civil and security presences". The Security Council therefore authorised "member States and relevant international organisations to establish the international security presence in Kosovo" and directed that there should be "substantial North Atlantic Treaty Organization participation" in the Force, which "must be deployed under unified command and control". In addition, Resolution 1244 authorised the Secretary-General of the United Nations to establish an international civil presence in Kosovo in order to provide an interim administration for Kosovo. The United Nations, through a Special Representative appointed by the Secretary-General in consultation with the Security Council, was to control the implementation of the international civil presence and coordinate closely with the international security presence (see *Behrami and Saramati*, cited above, §§ 3, 4 and 41). On 12 June 1999, two days after the Resolution was adopted, the first elements of the NATO-led Kosovo Force (KFOR) entered Kosovo.[913]

---

912  *Al-Jedda*, § 80.
913  *Behrami and Saramati*, § 83.

In *Hassan* the Court discussed jurisdiction at length, applying *Al-Skeini*, but did not rule separately on attribution.[914] Again, this was a detention case.

In *Jaloud* the Court established the Article 1 jurisdiction of the Netherlands, dismissing the suggestion that jurisdiction belonged exclusively to the United States and United Kingdom concurrently as 'occupying powers' or to the United Kingdom alone as 'lead nation' in south-eastern Iraq, the Dutch troops being subordinate to the British commander.[915] It then establishes attribution in the following terms:

> The facts giving rise to the applicant's complaints derive from alleged acts and omissions of Netherlands military personnel and investigative and judicial authorities. As such they are capable of giving rise to the responsibility of the Netherlands under the Convention[916]

– superfluously, in the view of Judges Spielmann and Raimondi whom we quoted at the beginning of this chapter, since in their view it is a 'non-issue' given the terms in which the judgment establishes jurisdiction.

### 8.3.2 *Attribution of Exercise of 'Hard Power' Committed within the Territory of a Contracting State*

The question of attribution also arises when a Contracting State tolerates on its territory acts contrary to the Convention committed by foreign agents. This was the situation in *El-Masri* and the four *Al Nashiri* and *Abu-Zubaydah* cases.

By 2014, when the first *Al Nashiri* and *Abu-Zubaydah* judgments were delivered, it was settled case-law that a State Party to the Convention must be regarded as responsible under the Convention for acts performed by foreign officials on its territory with the acquiescence or connivance of its authorities. In the Court's words:

> Taking into consideration all the material in its possession (...), the Court finds that there is abundant and coherent circumstantial evidence, which leads inevitably to the following conclusions:
> (a) that Poland knew of the nature and purposes of the CIA's activities on its territory at the material time and that, by enabling the CIA to use its airspace and the airport, by its complicity in disguising the movements of rendition aircraft and by its provision of logistics and services, including

---

914   *Hassan*, §§ 74-80.
915   *Jaloud*, §§ 142-152.
916   *Jaloud*, § 155.

ATTRIBUTION

the special security arrangements, the special procedure for landings, the transportation of the CIA teams with detainees on land, and the securing of the Stare Kiejkuty base for the CIA's secret detention, Poland cooperated in the preparation and execution of the CIA rendition, secret detention and interrogation operations on its territory;

(b) that, given that knowledge and the emerging widespread public information about ill-treatment and abuse of detained terrorist suspects in the custody of the US authorities, Poland ought to have known that, by enabling the CIA to detain such persons on its territory, it was exposing them to a serious risk of treatment contrary to the Convention (see also *El-Masri*, cited above, §§ 217-221).

Consequently, Poland was in a position where its responsibility for securing "to everyone within [its] jurisdiction the rights and freedoms defined ... in [the] Convention" set forth in Article 1 was engaged in respect of the applicant at the material time.[917]

This confirms that the Court considers witting toleration by a Convention State of unlawful acts by a non-Convention Government as falling under the direct responsibility of the Convention State – a form of complicity if one will – as is indeed logical.

Similarly, the removal of the applicants from Polish territory engaged the responsibility of Poland under Articles 3, 5 and 6 of the Convention.[918] On the latter point, however, the Court was careful to point out, as it had in *Soering*, that

While the establishment of the sending State's responsibility inevitably involves an assessment of conditions in the destination country against the standards set out in the Convention, there is no question of adjudicating on or establishing the responsibility of the destination country, whether under general international law, under the Convention or otherwise.

In so far as any liability under the Convention is or may be incurred, it is liability incurred by the sending Contracting State by reason of its having taken action which has as a direct consequence the exposure of

---

917  *Al Nashiri v. Poland*, § 442-43; *Husayn (Abu Zubaydah) v. Poland*, § 444-45.
918  *Al Nashiri v. Poland*, § 454-55; *Husayn (Abu Zubaydah) v. Poland*, no. 7511/13, § 454. See also *Abu Zubaydah v. Lithuania*, § 586, and *Al Nashiri v. Romania*, § 601 (same applicants, different respondents).

276                                                                    CHAPTER 8

an individual to proscribed ill-treatment or other violations of the Convention (...).[919]

This applies all the more, one might add, since the responsibility of the sending State flows not from an act which is in itself entirely in conformity with the Convention – in *Soering*, the extradition of a murder suspect to face trial – but from acquiescing in a situation that is illegal *per se*.

The cooperation of European Governments with the CIA rendition programme must rank among the darkest pages of the history of the Contracting States concerned since they joined the Council of Europe family of States. While of course their American allies were chiefly at fault as the active perpetrators, the Contracting States cannot escape attribution: their responsibility under the Convention is engaged, whether by virtue of their active connivance of their tacit consent.[920]

Let Senator Marty, whom we met in 6.3 above and who documented all the rendition cases thus far mentioned, have the last word:

> This situation is also due to the attitude of those European governments, which abandoned all control over the use of their own infrastructures they unconditionally put at the disposal of the American administration, in the wake of the acceptation of the implementation of Article 5 of the NATO treaty and of the operative measures accepted by the members of the alliance. In this way, the European governments effectively placed themselves in a position of reliance or even dependence on the good will of the American authorities.[921]

## 8.4 Involvement of Agents Other than Organs of the Contracting State

### 8.4.1 *General International Law*
In general international law, the position that a state is responsible for the acts of entities on its behalf is currently codified in Article 8 of the ILC's Articles on Responsibility of States for Internationally Wrongful Acts, which reads as follows:

---

919  *Al Nashiri v. Poland*, § 457; *Husayn (Abu Zubaydah) v. Poland*, § 454-55. See also *Abu Zubaydah v. Lithuania*, § 584, and *Al Nashiri v. Romania*, § 598.
920  *El-Masri*, § 206.
921  Third Marty report, § 14 (footnote references omitted).

ATTRIBUTION

> The conduct of a person or group of persons shall be considered an act of a State under international law if the person or group of persons is in fact acting on the instructions of, or under the direction or control of, that State in carrying out the conduct.

Within the terms of this provision two situations may be distinguished. The first is that in which the entity has been *instructed* to perform the acts in question. The second is that in which the entity is under the *direction* or *control* of the state concerned.[922]

The first situation, in which the entity – whatever its nature – has accepted instructions to act in a particular way, will normally give rise to few difficulties. In contrast, questions may arise as to the degree of direction or control required to deem the entity truly subordinate, and its acts attributable to the state.

The ILC calls it 'a matter for appreciation in each case whether particular conduct was or was not carried out under the control of a State, to such an extent that the conduct controlled should be attributed to it.'[923] Thus, in *Nicaragua*, the International Court of Justice held the United States accountable for acts of the *contras* 'only in certain individual instances ... based upon actual participation of and directions given by that State'; a 'general situation of dependence and support' would not of itself be sufficient.

In the *Bosnian Genocide* judgment, the International Court of Justice clarified this – and its understanding of the ILC's Article 8 – as follows:

> ... it is not necessary to show that the persons who performed the acts alleged to have violated international law were in general in a relationship of "complete dependence" on the respondent State; it has to be proved that they acted in accordance with that State's instructions or under its "effective control". It must however be shown that this "effective control" was exercised, or that the State's instructions were given, in respect of each operation in which the alleged violations occurred, not generally in respect of the overall actions taken by the persons or groups of persons having committed the violations.[924]

---

922   Crawford (2012), p. 144.

923   ILC Commentary on the Draft Articles, Article 8, § 5.

924   *Application of the Convention on the Prevention and Punishment of the Crime of Genocide (Bosnia and Herzegovina v. Serbia and Montenegro)*, Judgment, 26 February 2007, I.C.J. Reports 2007, § 400.

It would appear to matter little how the entity in issue sees itself. For example, the *contras* opposing the Sandinista government in Nicaragua, in issue in the Nicaragua case before the International Court of Justice,[925] may have aspired to government status, but it would have been clear to them that they never achieved it. In contrast, during the war of 1992-1995 the Republika Srpska, in issue in the *Bosnian Genocide* case,[926] saw itself as an independent state, having declared independence in April 1992. So also does the Turkish Republic of Northern Cyprus, cited as an example in the ILC Commentary itself,[927] view itself as an independent state, although its statehood is recognised only by Turkey.[928] The entity may even be a commercial company, state-owned or not.[929]

The ILC Commentary on Article 8 ends with a useful reminder:

> Article 8 uses the words "person or group of persons", reflecting the fact that conduct covered by the article may be that of a group lacking separate legal personality but acting on a *de facto* basis. Thus, while a State may authorize conduct by a legal entity such as a corporation, it may also deal with aggregates of individuals or groups that do not have legal personality but are nonetheless acting as a collective.[930]

### 8.4.2 *Private Agents: Case-law of the Court*

In its general case-law, the Court has held the use by the State of private agents to engage the State's responsibility. Thus, it has held in the context of Articles 6 and 8 of the Convention in relation to the use of covert means of criminal investigation that a Contracting State could not evade its responsibility under the Convention by allowing investigating authorities to relinquish control of events to private agents. For example, in *A. v. France*, it held that the covert use by police officers of a private agent to make a recording of an incriminating statement by a criminal suspect engaged the responsibility of the Contracting

---

925     *Military and Paramilitary Activities in and against Nicaragua (Nicaragua v. United States of America)*, Merits, Judgment, 27 June 1986, I.C.J. Reports 1986.

926     *Application of the Convention on the Prevention and Punishment of the Crime of Genocide (Bosnia and Herzegovina v. Serbia and Montenegro)*, Judgment, 26 February 2007, I.C.J. Reports 2007.

927     ILC Commentary, Article 8, § 5 and footnote 160 (reference to §§ 52 and 56 of *Loizidou (Merits)*).

928     Even to the point of entering into treaties with it, such as the treaty signed in New York on 21 September 2011 delimiting the maritime boundary between their respective continental shelves. Turkish Official Gazette, 12 July 2012, no. 28351.

929     ILC Commentary on the Draft Articles, Article 5, §§ 2 and 6.

930     ILC Commentary on the Draft Articles, Article 5, § 9.

ATTRIBUTION

State and violated Article 8 of the Convention.[931] It reached similar findings in the cases of *M.M. v. the Netherlands* and *Van Vondel v. the Netherlands*.[932] In *Allan v. the United Kingdom* it found a violation of Article 6 of the Convention in relation to the use in evidence of a statement made by a remand prisoner to a fellow inmate who had been instructed by the police to obtain from that prisoner a confession.[933]

It is submitted that this case-law is relevant to the use of private agents to exercise 'hard power' inasmuch as it illustrates that the use of private agents cannot suffice to relieve a Contracting State of its responsibility under the Convention.

### 8.4.3    *Private Military Security Contractors*
James Crawford calls the use of private military or security corporations hired by the state to engage in certain activities on its behalf 'a 'simple example' of private persons or entities acting on the instruction of a State within the meaning of Article 8 of the ILC Articles.[934]

Private military security contractors can offer advantages to Contracting States. For example, it may be more economical to outsource certain tasks to outside contractors on a temporary basis rather than create and maintain the required capacity as part of the standing armed forces of the State.[935]

### 8.4.3.1    On Land
The use of private contractors for tasks that were formerly seen as part of the traditional remit of the military is a phenomenon that has come to public notice only in recent years. For example, it was reported in 2007 that the Netherlands military in Afghanistan relied on private contractors for its catering and the supply of its rations and fuel; that the maintenance of military materiel was left to civilian mechanics; that armed Afghan contractors carried out guard duties around Dutch military bases; and that in training local security forces the

---

931    *A. v. France*, no. 14838/89, § 36, Series A no. 277-B.
932    *M.M. v. the Netherlands*, no. 39339/98, § 40, 8 April 2003; *Van Vondel v. the Netherlands*, no. 38258/03, § 49, 25 October 2007. The dissenting voices in the two Dutch cases – Judge Palm in *M.M.* and Judge Myjer in *Van Vondel*, commenting on *M.M.* – disagreed with the majority on the interpretation to be given to the facts of that case but not on the principle.
933    *Allan v. the United Kingdom*, no. 48539/99, § 52, ECHR 2002-IX.
934    Crawford (2013), p. 145.
935    AIV (*Adviesraad internationale vraagstukken*, Advisory Council on International Affairs,), *De inhuur van private militaire bedrijven, een kwestie van verantwoordelijkheid* (Employing private military companies, a question of responsibility), December 2007, pp. 12-14.

280                                                                      CHAPTER 8

Dutch military presence worked closely with a private party contracted by the American government.[936]

When such private contractors are entrusted with tasks that may entail the use of force, casualties can – and sometimes do – result, witness for example a shooting incident involving an American private military contractor that took place in Baghdad on 16 September 2007 and led to seventeen deaths among the local population.[937]

Private military and security contractors are bound by the local laws precisely because they are private parties not members of any government's armed forces. In principle, this does not change when they are in the pay of a foreign government, as in Afghanistan or Iraq.

In Iraq, however, the head of the Coalition Provisional Authority, Ambassador L. Paul Bremer III, decreed that private military contractors should be 'immune from Iraqi legal process with respect to acts performed by them pursuant to the terms and conditions of a Contract or any sub-contract thereto', although they remained bound to respect Iraqi laws, including in particular those promulgated by the Coalition Provisional Authority itself.[938]

In Afghanistan, the Technical Military Agreement between ISAF/NATO and the interim government of Afghanistan made the Convention on the Privileges and Immunities of the United Nations of 13 February 1946 concerning experts on mission applicable, *mutatis mutandis*, to the ISAF and supporting personnel – the latter being understood in practice to include private military contractors.[939]

It was not entirely clear in either case whether the contractors and their staff were subject to the jurisdiction of their sending state or their state of in-

---

936  AIV, *De inhuur van private militaire bedrijven, een kwestie van verantwoordelijkheid* (Employing private military companies, a question of responsibility), p. 5.

937  "Blackwater incident: what happened", BBC News, 8 December 2008, http://news.bbc. co.uk/2/hi/7033332.stm (accessed 17 April 2017); CBS News, "Blackwater guards found guilty in Baghdad mass shootings", 23 October 2014, http://www.cbsnews.com/news/ blackwater-case-former-guards-convicted-in-baghdad-mass-shootings (accessed 17 April 2017); The New York Times, "Ex-Blackwater Guards Given Long Terms for Killing Iraqis", 13 April 2015, https://www.nytimes.com/2015/04/14/us/ex-blackwater-guards-sentenced-to-prison-in-2007-killings-of-iraqi-civilians.html (accessed 17 April 2017).

938  Coalition provisional authority order number 17 (revised), 27 June 2004, section 4 (3) and (4).

939  David Nauta, *The International Responsibility of NATO and its Personnel during Military Operations: A study on international public law and international criminal law* (diss. Nijmegen 2016), Wolf Legal Publishers, p. 32.

corporation or nationality (if different).[940] In terms of the Convention, however, this distinction would not necessarily be decisive for the question of jurisdiction within the meaning of Article 1 of the Convention, which as we have seen concerns primarily the undertaking of the Contracting State to secure the rights and freedoms defined in the Convention and its Protocols (jurisdiction in terms of duty) rather than the power to legislate and enforce.[941]

As we have seen in paragraph 8.4.2 above, the Court has held in the context of criminal investigations that a Contracting State could not evade its responsibility under the Convention by allowing investigating authorities to relinquish control of events to private agents. Taking the reasoning further, this would mean that a State Party to the Convention that entrusts the use of force or coercive powers to private contractors would continue to be bound by its obligations under, at the very least, Articles 2, 3, 4 and 5. After all, on the ordinary meaning of the words, such contractors would surely be under the Contracting State's 'direction' and 'control'.[942]

The point is also made by the Dutch Government's Advisory Council on International Affairs that States retain the monopoly on the use of lawful force, and that consequently the Government remain answerable in law for the use of force on its behalf by private contractors on foreign soil.[943]

This means creating an appropriate regulatory framework, accompanied by the necessary supervision and the threat of penal sanctions, to prevent violations of Convention rights and providing access to domestic remedies.[944]

A joint initiative of the Swiss Federal Government and the International Committee of the Red Cross led to the publication, following consultations

---

940 For an interpretation of the situation with respect to the Netherlands, see Adviesraad internationale vraagstukken (Advisory Council on International Affairs), *De inhuur van private militaire bedrijven, een kwestie van verantwoordelijkheid* (Employing private military companies, a question of responsibility), December 2007, p. 18.

941 See 5.1 above.

942 *The New Shorter Oxford English Dictionary* (1993 ed.) gives definitions of "direction" including "1. The action or function of directing; guidance, instruction; management. lME. ... 3. An instruction on what to do, how to proceed, or where to go. Usually in *pl.* ..." and of "control" including "1. The act or power of directing or regulating; command, regulating influence. ...".

943 AIV, *De inhuur van private militaire bedrijven, een kwestie van verantwoordelijkheid* (Employing private military companies, a question of responsibility), p. 31. See also Ian M. Ralby, "Private Military Companies and the *Jus and Bellum*", in *The Oxford Handbook of the Use of Force in International Law* (Mark Weller, ed.), p. 1131 at pp. 1145-46.

944 See James Cockayne, "Private Military and Security Companies", in *The Oxford Handbook of International Law in Armed Conflict* (Andrew Clapham, Paola Gaeta, eds.), Oxford University Press 2014, p. 625, at pp. 640-643; Helen Duffy, *The 'War on Terror and the Framework of International Law*, pp. 111-112. See also 2.2.2 and 2.7 above.

282

CHAPTER 8

with governmental experts from countries including Convention States Parties Austria, France, Germany, Poland, Sweden Switzerland, the United Kingdom and Ukraine, of the 'Montreux Document on pertinent international legal obligations and good practices for States related to operations of private military and security companies during armed conflict' in September 2008.[945] As its name implies, it is addressed to states – 'Contracting States', meaning States that make use of private military and security contractors; 'Territorial States', meaning States on whose territory such contractors operate; and 'Home States', meaning States in which such contractors are based – setting out standards for them to establish 'effective oversight and control'. The standards it sets are derived from international humanitarian law and international human rights law. It is not an international treaty – it does not set binding rules – but states and international organisations can join as 'participating' states and organisations. So far, it has been joined by 54 states – including 34 States Parties to the Convention – and three international organisations.[946]

However, thus far it has been largely been left to the private military and security sector itself to regulate its conduct. An International Code of Conduct for Private Security Service Providers, concluded on 9 November 2010, invites private security contractors to subscribe to basic human rights standards as regards the use of force, the apprehending and detention of persons, sexual abuse and exploitation, human trafficking and slavery and child labour. Incidents are required to be reported to the 'Competent Authority' – defined as 'any state or intergovernmental organization which has jurisdiction over the activities and/or persons in question'. A public list of signatory companies is kept by the Swiss federal government.[947] The lack of precise government regulation is not without its critics.[948]

In a more recent development, the International Organization for Standardization (ISO) published an industry standard – ISO 18788 – entitled 'Man-

---

945    Montreux Document, https://www.icrc.org/eng/assets/files/other/icrc_002_0996.pdf (accessed on 26 March 2017).

946    All Council of Europe States have joined except Armenia, Andorra, Azerbaijan, Latvia, Malta, Montenegro, Moldova, Romania, Russia, San Marino, Serbia, Slovakia and Turkey. So have the European Union, the OSCE and NATO: https://www.eda.admin.ch/eda/en/home/foreign-policy/international-law/international-humanitarian-law/private-military-security-companies/participating-states.html (accessed on 26 March 2017). For a critical appraisal of the Montreux Document, see Ralby, pp. 1154 *et seq.*

947    International Code of Conduct for Private Security Service Providers, 9 November 2010, https://icoca.ch/en (English) (accessed on 26 March 2017).

948    Elke Krahmann, "Choice, Voice and exit: Consumer power and the self-regulation of the private security industry", 1 European Journal of International Security (2016) pp. 27-48.

ATTRIBUTION

agement system for private security operations – Requirements with guidance for use' in September 2015. This standard

> provides a business and risk management framework for organizations conducting or contracting security operations and related activities and functions while demonstrating:
> a) conduct of professional security operations to meet the requirements of clients and other stakeholders;
> b) accountability to law and respect for human rights;
> c) consistency with voluntary commitments to which it subscribes.[949]

### 8.4.3.2 At Sea

The use of private military and security contractors on board merchant ships to deter, and if necessary repel, attack by pirates deserves to be considered separately.

The argument has been made that States Party to the Convention are obliged to protect those on board ships flying their flag against any known risk of being injured, killed, or taken hostage by pirates. There is support in the Court's case-law for that position.[950] The corollary of this view is that any failure of a flag State Government to meet this obligation will accordingly be attributable to the flag State.

The deployment, by the flag state, of its own military forces on board ships flying its flag raises no problems of jurisdiction from a Convention perspective. The flag State has jurisdiction both because it is the flag state[951] and by dint of its command and control of its armed forces.[952] Some Governments are however baulked by the difficulties of deploying military forces on merchant vessels: the Dutch Minister of Defence, for example, has referred to 'logistical

---

949 International Organization for Standardization, https://www.iso.org/standard/63380. html (accessed on 27 March 2017).

950 Stefano Piedimonte Bodini, *Fighting Maritime Piracy under the European Convention on Human Rights*, (2011) 22 EJIL p. 829 at p. 839; Sofia Galani, *Somali piracy and the human right of seafarers*, (2016) 34 Netherlands Quarterly of Human Rights p. 71 at p. 81. See, *inter alia* and *mutatis mutandis, Osman v. the United Kingdom*, no. 23452/94, § 116, Reports 1998-VIII, and *Finogenov and Others v. Russia*, nos. 18299/03 and 27311/03, § 209, ECHR 2011 (Article 2); *Opuz v. Turkey*, no. 33401/02, §§ 130 and 159, ECHR 2009; *Rantsev v. Cyprus and Russia*, no. 25965/04, §§ 284 and 319 (Articles 4 and 5); and *Riera Blume v. Spain*, no. 37680/97, §§ 28-35, Reports 1997-VII (Article 5).

951 Article 94 of UNCLOS; see also generally Douglas Guilfoyle, "The Use Of Force Against Pirates", in *The Oxford Handbook of the Use of Force in International Law* (Mark Weller, ed.), Oxford University Press 2015, p. 1057 at pp. 1067-1071.

952 See above para. 5.5.2.1; see also Guilfoyle at p. 1066.

problems, legal restrictions and risks' that make such deployment impracticable.[953]

The International Maritime Organisation (IMO) strongly discourages the carrying and use of firearms for personal protection or protection of a ship, among other reasons because this 'may encourage attackers to carry firearms thereby escalating an already dangerous situation, and any firearms on board may themselves become an attractive target for an attacker'.[954]

For merchant ships to have any protection at all, if their own crews are unable for whatever reason to ensure their own defence, the remaining alternative is to engage the services of private security providers. IMO, 'while not endorsing the use of privately contracted armed security personnel',[955] offers guidance on the subject. IMO's circular notes that

> ... flag State jurisdiction and thus any laws and regulations imposed by the flag State concerning the use of PMSC [private maritime security companies] and PCASP [privately contracted armed security personnel] apply to their ships. Furthermore it is also important to note that port and coastal States' laws may also apply to such ships.[956]

– which brings us back to the matters discussed in paragraphs 5.3.1 and 5.4.1 above.

### 8.4.4 *Cyber-attacks as a New Problem of Attribution*
Cases arising from cyber-attacks have yet to reach the Court. The best a study such as this can do, therefore, is chart some of the likely dangers lurking beneath these uncertain waters.

The Tallinn Manual 2.0, which we have encountered above, states that

---

953 AIV, *Piraterijbestrijding op zee: een herijking van publieke en private verantwoordelijkheden* (Combating piracy at sea: a reassessment of public and private responsibilities), January 2010, p. 28.

954 IMO, "Piracy and armed robbery against ships: Guidance to shipowners and ship operators, shipmasters and crews on preventing and suppressing acts of piracy and armed robbery against ships", MSC/Circ.632/Rev.3, 29 May 2002, §§ 45-46.

955 IMO, "Revised interim guidance to shipowners, ship operators and shipmasters on the use of privately contracted armed security personnel on board ships in the high risk area" [sc. the waters off Somalia], MSC.1/Cric.1405/Rev.2, 25 May 2012, § 1.1.

956 *ibid.*, § 1.4.

> Cyber operations conducted by organs of a State, or by persons or entities empowered by domestic law to exercise elements of governmental authority, are attributable to the State.[957]

That is obvious enough. This rule derives directly from Articles 4 and 5 of the International Law Commission's Articles on State Responsibility. The Netherlands Royal Army's Defence Cyber Command and the French ANSSI (*Agence nationale de la sécurité des systèmes d'information*) are part of the defence forces of their respective states and their acts are attributable to the Netherlands and France respectively.[958] The Estonian Cyber Defence Unit is part of the Estonian Defence League, a volunteer unit with legal status under Estonian public law that coexists with the Estonian Defence Forces within the Estonian Defence Organisation and is placed under the orders of the Commander of the Estonian Defence Forces in wartime; there is little doubt that its acts, too, would be those of the Republic of Estonia.[959]

States may outsource cyber activities to private contractors, or to volunteer organisations without any official status under public law, simply because they lack the resources to set up agencies of their own. Again, there is little doubt that the acts of those contractors or organisations would be attributable to the State – at least as long as they were carried out on the State's behalf. Should those contractors or organisations act *ultra vires* but still generally within the scope of their duties, it would still be necessary for the State to accept attribution. Again, this is nothing novel: we are still within the ordinary rules governing State responsibility for internationally wrongful acts.[960]

However, experience suggests that those who carry out cyber-attacks on the assets and infrastructure of foreign States are likely to disguise their identities, perhaps by creating botnets – networks of robot devices – hacking computers of innocent third parties as 'zombies'. To complicate matters further, the attackers may disguise their identities by impersonating others, perhaps even a foreign government or an international organisation – 'spoofing'.[961] It may

---

957 Tallinn Manual 2.0, Rule 15 (p. 87).

958 Tallinn Manual 2.0, *ibid.*

959 Tallinn Manual 2.0, *ibid.*; NATO Cooperative Cyber Defence Centre of Excellence, *The Cyber Defence Unit of the Estonian Defence League* (2013), pp. 10-11.

960 Tallinn Manual 2.0, p. 90; see also Rule 17 on p. 94 and ILC Draft Articles 5 and 7 on State Responsibility for Internationally Wrongful Acts; see also Michael N. Schmitt, "The Use of Cyber Fore and International Law", in *The Oxford Handbook of the Use of Force in International Law* (Mark Weller, ed.), Oxford University Press 2015, p. 1110 at p. 1113.

961 Tallinn Manual 2.0, p. 91. Compare *Military and Paramilitary Activities in and against Nicaragua (Nicaragua v. United States of America)*, Merits, Judgment, 27 June 1986, I.C.J. Reports 1986, § 57.

286 CHAPTER 8

be very difficult to pin responsibility for a cyber-attack on any particular individual, organisation or government.

It is submitted, therefore, that Convention States bear a responsibility for preventing others from carrying out cyber-attacks from within their jurisdiction. The 'duty to establish, maintain, and safeguard international telecommunication infrastructure' identified by the Tallinn Manual 2.0 as its Rule 61[962] does not go far enough. In the same way that the State is required to do all that can be reasonably expected of it to secure the practical and effective exercise of the right to life – and as the WannaCry ransomware attack has demonstrated, human life may well be endangered by cyber-attacks[963] – the State is required to put in place an appropriate legislative framework that enables it to take effective preventive or corrective action when the situation so requires. It has long been settled case-law that the failure to provide effective deterrence through criminal law for attacks on basic values protected by the Convention engages the responsibility of the Contracting State.[964]

The Council of Europe Convention on Cybercrime (also known as the 'Budapest Convention')[965] represents an attempt to create an international framework for this purpose. It defines a number of computer-related crimes, some of them relevant to our discussion (illegal access, Article 2; illegal interception, Article 3; data interference, Article 4; system interference, Article 5; misuse of devices, Article 6) but its focus is on privacy, content (forgery and fraud, child pornography, infringement of intellectual property rights) and civil liability rather than on the prevention or prosecution of hostile acts or physical injury. Its provisions on mutual legal assistance, including exchange of information and extradition, add little that cannot be found in other instruments. Its value has been stated to be mostly symbolic.[966] Even so, what value it has lies in requiring States party to it to enact legislation criminalising misuse of a type that could lead to attacks of the type here in issue.[967] Its main weakness is perhaps

---

962 Tallinn Manual 2.0, p. 288.

963 See 6.4.7 above.

964 Among other authorities, *Mastromatteo v. Italy* (GC), no. 37703/97, § 67, ECHR 2002-VIII; *Osman v. the United Kingdom*, § 116; *Opuz v. Turkey*, no. 33401/02, §§ 129-30, ECHR 2009; and *Maiorano and Others v. Italy*, no. 28634/06, § 104, 15 December 2009. Compare also *X and Y v. the Netherlands*, no. 8978/80, § 27, Series A no. 91. See also footnote 950 above.

965 23 November 2001, ETS 185.

966 Nancy E. Macron, "The Council of Europe's Cyber Crime Treaty: An exercise in Symbolic Legislation", in *International Journal of Cyber Criminology*, Vol 4 Issue 1&2 (2010), pp. 699-712.

967 Compare for the Netherlands the following Articles of the Dutch Criminal Code (*Wetboek van Strafrecht*): Articles 138ab (hacking another's computer and/or using it as a "zombie"), 138b (distributed denial of service (DDOS) attack); 317 § 2 (ransomware attack); and 351

ATTRIBUTION 287

its very traditional territorial focus on domestic criminal jurisdiction: it enjoins States to establish such jurisdiction only over offences committed within their territory, on board of ships flying their flag and aircraft bearing their registration, or by their nationals if the offence is punishable under criminal law where it was committed or if the offence is committed outside the territorial jurisdiction of any State.[968] This would appear to leave it to the individual States whether or not also to extend their jurisdiction over foreigners hacking computers from outside the national territory to set up botnets composed of 'zombies' that cause harm in third countries.

### 8.4.5 *International Organisations*

8.4.5.1 International Organisations in General

International organisations[969] have existed since the nineteenth century. Governments set them up for purposes of multilateral cooperation, where a network of bilateral arrangements would be impracticable or unwieldy. In recent decades they have proliferated, and the number of international organisations now far outstrips the number of states.

A useful contemporary definition of an international organisation is given by Article 2a of the International Law Commission's 2011 Draft Articles on the Responsibility of International Organizations (hereafter DARIO):[970]

> "international organization" means an organization established by a treaty or other instrument governed by international law and possessing its own international legal personality. International organizations may include as members, in addition to States, other entities.

---

(*inter alia*, damaging or destroying cyber infrastructure). Section 5(2)(c)(2°) and (3°) of the Dutch International Crimes Act (*Wet internationale misdrijven*) – which provisions criminalise indiscriminate attacks on the civilian population and attacks on works or installations containing dangerous forces (dams, dykes and nuclear electrical generating stations) if such attacks may cause the release of dangerous forces and consequent severe losses among the civilian population, respectively, are also interesting from this perspective although their applicability is limited to international armed conflict.

968 Budapest Convention, Article 22 § 1.

969 For our purposes, the expression "international organisations" refers to international *intergovernmental* organisations (or IGOs), not non-governmental organisations or NGOs. Note that the International Committee of the Red Cross (ICRC) is an NGO governed by the Swiss Civil Code (see Article 2 of the Statutes of the International Committee of the Red Cross).

970 Crawford (2012), pp. 166-67.

In addition to international legal personality (recognised, at very least, by its member states), an international organization will enjoy the powers it requires to carry out the tasks and duties with which it is charged by the participating states. These may be particularly far-reaching: some international organisations exercise their authority over individuals and some even intervene in the domestic affairs of their member states.[971] Within the Council of Europe, the European Court of Human Rights itself provides an example: the Court adopts its own Rules of Court, which are binding on applicant and respondent parties and others (such as witnesses)[972] and of course its judgments are recognised as binding and executable by the Contracting States.[973]

International organisations enjoy privileges and immunities needed for them to function in independence. These tend to include immunity from domestic jurisdiction and execution; this is necessary in order that domestic courts not rule on the legality of acts of the organisations.[974] Detailed and potentially far-reaching immunities are usually the object of separate agreements between the organisation and its host state, often referred to as 'headquarters agreements'; an example is the headquarters agreement between NATO AF-SOUTH (based in Naples, Italy) and the Italian Republic successfully invoked by NATO in *Markovic and Others*.[975] Concomitantly, personnel of international organisations also enjoy immunity from domestic jurisdiction and execution, at minimum in respect of official acts.[976] Similar immunities tend to be recognised to state functionaries accredited to the organisation, such as Government representatives – usually the political decision-makers within such organisations[977] – and members of parliamentary bodies.[978]

The Court has had occasion to hold, in its general case-law,

> ... that where States establish international organisations in order to pursue or strengthen their cooperation in certain fields of activities, and

---

971   Crawford (2012), p. 170.

972   Article 25 (d) of the Convention.

973   Article 46 § 1 of the Convention.

974   Crawford (2012), pp. 174-76.

975   See 6.4.3.1.2 above. Other examples include the headquarters agreement between ICTY and the Netherlands: see *Galić*, § 23, and that between the Netherlands and the International Criminal Court: see *Djokaba Lambi Longa*, § 41, ECHR 2012. See also Lawson (1999), p. 288.

976   Crawford (2012), pp. 177-78.

977   For example, as members of the North Atlantic Council (Article 9 of the Washington Treaty) or the Committee of Ministers of the Council of Europe (Article 16 of the Statute of the Council of Europe).

978   Crawford (2012), pp. 178-79.

ATTRIBUTION

where they attribute to these organisations certain competences and accord them immunities, there may be implications as to the protection of fundamental rights. It would be incompatible with the purpose and object of the Convention, however, if the Contracting States were thereby absolved from their responsibility under the Convention in relation to the field of activity covered by such attribution. It should be recalled that the Convention is intended to guarantee not theoretical or illusory rights, but rights that are practical and effective.[979]

It is clear, therefore, that Contracting States cannot simply evade their Convention obligations by hiding behind the separate legal personality of international organisations of which they are members.

The above quotation is taken from the *Waite and Kennedy* judgment, which concerned the immunity of the European Space Agency from the domestic jurisdiction of its host states in respect of employment disputes between it and members of its staff. It is therefore natural that the Court should have considered the question whether European Space Agency staff had available to them 'reasonable alternative means to protect effectively their rights under the Convention' to be a 'material factor'.[980] However, the responsibility of Contracting States concerns not only procedural safeguards but also substantive guarantees.

In *Bosphorus Hava Yolları Turizm ve Ticaret Anonim Şirketi v. Ireland*, the Court was called upon to define the interrelation between, on the one hand, the transfer by Contracting States of sovereign powers to international or supranational organisations, and on the other, their responsibility under Article 1 of the Convention for 'all acts and omissions of its organs regardless of whether the act or omission in question was a consequence of domestic law or of the necessity to comply with international legal obligations'.[981] The dispute was occasioned by a decision of the Irish Government to impound an aircraft owned by the applicant company but leased to Yugoslav Airlines in pursuance of EEC Regulations themselves based on a resolution adopted by the United Nations Security Council under Chapter VII of the United Nations Charter imposing sanctions on the then Federal Republic of Yugoslavia. Here we have an

---

979    *Waite and Kennedy v. Germany* [GC], no. 26083/94, § 67, ECHR 1999-I.
980    *Waite and Kennedy*, § 68.
981    *Bosphorus Hava Yolları Turizm ve Ticaret Anonim Şirketi v. Ireland* ([GC], no. 45036/98, § 153, ECHR 2005VI.

example of 'economic sanctions', which, be it recalled, fall within the definition of 'hard power' given above no less than kinetic action.[982]

The applicant company complained of a violation of its property rights, as protected by Article 1 of Protocol No. 1 to the Convention.[983]

The Court held as follows:

154. In reconciling both these positions and thereby establishing the extent to which a State's action can be justified by its compliance with obligations flowing from its membership of an international organisation to which it has transferred part of its sovereignty, the Court has recognised that absolving Contracting States completely from their Convention responsibility in the areas covered by such a transfer would be incompatible with the purpose and object of the Convention; the guarantees of the Convention could be limited or excluded at will, thereby depriving it of its peremptory character and undermining the practical and effective nature of its safeguards (see *M. & Co. v. the Federal Republic of Germany* (no. 13258/87, Commission decision of 9 February 1990, Decisions and Reports (DR) 64, p. 138, and *Waite and Kennedy*, § 67, ...). The State is considered to retain Convention liability in respect of treaty commitments subsequent to the entry into force of the Convention (see, *mutatis mutandis*, *Matthews*, cited above, §§ 29 and 32-34, and *Prince Hans-Adam II of Liechtenstein v. Germany* [GC], no. 42527/98, § 47, ECHR 2001-VIII).

155. In the Court's view, State action taken in compliance with such legal obligations is justified as long as the relevant organisation is considered to protect fundamental rights, as regards both the substantive guarantees offered and the mechanisms controlling their observance, in a manner which can be considered at least equivalent to that for which the Convention provides (see *M. & Co.*, cited above, p. 145, an approach with which the parties and the European Commission agreed). By "equivalent" the Court means "comparable"; any requirement that the organisation's protection be "identical" could run counter to the interest of international cooperation pursued (...). However, any such finding of equivalence could not be final and would be susceptible to review in the light of any relevant change in fundamental rights protection.

156. If such equivalent protection is considered to be provided by the organisation, the presumption will be that a State has not departed from

---

982   See 1.2.3 above.

983   *Theory and Practice of the European Convention on Human Rights* (Pieter van Dijk, Fried van Hoof, Arjen van Rijn, Leo Zwaak, eds.), fifth edn., Intersentia, 2018, pp. 19-20.

ATTRIBUTION

the requirements of the Convention when it does no more than implement legal obligations flowing from its membership of the organisation.

However, any such presumption can be rebutted if, in the circumstances of a particular case, it is considered that the protection of Convention rights was manifestly deficient. In such cases, the interest of international cooperation would be outweighed by the Convention's role as a "constitutional instrument of European public order" in the field of human rights (see *Loizidou v. Turkey (preliminary objections)*, judgment of 23 March 1995, Series A no. 310, pp. 27-28, § 75).

The question of equivalence of the protection available arose with respect to the European Economic Community, since its regulation was directly applicable in Ireland; the Security Council Resolution, although admittedly the ultimate justification of the regulation, was not directly applicable as though it were domestic law.[984] In the event, the Court was able to find that, at a substantive level, fundamental rights were 'enshrined in the general principles of Community law protected by it, and that the Convention had a "special significance" as a source of such rights', and that at a procedural level, supervision by the domestic courts, coupled with the availability of the preliminary reference procedure.[985]

The Court has since restated the *'Bosphorus* presumption', as the presumption stated in paragraph 156 of the judgment has come to be called, not only with respect to the European Union[986] but also with respect to other international organisations, including the European Organisation for the Safety of Air Navigation ('Eurocontrol'),[987] NATO,[988] the European Patent Office,[989] the International Olive Oil Council,[990] the Council of Europe,[991] and – as we shall now see – the United Nations.

Lawson, writing well before the delivery of the *Bosphorus* judgment, suggested that if States of their own free choice transferred their authority in a

---

984   *Bosphorus*, § 145.

985   At the time, Article 177 of the Treaty establishing the European Economic Community (1957); now Article 267 of the Treaty on the Functioning of the European Union.

986   *Inter alia, Cooperatieve Producentenorganisatie van de Nederlandse Kokkelvisserij U.A. v. the Netherlands* (dec.), no. 13645/05, ECHR 2009; *Avotiņš v. Latvia* (GC), no. 17502/07, ECHR 2016, and *Lechouritou and Others v. Germany and 26 other member States of the European Union* (dec.), no. 37937/07, 3 April 2012.

987   *Boivin v. 34 member States of the Council of Europe* (dec.), no. 73250/01, ECHR 2008.

988   *Gasparini v. Italy and Belgium* (dec.), no. 10750/03, 12 May 2009.

989   *Rambus Inc. v. Germany* (dec.), no. 40382/04, 26 June 2009.

990   Now the International Olive Council. *Lopez Cifuentes v. Spain*, no. 18754/06, 7 July 2009.

991   *Beygo v. 46 member States of the Council of Europe* (dec.), no. 36099/06, 16 August 2009.

certain area to an independent entity – be it an international organisation, a federal unit or an independent organ of the State itself – then it should follow from the very freedom of that choice that a State should not be able to hide behind its independence to evade attribution of acts violating its international legal obligations.[992] The logic developed in the *Bosphorus* judgment may at first sight appear to run counter to this argument, in that it sets out the conditions that preclude attribution to the State; but on a second reading, the two are compatible. The link between the two is that the States that are members of an international organisation to which the *Bosphorus* presumption is applicable are found to have transferred to that organisation not only the means to violate the Convention but also legal means, equivalent even if not identical to those required by the Convention, to provide redress.

Lawson also suggests that it will be permissible to attribute all acts of an international organisation to its parent states if (a) the organisation has no international legal personality of its own, or (b) the organisation is set up *mala fide* for a purpose involving evading attribution of internationally wrongful acts of whatever description.[993] This must be correct.

### 8.4.5.2 The United Nations

#### 8.4.5.2.1 *Kosovo*

On 9 June 1999 a 'Military Technical Agreement' or MTA was signed between the Federal Republic of Yugoslavia (FRY), the Republic of Serbia and 'KFOR', the Kosovo Force (whose establishment was in fact to be announced the following day). This agreement provided for the withdrawal from Kosovo of FRY troops and the presence of an international security force following an appropriate UN Security Council Resolution. The Security Council Resolution, which was to be the basis for both KFOR and the civilian administration, United Nations Interim Administration in Kosovo or UNMIK, was adopted the next day.[994]

Security Council Resolution 1244 of 10 June 1999 provided for KFOR to be established by 'Member States and relevant international institutions', 'under UN auspices', with 'substantial NATO participation' but under 'unified command and control'. UNMIK was to be deployed under UN auspices; its implementation was to be supervised by a Special Representative to the Secretary General ('SRSG') to control its implementation. UNMIK was to coordinate closely with KFOR.

---

992 Lawson (1999), p. 304.

993 Lawson (1999), p. 341. On the latter point, compare Article 61 of DARIO (which is rather less absolute in its terms).

994 UN Security Council Resolution 1244 of 10 June 1999.

ATTRIBUTION

In March 2000 a group of young boys – including two sons of the applicant Behrami – found some cluster bomb units. These were from cluster bombs dropped by NATO aircraft in 1999 during the bombing campaign and had not yet been made safe. The boys played with them. One of them exploded, killing one of Mr Behrami's sons and maiming the other for life. The Court later found it established that responsibility for clearing up unexploded ordnance belonged with the United Nations Mine Action Co-ordination Centre or UNMACC, a body subordinate to UNMIK, although KFOR was involved as a 'service provider'.[995] At the relevant time, France was the 'lead nation' in the part of Kosovo where this unfortunate event took place. Before the Court, Mr Behrami and the surviving son later complained under Article 2 of the Convention that the French KFOR troops had failed to mark or defuse the cluster bomb units, even though their existence and whereabouts had been known.

Mr Saramati was arrested in April 2001 on suspicion of murder and illegal possession of a weapon. Released in June 2001 after the Supreme Court allowed his appeal, he was rearrested in July 2001. Mr Saramati's detention was ordered, and extended by the KFOR Commander ('COMKFOR'), who initially was a Norwegian officer and later a French one. Mr Saramati complained under Article 5 of the Convention that he had been detained extra-judicially.

The Court proceeded on the finding that issuing detention orders fell within the security mandate of KFOR and that the supervision of de-mining (including the removal of unexploded cluster bomb units) fell within the mandate of UNMIK.[996]

Answering the question whether France and Norway had exercised Article 1 jurisdiction at the relevant time, the Court found that Kosovo had been under the effective control of the 'international presences which exercised the public powers normally exercised by the Government of the FRY'.[997] The question was therefore 'less whether the respondent States exercised extra-territorial jurisdiction in Kosovo but far more centrally, whether this Court is competent to examine under the Convention those States' contribution to the civil and security presences which did exercise the relevant control of Kosovo'.[998]

As regards KFOR, the Court held as follows:

> UNSC [United Nations Security Council] Resolution 1244 gave rise to the following chain of command in the present cases. The UNSC was

---

995   *Behrami and Saramati*, § 125.
996   *Behrami and Saramati*, § 127.
997   *Behrami and Saramati*, § 70.
998   *Behrami and Saramati*, § 71.

to retain ultimate authority and control over the security mission and it delegated to NATO (in consultation with non-NATO member states) the power to establish, as well as the operational command of, the international presence, KFOR. NATO fulfilled its command mission via a chain of command (from the NAC [North Atlantic Council], to SHAPE [Supreme Headquarters Allied Powers Europe], to SACEUR [Supreme Allied Commander Europe], to CIC South [Commander in Chief of Allied Forces Southern Europe]) to COMKFOR, the commander of KFOR. While the MNBs [multinational brigades] were commanded by an officer from a lead TCN [troop contributing nation], the latter was under the direct command of COMKFOR. MNB action was to be taken according to an operational plan devised by NATO and operated by COMKFOR in the name of KFOR[999]

– from which it followed that, since KFOR was exercising lawfully delegated Chapter VII powers of the Security Council, the matters complained of, in so far as blamed on KFOR, were 'attributable' to the United Nations.

As regards UNMIK, the Court held that, whether it depended from the Secretary General or the Security Council, it was a subsidiary organ of the United Nations; the failure to make safe the cluster bomb units was therefore, in principle, 'attributable' to the United Nations in the same sense.[1000]

In so finding the Court took into account the International Law Commission's Draft Articles on the Responsibility of International Organisations (DARIO).[1001] It actually stated in the decision that it was using the expression 'attribution' in the same sense as the ILC did in Article 3 of DARIO.[1002]

The next question was whether to apply the presumption developed by the Court in the *Bosphorus* judgment. The presumption was that action taken by a State in compliance with obligations flowing from its membership of an international organisation to which it had transferred part of its sovereignty was 'justified as long as the relevant organisation [was] considered to protect fundamental rights, as regards both the substantive guarantees offered and the mechanisms controlling their observance, in a manner which [could] be considered at least equivalent to that for which the Convention [provided]'.[1003]

---

999    *Behrami and Saramati*, § 135.

1000  *Behrami and Saramati*, §§ 142-43.

1001  Report of the ILC, General Assembly Official Records, 55th session, Supplement No. 10 A/58/10 (2003).

1002  *Behrami and Saramati*, § 121.

1003  *Bosphorus*, § 155.

ATTRIBUTION

The United Nations was, however, an organisation to which fundamentally different parameters applied. Pursuant to Articles 25 and 103 of the UN Charter, the obligation of the Member States to obey the orders of the Security Council prevailed over 'any other international agreement'.[1004] Of even greater significance was the 'imperative nature of the principle [sic] aim' of the United Nations, namely the maintenance of international peace and security, for which purpose the UNSC was invested with the primary responsibility and the corresponding power to use coercive measures under Chapter VII:[1005]

> In the present case, Chapter VII allowed the UNSC to adopt coercive measures in reaction to an identified conflict considered to threaten peace, namely UNSC Resolution 1244 establishing UNMIK and KFOR.
>
> Since operations established by UNSC Resolutions under Chapter VII of the UN Charter are fundamental to the mission of the UN to secure international peace and security and since they rely for their effectiveness on support from member states, the Convention cannot be interpreted in a manner which would subject the acts and omissions of Contracting Parties which are covered by UNSC Resolutions and occur prior to or in the course of such missions, to the scrutiny of the Court. To do so would be to interfere with the fulfilment of the UN's key mission in this field including, as argued by certain parties, with the effective conduct of its operations. It would also be tantamount to imposing conditions on the implementation of a UNSC Resolution which were not provided for in the text of the Resolution itself. This reasoning equally applies to voluntary acts of the respondent States such as the vote of a permanent member of the UNSC in favour of the relevant Chapter VII Resolution and the contribution of troops to the security mission: such acts may not have amounted to obligations flowing from membership of the UN but they remained crucial to the effective fulfilment by the UNSC of its Chapter VII mandate and, consequently, by the UN of its imperative peace and security aim.[1006]

The cases were moreover clearly distinguishable from *Bosphorus*. The latter case had concerned the seizure of an aircraft, admittedly under an EU regula-

---

1004  *Behrami and Saramati*, § 147.
1005  *Behrami and Saramati*, § 148. See also Tobias Lock, "Beyond *Bosphorus*: The European Court of Human Rights' Case-Law on the Responsibility of Member States of International Organisations under the European Convention on Human Rights", in *Human Rights Law Review* 10:3 (2010), 529-545 at 532.
1006  *Behrami and Saramati*, § 149.

tion that was itself based on a Chapter VII resolution of the Security Council, but nonetheless directly by Irish domestic authorities on Irish territory. In contrast, the acts of KFOR and UNMIK were, as noted, those of the United Nations.[1007] Accordingly, since it had no jurisdiction over the United Nations, the Court declared both cases inadmissible *ratione personae*.

The *Behrami and Saramati* precedent has been applied since then in at least two cases decided by a Chamber, one against Greece, the other against Germany. The only feature of these cases worth noting is that in the German case the Serbian Government intervened as a third party under Article 36 of the Convention.[1008]

### 8.4.5.2.2 *Cyprus Buffer Zone*

In *Stephens* the applicant, who was the owner of a house situated in the United Nations-controlled buffer zone in Nicosia, complained of being denied access to it. She was advised by the Property Officer of the United Nations Peacekeeping Force in Cyprus (UNFICYP), which had control over the buffer zone, 'to contact the European Court of Human Rights to discover if it would be feasible to lodge a claim with them'.

Citing *Behrami and Saramati*, the Court noted that UNFICYP was a subsidiary organ of the UN. Its actions and inactions being therefore in principle attributable to the UN, it declared this complaint inadmissible *ratione personae*.[1009]

### 8.4.5.2.3 *Iraq*

In its *Al-Jedda* judgment, which we have come across already,[1010] the Court defined the interrelation between the Convention and Security Council resolutions in the following terms:

> 101. Article 103 of the Charter of the United Nations provides that the obligations of the members of the United Nations under the Charter shall prevail in the event of a conflict with obligations under any other international agreement. Before it can consider whether Article 103 had any application in the present case, the Court must determine whether there was a conflict between the United Kingdom's obligations under United

---

1007    *Behrami and Saramati*, § 151.
1008    *Kasumaj v. Greece* (dec.), no. 6974/05, 5 July 2007, and *Gajic v. Germany* (dec.), no. 31446/02, 28 august 2007.
1009    *Stephens v. Cyprus, Turkey and the United Nations* (dec.), no. 45267/06, 11 December 2008.
1010    See, in particular, 2.4 above.

ATTRIBUTION

Nations Security Council Resolution 1546 and its obligations under Article 5 § 1 of the Convention. In other words, the key question is whether Resolution 1546 placed the United Kingdom under an obligation to hold the applicant in internment.

102. In its approach to the interpretation of Resolution 1546, the Court has reference to the considerations set out in paragraph 76 above. In addition, the Court must have regard to the purposes for which the United Nations was created. As well as the purpose of maintaining international peace and security, set out in the first sub-paragraph of Article 1 of the Charter of the United Nations, the third sub-paragraph provides that the United Nations was established to "achieve international cooperation in ... promoting and encouraging respect for human rights and fundamental freedoms". Article 24 § 2 of the Charter requires the Security Council, in discharging its duties with respect to its primary responsibility for the maintenance of international peace and security, to "act in accordance with the Purposes and Principles of the United Nations". Against this background, the Court considers that, in interpreting its resolutions, there must be a presumption that the Security Council does not intend to impose any obligation on member States to breach fundamental principles of human rights. In the event of any ambiguity in the terms of a United Nations Security Council resolution, the Court must therefore choose the interpretation which is most in harmony with the requirements of the Convention and which avoids any conflict of obligations. In the light of the United Nations' important role in promoting and encouraging respect for human rights, it is to be expected that clear and explicit language would be used were the Security Council to intend States to take particular measures which would conflict with their obligations under international human rights law.[1011]

In the particular case, the Court held as follows:

105. The Court does not consider that the language used in this Resolution indicates unambiguously that the Security Council intended to place member States within the Multinational Force under an obligation to use measures of indefinite internment without charge and without judicial guarantees, in breach of their undertakings under international human rights instruments including the Convention. Internment is not explicitly referred to in the Resolution. ... Internment is listed in US Secretary of

---

1011 *Al-Jedda*, §§ 101-102.

State Powell's letter, as an example of the "broad range of tasks" which the Multinational Force stood ready to undertake. In the Court's view, the terminology of the Resolution appears to leave the choice of the means to achieve this end to the member States within the Multinational Force. Moreover, in the Preamble, the commitment of all forces to act in accordance with international law is noted. It is clear that the Convention forms part of international law, as the Court has frequently observed (...). In the absence of clear provision to the contrary, the presumption must be that the Security Council intended States within the Multinational Force to contribute towards the maintenance of security in Iraq while complying with their obligations under international human rights law.[1012]

The conclusion was that

in the absence of a binding obligation to use internment, there was no conflict between the United Kingdom's obligations under the Charter of the United Nations and its obligations under Article 5 § 1 of the Convention.[1013]

Milanović and Hadži-Vidanović have understood the Court's refusal in *Al-Jedda* to attribute the acts of American and British armed forces in Iraq to the United Nations as it had attributed the acts of KFOR in *Behrami and Saramati* as a correction of the latter decision. It is not. *Al-Jedda* itself points out that the British and American forces were already in theatre when the Security Council adopted its Resolution 1511; that resolution had not changed anything in their command structure or made them subsidiary to the Security Council as KFOR was. More importantly, the USA and the UK, through the CPA which they had established already at the start of the occupation, continued to exercise the powers of government in Iraq. The USA was requested to report periodically to the Security Council about the activities of the Multinational Force, but even so the United Nations did not thereby 'assume any degree of control over either the Force or any other of the executive functions of the CPA': the Security Council's request to the USA was just that, a request, not an order.[1014]

---

1012   *Al-Jedda*, § 105.
1013   *Al-Jedda*, § 109.
1014   *Al-Jedda*, § 80.

ATTRIBUTION

#### 8.4.5.2.4 *Switzerland*

Like *Bosphorus*, the cases of *Nada v. Switzerland* and *Al-Dulimi and Montana Management v. Switzerland* are examples of economic sanctions. They are moreover of importance in that they clarify the interrelation between Security Council resolutions and the Convention.

In *Nada* the applicant was a dual Egyptian and Italian national resident in Campione d'Italia, a small Italian exclave surrounded by the Swiss Canton of Ticino and separated from the rest of Italy by Lake Lugano. To travel to the rest of Italy over land he needed to cross Swiss territory.[1015]

In 1999, in response to the bomb attacks by Osama bin Laden and members of his network against the US embassies in Nairobi (Kenya) and Dar es Salaam (Tanzania) the previous year, the Security Council of the United Nations adopted, under Chapter VII of the United Nations Charter, Resolution 1267 (1999), providing for sanctions against the Taliban and created a committee to monitor the enforcement of that Resolution ('the Sanctions Committee'). By Resolution 1333 (2000) of 19 December 2000, the Security Council extended the sanctions regime. It was now also directed against Osama bin Laden and the al-Qaeda organisation, as well as the Taliban's senior officials and advisers. In both Resolutions 1267 (1999) and 1333 (2000), the Security Council requested the Sanctions Committee to maintain a list, based on information provided by States and regional organisations, of individuals and entities associated with Osama bin Laden and al-Qaeda. The applicant was added to this list on 9 November 2001.

In the meantime, in 2000, the Swiss Federal Council had adopted an ordinance to implement the sanctions regime. By the time of the events in issue, it prohibited entry into and transit through Switzerland for the individuals and entities concerned by the sanctions regime. In October 2003 the Canton of Ticino revoked the applicant's special border-crossing permit, making it impossible for the applicant to leave Campione d'Italia. This prevented the applicant from obtaining medical treatment and from consulting his lawyers.

The Court took the view that the case concerned the national implementation of United Nations Security Council resolutions. The matters complained of were therefore attributable to Switzerland.[1016]

Deciding whether the travel ban had constituted a violation of Article 8 of the Convention, the Court distinguished the case from *Al-Jedda* in the following terms:

---

1015   There is a ferry service across the lake that joins Campione d'Italia to the opposite shore which is Swiss.

1016   *Nada*, §§ 121-22.

# 300                                                                    CHAPTER 8

> ... in the present case it observes that, contrary to the situation in *Al-Jed-da*, where the wording of the resolution in issue did not specifically mention internment without trial, Resolution 1390 (2002) expressly required States to prevent the individuals on the United Nations list from entering or transiting through their territory. As a result, the above-mentioned presumption is rebutted in the present case, having regard to the clear and explicit language, imposing an obligation to take measures capable of breaching human rights, that was used in that Resolution (see also paragraph 7 of Resolution 1267 (1999), paragraph 70 above, in which the Security Council was even more explicit in setting aside any other international obligations that might be incompatible with the Resolution).

Even so, it emerged that the Security Council resolutions did not prevent the travel ban from being lifted 'where entry or transit [was] necessary for the fulfilment of a judicial process ...' and urged States to take restrictive measures 'where appropriate'. Taking its cue from the *Kadi I* judgment of the European Court of Justice,[1017] the Court therefore found that Switzerland had not made full use of what little discretion it had to improve the applicant's lot.[1018]

In *Al-Dulimi and Montana Management Inc. v. Switzerland* the applicants were identified by the Security Council as the head of finance for the Iraqi secret services under the regime of Saddam Hussein and a Panamanian company managed by him. The sanctions regime to which the applicants were subject were defined by Security Council Resolution 1483 – the same resolution that played such an important role in *Al-Skeini*, *Al-Jedda* and *Al-Saadoon and Mufdhi* – and after the Sanctions Committee set up to supervise the sanctions regime had placed them on the sanctions list (in April 2004), their assets in Switzerland were seized pursuant to an implementing ordinance adopted by the Federal Council. The applicants appealed to the Swiss courts, which verified that the applicants' names actually appeared on the lists drawn up by the Sanctions Committee and that the assets concerned belonged to them, then – citing Article 103 of the Charter of the United Nations and Article 30 § 1 of the Vienna Convention on the Law of Treaties – dismissed their appeals.

Before the Court, the applicants complained of a violation of their right of access to a court, as guaranteed by Article 6 § 1 of the Convention under its civil head.

---

1017  Court of Justice of the European Communities, *Yassin Abdullah Kadi and Al Barakaat International Foundation v. Council of the European Union and Commission of the European Communities* (joined cases C-402/05 P and C-415/05 P, 3 September 2008 (*"Kadi I"*).

1018  *Nada*, §§ 177-80.

ATTRIBUTION

The Court distinguished the case from *Nada* and *Al-Jedda* in that it did not concern either the essence of the substantive rights affected by the impugned measures or the compatibility of those measures with the requirements of the Convention, but merely the availability of 'appropriate judicial supervision' meeting the standards of Article 6 § 1.[1019]

It continued:

> 145. The Court notes, moreover, that the inclusion of individuals and entities on the lists of persons subject to the sanctions imposed by the Security Council entails practical interferences that may be extremely serious for the Convention rights of those concerned. Being drawn up by bodies whose role is limited to the individual application of political decisions taken by the Security Council, these lists nevertheless reflect choices of which the consequences for the persons concerned may be so weighty that they cannot be implemented without affording the right to appropriate review, which is all the more indispensable as such lists are usually compiled in circumstances of international crises and are based on information sources which tend not to be conducive to the safeguards required by such measures. In this connection, the Court would emphasise that the object and purpose of the Convention, a human rights treaty protecting individuals on an objective basis (see [*Neulinger and Shuruk v. Switzerland* [GC], no. 41615/07, § 145, ECHR 2010]), require its provisions to be interpreted and applied in a manner which makes its requirements practical and effective (see [*Artico v. Italy*, 13 May 1980, § 33, Series A no. 37]). The Court further observes that, the Convention being a constitutional instrument of European public order (see *Loizidou v. Turkey* (preliminary objections), 23 March 1995, § 75, Series A no. 310, and *Al-Skeini and Others*, cited above, § 141), the States Parties are required, in that context, to ensure a level of scrutiny of Convention compliance which, at the very least, preserves the foundations of that public order. One of the fundamental components of European public order is the principle of the rule of law, and arbitrariness constitutes the negation of that principle. Even in the context of interpreting and applying domestic law, where the Court leaves the national authorities very wide discretion, it always does so, expressly or implicitly, subject to a prohibition of arbitrariness (see *García Ruiz v. Spain* [GC], no. 30544/96, §§ 28-29, ECHR 1999-I, and *Storck v. Germany*, no. 61603/00, § 98, ECHR 2005-V).

---

1019   *Al-Dulimi and Montana Management Inc. v. Switzerland* (GC), no. 5809/08, §§ 143-44, ECHR 2016.

146. This will necessarily be true, in the implementation of a Security Council resolution, as regards the listing of persons on whom the impugned measures are imposed, at both UN and national levels. As a result, in view of the seriousness of the consequences for the Convention rights of those persons, where a resolution such as that in the present case, namely Resolution 1483, does not contain any clear or explicit wording excluding the possibility of judicial supervision of the measures taken for its implementation, it must always be understood as authorising the courts of the respondent State to exercise sufficient scrutiny so that any arbitrariness can be avoided. By limiting that scrutiny to arbitrariness, the Court takes account of the nature and purpose of the measures provided for by the Resolution in question, in order to strike a fair balance between the necessity of ensuring respect for human rights and the imperatives of the protection of international peace and security.

147. In such cases, in the event of a dispute over a decision to add a person to the list or to refuse delisting, the domestic courts must be able to obtain – if need be by a procedure ensuring an appropriate level of confidentiality, depending on the circumstances – sufficiently precise information in order to exercise the requisite scrutiny in respect of any substantiated and tenable allegation made by listed persons to the effect that their listing is arbitrary. Any inability to access such information is therefore capable of constituting a strong indication that the impugned measure is arbitrary, especially if the lack of access is prolonged, thus continuing to hinder any judicial scrutiny. Accordingly, any State Party whose authorities give legal effect to the addition of a person – whether an individual or a legal entity – to a sanctions list, without first ensuring – or being able to ensure – that the listing is not arbitrary will engage its responsibility under Article 6 of the Convention.[1020]

### 8.4.5.2.5 Conclusion: Security Council Resolutions under Chapter VII of the Charter of the United Nations

From the *Al-Jedda, Nada* and *Al-Dulimi and Montana Management* judgments we can conclude as follows.

*Firstly*, the obligations assumed by the Contracting States under Article 1 of the Convention do not override Security Council resolutions adopted under Chapter VII of the Charter. Consequently, when the two are in conflict, the latter prevail. There can be no doubt about this: it follows clearly from Article 103 of the Charter, which provision provides that in the event of a conflict between

---

1020   *Al-Dulimi and Montana Management Inc.*, §§ 145-47.

ATTRIBUTION

the obligations of the Members of the United Nations under the present Charter and their obligations under any other international agreement, their obligations under the Charter shall prevail. This rule is reinforced by Article 30 § 1 of the Vienna Convention on the Law of Treaties, which makes the hierarchy of treaty obligations set out in the remainder of that Article subordinate to Article 103 of the Charter.[1021]

*Secondly*, there is a presumption that the Security Council does not intend to impose any obligation on member States of the United Nations to breach fundamental principles of human rights. This follows from the very purpose and principles of the United Nations Charter itself. If a United Nations Security Council resolution is ambiguous its terms, the Court must therefore interpret the Security Council resolution so as to reconcile it as far as possible with the Convention. This enabled the Court to hold in *Al-Jedda* that the relevant Security Council resolution did not compel indefinite detention without the possibility of judicial review, and so to find violation of Article 5 of the Convention. *Thirdly*, the said presumption is rebuttable – but only to the extent that the Security Council resolution imposes direct obligations to adopt measures incompatible with the rights and freedoms guaranteed by the Convention. Even then, the Contracting States must nonetheless make use of what latitude remains to them to secure the rights and freedoms set out in the Convention.

It is only fair to mention that in this matter the way forward was shown already in 2008 by the Court of Justice of the European Communities in *Kadi I*.[1022]

### 8.4.5.2.6 *Anti-piracy Operations in the Western Indian Ocean*

As we have seen,[1023] the Security Council gave authority to States taking part in anti-piracy operations off the coast of Somalia to act, making use of its powers under Chapter VII of the UN Charter. It did not, however, express this authority in the form of a binding order.

In *Hassan and Others* the respondent Party, France, did not seek to deny jurisdiction on the ground that its acts were attributable to the UN and the Court did not examine the matter of its own motion.[1024] Now that European naval forces work together as EUNAVFOR [European Union Naval Force] Operation Atalanta, the question may arise at some point whether attribution should not rather be made to the European Union, whether alone – in which case, in pre-

---

1021 Lawson (1999), p. 148.
1022 See §§ 298-300 of that judgment (footnote 1017 above).
1023 See 6.4.5 above.
1024 Footnote 771 above.

304                                                                    CHAPTER 8

sent circumstances, Article 1 jurisdiction cannot be an issue[1025] – or together
with the Member State concerned.[1026]

### 8.4.5.3    International Organisations: the Problem of Accountability

Wrongful acts of whatever description, even when attributable to international organisations, are necessarily acts or omissions of human beings. In
the context of this study, they will often be the acts and omissions of persons
exercising functions as State organs placed at the disposal of international organisations to act in the name of the latter. We have seen that attribution to
international organisations may enable states to escape responsibility for such
acts and omissions, rightly or wrongly. This may leave the wronged individual
without any possibility to obtain redress.

The distinct legal personality of international organisations, separate from
that of their member states, precludes their being held to account under the
Convention in their own right. Likewise, it protects States from being held
responsible for acts attributable to the international organisations of which
they are members. It will not help applicants to cite as respondents all of the
organisation's member States, if these be at the same time parties to the Convention.[1027]

Thus, in *Markovic and Others* NATO invoked the immunity of its AFSOUTH
headquarters before the Italian domestic courts – successfully, inasmuch as
this caused the applicants to discontinue the proceedings against that organisation; but the Court accepted that it would have availed the applicants nothing to pursue them to their conclusion.[1028]

In *Behrami and Saramati* the Court used the term 'attribution' in the same
way as the ILC did in Article 3 of DARIO.[1029] So it did also in *Berić and Others*.[1030]

In *Stichting Mothers of Srebrenica and Others*, the Court noted the existence
of a jurisdictional void: a claims commission was supposed to have been set
up to hear claims against the United Nations, but it had not. This state of af-

---

1025   Footnote 618 above.
1026   Tullio Treves and Cesare Pitea, "Piracy, International Law and Human Rights", in *The Fron-
       tiers of Human Rights: Extraterritoriality and its Challenges, Collected Courses of the Acad-
       emy of European Law*, vol. XXIV/1, pp. 89-126 at pp. 108-112.
1027   Compare *Boivin v. 34 member States of the Council of Europe* (dec.), no. 73250/01, ECHR
       2008, and *Beygo v. 46 member States of the Council of Europe* (dec.), no. 36099/06, 16 Au-
       gust 2009. See also Lawson (1999), pp. 189-99.
1028   See 6.4.3.1.2 above; *Markovic and Others*, § 35.
1029   *Behrami and Saramati*, § 121.
1030   *Berić and Others*, § 28, 18 October 2007.

ATTRIBUTION

fairs, regrettable though it be, was not imputable to the Netherlands; nor was the Netherlands required by Article 6 of the Convention to step in itself.[1031] Domestic law can allow the State to be held to account, as the Dutch courts did in domestic civil proceedings in the Srebrenica litigation,[1032] but their jurisdiction over international organisations is very limited.

Commentators do not like this line of case-law. They tend to see *Stichting Mothers of Srebrenica and Others*, like *Behrami and Saramati*, as endorsement of a tendency on the part of States to use international organisations as a tool to evade accountability.[1033] One pair of authors goes so far as to call the decision 'lamentable'.[1034] Yet such is the current state of the law. Unless one takes the view that the law itself is wrong, it is difficult to find that the Court is plainly in error when it applies Article 3 of DARIO in these cases. The situation is little different from that of, for example, a State placing its organs at the disposal of a non-Convention State to whom the acts of the former would be attributable under Article 6 of the ILC's Articles on the Responsibility of States for Internationally Wrongful Acts;[1035] in such a case as in the case of an international organisation, there would most likely be no access to the Court in Strasbourg in the event that the non-Convention State failed to meet its human rights obligations.[1036]

Although *Al-Dulimi and Montana Management Inc.*[1037] must rank as one of the Court's boldest attempts until now to provide judicial guarantees where

---

1031    *Stichting Mothers of Srebrenica*, §§ 162-165.

1032    See 6.5.2.6 above.

1033    Alexander Breitegger, "Sacrificing the Effectiveness of the European Convention on Human Rights on the Altar of the Effective Functioning of Peace Support Operations: A Critique of *Behrami & Saramati* and *Al Jedda, International Community Law Review* 11 (2009) 155-183, *passim*; Heike Krieger, "A Credibility Gap: The Behrami and Saramati Decision of the European Court of Human Rights", *Journal of International Peacekeeping* 13 (2009) 159-180, *passim*; Marko Milanović and Vidan Hadži-Vidanović, "A Taxonomy of Armed Conflict" (January 20, 2012), *Research Handbook on International Conflict and Security Law*, Nigel White, Christian Henderson, eds., Edward Elgar, 2012. Available at SSRN: http://ssrn.com/abstract=1988915, p. 19; Crawford (2013), pp. 199-200; Andrew Drzemczewski, "Human Rights in Europe: An Insider's Views", [2017] E.H.R.L.R., issue 2, p. 134 at p. 143; PACE Resolution 1979 (2014), Accountability of international organisations for human rights violations, 31 January 2014, § 3; PACE Recommendation 2037 (2014), 31 January 2014, § 2.

1034    Milanović and Hadži-Vidanović, *loc. cit.*

1035    Report of the International Law Commission on the work of its Fifty-third session, Official Records of the General Assembly, Fifty-sixth session, Supplement No. 10 (A/56/10), chp.IV.E.1.

1036    Compare *Drozd and Janousek v. France and Spain* (see 5.5.4 above); James Crawford, *State Responsibility: The General Part*, Cambridge University Press 2013, p. 134-35.

1037    See 8.4.5.2.4 above.

306                                                                    CHAPTER 8

there are none, critics of the *Behrami and Saramati* and *Stichting Mothers of Srebrenica* decisions can derive little comfort from it. It is one thing to conceive of a remedy limited to testing the arbitrariness of continuing the domestic implementation of a sanctions regime targeting named individuals where such a remedy is not specifically excluded; it is quite another to create a judicial remedy that would allow the United Nations to be judged by domestic courts for the use by the Security Council of its powers under Chapter VII of the United Nations Charter – which would not only override an immunity granted by the world's most basic treaties[1038] but would of necessity involve recognising a substantive right to damages, and under domestic law to boot.

DARIO has been accepted in principle by the United Nations General Assembly,[1039] but unlike the ILC Articles on State responsibility for international wrongful acts, not yet formally endorsed. The Parliamentary Assembly of the Council of Europe has suggested that the Council of Europe itself, 'as an international organisation specialising in human rights', consider how the Draft Articles might apply to it.[1040]

There is a real need to make provision for international organisations wielding power to be accountable before independent organs with jurisdictional powers.[1041] In Kosovo, this need was recognised: an UNMIK Human Rights Advisory Panel was set up to examine complaints from any person or group of individuals claiming to be the victim of a violation by UNMIK of their human rights.[1042]

Although the creation of the UNMIK Human Rights Advisory Panel was a welcome development, it was not sufficient to solve the problem. It is known, for example, that KFOR military and UNMIK civilian personnel including police took part in human trafficking and forced prostitution, or used brothels staffed by victims of such practices, yet no prosecutions were ever authorised by either the commander of KFOR or national commanders and no immunity was ever waived by the Secretary General of the United Nations.[1043] Address-

---

1038   Article 105 of the Charter of the United Nations; Article II, section 2 of the Convention on the Privileges and Immunities of the United Nations, 13 February 1946.

1039   UNGA Res. 66/100, 9 December 2011, § 3.

1040   PACE Recommendation 2037 (2014), 31 January 2014, § 3.

1041   See also Heike Krieger, "A Credibility Gap: The *Behrami and Saramati* Decision of the European Court of Human Rights", *Journal of International Peacekeeping* 13 (2009) 159-180, p. 180.

1042   Human Rights Review Panel, Annual Report 2016, p. 45, http://www.hrrp.eu/docs/HRRP%20Annual%20Report%202016.pdf (accessed 15 March 2017).

1043   Nauta, pp. 24-29. The author was told of similar occurrences in Bosnia and Herzegovina during his time there.

ATTRIBUTION                                                                                           307

ing different issues, the presiding member of that Panel, Marek Nowicki, had
occasion in its final annual report to

> ... highlight again with deep regret the general structural problem that
> exists, namely the lack of implementation of the Panel's opinions, espe-
> cially with regard to UNMIK paying financial compensation to the com-
> plainants, as well as the lack of significant progress of EULEX or Kosovo
> law enforcement institutions' continuing investigations regarding the
> Panel's cases related to abductions, disappearances and killings'[1044]

– thus reflecting the inadequacy of a merely advisory body as a legal remedy,
whether preventive, compensatory or punitive.

In the meantime EULEX has assumed executive powers. The Human Rights
Advisory Panel has been replaced by a Human Rights Review Panel set up to

> review complaints from any person, other than EULEX Kosovo person-
> nel, claiming to be the victim of a violation of his or her human rights
> by EULEX Kosovo in the conduct of the executive mandate of EULEX
> Kosovo.[1045]

Its creation has been lauded by the Parliamentary Assembly of the Council
of Europe[1046] even though its terms of reference, or 'accountability concept',
remain classified.[1047]

The two Kosovo panels constitute a step in the right direction, however
timid.[1048] As matters stand, no other international panels than these two have
ever been given a mandate to hold international organisations operating in an
executive role in a conflict or post-conflict peacekeeping situation accountable for alleged human rights violations.[1049]

---

1044  Human Rights Advisory Panel, Annual Report 2015-16, pp. i-ii.
1045  Human Rights Review Panel, Annual Report 2016, p. 6, http://www.hrrp.eu/docs/
      HRRP%20Annual%20Report%202016.pdf (accessed 15 March 2017).
1046  PACE Resolution 1979 (2014), Accountability of international organisations for human
      rights violations, 31 January 2014, § 5.
1047  Human Rights Review Panel, Annual Report 2016, p. 6.
1048  The system has also received lukewarm praise from the Venice Commission in its Opinion
      on the existing mechanisms to review the compatibility with human rights standards of
      acts of UNMIK and EULEX in Kosovo, Opinion no. 545 / 2009, CDL-AD(2010)051, 21 De-
      cember 2010.
1049  Human Rights Review Panel, Annual Report 2016, p. 5

308 CHAPTER 8

## 8.5 Subordinate Pseudo-States

In the case-law of the Court thus far, there have been two situations of what has been called 'belligerent occupation'[1050] in which the Court has had to consider the value of a judicial remedy offered by a purportedly independent state that was in fact a client entity of one Contracting State set up on the territory of another.

### 8.5.1 *The 'Turkish Republic of Northern Cyprus'*

In *Cyprus v. Turkey* the Court was faced with the question whether the remedies offered by the courts of the 'TRNC' were to be exhausted in order to comply with then Article 26 of the Convention (now Article 35 § 1). The position of the Turkish Government, as expressed in the proceedings before the Commission (they did not appear before the Court), was that the 'TRNC' was 'an independent State established by the Turkish-Cypriot community in the exercise of its right to self-determination and possessing exclusive control and authority over the territory north of the United Nations buffer-zone'. The Cypriot Government argued strongly that they were not, pointing to the status of the 'TRNC' as an entity whose lawfulness was not recognised internationally except by Turkey; it followed that even Turkey did not regard the remedies of the 'TRNC' as domestic remedies of its own. Moreover, and submitting that the Turkish occupation of northern Cyprus was unlawful, they argued that the 'TRNC''s courts were not 'tribunals established by law'.

The Court, 'without in any way putting in doubt either the view adopted by the international community regarding the establishment of the "TRNC" (...) or the fact that the government of the Republic of Cyprus remains the sole legitimate government of Cyprus',[1051] dismissed both limbs of the Cypriot Government's arguments. This it did having regard to the 'Namibia principle':

> In general, the non-recognition of South Africa's administration of the Territory should not result in depriving the people of Namibia of any advantages derived from international co-operation. In particular, while official acts performed by the Government of South Africa on behalf of or concerning Namibia after the termination of the Mandate are illegal and invalid, this invalidity cannot be extended to those acts, such as, for instance, the registration of births, deaths and marriages, the effects of

---

1050 See 1.2.1 above.
1051 *Cyprus v. Turkey*, § 90.

ATTRIBUTION

which can be ignored only to the detriment of the inhabitants of the Territory.[1052]

After all,

> Life goes on in the territory concerned for its inhabitants. That life must be made tolerable and be protected by the *de facto* authorities, including their courts; and, in the very interest of the inhabitants, the acts of these authorities related thereto cannot be simply ignored by third States or by international institutions, especially courts, including this one. To hold otherwise would amount to stripping the inhabitants of the territory of all their rights whenever they are discussed in an international context, which would amount to depriving them even of the minimum standard of rights to which they are entitled.[1053]

Indeed,

> It appears ... difficult to admit that a State is made responsible for the acts occurring in a territory unlawfully occupied and administered by it and to deny that State the opportunity to try to avoid such responsibility by correcting the wrongs imputable to it in its courts. To allow that opportunity to the respondent State in the framework of the present application in no way amounts to an indirect legitimisation of a regime which is unlawful under international law.[1054]

In later judgments, the Court was to accept on this basis the lawfulness of the arrest of a Greek Cypriot by a 'TRNC' police officer and the trial of a Greek Cypriot – even its compatibility with Article 6 –by a 'TRNC' criminal court, it being implicit that both the arrest and the trial were attributable to Turkey.[1055]

---

1052  Legal Consequences for States of the Continued Presence of South Africa in Namibia (South West Africa) notwithstanding Security Council Resolution 276 (1970), *ICJ Reports* 1971, vol. 16, p. 56, § 125

1053  *Cyprus v. Turkey*, § 96. See also Fortin, pp. 294-95.

1054  *Cyprus v. Turkey*, § 101.

1055  *Foka v. Turkey*, no. 28940/95, § 83, 24 June 2008, and *Protopapa v. Turkey*, no. 16084/90, § 87, 24 February 2009, respectively.

310                                                                                                    CHAPTER 8

**8.5.2** *The 'Moldovan Republic of Transdniestria'*
In *Ilaşcu and Others* and again in *Mozer and Others* the Court expressed itself
as follows with regard to the court systems of the 'TRNC' and the 'MRT'.[1056]

> In certain circumstances, a court belonging to the judicial system of an
> entity not recognised under international law may be regarded as a tribu-
> nal "established by law" provided that it forms part of a judicial system
> operating on a "constitutional and legal basis" reflecting a judicial tradi-
> tion compatible with the Convention, in order to enable individuals to
> enjoy the Convention guarantees (see, *mutatis mutandis, Cyprus v. Tur-
> key*, cited above, §§ 231 and 236-237).

In *Ilaşcu and Others*, the Court found that this was not the case:

> The "Supreme Court of the MRT" which passed sentence [of death] on
> Mr Ilaşcu was set up by an entity which is illegal under international
> law and has not been recognised by the international community. That
> "court" belongs to a system which can hardly be said to function on a
> constitutional and legal basis reflecting a judicial tradition compatible
> with the Convention. That is evidenced by the patently arbitrary nature
> of the circumstances in which the applicants were tried and convicted,
> as they described them in an account which has not been disputed by
> the other parties (...), and as described and analysed by the institutions
> of the OSCE (...)[1057]

Thus, it was the dysfunction of the 'Supreme Court of the MRT' itself which
made it unlawful even by the relatively lenient standards of the *Namibia* principle as interpreted and applied in the 'TRNC' cases.
    In *Mozer* the Court confirmed this finding in no uncertain terms:

> 147. In the Court's view, it is in the first place for the Contracting Party
> which has effective control over the unrecognised entity at issue to show
> that its courts "form part of a judicial system operating on a constitution-
> al and legal basis reflecting a judicial tradition compatible with the Con-
> vention" (...). As the Court has already established (...), in the case of the
> "MRT" it is Russia which has such effective control. To date the Russian
> Government have not submitted to the Court any information on the or-

---

1056    *Ilaşcu and Others*, § 460; *Mozer*, § 141.
1057    *Ilaşcu and Others*, §§ 436 and 461.

ganisation of the "MRT" courts which would enable it to assess whether they fulfil the above requirement. Nor have they submitted any details of the "MRT" law which served as a basis for the applicant's detention. Furthermore, the Court notes the scarcity of official sources of information concerning the legal and court system in the "MRT", a fact which makes it difficult to obtain a clear picture of the applicable laws. Consequently, the Court is not in a position to verify whether the "MRT courts" and their practice fulfil the requirements mentioned above.

148. There is also no basis for assuming that there is a system reflecting a judicial tradition compatible with the Convention in the region, similar to the one in the remainder of the Republic of Moldova (compare and contrast with the situation in Northern Cyprus, referred to in *Cyprus v. Turkey*, cited above, §§ 231 and 237). The division of the Moldovan and "MRT" judicial systems took place in 1990, well before Moldova joined the Council of Europe in 1995. Moreover, Moldovan law was subjected to a thorough analysis when it requested membership of the Council of Europe (see Opinion No. 188 (1995) of the Council of Europe Parliamentary Assembly on the application by Moldova for membership of the Council of Europe), with amendments proposed to ensure compatibility with the Convention, which Moldova finally ratified in 1997. No such analysis was made of the "MRT legal system", which was thus never part of a system reflecting a judicial tradition considered compatible with Convention principles before the split into separate judicial systems occurred in 1990 (...).

149. The Court also considers that the conclusions reached above are reinforced by the circumstances in which the applicant in the present case was arrested and his detention was ordered and extended (see ... above, especially the order for his detention for an undefined period of time and the examination in his absence of the appeal against the decision to extend that detention), as well as by the case-law referred to by the applicant (...) and the various media reports which raise concerns about the independence and quality of the 'MRT courts' (...).[1058]

### 8.5.3    *Requirements Governing Remedies Offered by Subordinate Entities*

We see that the judicial fora existing even in internationally unrecognised entities may satisfy the Court for purposes of Articles 5 and 6 and accordingly also for purposes of Articles 13 and 35 § 1. It is however a requirement that such fora 'reflect a judicial tradition considered compatible with Convention principles' – as in the case of the 'TRNC' but not the 'MRT' – and meet the appropriate

---

1058    *Mozer*, §§ 147-149.

substantive standards. The latter requirement is crucial given that the domestic remedies are considered, from the Court's perspective, to be remedies offered by the respondent Party – Turkey or Russia, respectively, in the examples cited.

As in the case of the Dayton agreement setup for Bosnia and Herzegovina however, an important feature of the solution chosen is that it is in accordance with (or at least, not contrary to) general international law – in this case, the advisory opinion of the International Court of Justice in the *Namibia* case legitimises it.

The effect of applying the *Namibia* principle in these situations is not only to ensure that judicial protection is available to all those who find themselves under the control of the authorities of an unrecognised entity, important though that be. It is also that the European Court of Human Rights is not compelled to set itself up as the only recognised forum capable of offering the protection which Article 1 delegates to the Contracting Parties.

### 8.5.4 Ad hoc *Remedy: the 'Turkish Republic of Northern Cyprus'*

As we have seen above, in *Loizidou* (merits) and *Cyprus v. Turkey* the Court set out the principle that the continued failure by the respondent to allow persons displaced from Northern Cyprus to regain access to their immovable property and their homes constituted violations of 1 of Protocol No. 1 and Article 8 of the Convention, respectively. Pursuant to Article 159 of the Constitution of the 'TRNC' – adopted in 1985 – ownership of abandoned properties was vested in the 'TRNC' itself. A procedure was to be set up under which former owners could claim compensation.

In June 2003 the 'Parliament of the TRNC' rather belatedly enacted a law intended to set up such a procedure. Its adequacy as a remedy within the meaning of Article 13 of the Convention was put to the test in a pilot case, *Xenides-Arestis v. Turkey*.

The Court's finding was brief:

> As regards the application of Article 35 § 1 of the Convention to the facts of the present case, the Court notes at the outset that the compensation offered by Law no. 49/2003 in respect of the purported deprivation of the applicant's property is limited to damages concerning pecuniary loss for immovable property. No provision is made for movable property or non-pecuniary damages. Most importantly, however, the terms of compensation do not allow for the possibility of restitution of the property withheld. Thus, although compensation is foreseen, this cannot in the opinion of the Court be considered as a complete system of redress regu-

ATTRIBUTION                                                                313

lating the basic aspect of the interferences complained of (see, *mutatis mutandis*, *Brumărescu v. Romania* (just satisfaction) [GC], no. 28342/95, §§ 19-22, ECHR 2001-I, and *Papamichalopoulos and Others v. Greece* (Article 50), judgment of 31 October 1995, Series A no. 330-B, pp. 58-60, §§ 34-38).

In addition the Court would make the following observations concerning the purported remedy.

Firstly, the Law does not address the applicant's complaints under Article 8 and 14 of the Convention.

Secondly, the Law is vague as to its temporal application, that is, as whether it has retrospective effect concerning applications filed before its enactment and entry into force; it merely refers to the retrospective assessment of the compensation.

Finally, the composition of the compensation commission raises concerns since, in the light of the evidence submitted by the Cypriot Government, the majority of its members are living in houses owned or built on property owned by Greek Cypriots. In this connection, the Court observes that the respondent Government have not disputed the Cypriot Government's arguments on this matter and have not provided any additional information in their written and oral submissions. Further, the Court suggests that an international composition would enhance the commission's standing and credibility.[1059]

In its ensuing judgment on the merits, the Court restated its existing case-law and found violations of Articles 1 of Protocol No. 1 and 8 of the Convention, without it being necessary to go separately into the question of Article 14 in conjunction with Article 8. It further held, under Article 46 of the Convention, that Turkey should introduce a remedy that would secure

genuinely effective redress for the Convention violations identified in the instant judgment in relation to the present applicant as well as in respect of all similar applications pending before it, in accordance with the principles for the protection of the rights laid down in Article 8 of the Convention and Article 1 of Protocol No. 1 and in line with its admissibility decision of 14 March 2005.[1060]

---

1059   *Xenides-Arestis v. Turkey* (dec.), no 46347/99, 14 March 2005.
1060   *Xenides-Arestis v. Turkey* (merits), no 46347/99, § 40, 22 December 2005.

314                                                                              CHAPTER 8

In the meantime, in 2004, the then Secretary General of the United Nations, Mr Kofi Annan, had presented a plan for the establishment of a United Cyprus Republic ('the UCR'). The intention had been for this republic to include two constituent States: a predominantly Greek Cypriot one in the south, eventually comprising about 71% of the land area of Cyprus, and a predominantly Turkish Cypriot one in the north, comprising about 29% of the land area. Cypriots would be citizens both of the UCR and of the appropriate constituent State. This plan, which came to be known as the 'Annan plan', provided for the settlement of outstanding property claims. Put to referenda on both sides of the border, it failed to pass: although the Turkish Cypriots voted largely in favour, the Greek Cypriot side overwhelmingly voted to reject it.[1061]

A 'TRNC' law intended to cure the failings identified in *Xenides-Arestis* entered into force on 22 December 2005.[1062] It provided for an Immovable Property Commission before which all natural and legal persons who could prove title to immovable property as of 20 July 1974 (or who could prove that they were the heirs of such persons), or who could prove that they had owned movable property before 13 February 1975 and had been forced to abandon it due to conditions beyond their own volition, might bring claims. The law provided for a four-year window, which was later extended to six years. This Immovable Property Commission had the power to compel the submission of documents and the appearance of witnesses and its decisions were binding and executable similarly to judgments of a court. The Immovable Property Commission was composed of

> a president, a vice-president, and minimum five, maximum seven members, whose qualifications are specified below, .... At least two members of the [Immovable Property] Commission to be appointed shall not be nationals of the Turkish Republic of Northern Cyprus, [the] United Kingdom, Greece, [the] Greek Cypriot Administration or [the] Republic of Turkey. ...

Moreover,

---

1061   *Demopoulos and Others*, §§ 8-14.
1062   Law no. 67/2005 for the compensation, exchange and restitution of immovable properties which are within the scope of sub-paragraph (b) of paragraph 1 of Article 159 of the Constitution, as amended by Laws nos. 59/2006 and 85/2007. See *Demopoulos and Others*, §§ 35-37.

ATTRIBUTION

> Any persons directly or indirectly deriving any benefit from immovable properties on which rights are claimed by those who had to move from the north of Cyprus in 1974, abandoning their properties, cannot be appointed as members of the [Immovable Property] Commission

The two foreign members appointed were Mr Hans-Christian Krüger, former Secretary to the European Commission of Human rights and former Deputy Secretary General of the Council of Europe, and Mr Daniel Tarschys, a Swedish academic and politician and former Secretary General of the Council of Europe.

The Immovable Property Commission could order restitution of immovable property or compensation in lieu, or propose an exchange against immovable property held in the territory of the Republic of Cyprus but to which a citizen of the 'TRNC' held title.

An appeal against the decision of the Immovable Property Commission lay to the High Administrative Court of the 'TRNC'; an 'applicant' displeased with the decision of the latter could 'apply to the European Court of Human Rights'.

It was reported in the Court's *Demopoulos and Others* decision that

> As of the date of the hearing in November 2009, the number of cases brought before the IPC stood at 433. Of these, 85 had been concluded, the vast majority by means of friendly settlement. Only a handful of decisions not based on a settlement had been issued. In 4 cases, the IPC had ordered restitution and compensation; in 2 cases, exchange of property was agreed; and in 1 case the applicant agreed to restitution on resolution of the Cyprus problem. In more than 70 cases, compensation had been awarded. Some 361,493 square metres of property had been restituted and approximately 47 million euros paid in compensation.[1063]

The applicants submitted that the Immovable Property Commission was not a "remedy" to be exhausted for purposes of Article 35 § 1 of the Convention, both because of doubts as to its impartiality and effectiveness and because

> ... the [Immovable Property Commission] remedy was operated by the authorities of an entity widely resented and distrusted by Greek Cypriots and universally viewed (save in Turkey) as an unlawful occupier. Many

---

1063  *loc. cit.*, § 40.

property owners felt unable to submit to, or effectively collaborate with, an occupying power in such a way.[1064]

The Government of the Republic of Cyprus argued in addition that

> ... rather than being designed to provide redress for systemic violations and reinforce the effectiveness of the Court, it was an attempt to legitimise [the Turkish Government's] unlawful mass appropriation of Greek Cypriot properties

and that customary international law only required the applicants to exhaust Turkish remedies, whereas Turkey insisted that the IPC was a 'TRNC' remedy.[1065]

Addressing the argument that the 'TRNC' compensation law was not part of Turkish domestic law, the Court answered as follows:

> The Court considers this to be an artificial argument. Turkey has been held responsible for the acts and omissions of the authorities within the "TRNC" entity in numerous cases – otherwise the Court would not have had the competence to examine complaints brought by applicants against the respondent State concerning northern Cyprus. To the extent that any domestic remedy is made available by acts of the "TRNC" authorities or institutions, it may be regarded as a "domestic remedy" or "national" remedy vis-à-vis Turkey for the purposes of Article 35 § 1 (see *Cyprus v. Turkey*, cited above, §§ 101-02). It should also not be overlooked that Law no. 67/2005 and the IPC came into existence as the consequence of the Court holding in the *Xenides-Arestis* case (cited above) that Turkey had to introduce a remedy which secured the effective protection of the rights laid down in Article 1 of Protocol No. 1 in relation to the applicant as well as in respect of all similar applications pending before the Court. Accepting the functional reality of remedies is not tantamount to holding that Turkey wields internationally recognised sovereignty over northern Cyprus.

Answering the argument that argument that requiring exhaustion lent legitimacy to an illegal occupation, the Court reiterated the above-mentioned 'Namibia principle':

---

1064 *Demopoulos and Others*, § 58.
1065 *Demopoulos and Others*, §§ 63 and 64.

ATTRIBUTION

this, in brief, provides that even if the legitimacy of the administration of a territory is not recognised by the international community, "international law recognises the legitimacy of certain legal arrangements and transactions in such a situation, ... the effects of which can be ignored only to the detriment of the inhabitants of the [t]erritory" (Advisory Opinion of the International Court of Justice in the *Namibia* case (Legal Consequences for States of the Continued Presence of South Africa in Namibia (South West Africa) notwithstanding Security Council Resolution 276 (1970), *ICJ Reports* 1971, vol. 16, p. 56, § 125).[1066]

and:

95. Further, the overall control exercised by Turkey over the territory of northern Cyprus entails its responsibility for the policies and actions of the "TRNC" and that those affected by such policies or actions come within the "jurisdiction" of Turkey for the purposes of Article 1 of the Convention with the consequence that Turkey is accountable for violations of Convention rights which take place within that territory and is bound to take positive steps to protect those rights. It would not be consistent with such responsibility under the Convention if the adoption by the authorities of the "TRNC" of civil, administrative or criminal law measures, or their application or enforcement within that territory, were then to be denied any validity or regarded as having no "lawful" basis in terms of the Convention (see *Foka v. Turkey*, no. 28940/95, § 83, 24 June 2008, where arrest for obstruction of the applicant Greek Cypriot by a "TRNC" police officer was found to be lawful, and *Protopapa v. Turkey*, no. 16084/90, § 87, 24 February 2009, where a criminal trial before a "TRNC" court was found to be in accordance with Article 6, there being no ground for finding that these courts were not independent or impartial or that they were politically motivated).

96. In the Court's view, the key consideration is to avoid a vacuum which operates to the detriment of those who live under the occupation, or those who, living outside, may claim to have been victims of infringements of their rights. Pending resolution of the international dimensions of the situation, the Court considers it of paramount importance that individuals continue to receive protection of their rights on the ground on a daily basis. The right of individual petition under the Convention is no substitute for a functioning judicial system and framework for the

---

1066    *Demopoulos and Others*, § 93.

enforcement of criminal and civil law. Even if the applicants are not living as such under the control of the "TRNC", the Court considers that, if there is an effective remedy available for their complaints provided under the auspices of the respondent Government, the rule of exhaustion applies under Article 35 § 1 of the Convention. As has been consistently emphasised, this conclusion does not in any way put in doubt the view adopted by the international community regarding the establishment of the "TRNC" or the fact that the government of the Republic of Cyprus remains the sole legitimate government of Cyprus (see *Foka*, cited above, § 84). The Court maintains its opinion that allowing the respondent State to correct wrongs imputable to it does not amount to an indirect legitimisation of a regime unlawful under international law.

The *Demopoulos and Others* solution is a remedy created to address a single issue in a single context. That, however, does not make it unique. The same can be said about the '*legge Pinto*' or Pinto law enacted by Italy to provide a remedy for violations of Article 6 § 1 of the Convention caused by the excessive length of domestic civil proceedings.[1067]

Nor, as we have seen, is it unique in that it approves a legal remedy even though the entity that it to administer it is unrecognised except by the respondent State.

It is the combination of these two features that makes the *Demopoulos and Others* situation unique: the single-issue remedy administered by an entity whose very existence in law is, at the very least, a bone of contention.

The *Demopoulos* decision has been criticised for allowing *Realpolitik* to triumph over international humanitarian law, in particular the sixth paragraph of Article 49 of the Fourth Geneva Convention that forbids the Occupying Power to 'deport or transfer parts of its own civilian population into the territory it occupies'.[1068] Be that as it may, it offers a solution of sorts – and one that leaves the choice whether to seek compensation in the hands of the acknowledged owners, at that. Admittedly Greek Cypriots might resent going before a 'TRNC' body, but people do not necessarily like to go before their own domestic courts either; as the decision noted, those who preferred to hold out for return of their

---

1067   *Brusco v. Italy* (dec.), no. 69789/01, ECHR 2001-IX; *Giacometti and 5 others v. Italy* (dec.), no. 34939/97, ECHR 2001-XII.

1068   Aeyal Gross,"The Righting of the Law of Occupation", in *The Frontiers of Human Rights: Extraterritoriality and its Challenges* (Collected Courses of the Academy of European Law vol. XXIV/1, pp. 21-54 at p. 43.

ATTRIBUTION

property retained the option of doing nothing and waiting for the occupation to come to an end.[1069]

### 8.5.5 *Internationally Imposed Quasi-indigenous Institutions*
#### 8.5.5.1 Western Germany

It is possible to see certain aspects of the occupation regime in Western Germany after World War II as a distant ancestor of the Annex 6 setup in Bosnia and Herzegovina which we will discuss in greater detail below.

The applicants in *X v. Federal Republic of Germany* were German nationals before the Second World War. In 1932 the first applicant emigrated to what was then Palestine. The second applicant emigrated to England in 1936. The applicants had owned property in Wiesbaden, Germany, which was sold; they alleged, however, that the price had been well below market value and reduced still further by the so-called Flight Tax, an exit tax exacted from Jews seeking to flee Nazi persecution.

After the war Wiesbaden was in the American zone of occupation. The American occupying authorities enacted a law that created a presumption that property wrongfully taken 'for reasons of race, religion, nationality, ideology or political opposition to National Socialism', or from persons subject to persecution on those grounds, had in effect been confiscated. The presumption was rebuttable if a 'fair purchase price' had been paid or if 'the transaction as such and with its essential terms would have taken place even in the absence of National Socialism'.

After the war the applicants sought monetary compensation through the German courts but were met with a rejection on the ground that the first applicant had already been living outside Germany at the time of the sale (the implication being, presumably, that he had been under no constraint). Ultimately, in 1955, the case ended up in the Supreme Restitution Court, a body originally set up under an arrangement between the three Western allies (who as we have seen were at that time Occupying Powers in Western Germany) that had later been ratified by the Federal Republic.

Seized of the matter, the Commission came to the conclusion that the Supreme Restitution Court was an international court, subject neither to the jurisdiction of the Federal Republic of Germany nor to its sovereign power or control. True it might be that the Federal Republic of Germany had ratified the Convention before it ratified the arrangement that set up the Supreme Restitu-

---

1069  *Demopoulos and Others*, § 128.

tion Court, but it had done so shortly before recovering full sovereignty; the international status of the Supreme Restitution Court therefore prevailed.[1070]

### 8.5.5.2 Bosnia and Herzegovina[1071]

Following a NATO-led bombing campaign and the application of intense pressure by major powers (the United States and Russia in particular), the General Framework Agreement on Peace in Bosnia and Herzegovina[1072] was initialled in Dayton, Ohio (USA) on 21 November 1995. The signatories were the Republic of Bosnia and Herzegovina, as it existed at that time, the Republic of Croatia and the Federal Republic of Yugoslavia (the latter composed of Serbia and Montenegro). The General Framework Agreement will be referred to hereinafter by its more usual appellation, the Dayton Agreement.

Shortly afterwards, on 8 and 9 December 1995, a Peace Implementation Conference was held in London. It resulted in the establishment of a Peace Implementation Council ('PIC'), its Steering Board and a High Representative as the Chair of the Steering Board.[1073] While the PIC is composed of all the States, international organisations and agencies which attended the Conference, the Steering Board members are Canada, France, Germany, Italy, Japan, the Russian Federation, the United Kingdom, the United States, the Presidency of the European Union, the European Commission and Turkey (on behalf of the Organisation of the Islamic Conference). The Peace Implementation Council met on several occasions afterwards.

The Dayton Agreement entered into force upon signature on 14 December of the same year. It induced the warring factions to put a grudging end to the active hostilities in Bosnia and Herzegovina and, one may hope, created a basis for lasting peace in the country.

The Dayton Agreement sets up 'Bosnia and Herzegovina' (generally referred to as 'the State'[1074] – the name 'Republic' having come to be associated with one of the former warring factions) as a continuation of the former Republic. The State is composed of two Entities, the Federation of Bosnia and Herzegovina and the Serb Republic (more commonly known as the Republika Srpska).

---

1070  *X v. Germany*, Commission decision of 10 June 1958, no. 235/56, and Jewish Telegraphic Agency, 25 January 1956, http://www.jta.org/1956/01/25/archive/new-supreme-restitution-court-starts-functioning-in-germany (retrieved 12 April 2017).

1071  See generally Jessica Simor, "Tackling human rights abuses in Bosnia and Herzegovina: the Convention is up to it, are its institutions?", E.H.R.L.R. 1997, 6, 644-662.

1072  UN Document A/50/790 (General Assembly) – S/1995/999 (Security Council).

1073  UN Document S/1995/1029.

1074  The expression "the State" is often used for Bosnia and Herzegovina to disambiguate it from the Federation of Bosnia and Herzegovina, which is one of the two Entities.

ATTRIBUTION

The Federation is not so called because it unites Bosniak and Croat territorial entities (though it is easy to get that impression in practice), but because it is a 'federation' consisting of ten Cantons enjoying considerable autonomy; this federation was born of an earlier attempt at peace-making and nation-building, the Washington Agreement of 1 March 1994 (signed on 18 March 1994).[1075]

The Agreement itself comprises a brief preamble and eleven articles. Essentially the signatory parties – that is to say Bosnia and Herzegovina, Croatia and the Federal Republic of Yugoslavia – recognise each other's statehood and agree to conduct their relations in accordance with the applicable rules of international law. In addition, they 'welcome and endorse' the more detailed arrangements laid down in twelve Annexes (twelve, that is, taking Annexes 1-A and 1-B separately). The signatories to the Annexes are, in most cases, the State, the Federation of Bosnia and Herzegovina and the Republika Srpska.

We will examine those Annexes that are of interest to our study.

#### 8.5.5.2.1 *Military Aspects: Annex 1-A*

Annex 1-A, the 'Agreement on the Military Aspects of the Peace Settlement', the signatories – the State and the two Entities – 'welcome the willingness' of the international community to send a military force. The Security Council was invited to adopt a resolution by which it would authorise Member States or regional organisations and arrangements to establish a multinational military Implementation Force (to be known as 'IFOR') as the successor to UN-PROFOR; this force was to be led by NATO though it might include forces from non-NATO states.[1076] The Security Council did so, in a Chapter VII resolution, one day after the Dayton Peace Agreement entered into force.[1077] IFOR existed for one year, from 20 December 1995 to 20 December 1996.

Appended to Annex 1A were two Appendices, including one, Appendix B, which comprised a status of forces agreement between the State and NATO. This agreement provided that the Convention on the Privileges and Immunities of the United Nations of 13 February 1946 concerning experts on mission should apply to NATO IFOR personnel. Personnel enjoying privileges and immunities under this Appendix were to respect the laws of the Republic of Bosnia and Herzegovina insofar as it '[was] compatible with the entrusted tasks/mandate'[1078] – i.e. the latter took precedence over local laws – and 'under all

---

1075    To be found on the web site of the United States Institute of Peace, https://www.usip.org/files/file/resources/collections/peace_agreements/washagree_03011994.pdf (accessed on 1 May 2017).

1076    Article I (1) of Annex 1-A.

1077    S/RES/1031/1995 (15 December 1995), § 14.

1078    *loc. cit.*, § 3.

322                                                                                 CHAPTER 8

circumstances and at all times' were 'subject to the exclusive jurisdiction of their respective national elements in respect of any criminal or disciplinary offenses which may be committed by them in the Republic of Bosnia and Herzegovina'.[1079]

On 12 December 1996 the Security Council, again in a Chapter VII resolution, authorised the Stabilization Force (SFOR) to be set up as the legal successor to IFOR, initially for eighteen months.[1080] SFOR existed until 2 December 2004 when it was relieved by a European Union Force, known as EUFOR,[1081] embarking on its 'Operation Althea'.[1082] EUFOR is still in theatre, though its strength is now reduced to little more than symbolic levels.

#### 8.5.5.2.2   Civilian Structure

The post-war legal civilian structure of Bosnia and Herzegovina is based on further Annexes. Three of them are of particular interest here: Annex 4, Annex 6 and Annex 10.

##### Annex 4

Annex 4 is the Constitution of Bosnia and Herzegovina.[1083] It provides, in its first Article, that the Republic of Bosnia and Herzegovina continues its existence as simply 'Bosnia and Herzegovina'. It defines the powers of the Entities, which are all those not expressly reserved to the State, and the composition and powers of the institutions of the State – principally the Presidency, the Parliamentary Assembly, the Council of Ministers, the Constitutional Court and the Central Bank, though reference is made to bodies and organs created under other Annexes including the Human Rights Commission set up by Annex 6 which we shall meet anon.

Bosnia and Herzegovina is to 'ensure the highest level of internationally recognized rights and fundamental freedoms' (Article II (1)). More specifically, Article II (2) provides as follows:

> International Standards. The rights and freedoms set forth in the European Convention for the Protection of Human Rights and Fundamental

---

1079   loc. cit., § 7.

1080   S/RES/1088 (1996) of 12 December 1996, § 18.

1081   S/RES/1575 (2004) of 22 November 2004, § 10. The most recent extension of EUFOR's mandate at the time of writing is by S/RES/2315 (2016) of 8 November 2016, § 3.

1082   Named after Althea, the ancient Greek goddess of healing.

1083   See generally Mehmet Semih Gemalmaz, "Constitution, Ombudsperson and Human Rights Chamber in 'Bosnia and Herzegovina', Netherlands Quarterly of Human Rights, Vol. 17/3, 277-329, 1999, pp. 277-291.

ATTRIBUTION

Freedoms and its Protocols shall apply directly in Bosnia and Herzegovina. These shall have priority over all other law.

The Constitutional Court comprises nine members, two appointed by the Republika Srpska and four appointed by the Federation of Bosnia and Herzegovina[1084] (in practice, two Bosniacs and two Croats). The remaining three members, who may not be nationals of Bosnia and Herzegovina or of any neighbouring State (which rules out the former Yugoslav republics Croatia, Montenegro and Serbia), are appointed by the President of the European Court of Human Rights.[1085]

The Constitutional Court's constitutional jurisdiction, defined in Article VI (3), includes disputes arising under the Constitution between the Entities or between Bosnia and Herzegovina and an Entity or Entities, or between institutions of Bosnia and Herzegovina.

Its appellate jurisdiction is over issues under the Constitution arising out of a judgment of any other court in Bosnia and Herzegovina.

It is also empowered to give what amount to preliminary rulings on

issues referred by any court in Bosnia and Herzegovina concerning whether a law, on whose validity its decision depends, is compatible with this Constitution, with the European Convention for Human Rights and Fundamental Freedoms and its Protocols, or with the laws of Bosnia and Herzegovina; or concerning the existence of or the scope of a general rule of public international law pertinent to the court's decision.

In its various provisions defining the composition of the main political organs (the Parliamentary Assembly, the Presidency) the Annex 4 Constitution recognises only three 'constituent peoples': Serbs (to be elected from the Republika Srpska) and Bosniaks and Croats (to be elected from the Federation of Bosnia and Herzegovina). This is very much in keeping with the character of the Dayton Peace Agreement as an armistice agreement intended to put an end to active hostilities as quickly as may be. It is, however, unfair to all those who are not, or do not wish to identify as, members of one of those ethnic groups – for example, persons of mixed descent (of whom there were large numbers before the war and many remain) and members of other ethnic groups (such as Jews and Roma). This state of affairs has been challenged, even before the European Court of Human Rights, and with success: the Court has found a violation of

---

1084   Article VI (1) (a).
1085   Article VI (1) (a)-(b).

Article 14 of the Convention taken in conjunction with Article 3 of Protocol No. 1 on account of the ineligibility of persons not counted members of the 'constituent peoples' to stand for election to the House of Peoples of Bosnia and Herzegovina (the Lower House of Parliament) and the Presidency,[1086] or of the ineligibility of members of a minority constituent people within one of the Entities,[1087] to be elected from that Entity. In the Court's view, whatever the justification for such distinctions might have been at the time when the Annex 4 Constitution was adopted, it no longer existed at the time when the respective judgments were adopted.

The changes required by the Court's judgments have yet to be implemented.[1088] The fear is that any changes made to the Constitution will not be limited to this feature alone and that some will propose to amend it further so as to grant the Entities rights even more sweeping than those they enjoy already – even the right to secede, which in the present redaction is excluded.[1089] An external or supranational power with the competence to force through changes to the Constitution does not exist: responsibility lies entirely with the institutions of Bosnia and Herzegovina themselves.

The Constitutional Court ruled early on that it did not itself have jurisdiction to change either the Dayton Agreement or the Constitution:

> (...) the Constitutional Court is not competent to evaluate the constitutionality of the General Framework Agreement as the Constitutional Court has in fact been established under the Constitution of Bosnia and Herzegovina in order to uphold this Constitution (...) The Constitution of Bosnia and Herzegovina was adopted as Annex IV to the General Framework Agreement for Peace in Bosnia and Herzegovina, and consequently there cannot be a conflict or a possibility for controversy between this Agreement and the Constitution of Bosnia and Herzegovina.[1090]

It has, however, pointed the way forward:

---

1086    *Sejdić and Finci v. Bosnia and Herzegovina* (GC), nos. 27996/06 and 34836/06, ECHR 2009 (the applicants are a Rom and a Jew, respectively); *Zornić v. Bosnia and Herzegovina*, no. 3681/06, 15 December 2014 (the applicant does not declare affiliation with any of the "constituent peoples").

1087    *Pilav v. Bosnia and Herzegovina*, no. 41939/07, 9 June 2016.

1088    Committee of Ministers resolutions CM/ResDH(2011)291, 2 December 2011; CM/ResDH(2012)233, 6 December 2012; and CM/ResDH(2013)259, 5 December 2013.

1089    Article III (2) (a) of the Constitution of Bosnia and Herzegovina.

1090    Constitutional Court of Bosnia and Herzegovina, U-7/97, 22 December 1997.

ATTRIBUTION

Elements of a democratic state and society as well as underlying assumptions – pluralism, just procedures, peaceful relations that arise out of the Constitution – must serve as a guideline for further elaboration of the issue of the structure of BiH as a multi-national state. Territorial division (of Entities) must not serve as an instrument of ethnic segregation – on the contrary – it must accommodate ethnic groups by preserving linguistic pluralism and peace in order to contribute to the integration of the state and society as such. Constitutional principle of collective equality of constituent peoples, arising out of designation of Bosniacs, Croats and Serbs as constituent peoples, prohibits any special privileges for one or two constituent peoples, any domination in governmental structures and any ethnic homogenisation by segregation based on territorial separation. Despite the territorial division of BiH by establishment of two Entities, this territorial division cannot serve as a constitutional legitimacy for ethnic domination, national homogenisation or the right to maintain results of ethnic cleansing. Designation of Bosniacs, Croats and Serbs as constituent peoples in the Preamble of the Constitution of BiH must be understood as an all-inclusive principle of the Constitution of BiH to which the Entities must fully adhere, pursuant to Article III.3 (b) of the Constitution of BiH.[1091]

*Annex 6*

Annex 6, the 'Agreement on Human Rights' which we mentioned earlier,[1092] boldly states, in the first paragraph of its first article, that

The Parties shall secure to all persons within their jurisdiction the highest level of internationally recognized human rights and fundamental freedoms, including the rights and freedoms provided in the European Convention for the Protection of Human Rights and Fundamental Freedoms and its Protocols and the other international agreements listed in the Appendix to this Annex.

---

1091    Constitutional Court of Bosnia and Herzegovina, U-5/98 (Partial Decision Part 3), 1 July 2000.

1092    See generally Manfred Nowak, "The Human Rights Chamber for Bosnia and Herzegovina adopts its First Judgments", *Human Rights Law Review* 18 (1997) pp. 529-45; R. Aybay, "A New Institution in the Field: The Human Rights Chamber of Bosnia and Herzegovina", *Netherlands Quarterly of Human Rights*, Vol. 15/4, 529-558, and for a critical appraisal, Mehmet Semih Gemalmaz, "Constitution, Ombudsperson and Human Rights Chamber in 'Bosnia and Herzegovina', *Netherlands Quarterly of Human Rights*, Vol. 17/3, 277-329, 1999, pp. 291-329.

To 'assist in honoring their obligations under this Agreement', or as a cynic might say, to see to it that they all kept their word, the Parties set up a Commission on Human Rights composed of the Office of the Ombudsman and the Human Rights Chamber. Both had the same basic task, which was to consider

(a) alleged or apparent violations of human rights as provided in the European Convention for the Protection of Human Rights and Fundamental Freedoms and the Protocols thereto, or

(b) alleged or apparent discrimination on any ground such as sex, race, color, language, religion, political or other opinion, national or social origin, association with a national minority, property, birth or other status arising in the enjoyment of any of the rights and freedoms provided for in the international agreements listed in the Appendix to this Annex[1093]

– the agreements annexed including, significantly, the 1948 Convention on the Prevention and Punishment of the Crime of Genocide, the four Geneva Conventions, and the 1966 International Covenant on Civil and Political Rights with both of its Protocols. The Security Council, in the same resolution that authorised SFOR, called upon the State and the Parties to the Peace Agreement to cooperate with the Ombudsman and the Chamber.[1094]

The Human Rights Ombudsman and the Human Rights Chamber were intended, by Article III of Annex 6, to function as two limbs of a single body, sharing a single Executive Officer to manage their administration and staff. In actual fact the Commission never functioned as a single organisation: early on temperamental differences ensured that the Ombudsman and the Chamber went their separate ways. The first Human Rights Ombudsman, Dr Gret Haller, styled herself Ombudsperson, and it is under this name that her office became known.

In both bodies the international element predominated. The Human Rights Ombudsperson was a foreign national;[1095] of the fourteen members of the Chamber, eight were nationals of foreign countries, making the Chamber a hybrid court, and six were Bosnia and Herzegovina nationals appointed by the Entities (four appointed by the Federation of Bosnia and Herzegovina – in

---

1093   Article II (2) of Annex 6.
1094   S/RES/1088 (1996) of 12 December 1996, § 10.
1095   Article IV (2) of Annex 6.

ATTRIBUTION

practice, two Bosniaks and two Croats – and two appointed by the Republika Srpska).[1096]

Both the Office of the Ombudsperson and the Human Rights Chamber enjoyed support from the Strasbourg Institutions; in their first years, the Deputy Human Rights Ombudsperson and the head of the legal support staff of the Human Rights Chamber (known as the Registrar) were members of either the Secretariat of the European Commission of Human Rights or the Registry of the European Court of Human Rights, seconded by the Council of Europe.[1097] Both bodies had a mixed staff of Bosnia and Herzegovina citizens and foreign nationals, many of the latter seconded, or financed, by the governments of the States of which they were nationals.

The set-up was very much based on that of the European Commission and Court of Human Rights as it existed, at the time, under the European Convention on Human Rights of 1950: the Ombudsman was to investigate alleged violations of the Convention and report on them, forwarding the reports to the High Representative or initiating proceedings in the Human Rights Chamber as the case might require.[1098] A difference from the Convention set-up was that the Chamber was to receive cases, not only by referral from the Ombudsperson, but also

> directly from any Party or person, non-governmental organization, or group of individuals claiming to be the victim of a violation by any Party or acting on behalf of alleged victims who are deceased or missing.[1099]

The system established under Annex 6 was intended to be in existence for only five years after the Agreement entered into force, after which responsibility for its continued operation would pass to the parties unless otherwise agreed. The Ombudsperson became a domestic institution in 2001, after a State law that so provided was signed into force by the High Representative (although for a time the Ombudsperson continued to be a foreign national). Shortly before 14 De-

---

1096 For a thoughtful discussion of hybrid courts, drawing on the experience of the Human Rights Chamber for Bosnia and Herzegovina in particular, see Elizabeth M. Bruch, "Hybrid Courts: Examining Hybridity Through a Post-Colonial Lens", 28 *Boston University International Law Journal* 1 (2010). The author was the Human Rights Chamber's first Executive Officer.

1097 The present author among them. A member of the Registry of the European Court of Human Rights since 1992, he was seconded to the Human Rights Chamber in 1997-98 and again in 2000-2001. The latter secondment was financed by the Government of the Netherlands.

1098 Article V of Annex 6.

1099 Article VIII of Annex 6.

cember 2000, the day on which the five-year period was set to expire, the State and the two Entities – on the prompting of, in particular, the High Representative – reached an agreement that extended the existence of the Human Rights Chamber until the end of 2003.[1100]

While they were in existence, the Ombudsperson and the Human Rights Chamber were widely considered part of the international structure – as was only natural, considering their funding (which had to come, almost exclusively, from abroad), their predominantly international composition (as well as the proportion of non-Bosnia and Herzegovina nationals among their support staff) and the nature of the substantive law that they applied. Thus it was that in 1998 the Venice Commission, asked to express an opinion on whether the Chamber could be described as 'any other court' in Bosnia and Herzegovina, against whose decisions it was possible to appeal to the Constitutional Court, found on account of the Chamber's 'quasi-international (*sui generis*) and provisional character' that it was not.[1101] The Constitutional Court followed suit: when the Federation of Bosnia and Herzegovina attempted to challenge decisions of the Chamber before the Constitutional Court, the Constitutional Court held that the two jurisdictional bodies functioned in parallel.[1102]

In a decision echoing that of the Constitutional Court, the Human Rights Chamber held that it, too, lacked competence to review the decisions of other bodies created by the Dayton Agreement.[1103]

It is certain that during the years of their existence, the Ombudsperson and Human Rights Chamber enjoyed the confidence of the local population to a greater extent than domestic bodies, the latter being widely seen – so shortly after a bitter sectarian war – as protecting factional interests. In mid-2003 a spokesperson for Amnesty International was able to state that 'the Chamber [was] acting as a last and possibly only avenue of justice in Bosnia-Herzegovina'.[1104]

---

[1100]   For more detail, see Buyse (2008), pp. 284-301.

[1101]   Opinion of the Venice Commission on the admissibility of appeals against the Human Rights Chamber of Bosnia and Herzegovina, CDL-INF (98) 18.

[1102]   Constitutional Court of Bosnia and Herzegovina, U-7-11/98, 26 February 1999; see also Buyse (2008), p. 283.

[1103]   Human Rights Chamber for Bosnia and Herzegovina, CH/00/4441, *Merima Sijarić v. Federation of Bosnia and Herzegovina*, 6 June 2000, and CH/99/2327, *Momčilo Knežević v. Republika Srpska*, 11 October 2001; see also Buyse (2008), p. 283.

[1104]   Amnesty International UK Director Kate Allen, Amnesty International press release of 12 June 2003, "Bosnia-Herzegovina: Ashdown's proposal to abolish Human Rights Chamber leaves citizens unprotected".

ATTRIBUTION

Much of their success, of the Human Rights Chamber especially, came from the latter's use of its power to order binding provisional measures.[1105] 'Ethnic cleansing', to use a horrid expression coined during the war years, did not cease immediately when the Dayton Agreement entered into force; for some time afterwards local authorities in both Entities sought to consolidate the positions of one or other of the ethnic factions by evicting members of the other factions who had remained within their territories or who had returned to their original homes. The Chamber's orders for provisional measures, backed up by the executive force of other elements of the international community, helped to put a stop to this. Gradually, as the situation normalised, internally displaced persons who had taken up residence in dwellings abandoned by others and who were unwilling to return to their original homes sought provisional measures that would enable them to remain where they were; these were refused, an important premise of the Dayton peace process being precisely that people should as a rule return to where they had come from.[1106]

In time, after Bosnia and Herzegovina had acceded to the Convention, the question arose whether the Chamber, in particular, was 'another procedure of international investigation or settlement' within the meaning of Article 35 § 2 (b) of the Convention. It came up in the *Jeličić* case – the issue being the failure by one of the Entities to enforce a decision of the Human Rights Chamber.

Granted leave to intervene as a third party under Article 36 of the Convention, the Venice Commission submitted an *amicus curiae* opinion stating that proceedings before the Chamber must not be considered 'international' within the meaning of Article 35 § 2 (b) of the Convention. They must, on the contrary, be considered 'domestic' within the meaning of Article 35 § 1. The International Committee for Human Rights, a human rights NGO registered in Spain with its main office in Sarajevo which also intervened, stressed the transitional character of the Chamber and noted, among other things, that constituent units of Bosnia and Herzegovina were capable of being parties before it.

In its ensuing admissibility decision, the Court held that the Chamber 'constituted a part, albeit a particular part, of the legal system of Bosnia and Herzegovina' – a domestic body, not an international one.[1107] By this time the Chamber was safely defunct and it could no longer hurt its authority to deny its international status.

---

1105    Eva Rieter, *Preventing Irreparable Harm: Provisional Measures in International Human Rights Adjudication* (diss. Nijmegen), Intersentia, 2010, pp. 182-188.

1106    Rieter, pp. 508-509.

1107    *Jeličić v. Bosnia and Herzegovina* (dec.), no. 41183/02, ECHR 2005-XII.

*Annex 10*

Annex 10, or Agreement on Civilian Implementation of the Peace Settlement, contains a request to the United Nations Security Council for the appointment of a High Representative and defines the mandate of such a functionary.

The powers and duties of the High Representative include coordinating the work of civilian organisations providing aid and reporting on progress in the implementation of the peace agreement. The High Representative is 'the final authority in theater' regarding interpretation of the Dayton Agreement as regards its civilian aspects. It is specifically provided that the High Representative shall have no authority over the military.

The very day following the entry into force of the Dayton Agreement the Security Council adopted a resolution welcoming the conclusions of the Peace Implementation Conference held in London on 8 and 9 December 1995 (S/1995/1029), and in particular its decision to establish a Peace Implementation Council and its Steering Board and appointed the first High Representative, for whom the ground had been prepared by the Peace Implementation Conference. He was Carl Bildt, former prime minister of Sweden and former co-chairman of the Dayton Peace Conference itself.[1108]

On 10 December 1997, at its main meeting in Bonn, Germany, the Peace Implementation Council adopted a set of conclusions including the following:[1109]

### XI. High Representative

1. The Council commends the efforts of the High Representative and his staff in pursuing the implementation of the Peace Agreement. It emphasises the important role of the High Representative in ensuring the creation of conditions for a self-sustaining peace in Bosnia and Herzegovina and his responsibility for co-ordination of the activities of the civilian organisations and agencies in Bosnia and Herzegovina.

The Council reiterates that the Steering Board of the PIC will provide the High Representative with political guidance on peace implementation. It will continue to meet monthly, inviting representatives of relevant international organisations to attend as appropriate.

2. The Council welcomes the High Representative's agreement to continue reporting in accordance with Article II. 1 (f) of Annex 10 to the Peace Agreement.

---

1108   UN Security Council Resolution 1031 of 15 December 1995, para. 26.
1109   UN document S/1997/979.

ATTRIBUTION

The Council encourages the High Representative to report regularly on compliance by individual municipalities with the provisions of the Peace Agreement.

The Council welcomes the High Representative's intention to use his final authority in theatre regarding interpretation of the Agreement on the Civilian Implementation of the Peace Settlement in order to facilitate the resolution of difficulties by making binding decisions, as he judges necessary, on the following issues:

a. timing, location and chairmanship of meetings of the common institutions;

b. interim measures to take effect when parties are unable to reach agreement, which will remain in force until the Presidency or Council of Ministers has adopted a decision consistent with the Peace Agreement on the issue concerned;

c. other measures to ensure implementation of the Peace Agreement throughout Bosnia and Herzegovina and its Entities, as well as the smooth running of the common institutions. Such measures may include actions against persons holding public office or officials who are absent from meetings without good cause or who are found by the High Representative to be in violation of legal commitments made under the Peace Agreement or the terms for its implementation.

The Security Council endorsed these conclusions on 19 December 1997.[1110]

Since then, successive High Representatives have made use of their 'Bonn powers', as they are referred to, to impose or strike down legislation, to promote the implementation of decisions of the Human Rights Chamber or other authorities created by the Dayton Agreement when the State and the Entities were conspicuously dragging their feet, and to dismiss civil servants and even elected functionaries found to be obstructing the implementation, the letter or the spirit of the Dayton Agreement.

Thus, between June and December 2004 the then High Representative removed twenty-six individuals from their positions in public authority and political parties and barred them indefinitely from holding any such positions and standing for election thereafter for having obstructed arrests ordered by the ICTY Prosecutor. There being no legal remedy of any description available to them, they applied to the European Court of Human Rights, alleging violations of Articles 6 (under its criminal head), 11 and 13.

---

1110    UN Seurity Council 1144 (1997).

The Court declared their complaint inadmissible *ratione personae*, the decisions in issue having been lawfully taken by the High Representative under powers previously and explicitly delegated by the Security Council under Chapter VII of the United Nations Charter. Quoting §§ 146-149 of the *Behrami and Saramati* decision, it came to the conclusion that the same reasoning applied to 'the acceptance of an international civil administration in its territory by a respondent State'.[1111]

### 8.5.5.3    Kosovo

After the Federal Republic of Yugoslavia withdrew its troops from Kosovo and until Kosovo declared independence in 2008, the exercise of civilian jurisdiction was vested by UN Security Council Resolution 1244 (1999) in an interim administration established by the Secretary General of the United Nations.[1112] In his report of 12 June 1999 the Secretary General of the United Nations announced the setting up of the United Nations Interim Administration Mission in Kosovo (or UNMIK).[1113] One month later, he announced that UNMIK would be invested with '[a]ll legislative and executive powers, including the administration of the Judiciary'.[1114] This was in fact done by the very first UNMIK Regulation promulgated by the Special Representative of the Secretary General of the United Nations, in which the Special Representative vested these powers in himself – including the power to 'appoint any person to perform functions in the civil administration in Kosovo, including the judiciary, or remove such person'.[1115] A later UNMIK Regulation specified the law to be applied, which was, in order of precedence, the UNMIK regulations promulgated by the Special Representative and the law in force in Kosovo on 22 March 1989 (the date on which Kosovo had lost its autonomy within the SFRY).[1116] Moreover, in exercising their functions, all persons undertaking public duties or holding public office in Kosovo were to observe

---

[1111]    *Berić and Others*, §§ 26-30. This is now standing case-law: see *Kalinić and Bilbija v. Bosnia and Herzegovina* (dec.), nos. 45541/04 16587/07, 13 May 2008. See also Tobias Lock, "Beyond *Bosphorus*: The European Court of Human Rights' Case-Law on the Responsibility of Member States of International Organisations under the European Convention on Human Rights", in *Human Rights Law Review* 10:3 (2010), 529-545 at 532-33.

[1112]    UN Security Council Resolution 1244 (1999) of 10 June 1999, §§ 10 and 11.

[1113]    S/1999/672 (Report of the Secretary General pursuant to paragraph 10 of Security Council Resolution 1244 (1999).

[1114]    S/1999/779 (Interim administration mission in Kosovo), § 35.

[1115]    UNMIK Regulation 1999/1, Section 1.

[1116]    UNMIK Regulation 1999/24, Section 1(1).

internationally recognized human rights standards, as reflected in particular in:

(a) The Universal Declaration on Human Rights of 10 December 1948;

(b) The European Convention for the Protection of Human Rights and Fundamental Freedoms of 4 November 1950 and the Protocols thereto;

(c) The International Covenant on Civil and Political Rights of 16 December 1966 and the Protocols thereto;

(d) The International Covenant on Economic, Social and Cultural Rights of 16 December 1966;

(e) The Convention on the Elimination of All Forms of Racial Discrimination of 21 December 1965;

(f) The Convention on Elimination of All Forms of Discrimination Against Women of 17 December 1979;

(g) The Convention Against Torture and Other Cruel, Inhumane or Degrading Treatment or Punishment of 17 December 1984; and

(h) The International Convention on the Rights of the Child of 20 December 1989.[1117]

In 2004 the Venice Commission presented an opinion suggesting a Human Rights Court for Kosovo broadly based on the model of the Human Rights Chamber, but with an important difference:

> 105. Unlike the Human Rights Chamber for Bosnia and Herzegovina, the Human Rights Court for Kosovo should be empowered to accept applications lodged either by individuals or by the Ombudsperson on their behalf, with their agreement, concerning actions and omissions by the international authorities in Kosovo (when reviewing acts or omissions by UNMIK, the Chamber would have to sit in an exclusively international composition) and the agreement should therefore comprise a specific provision concerning the waiving of the immunity of the Special Representative and UNMIK personnel, and possibly also that of NATO. It would be a new phenomenon for a (quasi-) international court to hold jurisdiction over an international organisation to which it does not belong. However, the situation would be the same if the European Court were granted jurisdiction over UNMIK, or possibly KFOR, or for that matter once the European Union or European Community has acceded to the ECHR.[1118]

---

1117    UNMIK Regulation 1999/24, Section 1(3).

1118    Venice Commission, Opinion on human rights in Kosovo: Possible establishment of review mechanisms, CDL-AD (2004)033, 11 October 2004, § 105.

334

The suggestion was endorsed by the Parliamentary Assembly of the Council of Europe.[1119]

UNMIK still exists even after Kosovo's declaration of independence. It 'continues to implement its mandate in a status neutral manner and operate under Security Council resolution 1244 (1999)'.[1120]

The 2008 Constitution of Kosovo[1121] is largely based on the Comprehensive Proposal for the Kosovo Status Settlement,[1122] known as the 'Ahtisaari plan',[1123] to which it refers. Its Article 152 provides for Kosovo's Constitutional Court to be composed, temporarily, of six members appointed by the President of the Republic (their nationality is not specified) and three members, who shall be non-nationals, appointed by the International Civilian Representative (an official of the European Union), upon consultation with the President of the European Court of Human Rights.[1124]

The Court has recognised that the Republic of Serbia exercises no effective control over Kosovo and that consequently applications against Serbia alleging violations of the Convention by the authorities of Kosovo are inadmissible *ratione personae*.[1125]

Kosovo has not yet been universally recognised as an independent State; among States withholding recognition one finds Council of Europe Members including Serbia (unsurprisingly). The Court has taken to adding a footnote in judgments and decisions concerning Kosovo, stating that 'All reference to Kosovo, whether to the territory, institutions or population, in this text [should] be understood in full compliance with United Nations Security Council Resolution 1244 and without prejudice to the status of Kosovo'.

---

1119   PACE Resolution 1417 (2005), Protection of Human Rights in Kosovo (25 January 2005); see also PACE Doc. 10393, report of the Committee on Legal Affairs and Human Rights, rapporteur: Mr Lloyd.

1120   https://unmik.unmissions.org/mandate (accessed 14 May 2017).

1121   http://www.kushtetutakosoves.info/repository/docs/Constitution.of.the.Republic.of.Kosovo.pdf (accessed 14 May 2017).

1122   S/2007/168/Add.1, 26 March 2007.

1123   Martti Ahtisaari, former President of Finland, United Nations Special Envoy for Kosovo 2005-2007.

1124   Compare Article 6.1 of the Comprehensive Proposal for the Kosovo Status Settlement, fn. 1121 above.

1125   *Azemi v. Serbia (dec.)*, no. 11209/09, 5 November 2013.

## 8.6    Conclusion

Various ways are imaginable in which a Contracting State can seek to evade attribution to it of a violation of the Convention.

Setting up a subordinate pseudo-state has not proved successful in terms of escaping imputability under the Convention. The 'TRNC' and the 'MRT' are cases in point. That said, the 'TRNC' experience shows that a Contracting State may actually acquit itself of its Convention obligations by this means. It is interesting to note a certain ambivalence in this context: although in at least one recent case before the Court the Turkish Government have no longer raised a preliminary objection of inadmissibility *ratione loci*,[1126] in Turkish domestic legislation and international legal practice they apparently continue to maintain that the 'TRNC' is not an authority subordinate to the Republic of Turkey but a 'state' in its own right. At all events, demands of accountability under the Convention and the availability of effective domestic remedies have been found satisfied; thus is Turkey protected in a large measure against admissible applications.

As to the use of private agents, security contractors for example, it is unlikely that a State will escape accountability by mandating activities normally within its remit to them. Nonetheless, provided that proper regulatory and supervisory frameworks are in place and appropriate remedies exist to deal with any problems that may arise under the Convention this solution may be compliant.

International organisations – most notably the United Nations – may be of assistance to Contracting States from the perspective of accountability before the European Court of Human Rights. However, unless provision is made for the international organisation itself to be held to account, the risk is that a jurisdictional vacuum emerges that leaves the victim of a human rights violation without any remedy; this has been rightly noted. Moreover, as the Dutch experience of litigation in the Srebrenica cases shows, States may yet be held accountable in their own courts under domestic law.

The use of internationally imposed quasi-domestic institutions offers the best prospects of satisfying requirements of accountability while placing re-

---

1126   *Joannou v. Turkey*, no. 53240/14, § 61, 12 December 2017; see also the Chamber judgment in *Güzelyurtlu and Others v. Cyprus and Turkey*, no. 36925/07, § 184, 4 April 2018 (the preliminary objection of incompatibility *ratione loci* was however revived in the Grand Chamber proceedings: see *Güzelyurtlu and Others v. Cyprus and Turkey* (GC), no. 36925/07, § 172, 29 January 2019).

sponsibility elsewhere. Here we may turn to the lessons learned in Bosnia and Herzegovina.

There remains much to criticise about the Dayton setup for Bosnia and Herzegovina. In particular, it has failed to provide for a viable unitary state. There is still a perceived danger even now that part of the territory – whether the Republika Srpska or a part of the Federation of Bosnia and Herzegovina, if not both – may one day try to take itself out of the State, perhaps to become independent in its own right, perhaps to join a neighbouring state.

Nevertheless, the Dayton Agreement deserves credit for being what it was intended to be: an effective armistice agreement. It put an end to what remains, for the present, the bloodiest conflict on European soil since the Second World War and enabled a return to some semblance of normality. At the same time it made it possible for outside forces including European States to impose their will without themselves being held accountable under the Convention.

We can identify the following relevant features of the arrangement:

Firstly, compliance with general international law throughout. All coercive measures were agreed by the States involved beforehand and given the seal of legality by the Security Council. Failing permission of a local government enjoying international recognition, this is the *conditio sine qua non* for any solution that involves the use or threat of force or otherwise overrides the will of the warring factions if it is to be legal in terms of international law.

Secondly, the assumption of responsibility by quasi-domestic institutions that were not, as such, subordinate to the government or governments of any one or more of the Contracting States. This is the *conditio sine qua non* for the latter to avoid having to assume 'jurisdiction' within the meaning of Article 1 of the Convention, whether directly as Parties to the Convention (as in, for example, *Cyprus v. Turkey*, *Ilaşcu and Others* and *Jaloud*) or as 'occupying powers' within the meaning of Article 42 of the Hague Regulations (compare *Al-Skeini* and *Al-Jedda*).

A third, and extremely helpful, feature of the Dayton setup is that the substantive human rights standards of the Convention were incorporated in the solution chosen from the outset, even though Bosnia and Herzegovina was not to become a Party in its own right for many years yet. Although this was not in itself determinative for the jurisdiction of the Convention States involved in the rebuilding of post-war Bosnia and Herzegovina, it did enable the emergence of a Convention-based legal order that remains unique among newly-joined Contracting States without a strong indigenous human rights culture. The total number of applications lodged with the Court against Bosnia and Herzegovina, and put before a judicial formation, to date is relatively high – nearly as high as the number lodged against, for example, Austria and Greece,

ATTRIBUTION

which have been Parties for decades and have more than twice as many inhabitants – but the number of judgments finding at least one violation compares extremely favourably with both.[1127] This attests to the strength of the institutions in place protecting human rights, even as serious problems remain. The centrifugal forces that still threaten to tear the country apart will have to be challenged in the domestic political process; in this respect, the law, even the Convention, can be of but little assistance.

The least satisfactory feature of the Dayton setup is that it ignored the need to hold the international presence itself to account, which as the *Berić* decision demonstrates remains a concern. An attempt was made to apply the lessons learned in neighbouring Kosovo, although with little alacrity; even so, Kosovo leads the way for the present.[1128]

---

1127 European Court of Human Rights, Overview 1959-2016, available on the Court's internet web site (accessed 1 May 2017).

1128 See generally Tilmann Altwicker and Nuscha Wieczorek, "Bridging the Security Gap through EU Rule of Law Missions? Rule of Law Administration by EULEX", *Journal of Conflict and Security Law* (2016), Vol. 21 No. 1, 115-133.

CHAPTER 9

# Summary and Conclusions

### 9.1 Applicability of the Convention *Ratione Pacis Sive Belli*

The suggestion that the European Convention on Human Rights has no relevance outside peacetime can safely be laid to rest. The Convention applies to the application of 'hard power' by or on behalf of Contracting States, and it applies in situations of 'armed conflict', whether international or non-international. Its drafters and signatories intended it so. For proof we need look no further than the Convention itself, which unlike comparable human rights instruments (in particular the International Covenant on Civil and Political Rights) makes deliberate provision for derogation in time of war or other public emergency threatening the life of the nation (see Article 15 §§ 1 and 2). It is no coincidence either that the creation of the Convention, in 1949-1950, was largely contemporaneous with that of the four 1949 Geneva Conventions.[1129]

As used for the purposes of this study, the expression 'hard power', which we borrow from the language of international relations, is however not confined to armed conflict.

We have seen that the Convention is applicable to situations more conventionally addressed in terms of law enforcement than in terms of armed conflict, such as the prevention and suppression of terrorist activity[1130] and piracy.[1131]

We would argue that the Convention is applicable, potentially at least, also to cyber-attacks committed by the forces of a Contracting State or with the sponsorship of a Contracting State, whether or not these occur within an international or non-international conflict acknowledged as such.[1132]

Finally, we posit that it may be applicable to targeted assassination abroad, whether by the overt use of military hardware such as a drone or by stealth.[1133]

We include all of these situations in the understanding of 'hard power' adopted for the purposes of this study.

Substantive issues that have arisen under the Convention in connection with situations that can be considered to involve the exercise of 'hard power'

---

1129    See 4.3.1 above.
1130    See 2.2.1.1 and 4.5.1.8 above.
1131    See 6.6.2 above.
1132    See 6.4.7 above.
1133    See 6.4.6 above.

© KONINKLIJKE BRILL NV, LEIDEN, 2021 | DOI:10.1163/9789004425637_010

SUMMARY AND CONCLUSIONS

in this sense have, as one would expect, concerned mainly Articles 2 (right to life), 3 (prohibition of torture), 5 (liberty and security of person) and 8 of the Convention and 1 of Protocol No. 1 (in particular, the right to respect for home and the right of property).[1134] There must, however, be an effective domestic remedy before a national authority to entertain any claims by individuals that their rights under the Convention have been violated. Responsibility to secure the rights and freedoms belongs primarily to the Contracting States; so, consequently, does the primary responsibility to set right whatever is amiss.

These are the parameters within which we can now attempt to answer the question we set at the outset: what latitude do Contracting States have to tailor their Convention obligations to the situation in which the need to exercise 'hard power' presents itself to them, and how can they go about it?[1135]

To do so we will go over the 'defences' we identified in the first chapter.[1136]

## 9.2    The First Defence: No Violation

### 9.2.1    *Denying the Facts*
The most obvious defence is to deny the facts complained of. This means that the Court will have to establish the truth of any factual allegations levelled against the respondent before it can address any legal issues – which means assessing evidence, and may involve time-consuming efforts at fact-finding.[1137] The Court has however shown itself prepared to take a non-dogmatic approach to such matters as the distribution of the burden of proof and evidentiary standards, and indeed the disparity in power between applicants (individuals especially) and respondent Governments dictates such a course. Even so, like any other court of law in the world it must establish the facts to which it applies the law.[1138]

### 9.2.2    *The Possibilities of Derogation*
The possibility for Contracting States to take measures derogating from their obligations under the Convention was created specifically with 'hard power'

---

1134    See 2.5 above.

1135    See 1.3.1 above.

1136    See 1.3.2 above.

1137    On which subject, see, for example, *International Human Rights and Fact-Finding – An analysis of the fact-finding missions conducted by the European Commission and Court of Human Rights*, Philip Leach, Costas Paraskeva & Gordana Uzelac, Human Rights & Social Justice Research Institute, London Metropolitan University, February 2009.

1138    See 2.7 above.

340                                                                                    CHAPTER 9

situations in mind. However, it has until now rarely been invoked for purposes going beyond law enforcement.

Since waking up to the fact that human rights law is applicable even in situations in which international humanitarian law is also applicable, meaning that both may apply simultaneously, the International Court of Justice itself, and in its wake human rights treaty bodies, academics and practitioners, have attempted to define the interrelation between the two. The position that international humanitarian law applies in cases of armed conflict as *lex specialis* in relation to human rights law is logically untenable: the two are conceptually separate and unrelated subdivisions of international law, one is not *lex generalis* in relation to the other. So is the position that they are complementary: it is borne out in practice, and in the case-law of the Court, that they may clash. As regards the Convention specifically, it is our argument that there is no need to define the interrelation between the two in such unhelpful terms: the Convention itself makes express provision for the eventuality in which international humanitarian law needs to be applied. In this the Convention is unique among treaties of general application guaranteeing classical civil and political rights.

We have seen that Article 15 of the Convention makes it possible in case of 'war or other emergency threatening the life of the nation' for the State to adapt its liabilities under the Convention to the possibilities which it has to meet them.

Lawful derogation under Article 15 does not affect the existence or scope of the State's obligations to meet the human rights standards prescribed by the Convention: these continue to exist.[1139]

The effect of Article 15 derogation is not to limit the jurisdiction of the Court. A Government therefore cannot prevent the Court from reviewing acts imputable to the State under the Convention simply by means of a notice of derogation.[1140] The Court's review will encompass, firstly, an examination of the matters complained of as if no derogation were in place. If these are incapable of leading to a finding of a violation, then no issue under Article 15 need arise; only if they appear *not* to be permissible under the Convention *per se* will the Court need to consider whether the derogation invoked by the respondent Government is, firstly, valid, and secondly, sufficient to restore to that measure its acceptability.[1141]

Article 15 derogation is possible only '[i]n time of war or other public emergency threatening the life of the nation'. It is submitted that the expression

---

1139    See 4.2 above.
1140    See 4.2 above.
1141    See 4.2 above.

SUMMARY AND CONCLUSIONS

'war' should be construed in the same sense for present purposes as in international humanitarian law – that is, to mean either an international armed conflict or an armed conflict not of an international character between a State and a non-State actor but reaching the minimum intensity needed to trigger the applicability of international humanitarian law. For definitions it is convenient to borrow from the 1949 Geneva Conventions. Their common Article 2, first paragraph, defines *international* armed conflicts: these are 'all cases of declared war or of any other armed conflict which may arise between two or more of the High Contracting Parties, even if the state of war is not recognized by one of them' and 'all cases of partial or total occupation of the territory of a High Contracting Party, even if the said occupation meets with no armed resistance'. Not being dependent for its existence on the position of the parties, 'international armed conflict' is thus an autonomous concept in terms of the 1949 Geneva Convention – and also, we would submit, for the purpose of understanding the expression 'war' as used in Article 15 of the Convention. We read the expression to include international armed conflicts arising in peace operations outside the home territory of the State. On that understanding, it is possible, in principle, to derogate in respect of those if the need should arise.[1142]

*Non-international* armed conflicts, though referred to in common Article 3 of the four Conventions, are better understood as having the meaning given to them by Article 1 of Additional Protocol II: they are such as 'take place in the territory of a High Contracting Party between its armed forces and dissident armed forces or other organized armed groups which, under responsible command, exercise such control over a part of its territory as to enable them to carry out sustained and concerted military operations and to implement this Protocol'.[1143] Note that this definition, since it requires the 'dissident armed forces' or other non-State armed groups to be fighting the armed forces of a High Contracting Party, does not encompass the eventuality of two or more non-State armed groups fighting each other without involvement of Government forces; such a situation consequently cannot constitute a 'war' for purposes of Article 15 of the European Convention on Human Rights either (although it may develop into an 'emergency threatening the life of the nation' if it cannot be contained). We would however submit that a Contracting State would be entitled, if necessary, to derogate when participating in a peace operation intervening in a non-international armed conflict being fought abroad.[1144]

---

1142   See 4.3.3.4.3 above.
1143   See 4.3.1 above.
1144   See 4.3.3.4.3 above.

While on the wording of Article 15 it is clear that for an 'emergency' to warrant derogation it must 'threaten the life of the nation', there is ambiguity as to whether that requirement also applies to 'war'. A war fought by a State on its own territory in defence against a foreign aggressor would probably threaten 'the life of the nation' in any event; in such a case the question would be moot. A 'war' fought far from home, but with the prior authorisation of the Security Council of the United Nations, might not threaten 'the life of the nation' – but it would be illogical to deny the applicability of Article 15 in such cases. We submit, however, that an aggressor State would not be entitled to rely on Article 15. We argue provisionally that the expression 'threatening the life of the nation' does not qualify 'war' as long as the 'war' – understood as an international armed conflict – is being fought in accordance with Chapter VII of the Charter of the United Nations: that is, either in pursuance of a decision of the Security Council (Article 42) or, pending action by the Security Council, for individual or collective self-defence (Article 51).[1145]

Recognition by a State that a situation existing within its Article 1 jurisdiction qualifies as a 'non-international armed conflict' has its own dangers, which include the possibility that it may amount to recognition that law enforcement is inadequate and the insurgents need be taken seriously as enemy combatants. That may explain why Contracting States have been hesitant to go that far. Nevertheless, the presence on the territory of an organised armed force opposed to Government power may well give rise to an 'emergency threatening the life of the nation'; only rarely have the Commission and the Court not been willing to accept the judgment of the State's political leadership in this regard.[1146]

Measures derogating from the Convention must steer clear of the 'non-derogable rights', naturally. Non-derogable rights are not defined solely by Article 15 § 2; other rights are non-derogable by implication, whether as a consequence of their being the object of an appropriate guarantee offered by other binding international instruments – in particular instruments of international humanitarian law – or by virtue of their very nature.[1147]

Moreover, derogating measures may go no further than 'strictly required by the exigencies of the situation'. Views can – and do – differ from case to case, and depending on standpoint, as to what is 'the extent strictly required by the exigencies of the situation'. The words used suggest a strict necessity test; however, in practice the Court has shown itself more indulgent than that. The

---

1145   See 4.3.3 above.
1146   Actually, only once, in the *Greek Case*. See 4.5.1.3 above.
1147   See 4.7 above.

SUMMARY AND CONCLUSIONS

Court has until now generally accepted the necessity of derogating measures that were relevant to the crisis which they were intended to address and that were attended by appropriate safeguards both directly preventive of excesses and procedural.[1148]

Derogating measures must not be 'inconsistent with [the State's] other obligations under international law'. Neither *travaux préparatoires* nor case-law offer much in the way of guidance as to the 'other obligations under international law' with which derogating measures must remain consistent. We submit that that expression cannot be construed so as to import into Article 15 substantive provisions from other human rights treaties offering greater protection than the Convention itself. However, there is no room for discussion on the applicability in an armed conflict, be it international or non-international, of international humanitarian law. The importance of this statement derives from the fact that international humanitarian law admits of no further derogation: by its very nature, when it applies it sets the lowest permissible legal standard of rights protection.[1149]

It is a reasonable requirement that derogating measures be also of a nature to assist efforts towards a return to normality and therefore temporary: any other view would open the door to the indefinite application of derogating emergency measures. However, this is not to say that it can never be legitimate to extend notices of derogation repeatedly, even for a very long aggregate period; nor that such measures must be discontinued if the desired result is not achieved within a particular time frame.[1150]

As the application of Article 15 becomes a rather more common occurrence than has been the case previously, the dangers inherent in the hitherto lenient attitude the Court has adopted with regard to the applicable margin of appreciation are becoming clearer. The Court has recognised to States a wide margin of appreciation, both as regards the assessment whether an 'emergency threatening the life of the nation' exists and as regards the measures 'strictly required by the exigencies of the situation'. If it is an accurate observation that our continent is entering a period of prolonged instability, then it is reasonable to expect that the executive arm of Government may on occasion yield to the temptation to broaden its powers by adopting emergency measures even though the situation appears, to a dispassionate and disinterested observer, still manageable using ordinary legislation. The Court may soon have occasion

---

1148   See 4.8 above.

1149   See 4.4 and 4.9 above.

1150   See 4.8 above.

to take a stricter view of both the threat prayed in justification by the Government and the need for the measures actually taken.

Despite these reservations, it is our belief that derogating from the obligations assumed under the Convention offers possibilities that have not yet been tested to their limits. Although in *Hassan* the Court for the first time gave an interpretation of Article 5 of the Convention that would obviate the need to invoke Article 15 in an international armed conflict, we submit that use of that Article nonetheless remains the preferred way for Contracting States to derogate from their obligations. Not only was it so intended by the drafters of the Convention, but it is the only way compatible with the wording of the Convention itself. We also consider that appropriate use of Article 15 offers Contracting States all the latitude they may need in the legitimate use of 'hard power'. It does however require a formal act in the form of notification to the Secretary General of the Council of Europe.

## 9.3 The Second Defence: Denying the Jurisdiction of the Contracting State

### 9.3.1 *Existence of Article 1 Jurisdiction*
#### 9.3.1.1 Territorial Jurisdiction
We have seen that there are two aspects to the concept of 'jurisdiction'. Firstly, there is the state-centred concept understood in terms of legislative, executive and judicial power; this is the jurisdiction all States assert as a right. Secondly, and more relevantly for our purposes, there is the understanding of that expression from the point of view of the bearer of rights under the Convention, which rights the Contracting State has the duty under Article 1 of the Convention to protect; from the State's perspective, this is jurisdiction understood as a responsibility to be borne. The two are different, but not separate: what links them together is that the State has both the right and the duty to exercise its legislative, executive and judicial powers to secure Convention rights.[1151]

The concept of jurisdiction, in both senses, is 'primarily territorial'; indeed it is obvious that the jurisdiction of Contracting States is engaged on their respective European land territory. However, States can enjoy jurisdiction – in the first sense – elsewhere; it is therefore necessary to consider the implications for the exercise of jurisdiction in the second sense. We address this in terms of territorial and quasi-territorial jurisdiction.

---

1151    See 5.1 above.

SUMMARY AND CONCLUSIONS

Applicability of the Convention to the territories for whose international relations a Contracting State is responsible – including territorial possessions – is not automatic. Article 56 of the Convention – the 'colonial clause' – makes it dependent on a separate declaration, to be made by the mother country.[1152] The Court has rejected an interpretation *a contrario* of the 'colonial clause' to the effect that a Contracting State's Article 1 jurisdiction did not exist in relation to parts of its territory not actually under its control.[1153]

Treaty-based jurisdiction assimilated to territorial jurisdiction – in the first, state-centred, sense – exists over sea and airspace to the extent that particular treaties recognise them to be under the sovereignty of States. The existence of such jurisdiction, we submit, entails the existence of jurisdiction within the meaning of Article 1 of the Convention.[1154] In contrast, the exercise of national sovereignty in outer space, including on the moon and on other celestial bodies, is excluded.[1155]

Ships on the high seas are subject, in principle, to the exclusive jurisdiction of their flag State; other States may exercise jurisdiction over them with the permission of the flag State. Exceptionally, universal jurisdiction sufficient for purposes of the Convention would appear to exist under Articles 100-107 UNCLOS applied as customary international law in order to combat piracy.[1156]

States retain exclusive jurisdiction over spacecraft bearing their registration. More than that, States Parties to the Outer Space Treaty assume responsibility for the acts of their nationals, including private persons. At present spacecraft are almost without exception unmanned satellites; the only manned spacecraft are the International Space Station and the Russian delivery vehicles by which it is supplied. The International Space Station is subject to a legal regime unique to it.[1157]

The jurisdiction of a State over ships flying its flag or aircraft or spacecraft bearing its registration, being exclusive and linked to nationality, is actually exercised *within* that State's domestic limits; it is not properly 'extra-territorial'.[1158]

---

1152  Equivalent clauses are to be found in the various Protocols: Article 4 of Protocol No. 1; Article 5 of Protocol No. 4; Article 5 of Protocol No. 6; Article 6 of Protocol No. 7; Article 2 of Protocol No. 12 and Article 4 of Protocol No. 13.

1153  See 5.2.1 above.

1154  See 5.3.1 and 5.3.2 above.

1155  See 5.3.3 above.

1156  See 5.4.1 above.

1157  See 5.4.3 above.

1158  See 5.4 above.

346 CHAPTER 9

9.3.1.2 Extraterritorial Exercise of Jurisdiction

True extraterritorial Article 1 jurisdiction involves the exercise of State authority abroad. It is standard practice for States to exercise their jurisdiction over members of their own armed forces abroad, whether they be stationed or deployed on the territory of a foreign State with the latter's consent or not. An example of the former is the extraterritorial exercise of jurisdiction over troops stationed abroad with the consent of the receiving country in application of the NATO Status of Forces Agreement. Typically such an arrangement will also involve the exercise of jurisdiction over civilian auxiliaries or dependents. An example of the deployment of troops abroad without the consent of the foreign State concerned is, of course, an international armed conflict engaged on foreign soil, but such a situation may also arise in peacekeeping or peace-enforcing operations short of conflict.[1159]

Not every State act producing effects abroad constitutes exercise of extraterritorial jurisdiction. The deportation of aliens and the extradition of criminal suspects to a foreign country do not involve the extraterritorial exercise of territorial jurisdiction properly so-called. Likewise, a cross-border attack does not *ipso facto* constitute the exercise of jurisdiction extraterritorially: the Court has rejected the 'cause-and-effect' model.[1160]

### 9.3.2 Typology of Convention-relevant Exercise of Jurisdiction in 'Hard Power' Situations

9.3.2.1 Intraterritorial

As regards States acting on their own territory we distinguish, firstly, those cases in which States acknowledge the exercise of jurisdiction from those in which States deny the exercise of jurisdiction.

States applying 'hard power' to assert or reassert their authority over parts of their territory where it is threatened typically acknowledge jurisdiction – indeed, the exercise of jurisdiction is precisely the purpose of their actions. Such situations raise no questions with regard to Article 1 jurisdiction.[1161]

When States cannot readily assert their jurisdiction over part of their territory, for example because they must overcome the resistance of a secessionist force or even a foreign occupier to do so, the case-law of the Court does not absolve them from their Convention obligations for that reason alone. The question whether they exercise Article 1 jurisdiction is a question of fact, the presumption being that they do so throughout their territory. The presump-

---

1159 See 5.5.2 above.
1160 See 6.4.3.1 above.
1161 See 6.2.1 above.

SUMMARY AND CONCLUSIONS

tion is rebuttable: however, so far the only case of a State divested of its Article 1 jurisdiction over a part of its territory occupied by armed forces not under its own orders is that of Serbia in relation to Kosovo, where the Court accepted that there existed 'objective limitations' in the form of a United Nations administration that prevented the Contracting State from 'securing the rights and freedoms' itself.[1162]

For a Contracting State to tolerate or condone, let alone connive at, violations of the Convention committed on its soil by agents of a foreign State constitutes the exercise of Article 1 jurisdiction by that Contracting State, with the consequence that its responsibility under the Convention is engaged.[1163]

### 9.3.2.2 Extraterritorial

Military action abroad, that is the maintenance of a military presence on territory over which another State claims sovereignty or kinetic military action taking place, or producing effects, elsewhere than on home territory may be lawful or it may not. The State's responsibility under the Convention may be engaged in either case.[1164]

If a Contracting State acts on the territory of another Contracting State, then it is axiomatic that the former Contracting State assumes the Convention obligations of the latter: we have seen in the Cyprus-Turkey interstate case that any other view would create an unacceptable vacuum in human rights protection.[1165] A controlling Contracting State cannot evade its liability under the Convention by setting up a pseudo-state on occupied territory, as is shown by the Court's case-law in respect of the 'TRNC' (Northern Cyprus), the 'MRT' (Transdniestria), and the 'NKR' (Nagorno-Karabakh).[1166]

If the actions of the Contracting State take place, or the effects are felt, in a foreign State that is *not* a party to the Convention, the existence of Article 1 jurisdiction cannot be taken for granted. The mere fact that harm is suffered, and therefore a victim results, is not sufficient to create jurisdiction: that much is clear from *Banković*.[1167] The Court has confirmed this position in further case-law, including many years after *Banković* in *Al-Skeini* and *Jaloud*.

From the *Saddam Hussein* admissibility decision we learn, moreover, that mere participation of the armed forces of a Contracting State in a coalition deployed outside the territory of any Contracting State and that also includes

---

1162   See 6.2.2.4 above.
1163   See 6.3 above.
1164   See 6.4 above.
1165   See 6.4.1.1 above.
1166   See 6.4.2.1 - 6.4.2.3 above.
1167   See 6.4.3.1 above.

348    CHAPTER 9

forces of a non-Contracting State is not *per se* sufficient to establish Article 1 jurisdiction.[1168]

Conversely, the fact of holding a person captive does suffice to produce that effect: this we learn from *Al-Jedda* and *Al-Saadoon and Mufdhi*.[1169] So does a direct attempt on the life or safety of a specific individual by the overt use of military hardware, such as a shot fired at a targeted individual or, we would suggest, a targeted drone strike.[1170] We would further submit that the same would apply to murder by stealth[1171] or to a cyber-attack – in the latter case, provided that it can arguably be considered to target individuals.[1172]

The various strands are drawn together in *Al-Skeini*, in which two types of situations are identified that create extraterritorial Article 1 jurisdiction outside the Convention legal space. The first is 'State agent authority and control', in the sense of physical power and control over the person in question; this situation exists when that person is arrested or detained, or falls victim to the targeted use of force.[1173] The second is 'effective control over an area': this exists when, as a consequence of lawful or unlawful military action, a Contracting State exercises effective control of an area outside its national territory.[1174] It matters however which type of extraterritorial jurisdiction exists. In the first situation, that of 'State agent authority and control' over an individual, the Contracting State is under an obligation under Article 1 to secure to that individual the rights and freedoms under Section I of the Convention that are relevant to the situation of that individual: in this sense, to use a phrase that has gained some notoriety, the Convention rights can be 'divided and tailored'.[1175] In the second, that of 'effective control over an area', the obligation to secure the rights and freedoms set out in the Convention derives from the fact of such control, whether it be exercised directly, through the Contracting State's own armed forces, or through a subordinate local administration – even if, as may occur in the case of an occupation within the meaning of Article 42 of the Hague Regulations, it is the administration of the occupied State.[1176]

---

1168    See 6.5.1 above.
1169    See 6.5.2.1 above.
1170    See 6.4.6 above.
1171    See 6.4.6.3 above.
1172    See 6.4.7 above.
1173    See 6.5.2.3.1 above.
1174    See 6.5.2.3.2 above.
1175    See 6.5.2.3.1 above.
1176    See 6.5.2.3.2 above; see also 6.7 above.

SUMMARY AND CONCLUSIONS

The interrelation between the defining decisions and judgments – *Banković*, *Al-Skeini*, *Al-Jedda*, *Jaloud*, *Hassan* – has been much misunderstood; it can now be clarified.

We submit that there is no inconsistency between *Al-Skeini*, *Al-Jedda*, *Jaloud* and *Hassan* on the one hand and *Banković* on the other. In *Banković* Article 1 jurisdiction was not established because there was no territorial presence in Belgrade and the Court dismissed the 'cause-and-effect' interpretation of Article 1.[1177] We argue that the distinction between *Banković* and the other four lies in the fact that *Banković* did not involve the assertion of 'jurisdiction' understood in terms of the purposive exercise of power over individuals, unlike *Al-Jedda* and *Hassan*, which involved detention, and *Al-Skeini* and *Jaloud*, which involved the deliberate and targeted use of force.

To sum up, the Article 1 jurisdiction of a Contracting State will be established if that State is found to exercise 'effective control over an area'. If a Contracting State is to evade Article 1 jurisdiction in connection with the extraterritorial exercise of 'State agent authority and control' over an individual, as the Court's case-law now stands it will be necessary for that State to take all necessary measures to avoid all danger to individuals and to be prepared to prove that it has done so.

## 9.4 The Third Defence: Denying the Jurisdiction of the European Court of Human Rights

If a Contracting State cannot evade accountability under the Convention by denying Article 1 jurisdiction, then what about contesting the jurisdiction of the Court?

The Convention permits States to make reservations at the time of ratification (Article 57). The validity of such reservations, however, remains for the Court to consider. Thus far the Court has not accepted reservations intended generally to limit the applicability of the Convention itself. It has been suggested in legal literature that a reservation designed, to all appearances, to limit the scope of the Court's examination of emergency measures may be invalid because it is incompatible with the system itself of the Convention.[1178]

It may be possible for a Contracting Party to invoke Article 28 of the Vienna Convention on the Law of Treaties, which provides that treaties shall not bind a party 'in relation to any act or fact which took place or any situation which

---

1177   See 6.4.3.1.1 above.
1178   See 7.3 above.

350                                                                    CHAPTER 9

ceased to exist before the date of the entry into force of the treaty with respect to that party'. This was successfully done on at least one occasion in the early days of the Convention, but treaty obligations that may override the substantive provisions of the Convention will by now be rare indeed. Instead, it is more likely that the Convention – whose key provisions date from 1950 – will take precedence over more recent instruments, as the *Al-Saadoon and Mufdhi* judgment demonstrates.[1179]

### 9.5    The Fourth Defence: Denying Attribution

The case-law of the Court does not follow the same logic as Article 2 of the International Law Commission's Articles on State Responsibility. We have seen that the Court's consistent approach is first to establish Article 1 jurisdiction, then attribution.[1180] If Contracting States cannot evade the former, they may nonetheless be able to evade the latter.

Thus it is that, for example, Moldova is found to have Article 1 jurisdiction (as the territorial State) over Transdniestria, a territory over which it is unable to exercise authority effectively, but escapes blame for violations of the Convention for as long as it makes a real effort to secure Convention rights – the violations being imputable to the Russian Federation, which exercises extraterritorial jurisdiction in Transdniestria by maintaining an armed presence there and securing to that entity what viability it has.[1181]

Even so, the Court has held domestic remedies offered by both the 'TRNC' and the 'MRT' to be valid under the Convention – while stressing that these are remedies provided by Turkey and Russia respectively, through their subordinate entities.[1182] The *Demopoulos* example shows that a specialised remedy set up within the structures of a pseudo-state may be suitable for its parent Contracting State, if it is prepared to accept attribution on that basis, to discharge remedial obligations under the Convention.[1183]

The responsibility of Contracting States is engaged if they acquiesce or connive within their Article 1 jurisdiction violations of the Convention committed by foreigners. We have seen that this was so in the 'rendition' cases, in which individuals were subjected to treatment contrary to Articles 3 and 5 on the

---

1179    See 7.4 above.
1180    See 8.2.1 above.
1181    See 8.2.2 above.
1182    See 8.5.1 and 8.5.2 above.
1183    See 8.5.4 above.

SUMMARY AND CONCLUSIONS

territory of Contracting States but by agents of a State not Party to the Convention. Likewise, the Contracting State concerned remains responsible, under the *Soering* doctrine, for allowing such individuals to be removed to a place outside their own jurisdiction even though they cannot reasonably be unaware that the violations will continue.[1184]

We argue that a Contracting State is unlikely to escape attribution by the use of private military and security contractors, or by permitting their use by private parties. Contracting States choosing to engage the services of such contractors themselves remain answerable for the application of 'hard power' on their behalf, even by private agents.[1185] Contracting States who permit private parties to make use of privately contracted armed personnel – a situation that in practice is most likely to arise in relation to ship-owners seeking to protect their ships against pirate attack – remain responsible for creating and maintaining a suitable legislative framework attended by a suitable enforcement structure and legal remedies by virtue of their territorial or (in the case of the ship's flag state) quasi-territorial jurisdiction.[1186]

Acting under the aegis of the United Nations would appear to offer Contracting States better prospects of escaping attribution. We have seen that the Court was prepared to attribute to that organisation failings imputed to KFOR in Kosovo. KFOR was exercising lawfully delegated Chapter VII powers of the United Nations Security Council. With regard to the civilian authority established in Kosovo, UNMIK, the Court found that it was a subsidiary organ of the United Nations; its acts and omissions were therefore, in principle, 'attributable' to the United Nations.[1187] The position was the same with respect to UNFICYP, which controls the buffer zone in Cyprus.[1188]

We may therefore conclude that a Contracting Party may evade attribution by placing its forces under the orders of the Security Council in the lawful exercise of its powers under Chapter VII of the United Nations Charter or of a United Nations subsidiary organ. It is worth noting that United Nations peace operations are ordinarily subsidiary organs of the United Nations.[1189]

In contrast, in *Al-Jedda* the Court refused to attribute the acts of American and British armed forces in Iraq to the United Nations. At no time were the forces of the 'occupying powers' subsidiary to the Security Council; what was more, through the CPA which they had established already at the start of the

---

1184   See 6.3 and 8.3.2 above.
1185   See 8.4.3 above.
1186   See 8.4.3.2 above.
1187   See 8.4.5.2.1 above.
1188   See 8.4.5.2.2 above.
1189   See 4.3.3.4.3 above.

occupation they exercised the powers of government in Iraq, reporting to the Security Council but not bound by its orders.[1190] Although by virtue of Article 103 of the United Nations Charter a Security Council resolution overrides the Convention, the presumption is that the Security Council does not intend to impose on States obligations incompatible with human rights; this means that Contracting States must make use of whatever room for manoeuvre remains to them to avoid violating the Convention. The presumption is rebutted only if the Security Council resolution leaves Contracting States no other options whatsoever.[1191]

Transfer of responsibility to the United Nations does not remove the need to ensure accountability for human rights violations. Since the Convention cannot apply to the United Nations, propriety demands that alternative arrangements be set in place for this purpose.

Internationally imposed quasi-indigenous institutions – and here we look to the lessons learned in Bosnia and Herzegovina – would appear to offer the best prospects of satisfying requirements of accountability and placing it elsewhere. The arrangement set up in Bosnia and Herzegovina was characterised by the following features:

Firstly, general international law was complied with throughout. All coercive measures were agreed by the States involved beforehand and given the seal of legality by the Security Council. Failing permission of a local government enjoying international recognition, this is the *conditio sine qua non* for any solution that involves the use or threat of force or otherwise overrides the will of the warring factions.

Secondly, responsibility was borne by quasi-domestic institutions that were not, as such, subordinate to any government or group of governments of one or more Contracting States. This is the *conditio sine qua non* for the latter to avoid having to assume 'jurisdiction' within the meaning of Article 1 of the Convention.

Although it is not a *conditio sine qua non* for the legality of the arrangement, we have seen that imposing the substantive human rights standards of the Convention and other human rights instruments from the outset, together with an independent hybrid jurisdiction to enforce them, was highly beneficial in its effects. It did much to create awareness of human rights in Bosnia and Herzegovina and prepare that country for joining the Council of Europe. Herein lies perhaps another lesson for the future: the usefulness of human rights protection in state-building.

---

1190   See 8.4.5.2.3 above.
1191   See 8.4.5.2.5 above.

## 9.6 Final Observations

Even the Convention's most vocal critics recognise that basic standards of humanity and civilization should be maintained and that it is the primary responsibility of the individual State to enforce them. Nevertheless, the creation of international standards guarded by international human rights treaty bodies has proved a useful addition to domestic human rights protection.

One might think that the significance of international human rights systems could not be greater than in regulating the use of force by State agents, especially in situations involving the use of what we have termed 'hard power': inevitably these provide opportunities (and sometimes the temptation) to take the use of force further than would be permissible or even necessary in times of tranquillity. In the European setting, it is therefore right and proper that the European Court of Human Rights should have jurisdiction to maintain the standards set by the Convention in this respect.

The Court is a court of law, that is, a body vested with judicial power, offering the requisite guarantees of independence and impartiality and conducting its proceedings in accordance with a set procedure. Nevertheless, as in all international litigation, the parties to proceedings under the Convention are equal only if both are States. In cases brought by 'persons, non-governmental organisations or groups of individuals' claiming to be victims of violations of their human rights,[1192] they are not. The defensive position of the respondent Contracting State, though not impregnable, is a strong one.

From a substantive perspective, a respondent State will generally be able to argue, even if all formal admissibility conditions are met, that its actions are necessitated by the public weal. So the Court usually finds, without even being asked: it is not for nothing that it declares the overwhelming majority of individual applications inadmissible without even communicating them.

From a procedural perspective, as often as not the Contracting State holds the high ground in that it will be able, through its agents, to control access to vital evidence. It has to be recognised that good reasons may exist to keep certain information out of the public eye, especially in situations that may involve the use of 'hard power'. That said, it is the duty of the higher authorities of a State governed by the rule of law to monitor the acts of their subordinates in this respect and that of the Court to be alert to any abuses.

The basic text, the Convention itself, offers Contracting States an advantage that by its nature is denied individual applicants. It lies in the possibility, in case of 'war or other public emergency threatening the life of the nation', to

---

1192 Article 34 of the Convention.

shift the goal posts by making use of the possibility offered by Article 15 to limit the State's liability. In cases of armed conflict, whether international or non-international, the ultimate standards to be maintained would be those defined by international humanitarian law.

Our argument is that the possibilities of derogation have, until now, for whatever reasons, been underused in situations involving the use of 'hard power'. Derogation is, however, provided for by the Convention itself, and for the precise purpose of allowing the Contracting States to meet situations in which they cannot reasonably be required to secure the rights and freedoms defined in the Convention and its Protocols. Already for that reason it deserves to be considered in preference to tortuous solutions incompatible with the text of the Convention.

The Convention is an international legal instrument. It cannot be seen in isolation from other areas of international law. For purposes of the use of 'hard power', these would include the law of the United Nations. Participating in a United Nations peace operation has sometimes offered Contracting States protection against claims under the Convention. Past practice suggests that for such a solution to work, it will be necessary either that the peace operation itself be a subsidiary organ of the United Nations – as peace operations mandated by the Security Council generally are – or that any empowering Security Council resolution offer the Contracting State no other option than to act in a manner incompatible with the Convention. In either case, a lacuna in human rights protection will emerge which, while the Convention does not require it to be filled by the Contracting State, should be filled somehow: the restoration of a situation of normality, in which human rights are once again secured, is the very purpose of peace operations. This may be done by the creation of a remedy allowing claims to be brought against the subsidiary organ, or against the United Nations itself, or against the State for whose benefit the peace operation has been set up, as appropriate.

Such a course of action may involve the use of internationally imposed quasi-indigenous institutions. A particularly creative variant of this solution involves using such institutions to impose substantive human rights standards, perhaps those defined by the Convention itself: this serves the dual aim of furthering human rights protection and placing accountability for human rights violations where it belongs.

Thus we see that there is sufficient scope for Contracting States to tailor their obligations and liabilities under the Convention to the exigencies of situations involving the need to resort to 'hard power', provided always that they stay within the limits posed by general international law in choosing their means.

SUMMARY AND CONCLUSIONS

In other words, under this proviso, the law of the European Convention on Human Rights not only permits of finding a balance between the duty of the State, and hence its right, to resort to 'hard power' and the right of the individual, as protected by the Convention and its Protocols, to be shielded from its effects, but – more than that – leaves the State the room for manoeuvre needed to pursue its legitimate policy objectives.

# References

### Basic documents of the European Commission and Court of Human Rights

Statute of the Council of Europe, European Treaty Series, ETS 1[1193]

European Convention on Human Rights (Convention for the Protection of Human Rights and Fundamental Freedoms), ETS 5

Protocol No. 1 to the European Convention on Human Rights, ETS 9

Protocol No. 4 to the European Convention on Human Rights, ETS 46

Protocol No. 6 to the European Convention on Human Rights, ETS 55

Protocol No. 7 to the European Convention on Human Rights, ETS 114

Protocol No. 11 to European Convention on Human Rights, ETS 155, and explanatory report

Protocol No. 12 to the European Convention on Human Rights, ETS 177

Protocol No. 13 to the European Convention on Human Rights, ETS 187

Protocol No. 16 to the European Convention on Human Rights, CETS 214

Rules of Court of the European Court of Human Rights

Practice Direction "Requests for interim measures" (issued by the President of the Court in accordance with Rule 32 of the Rules of Court on 5 March 2003 and amended on 16 October 2009 and on 7 July 2011)

### Strasbourg case-law

#### *European Commission of Human Rights*

Decisions

*Greece v. the United Kingdom*, no. 176/56, 2 June 1956

*X v. Germany*, 10 June 1958, no. 235/56

*X, Y and Z v. Belgium*, 30 May 1961, Yearbook 1961 p. 260-70

*X v. Norway*, no. 2002/63, 2 July 1964, Collection 14, pp. 25-28

*X v. Norway*, no. 2369/64, 3 April 1967, Collection 23, pp. 21-25

*D.G.P. N.V. v. the Netherlands*, no. 5178/71, 12 October 1973, Collection 44, pp. 13-24

*X v. Germany*, no. 6742/94, 10 July 1974

---

[1193] Conventions and agreements opened for signature between 1949 and 2003 were published in the 'European Treaty Series' or ETS (Nos. 1 to 193 included). Since 2004, this Series is continued by the 'Council of Europe Treaty Series' or CETS (Nos. 194 and following).

*Cyprus v. Turkey (I) and (II)*, nos. 6780/74 and 6950/75, 26 May 1975, DR 2, p. 125

*Hess v. the United Kingdom*, no. 6231/73, 28 May 1975

*X v. the United Kingdom*, no. 7547/76, 15 December 1977, DR 12, p. 73

*Cyprus v. Turkey (III)*, no. 8007/77, 10 July 1978, DR 13, p. 85

*Freda v. Italy*, no. 8916/80, 7 October 1980, DR 21, p. 254

*Vearncombe and Others v. the United Kingdom and the Federal Republic of Germany*, no. 12816/87, 18 January 1989, DR 59, p. 186

*Chrysostomos, Papachrysostomou and Loizidou v. Turkey*, nos. 15299/89, 15300/89 and 15318/89, 4 March 1991, DR 68, p. 216

*Cyprus v. Turkey (IV)*, no. 25781/94, 28 June 1996, DR 86-A p. 104

*Touvier v. France*, no. 29420/95, 13 January 1997, DR 88-B p. 148

*P.N. v. Switzerland*, no. 26245/95, 11 September 1997

*Rigopoulos v. Spain*, no. 37388/97, 16 April 1998

*Ramirez Sanchez v. France*, no. 28780/95, 24 June 1996, DR 86-B p. 155

## Reports

*Greece v. the United Kingdom*, no. 176/56, 26 September 1958

*Greece v. the United Kingdom (no. 2)*, no. 299/57, 8 July 1959

*Lawless v. Ireland*, no. 332/57, 19 December 1959

*De Becker v. Belgium*, no. 214/56, 8 January 1960

*Denmark, Norway, Sweden and the Netherlands v. Greece*, nos. 3321/67, 3322/67, 3323/67 and 3344/67 (the *"Greek Case"*), 5 November 1969,

*Cyprus v. Turkey (I) and (II)*, nos. 6780/74 and 6950/75, 10 July 1976

*Cyprus v. Turkey (III)*, no. 8007/77, 4 October 1983

*Reinette v. France*, no. 14009/88, 2 October 1989, DR 63, p. 192

*Loizidou v. Turkey*, no. 15318/89, 8 July 1993

## *European Court of Human Rights*

### Advisory opinions

Decision on the competence of the Court to give an advisory opinion [GC], ECHR 2004 VI

Advisory opinion on certain legal questions concerning the lists of candidates submitted with a view to the election of judges to the European Court of Human Rights [GC], 12 February 2008

Advisory opinion on certain legal questions concerning the lists of candidates submitted with a view to the election of judges to the European Court of Human Rights (no. 2) [GC], 22 January 2010

## REFERENCES

### Decisions on admissibility

*Rigopoulos v. Spain* (dec.), no. 37388/97, ECHR 1999-II

*McGuinness v. the United Kingdom* (dec.), no. 39511/98, ECHR 1999-V

*Drieman and Others v. Norway* (dec.), no. 33678/96, 4 May 2000

*Öcalan v. Turkey* (dec.), no. 46221/99, 14 December 2000

*Xhavara v. Italy and Albania* (dec.), no. 39473/98, 11 January 2001

*Ilaşcu and Others v. Moldova and Russia* (GC) (dec.), no. 48787/99, 4 July 2001

*Marshall v. the United Kingdom* (dec.), no. 41571/98, 10 July 2001

*Brusco v. Italy* (dec.), no. 69789/01, ECHR 2001-IX

*Banković and Others v. Belgium and 16 Other Contracting States* (dec.) [GC], no. 52207/99,
§§ 59 and 61, ECHR 2001-XII

*Giacometti and 5 others v. Italy* (dec.), no. 34939/97, ECHR 2001-XII

*Papon v. France* (dec.), no. 54210/00, ECHR 2001-XII

*Kalogeropoulou and Others v. Greece and Germany* (dec.), no. 59021/00, ECHR 2002-X

*Garaudy v. France* (dec.), no. 65831/01, ECHR 2003-IX

*Markovic and Others v. Italy* (dec.), no. 1398/03, 12 June 2003

*Jeličić* v. Bosnia and Herzegovina (dec.), no. 41183/02, ECHR 2005-XII

*Puzinas v. Lithuania* (dec.), no. 63767/00, 13 December 2005

*Penart v. Estonia* (dec.), no. 14685/04, 24 January 2006

*Saddam Hussein v. Albania, Bulgaria, Croatia, Czech Republic, Denmark, Estonia, Hungary, Iceland, Ireland, Italy, Latvia, Lithuania, the Netherlands, Poland, Portugal, Romania, Slovakia, Slovenia, Turkey, Ukraine and the United Kingdom* (dec.), no. 23276/04, 14 March 2006

*Janković v. Bosnia and Herzegovina* (dec.), no. 5172/03, 16 May 2006

*Jeltsuyeva v. the Netherlands* (dec.), no. 39858/04, 1 June 2006

*Kolk and Kislyiy v. Estonia* (dec.), nos. 23052/04 24018/04, ECHR 2006-I

*Quark Fishing Ltd. v. the United Kingdom* (dec.), no. 15305/06, ECHR 2006-XIV

*Pavel Ivanov v. Russia* (dec.), no. 35222/04, 2 February 2007

*Collins and Akaziebie v. Sweden* (dec.), no. 23944/05, 8 March 2007

*Behrami and Behrami v. France and Saramati v. France, Germany and Norway* (dec.) (GC), nos. 71412/01 and 78166/01, 2 May 2007

*Pad and Others v. Turkey* (dec.), no. 60167/00, 28 June 2007

*Kasumaj v. Greece* (dec.), no. 6974/05, 5 July 2007

*Gajić v. Germany* (dec.), no. 31446/02, 28 August 2007

*Berić and Others v. Bosnia and Herzegovina* (dec.), nos. 36357/04, 36360/04, 38346/04, 41705/04, 45190/04, 45578/04, 45579/04, 45580/04, 91/05, 97/05, 100/05, 101/05, 1121/05, 1123/05, 1125/05, 1129/05, 1132/05, 1133/05, 1169/05, 1172/05, 1175/05, 1177/05, 1180/05, 1185/05, 20793/05 and 25496/05, 16 October 2007

*Boivin v. 34 member States of the Council of Europe* (dec.), no. 73250/01, ECHR 2008-IV

*El Morsli v. France* (dec.), no. 15585/06, 4 March 2008

*Kalinić and Bilbija v. Bosnia and Herzegovina* (dec.), nos. 45541/04 16587/07, 13 May 2008

*Andreou v. Turkey* (dec.), no. 45653/99, 3 June 2008

*Boumediene and Others v. Bosnia and Herzegovina* (dec.), nos. 38703/06 40123/06 43301/06 43302/06 2131/07 2141/07, 18 November 2008

*Cooperatieve Producentenorganisatie van de Nederlandse Kokkelvisserij U.A. v. the Netherlands* (dec.), no. 13645/05, ECHR 2009-I

*Stephens v. Cyprus, Turkey and the United Nations* (dec.), no. 45267/06, 11 December 2008

*Mangouras v. Spain*, no. 12050/04, 8 January 2009

*Galić v. the Netherlands* (dec.), no. 22617/07, 9 June 2009

*Rambus Inc. v. Germany* (dec.), no. 40382/04, 26 June 2009

*Al-Saadoon and Mufdhi v. the United Kingdom* (dec.), no. 61498/08, § 26, 30 June 2009

*Gasparini v. Italy and Belgium* (dec.). no. 10750/03, 12 May 2009

*Lopez Cifuentes v. Spain*, no. 18754/06, 7 July 2009

*Galić v. the Netherlands* (dec.), no. 22617/07, 9 June 2009

*Beygo v. 46 member States of the Council of Europe* (dec.), no. 36099/06, 16 August 2009

*Van Anraat v. the Netherlands* (dec.), no. 65389/09, 6 July 2010

*Demopoulos and Others v. Turkey* (dec.) (GC), nos. 46113/99, 3843/02, 13751/02, 13466/03, 10200/04, 14163/04, 19993/04 and 21819/04, ECHR 2010-I

*Mulder-van Schalkwijk v. the Netherlands* (dec.), no. 26814/09, 7 June 2011

*Chagos Islanders v. the United Kingdom* (dec.), no. 35622/04, 11 December 2011

*Georgia v. Russia* (II) (dec.), no. 38263/08, 13 December 2011

*Chiragov and Others v. Armenia* (dec.) (GC), no. 13216/05, 14 December 2011

*Lechouritou and Others v. Germany and 26 other member States of the European Union* (dec.), no. 37937/07, 3 April 2012

*Abdulkhanov v. Russia*, no. 14743/11, 2 October 2012

*Djokaba Lambi Longa v. the Netherlands* (dec.), no. 33917/12, ECHR 2012-IV

*Azemi v. Serbia* (dec.), no. 11209/09, 5 November 2013

*Stichting Mothers of Srebrenica and Others v. the Netherlands* (dec.), no. 65542/12, ECHR 2013-III

*H. and J. v. the Netherlands* (dec.), nos. 978/09 and 992/09, ECHR 2014-IV

*I.A.A. and Others v. the United Kingdom* (dec.), no. 25960/13, 8 March 2016

*Tagayeva and Others v. Russia* (dec.), nos. 26562/07, 14755/08, 49339/08, 49380/08, 51313/08, 21294/11 and 37096/11, 9 June 2016

*Lisnyy and Others v. Ukraine and Russia* (dec.), nos. 5355/15, 44913/15 and 50853/15, 5 July 2016

*Mustafić-Mujić and Others v. the Netherlands* (dec.), no. 49037/15, paras. 103-06, 30 August 2016

## Judgments

*Lawless v. Ireland (no. 3)*, no. 332/57, Series A no. 3

*De Becker v. Belgium*, no. 214/56, Series A no. 4

*Ireland v. the United Kingdom*, no. 5310/71, Series A no. 25

*Tyrer v. the United Kingdom*, no. 5856/72, Series A no. 26

*Klass and Others v. Germany*, no. 5029/71, Series A no. 28

*X and Y v. the Netherlands*, no. 8978/80, Series A no. 91

*Gillow v. the United Kingdom*, no. 9063/80, § 63, Series A no. 109

*Boyle and Rice v. the United Kingdom*, 27 April 1988, Series A no. 131

*Belilos v. Switzerland*, no. 10328/83, Series A no. 132

*Brogan and Others v. the United Kingdom*, nos. 11209/84, 11234/84, 11266/84 and 11386/85, Series A no. 145-B

*Soering v. the United Kingdom*, no. 14038/88, Series A no. 161

*Stocké v. Germany*, no. 11755/85, Series A no. 199

*Vilvarajah and Others v. the United Kingdom*, nos. 13163/87 13164/87 13165/87 13447/87 13448/87, Series A no. 215

*Pine Valley Developments Ltd. and Others v. Ireland*, no. 12742/87, Series A no. 222

*Drozd and Janousek v. France and* Spain, no. 12747/87, §§ 91 and 96, Series A no. 240

*Brannigan and McBride v. the United Kingdom*, nos. 14553/89 and 14554/89, Series A no. 258-B

*A. v. France*, no. 14838/89, Series A no. 277-B

*Karlheinz Schmidt v. Germany*, no. 13580/88, Series A no. 291-B

*Loizidou v. Turkey* (preliminary objections), no. 15318/89, Series A no. 310

*Fischer v. Austria*, no. 16922/90, Series A no. 312

*McCann and Others v. the United Kingdom* [GC], no. 18984/91, Series A no. 324

*Ribitsch v. Austria*, no. 18896/91, Series A no. 336

*Akdivar and Others v. Turkey* (GC), no. 21893/93, Reports 1996-IV

*Chahal v. the United Kingdom* (GC), no. 22414/93, Reports 1996-V

*Aksoy v. Turkey*, no. 21987/93, Reports 1996-VI

*Loizidou v. Turkey* (merits), no. 15318/89, Reports 1996-VI

*Ahmut v. the Netherlands*, no. 21702/93, Reports 1996-VI

*Findlay v. the United Kingdom*, no. 22107/93, Reports 1997-I, Reports 1997-I

*Stallinger and Kuso v. Austria*, nos. 14696/89 and 14697/89, § 48, Reports 1997-II

*Pauger v. Austria*, no. 16717/90, Reports 1997-III

*Coyne v. the United Kingdom*, no. 25942/94, Reports 1997-V

*Serves v. France*, no. 20225/92, Reports 1997-VI

*Aydın v. Turkey*, no. 23178/94, Reports 1997-VI

*Sakık and Others v. Turkey*, nos. 23878/94, 23879/94, 23880/94, 23881/94, 23882/94 and 23883/94, Reports 1997-VII

*Kurt v. Turkey*, 25 May 1998, Reports 1998-III

*Demir and Others v. Turkey*, nos. 21380/93, 21381/93 and 21383/93, Reports 1998-VI

*Matthews v. the United Kingdom* (GC), no. 24833/94, ECHR 1999-I

*Waite and Kennedy v. Germany* [GC], no. 26083/94, ECHR 1999-I

*Oğur v. Turkey* [GC], no. 21594/93, ECHR 1999-III

*Çakıcı v. Turkey* [GC], no. 23657/94, ECHR 1999-IV

*Tanrıkulu v. Turkey* [GC], no. 23763/94, ECHR 1999-IV

*Selmouni v. France* (GC), no. 25803/94, ECHR 1999-V

*Riera Blume and Others v. Spain*, no. 37680/97, ECHR 1999-VII.

*Taş v. Turkey*, no. 24396/94, 14 November 2000

*Thlimmenos v. Greece* (GC), no. 34369/97, ECHR 2000-IV

*Denizci and Others v. Cyprus*, nos. 25316-25321/94 and 27207/95, ECHR 2001-V

*Egmez v. Cyprus*, no. 30873/96, ECHR 2000-XII

*Kelly and Others v. the United Kingdom*, no. 30054/96, 4 May 2001

*Shanaghan v. the United Kingdom*, no. 37715/97, 4 May 2001

*Hugh Jordan v. the United Kingdom*, no. 24746/94, 4 May 2001

*Mills v. the United Kingdom*, no.35685/97, 5 June 2001

*McKerr and Others v. the United Kingdom*, no. 28883/95, ECHR 2001-III

*Cyprus v. Turkey* (merits) (GC), no. 25781/94, ECHR 2001-IV

*Prince Hans-Adam II of Liechtenstein v. Germany* [GC], no. 42527/98, ECHR 2001-VIII

*Al-Adsani v. the United Kingdom* (GC), no. 35763/97, ECHR 2001-XI

*Gentilhomme, Schaff-Benhadji and Zerouki v. France*, no. 48205/99 48207/99 48209/99, 14 May 2002

*McShane v. the United Kingdom*, no. 43290/98, 28 May 2002

*Demades v. Turkey*, no. 16219/90, 31 July 2002

*Papon v. France*, no. 54210/00, ECHR 2002-VII

*Mastromatteo v. Italy* (GC), no. 37703/97, ECHR 2002-VIII

*Allan v. the United Kingdom*, no. 48539/99, ECHR 2002-IX

*Mamatkulov and Abdurasulovic v. Turkey*, nos. 46827/99 and 46951/99, 6 February 2003

*M.M. v. the Netherlands*, no. 39339/98, 8 April 2003

*Elci and Others v. Turkey*, nos. 23145/93 and 25091/94, 17 June 2003

*Nuray Şen v. Turkey*, no. 41478/98, 17 June 2003

*Eugenia Michaelidou Developments Ltd and Michael Tymvios v. Turkey*, no. 16163/90, 31 July 2003

*Refah Partisi (the Welfare Party) and Others v. Turkey* (GC), nos. 41340/98, 41342/98, 41343/98 and 41344/98, ECHR 2003-II

*Djavit An v. Turkey*, no. 20652/92, ECHR 2003-III

*Finucane v. the United Kingdom*, no. 29178/75, ECHR 2003-VIII

*Aktaş v. Turkey*, no. 24351/94, ECHR 2003-V (extracts)

*Slivenko v. Latvia* (GC), no. 48321/99, ECHR 2003-X

*Yankov v. Bulgaria*, no. 39084/97, ECHR 2003-XII (extracts)

# REFERENCES

*Sadak v. Turkey*, nos. 25142/94 and 27099/95, 8 April 2004

*Yurttas v. Turkey*, nos. 25143/94 and 27098/95, 27 May 2004

*Abdülsamet Yaman v. Turkey*, no. 32446/96, 2 November 2004

*Issa and Others v. Turkey*, no. 31821/96, 16 November 2004

*Assanidze v. Georgia* (GC), no. 71503/01, ECHR 2004-II

*Aziz v. Cyprus*, no. 69949/01, Reports 2004-V

*Isayeva and Others v. Russia*, nos. 57947/00, 57948/00 and 57949/00, 24 February 2005

*Khashiyev and Akayeva v. Russia*, nos. 57942/00 and 57945/00, 24 February 2005

*Isayeva v. Russia*, no. 57950/00, 24 February 2005

*Tuquabo-Tekle and Others v. the Netherlands*, no. 60665/00, 1 December 2005

*Xenides-Arestis v. Turkey*, no. 46347/99, 22 December 2005

*Mamatkulov and Askarov v. Turkey* [GC], nos. 46827/99 and 46951/99, ECHR 2005-I

*Bubbins v. the United Kingdom*, no. 50196/99, ECHR 2005-II

*Öcalan v. Turkey* (GC), no. 46221/99, ECHR 2005-IV

*Storck v. Germany*, no. 61603/00, ECHR 2005-V

*Kolanis v. the United Kingdom*, no. 517/02, ECHR 2005-V

*Bosphorus Hava Yolları Turizm ve Ticaret Anonim Şirketi v. Ireland* (GC), no. 45036/98, ECHR 2005-VI

*Nachova and Others v. Bulgaria* [GC], nos. 43577/98 and 43579/98, ECHR 2005-VII

*Siliadin v. France*, no. 73316/01, ECHR 2005-VII

*Bilen v. Turkey*, no. 34482/97, 21 February 2006

*Bazorkina v. Russia*, no. 69481/01, 27 July 2006

*Martin v. the United Kingdom*, no. 40426/98, 24 October 2006

*Xenides-Arestis v. Turkey* (just satisfaction), no. 46347/99, 7 December 2006

*Blečić v. Croatia* (GC), no. 59532/00, ECHR 2006-III

*Ždanoka v. Latvia* (GC), no. 58278/00, ECHR 2006-IV

*Zarb Adami v. Malta*, no. 17209/02, ECHR 2006-VIII

*Salah v. the Netherlands*, no. 8196/02, ECHR 2006-IX

*Markovic and Others v. Italy* (GC), no. 1398/03, ECHR 2006-XIV

*Bitiyeva and X v. Russia*, nos. 57953/00 and 37392/03, 21 June 2007

*Van Vondel v. the Netherlands*, no. 38258/03, 25 October 2007

*Brecknell v. the United Kingdom*, no. 32457/04, 27 November 2007

*McCartney v. the United Kingdom*, no. 34575/04, 27 November 2007

*O'Dowd v. the United Kingdom*, no. 34622/04, 27 November 2007

*Reavy v. the United* Kingdom, no. 34640/04, 27 November 2007

*McGrath v. the United Kingdom*, no. 34651/04, 27 November 2007

*Ramsahai and Others v. the Netherlands* [GC], no. 52391/99, ECHR 2007-II

*Jorgić v. Germany*, no. 74613/01, § 68, ECHR 2007-III

*Harutyunyan v. Armenia*, no. 36549/03, ECHR 2007-III

*D.H. and Others v. the Czech Republic* (GC), no. 57325/00, ECHR 2007-IV

*Foka v. Turkey*, no. 28940/95, 24 June 2008.

*Solomou v. Turkey, no.* 36832/97, 24 June 2008

*Isaak v. Turkey*, no. 44587/98, 24 June 2008

*Korbely v. Hungary* (GC), no. 9174/02, ECHR 2008

*Saadi v. Italy* (GC), no. 37201/06, ECHR 2008

*Women on Waves and Others v. Portugal*, no. 31276/05, 3 February 2009

*Protopapa v. Turkey*, no. 16084/90, 24 February 2009

*Andreou v. Turkey*, no. 45653/99, 27 October 2009

*Opuz v. Turkey*, no. 33401/02, ECHR 2009-III

*Herri Batasuna and Batasuna v. Spain*, nos. 25803/04 and 25817/04, ECHR 2009

*A. and Others v. the United Kingdom* (GC), no. 3455/05, ECHR 2009-II

*Varnava and Others v. Turkey* (GC), nos. 16064/90, 16065/90, 16066/90, 16068/90, 16069/90 16070/90, 16071/90, 16072/90 and 16073/90, ECHR 2009-V

*Andrejeva v. Latvia* (GC), no. 55707/00, ECHR 2009-II

*Sejdić and Finci v. Bosnia and Herzegovina* (GC), nos. 27996/06 and 34836/06, ECHR 2009-VI

*Maiorano and Others v. Italy*, no. 28634/06, 15 December 2009

*Đokić v. Bosnia and Herzegovina*, no. 6518/04, 27 May 2010

*Medvedyev and Others v. France* (GC), no. 3394/03, ECHR 2010-III

*Rantsev v. Cyprus and Russia*, no. 25965/04, ECHR 2010-I

*Kononov v. Latvia* (GC), no. 36376/04, ECHR 2010-IV

*Gäfgen v. Germany* (GC), no. 22978/05, ECHR 2010-IV

*Palić v. Bosnia and Herzegovina*, no. 4704/04, 15 February 2011

*Brezovec v. Croatia*, no. 13488/07, 29 March 2011

*Khamzayev and Others v. Russia*, no. 1503/02, 3 May 2011

*Kerimova and Others v. Russia*, nos. 17170/04, 20792/04, 22448/04, 23360/04, 5681/05 and 5684/05, 3 May 2011

*Ivanţoc and Others v. Moldova and Russia*, no. 23687/05, 15 November 2011

*Finogenov and Others v. Russia*, nos. 18299/03 and 27311/03, ECHR 2011-VI

*Giuliani and Gaggio v. Italy* (GC), no. 23458/02, ECHR 2011-II

*Bayatyan v. Armenia* (GC), no. 23459/03, ECHR 2011-IV

*Al-Jedda v. the United Kingdom* (GC), no. 27021/08, ECHR 2011-IV

*Al-Skeini and Others v. the United Kingdom* (GC), no. 55721/07, ECHR 2011-IV

*Harkins and Edwards v. United Kingdom*, nos. 9146/07 and 32650/07, 17 January 2012

*Esmukhambetov and Others v. Russia*, no. 23445/03, 29 March 2011

*Mago and Others v. Bosnia and Herzegovina*, nos. 12959/05, 11706/09, 19724/05, 47860/06, 8367/08 and 9872/09, 3 May 2012

*Nada v. Switzerland* (GC), no. 10593/08, ECHR 2012-V

*Hirsi Jamaa and Others v. Italy* (GC), no. 27765/09, ECHR 2012-II

REFERENCES

*Catan and Others v. the Republic of Moldova and Russia* (GC), nos. 43370/04, 18454/06 and 8252/05, ECHR 2012

*Othman (Abu Qatada) v. the United Kingdom*, no. 8139/09, ECHR 2012-I

*El-Masri v. "the Former Yugoslav Republic of Macedonia"* (GC), no. 39630/09, ECHR 2012

*Maskhadova and Others v. Russia*, no. 18071/05, 6 June 2013

*Mustafa Tunç and Fecire Tunç v. Turkey*, no. 24014/05, 25 June 2013

*Sabanchiyeva and Others v. Russia*, no. 38450/05, ECHR 2013

*McCaughey and Others v. the United Kingdom*, no. 43098/09, ECHR 2013

*Vinter and Others v. the United Kingdom* (GC), nos. 66069/09, 130/10 and 3896/10, ECHR 2013

*Kasap and Others v. Turkey*, no. 8656/10, 14 January 2014

*Ziaunys v. Moldova*, no. 42416/06, 11 February 2014

*Husayn (Abu Zubaydah) v. Poland*, no. 7511/13, 24 July 2014

*Al Nashiri v. Poland*, no. 28761/11, 24 July 2014

*Ali Samatar and Others v. France*, nos. 17110/10 and 17301/10, 4 December 2014

*Hassan and Others v. France*, nos. 46695/10 and 54588/10, 4 December 2014

*Zornić v. Bosnia and Herzegovina*, no. 3681/06, 15 December 2014

*Cyprus v. Turkey* (just satisfaction) (GC), no. 25781/94, ECHR 2014-II

*Jones and Others v. the United Kingdom* (GC), nos. 34356/06 and 40528/06, ECHR 2014-I

*Jaloud v. the Netherlands* (GC), no. 47708/08, ECHR 2014-VI

*Mocanu and Others v. Romania* (GC), nos. 10865/09, 45886/07 and 32431/08, ECHR 2014-V

*Hassan v. the United Kingdom* (GC), no. 29750/09, ECHR 2014-VI

*Trabelsi v. Belgium*, no. 140/10, ECHR 2014-V

*Marguš v. Croatia* (GC), no. 4455/10, ECHR 2014-III

*Gross v. Switzerland* (GC), no. 67810/10, ECHR 2014-IV

*Plechkov v. Romania*, no. 1660/03, 16 September 2014

*Sõro v. Estonia*, no. 22588/08, 3 September 2015

*Chiragov and Others v. Armenia* (GC), no. 13216/05, ECHR 2015-III

*Vasiliauskas v. Lithuania* (GC), no. 35343/05, ECHR 2015-VII

*Sargsyan v. Azerbaijan* (GC), no. 40167/06, ECHR 2015-IV

*Bouyid v. Belgium* (GC), no. 23380/09, ECHR 2015-V

*Nasr and Ghali v. Italy*, no. 44883/09, 23 February 2016

*Mozer v. Moldova and Russia* (GC), no. 11138/10, 23 February 2016

*Armani da Silva v. the United Kingdom* (GC), no. 5878/08, ECHR 2016

*Ibrahim and Others v. the United Kingdom* (GC), nos. 50541/08, 50571/08, 50573/08 and 40351/09, ECHR 2016

*Paposhvili v. Belgium* (GC), no. 41738/10, ECHR 2016

*Murray v. the Netherlands* (GC), no. 10511/10, ECHR 2016

*Avotiņš v. Latvia* (GC), no. 17502/07, ECHR 2016

*Al-Dulimi and Montana Management Inc. v. Switzerland* (GC), no. 5809/08, ECHR 2016

*Khlaifia and Others v. Italy* (GC), no. 16483/12, ECHR 2016

*Güzelyurtlu and Others v. Cyprus and Turkey*, no. 36925/07, 4 April 2017

*Tagayeva and Others v. Russia*, nos. 26562/07, 14755/08, 49339/08, 49380/08, 51313/08, 21294/11 and 37096/11, 13 April 2017

*Khlebik v. Ukraine*, no. 2945/16, 25 July 2017

*Chiragov and Others v. Armenia (just satisfaction)* (GC), no. 13216/05, 12 December 2017

*Sargsyan v. Azerbaijan (just satisfaction)* (GC), no. 40167/06, 12 December 2017

*Joannou v. Turkey*, no. 53240/14, 12 December 2017

*Merabishvili v. Georgia* (GC), no. 72508/13, ECHR 2017 (extracts)

*Ireland v. the United Kingdom*, no. 5310/71, 20 March 2018

*Mehmet Hasan Altan v. Turkey*, no. 13237/17, 20 March 2018

*Şahin Alpay v. Turkey*, no. 16538/17, 20 March 2018

*Pocasovschi and Mihaila v. Moldova and Russia*, no. 1089/09, 29 May 2018

*Abu Zubaydah v. Lithuania*, no. 46454/11, 31 May 2018

*Al Nashiri v. Romania*, no. 33234/12, 31 May 2018

*Big Brother Watch and Others v. the United Kingdom*, nos. 58170/13, 62322/14 and 24960/15, 13 September 2018

*Güzelyurtlu and Others v. Cyprus and Turkey* (GC), no. 36925/07, 29 January 2019

## Communicated applications

*Carter v. Russia*, no. 20914/07, 24 November 2010

*Al Nashiri v. Romania*, no. 33234/12, 18 September 2012 and 26 May 2015

*Big Brother Watch and Others v. the United Kingdom*, no. 58170/13, 7 January 2014

*Ukraine v. Russia (I)*, no. 20958/14, 25 November 2014

*Ukraine v. Russia (II)*, no. 43800/14, 25 November 2014

*The Bureau of Investigative Journalism and Alice Ross v. the United Kingdom*, no. 62322/14, 5 January 2015

*Ukraine v. Russia (re Crimea)*, no. 20958/14, 25 November 2014 and 29 September 2015

*Ukraine v. Russia (re Eastern Ukraine)*, no. 42410/15, 29 September 2015

*10 Human Rights Organisations and Others v. the United Kingdom*, no. 24960/15, 24 November 2015

## Other Court document

*Banković and Others v. Belgium, the Czech Republic, Denmark, France, Germany, Greece, Hungary, Iceland, Italy, Luxembourg, the Netherlands, Norway, Poland, Portugal, Spain, Turkey and the United Kingdom*, no. 52207/99, observations of the applicants, 20 October 1999

## Council of Europe

### Committee of Ministers of the Council of Europe

*The "Greek Case"*, nos. 3321/67, 3322/67, 3323/67 and 3344/67, Resolution DH(70)1, 15 April 1970

*Assanidze v. Georgia*, no. 71503/01, Resolution DH(2006)53, 2 November 2006

*Sejdić and Finci v. Bosnia and Herzegovina* (GC), nos. 27996/06 and 34836/06, Resolutions DH(2011)291, 2 December 2011; DH(2012)233, 6 December 2012; and DH(2013)259, 5 December 2013

### Parliamentary Assembly of the Council of Europe

Resolution 1417 (2005), *Protection of Human Rights in Kosovo*, 25 January 2005

Committee on Legal Affairs and Human Rights, *Alleged secret detentions and unlawful inter-state transfers involving Council of Europe member states*, Doc. 10957, 12 June 2006 (first Marty report)

Committee on Legal Affairs and Human Rights, *Secret detentions and illegal transfers of detainees involving Council of Europe member states: second report*, Doc. 11302, 11 June 2007 (second Marty report)

Resolution 1782 (2011), *Inhuman treatment of people and illicit trafficking in human organs in Kosovo*, 7 January 2011

Committee on Legal Affairs and Human Rights, *Abuse of state secrecy and national security: obstacles to parliamentary and judicial scrutiny of human rights violations*, Doc. 12714, 16 September 2011 (third Marty report)

Recommendation 2037 (2014), *Accountability of international organisations for human rights violations*, 31 January 2014

Resolution 1979 (2014), *Accountability of international organisations for human rights violations*, 31 January 2014

Resolution 2051 (2015), *Drones and targeted killings: the need to uphold human rights and international law*, 23 April 2015

### Secretary General

*Note verbale* from the Ukrainian Permanent Representative to the Secretary General of the Council of Europe, Declaration of the Verkhovna Rada of Ukraine on Derogation from Certain Obligations under the International Covenant on Civil and Political Rights and the Convention for the Protection of Human Rights and Fundamental Freedoms, 5 June 2015

Letter from the Turkish Permanent Representative to the Secretary General withdrawing the derogation notified on 21 July 2016, 8 August 2018

### Registrar of the European Court of Human Rights

"La Cour européenne des droits de l'homme fait droit à une demande de mesures provisoires", press release, 12 August 2008
*Derogation in time of emergency*, factsheet by the Press Unit of the Court's Registry, July 2016
*Overview 1959-2016* (prepared by the Jurisconsult), 2017

### Travaux préparatoires *of the European Convention on Human Rights*

Extract from the annotation on the draft International Covenants prepared by the United Nations Secretary-General (UN Doc. A/2929), DH (56) 4, Annex I
Pierre-Henri Teitgen, Consultative Assembly, Plenary Sitting of 7 September 1949, *Collected edition of the travaux préparatoires*, CDH (69) 12, p. 14
Article 1, Cour (77) 9

### European Commissioner for Human Rights

Opinion of the European Commissioner for Human Rights, Mr Alvaro Gil-Robles, on certain aspects of the United Kingdom 2001 derogation from Article 5 par. 1 of the European Convention on Human Rights, CommDH(2002)7, 28 August 2002

### European Commission for Democracy through Law ("Venice Commission")

Opinion on the admissibility of appeals against the Human Rights Chamber of Bosnia and Herzegovina, CDL-INF (98) 18
Opinion on human rights in Kosovo: Possible establishment of review mechanisms, CDL-AD (2004)033, 11 October 2004
Opinion no. 363 / 2005 on the international legal obligations of Council of Europe Member States in respect of secret detention facilities and inter-state transport of prisoners, CDL-AD(2006)009
Opinion no. 545 / 2009 on the existing mechanisms to review the compatibility with human rights standards of acts of UNMIK and EULEX in Kosovo, CDL-AD(2010)051, 21 December 2010
Opinion on the protection of human rights in emergency situations, CDL-AD(2006)015
Rule of Law Checklist, CDL-AD(2016)007

## REFERENCES

369

### *Steering Committee for Human Rights (CDDH)*

*The longer-term future of the system of the European Convention on Human Rights*, Report adopted on 11 December 2015

### Treaties

Hague Convention (III) on the Opening of Hostilities, 18 October 1907

Hague Convention (IV) Respecting the Laws and Customs of War on Land, 18 October 1907

Charter of the International Military Tribunal (Nuremberg Tribunal), annexed to the London Agreement of 8 August 1945

Convention on International Civil Aviation ("Chicago Convention"), 7 December 1944; Ninth Edition, 2006

Charter of the United Nations, 26 June 1945

Convention on the Privileges and Immunities of the United Nations, 13 February 1946

North Atlantic Treaty ("Washington Treaty"), 4 April 1949

Geneva Convention (I) on Wounded and Sick in Armed Forces in the Field, 12 August 1949

Geneva Convention (II) on Wounded, Sick and Shipwrecked of Armed Forces at Sea, 12 August 1949

Geneva Convention (III) on Prisoners of War, 12 August 1949

Geneva Convention (IV) on Civilians, 12 August 1949

NATO Status of Forces Agreement, 19 June 1951

Antarctic Treaty, 1 December 1959

Additional Protocol (I) to the Geneva Conventions of 12 August 1949, and relating to the Protection of Victims of International Armed Conflicts, 8 June 1977

Additional Protocol (II) to the Geneva Conventions of 12 August 1949, and relating to the Protection of Victims of Non-International Armed Conflict, 8 June 1977

Convention on the Prevention and the Punishment of the Crime of Genocide, 12 January 1951

Treaty establishing the European Economic Community, 25 March 1957

Convention on the High Seas, 29 April 1958

Convention on Offences and Certain other Acts Committed On Board Aircraft ("Tokyo Convention"), 14 September 1963

Treaty on Principles Governing the Activities of States in the Exploration and Use of Outer Space, including the Moon and Other Celestial Bodies ("Outer Space Treaty"), 27 January 1967

Vienna Convention on the Law of Treaties, 23 May 1969

International Convention on Civil Liability for Oil Pollution Damage (CLC), 29 November 1969

Convention for the Suppression of Unlawful Acts Against the Safety of Civil Aviation, 23 September 1971

International Convention for the Safety of Life at Sea (SOLAS), 1974 (5th version, as amended)

Convention on Registration of Objects Launched into Outer Space, 12 November 1974

International Convention on Standards of Training, Certification and Watchkeeping for Seafarers (STCW), 7 July 1978

Agreement Governing the Activities of States on the Moon and Other Celestial Bodies, 18 December 1979

United Nations Convention on the Law of the Sea, 10 December 1982

Washington Agreement (Republic of Bosnia and Herzegovina and "Croatian Republic of Herzeg-Bosna"), 1 March 1994 (signed on 18 March 1994)

Convention against Torture and Other Cruel, Inhuman or Degrading Treatment or Punishment, 4 February 1985

United Nations Convention against Illicit Traffic in Narcotic Drugs and Psychotropic Substances, 20 December 1988

General Framework Agreement for Peace in Bosnia and Herzegovina ("Dayton Peace Agreement") and Annexes 1-10, 14 December 1995

Agreement on partnership and cooperation establishing a partnership between the European Communities and their Member States, of one part, and the Russian Federation, of the other part, Official Journal of the European Communities L 327, 28 November 1997

Agreement among the Government of Canada, Governments of Member States of the European Space Agency, the Government of Japan, the Government of the Russian Federation, and the Government of the United States of America concerning co-operation on the Civil International Space Station ("the Intergovernmental Agreement"), 29 January 1998

Agreement between the Government of the United Kingdom of Great Britain and Northern Ireland and the Government of the Kingdom of the Netherlands concerning a Scottish trial in the Netherlands (with annexes), 18 September 1998

Rome Statute of the International Criminal Court, 17 July 1998, corrected by *procès-verbaux* of 10 November 1998, 12 July 1999, 30 November 1999, 8 May 2000, 17 January 2001 and 16 January 2002

International Convention for the Suppression of the Financing of Terrorism, 10 January 2000

Council of Europe Convention on Cybercrime ("Budapest Convention"), 23 November 2001, ETS 185

REFERENCES 371

Treaty on the Functioning of the European Union (consolidated version), Official Journal C 326, 26 October 2012

## United Nations

### *International Court of Justice*

*Legal Consequences for States of the Continued Presence of South Africa in Namibia (South West Africa) notwithstanding Security Council Resolution 276 (1970)*, Advisory Opinion, 21 June 1971, I.C.J. Reports 1971

*Military and Paramilitary Activities in and against Nicaragua (Nicaragua v. United States of America)*, Merits, Judgment, 27 June 1986, I.C.J. Reports 1986

*Legality of the Threat or Use of Nuclear Weapons*, Advisory Opinion, 8 July 1996, I.C.J. Reports 1996

*Legal Consequences of the Construction of a Wall in the Occupied Palestinian Territory*, Advisory Opinion, 9 July 2004, I.C.J. Reports 2004

*Armed Activities on the Territory of the Congo (Democratic Republic of the Congo v. Uganda)*, Judgment, 19 December 2005, I.C.J. Reports 2005

*Armed Activities on the Territory of the Congo (Democratic Republic of the Congo v. Rwanda)*, Judgment, 3 February 2006, I.C.J. Reports 2006

*Application of the Convention on the Prevention and Punishment of the Crime of Genocide (Bosnia and Herzegovina v. Serbia and Montenegro)*, Judgment, 26 February 2007, I.C.J. Reports 2007

*Accordance with International Law of the Unilateral Declaration of Independence in Respect of Kosovo*, Advisory Opinion, 22 July 2010, I.C.J. Reports 2010

*Jurisdictional immunities of the State (Germany v. Italy: Greece intervening)*, Judgment, 3 February 2012, I.C.J. Reports 2012

*Questions relating to the Obligation to Prosecute or Extradite (Belgium v. Senegal)*, Judgment, 20 July 2012, I.C.J. Reports 2012

### *Security Council*

#### Security Council Resolutions

S/Res/83, 27 June 1950, Complaint of aggression upon the Republic of Korea

S/Res/84, 7 July 1950, Complaint of aggression upon the Republic of Korea

S/Res/541, 18 November 1983, Cyprus

S/Res/550, 11 May 1984, Cyprus

S/Res/1031, 15 December 1995, Bosnia and Herzegovina

S/Res/1144, 19 December 1997, The situation in Bosnia and Herzegovina

S/Res/1244, 10 June 1999, The situation in Kosovo

S/Res/1267, 15 October 1999, Afghanistan

S/Res/1368, 12 September 2001, Threats to international peace and security caused by terrorist acts

S/Res/1390, 16 January 2002, Afghanistan

S/Res/1440, 24 October 2002, Threats to international peace and security caused by terrorist acts

S/Res/1483, 22 May 2003, Situation between Iraq and Kuwait

S/Res/1511, 16 October 2003, Situation between Iraq and Kuwait

S/Res/1674, 28 April 2006, Protection of civilians in armed conflict

S/Res/1706, 31 August 2006, The situation in Sudan

S/Res/1816, 2 June 2008, The situation in Somalia

S/Res/1894, 11 November 2009, Protection of civilians in armed conflict

## Other Security Council documents

S/1995/1029, Conclusions of the Peace Implementation Conference held at Lancaster House, London, on 8 and 9 December 1995

S/1997/979, Conclusions of the Peace Implementation Conferences held in Bonn on 9 and 10 December 1997

S/1999/672, 12 June 1999, Report of the Secretary General pursuant to paragraph 10 of Security Council Resolution 1244 (1999)

S/1999/779, 12 July 1999, Report of the Secretary General of the United Nations: Interim administration mission in Kosovo

S/2007/168/Add.1, 26 March 2007, Comprehensive Proposal for the Kosovo Status Settlement

S/2015/928, Letter dated 3 December 2015 from the Permanent Representative of the United Kingdom of Great Britain and Northern Ireland to the United Nations addressed to the President of the Security Council

S/2015/946, Letter dated 10 December 2015 from the Chargé d'affaires a.i. of the Permanent Mission of Germany to the United Nations addressed to the President of the Security Council

S/2016/34, Letter dated 11 January 2016 from the Permanent Representative of Denmark to the United Nations addressed to the President of the Security Council

S/2016/132, Letter dated 10 February 2016 from the Chargé d'affaires a.i. of the Permanent Mission of the Netherlands to the United Nations addressed to the President of the Security Council

S/2016/513, 3 June 2016 Letter dated 3 June 2016 from the Permanent Representative of Norway to the United Nations addressed to the President of the Security Council

REFERENCES                                                                                    373

S/2018/53, Identical letters dated 20 January 2018 from the Chargé d'affaires a.i. of the
    Permanent Mission of Turkey to the United Nations addressed to the Secretary-
    General and the President of the Security Council

### General Assembly

A/Res/95 (I), 11 December 1946, Affirmation of the Principles of International Law rec-
    ognized by the Charter of the Nürnberg Tribunal
A/2929, 1 July 1955, Annotations on the text of the draft International Covenants on
    Human Rights (prepared by the Secretary-General)
A/Res/2444 (XIII), Respect for Human Rights in Armed Conflict, 19 December 1968.
A/Res/ 3314 (XXIX), 14 December 1974, Definition of Aggression
A/Res/51/210, 16 January 1997, Measures to Eliminate International Terrorism
A/Res/56/83, Responsibility of states for internationally wrongful acts
A/Res/60/1, 2005 World Summit Outcome
A/Res/66/100, 9 December 2011, Responsibility of international organizations

### Secretary General

UN Doc. C.N.416.2015.TREATIES-IV.4, Depositary Notification by the Secretary General
    of the United Nations, Declaration of the Verkhovna Rada of Ukraine on Derogation
    from Certain Obligations under the International Covenant on Civil and Political
    Rights and the Convention for the Protection of Human Rights and Fundamental
    Freedoms, 5 June 2015

### International Criminal Court

International Criminal court, Office of the Prosecutor, Report on Preliminary Exami-
    nation Activities 2016

### Economic and Social Council

UN Doc. E/CN.4/353/Add.2, 7 January 1950, Comments of Governments on the draft
    International Covenant on Human Rights and measures of implementation

### United Nations Commission on the Limits of the Continental Shelf

Partial Submission of the Government of the Kingdom of Denmark together with
    the Government of Greenland to the Commission on the Limits of the Conti-
    nental Shelf, The Northern Continental Shelf of Greenland (executive summary,

15 December 2014), https://www.un.org/Depts/los/clcs_new/submissions_files/dnk76_14/dnk2014_es.pdf

Partial revised submission of the Russian Federation to the Commission on the Limits of the Continental Shelf in respect of the continental shelf of the Russian Federation in the Arctic Ocean (executive summary, 3 August 2015), https://www.un.org/depts/los/clcs_new/submissions_files/rus01_rev15/2015_08_03_Exec_Summary_English.pdf

Progress of work in the Commission on the Limits of the Continental Shelf - Statement by the Chair - Forty-sixth session, UN Doc. CLCS/103 (8 April 2018) and UN Doc. CLCS/103/Corr.1 (9 May 2018)

UN Doc. CLCS/102, 6 February 2018, Agenda for the forty-sixth session (New York, 29 January-6 March 2018)

## *International Tribunal for the Prosecution of Persons Responsible for Serious Violations of International Humanitarian Law Committed in the Territory of the Former Yugoslavia since 1991 (International Criminal Tribunal for the former Yugoslavia, "ICTY")*

Appeals Chamber, *Prosecutor v. Duško Tadić*, IT-94-1-T, judgment, 7 May 1997

Final Report to the Prosecutor by the Committee Established to Review the NATO Bombing Campaign Against the Federal Republic of Yugoslavia, 13 June 2000

Appeals Chamber, *Prosecutor v. Kunarac, Kovač and Vuković*, IT-96-23 and IT-96-23/1, judgment, 12 June 2002

## *International Criminal Tribunal for Rwanda ("ICTR")*

Trial Chamber, *Prosecutor v. Kayishema and Ruzindana*, ICTR-95-1-T, judgment, 21 May 1999

Appeal Chamber, *Prosecutor v. Kayishema and Ruzindana*, ICTR-95-1-T, judgment, 1 June 2001

## *International Tribunal for the Law of the Sea ("ITLOS")*

*Request for an advisory opinion submitted by the Sub-Regional Fisheries Commission (SRFC) (Case No. 21), Advisory Opinion, 2 April 2015*

REFERENCES 375

### *International Law Commission*

Principles of International Law Recognized in the Charter of the Nürnberg Tribunal and in the Judgment of the Tribunal ("Nuremberg Principles"), *Yearbook of the International Law Commission*, 1950, Vol. II, para. 97

Report of the International Law Commission on the work of its Fifty-third session, Official Records of the General Assembly, Fifty-sixth session, Supplement No. 10 (A/56/10)

Report of the ILC, General Assembly Official Records, 55th session, Supplement No. 10 A/58/10 (2003)

### *Human Rights Committee*

General Comment no. 29, States of Emergency (Article 4), CCPR/C/21/Rev.1/Add.11, 31 August 2001

General Comment No. 31, The Nature of the General Legal Obligation Imposed on States Parties to the Covenant, CCPR/C/21/Rev.1/Add.13, 26 May 2004

### *Committee on the Elimination of Racial Discrimination*

Concluding observations on the United Kingdom of Great Britain and Northern Ireland, CERD/C/63/CO/11, 4-22 August 2003

### *International Conference on Human Rights (Teheran, April-May 1968)*

Human Rights in Armed Conflicts, Resolution XXIII, 12 May 1968

### Other international organisations

### *European Space Agency*

*Galileo Full Operational Capability Procurement factsheet*, http://download.esa.int/docs/Galileo_IOV_Launch/FOC_factsheet_20111003.pdf, accessed on 5 October 2015

*EGNOS brochure*, http://www.egnos-pro.esa.int/Publications/ESA_EGNOS_br284_2009.pdf, accessed on 5 October 2015

### European Union

Court of Justice of the European Communities,[1194] *Yassin Abdullah Kadi and Al Barakaat International Foundation v. Council of the European Union and Commission of the European Communities* (joined cases C-402/05 P and C-415/05 P), 3 September 2008

Court of Justice of the European Union, *Opinion 2/13 on accession to the Convention*, 18 December 2014

General Court, judgment of 15 June 2017, Case T-262/15, *Kiselev v. Council*

### International Commission on Intervention and State Sovereignty

*The Responsibility to Protect*, issued by the International Government Research Centre, Ottawa, December 2001

### International Maritime Organization

"Piracy and armed robbery against ships: Guidance to shipowners and ship operators, shipmasters and crews on preventing and suppressing acts of piracy and armed robbery against ships", MSC/Circ.632/Rev.3, 29 May 2002

"Revised interim guidance to shipowners, ship operators and shipmasters on the use of privately contracted armed security personnel on board ships in the high risk area" [sc. the waters off Somalia], MSC.1/Cric.1405/Rev.2, 25 May 2012

### International Organization for Standardization

ISO 18788:2015, Management system for private security operations – Requirements with guidance for use

### North Atlantic Treaty Organisation (NATO)

Statement by the North Atlantic Council, NATO press release (2001)124, 12 September 2001, http://www.nato.int/docu/pr/2001/p01-124e.htm (accessed 28 July 2015)

Wales Summit Declaration, NATO press release (20014)120, 5 September 2014, https://www.nato.int/cps/en/natohq/official_texts_112964.htm (accessed on 27 November 2017)

---

1194 The Court of Justice of the European Communities became the Court of Justice of the European Union on 1 January 2009.

# REFERENCES

## Domestic case-law

### *Corpus Iuris Civilis*

D.50.17.185

### *Bosnia and Herzegovina*

Human Rights Chamber for Bosnia and Herzegovina, Cases nos. CH/02/8679, CH/02/8689, CH/02/8690 and CH/02/8691, *Hadˋ BOUDELLAA, Boumediene LAKH-DAR, Mohamed NECHLE and Saber LAHMAR against Bosnia and Herzegovina and the Federation of Bosnia and Herzegovina*, 11 October 2002

Human Rights Chamber for Bosnia and Herzegovina, CH/00/4441, *Merima Sijarić v. Federation of Bosnia and Herzegovina*, 6 June 2000

Human Rights Chamber for Bosnia and Herzegovina CH/99/2327, *Momčilo Knežević v. Republika Srpska*, 11 October 2001

Constitutional Court of Bosnia and Herzegovina, U-7/97, 22 December 1997

Constitutional Court of Bosnia and Herzegovina, U-7-11/98, 26 February 1999

### *Netherlands*

Supreme Court (*Hoge Raad*), judgment of 7 May 2004, ECLI:NL:HR:2004:AF6988, also published in NJ 2007/276 with an annotation by A.H. Klip

Supreme Court, 4 April 2017, ECLI:NL:HR:2017:574, also published in NJ 2018/106

Supreme Court, 4 April 2017, ECLI:NL:HR:2017:574, also published in NJ 2018/107

Supreme Court, 4 April 2017, ECLI:NL:HR:2017:577, also published in NJ 2018/108, with an annotation by E. van Sliedregt

Supreme Court (*Hoge Raad*), *State v. Nuhanović*, 6 September 2014, ECLI:NL:HR:2013:BZ9225

Supreme Court, *State v. Mustafić-Mujić and Others*, 6 September 2014, ECLI:NL:HR:2013:BZ9228, also published in NJ 2015/376 with an annotation by N.J. Schrijver

### *Russian Federation*

Constitutional Court of the Russian Federation, Judgment of 31 July 1995 on the constitutionality of the Presidential Decrees and the Resolutions of the Federal Government concerning the situation in Chechnya (translation by Federal News Service Group, Washington D.C., published by the Venice Commission on 10 January 1996 as CDL-INF (96) 1)

378                                                                      REFERENCES

### Serbia

Supreme Court of Serbia, judgment of 23 May 2007 (case no. 1251/07)
Constitutional Court of Serbia, judgment of 1 April 2010 (case no. 531/2008)

### United Kingdom

House of Lords, *R (on the application of Al-Jedda) (FC) (Appellant) v Secretary of State for Defence (Respondent)*, [2007] UKHL 58, [2008] 1 AC 332

Supreme Court, *Abd Ali Hameed Al-Waheed (Appellant) v Ministry of Defence (Respondent) and Serdar Mohammed (Respondent) v Ministry of Defence (Appellant)* (per Lord Sumption), 17 January 2017, [2017] UKSC 2

## Books and book articles

Bellal, A., *The War Report* 2016, https://armedgroupsinternationallaw.files.wordpress.com/2017/05/the-war-report-2016.pdf (accessed on 27 May 2017).

Bellal, A., *The War Report* 2017, https://www.geneva-academy.ch/joomlatools-files/docman-files/The%20War%20Report%202017.pdf (accessed on 11 August 2018)

Bethlehem, Sir D., "When is an act of war lawful?", in *The Right to Life under Article 2 of the European Convention on Human Rights: Twenty Ywars of Legal Developments since McCann v. the United Kingdom (In honour of Michael O'Boyle)*, p. 231

Buyse, A., *Post-Conflict Housing Restitution: The European human rights perspective, with a case study on Bosnia and Herzegovina* (diss. Leiden 2008), Intersentia, 2008, pp. 275-281

Casey-Maslen S. (Editor), *Weapons Under International Human Rights Law*, Cambridge University Press 2014

Chadwick, E., *Self-Determination, Terrorism and the International Humanitarian Law of Armed Conflict*, Martinus Nijhoff 1996

Chernishova, O., "Right to the truth in the case-law of the European Court of Human Rights", in in *The Right to Life under Article 2 of the European Convention on Human Rights: Twenty Years of Legal Developments since McCann v. the United Kingdom (In honour of Michael O'Boyle)*, pp. 145-160

Cockayne, J., "Private Military and Security Companies", in *The Oxford Handbook of International Law in Armed Conflict* (Andrew Clapham, Paola Gaeta, eds.), Oxford University Press, 2014

Costa, J.-P., and O'Boyle, M., "The European Court of Human Rights and International Humanitarian Law", in *The European Convention on Human Rights, a living instrument, Essays in Honour of Christos L. Rozakis* (Bruylant, 2011), p. 107

# REFERENCES

Cuyckens, H., "The Law of Occupation" in *Armed Conflicts and the Law*, Jan Wouters, Philip De Man, Nele Verlinden (eds.), Intersentia, 2016

Crawford, J., *Brownlie's Principles of Public International Law*, Oxford University Press, 8th edn. 2012 (Crawford (2012))

Crawford, J., *State Responsibility: The General Part*, Cambridge University Press 2013 (Crawford (2013))

Czech, P., "European Human Rights in International Military Operations", 15 *European Yearbook on Human Rights* (2015) p. 391

Dinstein, Y., *The Conduct of Hostilities under the Law of International Armed Conflict*, Cambridge University Press, 3rd ed. 2016

Dijk, P. van; Hoof, F. van; Rijn, A. van; Zwaak, L. (eds.), *Theory and Practice of the European Convention on Human Rights*, fifth edn., Intersentia, 2018

Doswald-Beck, L., *Human Rights in Times of Conflict and Terrorism*, Oxford University Press 2011

Droege, C., and Arimatsu, L., "The European Convention on Human Rights and international humanitarian law: Conference report", *Yearbook of International Humanitarian Law* volume 12 – 2009 – pp. 435-449

Duffy, H., *The 'War on Terror' and the Framework of International Law* (2nd edition), Cambridge University Press 2015 (Duffy (2015))

Duffy, H., and Kostas, S.A., "'Extraordinary Rendition': A Challenge for the Rule of Law", in *Counter-Terrorism: International Law and Practice* (Ana María de Frías, Katja L.H. Samuel, Nigel D. White, eds.), Oxford University Press 2011 p. 539

Duranti, M. *The Conservative Human Rights Revolution*, Oxford University Press 2017

Fachataller, T., "Hassan v. United Kingdom and the Interplay Between International Humanitarian Law and Human Rights Law in the Jurisprudence of the European Court of Human Rights", *EYIL* 2016 p. 345

Fortin, K., *The Accountability of Armed Groups under Human Rights Law*, diss. Utrecht 2015

Gill, T.D., "Some Thoughts on the Relationship Between International Humanitarian Law and International Human Rights Law: A Plea for Mutual Respect and a Common-Sense Approach", in [2013] 16 *Yearbook of International Humanitarian Law* p. 251

Gillard, E-C, "International Humanitarian Law and Extraterritorial State Conduct", in *Extraterritorial Application of Human Rights Treaties*, edited by Fons Coomans and Menno Camminga (Intersentia, 2004), pp. 25-40

Gross, A. "The Righting of the Law of Occupation", in *The Frontiers of Human Rights: Extraterritoriality and its Challenges* (Collected Courses of the Academy of European Law vol. XXIV/1, pp. 21-54

Grotius, H. *De iure belli ac pacis* (1625)

Harris, D., O'Boyle, M., and Warbrick, C., Buckley, C., *Harris, O'Boyle and Warbrick: Law of the European Convention on Human Rights*, 3rd edition Oxford University Press 2014

Have, N. van der, *The prevention of gross human rights violations under international human rights law* (diss. Amsterdam 2017)

Haeck, Y., and Burbano Herrera, C., "The Use of Interim Measures by the European Court of Human Rights in Times of War or Internal Conflict", in *Margins of Conflict: The ECHR and Transitions to and from Armed Conflict*, Antoine Buyse, ed., Intersentia, 2011, pp. 77-129

Heijer, M. den, and Lawson, R., "Extraterritorial Human Rights and the Concept of 'Jurisdiction'", in M. Langford a.o. (eds.), *Global Justice, State Duties* (Cambridge University Press 2013), p. 153

Jankowska-Gilberg, M., *Extraterritorialität der Menschenrechte: Der Begriff der Jurisdiktion im Sinne von Art. 1 EMRK* (diss. Regensburg 2007), Nomos, 2008

Kalshoven, F., and Zegveld, L., *Contraints on the waging of war: an introduction to international humanitarian law* (fourth edition), Cambridge University Press/ICRC 2011

Kittrie, O.F., *Law as a weapon of war*, Oxford University Press 2016

Kolb, R., "Human Rights and Humanitarian Law", *Max Planck Encyclopedia of Public International Law* (2012) (Kolb (2012))

Kruit, van der, P. (ed.), *Handboek Militair Recht*, published by *Nederlandse Defensie Academie* (Netherlands Defence Academy), 2nd edition 2009

Kjetil Mujezinović Larsen, *The Human Rights Treaty Obligations of Peacekeepers*, Cambridge University Press 2012

Lawson, R., "Out of Control: State Responsibility and Human Rights: Will the ILC's Definition of the 'act of State' meet the Challenges of the 21st Century?" in M. Castermans, F. van Hoof and J. Smiths (eds.), *The Role of the Nation State in the 21st Century – Essays in Honour of Peter Baehr* (Kluwer Law International, 1998) (Lawson (1998))

Lawson, R., *Het EVRM en de Europese Gemeenschappen: Bouwstenen voor een aansprakelijkheidsregime voor het optreden van internationale organisaties*, diss. Leiden 1999 (Lawson (1999))

Lawson, R., *Life after Bankovic: On the Extraterritorial Application of the European Convention on Human Rights*, in Extraterritorial Application of Human Rights Treaties (Fons Coomans and Menno T. Kamminga, eds.), Intersentia, 2004, pp. 83 *et seq.* (Lawson (2004))

Lawson, R., *Really out of sight? Issues of Jurisdiction and Control in Situations of Armed Conflict under the ECHR*, in *Margins of Conflict: The ECHR and Transitions to and from Armed Conflict* (Antoine Buyse, ed.), Intersentia, 2011, pp. 57-76 (Lawson (2011-1))

Lawson, R., "The Extra-Territorial Application of the European Convention on Human Rights", *European Yearbook of International Law* 2011, pp. 427-444 (Lawson (2011-2))

REFERENCES                                                                    381

*Leuven Manual on the International Law Applicable to Peace Operations* (T. Gill, D. Fleck, W. Boothby and A. Vanheusden, general eds; M. Benatar and R. Jorritsma, assistant eds.), Cambridge University Press 2017

Loof, J.-P., *Mensenrechten en staatsveiligheid: verenigbare grootheden?* (diss. Leiden 2005) Wolf Legal Publishers 2005

Macdonald, R. St.J., "The Margin of Appreciation in the Jurisprudence of the European Court of Human Rights", *Collected Courses of the Academy of European Law* (1990), Vols. I-II (Macdonald (1990))

Melzer, N., *Targeted killing in international law*, Oxford University Press 2008

Meredith, C., and Christou, T., "Not in my Front Yard: Security and Resistance to Responsibility for Extraterritorial State Conduct", in *War or Crime? National Legal Challenges in Europe to the War in Iraq* (Elspeth Guild, editor), Wolf Legal Publishers, 2009

Milanovic, M., *Extraterritorial application of human rights treaties*, Oxford University Press 2011/2013 (Milanovic (2011/13))

Milanovic, M., "Extraterritorial Derogations from Treaties in Armed Conflict", in *The Frontiers of Human Rights: Extraterritoriality and its Challenges, Collected Courses of the Academy of European Law*, vol. XXIV/1, p. 55-88 (Milanovic (2016-1))

Milanović, M., and Hadži-Vidanović, V., *A Taxonomy of Armed Conflict* (January 20, 2012). *Research Handbook on International Conflict and Security Law*, Nigel White, Christian Henderson, eds., Edward Elgar, 2012

Mills, A., "Rethinking Jurisdiction in International Law", *The British Yearbook of International Law* (2014), Vo. 84 No. 1, 187-239

Monash, Lieutenant General Sir J., *The Australian Victories in France* (London, Hutchinson & Co., 1920)

Murphy, M., Hoffman, F., Schaub, G., *Hybrid Maritime Warfare and the Baltic Sea Region*, University of Copenhagen, Centre for Military Studies, November 2016

Murray, D., *Practitioner's Guide to Human Rights Law in Armed Conflict*, Chatham House/Oxford University Press 2016 (Murray 2016)

Myjer, E., "Human Rights Without Peace? The European Court of Human Rights and Conflicts Between High Contracting Parties", in *Margins of Conflict: The ECHR and Transitions to and from Armed Conflict*, Antoine Buyse, ed., Intersentia, 2011, pp. 1-32 (Myjer (2011))

Myjer, E., "About court jesters: Freedom of expression and duties and responsibilities of journalists", in *Freedom of expression: Essays in honour of Nicolas Bratza*, Wolf Legal Publishers 2012 (Myjer (2012))

Nauta, D., *The International Responsibility of NATO and its Personnel during Military Operations: A study on international public law and international criminal law* (diss. Nijmegen 2016), Wolf Legal Publishers

Nye, J., 'Hard, Soft, and Smart Power', in *The Oxford Handbook of Modern Diplomacy* (Andrew F. Cooper, Jorge Heine, Ramesh Thakur, Eds.), Oxford University Press 2013, pp. 559-574

O'Boyle, M., "The European Convention on Human Rights and Extraterritorial Jurisdiction: A Comment on Life After Bankovic'", in *Extraterritorial Application of Human Rights Treaties*, Fons Coomans and Menno T. Kamminga, eds., Intersentia, 2004, pp. 125-139 (O'Boyle (2004))

Ovey, C., "Application of the ECHR during International Armed Conflicts", in *The UK and European Human Rights: A Strained Relationship?* (Katja S Ziegler, Elizabeth Wicks and Loveday Hodson, eds.), Hart Publishing, 2015, pp. 225-245

Paulsson, L., *Delegation of powers to United Nations Subsidiary organs*, Master's thesis, Lund 2004

Pejic, J., "Armed Conflict and Terrorism: There Is A (Big) Difference", in *Counter-Terrorism: International Law and Practice* (Ana María de Frías, Katja L.H. Samuel, Nigel D. White, eds.), Oxford University Press 2011 p. 171

Pouw, E., *International Human Rights Law and the Law of Armed Conflict in the Context of Counterinsurgency - With a Particular Focus on Targeting and Operational Detention* (diss. UvA 2013)

Rainey, B., Wicks, E., and Ovey, C., *Jacobs, White, and Ovey, The European Convention on Human Rights*, 7th edition Oxford University Press 2017

Ralby, I., "Private Military Companies and the *Jus and Bellum*", in *The Oxford Handbook of the Use of Force in International Law* (Mark Weller, ed.), p. 1131

Raymond, D., "Military Means of Preventing Mass Atrocities", in *Reconstructing Atrocity Prevention* (Sheri P. Rosenberg, Tibi Galis, Alex Zucker, eds.), Cambridge University Press 2016, pp. 295-318

Reydams, L., and Wouters, J., "A la guerre comme à la guerre", in *Armed Conflicts and the Law*, Jan Wouters, Philip De Man, Nele Verlinden (eds.), Intersentia, 2016, pp.1-27

Rieter, E., *Preventing Irreparable Harm: Provisional Measures in International Human Rights Adjudication* (diss. Nijmegen), Intersentia, 2010

Schokkenbroek, J.G.C. , *Toetsing aan de vrijheidsrechten van het Europees verdrag tot bescherming van de rechten van de mens* (diss. Leiden 1996)

Shubber, S., *Jurisdiction over crimes on board aircraft*, Martinus Nijhoff, 1973

Tallinn Manual 2.0 on the international law applicable to cyber operations (2nd edition), Cambridge University Press 2017

*The New Shorter Oxford English Dictionary* (1993 ed.)

Voetelink, J., *Militair Operationeel Recht* (Wolf Legal Publishers, 2013)

Young, Commander T.C., *Maritime Exclusion Zones: A Tool for the Operational Commander?*, Naval War College, Newport, Rhode Island, USA, 18 May 1992

Zegveld, L., *The Accountability of Armed Opposition Groups in International Law*, Cambridge University Press 2002

## Journal articles, papers and lectures

Abbott, K., "A brief overview of legal interoperability challenges for NATO arising from the interrelationship between IHL and IHRL in light of the European Convention on Human Rights", *International Review of the Red Cross*, vol. 96, no. 893, pp. 107-37

Altwicker, T., and Wieczorek, N., "Bridging the Security Gap through EU Rule of Law Missions? Rule of Law Administration by EULEX", *Journal of Conflict and Security Law* (2016), Vol. 21 No. 1, 115-133

Austin, A., Contribution to a seminar held at the University of Toulouse in March 2016

Aybay, R., "A New Institution in the Field: The Human Rights Chamber of Bosnia and Herzegovina", *Netherlands Quarterly of Human Rights*, Vol. 15/4, 529-558,

Baldovin, A., "Impact de la jurisprudence récente de la Cour européenne des droits de l'Homme sur la planification et l'exécution des opérations militaires à venir : Application extraterritoriale de la Convention, imputabilite des faits des troupes et fragmentation du droit international", in *Military Law and the Law of War Review* 50/3-4 (2011), pp. 369-418

Benvenuti, P., "The ICTY Prosecutor and the Review of the NATO Bombing Campaign against the Federal Republic of Yugoslavia", in *EJIL* (2001), Vol. 12 No. 3, 503–529

Besson, S., "The extraterritoriality of the European Convention on Human Rights: why human rights depend on jurisdiction and what jurisdiction amounts to", *Leiden Journal of International Law* 2012, 25(4), 857-884 at p. 868

Bjorge, E., "What is living and what is dead in the European Convention on Human Rights? A Comment on Hassan v. United Kingdom", *Questions of International Law Zoom-In* 15 (2015), 23-36

Borelli, S., "*Jaloud v. Netherlands* and *Hassan v. United Kingdom*: Time for a principled approach in the application of the ECHR to military action abroad", *QIL, Zoom-in* 16 (2015) 25-43

Bowring, B. (2008) – "How will the European Court of Human Rights deal with the UK in Iraq?: lessons from Turkey and Russia" - London: Birkbeck ePrints. Available at: http://eprints.bbk.ac.uk/859

Breitegger, A., "Sacrificing the Effectiveness of the European Convention on Human Rights on the Altar of the Effective Functioning of Peace Support Operations: A Critique of *Behrami & Saramati* and *Al Jedda*, *International Community Law Review* 11 (2009) 155-183

Bruch, E., "Hybrid Courts: Examining Hybridity Through a Post-Colonial Lens", 28 *Boston University International Law Journal* 1 (2010).

Cassese, A., "*Ex iniuria ius oritur*: Are We Moving towards International Legitimation of Forcible Humanitarian Countermeasures in the World Community?", in *EJIL* 10 (1999), 1-22, pp. 23-40

Comae Technologies, 28 June 2017, 'Petya.2017 is a wiper not a ransomware', https://blog.comae.io/petya-2017-is-a-wiper-not-a-ransomware-9ea1d8961d3b (accessed 25 August 2017);

Correia, V., "L'adage *lex specialis derogat generali* : Réflexions générales sur sa nature, sa raison d'être et ses conditions d'application", https://www.academia.edu/25191057/L_adage_lex_specialis_derogat_generali_R%C3%A9flexions_g%C3%A9n%C3%A9rales_sur_sa_nature_sa_raison_d_%C3%AAtre_et_ses_conditions_d_application (accessed on 13 August 2018)

De Koker, C., "Hassan v United Kingdom: The Interaction of Human Rights Law and International Humanitarian Law with regard to the Deprivation of Liberty in Armed Conflicts", *Utrecht Journal of International and European Law* 31(81), pp.90-96

Donald, A. and Leach, P., 'A Wolf in Sheep's Clothing: Why the Draft Copenhagen Declaration Must be Rewritten', *EJIL:Talk!*, 21 February 2018

Doswald-Beck, L., and Vité, S., "International Humanitarian Law and Human Rights Law", *International Review of the Red Cross*, 30 April 1993, no. 293

Droege, C., "Elective affinities? Human rights and humanitarian law", *International Review of the Red Cross*, September 2008, vol. 90, no. 871, pp. 501-547

Drzemczewski, A., "Ireland v. U.K.", [1978] 12 *The Law Teacher* 1 p. 49 (Drzemczewski (1978))

Drzemczewski, A., "Human Rights in Europe: An Insider's Views", [2017] E.H.R.L.R., issue 2, p. 134 (Drzemczewski (2017))

Duffy, H., "Strategic Human Right Litigation: 'Bursting the Bubble on the Champagne Moment', inaugural lecture (University of Leiden), 13 March 2017, https://www.universiteitleiden.nl/binaries/content/assets/rechtsgeleerdheid/instituut-voor-publiekrecht/grotius-centre/oratie-helen-duffy-spreekversie.pdf (accessed 27 March 2017) (Duffy (2017))

Duffy, H., "Trials and Tribulations: Co-Applicability of IHL and Human Rights in an Age of Adjudication" in Bohrer, Dill and Duffy, *Law Applicable to Armed Conflict*, Cambridge University Press 2020 (Duffy (2018))

Duttwiler, M., "Authority, Control and Jurisdiction in the Extraterritorial Application of the European Convention on Human Rights, *Netherlands Quarterly of Human Rights*, Vol. 30/2, 137-162, 2012

Ekins, R.; Morgan, J.; Tugendhat, T., *Clearing the Fog of Law: Saving our armed forces from defeat by judicial diktat*, Policy Exchange, 30 March 2015

Fallon, M., speech at the Policy Exchange seminar 'Clearing the "Fog of Law"', 8 December 2014, https://www.gov.uk/government/speeches/clearing-the-fog-of-law-policy-exchange-seminar

Ferraro, T., "The applicability and application of international humanitarian law to multinational forces", in *International Review of the Red Cross* (2013), 95 (891/892), pp. 561-612

Focarelli, C., "The Responsibility to Protect Doctrine and Humanitarian Intervention: Too Many Ambiguities for a Working Doctrine", *Journal of Conflict and Security Law* (2008), Vol. 13 No. 2, 191-213

Frostad, M., "The 'Colonial Clause' and Extraterritorial Application of Human Rights: The European Convention on Human Rights Article 56 and its Relationship to Article 1", *Arctic Review on Law and Politics*, vol. 4, 1/2013

Frumer, P., "Quand droits de l'homme et droit international humanitaire s'emmêlent – Un regard critique sur l'arrêt Hassan c. Royaume-Uni", *Rev. tr. d.h.* 102/2015 p. 481

Gemalmaz, M.S., "Constitution, Ombudsperson and Human Rights Chamber in 'Bosnia and Herzegovina', *Netherlands Quarterly of Human Rights*, Vol. 17/3, 277-329, 1999, pp. 291-329.

Goldsmith, J., "How Cyber Changes the Laws of War", *EJIL* (2013), Vol. 24 No. 1, 129-138

Gross, O., and Ní Aoláin, F., "From Discretion to Scrutiny: Revisiting the Application of the Margin of Appreciation Doctrine in the Context of Article 15 of the European Convention on Human Rights", *Human Rights Quarterly* 23 (2001) 625-649

Guilfoyle, D., "The Use Of Force Against Pirates", in *The Oxford Handbook of the Use of Force in International Law* (Mark Weller, ed.), p. 1057

Habteslasie, A., "Detention in times of war: Article 5 of the ECHR, UN Security Council Resolutions and the Supreme Court decision in Serdar Mohammed v. Ministry of Defence", E.H.R.L.R. 2017, 2, 180-191

Haijer, F.A. and Ryngaert, C.M.J., "Reflections on *Jaloud v. the Netherlands* – Jurisdictional Consequences and Resonance in Dutch Society", *Journal of International Peacekeeping* 19 (2015), pp. 174-189

Hakimi, M., and Katz Cogan, J., A Role for the Security Council on Defensive Force?, *Ejil:Talk!*, 21 October 2016

Hampson, F.J., "The relationship between international humanitarian law and human rights law from the perspective of a human rights treaty body", *International Review of the Red Cross*, September 2008, vol. 90, no. 871, pp. 549-572 (Hampson (2008))

Hampson, F.J., written statement in *The use of force in armed conflicts: interplay between the conduct of hostilities and law enforcement paradigms*, Expert meeting held in 2012, ICRC, November 2013, pp. 69-80 (Hampson (2012))

Hampson, F.J., "Article 2 of the Convention and military operations during armed conflict", in *The Right to Life under Article 2 of the European Convention on Human Rights: Twenty Years of Legal Developments since McCann v. the United Kingdom (In honour of Michael O'Boyle)* (Hampson (2017))

Happold, M., „Bankovic v. Belgium and the territorial scope of the European Convention on Human Rights", Human Rights law Review 2003, Volume 3, Number 1, pp. 77-90;

Henderson, C., "The use of cyber force: Is the *jus ad bellum* ready?", in *QIL*, Zoom-in 27 (2016), pp. 3-11

Henriksen, A., "The Poisoning of Alexander Litvinenko and the Geographical Scope of Human Rights Law", *Just Security*, https://www.justsecurity.org/29238/poisoning-litvinenko-scope-human-rights/, accessed 14 February 2016

Herik, L. van den, and Duffy, H., *Human Rights bodies and International Humanitarian Law: Common but Differentiated Approaches*, Grotius Centre Working Paper 2014/020-IHL

Hervieu, N., « La jurisprudence européenne sur les opérations militaires à l'épreuve du feu », *La Revue des droits de l'homme* (en ligne), placed online on 20 October 2014

Herzog, S., "Revisiting the Estonian Cyber Attacks: Digital Threats and Multinational Responses", in *Journal of Strategic Security*, Vol. 2, No. 4 (Summer 2011), pp. 49-60

Heyns, C.; Akande, D.; Hill-Cawthorne, L.; and Chengeta, T., "The International Framework Regulating the Use of Armed Drones", *ICLQ* vol 65, October 2016 pp 791–827

Hill-Cawthorne, L., "The Grand Chamber Judgment in Hassan v UK", *Ejil:talk!* 16 September 2016

Hura, M., McLeod, G., Larson, E., James Schneider, J., Gonzales, D., Norton, D., Jacobs, J., O'Connell, K., Little, W., Mesic, R., and Jamison, L., *Interoperability: A Continuing Challenge in Coalition Air Operations*. Santa Monica, CA: RAND Corporation, 2000. https://www.rand.org/pubs/monograph_reports/MR1235.html (accessed on 22 August 2018).

"Hybrid war – does it even exist?", NATO review, http://www.nato.int/docu/review/2015/Also-in-2015/hybrid-modern-future-warfare-russia-ukraine/EN/index.htm (accessed 7 June 2016)

Jones, Lieutenant K.M., USN, *Cyber War: The Next Frontier For NATO*, Progressive Management, 2016, pp. 20-23

Keating, V.C., "The anti-torture norm and cooperation in the CIA black site programme", *The International Journal of Human Rights*, 2016, Vol. 20, No. 7, 935-955

Kolb, R., "The relationship between international humanitarian law and human rights law: A brief history of the 1948 Universal Declaration of Human Rights and the 1949 Geneva Conventions", *International Review of the Red Cross*, September 1998, no. 324, pp. 409-419 (Kolb(1998))

Krahmann, E., "Choice, Voice and exit: Consumer power and the self-regulation of the private security industry", 1 *European Journal of International Security* (2016) pp. 27-48

Krieger, H., "A Credibility Gap: The Behrami and Saramati Decision of the European Court of Human Rights", *Journal of International Peacekeeping* 13 (2009) 159-180

Lock, T., "Beyond *Bosphorus*: The European Court of Human Rights' Case-Law on the Responsibility of Member States of International Organisations under the European Convention on Human Rights", in *Human Rights Law Review* 10:3 (2010), 529-545

Loucaides, L., "The Judgment of the European Court of Human Rights in the Case of Cyprus v. Turkey", 15 *Leiden Journal of International Law* 225-236

Macdonald, R. St.J., "Derogations under Article 15 of the European Convention on Human Rights", [1997] 36 *Columbia Journal of Transnational Law* p. 225 (Macdonald (1997))

Macron, N.E., "The Council of Europe's Cyber Crime Treaty: An exercise in Symbolic Legislation", *International Journal of Cyber Criminology*, Vol 4 Issue 1&2 (2010)

Mačkić, J., "Het onzichtbare bewijzen: Over de mogelijkheden om de bewijslast te verschuiven van klager naar de verwerende staat in zaken van discriminatoir geweld voor het Europese Hof voor de Rechten van de Mens", NTM/NJCM-bulletin jrg. 42 [2017], nr. 4, pp. 477-494

Mariniello, T., "Prolonged Emergency and Derogation of Human Rights: Why the European Court Should Raise Its Immunity System", to appear in *German Law Journal* (forthcoming 2019), available on https://www.academia.edu/ (last accessed 26 June 2018).

Milanovic, M., "A Few Thoughts on Hassan v. United Kingdom", *Ejil:talk!* 22 October 2014 (Milanovic (2014))

Milanović, M., "Ukraine Derogates from the ICCPR and the ECHR, Files Fourth Interstate Application against Russia", *EJIL:Talk!*, 5 October 2015 (Milanovic (2015))

Milanovic, M., "Belgium's Article 51 Letter to the Security Council", EJIL:Talk!, 17 June 2016 (Milanovic (2016-2))

Moreno-Lax, V., "*Hirsi Jamaa and Others v. Italy* or the Strasbourg Court versus Extraterritorial Migration Control?", *Human Rights Law Review* 12:3(2012), 574-598

Munoz Mosquera, A., and Bachmann, S., "Lawfare in Hybrid Wars: The 21st Century Warfare", in *Journal of International Humanitarian Legal Studies* 7 (2016) 63-87

Muzny, P., "Bayatyan v Armenia: The Grand Chamber Renders a Grand Judgment", *Human Rights Law Review* 12:1(2012), 135-147

NATO Cooperative Cyber Defence Centre of Excellence, *The Cyber Defence Unit of the Estonian Defence League* (2013)

Nowak, M., "The Human Rights Chamber for Bosnia and Herzegovina adopts its First Judgments", *Human Rights Law Review* 18 (1997) pp. 529-45;

Nußberger, A., "The Concept of 'Jurisdiction' in the Jurisprudence of the European Court of Human Rights", [2012] Current Legal Problems 65 p. 241

O'Boyle, M., "The Margin of Appreciation and Derogation under Article 15: Ritual Incantation or Principle?", 19 HRLJ (1998) p. 23 (O'Boyle (1998))

O'Boyle, Michael, "Emergency Government and Derogation under the ECHR", [2016] E.H.R.L.R. p. 331 (O'Boyle (2016))

Paige, T., "The Impact and Effectiveness of UNCLOS on Counter-piracy Operations", in *Journal of Conflict & Security Law* (2017), Vol. 22 No. 1, pp. 97-123

Papua Heritage Foundation, *Head Hunting on the South Coast*, http://www.papuaerfgoed.org/en/Head_Hunting_on_the_South_Coast (translated from the Dutch) (retrieved on 3 April 2016)

Pastre-Belda, B., « L'interprétation surprenante de l'article 5 à la lumière du droit international humanitaire », *La semaine juridique* 2014, page 1796

Peters, A., *Surveillance without Borders: The Unlawfulness of the NSA Panopticon, Part II*, *EJIL:Talk!*, 4 November 2013 (Peters 2013)

Peters, A., "The Turkish Operation in Afrin (Syria) and the Silence of the Lambs", *EJIL:Talk!*, 30 January 2018 (Peters 2018)

Piedimonte Bodini, S., *Fighting Maritime Piracy under the European Convention on Human Rights*, *EJIL* (2011), Vol. 22 No. 3, 829-848

Rooney, J.M., "Extraterritorial derogation from the European Convention on Human Rights in the United Kingdom", E.H.R.L.R. 2016, 6, pp. 656-663

Rossi d'Ambrosio, D., *Hassan v. the United Kingdom*, 23 European Human Rights Advocacy Centre Bulletin (Summer 2015) p. 4

Ryniker, A., 'The ICRC's position on "humanitarian intervention', *International Review of the Red Cross*, June 2001, vol. 83, no. 842, pp. 527-532

Sari, A., "Untangling Extra-Territorial Jurisdiction from International Responsibility in *Jaloud v. the Netherlands*: Old Problem, New Solutions?" in *Military Law and the Law of War Review* 53/2 (2014) pp. 287-316

Sassòli, M., "The Role of Human Rights and International Humanitarian Law in New Types of Armed Conflicts", in Orna Ben-Naftali (ed.), *International Humanitarian Law and International Human Rights Law: Pas de Deux*, Collected Courses of the Academy of European Law vol. XIX/1, Oxford University Press 2011, pp. 34-94

Sayapin, S., "Russia's Withdrawal of Signature from the Rome Statute Would not Shield its Nationals from Potential Prosecution at the ICC", *EJIL:Talk!*, 21 November 2016

Scheinin, M., "Extraterritorial effect of the International Covenant on Civil and Political Rights", in *Extraterritorial Application of Human Rights Treaties* (Fons Coomans and Menno T. Kamminga, eds.), p. 73 *et seq.*

Schmitt, M., "International Law and Military Operations in Space", in *Max Planck Yearbook of United Nations Law*, Volume 10, 2006 (A. von Bogdandy and R. Wolfrum, eds.), pp. 89-125 (Schmitt (2006))

Schmitt, M., "The Use of Cyber Fore and International Law", in *The Oxford Handbook of the Use of Force in International Law* (Mark Weller, ed.), Oxford University Press 2015, p. 1110 (Schmitt (2015))

Sicilianos, L.-A., "The European Court of Human Rights at a time of crisis in Europe", SEDI/ESIL Lecture, European Court of Human Rights, 16 October 2015 (Sicilianos (2015))

Sicilianos, L.-A., "La Cour européenne des droits de l'homme et le droit international humanitaire : une ouverture progressive", in *Human Rights in a Global World: Essays in Honour of Judge Luis López Guerra* (Guido Raimondi, Iulia Motoc, Pere Pastor Vilanova, Carmen Morte Gómez, eds.; Wolf Legal Publishers, 2018), pp. 373-386 (Sicilianos (2018))

Simma, B., "NATO, the UN and the Use of Force: Legal Aspects", in *EJIL* 10 (1999), 1-22

Simor, J., "Tackling human rights abuses in Bosnia and Herzegovina: the Convention is up to it, are its institutions?", *E.H.R.L.R.* 1997, 6, 644-662

Sloot, B. van der, "Is All Fair in Love and War? An Analysis of the Case Law on Article 15 ECHR", in *Military Law and the law of War Review* 53/2 (2014), pp. 319-358

Sperotto, F., "Beyond Bankovic: Extraterritorial Application of the European Convention on Human Rights", *Human Rights & Human Welfare*, working paper no. 38, 13 November 2006;

Todeschini, V., 'The ICCPR in Armed Conflict: An Appraisal of the `Human Rights Committee's Engagement with International Humanitarian Law', in *Nordic Journal of Human Rights* (2017 Vol. 35, Issue 3

Tomuschat, C., "Human Rights and International Humanitarian Law", *EJIL* (2010), Vol. 21 No. 1 15-23

Treves,T., and Pitea, C., "Piracy, International Law and Human Rights", in *The Frontiers of Human Rights: Extraterritoriality and its Challenges, Collected Courses of the Academy of European Law*, vol. XXIV/1, pp. 89-126

Tugendhat, T., and Croft, L., *The Fog of Law: An introduction to the legal erosion of British fighting power*, Policy Exchange, 2013, www.policyexchange.org.uk

Tugendhat, T., "Human rights lawyers now present a real threat to British troops at war", *The Telegraph*, 19 September 2016, http://www.telegraph.co.uk/news/2016/09/19/ human-rights-lawyers-now-present-a-real-threat-to-british-troops/

Twomey, M., "Muddying the waters of maritime piracy or developing the customary law of piracy? Somali piracy and Seychelles", (2014) 20 *CLJP/JDCP* pp. 137 *et seq.*

Evangelia Vasalou, "Les rapports normatifs entre le droit international humanitaire et la Convention europeenne des droits de l'homme : Le droit international humanitaire, une lex specialis par rapport a la Convention europeenne des droits de l'homme ?", *Revue trimestrielle des droits de l'homme* (112/2017), pp. 953-987

Verhoeven, S., "International and non-international armed conflicts", in *Armed Conflicts and the Law*, Jan Wouters, Philip De Man, Nele Verlinden (eds.), Intersentia, 2016, pp. 151-185

Wilson, E., "Hard Power, Soft Power, Smart Power" in *The Annals of the American Academy of Political and Social Science* 2008; 616; p. 110-24

Yaeger, J., "The Human Rights Chamber for Bosnia and Herzegovina: A Case Study in Transitional Justice", 14 *International Legal Perspectives* (Spring 2004)

Zimnitskaya, H., and von Geldern, J., "Is the Caspian Sea a sea; and why does it matter?", *Journal of Eurasian Studies* 2 (2011) 1-14

## Domestic legislation

### France

Loi n° 99-882 du 18 octobre 1999 relative à la substitution, à l'expression « aux opérations effectuées en Afrique du Nord », de l'expression « à la guerre d'Algérie ou aux combats en Tunisie et au Maroc », *Journal officiel* n° 244, 20 October 1999

Loi n° 55-385 du 3 avril 1955 pour la déclaration de l'état d'urgence (Law No. 55-385 of 3 April 1955 on the state of emergency), *Journal officiel* n° 85, 7 April 1955

### Iraq

Coalition provisional authority order number 17 (revised), 27 June 2004

### Kosovo

UNMIK Regulation 1999/1
UNMIK Regulation 1999/24
Constitution of Kosovo
Kosovo Law No. 05/L-53 on the Specialist Chambers and Specialist Prosecutor's Office

### Netherlands

Criminal Code (*Wetboek van Strafrecht*): Articles 138ab, 138b, 317 para. 2 and 351
International Crimes Act (*Wet internationale misdrijven*) Section 5(2)(c)(2°) and (3°) and 5(5)(d)

### Saarland

Constitution of Saarland of 15 December 1947, Preamble

### Turkey

Law no. 6344 of 29 June 2011, Approval of the Treaty of New York of 21 September 2011 between the Republic of Turkey and the Turkish Republic of Northern Cyprus on the delimitation of the continental shelf, Turkish Official Gazette, 12 July 2012, no. 28351

## REFERENCES

### 'Turkish Republic of Northern Cyprus' ('TRNC')

Law no. 67/2005 for the compensation, exchange and restitution of immovable properties which are within the scope of sub-paragraph (b) of paragraph 1 of Article 159 of the Constitution, as amended by Laws nos. 59/2006 and 85/2007

### United Kingdom

Human Rights Act 1998

## Domestic governmental documents other than case-law or legislation

### Bosnia and Herzegovina

Commission for Real Property Claims of Displaced Persons and Refugees and United Nations High Commissioner for Refugees, *Return, Local Integration and Property Rights*, Sarajevo, November 1999

### Greece

"Territorial sea – Casus belli", web site of the Ministry of Foreign Affairs of the Hellenic Republic, http://www.mfa.gr/en/issues-of-greek-turkish-relations/relevant-documents/territorial-sea-casus-belli.html (accessed on 6 October 2015)

### Kosovo

Human Rights Advisory Panel, Annual Report 2015-16
Human Rights Review Panel, Annual Report 2016

### Netherlands

#### Parliament

Lower House of Parliament (*Tweede Kamer der Staten-Generaal*), Parliamentary Year 2015-16, appendix to the parliamentary proceedings, no. 2640, question by the member of Parliament Ms. S. Belhaj to the Minister of Defence (submitted on 3 May 2016) and the Minister's reply (received on 26 May 2016)

## Openbaar ministerie (public prosecution service)

*Vijf Somaliërs wegens zeeroof vervolgd*, press release 5 December 2010, https://www.om.nl/actueel/nieuwsberichten/@28465/vijf-somaliers/ (accessed 23 April 2017)

## Ministry of Defence

Press release 8 December 2010 (in English), *The Netherlands picks up 5 Somalis*, https://www.defensie.nl/english/latest/news/2010/12/08/the-netherlands-picks-up-5-somalis (accessed 23 April 2017)

*De Britse reactie op claims van mensenrechtenschendingen door Britse militairen gedurende de militaire aanwezigheid in Irak: een analyse van het Iraq Historic Allegations Team* (The British reaction to claims of human rghts violations by British military personnel during the military presence in Iraq: an analysis of the Iraq Historic Allegations Team), published by the Dutch Ministry of Defence on 28 August 2017, last updated on 19 March 2018, http://puc.overheid.nl/doc/PUC_88361_11 (accessed on 4 September 2018)

## Adviesraad internationale vraagstukken (Advisory Council on International Affairs, "AIV")

*De inhuur van private militaire bedrijven, een kwestie van verantwoordelijkheid* (Employing private military companies, a question of responsibility), no. 59, December 2007

*Piraterijbestrijding op zee: een herijking van publieke en private verantwoordelijkheden* (Combating piracy at sea: a reassessment of public and private responsibilities), no. 72, January 2010

*Nederland en de 'Responsibility to protect': De verantwoordelijkheid om mensen te beschermen tegen massale wreedheden* (The Netherlands and the Responsibility to Protect: The responsibility to protect people from mass atrocities), no. 70, June 2010

*Digitale oorlogvoering* (Cyber Warfare), no. 77, December 2011

*Azië in opmars: Strategische betekenis en gevolgen* (Asia on the rise: Strategic significance and implications), no. 86, December 2013

## Commissie van onderzoek besluitvorming Irak (Committee to Investigate Decision-Making concerning Iraq)

*Rapport Commissie van onderzoek besluitvorming Irak* (Report of the Committee to Investigate Decision-Making concerning Iraq), Uitgeverij Boom 2010

## Turkey

"The Breadth of Territorial Waters", website of the Ministry of Foreign Affairs of the Republic of Turkey, http://www.mfa.gov.tr/the-breadth-of-territorial-waters.en.mfa (accessed on 6 October 2015)

# REFERENCES

"The Delimitation of the Aegean Continental Shelf", and http://www.mfa.gov.tr/the-delimitation-of-the-aegean-continental-shelf.en.mfa (accessed on 6 October 2015)

## *United Kingdom*

Joint Parliamentary Committee on Human Rights, Second Report of the Session 2001-02, and Sixth Report of the Session 2003-04

Privy Councillor Review Committee, Anti-terrorism, Crime and Security Act 2001 Review, Ordered by The House of Commons to be printed 18th December 2003

Memorandum Of Understanding Between The United Kingdom Of Great Britain And Northern Ireland Contingent Of Multinational Forces-Iraq And The Ministries Of Justice And Interior Of Iraq Regarding Criminal Suspects, published by the House of Commons Foreign Affairs Committee with evidence taken jointly with the Defence Committee on Iraq and Afghanistan on 28 October 2008, HC (2007-08) 1145-I

Statement by the United Kingdom Government, quoted by the House of Commons Foreign Affairs Committee, Human Rights Annual Report for 2008 (Seventh Report of Session 2008-09)

House of Commons Foreign Affairs Committee, Human Rights Annual Report for 2008, sent for printing on 21 July 2009 and published on 9 August 2009

UK Armed Forces Personnel and the Legal Framework For Future Operations, Written Evidence from Dr Aurel Sari, Lecturer in Law University of Exeter, submitted to the House of Commons (Session 2013-2014)

House of Lords, Select Committee on Soft Power and the UK's Influence – First Report: Persuasion and Power in the Modern World, ordered by the House of Lords to be printed on 11 March 2014

Report of the Iraq Inquiry ("Chilcot Report"), 6 July 2016, Executive Summary

House of Lords and House of Commons, Joint Committee on Human Rights, *The Government's policy on the use of drones for targeted killing*, Second Report of Session 2015–16

The Litvinenko Inquiry: Report into the death of Alexander Litvinenko, presented to the House of Commons on 21 January 2016 (HC 695), and Statement by the Chairman

*Syria action – UK government legal position*, policy paper published on 14 April 2018

Iraq Historic Allegations Team, https://www.gov.uk/government/groups/iraq-historic-allegations-team-ihat (accessed 4 September 2018)

## United States of America

US Government, National Commission on Terrorist Attacks Upon the United States, *The 9/11 Commission Report*, http://govinfo.library.unt.edu/911/report/911Report.pdf (accessed 28 July 2015

## Educational and non-governmental bodies

### Amnesty International

"Bosnia-Herzegovina: Ashdown's proposal to abolish Human Rights Chamber leaves citizens unprotected", press release, 12 June 2003

### International Code of Conduct Association

International Code of Conduct for Private Security Service Providers, 9 November 2010, https://icoca.ch/en (English) (accessed on 26 March 2017)

### International Committee of the Red Cross (ICRC)

International Committee of the Red Cross, Convention (IV) relative to the Protection of Civilian Persons in Time of War. Geneva, 12 August 1949, Commentary of 1958

International Committee of the Red Cross, Convention (III) relative to the Treatment of Prisoners of War. Geneva, 12 August 1949, Commentary of 1960

*How is the Term "Armed Conflict" Defined in International Humanitarian Law?*, Opinion Paper, March 2008

Montreux Document on pertinent internatarkional legal obligations and good practices for States related to operations of private military and security companies during armed conflict (with the Swiss Federal Department of Foreign Affairs) August 2009

IHL Database, https://ihl-databases.icrc.org/customary-ihl/eng/docs/home (accessed on 5 September 2018)

International Committee of the Red Cross, Convention (I) for the Amelioration of the Condition of the Wounded and Sick in Armed Forces in the Field, Commentary of 2016

Statutes of the International Committee of the Red Cross, adopted on 21 December 2017, in force 1 January 2018

### Durham University

IBRU Centre for Borders Research, Durham University, Maritime jurisdiction and boundaries in the Arctic region, https://www.dur.ac.uk/resources/ibru/resources/Arcticmap04-08-15.pdf (accessed on 3 September 2016)

### London Metropolitan University

*International Human Rights and Fact-Finding – An analysis of the fact-finding missions conducted by the European Commission and Court of Human Rights*, Philip Leach, Costas Paraskeva & Gordana Uzelac, Human Rights & Social Justice Research Institute, London Metropolitan University, February 2009

### Drone Wars UK

"Fallon to face questions on drone targeted killing – but will there be answers?", 14 December 2015, https://dronewars.net/2015/12/14/fallon-to-face-questions-on-drone-targeted-killing-but-will-there-be-answers/ (retrieved on 9 March 2016)

### Press items

Jewish Telegraphic Agency, 25 January 1956, http://www.jta.org/1956/01/25/archive/new-supreme-restitution-court-starts-functioning-in-germany (retrieved 12 April 2017).

*The Daily Telegraph*, 1 September 2014, "British jihadists to be forced to attend deradicalisation programmes, says Cameron", http://www.telegraph.co.uk/news/uknews/terrorism-in-the-uk/11068878/British-jihadists-to-be-forced-to-attend-deradicalisation-programmes-says-Cameron.html (accessed 26 August 2017)

*The Sun*, "European Court of Killers' Rights; EXCLUSIVE: Third of cases won by terrorists, murderers and lags", 17 August 2015, updated 5 April 2016, https://www.thesun.co.uk/archives/politics/204465/european-court-of-killers-rights/ (retrieved 20 April 2017)

BBC, "Islamic State conflict: Two Britons killed in RAF Syria strike", 7 September 2015, http://www.bbc.com/news/uk-34178998 (accessed on 3 September 2017)

*De Volkskrant*, http://www.volkskrant.nl/buitenland/somali-victims-of-us-drone-strike-take-legal-action-against-the-netherlands~a4196845/ (English), http://www.volkskrant.nl/buitenland/somalische-droneslachtoffers-klagen-nederlandse-staat-aan~a4196859/ (Dutch), 28 November 2015 (accessed 3 September 2017)

RTL Nieuws, "Somalische slachtoffers drone-aanval klagen Nederland aan", https://www.youtube.com/watch?v=CMmu5mPNGic, 28 November 2015 (accessed 3 September 2017)

TASS, "Kremlin does not perceive Litvinenko death investigation results as verdict", 21 January 2016, quoting an official spokesperson of the Russian Foreign Ministry; http://tass.com/politics/851376, accessed on 3 September 2016

*Tirana Times*, "Albania wants Greece to repeal state of war", 19 February 2016

Radio Canada International, "Canada to submit its Arctic continental shelf claim in 2018", 3 May 2016, http://www.rcinet.ca/en/2016/05/03/canada-to-submit-its-arctic-continental-shelf-claim-in-2018/ (accessed on 3 September 2016)

BBC News, "NHS cyber-attack: GPs and hospitals hit by ransomware", 13 May 2017, http://www.bbc.com/news/health-39899646 (accessed 28 May 2017)

Brenner, B., "Experts doubt Russian government launched DDoS attacks", 18 May 2017, http://searchsecurity.techtarget.com/news/1255548/Experts-doubt-Russian-government-launched-DDoS-attacks (accessed 28 May 2017)

The Independent, "'Petya' cyber attack: Chernobyl's radiation monitoring system hit by worldwide hack', 27 June 2017, http://www.independent.co.uk/news/world/europe/chernobyl-ukraine-petya-cyber-attack-hack-nuclear-power-plant-danger-latest-a7810941.html (accessed 25 August 2017)

CNN, 'Chernobyl monitoring system hit by global cyber attack', 28 June 2017 http://edition.cnn.com/2017/06/27/europe/chernobyl-cyber-attack/index.html (accessed 25 August 2017)

International Business Times, 'Petya ransomware: What were the hackers' motives and how much money have they raked in so far?', 29 June 2017, http://www.ibtimes.co.uk/petya-ransomware-what-were-hackers-motives-how-much-money-have-they-raked-so-far-1628223 (accessed 25 August 2017)

BBC News, "Blackwater incident: what happened", 8 December 2008, http://news.bbc.co.uk/2/hi/7033332.stm, (accessed 17 April 2017)

CBS News, "Blackwater guards found guilty in Baghdad mass shootings", 23 October 2014, http://www.cbsnews.com/news/blackwater-case-former-guards-convicted-in-baghdad-mass-shootings (accessed 17 April 2017)

*The New York Times*, "Ex-Blackwater Guards Given Long Terms for Killing Iraqis", 13 April 2015, https://www.nytimes.com/2015/04/14/us/ex-blackwater-guards-sentenced-to-prison-in-2007-killings-of-iraqi-civilians.html (accessed 17 April 2017)

*Balkan Insight*, 22 March 2016, http://www.balkaninsight.com/en/article/albania-and-greece-agree-to-abolish-the-war-law-03-22-2016 (retrieved 6 November 2016)

Gov.uk, "Government to protect Armed Forces from persistent legal claims in future overseas operations", 4 October 2016, https://www.gov.uk/government/news/government-to-protect-armed-forces-from-persistent-legal-claims-in-future-overseas-operations (accessed 29 August 2018)

# Index

9/11 attack (New York and Washington D.C., 2001)   7-8, 89, 90, 91, 103, 105, 106
Abbott, Kirby   12-13
abduction   137
Abkhazia   90
abortion   157
access to court (Article 6 § 1)   218-19, 300,
Action Directe   195
Aden Colony   152
Aden, Gulf of   199, 224
*ad hoc* domestic tribunal   177
administrative detention   94, 96, 102, 138
Aegean Sea   156
African Charter of Human and Peoples' Rights   11
Afghanistan   8, 29, 75, 80, 91, 196, 197, 198, 199, 263, 279, 280
African Charter on Human and People's Rights   11, 38, 123
Afrin (Syria)
   Turkish military operation   7, 146
aggression   74, 85, 87, 187
aggressor states   85-87
Agreement Governing Activities of States on the Moon and Other Celestial Bodies (Moon Treaty), 18 December 1979   161
Ahtisaari, Martti   334 (fn. 1123)
aircraft   12, 70, 158, 162, 166, 169, 172, 195, 204, 239, 245-246, 252, 274, 287, 289
   attack   69, 211, 213, 217, 293, 295, 345
   criminal jurisdiction   169-70
   hijack   195
   military   12, 70, 171, 211, 213, 217
   nationality of   162, 166, 169, 172, 252, 345
   rendition   201, 274, 293
   State –   170
   unmanned remotely piloted (drone) *see* drone
air force
   Argentinian   70
   United Kingdom (Royal Air Force)   226
airspace   160, 201, 274, 345
AIV (*Adviesraad internationale vraagstukken*, Advisory Council on International Affairs)   9 (fn. 35), 232

(fn. 803), 279 (fn. 935), 280 (fn. 936), 281, 284 (fn. 953)
Ajaria (Georgia)   186
al-Qaeda   7, 8, 91, 112, 114, 196, 199, 226, 299
Alderney   152
Algeria   78, 81, 176, 198
   see also *Guerre d'Algérie*
aliens   175, 179, 181, 212, 346
   civilians   135
   protected persons   135
   who owe allegiance to the enemy   134
Allied Powers (post-World War II occupation of Germany)   206-07, 260
Althea, Operation   322
American Convention on Human Rights   38, 123,133
*amicus/amici curiae*   121, 329
amnesty   61, 62, 76, 100, 132
Amnesty International   121, 328
Angola   81
Anguilla   53
Annan, Kofi   314
Annan plan (Cyprus)   314
ANSSI (*Agence nationale de la sécurité des systèmes d'information*, France)   285
Antarctica   154
Antarctic Treaty, 1 December 1959   154
archipelagic waters   158
Arctic   159
armed conflict   4, 10, 11, 42, 50, 69, 72, 73, 74, 77, 83
armed conflict, law of *see* International humanitarian law
Armenia, support for 'Republic of Nagorno-Karabakh'   210-11
armistice agreement   33, 178, 323, 336
   *see also* General Framework Agreement for Peace in Bosnia and Herzegovina
arrest *see* liberty and security, right to (Article 5 of the Convention)
artillery   190
Aruba   152
assembly, freedom of *see* freedom of assembly

398 INDEX

Assize Court (Turkey)  116
asylum  165, 171, 199, 229
Atalanta, Operation  303
attack, definition (Article 49 § 1 of Additional
    Protocol I (1977))  234
Attack on foreign territory  181
attribution
    distinct from jurisdiction  267-269
    implementation of Security Council
        resolutions  292-303
    of acts committed by foreign agents  274-
        276
    of acts committed by private agents  278-
        79, 281, 335, 351
    of acts committed by private military
        security contractors  279-84, 285,
        335, 351
    of cyber-attacks  284-287
    to Netherlands (Iraq)  274
    to Russian Federation
        (Transdniestria)  269-271
    to Turkey (Northern Cyprus)  269
    to United Kingdom (Iraq)  272-273
    to United Nations (Kosovo)  273
Axis (World War II)  129
Azores  153

Ba'ath party (Iraq)  52
Bahamas  152
Balearic Islands  153
Baltic Sea  156
Baltic States  247
banditry  73
Barbados  152
baseline  156, 158
Basutoland (now Lesotho)  152
Bechuanaland (now Botswana)  152
Belgian Congo  152
belligerent occupation see occupation
Berlin, post-World War II occupation  206-
    207
Bermuda  152, 153
Beslan school massacre  185
Bianku, Ledi, Judge of the Court  55
Bildt, Carl  330
Bin Laden, Osama  299
bird flu  90
bitcoin  231
Black Sea  156

Black September  195
black site  27 (fn. 86), 199, 202
    see also rendition
bomb attack
    aerial  68-69, 185, 211, 216, 217, 293, 320
    EOKA  92
    Lockerbie  177
    mainland United Kingdom  112, 120
    Northern Ireland  101
Bonaire  152 (fn. 530)
Borelli, Silvia  59
Borneo, British North  80, 152
Bosnia and Herzegovina  75
    application of Convention and Protocols
        as primary source of law  34
    constituent peoples  323-325
    Convention-based legal order  336
    Republic of  320-22
    the State  320, 321, 322, 326, 327, 328
    war 1992-1995  7, 32
botnets  285, 287
boycotts  10
Bratza, Sir Nicolas, judge of the Court  263
Bremer, L. Paul – III  238, 280
Brigate Rosse see Red Brigades
British Antarctic Territory  153
British Empire  151
British Guiana (now Guyana)  152
British Indian Ocean Territory  152
British Honduras (now Belize)  152
British India  3
British Solomon Islands (now Solomon
    Islands)  152
British Virgin Islands  153
buffer zone (Cyprus)  209, 222, 223, 225, 296,
    308, 351

Cambodia  166-68
Canada  12, 160, 173, 174, 320
Canary Islands  153
cannibalism  151
canon law  41
Caspian Sea  155, 156
Cassin, René  39
casualty, casualties  185 (fn. 665), 212, 253,
    280
casus belli  74, 156 (fn. 540)
Caucasus, Northern (Russian)  7, 18, 68, 185

INDEX 399

cause-and-effect model of extraterritorial jurisdiction 181, 213, 214 (fn. 746), 221, 227, 234, 244, 253, 346, 347, 349
Cayman Islands 153
ceasefire 187, 188, 190, 210, 224
censorship 97, 138
Central African Republic 176
Chagos Islands 153
Channel Islands 152
Chapter VI (United Nations Charter) 82
Chapter VII (United Nations Charter) 4, 60, 82, 84, 85, 86, 88, 106, 139, 144, 223, 289, 294, 295, 296, 299, 302, 303, 306, 321, 322, 332, 342, 351
Chapter VIII (United Nations Charter) 86, 88
Chapter XII (United Nations Charter) 150
Chechen Republic (Chechnya) (Russian Federation) 7 (fn. 26), 77, 185
Chechen separatists 7, 185
Chechen War, First 7 (fn. 26), 77
Chechen War, Second 7 (fn. 26)
checkpoint 225, 244, 245
chemical weapon 61
Chernishova, Olga 22
Chernobyl nuclear power plant 232, 233,
Chicago Convention see Convention on International Civil Aviation
Chilcot Report (Report of the Iraq Inquiry, United Kingdom) 86-87
children
    right to protection 27
CIA (Central Intelligence Agency, USA) 27, 29, 30, 180, 196, 197, 198, 199, 201, 202, 274, 275, 276
CIC South (Commander in Chief of Allied Forces Southern Europe) 294
civic obligations 128
civil proceedings 24, 192, 218, 228
Civil War
    American 39
    Spanish 39
clandestine murder 229-231, 252, 338, 348
classified information 101, 199-200, 229, 307
    see also secret information
cluster bomb units 293-294
Coalition of the Willing 235

Coalition Provisional Authority (Iraq) 235, 238, 241, 244, 249, 260, 272-73, 280, 298, 351
collective punishment 94-95
conflicting international obligations 258
    ius cogens 258
    prior treaty obligation 260, 263, 349-50
    subsequent treaty obligation 260-263, 265, 350
colonial clause (Article 56, former Article 63) 92, 150-155, 265, 345
    effect of not making declaration 265
    interpretation a contrario 155, 345
    jurisdiction over overseas territory in absence of declaration 154
    separate for Protocols 153-54
Colonial Office (United Kingdom) 151
colonial wars 78, 80, 81
collateral damage 212, 253
combatant 50, 123, 125
    enemy 51, 52, 342
    status 145
Commission for Real Property Claims (Bosnia and Herzegovina) 33
Commission on Human Rights (Bosnia and Herzegovina) 33, 34, 326
Committee Established to Review the NATO Bombing Campaign Againstthe Federal Republic of Yugoslavia (reporting to ICTY Prosecutor) 211-12
Committee on the Administration of Justice 100, 121
Commonwealth of Independent States (CIS) 187
Communist, Communists 77, 93, 97, 129
compensation 32, 307, 312, 313, 315, 318,
    claim for 35, 219, 312, 316, 319
    enforceable right to (Article 5 § 5) 31
    right to 219, 261
Congo, Belgian see Belgian Congo
conscience, freedom of see freedom of thought, conscience and religion
conscientious objections/objectors 127-28, 132
Constitutional Court
    Bosnia and Herzegovina 33-34, 178, 322, 323, 324, 328,
    Croatia 61
    Kosovo 334

Russian Federation 7, 77
Serbia 192
Turkey 115, 116
contiguous zone 157-158
Italy 164
continental shelf 158
Denmark (Greenland) 159-60
Norway 159
Russia 159-60
*contras* (Nicaragua) 277-278
Convention against Illicit Traffic in Narcotic
Drugs and Psychotropic Substances, 20
December 1988 168
Convention against Torture and Other Cruel,
Inhuman or Degrading Treatment or
Punishment 26, 62, 130, 148, 333
Convention on Elimination of All Forms of
Discrimination Against Women, 17
December 1979 333
Convention on the Elimination of All Forms
of Racial Discrimination, 21 December
1965 333
Convention for the Suppression of Unlawful
Acts Against the Safety of Civil
Aviation (Montreal Convention), 23
September 1971 169-170
Convention legal space (*espace
juridique*) 15, 55, 56, 215, 237, 241, 249,
267, 348
Convention on Cybercrime (Budapest
Convention), 23 November 2001 286
Convention on International Civil Aviation
(Chicago Convention), 7 December
1944 160, 169, 170
Convention on Offences and Certain other
Acts Committed On Board Aircraft
(Tokyo Convention), 14 September
1963 169
Convention on the Law of the Sea (UNCLOS),
10 December 1982 155-160, 162-63, 167,
168, 223, 345
Convention on the Prevention and
Punishment of the Crime of Genocide,
9 December 1948 62, 130, 326
Convention on the Privileges and Immunities
of the United Nations, 13 February
1946 280, 306 (fn. 1038), 328,

Convention to Suppress the Slave Trade
and Slavery (Slavery Convention), 25
September 1926 127
Co-Princes (Andorra) 177
corporal punishment 94
correspondence, respect for *see* respect for
correspondence
Costa Rica 171
Council of Europe 15, 33, 43, 114, 130, 150,
192, 241, 254, 276, 288, 291, 306, 311, 315,
327, 344, 352
Commissioner for Human Rights 108,
201
Committee of Ministers 98, 187, 207
Deputy Secretary General 315
Parliamentary Assembly 178, 196, 197,
306, 307, 311, 334
Secretary General 66, 67, 92, 95, 96, 97,
99, 105, 114, 142, 150, 315
Statute of 1, 288
Steering Committee for Human
Rights 14
*coup d'état* 90, 98, 114-16, 122, 141, 142, 143
Court of Appeal
England 109, 236, 264
Netherlands 242-43
Court of Cassation (Italy) 217-19, 244
Court of Justice of the European
Communities 300, 303
Court of Justice of the European Union 174
(fn. 618)
Covert use of force 8, 9, 79
CPA *see* Coalition Provisional Authority (Iraq)
Crimea 74, 90, 145
crimes against humanity 74, 84, 85, 128, 129-
130, 178, 260
criminal armed groups 8
Croft, Laura 144
Crown Colony (United Kingdom) 89, 91, 153
Curaçao 152
curfews 94, 138
customary international law 140, 243
abolition of the death penalty 131
Articles on State Responsibility for
Internationally Wrongful
Acts 268
exhaustion of domestic remedies 316
implied non-derogable rights 137
immunity of State aircraft 170

INDEX 401

international humanitarian law  5
law of the sea  168, 345
cyber-attack  79, 118, 231-235, 284-287, 338, 348
  attribution  284-287
  definition  233
  DDoS (distributed denial-of-service)  231
  disguised identity  285-86
  malware  232
  ransomware  231-232, 286
  using botnets *see* botnets
  using zombies *see* zombies
Cyber Defence Unit (Estonia)  285
Cyprus (British Crown Colony)  89, 91, 152
Cyprus, Northern 4, 31, 32, 191, 194, 203, 205,
    207, 208, 209, 212, 215, 231, 247, 250, 252,
    255, 308, 311, 312, 316, 317,
  buffer zone  222-223
  *see also* 'Turkish Republic of Northern
    Cyprus'
Czech, Philip  59

Dagestan (Russian Federation)  185
Darfur  85
DARIO *see* Draft Articles on the
    Responsibility of International
    Organizations
Dayton Peace Agreement *see* General
    Framework Agreement on Peace in
    Bosnia and Herzegovina
Daesh *see* Deash [sic]
Deash [sic] (also Daesh; Islamic State)  146
Dar es Salaam, attack on US embassy
    (1998)  199
death penalty  19, 123, 235, 261, 263, 264
  abolition *de facto*  131
  prohibition (Protocols Nos. 6 and
    13)  130-132
  sentence  202
declaration of war  70, 71, 91, 341
  Greek declaration of war on Albania
    (1940)  70
Defence Cyber Command (Royal Army,
    Netherlands)  285
De Koker, Cedric  58
democracy  3, 65, 119
deportation  92, 94, 106-111, 129, 137, 179, 180,
    181, 212, 318, 346
  *see also* expulsion

deradicalisation (of jihadist fighters)  30-31
derogation  65-146
  Albania  70, 89
  Armenia  131
  France  78, 81, 90, 109, 111, 141, 144, 145
  Georgia  90
  Turkey  75, 89, 90, 104, 105, 114, 115-116, 118,
    141, 142, 145, 146
  Ukraine, 5 June 2015  74
  United Kingdom
detention
  administrative *see* administrative
    detention
  incommunicado *see* incommunicado
    detention
  unacknowledged *see* unacknowledged
    detention
  *see also* Liberty and security, right to
    (Article 5 of the Convention)
diplomatic or consular activity  175-76
diplomatic assurances  198, 261, 263-64
disappearance without trace  29
displaced persons
  Bosnia and Herzegovina  33, 329
  former Socialist Federative Republic of
    Yugoslavia  32
  Nagorno-Karabakh  190, 210
  Northern Cyprus  205, 209, 312,
displacement of populations  137
discrimination
  Article 14  133
  Article 1 of Protocol No. 12  133
  between States Parties  186
  freedom from (non-derogable
    nature)  132-134
  in Annex 6 to the Dayton Peace
    Agreement  326
  incitement to  137
  notion of  134
  objective and reasonable
    justification  134
Dominica  152
'Donetsk People's Republic'  6
Draft Articles on the Responsibility
    of International Organizations
    (DARIO)  287, 292, 294, 304, 305, 306
drone attack  126, 226-229, 338, 348
dual use target  211
Dubrovka theatre attack  7 (fn. 27), 185

Duffy, Helen 47

Eastern Ukraine 145
  see also 'Donetsk People's Republic' and
    'Luhansk People's Republic'
economic collapse 145
economic crisis 118, 140
economic sanctions 10, 289-90, 299-302, 306
effective control of foreign State or non-state
    actor 190, 191, 215, 310
effective enquiry 21-24
effective remedy, right to (Article 13 of the
    Convention) 34-35, 132, 338
EGNOS see European Geostationary
    Navigation Overlay Service
Egypt 199
election, right to vote and stand for (Article 3
    of Protocol No. 1) 205
Ellice Islands (now Tuvalu) 152
emergency powers 10, 65
emigration, uncontrollable 118
environmental disaster 145
EOKA (*Εθνική Οργάνωσις Κυπρίων Αγωνιστών*,
    National Organisation of Cypriot
    Struggle, 1954-59) 89, 91-93
epidemic 118
Erdoğan, Recep Tayyip (President of
    Turkey) 122
ESA see European Space Agency
*espace juridique* see Convention legal space
Estonian Defence League 285
estoppel 110, 237
ethnic cleansing 32, 84, 85, 325, 329
EUFOR (European Union force) 322
EUNAVFOR 303
European Commission 231, 290, 320,
European Commission for Democracy
    through Law (Venice
    Commission) 65, 117, 328, 329, 333
European Commission of Human Rights
  right of individual petition 254
  Secretariat 327
  Secretary 315
European Court of Human Rights
  court of law 37, 57, 140, 339, 353
  President 178, 323, 334
  Registry 327
  supervisory role of 1
  Vice-President 4

European Economic Community
    (EEC) 289, 291
European Geostationary Navigation Overlay
    Service (EGNOS) 174
EULEX (European Rule of Law Mission in
    Kosovo) 307
European Space Agency (ESA) 173-174, 289
European Union
  accession to Convention 174, 333
  armed presence in Bosnia and
    Herzegovina 2004-present
    (EUFOR) 322
  attribution to 303
  Convention on the law of the Sea 155
  Kosovo 334
  naval force see EUNAVFOR
  Peace Implementation Council 320
  presumption of equivalent
    protection 291
evidentiary principles see proof
exclusive economic zone 157-58, 163-64
  Denmark (Greenland) 159-60
  Norway 159
  Romania 159
  Russia 159-60
  Spain 159
  United Kingdom (South Georgia and
    South Sandwich Islands) 159
exigencies of the situation (Article 15 §
    1) 56, 64, 66, 67, 89, 95, 96, 98, 99, 100,
    104, 109, 113, 116, 119, 134, 137138-139, 257,
    342, 343, 354
*ex iniuria ius non oritur* 85
expression, freedom of see freedom of
    expression
expulsion 25, 179-181
  see also deportation
extradition 179-181, 193-195, 199, 212, 258,
    259, 262, 276, 286, 346,

Fachataller, Tanja 59
fact-finding 200-201, 339
Faeroe Islands 153
fair trial guarantees (Article 6)
  implied non-derogable rights 135-137
Falkland Islands 6, 70, 82, 152, 153
Argentinian allegation of belligerent
    occupation by United Kingdom 6

# INDEX

Fallon, The Rt Hon Sir Michael   2, 227 (fn. 782)
family life, respect for *see* respect for family life
Federation of Bosnia and Herzegovina (Entity of Bosnia and Herzegovina)   320, 321, 323, 326, 328, 336,
female genital mutilation   151
FETÖ/PDY ('Gülenist Terror Organisation/ Parallel State Structure')   115
Fiji   152
firearms   20, 95, 284
First World War *see* World War I
flag state (ships)   162-68, 283-84, 345, 351
Flagrant denial of justice   180, 202
foreign agents   199, 252, 274
foreign judges
    Andorra   177
    Bosnia and Herzegovina   178
    Kosovo   178
    Liechtenstein   178
formalism   141
Franco-Prussian War   39
freedom of assembly (Article 11)   89-90
freedom of expression (Article 10)   115-116, 157
freedom of information (Article 10)   89
freedom of movement (Article 2 of Protocol No. 4)   89-90
freedom of thought, conscience and religion (Article 9)   128, 140
Frumer, Philippe   59
FSB (Federal Security Service, Russian Federation)   229

Galileo (European satellite system)   174
Gambia   152
General Framework Agreement on Peace in Bosnia and Herzegovina   33
    Annex 1-A (Agreement on the Military Aspects of the Peace Settlement)   321
    Annex 4 (Constitution of Bosnia and Herzegovina)   33-34, 178, 322-325,
    Annex 6 (Agreement on Human Rights)   33-34, 198, 319, 322, 325-329
    Annex 7 (Agreement on Refugees and Displaced Persons)   33

Annex 10 (Agreement on Civilian Implementation of the Peace Settlement)   322, 330-331
    as armistice agreement   33, 178, 323, 336
general principles of law   130
    European Economic Community   291
    international law   50, 53
    recognised by civilised nations   128
Geneva Academy (of International Humanitarian Law and Human Rights)   5-7
Geneva Conventions, pre-1929   74
Geneva Conventions (1929)   5, 74
Geneva Conventions (1949)   5, 71, 73, 74
    Common Article 1   43 (fn. 152)
    Common Article 2   71 (fn. 240), 341
    Common Article 3   5, 43 (fn. 152), 62, 71 (fn. 242), 72, 129, 132, 341
    Geneva Convention (I) for the Amelioration of the Condition of the Wounded and Sick in Armed Forces in the Field, 12 August 1949   62
    Geneva Convention (II) for the Amelioration of the Condition of Wounded, Sick and Shipwrecked Members of Armed Forces at Sea, 12 August 1949   62
    Geneva Convention (III) on Prisoners of War, 12 August 1949   28, 30, 52-54, 62, 88
    Geneva Convention (IV) on Civilians, 12 August 1949   28, 30, 51-54, 60, 61, 62, 88
    Protocol Additional to the Geneva Conventions of 12 August 1949, and relating to the Protection of Victims of International Armed Conflicts (Protocol I), 8 June 1977   61
    Protocol Additional to the Geneva Conventions of 12 August 1949, and relating to the Protection of Victims of Non-International Armed Conflicts (Protocol II), 8 June 1977   5, 47, 62, 72, 77
genocide   84, 85, 258, 260
German High Command (*Oberkommando der Wehrmacht*)   206
Germany, 1949-1990

404 INDEX

Allied occupation 206-207
German Democratic Republic 206
Federal Republic of (Western
Germany) 206
Gibraltar 152, 153
Gilbert islands (now Kiribati)
GLONASS 172, 174
GPS (Global Positioning System) 174
*Guerre d'Algérie* 78
Gold Coast (now Ghana) 152
Governing Council of Iraq 238
Grand National Assembly (Turkey) 105, 115
Greek colonels (military dictatorship, 1967-74) 89, 96-98
Greenland 153, 160 (fn. 560)
Greenpeace 158
Grenada 152
Grotius, Hugo 71
Guantánamo Bay (American military base and detention site) 180, 198, 199, 200, 202
Guernsey, Bailiwick of 152
Guinea, Portuguese 81
Gülen, Fetullah 115

*habeas corpus* 28, 31
Hadži-Vidanović, Vidan 298
Hague Conventions (1899 and 1907) 5, 74
Hague Convention (III) relative to the Opening of Hostilities, 18 October 1907 70
Hague Convention (IV) Respecting the Laws and Customs of War on Land, 18 October 1807 43
Hague Regulations on the Laws and Customs of Law on Land 248-251, 336, 348
Haller, Gret 326
Hampson, Françoise 44, 47-48, 63
Happold, Matthew 216
Hard power 1-3, 4, 8-10, 11, 14, 16, 17, 18, 34, 37, 80, 87, 149, 181, 182, 183, 202, 254, 272, 274, 279, 290, 338, 339, 344, 346, 351, 353, 354, 355
head-hunting 151
helicopters 222, 246
Hess, Rudolf 206, 260
hijack (aircraft) 195
High Representative (Bosnia and Herzegovina) 320, 327, 328, 330-32

'Bonn powers' 330-331, 332
Hill-Cawthorne, Lawrence 59
Hitler, Adolf 206
Hoffmann, The Rt Hon. The Lord 109, 112, 120
home, right to respect for *see* respect for home
Hong Kong 81, 153
hostages, taking of 36, 137, 283
House of Commons 82, 102, 125, 226, 228, 229, 263
House of Lords 109-114, 125, 228, 273,
human dignity 25-26, 137
humanitarian intervention 83
Human Rights Advisory Panel (Kosovo) 306-07
Human Rights Chamber for Bosnia and Herzegovina 33, 198, 326-329, 331, 333
Human Rights Committee 46, 119, 137, 220
Human Rights Court for Kosovo (Venice Commission proposal) 333
human rights instrument, particular importance of Convention as 263
human rights obligations of the State, serviceman's duty to comply with 37
Human Rights Review Panel (Kosovo) 307
Human Rights Watch 210, 211
Hungary, 1956 uprising 61, 77, 92, 128
hybrid court 326, 327, 352
hybrid warfare 79

ICTY (International Tribunal for the Prosecution of Persons Responsible for Serious Violations of International Humanitarian Law Committed in the Territory of the Former Yugoslavia since 1991, *also* International Criminal Tribunal for the Former Yugoslavia) 24, 72, 233
Prosecutor 211, 331
IFOR (Implementation Force, Bosnia and Herzegovina) 321-322
IHAT (Iraq Historic Allegations Team, United Kingdom) 22-23
immigration, uncontrollable 118
imminence, requirement of 112, 117
Immovable Property Commission ('Turkish Republic of Northern Cyprus') *see* 'Turkish Republic of Northern Cyprus'

INDEX 405

('TRNC'), Immovable Property Commission

Imperial Persia 156

Imperial Russia 156

*impossibilium nulla obligatio est* (Corpus Iuris Civilis D.50.17.185) 144

incommunicado detention 28-29, 60

incursion into foreign territory 220-223

independent and impartial tribunal
   court martial (United Kingdom) 177
   implied non-derogable right 132

India 3, 25

individual petition, right of
   (Article 34) 132, 151, 152, 154, 204, 254-256, 317
   (former Article 25) 141

information, freedom of *see* freedom of information

Ingushetia (Russian Federation) 185

inhuman or degrading treatment 25, 27, 29, 126, 179, 198, 262, 264,
   distinction from torture 26

INMARSAT 172

innocent passage 157

Inter-American Commission of Human Rights 220

Interights 100, 121

interim measure *see* provisional measure

internal waters 156-157

international armed conflict 5, 6, 10, 11, 14, 18, 28, 30, 42, 48, 51-60, 69, 71, 74-75, 83, 88, 123, 124, 125, 134, 135, 144, 146, 341, 342, 344, 346

International Civilian Representative (Kosovo) 334

International Committee for Human Rights 329

International Committee of the Red Cross 43, 73, 281

International Conference on Human Rights 43

International Convention for the Safety of Life at Sea (SOLAS) 162

International Convention on the Rights of the Child, 20 December 1989 333

International Court of Justice 11, 40-41, 44-46, 53-54, 58, 88, 233, 271, 277, 278, 312, 317, 340

International Covenant on Civil and Political Rights, 16 December 1966 3, 11, 38, 39-41, 44-46, 53, 57, 81, 88, 102, 119, 123, 129, 132-133, 136, 137, 140, 141, 143, 147, 243, 252, 326, 333, 338

International Covenant on Economic, Social and Cultural Rights, 16 December 1966 333

International Covenant on Human Rights 147

International Criminal Court
   Office of the Prosecutor 146 (fn. 512)
   Rome Statute of 130, 140

International Criminal Tribunal for the Former Yugoslavia *see* ICTY

International Crisis Group 210

international humanitarian law 4, 5, 10, 11, 12, 13, 15, 16, 28, 37, 38-64, 69, 71, 73, 83, 88, 89, 124, 125, 132, 135, 139, 144, 145, 233, 247, 251, 282, 318, 340, 341, 342, 343, 354

International Labour Organisation (ILO)
   basic human rights conventions 140

international law
   compliance with 95, 336, 354
   general 15, 42, 137, 147, 179, 203, 237, 263, 268, 271, 275, 276, 312, 336, 352, 354
   human rights law as subdivision 3, 42
   international humanitarian law as a subdivision 4, 42
   law of international organisations as a subdivision 3

International Law Commission 130, 216, 268, 285, 287, 294, 350

International Maritime Organisation 163 (fn. 571), 284

international organisation
   accountability 304-307
   definition 287
   Draft Articles on Responsibility *see* DARIO
   presumption of equivalent protection ('*Bosphorus* presumption') 290-292
   privileges and immunities 288-289

International Space Station 173-74, 345

International Tribunal for the Prosecution of Persons Responsible for Serious Violations of International Humanitarian Law Committed in the

406 INDEX

Territory of the Former Yugoslavia
since 1991 *see* ICTY
internationally wrongful act   267, 268, 285,
292, 304,
Articles on *see* State responsibility for
Internationally Wrongful Acts,
Articles on
internment   29
for reasons of security   28, 52, 88,
legal basis in Security Council
resolution   144, 297-298, 300
under international humanitarian
law   56, 57
obligation to hold someone in   297
peacetime   54
review of   139
wartime   57
without charge   111, 297
interoperability   12
legal   12-13
Interpol   194
interrogation   26, 127, 196-201, 275
'enhanced – techniques'   27
interstate application   92, 97
interstate case   15, 31, 85, 184, 208-209, 231,
347
IRA (Irish Republican Army)   19, 89, 95-96,
183, 184
Iran   156, 221-222
*see also* Imperial Persia
Iran-Iraq War, 1980-88   61
Iraq   4, 7, 18, 22-23, 29, 36, 51, 56, 61, 80, 86-
87, 88, 144, 146, 220-221, 235-238,241,
244, 249-250, 260-263, 272-274, 280, 296,
298, 351, 352
Iraqi High Tribunal (IHT)   236, 260-261,
263-264
ISAF (International Security Assistance
Force)   280
Islamic State *see* Deash [sic]
Islamist   199
Isle of Man   152
*ius ad bellum*   3, 4, 46
*ius cogens*   86, 132, 258,
*ius in bello*   3, 4, 124

Jama'a al-Islamiya   199
Jamaica   152
Jan Mayen Island   153

Jersey, Bailiwick of   152
Jews   319, 323
Joint Committee on Human Rights of the
House of Lords and the House of
Commons (United Kingdom)   125, 128
jurisdiction (of the Court)
acceptance (former Article 46)   254
*Kompetenz-Kompetenz*   254
territorial limitations   254-256, 265
jurisdiction (of the State)
accountability   149
acknowledging   183-185
Al-Skeini rule (extraterritorial
jurisdiction)   238-241
as an autonomous concept   250
asserted as a right   147-149
assertion of   217, 349
attributes of sovereignty   147
borne as a responsibility   148-149
distinct from attribution   267-69
effective control over an area   154, 193,
204, 212, 214, 216, 227, 230, 237, 238,
240-241, 249, 250, 267, 293, 334, 348,
349
obligations divided and tailored   214,
239, 251, 348
over armed forces   176-177
over overseas territory in absence of
Article 56 declaration   154
presumption of territorial   186, 190-91,
346
quasi-territorial   155-174
State agent authority and control   51, 154,
167, 171, 217, 220-221, 226, 227, 228,
231, 234, 238-240, 241, 245, 249-251,
252, 267, 271, 272, 294, 348, 349
territorial   149-155
threshold criterion   149
universal   168, 345
unlawful   203
just satisfaction (Article 41)   31, 32

Kalaydjieva, Zdravka, Judge of the Court   55
Kazakhstan   156
Kenya   80, 152, 170, 245-46, 299
KFOR (Kosovo Force)   191, 273, 292-98, 306,
333, 351
Commander (COMKFOR)   293, 294
kinetic warfare   5, 8, 78, 79, 214, 290, 347

INDEX

KLA (Kosovo Liberation Army *see* UÇK
*Koninklijke Marechaussee* (Netherlands) *see* Royal Military Constabulary
Korean War   82, 87
Kosovo   4, 7, 75, 178, 191-193, 211, 273, 292-293, 306-07, 332-34, 337, 347, 351
    exercise of jurisdiction by Serbia   192-93
    independence   192
    international recognition status   334
    statehood   192-193
    Status Settlement, Comprehensive Proposal (Ahtisaari Plan) 334
Kosovo Liberation Army (KLA) *see* UÇK
Krüger, Hans-Christian   315

Lake Success   147
law enforcement   5, 10, 11, 12, 19, 20, 28, 40, 48, 77, 123, 211, 307, 338, 340, 342,
    paradigm   5, 12, 40, 50, 77, 123
Law of the Sea Conventions (Convention on the Territorial Sea and the Contiguous Zone; Convention on the High Seas; Convention on Fishing and Conservation of the Living Resources of the High Seas; Convention on the Continental Shelf), 29 April 1958   155
laws of war *see* International humanitarian law
Lawson, Rick   186 (fn. 666), 216-17, 291-92
League of Nations   150
Leeward islands   152
lethal force   2, 9, 19, 126, 225, 228, 240, 244
*lex posterior derogat legi priori*   42 (fn. 144)
*lex specialis* (international humanitarian law in relation to human rights law)   40-47, 51, 52, 58, 63, 340
*lex specialis derogat legi generali*   41
Liberty (non-governmental organisation)   100, 121
liberty and security, right to (Article 5 of the Convention)   28-31
    Court case-law on international humanitarian law   51-60
    deprivation of liberty   28-31
    enforceable right to compensation (in case of violation)   31
    procedural obligations   31
    substantive obligations   28-30

supervision by judge or similarly qualified functionary   28
Libya   165-166
life of the community   96, 98, 103, 117
life, right to (Article 2 of the Convention)   19-24
    active deprivation of life   19-20
    Court case-law on international humanitarian law   50-51
    positive obligations   20-21
    procedural obligations   21-24
    substantive obligations   19-20
life of the nation *see* threat to the life of the nation
*Limburg* attack (2002)   199
Litvinenko, Alexander   229-230
Lockerbie bombing (Pan Am flight 103)   177
looters   130
loyalist paramilitaries (Northern Ireland)   184
    Ulster Defence Association   195
    Ulster Volunteer Force   195
'Luhansk People's Republic'   6

Madeira Islands   153
Makarios III, Archbishop   92,94
Malaya, British   81, 152
Malaysia   152
Man, Isle of *see* Isle of Man
mandate territories   150
margin of appreciation   97, 100, 104, 111-12, 118, 121, 138-39, 143, 343
Maritime Exclusion Zone (Falklands War, 1982)   70
Marty Report
    First   196, 197
    Second 197, 200 (fn. 695)
    Third   276
Marty, Senator Dick   196, 201, 276,
Maslow's hierarchy of needs   34
Mauritius   152
medical assistance to wounded   50
medical care in detention   270
Memorandum of Understanding between the United Kingdom of Great Britain and Northern Ireland Contingent of Multinational Forces-Iraq and the Ministries of Justice and Interior of

408 INDEX

Iraq regarding criminal suspects   236, 260-61, 263
merchant ship   166, 283-84
    oil tanker   159, 199
metadata   228
Middle East   6, 30, 75, 108, 151, 195
Milanović, Marko   151, 298,
Military Commission (USA)   199
Military Administration (Soviet Union, in German Democratic Republic)   206
Military Governor (Soviet Union, in German Democratic Republic)   206
military necessity   140
military objectives   140
military service   127-128, 132
Military Technical Agreement (Kosovo)   292
MINUSMA (*Mission multidimensionnelle intégrée des Nations unies pour la stabilisation au Mali*)   6
missile attack   211, 235, 252
MIVD (Netherlands military intelligence service)   228
Moldavian Soviet Socialist Republic   187
Moldova, Soviet Socialist Republic   187
'Moldovan Republic of Transdniestria' (MRT') see Transdniestria
monetary crisis   118
Montserrat   153
MONUSCO (*Mission de l'Organisation des Nations unies pour la stabilisation en République démocratique du Congo*)   6-7
Moon Treaty see Agreement Governing Activities of States on the Moon and Other Celestial Bodies
Morocco   111, 199, 200
movement, freedom of see freedom of movement
Mozambique   81
Multinational Brigade (MNB), Kosovo   294
Multinational Force, Iraq   22-23, 237, 260, 261, 272, 273, 297-98
murder   22, 120, 128, 176, 193-195, 203, 276, 293
    Clandestine (as exercise of 'hard power') see Clandestine murder
Murray, Daragh   47
Muslim, Muslims   114, 120, 175, 242

Nagorno-Karabakh   4, 32, 190, 210, 347
'Nagorno-Karabakh, Republic of' see Nagorno-Karabakh
Namibia principle (legal acts of unrecognised authority)   308-309, 310, 312, 316
Napoleonic Wars   39
nation (expression)   92, 95
National Security Agency (USA)   264
National Socialism   319
    see also Nazi, Nazis *and* Nazi Germany
Nairobi, attack on US embassy (1998)   299
NATO (North Atlantic Treaty Organization)   3, 4, 6, 8, 12-13, 79-80, 90, 91, 176-177, 191, 211-13, 217, 231, 273, 280, 288, 292-294, 304, 320, 321, 333
    AFSOUTH   217, 288, 304
    Cooperative Cyber Defence Centre of Excellence   233
    immunity   217
    Status of Forces Agreement   176-77, 217, 321 (Bosnia and Herzegovina)   346
natural disaster   118, 140
naval attack (Indonesian, on Netherlands New Guinea, 1962)   80
naval command   203
naval forces   9, 70, 155, 164, 167, 223
    Argentinian   70
    European see EUNAVFOR
naval vessel   164, 165, 167, 224
Navstar   174
navy see naval forces
Nazi, Nazis   129-130, 206, 246, 260, 319
    see also National Socialism *and* Nazi Germany
Nazi Germany
    aggression   85
    occupation   61, 246
    see also National Socialism *and* Nazi, Nazis
*ne bis in idem* see Not to be tried or punished twice, right (Article 4 of Protocol No. 7)
Netherlands Antilles   152
Netherlands East Indies   3, 80, 81
Netherlands New Guinea   80, 151, 152
New Caledonia   153
Nicolaou, George, Judge of the Court   55
Nigeria   152
NIOD Institute for War, Holocaust and Genocide Studies (Netherlands)   24
no punishment without law   122, 128-130

# INDEX

Court case-law on international
humanitarian law   60-61
non-derogable rights   41, 45, 67, 66, 67, 97,
122-137, 140, 342
by implication   132-137, 342
non-international armed conflict   5, 6, 7, 8,
10, 11, 42, 43, 48, 60, 62, 69, 71, 73-74, 75-
77, 82-83, 123, 124, 136, 137, 341, 342
non-self-governing territory   81, 92, 153
Non-State actor, actors   15, 91, 172, 341
Normality
return to   103, 138, 336, 343
restoration of   354
North Atlantic Council   90-91, 211, 294
North Borneo *see* Borneo, British North
Northern Rhodesia (now Zambia)   152
not to be tried or punished twice, right
(Article 4 of Protocol No. 7)   123
Court case-law on international
humanitarian law   61
*note verbale*   74, 90, 92, 142, 246
Notice of derogation (Article 15 § 3)   56, 68,
69, 74, 88, 90, 92, 94, 95, 97, 99, 102, 103,
105, 111, 114, 120, 122, 141-143, 144, 145, 146,
183, 258, 340, 343
*nulla poena sine lege* see no punishment
without law
Nuremberg Charter   130
Nuremberg Principles   130
Nuremberg Tribunal   129, 206
Nyasaland (now Malawi)   152

O'Boyle, Michael   143, 216, 258
*Oberkommando der Wehrmacht* see German
High Command
Ocean Shield, Operation   228
occupation
belligerent   6, 71, 74, 214, 308, 341
expression   246
foreign   191
Germany (by Allied powers)   206, 319
High Contracting Party, territory of   341
illegal   316
in international humanitarian law   247-
248, 251, 348
Iraq   86, 235, 272, 352
lending legitimacy to   316-18
military   214, 270
Moon and other celestial bodies   161

Nagorno-Karabakh   257
Nazi Germany   246
outer space   161
Soviet Union   247
'Turkish Republic of Northern
Cyprus'   247, 308, 316-319
Ukrainian territory by the Russian
Federation, posited by Ukraine   74,
90
Occupying power   136, 207, 237, 241, 316, 318,
319, 336, 351
Status of   246-274
Öcalan, Abdullah   170, 245-46
Olympic Games 1972 (Munich), Black
September attack   195
Ombudsperson (Human Rights Ombudsman,
Bosnia and Herzegovina)   33, 326-329,
333
operational choices   20
Operation Althea *see* Althea, Operation
Operation Atalanta *see* Atalanta, Operation
*opinio iuris*   234
*ordre public* see Public order, European
Ossetia, northern   185
Ossetia, South *see* South Ossetia
other obligations under international law
(Article 15 § 1)   38, 56, 66, 67, 88, 89,
95, 102, 139-140, 343
Ottoman Empire   91
Outer space   161
Outer Space Treaty *see* Treaty on Principles
Governing the Activities of States
in the Exploration and Use of Outer
Space, including the Moon and Other
Celestial Bodies
overthrow of Government   92, 114, 115, 117,
122
Ovey, Clare   221, 241

Pakistan   3, 199
Palestinian hanging (torture technique)   27
paratroops   176
parliamentary enquiry   24
Pastre-Belda, Beatrice   59
peace enforcement   82-83, 235, 246, 346
peacekeeping   13, 23, 24, 82-83, 189, 235, 296,
307, 346
peacekeeping force   23, 24, 296

410 INDEX

Peace Implementation Conference (Bosnia and Herzegovina)   320, 330
Peace Implementation Council (Bosnia and Herzegovina)   320, 330
Pearl Harbor attack (1941)   195
Persia, Imperial *see* Imperial Persia
Peters, Anne   264-265
pillaging   140
Pinto law (Italy)   318
piracy   8-9, 10, 168, 223-24, 228, 246, 283, 303, 338, 345, 351
Pitcairn Islands   153
PKK (*Partiya Karkerên Kurdistanê*, Workers' Party of Kurdistan)   6, 89, 104, 146, 184, 245
police   18, 19-20, 25, 27, 31, 73, 99, 101, 170, 172, 194-195, 205, 226, 278, 279, 306
  action   20
  custody   99
  investigations   104
  military (Netherlands)   36 *see also* Royal Military Constabulary
  military (Royal Military Police, United Kingdom)   23, 236, 260
  operations   7
  Revenue – and Coastguard (Italy)   177
  stations   92
  work   22, 120
policing   157, 223
polonium-210   229
post-conflict situation   51, 238, 307
presumption of innocence   136-137
preventive detention   29-30, 111
prison   18, 189-90, 196, 198, 200, 245
  İmralı   245
  military   272
  Spandau   206, 260
prison work   128
prisoners of war   26, 28, 51, 52, 54-56, 60, 88, 260
  *see also* Geneva Convention (III) on Prisoners of War, 12 August 1949
private agents   278-279, 281, 335, 351
private military security contractors   279
  agreement between ISAF/NATO and Afghanistan   280
  bound by local laws   280
  cyber-attacks   285
  in Iraq   280

International Code of Conduct for Private Security Service Providers   282
  ISO 18788   282
  Montreux Document   282
  use by Netherlands in Afghanistan   279-80
  use by US in Afghanistan   280
Privy Council (United Kingdom)   86, 108
procedural provisions of the Convention   132
proof (procedure of the European Court of Human Rights)   35-37
  admissibility of evidence   35
  beyond reasonable doubt (standard of proof)   35, 339
  burden of proof   36, 37, 339
  evidentiary principles   35-36
  free evaluation of evidence   35
  inferences which may be unfavourable for the respondent Government   36
  presumptions of fact   36
propaganda for war   137
property   140, 169, 175, 204, 248, 290, 319
  immovable   205, 208-209, 255, 312-319 *see also* Real estate
  intellectual   286
  religious, charitable, educational and cultural   248
  right to respect for (Article 1 of Protocol No. 1)   31-34, 339
  status (discrimination)   326
Protecting Power   135
protectorate   150, 151
provisional measure
  of the Court (Rule 39 of the Rules of Court)   123 (fn. 420), 236, 261
  Human Rights Chamber for Bosnia and Herzegovina   198, 329
proxy government   207, 209
pseudo-interstate cases   85
pseudo-state   308, 335, 347, 350
public emergency
  officially proclaimed   39, 92, 102, 141, 143
  threatening the life of the nation (Article 15 § 1)   9, 39, 42, 52, 64, 66, 67, 74, 78, 91, 92, 95, 96, 97, 100, 101, 103, 104, 106, 109, 111, 112, 115, 117, 119, 126, 127, 214, 338, 340, 353
public order (safety)   89, 104, 248

INDEX                                                                                          411

public order, European (also *ordre
    public*)   208, 241, 256, 29, 301,
puppet state   207

quasi-indigenous institutions   319, 335, 352,
    354
questioning *see* Interrogation

racism   22
radiation syndrome   229
Radio Televizije Srbije (RTS)   211, 212, 217,
    239
Raimondi, Guido, judge of the Court   267,
    274
*raison d'état*   149
rape (as torture technique)   27
*ratione loci* (competence of the Court)   149,
    203, 218, 225, 335
*ratione materiae* (competence of the Court)
    49, 263
*ratione pacis sive belli* (applicability of the
    Convention)   338
*ratione personae* (competence of the
    Court)   207, 218, 296, 332, 334
*ratione temporis* (competence of the
    Court)   75, 198, 266
real estate   31-34 *see also* property,
    immovable
*Realpolitik*   318
Red Army Faction (*Rote Armee Fraktion*)   195
Red Brigades (*Brigate Rosse*)   195
Red Partisan   61
refugees   33, 165
registration, state of *see* state of registration
    (aircraft and spacecraft)
religion, freedom of *see* freedom of thought,
    conscience and religion
remedy
    offered by subordinate entity *see*
        subordinate entity, remedy offered
        by
    single-issue   318
    *see also* effective remedy, right to
rendition   30, 180, 197, 201, 274-76, 350
    European collusion   197, 350-351
Republika Srpska (Entity of Bosnia and
    Herzegovina)   278, 320, 321, 323, 327,
    336
reservation (Article 57)   69, 256-58, 265, 349

Azerbaijan   257
France   257
invalid   258, 349
Moldova   256-257
Resolute Support (mission in
    Afghanistan)   8
respect for correspondence (Article 8)   240
respect for family life (Article 8)   175, 260
respect for home (Article 8)   31-34, 210, 312,
    339
responsibility to protect   76, 83-85
return to normality *see* Normality, return to
rifle fire   225, 227, 231, 244, 253
right of individual petition *see* Individual
    petition, right of
rights and actions of nationals of hostile
    party   140
riots   72-73, 89, 93, 123
    rioters   130
Roma   323
Roman law   41
Rome Statute of the International Criminal
    Court *see* International Criminal
    Court, Rome Statute of
Rossi d'Ambrosio, Dario   59
*Rote Armee Fraktion* see Red Army Faction
Royal Army (Netherlands)   23-24, 244, 285
Royal Military Constabulary (*Koninklijke
    Marechaussee*, Netherlands)   36
rule of law   1, 3, 65, 116, 313, 353,
Russia
    armed forces   74
    support of 'Moldovan Republic of
        Trandsniestria'   209-210
    Imperial *see* Imperial Russia
    incursion into Abkhazia and Southern
        Ossetia   90
    internal waters   156
    irregular forces allegedly under Russian
        control   74
Russian Operational Group   187-188, 209
Rwanda-Urundi   150

saboteur, saboteurs   60, 136, 248
Saarland   151
Saba   152 (fn. 530)
SACEUR (Supreme Allied Commander
    Europe)   294
Saint Martin *see* Sint Maarten

## INDEX

Sarawak 152
Sark 152
SAS (Special Air Service, United Kingdom) 19
satellites (unmanned spacecraft) 172-174, 345
Scottish Court in the Netherlands 177
secession
    Algeria 78
    force 346
    overseas territories 81
    separatist 191
    'Turkish Republic of Northern Cyprus' 207
Second World War *see* World War II
secret agreements 264
secret detention facility 197, 200, 275
secret information 199-200
    *see also* classified information
self-defence
    Article 51 of the Charter of the united Nations 8, 74, 79, 82, 86, 87, 146, 342
self-determination 81, 93, 308
separatists
    Azerbaijan 190
    control over territory 186, 190, 191
    Moldova 187-188, 209-210
    Russia 7, 18, 185
    Turkey 105
    Ukraine 90
servitude 122, 127
Seychelles 92, 94, 152
SFOR (Stabilization Force, Bosnia and Herzegovina) 322, 326
SHAPE (Supreme Headquarters Allied Powers Europe) 294
shot fired across the border 224, 227, 231, 348
Sicilianos, Linos-Alexandre (Vice-President, now President of the European Court of Human Rights) 4, 58
Sierra Leone 152
signals intelligence 234
Singapore 152
Sint Eustatius 152 (fn. 530)
Sint Maarten/Saint Martin 152
SISMi (Italian intelligence service)
slavery 122, 127, 282

Slavery Convention *see* Convention to Suppress the Slave Trade and Slavery
smart power 9
soft power 9
SOLAS *see* International Convention for the Safety of Life at Sea
Somaliland
    British 150, 152
    Italian 150
South Ossetia 90
Southern Rhodesia (now Zimbabwe) 152
Sovereign rights (marine areas) 156
Sovereignty
    Andorra (Co-Princes) 177
    assertion of 181
    attributes: legislative, executive and judicial power 147
    Chinese, reversion of Hong Kong to 153
    colonial 151
    Cyprus (Northern Cyprus) 193
    domestic 179
    exercise of criminal jurisdiction as feature of 195
    Federal Republic of Germany, recovery of– 318-19
    international legal personality 147
    jurisdiction 149, 195, 203
    Kenya 245
    lack of 167
    quasi-territorial 175
    Russian (Northern Caucasus) 19, 185
    sea, airspace and outer space 155-161, 345
    State 84
    status of Occupying Power does not confer 249
    territorial 175
    territory over which – is disputed 131, 202, 347
    transfer of – to international organisation 290, 294
    Turkey (supposed constructive recognition of – over Northern Cyprus) 194, 316
    Turkey (south-eastern Turkey) 18
    United Kingdom (Falkland Islands) 82
    United Kingdom (Northern Ireland) 183
Soviet Union (1922-1991) 3, 129-30, 156, 185, 187, 190, 206, 209, 210, 247, 260
spacecraft 161, 162, 172-73, 345,

# INDEX

Spano, Robert, judge of the Court    55-57
Special Immigration Appeals Commission
    (SIAC) (United Kingdom)    109, 112
Special Representative of the Secretary
    General (Kosovo)    191-92, 273, 292,
    332, 333
Sperotto, Federico    216
Spielmann, Dean, judge of the Cour    t267,
    274
spy, spies    60, 127, 136, 248
Srebrenica massacre    24, 242
St. Helena    152, 153
St. Lucia    152
St. Vincent    152
state-building    352
state of emergency    89, 90, 92, 100, 102, 104,
    114-116, 119, 141, 142, 258
state of registration (aircraft and
    spacecraft)    161, 162,169, 172, 173, 345
State Responsibility for Internationally
    Wrongful Acts, Articles on    216, 268,
    272, 276-77, 286 (fn. 960), 305, 306,
straits    158
strict necessity test    138, 342
subordinate entity, remedy offered by    311-
    312
Sudan    171
Supreme Court
    Croatia    61
    Georgia    186
    Kosovo    293
    'Moldovan Republic of Transdniestria'
        ('MRT')    310
    Netherlands (*Hoge Raad*)    242-244
    Serbia    192
    United Kingdom    60, 110
Supreme Restitution Court (occupied West
    Germany)    319-320
Suriname    152
Svalbard    153
Swaziland    152
Syria    6, 7, 18, 146, 226, 245
systemic violations    316

Taliban 299
Tallinn Manual on the International Law
    Applicable to Cyber Operations    233-
    235
Tanganyika    152

Tanzania    299
targeted killing    126, 224-253, 338, 348
Tarschys, Daniel
territorial sea    157-158, 164
    Argentina    70
    Greece    156
    Italy    164
    Somalia    223
    Turkey    156
*territorium nullius*    162
terrorism
    combating    18, 21, 103, 133
    definition    76-77, 122
    distinct from armed conflict    8, 18
    Europe    195
    international    21, 106, 109, 196,
    keep public safe from    2
    Northern Ireland    99, 102-103
    South-East Turkey    105
    United Kingdom    106, 109
terrorist activity    73, 104, 108, 183, 338
terrorist acts
    aftermath of July 206 coup attempt in
        Turkey    114, 122, 142-143
    duty of the State to protect against    21
*testimonium paupertatis*    76
Thailand    199
threat to the life of the nation    39, 42, 52, 64,
    66, 67, 74, 77-88, 89, 91-122, 127, 130, 138,
    142-44, 338, 340, 341, 342, 343, 353
Tonga, Kingdom of    152, 153
torture, prohibition of (Article 3 of the
    Convention)    25-28
    absolute nature of    25
    positive obligations    27
    procedural obligations    27
    substantive obligations    25-27
torture
    as distinct from 'inhuman or degrading
        treatment'    25
    techniques    27
    use to extract confession    25
Total Exclusion Zone (Falklands War,
    1982)    70
thought, freedom of *see* freedom of thought,
    conscience and religion
Transdniestria    4, 187, 188-189, 191, 210 269-
    270
    jurisdiction over    191, 350

414 INDEX

'Moldovan Republic of –' ('MRT')   187, 269

remedies offered by 'MRT' courts   188, 310

Russian Federation's responsibility   209-210

pseudo-state   204, 347

separatist forces   187, 188

*travaux préparatoires*

Convention   39, 343

International Covenant on Civil and Political Rights   39

Treaty on Principles Governing the Activities of States in the Exploration and Use of Outer Space, including the Moon and Other Celestial Bodies ("Outer Space Treaty"), 27 January 1967   161

tribunal established by law (Article 6 § 1)   135, 380, 310

'Turkish Republic of Northern Cyprus' ('TRNC')

*ad hoc* remedy   312-319

attribution to Turkey   308-309

domestic remedies of   308-309, 310, 311, 350

High Administrative Court   314

Immovable Property Commission   314-315

legal assistance in criminal matters (Cyprus)   193-195

proxy government   207-209

pseudo-state   335, 347

status in international law   278, 308

Turkey's meeting of Convention obligations   335

Turkish jurisdiction   193-95, 221-22, 224-26, 227, 231

Turkish overall control   208

Turkish support for   193

Turkish territorial limitation on acceptance of jurisdiction of the Court   255

Trinidad   152

troop contributing nation   294

trust, territories held in   150

truth, right of surviving kin to know the–   22

Tugendhat, Tom   2, 68, 144

Turkmenistan   156

Turks and Caicos Islands   153

UCR (United Cyprus Republic) *see* Annan plan

UÇK (*Ushtria Çlirimtare e Kosovës*, Kosovo Liberation Army (also KLA))   178

Uganda (British protectorate 1894-1962)   152

unacknowledged detention   29, 137, 185

UNCLOS *see* Convention on the Law of the Sea

uniforms   221, 225, 269

United Nations Organization   3, 39, 43

attribution to   351-52, 292-303, 351-52

Charter   4, 30, 40, 46, 60, 74, 82, 86, 87, 88

claims commission, absence of   304-305

Commission on the Limits of the Continental Shelf   160

Committee on the Elimination of All Forms of Racial Discrimination   108

Convention against Illicit Traffic in Narcotic Drugs and Psychotropic Substances *see* Convention against Illicit Traffic in Narcotic Drugs and Psychotropic Substances

Convention on the Law of the Sea *see* Convention on the Law of the Sea

flag   82

General Assembly   43, 84

peace operations   82-83, 87

Sanctions Committee   299-300

Secretary General   24, 38

Security Council   3, 29, 30, 60,79, 82-88, 106, 144, 146, 191, 192, 207, 211, 223-224, 237, 249, 260, 272-73, 289, 291, 292-303, 306, 317,321-22, 326, 330-32, 334, 336, 342, 351-52, 354

Special Representative of the Secretary General   191-192, 273, 292, 332-333

subsidiary organ (peace operation)   83, 294, 296, 298, 351, 354

Treaty Series   265

United Nations Security Council Resolutions:

1031 (1995)   321, 330

1244 (1999)   191, 192, 273, 292, 293, 295, 332, 334

1267 (1999)   299

1333 (2000)   299

1368 (2001)   106

1373 (2001)   106

1441 (2002)   88

INDEX
415

1483 (2003)  237, 249, 260, 272, 300, 302
1511 (2003)  237, 272, 298
1546 (2004)  29, 30, 297
Universal Declaration of Human Rights, 10
  December 1948  333
UNFICYP (United Nations Peacekeeping
  Force in Cyprus)  194, 222-224, 296,
  351
Union of Socialist Soviet Republics see Soviet
  Union
United Cyprus Republic (UCR) see Annan
  plan
UNMACC (United Nations Mine Action Co-
  ordination Centre, Kosovo)  293
UNMIK (United Nations Mission in
  Kosovo)  191-92, 292-296, 306-07, 332-
  34, 351
UNPROFOR (United Nations Protection
  Force, Bosnia and Herzegovina/
  Croatia)  242, 321
USA (United States of America)  12
use of force
  by law enforcement officials  20
  monopoly of the State  2, 22, 75
USS Cole attack (2000)  199
USSR (Union of Socialist Soviet Republics)
  see Soviet Union

vacuum in human rights protection  209,
  215, 227, 238, 241, 251, 317, 335, 347
Venice Commission see European
  Commission for Democracy through
  Law
Vienna Convention on the Law of
  Treaties  52, 258, 259, 262, 300, 303,
  349
Vietnam War  226
Volga  156
volunteer organisations  285
vulnerable persons
  right to protection  27

war
  other international legal obligations  139
  calamity falling short of  130
  declaration of see Declaration of war
  expression  4, 5, 38, 39-40, 66, 67, 69, 74,
    78, 79, 341
  imminent threat of  130

lawful acts of  45, 62, 63, 66, 122, 124, 125,
  126
political decision to go to  125
state of  70
threat to the life of the nation  77-88, 342
war crime  61, 62, 74, 84, 85, 130, 178, 229,
  236, 260
war criminals  129, 132
War on Terror  8, 77, 195
warship see naval vessel
Washington, burning by British (1814)  195
Washington Agreement (Confederation
  Agreement Between The Bosnian
  Government And Bosnian Croats) 1
  March 1994  321
Washington Treaty
  Article 5 of  8, 79-80, 276,
  entry into force  3
water-boarding  27, 199
White Sea  156
Windward Islands  152
World Summit Outcome  84
World War I  39
World War II  2, 5, 39, 43, 57

Yugoslavia
  Federal Republic of (FRY) (1992-
    2006)  191, 211, 215, 292, 293, 320,
    321, 332
  former Socialist Federative Republic of
    (SFRY) (1945-1992)  4, 18, 32, 192,
    332

Zanzibar  152
zombies see botnets